THE CAMBRIDGE COMPANION TO
MEDIEVAL JEWISH PHILOSOPHY

From the ninth to the fifteenth centuries Jewish thinkers living in Islamic and Christian lands philosophized about Judaism. Influenced first by Islamic theological speculation and the great philosophers of classical antiquity, and then in the late medieval period by Christian Scholasticism, Jewish philosophers and scientists reflected on the nature of language about God, the scope and limits of human understanding, the eternity or createdness of the world, prophecy and divine providence, the possibility of human freedom, and the relationship between divine and human law. Though many viewed philosophy as a dangerous threat, others incorporated it into their understanding of what it is to be a Jew. This *Companion* presents all the major Jewish thinkers of the period, the philosophical and non-philosophical contexts of their thought, and the interactions between Jewish and non-Jewish philosophers. It is a comprehensive introduction to a vital period of Jewish intellectual history.

Daniel H. Frank is Professor of Philosophy and Director of the Judaic Studies Program at the University of Kentucky. Among recent publications are *History of Jewish Philosophy* (edited with Oliver Leaman, 1997), *The Jewish Philosophy Reader* (edited with Oliver Leaman and Charles Manekin, 2000), and revised editions of two Jewish philosophical classics, Maimonides' *Guide of the Perplexed* (1995) and Saadya Gaon's *Book of Doctrines and Beliefs* (2002).

Oliver Leaman is Professor of Philosophy and Zantker Professor of Judaic Studies at the University of Kentucky. He is the author of *An Introduction to Classical Islamic Philosophy* (2002), *Evil and Suffering in Jewish Philosophy* (1995), and is editor of *Encyclopedia of Asian Philosophy* (2001) and *Companion Encyclopedia of Middle Eastern and North African Film* (2001). He is co-editor, with Glennys Howarth, of *Encyclopedia of Death and Dying* (2001).

The Cambridge Companion to

MEDIEVAL JEWISH PHILOSOPHY

Edited by

Daniel H. Frank and Oliver Leaman
University of Kentucky

CAMBRIDGE
UNIVERSITY PRESS

PUBLISHED BY THE PRESS SYNDICATE OF THE UNIVERSITY OF CAMBRIDGE
The Pitt Building, Trumpington Street, Cambridge CB2 1RP, United Kingdom

CAMBRIDGE UNIVERSITY PRESS
The Edinburgh Building, Cambridge, CB2 2RU, UK
40 West 20th Street, New York, NY 10011–4211, USA
477 Williamstown Road, Port Melbourne, VIC 3207, Australia
Ruiz de Alarcón 13, 28014 Madrid, Spain
Dock House, The Waterfront, Cape Town 8001, South Africa

http://www.cambridge.org

First published 2003

Printed in the United Kingdom at the University Press, Cambridge

Typeface Trump Medieval 10/13 pt.   *System* LATEX 2$_\varepsilon$ [TB]

A catalogue record for this book is available from the British Library

Library of Congress Cataloguing in Publication data
The Cambridge companion to medieval Jewish philosophy / edited by
Daniel H. Frank and Oliver Leaman.
    p.   cm. – (Cambridge companions to philosophy)
Includes bibliographical references and index.
ISBN 0 521 65207 3 – ISBN 0 521 65574 9 (paperback)
1. Philosophy, Jewish.   2. Philosophy, Medieval.
3. Judaism–History–Medieval and early modern period, 425–1789.
I. Frank, Daniel H., 1950–   II. Leaman, Oliver, 1950–   III. Series.
B755.C36   2003
181'.06 – dc21   2003041200

ISBN 0 521 65207 3 hardback
ISBN 0 521 65574 9 paperback

CONTENTS

CONTRIBUTORS

ARI ACKERMAN is Lecturer in Jewish Thought and Philosophy of Education at the Schechter Institute in Jerusalem. In addition to his doctoral dissertation, "The Philosophic Sermons of Zerahia ben Isaac Halevi Saladin: Jewish Philosophic and Sermonic Activity in Late 14th and Early 15th Century Aragon" (Hebrew University of Jerusalem, 2000), he has published articles on other aspects of late medieval Jewish philosophy, including "The Composition of the Section on Divine Providence in [Crescas'] *Or Hashem*," *Da'at* 32–3 (1994), 37–45.

SEYMOUR FELDMAN is Professor of Philosophy Emeritus at Rutgers University. Among his publications are a complete translation of and commentary on Gersonides' *Wars of the Lord* (3 vols. 1984–99), articles on several medieval Jewish philosophers and on Spinoza, and *Philosophy in a Time of Crisis: Don Isaac Abravanel, Defender of the Faith* (2003).

PAUL B. FENTON is Professor of Hebrew Language and Literature at the Sorbonne. He has published extensively on Jewish civilization in the Islamic world, especially on the mystical tradition. Among recent publications is *Philosophie et exégèse dans le jardin de la métaphore* (1997), dealing with the Golden Age in Spain.

DANIEL H. FRANK is Professor of Philosophy at the University of Kentucky. Among recent publications are *History of Jewish Philosophy* (edited with Oliver Leaman, 1997), *The Jewish Philosophy Reader* (edited with Oliver Leaman and Charles H. Manekin, 2000), and revised editions of two Jewish philosophical classics,

Maimonides' *Guide of the Perplexed* (1995) and Saadya Gaon's *Book of Doctrines and Beliefs* (2002).

STEVEN HARVEY is Professor of Philosophy at Bar-Ilan University. He has published extensively on the medieval Jewish and Islamic philosophers, with special focus on Averroes' commentaries on Aristotle and on the influence of the Islamic philosophers on Jewish thought. He is the author of *Falaquera's "Epistle of the Debate": An Introduction to Jewish Philosophy* (1987) and editor of *The Medieval Hebrew Encyclopedias of Science and Philosophy* (2000).

BARRY S. KOGAN is Clarence and Robert Efroymson Professor of Philosophy and Jewish Religious Thought at Hebrew Union College–Jewish Institute of Religion, Cincinnati. The author of *Averroes and the Metaphysics of Causation* (1985) and of articles on medieval Jewish and Islamic philosophy, he is currently preparing for the Yale Judaica Series a new English translation of Judah Halevi's *Kuzari*.

JOEL L. KRAEMER is John Henry Barrows Professor in the Divinity School and the Committee on Social Thought at the University of Chicago. He has written on the transmission of the intellectual heritage of Greek antiquity to Islamic civilization. Among his major publications are *Humanism in the Renaissance of Islam: The Cultural Revival during the Buyid Age* (2nd rev. ed. 1992) and *Philosophy in the Renaissance of Islam: Al-Sijistani and his Circle* (1986). His more recent interests concern the interplay of cultural and religious themes within Islam and Judaism.

TZVI LANGERMANN is Associate Professor of Arabic at Bar-Ilan University. His recent books include *Yemenite Midrash: Philosophical Commentaries on the Torah* (1997) and *The Jews and the Sciences in the Middle Ages* (1999).

OLIVER LEAMAN is Professor of Philosophy and Zantker Professor of Judaic Studies at the University of Kentucky. He has published extensively on Islamic and Jewish philosophy. He is the author of *An Introduction to Classical Islamic Philosophy* (2002) and *Evil and Suffering in Jewish Philosophy* (1995), and editor of *Encyclopedia of*

Asian Philosophy (2001) and *Companion Encyclopedia of Middle Eastern and North African Film* (2001).

MENACHEM LORBERBAUM is Senior Lecturer in Jewish Philosophy at Tel Aviv University and a research associate at the Shalom Hartman Institute, Jerusalem. He is the author of *Politics and the Limits of Law: Secularizing the Political in Medieval Jewish Thought* (2001) and co-editor, with Michael Walzer and Noam Zohar, of the multi-volume *The Jewish Political Tradition* (2000–).

CHARLES H. MANEKIN is Associate Professor of Philosophy at the University of Maryland at College Park. He is the author of *On Maimonides* (2003), and a co-editor of *The Jewish Philosophy Reader* (2000) and *Freedom and Responsibility: General and Jewish Perspectives* (1997).

SARAH PESSIN is Assistant Professor of Philosophy at California State University, Fresno. Her research interests focus on medieval Jewish and Islamic Neoplatonism, and she is currently completing a book on Solomon ibn Gabirol. Among her recent publications are "Hebdomads: Boethius Meets the Pythagoreans," *Journal of the History of Philosophy* 37 (1999) and "Matter, Metaphor, and Private Pointing: Maimonides on the Complexity of Human Being," *American Catholic Philosophical Quarterly*, special Maimonides issue, ed. D. H. Frank (2002).

JAMES T. ROBINSON is Assistant Professor of the History of Judaism in the Divinity School at the University of Chicago. He is the author of *Philosophy and Exegesis in Samuel ibn Tibbon's Commentary on Ecclesiastes* (forthcoming). Recent articles include "The First References in Hebrew to al-Bitruji's *On the Principles of Astronomy*," *Aleph* 3 (2003).

T. M. RUDAVSKY is Professor of Philosophy at Ohio State University. She is the author of *Time Matters: Time, Creation, and Cosmology in Medieval Jewish Philosophy* (2000), and editor of *Gender and Judaism: Tradition and Transformation* (1995) and *Divine Omniscience and Omnipotence in Medieval Philosophy* (1985).

DAVID SHATZ is Professor of Philosophy at Yeshiva University. He has published extensively on both Jewish and general philosophy. His work in general philosophy focuses on epistemology, free will, and philosophy of religion, while his work in Jewish philosophy focuses on Maimonides and on twentieth-century figures. He has recently edited *Philosophy and Faith: A Philosophy of Religion Reader* (2002) and co-edited, with Steven M. Cahn, *Questions about God: Today's Philosophers Ponder the Divine* (2002).

GREGG STERN is Lecturer in the Study of Religions at the School of Oriental and African Studies, University of London, and Sam and Vivienne Cohen Fellow at the London School of Jewish Studies. Among his recent publications is "Philosophic Allegory in Jewish Culture: The Crisis in Languedoc (1304–6)," in *Interpretation and Allegory: Antiquity to the Modern Period*, ed. J. Whitman (2000).

SARAH STROUMSA is Professor of Arabic Language and Literature and Jewish Thought at the Hebrew University of Jerusalem. Her recent publications include *The Beginnings of the Maimonidean Controversy in the East: Yosef ibn Shim'on's Silencing Epistle concerning the Resurrection of the Dead* (1999) and *Freethinkers of Medieval Islam: Ibn al-Rawandi, Abu Bakr al-Razi, and their Impact on Islamic Thought* (1999).

HAVA TIROSH-SAMUELSON is Associate Professor of History at Arizona State University. The author of *Between Worlds: The Life and Thought of Rabbi David ben Judah Messer Leon* (1991) and *Happiness in Premodern Judaism: Virtue, Knowledge, and Well-being* (2003), she has edited *Judaism and Ecology: Created World and Revealed Word* (2002). Among recent articles are "Nature in the Sources of Judaism," *Daedelus* 130 (2001) and "Theology of Nature in Sixteenth-Century Italian Jewish Philosophy," *Science in Context* 10 (1997).

From the ninth through the fifteenth centuries, some six hundred years, Jewish philosophers living in both Islamic and Christian lands philosophized about Judaism, hoping thereby to put their religion on a sound intellectual footing. Influenced first by Islamic theological speculation and by the great Greek philosophers and their Islamic successors, and then in the late medieval period by Christian Scholasticism, Jewish philosophers reflected on the nature of language about God, the scope and limits of human understanding, the eternity or createdness of the world, prophecy and divine providence, the possibility of human freedom, and the relationship between divine and human law. During the medieval period philosophy was often viewed as dangerous, but for those intent on such speculation the opportunity presented itself to prove that Judaism and human wisdom are compatible with one another. The essays in this volume present all the major Jewish thinkers of the medieval period, the philosophical and non-philosophical contexts of their thought, and the interactions between Jewish and non-Jewish philosophy.

This companion to medieval Jewish philosophy is a bit of an anomaly in the Cambridge series of companions to the major philosophers. First, while volumes in the series are in the main devoted to single authors, ours is devoted to a host of thinkers from the Jewish middle ages. Second, and in our view most important, this Companion extends to non-European locales (Baghdad and Cairo) and Semitic tongues (Arabic and Hebrew). We commend the Press for seeing the need to include within the ambit of a series devoted to "Western" philosophy, the philosophers of medieval Jewry. Before the thirteenth century the best work was done in Arabic and in Arabic lands, including of course Muslim Spain. But, as is increasingly recognized, the work of such philosophically minded Jews, indeed Jewish and Islamic philosophy generally, is part and parcel of "Western" philosophy, the tradition that commenced with the ancient Greeks. Jews and Arabs saw in Plato, Aristotle, Alexander of Aphrodisias, Themistius, Galen, John Philoponus, and Plotinus much that was of value for better understanding and interpreting their own monotheistic traditions. And in so using and revivifying the ancients for their own purposes they bequeathed to future generations of philosophers in medieval Christendom a rich supply of arguments and, as importantly, a non-parochial outlook, an openness, which saw Aquinas look respectfully to Averroes as the Commentator (on Aristotle) and to Maimonides as Rabbi Moyses.

One runs the risk of looking at the Jewish philosophers and their use of the past for present concerns as quite unoriginal, as merely middlemen in the transport of ideas from ancient Greece to medieval Christendom. Such a view bears its Christian triumphalism clearly, and should be stoutly resisted. Judaism did not end with Jesus, and one should likewise realize that Jewish philosophy continued unabated long after Aquinas, often seemingly uninfluenced by Christian philosophical trends. It would be very wrong in fact to read medieval Jewish philosophy in isolation from the host cultures in which it invariably found itself, but it would be equally misguided to lose sight of it as a rich source of philosophical argumentation just because it looked to extra-Jewish sources as a means by which to explicate its own monotheistic traditions. It is our hope that the reader will come away with an appreciation of a diverse set of thinkers, often at odds with each other, whose originality consists precisely in its creative use and constant adaptation of traditional texts and norms.

Production of this volume has been a pleasingly international project, bringing together scholars from America, Europe, and Israel. We have been aided in our editorial task by the timeliness of our contributors and by the helpful team at Cambridge University Press (UK), especially Kevin Taylor. Our thanks to all.

DANIEL H. FRANK
OLIVER LEAMAN

7 July 2003
7 Tammuz 5763

CHRONOLOGY OF PERSONS AND EVENTS

The following chronology attempts to take into account influences within certain time spans, even if a strict chronology is occasionally forsaken. All dates are CE; acronyms and important texts are in parentheses.

c. 500	Babylonian Talmud complete
622	The *Hijra*: Muhammad's migration from Mecca to Medina
632	Death of Muhammad
711–715	Muslim conquest of Spain
762–767	Karaite movement (see Glossary) begins
813–833	Reign of caliph al-Maʾmun in Baghdad and vigorous translation movement of Greek philosophical and scientific texts into Arabic
d. c. 866	Al-Kindi
820–890	Daud al-Muqammis
850–c. 932	Isaac Israeli
c. 870–950	Al-Farabi
882–942	Saadya Gaon (*Book of Doctrines and Beliefs*)
980–1037	Ibn Sina (Avicenna)
1021–c. 1058	Solomon ibn Gabirol (*Fons Vitae*)
fl. 1080	Bahya ibn Paquda (*Duties of the Heart*)
1040–1105	Rashi (preeminent medieval biblical commentator)
1058–1111	Al-Ghazali
1085	Capture of Toledo in Muslim Spain by Christians
1095	First Crusade
c. 1075–1141	Judah Halevi (*The Kuzari*)

d. c. 1136	Abraham bar Hiyya
1089–1164	Abraham ibn Ezra
d. 1138	Ibn Bajja (Avempace)
1147–1149	Second Crusade
1148	Almohads conquer Cordova
1110–1180	Abraham ibn Daud (*The Exalted Faith*)
d. 1185	Ibn Tufayl
c. 1120–1190	Judah ibn Tibbon (translator of Saadya's *Book of Doctrines and Beliefs*, Bahya's *Duties of the Heart*, and Halevi's *Kuzari* from Arabic into Hebrew)
1126–1198	Ibn Rushd (Averroes)
1135/8–1204	Maimonides (Rambam) (*The Guide of the Perplexed*)
1189–1192	Third Crusade
1186–1237	Abraham ibn Maimonides (son of Rambam)
c. 1160–1230	Samuel ibn Tibbon (translator of Maimonides' *Guide* from Judeo-Arabic into Hebrew in 1204)
c. 1160–1235	David Kimhi (Radak)
1194–1270	Nahmanides (Ramban)
1232	Maimonides' *Guide* and *Book of Knowledge* from his *Mishneh Torah* (see Glossary) are condemned by the rabbis of Northern France and burned by the Dominicans
1240	Disputation of Paris
1242	Talmud burned by Church authorities in Paris
fl. 1230	Jacob Anatoli
fl. 1250	Moses ibn Tibbon
1263	Disputation of Barcelona
1221–1274	Bonaventure
c. 1214–1292	Roger Bacon
1224/5–1274	Thomas Aquinas
c. 1240–1284	Siger of Brabant
1277	Condemnation of 219 philosophical propositions by Bishop Stephen Tempier in Paris
c. 1225–1295	Shem Tov ibn Falaquera
fl. 1250	Isaac Albalag
1240–c. 1291	Abraham Abulafia

c. 1240–1305	Moses de Leon (*Zohar* [see Glossary])
1235–1310	Solomon ibn Adret (Rashba)
fl. 1300	Abba Mari of Montpellier
1249–1316	Menahem Meiri
1305	Greco-Arabic works of physics and metaphysics condemned by Rashba in Barcelona
1265–1308	Duns Scotus
1265–1321	Dante Alighieri
fl. 1275	Hillel of Verona
c. 1280–1325	Judah Romano
c. 1270–1340	Yedayah Bedersi ha-Penini
c. 1275–1342	Marsilius of Padua
c. 1280–1349	William of Ockham
c. 1270–1340	Abner of Burgos
fl. 1300	Isaac Pollegar
1279–1340	Joseph ibn Kaspi
1288–1344	Gersonides (Ralbag) (*The Wars of the Lord*)
d. c. 1362	Moses Narboni
1332–1406	Ibn Khaldun
c. 1310–1375	Nissim Gerondi (Ran)
c. 1320–1382	Nicholas Oresme
1391	Anti-Jewish riots and massacres in Castile and Aragon
c. 1340–1410/11	Hasdai Crescas (*Light of the Lord*)
1413–1414	Disputation of Tortosa
1361–1444	Simeon ben Zemah Duran
d. 1444	Joseph Albo (*Book of Principles*)
1401–1464	Nicholas of Cusa
1400–1460	Joseph ben Shem Tov ibn Shem Tov
d. c. 1489	Abraham Bibago (*The Way of Belief*)
c. 1420–1494	Isaac Arama
d. 1492	Abraham Shalom
1437–1509	Isaac Abravanel (*Principles of Faith*)
1492	Expulsion of the Jews from Spain
1497	Expulsion of Jews from Portugal
1433–1499	Marsilio Ficino
1434–1504	Yohanan Alemanno
c. 1460–1493	Elijah del Medigo (*The Examination of Religion*)
1462–1525	Pietro Pomponazzi

1463–1494	Pico della Mirandola
1469–1527	Machiavelli
c. 1460–1530	David ben Judah Messer Leon
c. 1460–1523	Judah Abravanel (Leone Ebreo) (*Dialogues of Love*)
1466–1536	Erasmus
1483–1546	Martin Luther
1488–1575	Joseph Karo (*Shulhan Arukh* [see Glossary])
1522–1570	Moses Cordovero
1534–1572	Isaac Luria
c. 1530–1593	Judah Moscato
1548–1600	Giordano Bruno
1561–1626	Francis Bacon
1564–1642	Galileo
1591–1655	Joseph del Medigo (Yashar)
1588–1679	Hobbes
1596–1650	Descartes
1626–1676	Shabbetai Zevi
1632–1677	Spinoza (*Tractatus Theologico-Politicus*)

NOTE ON TRANSLITERATION

We have not sought to impose a common system of transliteration on the whole text, but have used those versions of terms and names which are most generally recognizable. We have omitted all macrons and diacritics. In general, for Arabic we have distinguished between 'ayn (') and hamza ('). Likewise for Hebrew, we have distinguished between 'ayin (') and aleph (').

GLOSSARY OF SOME SIGNIFICANT TERMS AND TEXTS IN JEWISH CULTURE

Aggadah	Rabbinic collection of narratives stemming from the Second Temple period to c. 500 CE, not legally binding but still significant in issues of interpretation.
Aqedah	The binding of Isaac, preparatory to his sacrifice.
Ashʿariyya	Islamic theological school, emphasizing the overwhelming power of God and the subjectivity of ethics.
Devequt	Cleaving to God, particularly discussed in the kabbalistic tradition, and resulting from prayer and meditation.
Dhikr	Sufi concept of remembrance, often instilled via mystical practices and exercises.
Falsafa/falasifa	Peripatetic philosophy in the Islamic world.
Gaon (pl. geonim)	Head of the Babylonian academies, which prevailed between the sixth and eleventh centuries CE in Iraq, and who were the most significant religious authorities in the exile community.
Halakhah	Rabbinic law, as distinct from Aggadah, covering all aspects of Jewish life, religious and civil, public and personal.
Judeo-Arabic	Arabic written in Hebrew characters, the method of writing of many Jews in the Islamic world.

Kabbalah	Series of mystical texts and the school associated with it. Typically the approach is to seek the esoteric meaning of biblical texts.
Kalam	Literally "speech" in Arabic, became synonymous with theology.
Karaites	School of interpretation starting in the eighth century CE and arguing in favor of the written as opposed to the oral law.
Midrash	Interpretation of biblical and legal texts, often with an emphasis on ethical ideas.
Mishnah	Compilation of oral law stemming from second century CE and attributed to Judah ha-Nasi.
Mishneh Torah	Maimonides' codification of Jewish law.
Mutakallimun, see *kalam*	Theologians.
Mu'tazila	Islamic school of theology, emphasizing the objectivity of ethics and the ubiquity of justice.
Rabbanites	Those who accept the authority of the oral law, in opposition to the Karaites.
Sefer ha-Bahir	Kabbalistic work describing the organization of the *sefirot* (celestial spheres), probably written in the late twelfth century CE.
Sefer Yetzirah	*Book of Creation*, an important and very early mystical text, commented on by Saadya, amongst others.
Shekhinah	God's presence in the world.
Shulhan Arukh	Authoritative Jewish legal code, compiled by Joseph Karo and first printed in Venice in 1565.
Sifra (pl. *sifrei*)	Aramaic midrash on parts of the Five Books of Moses (Torah).
Sufism	Islamic form of mysticism, emphasizing the significance of religious experience.
Talmud	Extensive discussion of the Mishnah, and a prime source of ideas and concepts in

	Judaism. There is a smaller Palestinian and a larger Babylonian version.
Targum (pl. Targumim)	Translation of the Bible into Aramaic.
Zohar	Kabbalistic work, literally "Splendor," commenting on the Bible esoterically, probably composed in the 1280s by Moses de Leon of Castile.

Part I
Background and Context

1 Introduction to the study of medieval Jewish philosophy

Philosophers sometimes argue that there are particular expressions that are so frequently fought over that they are best characterized as "essentially contested concepts." The concept of Jewish philosophy is just such a concept. There has always been a lot of controversy about what it is, and whether it is anything at all. This is not a problem for Jewish philosophy alone, of course, but affects all philosophies that are described in religious and ethnic terms, and familiar issues of definition then enter the discussion. Is Jewish philosophy philosophy by Jews? That is not such a simple question either, since the whole issue of who is a Jew is complex, and although at the time of the Third Reich the Nazis thought they had a neat definition of the Jewish race, we would probably hesitate to call Catholic priests Jewish thinkers merely on the basis of the fact that they had one Jewish grandparent. On the other hand, it would be wrong to define as a Jewish philosopher only those Jews who had a commitment to Judaism itself, since we know that many people feel themselves to be Jewish and are ethnically Jewish without sharing any religious beliefs at all with their more observant coreligionists. Yet they may have interesting views on religion and philosophy and it seems wrong to disqualify their work as potentially being Jewish philosophy. On the other hand, perfectly observant Jews may write on topics in philosophy that have nothing to do with Judaism, and it would be strange to classify what they do as Jewish philosophy. We seem to be getting back to the idea of Jewish science, a doctrine popular with racists but without much to be said for it otherwise. There is also a good deal of Jewish thought that is close to philosophy (theology, law, discussions of ritual) which is not philosophy, although it is capable of philosophical interest. One would not want to draw the boundaries

of Jewish philosophy too restrictively, yet a wide definition that allowed in all sorts of linked but distinct disciplines is not likely to be
productive.

In fact, when we look at the different traditions of philosophical activity that have been called Jewish philosophy, we see much
debate over the nature of Jewish philosophy, but not much disagreement about who the Jewish philosophers were. The main characters
form a distinct group ranging from Philo right up to contemporary
figures such as Levinas. What makes them all Jewish philosophers?
One explanation is the nature of the issues they considered, issues
that are both philosophical and that treat seriously the view of the
world that can be extracted from the Jewish texts. (Actually, on such
an account we can justify calling the early work of Levinas philosophy, and his later work Jewish philosophy.) This is reasonable as a
starting position, and avoids the suggestion that Jewish philosophy
has to accept what might be taken to be the principles of Judaism
itself.

What is wrong with this presupposition? There are at least two
problems with it. One is the issue as to whether there are principles of Judaism at all, something that has been very controversial
in Jewish history. Some thinkers do argue for a set of basic principles, although there is then much discussion about what this set
actually contains, but others argue that there is no such set at all,
that Judaism is quite open when it comes to basic principles. This
is not the more important problem, though. That is the difficulty of
combining the universality of philosophy with the particularity of a
religious faith. If it is the case that a philosopher was restricted in her
work due to the imposition of a religious straitjacket, as it were, then
we should hardly call what she did philosophy. Much of the scholarship that has taken place in the field suggests that this is in fact
the precise model we should accept of Jewish philosophy. Individual
thinkers are committed both to general philosophical principles of
one kind or another (depending on where they live, what is in fashion at the time) and also to Judaism, and then they have to reconcile
what might seem to be inconsistencies between these two sorts of
commitment.

The medieval period is one in which the debate between philosophy and religion is regarded as having dominated the cultural atmosphere of the times. The main arena of intellectual life was the

Iberian peninsula, and especially al-Andalus, the Islamic territories on the peninsula, with its large and well-integrated Jewish community. This is often referred to as a Golden Period in which the three religions of Christianity, Islam, and Judaism flourished and regarded each other with mutual toleration, but this is a wide exaggeration of the reality. In fact the Middle Ages in the Iberian peninsula were marked by constant strife and interreligious conflict, with occasional periods of relative peace, and intellectual life was difficult even within each religious community, let alone between the different communities. For example, one of the main problems for Jews was the internecine conflicts within the Islamic world, and the changes of regime in al-Andalus had an impact on the lives of the other communities, even the *kitabi* (monotheistic) ones. The conflict between the Christians and the Muslims led to the Jews sometimes being courted as useful allies, but sometimes being persecuted by both sides as dubious elements in the state. One also assumes that then as now large numbers of Jews were converted to other religions, and assimilated thoroughly into the larger and more powerful communities that surrounded them, and in fact it is the debate between the religions that was much more important for Jews in the medieval period rather than the debate within Jewish philosophy. After all, Jewish philosophy was only available to a relatively small part of the community, those who were both sufficiently educated to participate in intellectual debates and who were interested in the particular sort of issues that arise in philosophy as compared with the other theoretical pursuits of Jews, such as the Bible, Talmud, and so on. On the other hand, from the fact that so many translations were made into Hebrew from Arabic and Judeo-Arabic during the medieval period, and well after into the Renaissance, we have to conclude that there was a fairly wide interest in philosophy within a Jewish context, and many individuals within the wider Jewish community must have felt the need to be aware of the sorts of debates that went on in the philosophical world.

One danger we should not fall into is that of treating medieval Jewish philosophy as though it was regarded at the time as just like a subdivision of philosophy itself. It was not, because at the time the concept of philosophy as a discrete academic discipline did not exist. In Arabic the word *hikma* was used far more for philosophy than the specific term *falsafa*, and similarly in Jewish philosophy the subject was more identified with "wisdom" in its widest sense than with something more specialized. While the educated individual might have wished to know something about philosophy, he would also have wanted to know about science (the first book of Aristotle to be translated into Hebrew is his *Meteorology*) and about a range of other secular types of knowledge. He would have been interested in ideas, the sort of ideas he did not find explicitly mentioned in Jewish works like the Bible and Talmud, and he would have wished to show his sophistication by displaying this interest and a degree of competence at operating with these ideas. It is within this cultural context that Jewish philosophy features in the medieval period.

What are the chief contributions of medieval Jewish philosophy to philosophy itself? Historically there are two important contributions that should be mentioned here. One is that Jewish philosophy played the role of intermediary between Islamic philosophy, and the Greek philosophy it incorporated, and the Christian world. The Jews were the intellectual intermediaries, and often the translators, who made the cultural transmission that played such an important role in the creation of the Renaissance and eventually the Enlightenment possible. Ethnic groups that are international often play this role, since they have the linguistic skills and the transnational links that make it feasible.

The other contribution is not to philosophy as a whole, but to Jewish thought. Due to the influence of Maimonides (d. 1204) philosophy really did enter the Jewish intellectual world in a firm manner, and although many Jews determinedly turned their back on this cuckoo in the nest, the status of Maimonides as a legal thinker imported philosophical ideas into Judaism, albeit rather surreptitiously, through the form of his legal ideas. And although the Jewish community throughout the world has never been large, it has had a large effect on the development of culture in general, through the overrepresentation (in relation to absolute population numbers) of Jews in public and intellectual life, so medieval Jewish philosophy has been significant in the history of ideas.

From a philosophical point of view medieval Jewish philosophy is based on two main principles. Neither principle is original to it, but became definitive. The first principle is that one should pay a lot of attention to the different ways of speaking and of expressing truth. That is, the rules of theology are different from the rules of political speech, and the rules of prophecy are different from the rules of philosophy. The implication of this thesis is that the idea of truth is far more complex than might appear superficially. This is not an original discovery of Jewish philosophy but comes from al-Farabi, and he developed this thesis after thinking about Aristotle. Yet it is an idea that was turned into a major theme by Maimonides and by many other Jewish thinkers.

The other main point shared by most medieval Jewish philosophers is the issue of theological realism, an issue they felt had to be addressed, and in the case of Maimonides quite decisively so. Maimonides argued against realism, interpreting (some would say reinterpreting) Scripture so that it would fit in with his naturalistic understanding of the character of the universe and its creator. It is often said that we should distinguish between Maimonides the philosopher and Maimonides the Jewish thinker, but nothing could be further from the truth. His philosophical attention is directed almost exclusively on the texts of Judaism, and his religious works are replete with his philosophical views. The challenge of medieval Jewish philosophy is whether a role can be found for God that makes a real difference or whether the name "God" is merely a way of referring to a range of natural events and their organization that has no place for the autonomy of a particular individual.

Linked to this issue, and often less directly addressed, is the significance of being a member of a particular religion, in this case the Jewish religion. Does being Jewish make a real difference, or is it as Christians and Muslims claim stubbornly resisting later revelations that incorporate Judaism and make Judaism redundant? This is a related topic since it might be argued that if there were no real difference between the Jewish understanding of the facts that underlie reality and the interpretation of other faiths, since realism in theology is ruled out, then the point of adhering to a particular faith is difficult to grasp. After all, it is not as though that faith represents the facts accurately, as compared with other competing faiths. On the contrary, we are told that the facts themselves are not important, what is important is what is made of them. This was taken up enthusiastically by Maimonides' opponents, who suggested that, if Maimonides were right in his interpretation of the Bible, then one might as well change from being Jewish when this became inconvenient. After all, being Jewish is just seeing the world from a particular point of view, and if that point of view is not solidly based on fact, more solidly based than other points of view, then one might as well abandon Judaism if being Jewish is no longer propitious. As we know, many Jews then and indeed today follow the logic of this to abandon their religion, although they find it much harder to change their ethnicity. This argument for conversion is certainly not one Maimonides himself adopted; on the contrary he argued for the preservation of one's faith regardless of the political and personal consequences. But it is an implication of much of his metaphysical system that this is at the very least a question that demands to be asked. What distinguishes being Jewish from adhering to a different religion is the character of Judaism, its many excellences, and its important role in the history of the world, but not for Maimonides a particularly close connection with the truth. This rather subtle argument for a faith, based on its internal rather than external features, did not find universal favor in the Jewish intellectual community, but again it set an agenda, and the question of the grounds of faith had to be discussed and defended in one way or another.

Perhaps a more minor offshoot of this theme was the discussion as to whether there are principles of Judaism, something that came to be energetically argued since the Middle Ages. Given his orientation towards the coherence of Judaism it is hardly surprising that Maimonides stressed the significance of what he took to be the central principles of the faith (and indeed these have entered the liturgy of the synagogue through the hymn "Yigdal elohim hai"). Although this issue is certainly mentioned in earlier rabbinic literature, it was possibly the frenetic marketplace in conversions that led to the need to define the bases of Judaism, so that potential waverers would know what the principles of their faith were and thus how they could defend the faith more efficiently.

This brings out a feature of philosophy of which we should remain constantly aware, and that is how different its pursuit was in the Middle Ages than is the case today. Philosophy was not an academic discipline alongside other disciplines to be chosen or not by a variety of students. It was a set of doctrines, and most importantly techniques, that were intimately tied in with natural science, theology, law, medicine, and intellectual life in general. Thinkers could reject philosophy, but to reject it they had to use it to show why it should be set aside, something with which we are familiar in Islamic philosophy in the cases of al-Ghazali and Ibn Taymiyya. Philosophy was part and parcel of the increasingly desperate attempts of Islam and Christianity to overwhelm and incorporate the Jewish remnant into their ranks, and became a part of the resistance also. After all, philosophy represents at its purest the rules of argument, and these were vital in the conversion process. (One might be cynical and suggest that most conversions had nothing to do with argument, but were either due to compulsion or to the perceived self-interest of the target group itself. On the other hand, from historical reports it seems that great attention was paid to producing strong arguments for one faith and against others, so one must assume that argument played more than just a cosmetic part in the process.) Argument remains significant for any individual who is aware of a variety of possible interpretations of the facts and the texts that represent those facts, and the increasing sophistication of the Jewish community led to its inevitable involvement in the study of the principles of interpretation themselves. There is a lot of evidence that, even in the rabbinic literature of the Talmud and Mishnah, Greek philosophy plays a role. It is hardly surprising in the Middle Ages, when philosophy came to take on such a large role in intellectual life as a whole, that Greek-inspired thought should come to have an important place again in the Jewish community.

Let us now consider some of the strategies that were employed in dealing with these key issues, and the implications of those strategies.

THE SIGNIFICANCE OF TECHNIQUE

When philosophy first entered the Islamic world in the ninth century, a debate arose about the respective merits of Greek-inspired thought versus the local Arabic disciplines of grammar, law, theology, and the other Islamic sciences. This debate would have been familiar to Plato, who saw himself as part of a struggle against the sophists in the Greek world. The sophists also thought that they had available to themselves a range of techniques that were appropriate for settling any theoretical and indeed practical issues that might arise. And the advantage of these techniques, of course, is that they were local, they were part and parcel of the local culture and so embodied the view of that culture on any problems that arose. Now, there is a great temptation within any culture to come to such a view, and the temptation certainly arose within Jewish culture, which also had an extensive and rich tradition of religious sciences and techniques to resolve any and every problem as it arose. In fact, when one looks at the Talmud one sees discussions of problems that reflect issues of relevance when the Temple was operating! So the idea that the local theological sources of understanding how to behave and act, and generally how to understand the world around us, are insufficient for the tasks at hand seemed wrong to many Jews, as it had to many Muslims, and no doubt to many Greeks also.

To naturalize philosophy a number of approaches may be adopted. One is to claim that philosophy is in fact the descendant of religion, and there were stories to that effect, although it is difficult to know how seriously they were expected to be taken. The more plausible approach is to show how valuable philosophy is when applied to religious and other issues, since philosophy is capable of distinguishing clearly between different ways of looking at an issue and adjudicating between those ways. Now, when one looks at religious texts this is far from the case. When one looks at the Talmud, for instance, it is often very difficult to tell what view is the view one should accept or that has the greater plausibility. That is one of the delights of Talmud, that one may construct a wildly unlikely argument out of the sources available in the text, and other sources one may argue are linked to the text, and construct a thesis that at the same time looks as though it should be accepted while obviously being unacceptable. It is just this sort of approach that philosophy will attack, since it will link texts to each other not in terms of weak connectors such as allusion, analogy, and propinquity between passages, but between the logical relationships between terms. It was this conceptual strength of philosophy that made it so significant in various cultures despite its apparent foreignness and the potential danger of allowing rationality to peer into areas that might be better left in the dark, in the view of many. Like Pandora's box, once the ideas are out in the open, it is difficult if not impossible to put them back again, and this happened with philosophy. Once the ideas are out, the only way of getting them back is to use other ideas to carry out the operation, which defeats the whole purpose of the exercise.

The realization that there are many different kinds of writing, and so different techniques need to be applied to assess them, is of major importance. It implies that there is a range of ways of expressing the truth, and that it is only if one understands the range that one will grasp the nature of the different forms of expression. This point was emphasized by Aristotle, and taken up with alacrity in Islamic philosophy by al-Farabi, whose works were much admired by Jewish philosophers, and especially by Maimonides. When the latter goes through the terms in the Torah that he finds problematic and then analyzes them in accordance with his theory of naturalism, he has to explain why the Torah uses words that imply that God is a person and that he is literally an agent. He suggests that these different forms of expression are there to represent truths vividly to an audience that on the whole is not able to recognize those truths unless they are represented imaginatively and figuratively. There is nothing wrong with presenting the truths in this way; on the contrary, this is the right way to present them to a general audience. It follows that the language in the prayer book, and by commentators in the rabbinic literature, replicates this sort of language, although often with greater sophistication, and the more one studies it the more one appreciates the variety one finds within it. This enables the intelligent reader to ask questions about what is not said as well as about what is said. For example, Maimonides thinks it is significant that in the book of Job, Job himself is never called "wise," which Maimonides argues is a signal to readers that he is not taken to be wise, and so his early complaints are to be seen as a reflection of his lack of wisdom. The question then arises: If Job is to be seen as not wise, why did not the text make this clear? Perhaps because his words are not to be seen as so obviously foolish that they are not worth considering. Indeed, they are worth thinking about like everything else in the Bible, but the more alert reader will understand that the intelligence of Job's critique of divine justice masks the underlying shallowness of his presupposition, that God's justice must replicate our notion of justice. This approach to the text, whatever one thinks about its credibility in this particular instance, has radical implications for how to look at texts as a whole. It was not present in any definite way before Maimonides, but it became a firm part of the agenda of Jewish philosophy ever since his works became well known and influential.

THE SCOPE OF THEOLOGICAL REALISM

Maimonides also played a decisive role in placing the topic of theological realism firmly on the philosophical and rabbinic agenda. This is because he was the first Jewish philosopher to grasp completely the implication of philosophy as part of an understanding of religion. The idea that religion is true because it represents the truth is not acceptable in that form once it is analyzed philosophically, although of course it may be accepted once it is examined by the appropriate philosophical conceptual machinery. The point is that the appropriate understanding of such claims is not one that can be ignored or regarded as unproblematic, but as one that must be investigated and resolved in some way. Yet the Torah itself does not display much doubt about the truth of the claim of realism. On the contrary, it constantly reiterates the literal truth of what it describes. It is first of all the rabbinic commentaries and then the philosophers who start to investigate what these claims actually mean, who point to apparent inconsistencies and who ask for explanations of the precise formulation of the religious texts. This is obviously linked to the first item on the philosophical agenda, the discussion of different kinds of literary expression in the Torah, but the realism issue was much discussed even before Maimonides took such control of the discipline. One tends to link the issue with him because it was only his *Guide* and other related works that provided Jewish philosophy with the technical resources to deal with the issue in a decisive sort of way. Maimonides did set off the debate in a new and far more nuanced manner, and it has remained ever since firmly part of the Jewish intellectual curriculum. (One might even say that it is not mere chance that such a large proportion of the protagonists of postmodernism and deconstructionism are Jewish!)

THE "WHY BE JEWISH?" DEBATE

This was the issue that really resonated with the lives of all Jews during the Middle Ages. They were under sustained pressure to convert, by both Muslims and Christians, and even in Spain this was hardly a Golden Age. Even after conversion their loyalty to their new faith remained suspect for some time in Christian Europe. Most Jews probably made their decision on what to do on purely prudential reasons (if they converted) or in order to remain within the faith with which they were familiar (if they did not). Argument played little part in the decision, but argument was undoubtedly important for the intellectual elite in the community who were troubled not only by the strength of competing faiths, but also by the apparent conceptual difficulties of traditional religion when it comes into apparent conflict with modernity, with science, and philosophy. (This was a pressure that of course was also felt by Christians and Muslims, but in most cases without the additional pressure to convert.) The attack on realism by Maimonides makes the conversion question harder to resist, in some ways, given that the only things to be said in favor of one religion are internal features, which might be thought to be a rather unrobust response to the enemies of one's faith.

HOW NOT TO ARGUE FOR THE DISTINCTIVENESS OF MEDIEVAL JEWISH PHILOSOPHY

A good example of the sort of argument in support of the distinctiveness of medieval Jewish philosophy is the discussion of the popularity in Jewish philosophy of Plato's *Republic*, as compared with Aristotle's *Politics*. Despite the (late) encroachment of Scholastic philosophy into the Jewish world, there seems to have been little enthusiasm for works on political philosophy that made a sharp demarcation between the theological and the political, as characterized in the Christian tradition by the enthusiasm for Aristotle's *Politics* and by works such as Dante's *On Monarchy*, Hobbes' *Leviathan*, and Machiavelli's *Prince*. It is sometimes argued that the difference between Christianity, on the one hand, and Judaism and Islam on the other, is that the former made a separation between law and religion, between the state and God, while the other religions did not. However, Christianity also sees the state as an appropriate site for religious influence, and in that sense is not less holistic than Judaism and Islam. It is certainly true, though, that the concept of political revelation, so important in the latter pair, is largely absent in Christianity, which accordingly developed a rather secular notion of the state. Christian thinkers went on to present accounts of the state that are discussions and descriptions of actual states divorced from any particular theological background, while Judaism and Islam saw political philosophy as very much part of jurisprudence, as part and parcel of the explanation of why and how religious law structures the everyday lives of its participants. One effect of this distinction is that the Christian world got on very well without the *Republic* until the early Renaissance, while the Jewish and Islamic world ignored Aristotle's *Politics*. By contrast, the *Nicomachean Ethics* found a ready home in the Jewish and Islamic world, which often saw it as the prelude to the *Republic,* standing in as it did for the missing *Politics*. Christianity, it is argued, saw the temporal state as merely a prelude to the next life, and so the arrangements in this world are of no great salvific significance. For Judaism and Islam, though, the actual state is the site of God's influence in the world, and it is incumbent on the believer to work within that state and try to bring it close to divine law. As there are no priests in (post-Temple) Judaism to embody spiritual purity, such purity becomes part of the community and part of the task of the community. In this way political and religious life form a seamless web, and there is nothing in principle to prevent the spiritual leader from being the political leader, and in fact it is highly desirable that he is! The emphasis on practice in Judaism meant that God could not be worshiped merely as an idea or concept abstracted from everyday life. There has to be some route to understanding him if we are to imitate him, and that route comes through political life.

One impact of the *Republic* in early Jewish philosophy could be the construction of the persona of the "king" as both the intellectual and political head of the state, a concept we find in both Saadya Gaon (d. 942) and Halevi (d. 1141). The latter argues that such a king would choose Judaism as the best religion since it combines most acceptably the theoretical and the political, and contrasts markedly with other religions such as Christianity that only address themselves to a limited part of our lives as human beings. This is very much taken up by Maimonides himself who compared *nomos* (custom) and Shariʿa/Torah (religious law) by claiming that the former is directed exclusively to our physical being, while the latter is directed both at this and at our spiritual being. One might contrast this with theories that would regard the spiritual as the only important part of us. One of the reasons why this law can do both is because of the way it has been devised, namely, to appeal both to our everyday interests and to guide and extend them until we are well on the route to self-perfection. The ruler has a vital role as educator here, something that of course is part of the *Republic*, and one of the leading reasons for the ruler's ability to move people emotionally and physically is his capacity to understand how to talk to them, how to inspire them, and make them feel that, although they only understand part of the whole, there is a whole that their actions are working to establish and that is ultimately in their best interests, even though they may not understand why or how. Yet we should observe that the arguments for Judaism here as elsewhere are not based on its truth, but on its internal characteristics, and it could be argued that this orientation of medieval Jewish philosophy came to characterize much Jewish philosophy that followed, and indeed had a wider influence in philosophy and theology also.

2 The biblical and rabbinic background to medieval Jewish philosophy*

Medieval Jewish philosophy is in large measure an interpretation in philosophical terms of beliefs, concepts, and texts bequeathed to medieval Jews by the Bible and by rabbinic literature. Thus, much of the agenda of medieval Jewish philosophy is set by ideas featured in the Bible, Talmud, and midrash: God, creation, prophecy, providence, miracles, commandments, and more. For this reason, although there is a need here to present the biblical and rabbinic background to medieval Jewish philosophy, the discussion will largely be an exposition of one aspect of medieval Jewish philosophy itself: namely, its ambition to provide an exegesis of biblical and rabbinic texts, along with explications of their concepts, that would demonstrate the value of philosophy in earlier Judaism and would unearth rigorous philosophical propositions contained in the ancient works.

Examples abound. Saadya Gaon (882–942), head of the academy in Babylonia and the father of medieval Jewish philosophy, and Levi ben Gershom (Gersonides) (1288–1344), an eminent philosopher, logician, and scientist, authored biblical commentaries – Gersonides' cover a very substantial part of the Bible – that are controlled by a view of the book as shot through with philosophical truth and as standing in agreement with the conclusions of human reason. While the less illustrious rationalist Joseph ibn Kaspi (1279–1340) authored a commentary on the Bible that is controlled not by the assumption of an underlying philosophical truth, but instead by a historicist view, he is an exception among medieval rationalists.[1] Exegesis, furthermore, is found not only in formal commentaries

---

* I thank David Berger, Shalom Carmy, and Warren Zev Harvey for commenting on an earlier draft of this chapter.

but also in works that aim to develop philosophical positions. Moses Maimonides (1138–1204), the greatest of the medieval Jewish thinkers, describes the aim of his *Guide of the Perplexed* as the interpretation of problematic biblical terms and parables, and he supplies in the book's first part a philosophical lexicon of biblical terms. He also informs us in the work's introduction that he considered authoring a commentary on problematic rabbinic texts. Likewise, works by the Neoplatonist Solomon ibn Gabirol, Abraham ibn Daud, Abraham bar Hiyya, Bahya ibn Paquda, and Joseph Albo weave together exegesis and philosophy; and commentators like David Kimhi, Moses Nahmanides, and Isaac Abravanel incorporate elements of philosophy (reflecting in particular knowledge of the Maimonidean matrix), even while refusing to accord it supremacy as a method for acquiring true knowledge. Medieval Jewish philosophers also adduce and interpret a substantial number of rabbinic texts.

In brief, had there been no Bible and rabbinic literature to supply core concepts and to serve as a focus for exegetical activity, medieval Jewish philosophy would either not have existed at all or would have been dramatically different in character from what it actually was. Notwithstanding this dependency, a frequently noted feature of medieval Jewish philosophy is its prima facie lack of continuity with biblical and rabbinic Judaism; its closest analogues, it seems, are works produced by Jews in Hellenistic cultures of the first and second centuries. The medieval philosophers, as mentioned, understood both the Bible and the rabbinic corpus as a repository of philosophical and scientific truths. But the philosophical views advocated by the medieval philosophers entered Judaism via contact between Jews and other cultures: from the early tenth through late twelfth centuries, contact with Islamic civilization in Spain; from the late twelfth through early sixteenth centuries, contact with Christian culture by Jews in Christian Spain, Provence, and Italy. After their extended conquests beginning with the seventh century, the Muslims translated works of Greek philosophy, composed commentaries on them, and developed their own philosophical-theological systems with categories and principles that originated with the Greeks. (Some works of Plotinus were mistakenly attributed to Aristotle, leading to a hybrid known as Neoplatonized Aristotelianism.) Jews familiar with Islamic thought admired and appropriated many of these categories and principles. The resultant views, however, do not seem to be characteristic of either biblical or rabbinic thought.

First and foremost among the ostensible differences is the presence of anthropomorphic and anthropopathic language in biblical and rabbinic texts. The texts ascribe bodily characteristics, emotions, and personality to God; he has physical form, affect, and personality.[2] Yet philosophers held that God cannot have a body and that having emotions would be inconsistent with his changeless and self-sufficient nature. Next, traditional Judaism taught that the world was created *ex nihilo*; the Greeks denied that: Aristotle held the world was eternal, Plato that it was made by the demiurge from preexistent matter. Again, in the Bible and rabbinic literature divine intervention in the world is frequent, but philosophers believed in a mostly or totally naturalistic system. Prophecy in the Bible would seem to be a direct communication from God to a human being; philosophers thought that prophecy is a natural result of perfecting the intellect and imagination. The human ideal in the traditional texts would seem to be a life of right action, as in Jeremiah 9:22–23; for the philosophers, the *summum bonum* is intellectual contemplation of scientific and metaphysical truths, and Jeremiah 9:22–23 is invoked to support this claim.[3] Rabbinic Judaism puts forth a doctrine of bodily resurrection; philosophers, owing to their devaluation of the body and their reluctance to posit miracles, endorse the immortality of the soul, while often remaining ambiguous at best about resurrection of the body. The philosopher's emphasis on critical rational inquiry, finally, reflects a method of acquiring truth that is quite different from an appeal to revelation and authority. Given these conflicts, medieval attempts at harmony seem strained.

Notwithstanding this ostensible absence of continuity, medieval Jewish philosophers vigorously affirmed its existence. They explained that the original philosophical content of Torah was lost through centuries of persecution. Maimonides maintains that the tradition's having been passed down only orally made it vulnerable to such loss, and this seems to propel him to write the truth down – just as the Talmud relates that Rabbi Judah the Prince (in 200 CE) compiled the body of teaching known as the Mishnah because in his time the oral legal tradition was in danger of being forgotten (*Guide* 1:71, 2:11). Some Jews, such as Shem Tov ibn Falaquera (*Book of Degrees*, introduction), went so far as to say that the non-Jewish world learned or even stole philosophy from the Jews, necessitating now Jewish reliance upon non-Jewish philosophers.[4] Invoking an ancient tradition was a means of legitimating philosophical study. Even Judah Halevi (d. 1141), whose *Kuzari* is an extended polemic against grounding a Jewish religious outlook in Greek philosophy rather than tradition, states that the Greeks received philosophy from the Persians, who took it from the Chaldeans (*Kuzari* 1:63). Viewing them as authentic components of Jewish belief, he endorses numerous of the claims and assumptions of the philosophers' metaphysical schemes. In short, the medieval Jewish philosophers present themselves as champions, continuators, or one might even say resurrecters of the true biblical and rabbinic traditions.

Such claims of continuity have seemed implausible to modern scholars, so much so that, in contrast to medieval interpreters, some even doubt Maimonides' sincerity in putting them forth.[5] Arguably these modern scholars have underestimated the degree to which Maimonides and, even more evidently, Saadya and Gersonides pursued their projects out of a conviction of Torah's truth. Scholars have not doubted the sincerity of the latter two, which implies that it was possible for an interpreter not to be conscious of a gap. Medieval philosophers could not help appreciating the general richness of Islamic culture, and because they regarded the philosophers' systems as true, they understandably wanted to see their religion embrace these truths.[6] It is precisely their fidelity to the truth of Torah, not their disloyalty, that propelled the medievals' project, inducing them to interpret Torah in a way that would make its claims always emerge as true, an extreme illustration of what analytic philosophers such as W. V. O. Quine and Donald Davidson today call the Principle of Interpretive Charity.[7] Modern writers tend to share Spinoza's view in the *Theologico-Political Treatise* (ch. 2) that the prophets were neither scientists nor philosophers, and they impute that view anachronistically to Spinoza's predecessors. We can appreciate the gap whose existence propels the charge of insincerity, but ultimately the assumptions of earlier interpreters cannot be judged by the premises of readers a millennium later. In fact, ours is an age that is more conscious and more approving than any other of the role that background beliefs play in the hermeneutical enterprise, and to that extent the cited criticism itself is out of tenor with today's times.

Perhaps more critically, the notion of *sitrei Torah* (hidden aspects of Torah that should not be publicized) was promulgated by the rabbis themselves (Mishnah *Hagigah* 2:1); and they comment on the value of riddles and parables (for example, "Great is the power of the prophets because they compare a created thing to its creator," i.e. they describe God in anthropomorphic terms [*Genesis Rabbah* 26, cited by Maimonides, *Guide*, 1:46]). Finally, it should be noted that a philosophically laden reading of a text may well have its roots in rabbinic midrashim, and Maimonides not infrequently cites such a source.[8] In what follows I shall elaborate on the general approach to biblical and rabbinic literature on the part of the medievals, note some attitudes toward the continuity problem, and give a sampling, hopefully not random, of how they interpreted key texts of the tradition. Due to limitations of space I shall deal exclusively with medieval rationalism, leaving aside, save for brief references, exegetical approaches of Neoplatonists like Gabirol as well as of kabbalists like Nahmanides who, for example, interpret the creation narrative in Genesis 1 in accordance with their own metaphysical opinions. Insofar as Maimonides bestrides the medieval world like a colossus, his approach to interpretation is the one to which I will refer most often.

PHILOSOPHIC EXEGESIS OF THE BIBLE

The key to the medieval philosophical approach to biblical and rabbinic texts is the notion of a two-layered text: one outer, exoteric, geared to the multitude; the other inner, hidden, esoteric, aimed at the philosopher. The task of the philosophical exegete is to pierce through the exoteric layer, whose truth is either unacceptable or inferior, and get at the rich esoteric truth. So, while resisting total allegorization of the stories and laws in the Bible, medieval Jewish philosophers understand the vision of the wheels, angels, and chariots in Ezekiel 1 and 10 to present an Aristotelian-cum-Neoplatonic cosmology. Similarly, Maimonides and Gersonides find the characters in Job to be espousing positions held by the great philosophical schools like those of Epicurus and Aristotle. The love between a man and a woman depicted in Song of Songs, construed by the sages and, in more systematic fashion, Rashi and Ibn Ezra, as a *mashal* (parable) for the mutual love between God (anthropopathically depicted) and

Israel, becomes for Maimonides a model for the individual's intellectual love of God (*Mishneh Torah*, Laws of Repentance 10:6), and
for Gersonides a dialogue between the passive and active intellects.
"God created man in His image [*tzelem*]" (Genesis 1:27) becomes
a way of saying that the form or essence of the human being is,
like God's essence, intellect; the elements described in Genesis 1:2
are none other than the four elements of Greek cosmology; King
Solomon's proverbs about a seductress become a depiction of the
harm matter wreaks upon the intellect, while Proverbs 31 is taken
to express how rare it is for a person to find the "woman of valor" –
matter that will not corrupt him. Adam's sinning at Eve's suggestion
represents form's being brought down by the seductive attractions
of matter; Jacob's dream of angels ascending and descending a ladder
and God speaking to him represents the prophets and the separate
intellects (*Guide* 1:15). Gersonides read into the *Aqedah* (the binding of Isaac, Genesis 22) his controversial denial that God knows
future contingents. Figures like Abraham and Moses are represented
by medieval philosophical exegetes as philosopher-scientists. "You
shall love the Lord your God" (Deuteronomy 6:5) and "You should
know this day and commit to your heart that the Lord is God..."
(Deuteronomy 4:39) are construed as calls to study philosophy and
science.

The simplicity of the idea of a two-layered text is seductive and
masks significant ambiguities. Does the exoteric layer have value,
and if so, in what does that value consist? Why does the exoteric
layer exist at all? Our formulation also conceals the fact that almost
side by side with the notion of a two-layered text we find the thesis
that in some cases there is but one layer, whose only true meaning in
the context is philosophical. I proceed to elaborate on these issues,
beginning with the question of why the exoteric layer exists at all –
why the Bible does not state philosophic truth directly and explicitly.

"The Torah Speaks in the Language of Humans"

Beginning with the geonim, Babylonian authorities of eighth–tenth-
century Babylonia, medieval Jewish philosophers are wont to cite the
talmudic dictum, "the Torah speaks in the language of *benei adam*,
human beings" (*Sifre*, Numbers 112; Babylonian Talmud, *Yevamot*
71a). They maintain that anthropomorphic and anthropopathic

verses are used because the masses need concrete, visual images to think about theology (*Guide* 1:26, 48). Picturesque language makes for good pedagogy. Further, the stories of God's providence and the ascription to him of emotions like anger and love are politically useful: they will induce the simpleminded masses to be obedient and will promote social order (*Guide* 3:28). Finally, were the masses taught the truth they would think it undermines Scripture and might reject Scripture as a source of truth (Maimonides, *Commentary to the Mishnah, Hagigah* 2:1). Maimonides adopts a more precise understanding of "the Torah speaks in the language of man" when he declares that the term "adam" (man or human), in one of its meanings, refers to the multitude, the philosophically ignorant (*Guide* 1:14). The Torah, the great teacher, is addressed to the community and must serve even its lowest intellectual rung.[9]

Interestingly, the rationalists' use of the phrase "the Torah speaks in the language of human beings" to guide philosophic reinterpretation of Scripture, is itself an example of their highly creative deployment of texts. In the original talmudic context of "the Torah speaks in the language of human beings," Rabbi Akiva and Rabbi Ishmael (second century CE) are debating a point about legal contexts in the Bible. At issue is whether in such contexts the Bible's repetition of a term – a doubling of a verb, for example – should be used to derive a new legal conclusion that is not explicit in the biblical text. Whereas Rabbi Akiva regularly derives laws in this way, Rabbi Ishmael, following his teacher Rabbi Elazar ben Azaryah, states, "the Torah speaks in the language of human beings" – meaning (roughly), do not make such inferences, for the Torah merely uses the device of repetition for stylistic emphasis or ornamentation. When medieval rationalists apply Rabbi Ishmael's phrase to theological expressions rather than legal ones, or perhaps more accurately, in addition to them, and to features of verses other than repetition, they are extending it beyond its original scope. Notice, moreover, that Rabbi Ishmael is prescribing a conservative approach to exegesis, limiting our right to derive ideas that are not explicit in the text; in the hands of Saadya Gaon or Maimonides the phrase becomes the opposite (albeit without an implication this was the original meaning): a license for creating new interpretations of the Bible's anthropomorphic and anthropopathic descriptions.[10] Interpretations that deviate from the plain meanings of verses are common among the rabbis of the Talmud, and it is interesting that medieval Jewish philosophers saw their own method of reinterpretation as duplicating the sages', even as the latter's use of figurative language emulates the Bible's. Notably, some philosophers regarded at least some of the sages' *midreshei halakhah*, interpretations that carry legal consequences, as ornamental props or supports rather than actual meanings, but their philosophical readings of the Bible were not qualified in this way.

The Bible's communicative strategy as seen by the rationalists should be understood in terms of a theory of prophecy formulated by the Islamic philosopher al-Farabi (d. 950), an important influence on Maimonides.[11] Al-Farabi maintained that philosophy precedes religion temporally. The prophet is someone who has passed through the stage of philosophy and now exercises his faculty of imagination – the faculty that receives visual images and creates mental pictures and symbols – in order to translate these truths from abstract to concrete terms, from philosophical propositions to metaphors and parables. Prophecy is thus the apprehension and imaginative translation of philosophical truth, and the formulations of the prophets in the Bible express the scientific and philosophic truths the latter have attained. Maimonides appropriated al-Farabi's views on prophecy, and it is this concept of prophecy that guides his understanding of biblical texts. (Some interpreters believe that the symbols are needed not only for communication to the masses but for the prophet's own apprehension.)

By appraising the exoteric layer as a sop to the masses, the "language of humans" model gives little credit to that exoteric layer as a source of truth, except to the extent that it implies general ideas like the existence of God and the operation of providence. There is, however, another model of the multiple layers to consider, one featured in Maimonides' introduction to The Guide of the Perplexed: "apples of gold in filigrees of silver is a word fitly spoken" (Proverbs 25:11). Maimonides has in mind parables, of the kind King Solomon presents in the biblical book of Proverbs. A saying uttered with two meanings – an exoteric and an esoteric – is like an apple of gold overlaid with small holes, as in filigree work, through which one can glimpse the inner deeper meaning. In this imagery the external meaning of a figure of speech or parable is valuable like silver, and is not a mere concession to the multitude, devoid of intrinsic merit.

Still, this is not to say that the outer layer conveys truth. Rather, Maimonides implies that the outer meaning contains wisdom that is politically useful, conducing to an ordered society; the inner meaning, in contrast, contains "wisdom that is useful for beliefs concerned with the truth as it is."[12]

Besides the "language of humans" and "filigrees of silver" assessments of the exoteric layer, there is yet a third approach to the text, one that at least implicitly denies that we always have two layers in texts that trouble the philosopher. In the early chapters of the *Guide*, the lexicographic chapters, Maimonides shows that specific terms which people tend to construe as anthropomorphic or anthropopathic in truth have multiple meanings that vary according to context. And here is the rub: the correct, literal meaning of such supposedly anthropomorphic and anthropopathic expressions is in their context, that is, given the subject of which those terms are predicated, non-anthropomorphic and non-anthropopathic. The term applied to God is "borrowed" from another context, in this case the human one, but its meaning is adjusted in accordance with the difference in the subject of predication. For example, when predicated of God, "standing" means "permanent" and enduring, "sitting" means changeless (when God is said to "sit for all eternity"). (This method is known in Hebrew as *hash'alah*, borrowing a term, in contrast to *mashal* or parable.[13]) Maimonides uses this type of interpretation when he depicts the activity of the Targumim, to be discussed shortly: he hints that their (allegedly) anti-anthropomorphic renditions are simply the result of a good understanding of Hebrew.

In most cases of *mashal*, according to Maimonides, the *mashal* is not fully allegorical, that is, not every word is to be assigned either a figurative or a "borrowed" meaning. Rather, in most cases, many of the terms in the parable serve only to embellish the *mashal*. When Solomon describes at length a married harlot who is supposed to represent matter (Proverbs 7), most of the specifics supplied are simply descriptions of a harlot rather than figurative allusions to specific features of matter. And in the book of Job many details are needed just to flesh out the plot line. Departing from the usual interpretation of Song of Songs, Maimonides did not think that the details had to be interpreted figuratively; it was enough for the book to depict a man and woman in love in the ways characteristic of wooing.

Allegorization carries dangers. If not held in check, it can lead to radical assertions, even heresies. For this reason medieval philosophers usually cautioned that figurative interpretations of Scripture are not to be adopted unless a specific reason exists to depart from the literal meaning of a verse. Saadya Gaon identifies four such cases: the literal reading yields a thesis contrary to reason, which means its falsehood is subject to demonstration; it contradicts human experience; it contravenes accepted tradition; or it contradicts other verses (*Book of Doctrines and Beliefs*, 7:2). Maimonides furnishes a nuanced example of how conflict between Scripture and reason should be approached. He presents three possible views of the origin of the world: creation *ex nihilo* (the Torah view); made from preexistent eternal matter (Plato); eternal (Aristotle). The scriptural text, he says, could be read either literally as creation *ex nihilo* or figuratively to accord with a Platonic or Aristotelian view – the "gates of figurative interpretation" are not "shut in our faces." But, unlike the case of anthropomorphic language, there is no adequate philosophical reason to depart from literalism, no demonstration of a different side; if there were, a figurative interpretation could be accepted. Maimonides imposes a further restriction: any interpretation that would deny the possibility of miracles must be rejected – and that means that Aristotle's view could never supply the proper interpretation.

Notwithstanding Maimonides' insistence on the unacceptability of Aristotle's view, medieval philosophers arguably did not treat satisfactorily the question of just where the line should be drawn between admissible and inadmissible interpretations. Interpreters of Maimonides have long suspected he secretly endorsed Aristotle's view, or, alternatively, that secretly he felt Aristotle's view was compatible with Torah; these secret beliefs would be proof for some that the figurative method is too liberal. There is a radical strain of biblical interpretation in medieval philosophy. Gersonides claimed that the Platonic view could be demonstrated, and that Genesis 1 was best read in line with this view, even on the literal level. Other radical readers include Samuel ibn Tibbon, Rabbi Nissim of Marseilles and Joseph ibn Kaspi. Against philosophical readings of Scripture, Yitzhak Arama raised the criticism that the rationalists do not learn anything from the biblical text itself. They accept only

those propositions that accord with philosophy and interpret figuratively those that do not, so what they knew after the revelation is identical with what they knew before, and revelation teaches
nothing.

Worthy of mention as well is the question: If the Torah is allegorical, why should Jews not allegorize the laws as well as the narratives? This antinomian argument was frequently brought up in
Jewish–Christian polemics.

The Question of Precedent

The notion of a two-layered text and the use of allegorical interpretation is found abundantly in Christian thought, most notably in
Augustine, and the idea of a two-layered text was championed by
Muslim thinkers as well, notably Averroes. But is there precedent in
premedieval Judaism for interpreting biblical texts as metaphors or
parables?

Various midrashim are fairly categorized as allegorical and thus afford a precedent, as when "the earth was *tohu va-vohu* [unformed]"
in Genesis 1:2 is explained by the midrash as referring to foreign
powers and the deeds of the wicked. In addition, Aristobulus in
the second century BCE interpreted references to God's body as referring to noncorporeal things (hand–power; standing–permanence;
descending–revelation; speech–establishing of things). Nevertheless,
the founding of a systematic Jewish figurative interpretation of Scripture based on philosophy is usually credited to Philo of Alexandria
(c. 20 BCE–50 CE). Philo understood the Bible, particularly Genesis,
as Greek philosophers troubled by Homer's gods understood Homer:
as an allegory to be construed via the principles of Hellenistic
thought, in his case middle Platonic thought in particular. So, for example, Philo's reading of Genesis adapts Plato's account of creation
in the *Timaeus* and states that God's first creation was the Ideas
(Forms). Different biblical characters represent different personal
characteristics or faculties: Adam, spirituality; Eve, feeling; Noah,
righteousness. Places, animals, and plants likewise are symbols.
Philo stresses the need for human beings to break from materiality and apprehend the intelligible world. Moses, for Philo, is
a great philosopher. Philo influenced Christianity far more than
Judaism and was not known to medieval thinkers; yet medieval

Jewish philosophers accept Greek wisdom, holding many of the same views about God and the value of reason as does Philo, owing perhaps to his indirect influence.

Philo believed in the historical truth of some of the biblical stories, but viewed others as purely allegorical and non-historical. Jewish philosophers did not generally question the historicity of the biblical narratives. Still, rationalists were accused of understanding "Abraham and Sarah as matter and form, the twelve tribes as the twelve constellations, the alliance of four and five kings in Genesis 14 as the four elements and five senses, and Amalek as the evil inclination."[14] Some statements of Maimonides struck his interpreters as denying historicity and thus using allegory objectionably. Specifically, one son of Adam, Cain, is said by Maimonides to represent the acquisitive instinct, the other, Seth, intellectual attainment (*Guide* 2:30); and, as in Philo, who draws from Plato's identification of reason (form) with man and matter with woman, Adam seems to represent form (intellect), while Eve represents matter, which distracts Adam and leads to his sinning (*Guide* 1:17).

Turning now from Philo, two important figures in our context are Onkelos "the proselyte" and Yonatan ben Uziel, whom Jewish tradition views as authors of the Aramaic translations of the Bible known as Targumim. An Amoraic statement reads: "Onkelos the proselyte said the [Aramaic] translation of the Torah [Pentateuch][comes] from the mouth of R. Eliezer and R. Joshua; Yonatan ben Uziel said the translation of the books of the prophets [comes] from the mouth of [the prophets] Haggai, Zechariah, and Malakhi" (*Megillah* 3a). (Modern scholars dispute this traditional view of the Targumim's authorship.) Now according to Maimonides,

Onkelos the proselyte was very perfect in the Hebrew and Syrian languages and directed his effort toward the abolition of the belief in God's corporeality. Hence he interprets in accordance with its meaning every attribute that Scripture predicates of God and that might lead toward the belief in corporeality.

"The Lord will descend" is rendered as "the Lord will manifest himself"; "the Lord heard" as "it was heard before God and received" (*Guide* 1:47). When motion is attributed to the deity, Onkelos – according to Maimonides – attributes it to a created entity, the Shekhinah (lit. indwelling) which medieval rationalists view not as a name of God but as a term denoting a created thing, either a form (Saadya, *Doctrines and Beliefs* 2) or a created light whose presence in a place is a mark of that place's distinction (Maimonides, *Guide* 1:21).[15]

The Targumim are important for the rationalists for several reasons. First, as the quotation from *Megillah* 3a suggests, the authors of the Targumim studied with sages or even prophets. This implies that their work represents the views of the sages or prophets, and so the rationalists' modes of interpretation are not radical breaks with the past but on the contrary boast an ancient and authoritative pedigree. Second, the availability of the Targumim means that the average person from among the masses cannot justify or excuse being an anthropomorphist. Consider in particular the argument of Abraham ben David (Rabad) protesting Maimonides' categorization of an anthropomorphist as a heretic in *Mishneh Torah, Laws of Repentance* 3:7: "People greater and better than he have followed this opinion, based on what they saw in scriptural texts and in the words of the Aggadah, which corrupt opinions." Contrary to Rabad's gloss, Maimonides in the *Guide* claims that this excuse is not valid because, inter alia, the Targumim exist to dispel false notions (1:36). Finally, it is interesting that Maimonides praises Onkelos' knowledge of languages but not his knowledge of philosophy. This suggests that when Onkelos translates phrases in a non-anthropomorphic way, he is rejecting an alternative approach that would translate terms anthropomorphically but understand them non-anthropomorphically. In this formulation, even the "literal" meaning of the relevant terms is non-anthropomorphic.

Maimonides' portrait of Onkelos is energetically disputed by Moses Nahmanides (1194–1270), a major kabbalist, legal scholar, and biblical commentator. In his commentaries to Genesis 46:1 and Exodus 20:16, Nahmanides argues that, while Onkelos may remove the anthropomorphic flavor of words denoting motion and hearing, he translates terms connoting divine speech with their literal Aramaic equivalents ("God said," "God spoke," "God called"). Likewise Onkelos translates verbs connoting sight in a way that does not remove the anthropomorphism. Elsewhere Onkelos preserves in his translation biblical references to the Lord's hand and finger. Nahmanides' alternative account of Onkelos' method is obscure insofar as it is steeped in kabbalah, but his critique of Maimonides' reading of Onkelos is powerful. In addition to being denied by Nahmanides, the notion that Shekhinah refers to a created thing has been disputed by modern scholars such as Ephraim Urbach, who argue that the term does denote the presence or nearness of God.

TALMUDIC AND MIDRASHIC LITERATURE

When we turn to dicta of the sages of the talmudic-midrashic era, and more specifically to the non-legal sections of the Talmud and midrash known collectively as the Aggadah, we find on the one hand numerous elements – or at least fragments – of a theology, enough to have generated several lengthy scholarly studies of the sages' theology.[16] The impact of philosophical schools, specifically Stoicism, on rabbinic thought is evident in teachings that the soul fills and vitalizes the body as God fills the world, that all humans have is borrowed from God, that God builds and destroys worlds, and that the soul is estranged in this world. Parallels to Platonic thought include the suggestion that there is knowledge prior to birth (albeit this is knowledge of the Torah, not the Forms) and the notion that God created the world by looking into the Torah.[17] But on the other hand we find no evidence of extensive involvement with philosophy (the borrowings are from popular versions of Stoicism and Platonism), and we even encounter statements that could be construed as opposed to "Greek wisdom," "the wisdom of the nations," and "logic."[18] Unlike the case with legal idioms, there are no borrowings of philosophical vocabulary. Oddly, the rabbis record debates with non-Jews and heretics over issues like creation without adducing philosophical arguments that were used by their side.[19] As well, according to an eminent scholar of the period, "none of [the rabbinic sources] provides systematic treatment of the subject of beliefs and conceptions, and there are almost no continuous discourses dealing with a single theme."[20]

Were the rabbis not literate in philosophy? Not interested in philosophy? Were they fearful of it? Did they engage in philosophical discussion at all? Warren Zev Harvey has argued that in all likelihood when the rabbis engaged in disputes with non-Jews and heretics, some of which we are told were quite protracted, they utilized philosophical arguments. Nevertheless, in summarizing those debates in a short space, they eschewed philosophical vocabulary and argumentation. Harvey maintains further that particular views of the sages, for instance, that God builds and destroys worlds, reflect knowledge of Stoic and Epicurean views of cosmogony, even while (1) breaking from both Stoic determinism and Epicurean chance and in addition (2) asserting, unlike either of those schools, that this world will not be destroyed. Such awareness of philosophical schools was found in the land of Israel, where Hellenism flourished, but not in Babylon. Harvey suggests that the rabbis "considered philosophy to be foreign to their concerns not because they did not know what it was, but rather because they did know."[21]

Be that as it may, we must return to the challenge confronting the medieval philosophers. For all the convergence in ideas about a transcendent deity who exercises providence and gave the Torah, rabbinic views and dicta were not infrequently contrary to philosophical wisdom.

In the Aggadah, God wears phylacteries and dons a prayer shawl, roars like a lion yet also sheds tears, studies Torah, and suffers over the tribulations of Israel that he brought on, sharing in their exile (see *Avodah Zarah* 3b, *Berakhot* 9b, *Sifre be-Midbar* 84). At times a seemingly anthropomorphic theology even influences law, or at least the rabbis' understanding of it. A person blind in one eye need not make the festival pilgrimage, because just as the man who comes to the holy place must be seen by God with two eyes, so must he see God with two eyes (*Hagigah* 2a). Again, when the Bible prescribes that the body of a criminal executed by hanging must be buried before sunset (Deuteronomy 22:21), the rabbis explain that the law's purpose is to prevent people from thinking that the king himself is hanging instead of his twin (*Sanhedrin* 46b). Philosophy seems not to be a valuable objective: the statement "the holy one has nothing in his world but the four ells of halakhah [Jewish law]" (*Berakhot* 8a) prima facie cuts against the rationalist claim that non-legal disciplines such as science and philosophy represent, as per Aristotle, the highest human achievement. As a corollary, the motifs of Israel's election and the need for *mitzvot*, salient in biblical and rabbinic thought, are problematic for the philosopher who stresses scientific and philosophical pursuits that cut across ethnic and religious divisions.

Critics of rabbinic Judaism – from Karaites, to Christians and Moslem polemicists, to skeptical thinkers from within – assailed rabbinic thought as absurd and, as in the case of anthropomorphism, even blasphemous.[22] The philosophical problems in the Aggadah led the geonim to pioneer two distinct approaches vis-à-vis the rabbinic statements: rejection and reinterpretation. The first was used by Hai Gaon and Sherira Gaon on a limited basis,[23] and much later was employed by Nahmanides when he needed to rebut allegations of a Christian interlocutor in a public disputation. Citing his father, Abraham Maimonides endorses occasional rejection of Aggadot. Rabbinic dicta are not the product of prophecy as biblical teachings are, and rejection is therefore more of an option.[24]

That said, the second approach – reinterpreting problematic statements to protect the view of the sages as wise men – seemed more desirable. Like the Bible, the rabbis were said (Abraham bar Hiyya being perhaps the first to claim this) to speak in the language of human beings. They used symbols and stories in figurative fashion, and at times anthropomorphic depictions of God were mere descriptions of scenes and objects beheld in a vision. In his introduction to his commentary to ch. 10 of *Mishnah Sanhedrin*, Maimonides alleges that scientifically knowledgeable people who take the sages' problematic statements literally, and on that basis reject those statements, lack an understanding of pedagogy. Teaching difficult matters must proceed through parables and other figurative techniques. Although Maimonides, as noted earlier, gave up on an earlier plan to provide a decoding of rabbinic texts, his rereadings of rabbinic texts, like his interpretations of biblical verses, constitute an exceptionally rich achievement. Not only did he engage offending statements, but he construed relatively benign ones in philosophical categories. While on occasion Maimonides ignored or even rejected problematic rabbinic statements, the cumulative effect of his hermeneutic achievements was an impression that the very project of the rabbis was the same as his – to give expression to the metaphysical and ethical assertions of Aristotelian philosophy.

What follows is a variety of examples of rabbinic texts to which rationalists, especially Maimonides, gave a philosophical spin:

1. In the tractate *Hagigah* 2:1, the Mishnah places restrictions on the study of "the work of creation" and "the work of the chariot." Probably these terms originally referred to certain mystical teachings. Maimonides holds they convey a limitation on teaching the esoteric subjects of natural science and metaphysics, and he uses the Mishnah's restrictions on how esoteric material should be taught

as a guideline for his own method of composition (introduction to *Guide of the Perplexed*).

2. Angels mentioned in the Talmud are said to refer to the ten separate intellects of medieval cosmology.

3. R. Haninah (*Berakhot* 33b) rebuked a prayer reader for augmenting established adjectives for God in the liturgy with additional laudatory ones. This is not, Maimonides tells us, because the man did not use enough adjectives. Rather, it is because no affirmative attributes pertain to God at all. This position Maimonides holds on the basis of various philosophical considerations such as the unity of the divine being. The pivotal anti-Aristotelian Hasdai Crescas (author of *Light of the Lord*) objected to this reading, and thought that the problem is that the list of positive laudatory attributes was too long.

4. The Mishnah in *Avot* (5:6) states that God created certain miracles on the twilight of the first Sabbath eve before the creation of Adam and Eve. Maimonides construes this and other texts as saying that miracles are part of the original creation. All events are located in the natural order, reflecting the dominance of divine wisdom as opposed to divine will (*Commentary to Avot; Guide* 2:29).

5. "Moses died with a kiss" (*Bava Batra* 17a). The Maimonidean reading is that, with his sensory and imaginative faculties enfeebled with age, Moses could focus on intellectual matters exclusively, and he died with the pleasure of intellectual apprehension (*Guide* 3:51).

6. *Hagigah* 15a relates: "Four entered Pardes..." For Maimonides, "Pardes" refers to wisdom – specifically, natural science plus metaphysics (= work of the creation plus work of the chariot). The point of the passage is that only R. Akiva emerged in peace because only he had grasped the fact that the human intellect is limited and not all truths can be demonstrated (Guide 1:32).

7. "Service of the heart," a biblical idiom construed by the sages to denote prayer (*Taanit* 2a) comes to refer, in Maimonides' thought, to a nonverbal intellectual contemplation, the highest form of prayer. (The heart signifies mind in medieval writing.)

8. The rabbis at times denigrate "this world" and affirm the importance and value of "the world to come." In rabbinic parlance, these terms refer to stages in history; Maimonides used the terms to denote the contrast between existence in the physical world – in which matter can wreak havoc upon human intellectual apprehension and upon concentration on scientific and metaphysical subjects – and

a higher disembodied existence in the afterlife. Now the sage Rav declared (*Berakhot* 17a): "In the world to come there is no eating, drinking, or intercourse. Rather, the righteous sit with crowns on their heads." The second sentence of the quotation suggests that the afterlife in the rabbinic conception is corporeal, contrary to the philosophers' devaluation of embodied existence. Maimonides understands the "righteous sitting with crowns on their heads" figuratively, as connoting a state of knowledge that brings peace. The first quoted statement, which denies the occurrence of corporeal activities in the afterlife, is used by Maimonides to argue that the future existence will be bodiless. Critics pointed out that existence could be embodied while the bodies could have needs different from those in this world. In any event, as a result of his portrait of the afterlife as disembodied, Maimonides was accused of denying resurrection of the body altogether, a charge he later denied in his *Treatise on Resurrection*.

9. We have already noted the significance for Maimonides of the Aramaic translations of the Bible.

10. R. Haninah states (*Hullin* 7a): "A person does not bruise his finger below unless it has been decreed from above." Maimonides holds that when the prophets speak of God doing x, what this means is that x occurs according to the laws of nature that God willed. Extending this to the rabbis, the statement now means that all bruises are the result of natural law. (On this reading, it is unclear what view the *Hullin* statement was designed to counter.)

A medieval critic considered such exegeses to be "like one who makes for a great king a crown of clay," and nonliteral interpretations of Aggadah were a major flashpoint in the Maimonidean controversy.[25] But for rationalists, rabbinic texts would have been an embarrassment to Jews if understood literally. Read figuratively, they represent "apples of gold in filigrees of silver" (Proverbs 25:11). In *Guide* 3:43, Maimonides suggests that such midrashim are poetical conceits that do not need all their details interpreted.

A SAMPLE ISSUE: DIVINE PROVIDENCE

Notwithstanding the difficulties in Maimonides' and other rationalists' interpretations of rabbinic texts, rabbinic thought is reactive to philosophical ideas and in some respects displays a surprising degree of convergence with medieval philosophy. By way of illustration let us consider the subject of divine providence.

Medieval Jewish philosophers considered prophecy and providence to be natural phenomena dependent on the level of a person's intellectual development. In contrast to philosophical naturalism, the world of the sages seems punctuated by frequent divine interventions. This is clear both from stories told and statements issued: for instance, the already cited "a person does not bruise his finger below unless it has been decreed from above..." and "all is in the hands of heaven, save for the fear of heaven" (*Berakhot* 33b).

Close examination reveals, however, that the rabbis were far from oblivious of natural causation. In one talmudic story, a poor widower, unable to afford a wet-nurse, miraculously grows breasts to nurture his child; while one sage takes this to signal the man's greatness, another declares "on the contrary, how inferior is this man, that the natural order was changed for him" (*Shabbat* 53b).[26] More strikingly, the Amora Rav declares that children, longevity, and sustenance depend upon *mazzal*, or astrological flow, rather than on the individual's merits. Even the view in the Talmud that "Israel is immune from mazzal" means not that astrology does not affect Jews at all, but rather that exceptional Jews like Abraham and R. Akiva can counteract the *mazzalot* through their good deeds (*Shabbat* 156a–b). When Abraham frets that the constellations augur that he will not have an heir, God tells him that he can alter the position of the planets. Thus even the result that is contrary to the *mazzal* is achieved by exploiting astrological laws, not canceling them. Ironically, the rabbinic statement "the world follows its natural course" (*Avodah Zarah* 54a), quoted by medieval philosophers to corroborate the existence of a natural order, actually suggests, in context, that God directly shapes the human embryo. Thus statements that sound naturalistic are embedded in a non-naturalistic framework, and statements that sound non-naturalistic reflect a naturalism. The idea that nature by itself is wondrous occurs frequently.

A common misconception about rabbinic thought is that it subscribes to a simple doctrine that suffering and death (or at least the timing of a death) are always punishment for sin. Yet in the one place in the Talmud where a sage (R. Ami) asserts this explicitly, his view is rejected (for reasons, moreover, that are less than powerful), suggesting that the Talmud is far from satisfied with such a theodicy (*Shabbat* 55a). Yaakov Elman argues that Babylonian and

Israel-based sources evince differing approaches to theodicy. In contrast to sages of the Jerusalem Talmud, those in Babylon held that "divine providence in the private lives of even the righteous is the exception rather than the rule." The Babylonian Talmud invokes a range of explanations of unmerited suffering: "a time of anger," "sufferings of love," "vicarious atonement," and others. In post-talmudic times such explanations were often ignored or minimized, and other accounts developed.[27] For example, to explain certain anomalies, Gersonides developed an intriguing doctrine of inherited providence.[28]

NOTES

1. See I. Twersky, "Joseph ibn Kaspi: Portrait of a Medieval Jewish Intellectual," in *Studies in Medieval Jewish History and Literature*, ed. I. Twersky (Cambridge, Mass.: Harvard University Press, 1979), 231–57, esp. 238–42.

2. See Y. Muffs, "Of Image and Imagination in the Bible," in *Biblical Paintings*, ed. J. Tisso (New York: The Jewish Museum, 1982), 8–10.

3. See A. Melamed, "Philosophical Commentaries to Jeremiah 9:22–23 in Medieval and Renaissance Jewish Thought" [Hebrew], *Jerusalem Studies in Jewish Thought* 4 (1985), 31–82.

4. See N. Roth, "The 'Theft of Philosophy' by the Greeks from the Jews," *Classical Folia* 22 (1978), 53–67. Moses Nahmanides held the same historical thesis, but did not infer therefrom the legitimacy of studying philosophy; see D. Berger, "Judaism and General Culture in Medieval and Early Modern Times," in G. Blidstein, D. Berger, S. Z. Leiman, and A. Lichtenstein, *Judaism's Encounter with Other Cultures: Rejection or Integration* (Northvale N.J.: Jason Aronson, 1997), 79.

5. Noted by A. Ravitzky, "The Secrets of the Guide of the Perplexed: Between the Thirteenth and the Twentieth Centuries," in *Studies in Maimonides*, ed. I. Twersky (Cambridge, Mass.: Harvard University Press, 1990), 177–82; see, for example, S. Pines, "Translator's Introduction" to *Guide of the Perplexed* (Chicago: University of Chicago Press, 1963), cxx; cf., however, S. Rosenberg, "On Biblical Interpretation in the Guide of the Perplexed" [Hebrew], *Jerusalem Studies in Jewish Thought* 1 (1981), 88–94.

6. See Berger, "Judaism and General Culture," 61–84.

7. See M. Halbertal, *Interpretative Revolutions in the Making* [Hebrew] (Jerusalem: Magnes Press, 1997), ch. 8; M. Halbertal, *People of the Book: Canon, Meaning, and Authority* (Cambridge, Mass.: Harvard University Press, 1997), 27–32.

8. See J. Cohen, "Philosophical Exegesis in Historical Perspective: The Case of the Binding of Isaac," in *Divine Omniscience and Omnipotence in Medieval Philosophy*, ed. T. Rudavsky (Dordrecht: Reidel, 1985), 135–42, esp. 136; W. Harvey, "On Maimonides' Allegorical Readings of Scripture," in *Interpretation and Allegory: Antiquity to the Modern Period*, ed. J. Whitman (Leiden: Brill, 2000), 181–88; S. Klein-Braslavy, *Maimonides' Interpretation of the Story of Creation* [Hebrew] (Jerusalem: Reuben Maas, 1987), chs. 1–2.

9. For Ibn Kaspi's distinctive reading, see Twersky, "Joseph ibn Kaspi," 38–42.

10. J. Stern, "Language," in *Contemporary Jewish Religious Thought*, ed. A. Cohen and P. Mendes-Flohr (New York: Charles Scribner's Sons, 1987), 549–50.

11. See, inter alia, L. Berman, "Maimonides, The Disciple of Alfarabi," *Israel Oriental Studies* 4 (1974), 154–78.

12. *Guide*, trans. Pines, introduction, 12; see also 2:47. See J. Stern, *Problems and Parables of Law: Maimonides and Nahmanides on Reasons for the Commandments* (Albany: State University of New York Press, 1998), 7–13; cf. Klein-Braslavy, *Maimonides' Interpretation*, 47–59.

13. See M. Cohen, "Radak's Contribution to the Tradition of Figurative Biblical Exegesis," Ph.D. dissertation, Yeshiva University, 1994.

14. Berger, "Judaism and General Culture," 102.

15. See G. F. Moore, "Intermediaries in Jewish Theology," *Harvard Theological Review* (1922), 41–8; E. Urbach, *The Sages: Their Concepts and Beliefs*, trans. I. Abrahams (Cambridge, Mass.: Harvard University Press, 1987), 40–5.

16. For example: S. Schechter, *Aspects of Rabbinic Theology* (New York: Schocken Books, 1961); G. Moore, *Judaism in the First Centuries of the Christian Era*, 3 vols. (Cambridge, Mass.: Harvard University Press, 1927–30); Urbach, *The Sages*.

17. See J. Guttmann, *Philosophies of Judaism*, trans. D. W. Silverman (New York: Schocken Books, 1964), 45–6.

18. Analyzed by G. Blidstein, "Rabbinic Judaism and General Culture: Normative Discussion and Attitudes," in Blidstein, Berger, Leiman, and Lichtenstein, *Judaism's Encounter*, 9–26.

19. See S. Lieberman, "How Much Greek in Jewish Palestine?," in *Biblical and Other Studies*, ed. A. Altmann (Cambridge, Mass.: Harvard University Press, 1962); W. Harvey, "Rabbinic Attitudes toward Philosophy," in *"Open Thou Mine Eyes": Essays on Aggadah and Judaica Presented to William G. Braude on his Eightieth Birthday and Dedicated to his Memory*, ed. H. Blumberg (Hoboken: Ktav, 1992), 83–101.

20. Urbach, *The Sages*, 4.

21. Harvey, "Rabbinic Attitudes," 101.

22. See M. Saperstein, *Decoding the Rabbis: A Thirteenth-Century Commentary on the Aggadah* (Cambridge, Mass.: Harvard University Press, 1980), ch. 1, which aided me in compiling the examples that follow.

23. R. Sherira Gaon, *Sefer ha-Eshkol* 2:47 and R. Hai Gaon, in *Otzar ha-Geonim: Yom Tov, Hagigah u-Mashkin* 2:59.

24. See Rosenberg, "On Biblical Interpretation," 143–51, on the possibility of prophets making errors.

25. See B. Septimus, *Hispano-Jewish Culture in Transition: The Career and Controversies of Ramah* (Cambridge, Mass.: Harvard University Press, 1982), 39–103.

26. But see Urbach, *The Sages*, 110.

27. See Y. Elman, "The Contribution of Rabbinic Thought to a Theology of Misfortune," in *Jewish Perspectives on the Experience of Suffering*, ed. S. Carmy (Northvale, N.J.: Jason Aronson, 1999), 155–212, and Elman's other articles cited there; cf. R. Goldenberg, "Early Rabbinic Explanations of the Destruction of Jerusalem," *Journal of Jewish Studies* 33 (1982), 517–26; D. Kraemer, *Responses to Suffering in Classical Rabbinic Literature* (New York and Oxford: Oxford University Press, 1995).

28. See R. Eisen, *Gersonides on Providence, Covenant, and the Chosen People: A Study in Medieval Jewish Philosophy and Biblical Commentary* (Albany: State University of New York Press, 1995).

3 The Islamic context of medieval Jewish philosophy

In memory of Franz Rosenthal

INTRODUCTION

Medieval Jewish thought flourished under the aegis of Islamic civilization from the ninth through the thirteenth centuries when the venue shifted to the Christian West. Its language was Arabic, its concerns determined by issues raised in the context of Islamic thought. The same issues (e.g. the nature of the divine, creation, prophecy, providence, human perfection, and immortality) were later pondered by Jewish thinkers in the Christian milieu, and Hebrew scientific terminology was modeled on Arabic.

For Islam, as for Judaism, the religious law is paramount, a comprehensive guide to life in all its aspects. Study of Qurʾan, tradition (*hadith*), theology (*kalam*) and jurisprudence (*fiqh*) dominated Muslim intellectual life. The *ʿulamaʾ* (clerics) regarded "the ancient sciences" as alien and useless, as an insidious threat to religious faith.[1]

Ibn Rushd (Averroes) (d. 1198), a philosopher and jurist, justified philosophy as a religious obligation, but his opinion had no effect on the career of philosophy in Islam, which was emphatically rejected by religious authorities. Even the Tunisian historian Ibn Khaldun (d. 1406) felt the need to refute philosophy.

The medieval Islamic world had no universities as did Europe, where philosophy was taught alongside theology. Muslim rulers sponsored scientific research, which was institutionalized in libraries, hospitals, and observatories. Philosophers taught privately or to circles that met in their homes or in other venues such as bookstores.

Philosophy and science were cultivated from the ninth through the twelfth centuries in the heartlands of Islam, as well as in Andalusia and the Maghreb. By the thirteenth century, however, an intellectual decline had set in as the result of socio-economic and military disasters (the Crusades, a "feudal" economy, the Mongol invasion of Iraq, plagues and famine in Egypt). This decline deepened in the later Middle Ages just as European intellectuals were awakening to the new spirit of the Renaissance, the scientific revolution, and the Enlightenment.[2]

Contrary to orthodox Islam, Christianity adopted philosophy at an early stage, making it a handmaiden to theology. Philosophy was a vital component of the officially sanctioned and required training of the student of *sacra doctrina*. Thomas Aquinas justifies the study of theology before the bar of philosophy. It is necessary, he says, that besides the philosophical sciences investigated by reason there should be a sacred doctrine based on divine revelation (*Summa Theologica*, First Part, 1:1).

The precarious status of philosophy in the Islamic milieu guaranteed its private, reclusive character and its freedom from state or clerical control. When philosophy receives official sanction, as in Christendom, it may serve ulterior purposes. Philosophy for the Christian Aristotelianism of Albert the Great and Thomas Aquinas was an *ancilla theologiae*. The reception of philosophy in the Christian world meant its subservience to ecclesiastical supervision.[3] This supervision was gradually broken with Galileo and the rise of modern science in the seventeenth century.

FROM GREEK INTO ARABIC

Classical culture, belonging to the *Kulturkreis* of the Mediterranean, was not considered alien wisdom by Islamic philosophers, who felt themselves affiliated with "the sciences of the ancients" – in the widest sense, the Greeks, Indians, and Persians. They believed that the Greeks derived their wisdom from the East (*ex oriente lux*), so that the study of ancient thought was a renovation rather than an innovation. Al-Farabi (Alfarabi) (d. 950) located the birthplace of philosophy in Iraq, whence it was transmitted to Egypt, then to Greece, and finally rendered into Syriac and Arabic. He envisioned a rebirth of philosophy in its original home, ancient wisdom thus coming full circle.

The Islamic philosophers (*falasifa*), reflecting ancient and Hellenistic lore, believed that the Presocratic philosophers acquired their wisdom from the Orient. Thales, they claimed, received instruction in Egypt, and Empedocles studied with Luqman the sage at the time of the prophet David. Pythagoras studied physics and metaphysics with Solomon's disciples in Egypt. He learned geometry from the Egyptians, receiving the sciences from the "niche of prophecy" (*mishkat al-nubuwwa*).[4] Solomon transferred the sciences to Greece. Scientific knowledge was thus legitimized as an indigenous growth, as Hellenistic and medieval Jewish thinkers also portrayed Abraham, Solomon, and Moses as philosophers from whom Greek wisdom was derived.

The Islamic philosophers were heirs to a late Hellenistic syllabus of Greek learning.[5] They integrated Aristotelian logic, physics, and ethics, Neoplatonic metaphysics, Platonic political philosophy, Ptolemaic astronomy, Euclidian geometry, and Galenic medicine into a cohesive structure, thereby transforming the eclectic diversity of late Hellenistic thought into a coherent system of cumulative knowledge within the broad framework of a Neoplatonic Aristotelianism.

True doctrine was associated with antiquity, and philosophy was pursued mainly by exegesis of ancient texts, by questioning them and by progressing to knowledge beyond them.

The cultural adaptation of the Greek heritage was not a passive reception of a foreign legacy but an act of creative appropriation.[6] The prominence of critical works (e.g. Abu ʿAli ibn al-Haytham's [d. 1039] *Doubts on Ptolemy* and Abu Bakr al-Razi's [d. 925] *Doubts on Galen*) underscores the ingenuity of Islamic science. Even Aristotle, a towering authority, was studied critically by readers attentive to obscurities and puzzles in his works. Islamic learning – with original contributions in astronomy, mathematics, medicine, and optics – was not merely a transitional link between Greek antiquity and medieval Europe but a dramatic chapter in the progress of human knowledge.

The transmission of learning from Greek into Arabic, and then from Arabic into Hebrew, Latin, and other European languages, was a momentous achievement of human civilization, and it was

formative of the "Western" consciousness. Medieval European intellectuals, Christian and Jewish, studied Muslim thinkers such as
al-Kindi (d. c. 866), al-Farabi, Ibn Sina (Avicenna) (d. 1037), al-Ghazali
(Alghazali) (d. 1111), and Ibn Rushd (Averroes), and early (ninth- and
tenth-century) scientists such as Masha'allah, Abu Ma'shar al-Balkhi
and Abu 'Abdallah al-Battani. Translators in Sicily and Toledo rendered Arabic works into Latin, French, Spanish, and Hebrew without
a substantial loss of meaning, thereby creating a true international-
ity of sciences. Medieval thinkers – Christian, Jewish, and Muslim –
confronted identical philosophical issues, refracted through different linguistic prisms, their methods and basic postulates being similar. Without the intense Greco–Arabic translation activity in the
Islamic world and transmission of these texts into Hebrew and Latin,
medieval Jewish thought and Latin Scholasticism are inconceivable.

The extent of texts translated from Greek into Arabic is
breathtaking in scope: the Presocratics, Plato, Aristotle, Euclid,
Ptolemy, Galen, Plotinus, Porphyry, Proclus, Alexander, Themistius,
Nicomachus of Gerasa, and others.[7]

The Greco–Arabic translation movement began in full vigor under the caliph al-Ma'mun (813–33), and was centered at the Bayt
al-Hikma (House of Wisdom) in Baghdad. This was a library containing writings on philosophy and science, including manuscripts
brought from the Byzantine empire. It served as a place for scholars to convene, and had an astronomical observatory. Here the
Nestorian Hunayn b. Ishaq and his colleagues translated Greek
philosophy and science, particularly medicine, into Syriac and
Arabic, using sound philological method, hunting down and col-
lating Greek manuscripts. The philosopher Abu Yusuf Ya'qub al-
Kindi helped foster this enterprise. The Nestorian medical school in
Persian Gondeshapur produced physicians and translators who contributed to the rise of scientific and intellectual pursuits in Islamic
civilization.

A second wave of translation activity, mainly from Syriac versions, took place in the tenth century, with the Nestorian Matta b.
Yunus and the Jacobite Yahya b. 'Adi in the forefront. These scholars,
along with other Christian and Muslim philosophers in Baghdad,
wrote commentaries on Aristotelian works. The Alexandrian tradition of Aristotle studies was transferred by Syriac-speaking
Christians to intellectual centers in Antioch and Baghdad.

The accommodation to Christian beliefs in the Neoplatonic school of Alexandria served as a model for Islamic philosophers. Christian philosophers (such as the sixth-century John Philoponus) presented Aristotle in a light favorable to Christianity. Philoponus' rejection of Aristotelian cosmology provided Islamic theologians with effective arguments. Greek and Syriac Christian theological inquiry is considered to have been a main source of Islamic *kalam*.

The school tradition of the (pagan) Platonic Academy in Athens (Plutarch, Syrianus, Iamblichus, Proclus, Damascius, Simplicius) was also transmitted to the Islamic milieu. The Athenian school had been hostile to Christianity and rejected Alexandrian concessions to it. The philosophical interpretation of pagan mythology by Iamblichus and Proclus, like the philosophical hermeneutics of Plotinus and Porphyry, served as a model for monotheistic demythologizing of sacred texts. The Athenian school was more disposed than its Alexandrian counterpart to admit revealed knowledge and supernatural insight. Along these lines, the Muslim philosopher al-Kindi believed that prophetic revelation is superior to human knowledge.

Arabic translators rendered Greek terms by functionally equivalent idioms, recontextualizing them and making them rhetorically effective in their new socio-cultural context. Translation is not a mere transference of lexical items from source to target language but a communicative process of adaptation, a cultural transfer from source to target culture, a transmission from one language and cultural context to another.

The translators accommodated Greek locutions to an Islamic setting by using Arabic expressions with a religious nuance and a congenial semantic load. They rendered Greek *nomos* ("[civil] law," "custom") by the Islamic terms *Shariʿa* ("religious law") and *sunna* ("custom," "tradition"), although the word *namus* was also used. Greek *nomothetes* ("lawgiver," "legislator") was regularly translated by *wadiʿ al-Shariʿa* or *al-Sunna* – "one who posits the religious law."[8] The translators purged pagan vestiges from ancient texts by substituting "God" or "angels" for "gods." The Aristotelian First Mover was expediently equated with "Allah." Greek *enthousiasmos* was translated by religious terms for inspiration and prophecy like *ilham*, *wahy*, and *nubuwwa*, referring to the ultimate human knowledge. The Platonic philosopher-king became "Imam" (the head of the Islamic community). The struggle to convert the world to the rule of philosophy and the sovereignty of reason is called *jihad*. This communication of Greek philosophical concepts in Islamic terms comports with the view of the *falasifa* that religious symbols are a mimesis of philosophical truths.

PLATO ARABUS

As the Platonic dialogues were not translated intact, the dialogue form and dramatic setting were lost. Plato's *Republic, Timaeus*, and *Laws* were accessible, and select passages from the *Crito, Phaedo*, and *Symposium* survive in Arabic. Socrates was viewed as a model of the philosophical way of life, his death cited as paradigmatic of the conflict between philosophy and the city. Passages from commentaries on Plato (e.g. Olympiodorus, Proclus) were available, as were Galen's synopses of the *Timaeus, Republic*, and *Laws*.

Plato's *Republic* was the basic text for theorizing about politics. It induced an understanding of the prophet as a guide of society along the lines of a philosopher-king. The Islamic philosophers understood political science to be an examination of the best polity, ideal rule, types of regime, justice, and human happiness. The study of prophecy and the law was subsumed under this science.

Plato's *Republic* is a model for al-Farabi's *Opinions of the Inhabitants of the Virtuous City* and is decisive for all his political writings. He wrote a commentary on the *Republic*, known from Averroes' citations in his own commentary.[9] Averroes appealed to the *Republic* for thinking about politics because, he says, he could not find an Arabic version of Aristotle's *Politics*, which he heard was available in the Muslim East. In his commentary, Averroes envisions the transformation of the Muslim state into Plato's ideal regime through a series of enlightened rulers who would gradually reform their societies.

Al-Farabi's summary of Plato's philosophy presented the dialogues in thematic sequence, stressing their political aspect and excluding Neoplatonic doctrines. It was the centerpiece of a trilogy beginning with the *Attainment of Happiness* and ending with the *Philosophy of Aristotle*.[10] In the *Attainment* al-Farabi gives his (and ancient) views on philosophy and religion. Philosophy is prior to religion in time, and religion is a *mimesis* of philosophy. The perfect philosopher, like the supreme ruler, teaches the populace and forms their character so they may reach the happiness they are capable of attaining. In the next two parts he expounds the ideas of Plato and Aristotle, only rarely trying to harmonize them, which he does elsewhere.

Leo Strauss viewed the *Philosophy of Plato* as the key for unlocking al-Farabi's thought, on the assumption that he taught his own most personal views chiefly under the camouflage of interpreter. By omitting distinctive Platonic themes (theory of ideas, immortality) in a summary of Plato's entire philosophy, Strauss argued, he was intimating a veiled teaching. The editors of the *Philosophy of Plato* rather traced this politically oriented portrait of Plato to a presumed Middle Platonic source.[11]

In another interpretive work, the summary of Plato's *Laws*, al-Farabi shows how the Greek notion of divine law helps one understand divine laws in general. Plato's *Laws* represents the authoritative philosophic teaching on prophecy and the revealed laws.[12] Al-Farabi subsumed the study of religion, jurisprudence (*fiqh*), and theology (*kalam*) under the heading of political science.[13] Avicenna followed suit by making practical philosophy, including Plato's *Laws*, the starting point for the study of prophecy and the religious law.[14]

The *falasifa* also read Plato through the prism of a Neoplatonic tradition, that is, as interpreted by Plotinus, Porphyry, and Proclus. Shihab al-Din al-Suhrawardi and the Islamic Illuminationist philosophers (Ishraqiyyun) stressed the mystical aspects of Neoplatonism and revered Plato ("the divine") as the greatest of ancient sages, the *imam* and *ra'is* (chief) of wisdom. Reviving an ancient philosophical tradition, as he claimed, al-Suhrawardi established an intellectual affiliation with Hermes (who preceded Plato) and with the great sages, "the pillars of wisdom," like Pythagoras, Empedocles, Socrates, Plato, and Aristotle, along with sages of ancient Persia and India, and a number of Sufis in the same *silsila* (chain of spiritual descent).

NEOPLATONISM

The Legacy

Plotinus was transmitted to the Islamic milieu in the guise of the *Theology of Aristotle*, a paraphrase of parts of Books 4–6 of the *Enneads*, as well as in texts ascribed to "the Greek Sage," and in a work entitled the *Divine Science*.[15] The *Theology of Aristotle* exists in a short recension ascribed to al-Kindi and in a long version, evidently an expansion of it.

The aim of the al-Kindi circle, in which the *Plotiniana Arabica* emerged, was to disseminate a natural theology transcending sectarian doctrine by using Islamic concepts to convey a philosophical monotheism appealing to intellectuals.[16]

The long version of the *Theology* was translated into Hebrew and Italian by Moses Arovas, a Cypriot Jewish physician, who was also influential in having it rendered into Latin. This version is intriguing, as it introduces a *logos* doctrine – "the word," also called God's "power" and "will" – between the Plotinian One and the First Intelligence. It also depicts one who creates the world *ex nihilo* (*la min shay'*).[17]

The supersensible substances in the Arabic Plotinus, as in the *Enneads*, are the One, Intelligence (Mind), Soul, and Nature. Plotinus regarded the One as "beyond being," as Plato's Good is beyond being (*Republic* 6:509b). The Arabic Plotinus, like Porphyry, portrays the One as pure being, being itself, or absolute being, not a limited, determinate being.

Proclus' *Elements of Theology* was reworked in Arabic with monotheistic modifications as *Kitab al-Idah (Kalam) fi mahd al-khayr* (*Discourse on the Pure Good*), known in the West as *Liber de Causis*, and generally taken to be by Aristotle.[18] It comes from the same al-Kindi milieu as the *Theology of Aristotle*. Neoplatonic emanation is presented as an act of origination (*ibda'*). The First Cause is the Pure Good and the Originator of Intelligence and of all other things in the world through its mediation. The Pure Good causes good things to permeate throughout the world, each existent entity receiving in accordance with its potentiality. Since "everything is in everything but in a manner appropriate to each,"[19] the observable horizons in the world reflect invisible levels of being.

Proclus' system substitutes for Plotinus' Intelligence a triad of Being–Life–Intelligence. He bridges the gap between the One and Being with a series of principles of individuality called *henads* ("ones"). These are derivative unities, identified by Proclus with the Hellenic gods. They mediate between the One and lower realities and exercise providence in the world. The Arabic version displaces the many divine *henads* with the First Good. It is pure being (*anniyya faqat*), the One, the Real,[20] and it is above eternity, without qualification, name, or form.

Neoplatonism is combined with monotheistic creationism in texts ascribed to Presocratic philosophers in Arabic doxographic and gnomological collections. Thales is said to have held a doctrine of *creatio ex nihilo*. That is, originally only the creator (*mubdi*ʿ) existed, and he created without the presence of a form along with him. Before creation he alone existed, and all attributes were contained in his unique self-identity, "he is he" (*huwa huwa*).[21] Pseudo-Ammonius' *Araʾ al-falasifa* defines creation, or origination (*ibdaʿ*), as making something exist that had not existed before (*taʾyyis shayʾ mimma lam yakun*).[22] Empedocles is said to have held that only God's being has always existed as eternally his own essence (*huwiyyatuhu*). He is pure knowledge, pure will, bounty, power, justice, goodness, and truth, all these powers belonging to his essence. This Empedoclean doctrine of divine attributes influenced the early Muʿtazili theologian, Abu l-Hudhayl al-ʿAllaf. The first simple intelligible entity produced by the Creator (*al-mubdiʿ*) is the primordial element or first matter (*al-ʿunsur al-awwal*).[23] Empedocles states that worldly beings have only possible existence (*al-wujud al-imkani*) insofar as they are produced, whereas God's essence is unique in having necessary existence (*wajib al-wujud*) independent of production.[24]

The ancient sciences that came to the Islamic milieu in Neoplatonic guise were bound up with the religious and pseudo-scientific heritage of late antiquity – alchemy, astrology, magic, and theurgy. Theurgic praxis, as followed by Proclus and Iamblichus, blended with Egyptian and Hermetic themes. The Sabians of Harran, in the Islamic period, heirs of the Platonic school of Athens, many of them outstanding astronomers and mathematicians, were astrolators who aspired to reach the spiritual beings (*ruhaniyyat*) by means of the planets, the celestial temples.

Astrology was widely accepted by intellectuals in the Islamic environment. It required sound knowledge of astronomy for making calculations of the positions of the various planets in the twelve constellations of the zodiac. Judicial astrology, which assesses the astral influences on human destiny, includes conjecture on dynastic fates and the advent of the Mahdi. These predictions were based on conjunctions of the planets Saturn and Jupiter in cycles of 20, 240 or 260, and 960 years. The forecasts gave rise to *malahim* (or *hidthan*) works – books of oracles of an eschatological nature. These were popular among sectarian groups, such as Shiʿi Muslims and Jews, who envisioned the end of Sunni Muslim domination, as they were also among Sunnis.

Alchemy was often treated allegorically in mystical speculation, where transmutation of base to precious metals was interpreted as a symbol of human transformation into a divine nature.

Responses to Neoplatonism

Neoplatonism is a religious movement and a doctrine of salvation as well as a philosophical system. As such, its basic postulates conflict with the monotheistic faiths: an impersonal One and necessary emanation rather than voluntary creation, mystical illumination instead of revelation, a soteriology (including metempsychosis) submerging the individual soul in the universal soul.

These barriers were not, however, insurmountable. The method of figurative interpretation, cultivated by ancient Neoplatonists (as by Pythagoreans and Stoics) to identify pagan myths with rational concepts (as Proclus identified the *henads* with the gods of mythology), was used by the *falasifa* to apply a philosophical hermeneutics to Scripture. We have seen how creation became a metaphor for eternal procession. Prophecy and supernatural knowledge are presented in terms akin to illumination and vision in *Enneads* 5:3.17 and 5:5.8. The celebrated passage on ecstasy in the *Theology of Aristotle*, based on *Enneads* 4:8.1, is frequently cited: "Often have I been alone with my soul and have doffed my body and laid it aside and become as if I were naked substance without body, so as to be inside myself, outside all other things."[25]

Neoplatonism was congenial to religious sentiment. Assimilation to the divine (*homoiosis theoi*) was a goal of philosophy in the Neoplatonic introductions to Aristotle ("assimilation to God as far as attainable for man"), traceable to a famous passage in Plato's *Theaetetus* (176a). The intense spirituality of Neoplatonism inspired the kind of synthesis with religious feeling that we find in the intellectual mysticism of Avicenna, Ibn Tufayl, and al-Suhrawardi. Thinkers influenced by Neoplatonism and Sufism regarded human reason as limited and viewed mystical experience as a way to a higher awareness. Experience rather than reason is the path to the mysterious

One beyond being and intelligibility. Unlike these mystically in-clined sages, *falasifa* like al-Farabi and Averroes regarded prophecy as contact between the supreme human intelligence and a cosmic, divine intelligence beyond it, the Agent Intellect (*al-'aql al-fa''al/ nous poietikos*).

Neoplatonism has a dual aspect: a downward way of emanation from the One and an upward way by the soul's ascent to Intelligence and through love to ultimate union with the One. The soul's return to a blissful union with the divine is realized consummately in the afterlife.

None of the Muslim *falasifa*, except perhaps al-Kindi, accepted the doctrine of creation from nothing. Most presented emanation-ist doctrine in creationist language. The Platonic idea of a demiurge bringing the visible world from disorder to order (*min la nizam ila nizam/eis taxin ek tes ataxias*) (*Timaeus* 30a) – a *formatio mundi* – was appealing to the *falasifa* and agreeable to religious sentiment as a divine transformation of chaos into the order of creation.[26] The Arabic version of Galen's compendium of the *Timaeus* uses the language of creation, with Plato's demiurge becoming "Allah" and *al-khaliq* (the creator). The Platonic model, having the demiurge as efficient cause, was fused with Neoplatonic emanation, giving rise to a theory of eternal creation. This idea conformed with Qur'anic verses depicting Allah as the Creator who does not cease to create (*al-khallaq*) (10:4, 34; 30:11; 36:81).

When the philosophers spoke of creation, they usually meant some mode of dependence of the world on God, its eternal sus-tainer. Spoken figuratively it was temporal creation, but in the real sense it was an eternal process. The term *ibda'* (creation, in-novation, origination), introduced into the philosophical lexicon by Pseudo-Ammonius in *Ara' al-falasifa*, means bringing into ex-istence of the supernal simple substances, or the first innovated (*al-mubda' al-awwal*), by "an eternal, timeless existentiation."[27] *Ibda'* is conveniently reminiscent of Qur'anic *badi'*, "creator" (2:117; 6:101).

For Ibn 'Arabi and other mystical thinkers influenced by Neo-platonism, creation is a manifestation (*tajalli*) of God, as existent entities mirror the divine essence. The metaphor of light in Neopla-tonist and Sufi texts was evocative of Qur'anic references to God as "Light upon Light" (24:35).

Islamic philosophers spoke of creation *a nihilo*, where by "nothing" they meant the One beyond being and attributes. God is called "nothing"/"no thing" because of his incomprehensibility and ineffability. The world is created from the essence of God (*creatio ex essentia Dei*) as for Dionysius the Areopagite and John Scotus Eriugena. Porphyry had expressed this by saying that God generates things from himself, and Plotinus spoke of being coming from the One. By "nothing" (*al-ʿadam*) the *falasifa* occasionally intended matter, which for Plotinus is non-being (*me on*).

Islamic Neoplatonism was multifaceted, as Neoplatonism was not simply an amplification of Plato. Plotinus had already adopted into his system aspects of Aristotelianism, Pythagoreanism, and Stoicism. Porphyry received Aristotle's corpus within the Neoplatonic curriculum. The school of Alexandria devoted much effort to commentaries on Aristotle. And while Neoplatonism combined philosophy with mysticism, it was also concerned with logical and semantic method, mathematics, epistemology, theories of space and time, and ethics.[28]

The Neoplatonic harmonization (by Ammonius Saccas, Plotinus, Porphyry, and Simplicius) of Plato and Aristotle influenced the course of Neoplatonism in the Islamic milieu. Al-Farabi's *Harmonization of the Opinions of the Two Wise Men: Plato, the Divine and Aristotle* sets out to prove this. In a deeper sense, however, it is a defense of philosophy against criticism that philosophers contradict one another and undermine philosophy's validity. Al-Farabi asserts that the two sages concur on the main issues, such as creation and immortality, and that their ideas do not conflict with religious beliefs.[29]

In the *Harmonization*, al-Farabi presents Aristotle as believing in creation. He argues that Aristotle does not affirm eternity in the *De Caelo* as is commonly believed. What Aristotle meant there was that the universe has no temporal beginning because time results from the movement of the sphere.[30] The creator creates the sphere in a single instant of time without temporal duration, and time results from the sphere's movement. Al-Farabi ostensibly accepts Aristotle's authorship of the *Theology of Aristotle* as proving the existence of an artisan who creates the world by his will. Accordingly, God is the efficient cause, the One, the Real, creator of everything. This, says al-Farabi, accords with Plato's teaching in the *Timaeus* and *Republic*.

Al-Farabi shows, following a late Hellenistic motif, that the divergent literary styles of Plato and Aristotle have the same aim.[31] Plato refrained from inscribing the sciences in books, favoring pure hearts and congenial minds (see *Phaedrus* 275ff.). When he was old and afraid of forgetting (*Seventh Letter* 344e), he wrote things down, but used parables (*rumuz*) and enigmas (*alghaz*) so that only the deserving would understand.[32] Aristotle, however, communicated in writing by elucidation and exhaustive discussion, thereby making philosophy accessible, to which Plato allegedly objected. It is explained that Aristotle's style was nevertheless abstruse, obscure, and complicated despite its apparent clarity.[33]

Alexandrian introductions to Aristotle, which were known in the Islamic environment, elucidated that the aim of Aristotle's obscurity was to exclude the unworthy, like curtains in temples. The writings of the "pillars of wisdom" (Empedocles, Pythagoras, Socrates, Plato) are filled with symbols and enigmas. They employed this style because (1) they were averse to having the unworthy delve into the secrets of wisdom and come to harm; (2) so that the lover of wisdom spare no effort to acquire it, however difficult, and so that the lazy shun it because of its abstruseness; (3) to discipline nature by taxing the mind, so that the student not be lax and complacent, and so that he strives to understand what is complex and intricate.[34]

ARISTOTELES ARABUS

The Legacy

Aristotle is called in Arabic philosophical texts "the philosopher," "the first teacher" (al-Farabi being the second), and is considered the ultimate in human perfection.[35] The Arabic Aristotle is not a dogmatic authority, as he is often portrayed later in the West, but a seeker of truth, tentatively promulgating plausible theories. Aristotle held that philosophy begins with problems and puzzles, and thrives by unraveling difficulties. Following this line, the masters of arts in thirteenth-century Paris found in Aristotle a model scientist and researcher who poses questions qua hunter (*Prior Analytics* 1:30, 46a11), discoverer (*Nicomachean Ethics* 3:3, 1112b19), and investigator (*Metaphysics* 1:2, 983a23).[36]

The Arab translators rendered into Arabic the bulk of the Aristotelian corpus, except for the *Politics*, the *Eudemian Ethics*, *Magna Moralia*, and the dialogues. They translated the entire *Organon* and Porphyry's *Isagoge*, which was used as an introduction to it. The *Rhetoric* and *Poetics* were included in the logical works, so that rhetorical and poetical statements were treated alongside demonstrative and dialectical propositions.[37] The Arabic *Physics* was transmitted intact with citations from classical commentators and glosses by members of the tenth-century Baghdad school of Aristotle studies. The Islamic philosophers also had access to the *De Caelo*, *De Generatione et Corruptione*, *Meteorology*, *De Partibus Animalium*, *De Anima*, *De Sensu*, *Metaphysics*, and *Nicomachean Ethics*. Aristotle was studied along with his commentators, in particular Alexander of Aphrodisias, Porphyry, John Philoponus, and Themistius. Some of their writings not extant in Greek are preserved in Arabic.

Averroes wrote many commentaries on Aristotle, including a middle commentary on the *Nicomachean Ethics* and long commentaries on the *Metaphysics* and the *De Anima* (the last extant only in Latin). Averroes'commentaries were done in three possible recensions, known as short, middle, and great, serving as a gradual initiation into Peripatetic thought. In the great commentaries (called *tafsir*), he comments on the text by paragraph and by citing lemmata in extenso, and using commentaries by predecessors like Alexander.

Responses to Aristotelianism

Aristotle's system contradicts the monotheistic revealed religions on the issues of creation, divine providence, and the hereafter. God is for Aristotle intelligence knowing intellection itself, *noesis noseos*. He is simultaneously thought (*'aql*), thinking (*'aqil*) and object of thought (*ma'qul*). Aristotle's God is the final cause of the universe, not the efficient cause of its existence (although commentators disagreed on this last point). The Aristotelian idea of an eternal universe and permanent world order – his belief that the universe is static, with no beginning or end – conflicts with the Islamic doctrine of God as Creator of the world by a free act of will (Qur'an 2:117, 3:47, 16:40, etc.).[38]

Averroes, a devoted Aristotelian, affirmed the existence of an eternal world order, and was convinced that *creatio ex nihilo* undermines natural causation and thereby precludes natural science. Yet he too used the language of creation or innovation. The world is coeternal with God as eternally moved by God (a non-temporally prior cause) in a process of eternal innovation. Existent beings are innovated as brought from potentiality to actuality. Averroes can describe this eternal process in the language of creation because God is the cause of the continuous motion of the heavenly spheres and thereby the cause of the existence of all other beings. God is an intelligent, creative agent which eternally brings the world from the non-being of potentiality to the being of actual existence.[39] This realization of being Averroes calls "creation."

Averroes' *Tahafut al-Tahafut*, directed against al-Ghazali's critique of the Aristotelian tradition (*Tahafut al-falasifa*), was at the same time aimed against Avicenna's Neoplatonic emanationism. Averroes carefully pruned Neoplatonic branches from his Aristotelian tree, discarding emanationism as crypto-creationism, and propounding a more naturalistic Aristotelianism.[40]

Ibn Tufayl's *Hayy ibn Yaqzan* regards arguments for creation and eternity as equivalent truth claims. Both the assumption of the universe's eternity and its innovation entail anomalies of reason. However, it is argued, the implications of both arguments are the same, for a created world must have an agent, and an eternal world having eternal motion implies a First Mover. As proofs for creation and eternity are equivalent, one's commitment to one over the other results from a decision of the will.

Averroes believed that arguments for the eternity of the universe are dialectical, and that Aristotle himself regarded them as no more than plausible. When Aristotle says that the question whether the universe is eternal or not is too vast for us to solve with convincing arguments (*Topics* 1:11, 104b1–105a9), al-Farabi understands this to mean that the issue whether the world is eternal or not is dialectical, and that no solution based upon a demonstrative syllogism exists. The physician Galen, al-Farabi observes, could not find his way to demonstrating eternity, for all the demonstrations are of equal value.[41]

The *falasifa* did not rest their proofs for God's existence on the premise of creation as did the *mutakallimun*. In Avicenna's classic formulation – which reverberated through the centuries, and appealed to Descartes, Leibniz, and Spinoza – God is the Necessary

Being whose essence implies existence. For God, essence and existence are identical, whereas for all other beings, essence and existence are distinct, such that existence is an accident that may or
may not accrue to essence.[42] God is self-caused, whereas existent
beings always have the possibility of not being.[43]

Avicenna's cosmological proof for God's existence starts with our
certainty that something exists.[44] This major premise, "something
exists," is a simple postulate acceptable to everyone. Now this entity
does not exist by necessity but is contingent, that is, there is no
contradiction in its non-existence. It must therefore have a cause
that actualizes its being. This cause may be necessary or contingent.
If contingent, we must seek a prior cause and follow a series of causes
until we come to a Necessary Being, for there cannot be an infinite
series of causes bringing about an effect. There must therefore exist a
Necessary Being (cf. *Metaphysics* 12:7, 1072b10–13). The existence
of the Necessary Being is logically necessary such that its denial
would involve a contradiction. Avicenna goes on to assert that this
Necessary Being is equivalent to God.[45]

The Necessary Being produces a single Intelligence (following the
Neoplatonic principle that "from the One can come only one"),
which is the first innovated being. From Intelligence, by a process
of emanation, a series of intelligences, celestial souls, and celestial spheres proceed until the tenth intelligence, the agent intellect,
which presides over the terrestrial world.[46] In his description of God,
Avicenna espoused the doctrine of negative attributes, that essential
attributes ascribed to God (existing, one, wise, powerful) do not have
a positive sense but must be understood as denials of their opposites.

Avicenna rejected the Aristotelian proof from motion because it
does not establish the One, the Real, the ultimate principle of all
existence, but only the principle of the motion of the celestial sphere,
not the principle of its existence.[47] Averroes favored the proof from
motion and opposed Avicenna's argument for a Necessary Being and
its presumption that existence is an attribute superadded to essence.
Averroes regarded the Aristotelian proof for a First Mover as the only
convincing argument. The First Mover can be proven to exist only
by reference to physics, its starting point being physical data like
motion. The arguments of Avicenna and Averroes have in common
that they are cosmological arguments and postulate the impossibility
of an infinite regress of causes.

For Avicenna, the Necessary Being is proven to exist in the metaphysical realm, beyond nature. Avicenna's Necessary Being is transcendent, outside the cosmos and distinct from the intellect of the outer sphere. Averroes' deity is proven to exist in nature, and is identical with the intellect of the outer sphere, enmeshed in the workings of nature.

The world, for Islamic Aristotelians, is governed proximately by the Agent Intellect, the tenth intelligence, of the lowest celestial sphere (of the moon), which gives particular forms to sublunar physical objects and universal forms to the human soul. The *falasifa* identify the Agent Intellect with the angel of revelation, or Gabriel, *malakut*, "the spirit of holiness," and "the trustworthy spirit."

Essences, or forms, exist as paradigms in the Agent Intellect, abstractly in the human mind and concretely in objects. The truth is therefore defined by a correspondence theory, the intelligible forms in the mind conforming to forms in sensible objects. The correspondence between mind and the world order is thus both noetic and ontological. The universe is rational and can be understood by the human mind. There is a commensurability and reciprocal linkage between human beings and the universe.

The Agent Intellect is based upon an obscure passage in *De Anima* 3:5, 430a13–15, where Aristotle refers to a *nous* that becomes all things and a *nous* that makes all things, as light makes potential colors into actual colors. The commentators Alexander (and pseudo-Alexander), Themistius, and (pseudo-)Philoponus, with some variation of details, account for human cognition by distinguishing different stages. On its own the mind attains sensation and imagination. Understanding the intelligible, however, involves the following dynamism: (1) There is a potential intellect, called also "material intellect", a pure potentiality for intellection. The potential intellect comprehends all forms, receives all ideas and, like Aristotle's prime matter, is a universal potentiality that can become all things. (2) There is an Agent Intellect, which makes all things by giving forms to objects and to the human intellect. It enters the soul from outside, actualizes, or illumines, the potential intellect, and abstracts forms from their matter, making them known and producing thought. (3) When the Agent Intellect enters the human mind and creates a habitus (*hexis*) of intelligible thinking, it becomes the acquired intellect (*al-ʿaql al-mustafad*/*nous epiktetos*), capable of apprehending intelligibles even when corresponding sensibles are absent. (4) When the acquired intellect performs its competence to intelligize it is said to be *in actu* (*bil-fiʿl/kat' energeian*).[48]

We humans think by means of the same (Agent) Intellect, as though our minds were our personal computers tapping into a main-frame computer, the cosmic mind, or Agent Intellect. How else could we comprehend reality if we did not access the mind of the universe? The universe has a mind and we think with it. The universe is ratio-nal and knowable because the same cosmic mind that determines its order (the laws of nature) illumines human intelligence. The cosmos is mind-like, and so human beings can understand it and find in it a source of delight. Humans find meaning and order in life and nature because in the closed world of medieval astronomy everything had its natural place and purpose. The universe is not only intelligible but intelligent.

The Agent Intellect is separate, pure, and impassive, and it thinks incessantly (*De Anima* 3:5, 430a22). Alexander of Aphrodisias identified it with the divine intelligence itself, the First Cause of *Metaphysics* 12. Others (Themistius and Philoponus) did not equate the Agent Intellect with God. The Agent Intellect is akin to the Neoplatonic Intelligence, which emanates from the One, and they have similar noetic functions as actualizing thought. The Neopla-tonic *nous*, however, is hypercosmic, whereas the Agent Intellect is encosmic as belonging to the lowest celestial sphere.

Averroes held that the faculty of intellection – the passive, or ma-terial, intellect – is universal and the same for all humankind, par-ticipated in by the individual person. This faculty is permanently actualized in the totality of humankind, so that humans are never without it. The human species is eternal, and immortality is col-lective and relates to this one human intellect.[49] The unity of the intellect (what Leibniz later calls "monopsychism") implies a denial of individual immortality. This thesis and others of Averroes and Aristotle were condemned in Paris in 1270 and in 1277.[50]

Immortality for the *falasifa* is the survival of the rational part of a human being, a boon for the happy few. Intellect when iso-lated as its true self is immortal and eternal (*De Anima* 430a23; cf. *De Generatione Animalium* 736b27). It is the point of contact between the human and divine. The *falasifa* regarded the religious idea of personal immortality and the belief in physical resurrection as

socially beneficial myths. For philosophers and mystics immortality is a spiritual ascension and return to God rather than a continued
existence in a quasi-physical paradise as depicted in the Qur'an. Contact, or "conjunction" (*ittisal*), between the individual intellect and
the divine intellect is a blissful enlightenment leading to immortality. It is the philosophical counterpart of the Sufi *unio mystica*
(*ittihad*) where the union is with God.[51]

The Islamic philosophers, following Aristotle, saw the *summum
bonum* as consisting in theoretical contemplation. They depicted
supreme perfection as the conjoining of the human intellect with
the cosmic intellect, or the realm of spiritual forms. Aristotle suggests a kinship between the divine and the human intellect by
saying that during intellection the subject becomes one with its object, intellect becoming its intelligible, like the Unmoved Mover
(*Metaphysics* 12:9, 1074b34), which is self-intelligized intelligence.

Ibn Bajja (Avempace) and Ibn Tufayl present the ideal philosophical life as withdrawal (emigration) from imperfect cities and isolation from humankind in pure contemplation of the intelligible.
This individualistic ethos differs from the ethical systems of other
falasifa (al-Farabi, Miskawayh, Averroes) which stressed the human
need for society and political order and the importance of love
and friendship. Aristotle's well-known dictum, often cited by the
falasifa, "Man is by nature a political animal" (*Nicomachean Ethics*
1:7, 1097b12 and *Politics* 1:2, 1253a2), defined human nature for
them.

Islamic ethical theory, like its classical forbear, is virtue based, as
it was concerned with moral education, character, goodness, and nobility, the whole of life and its purpose.[52] The *falasifa* saw supreme
happiness, following Aristotle, as being activity in accordance with
reason. Theoretical reason is the divine element in humankind, and
it above all else *is* what we as humans are (*Nicomachean Ethics*
10:7, 1177a12–28, 1178a6–7). Supreme happiness does not reside in
the exercise of ethical virtue, justice, courage, liberality, or temper-
ance; for the most felicitous human activity and that most akin to
the divine is contemplation (*Nicomachean Ethics* 10:8, 1178b7–23).
The object of the deity's contemplation is necessarily himself, the
most prefect being (*Metaphysics* 12:9, 1074b33–35). The life of this
First Mover is the best we enjoy, but for a brief time (*Metaphysics*
12:7, 1072b14–15). This elitist and intellectualist formulation of the

finis ultimus as a life of pure contemplation contrasts with another Aristotelian formulation that defines the aim of human existence as the organization of the broad range of human activity in a well-ordered and comprehensively planned life in accordance with ethical virtue and practical wisdom (*phronesis*). Both formulations are represented in Islamic ethical thought.

PHILOSOPHY AND THEOLOGY

Philosophy had its starting point in research and theory, whereas theology (*kalam*) began with principles of religious belief. Its aim was defensive, its energies directed against non-believers, heretics, and free-thinkers such as the Mazdeans, Manicheans, and Dahriyya. The theologians wanted to prove creation and infer therefrom the existence of a creator, whilst the philosophers denied that a proof could be adduced for creation.[53]

The *falasifa* rejected the theologians' attempt to defend religious belief with rational arguments. The philosophers claimed that the theologians were ultimately apologists, disputatious and eristic, and they condemned the attempt by the theologians to enlighten the many, to publicly debate fundamental articles of faith, like creation and the existence of God and his attributes. The philosophers favored the certainty of science over the uncertainty of theology.

The theologians, for their part, regarded philosophy as threatening to religious belief. They considered the philosophers heretics, thereby obliterating the distinction between philosophers who sustained religious faith and real heretics.

The heretics, or free spirits, such as Abu Bakr al-Razi and Ibn al-Rawandi, advocated a rational enlightenment devoid of revealed religion.[54] Al-Razi accepted the Stoic principle that all human beings are capable of reasoning, not just a select few. They can dispense with religion, which is based on blind adherence to authority and blighted by internal contradiction, ignorance, and falsehood. Religion incites fanatic hatred, divisions among humankind, and warfare. The prophets Moses, Jesus, and Muhammad are "the three great imposters" (*tres impostoribus*). Al-Razi's direct Epicurean defiance of religion was a path that few of his fellow intellectuals were ready to take, however, and most shunned this brand of candid expression. But al-Razi was not alone. Free thinkers called Dahriyya (eternalists or materialists) were said to believe in the eternity of the world, and to deny creation, resurrection, and a future life.

Kalam – especially the Mu'tazili school – was rationalist in its approach. The Mu'tazilis believed that human beings have the capacity to apprehend God, his nature, and justice through reason independently of revelation. They affirmed a pristine monotheism (*tawhid*) and divine transcendence, negating by *tanzih* (*via remotionis*) God's likeness to created entitities (cf. Qur'an 23:91, 42:11). They ascribed to God only attributes of action, and considered attributes such as knowledge, power, and speech as identical with the divine essence. They consequently used symbolic interpretation (*ta'wil*) to explain metaphorically Qur'anic anthropomorphisms (face, eyes, hands, movement, sitting on a throne). A second principle was God's justice (*'adl*). The Mu'tazilis held the objectivist view that good and evil (*hasan, qabih*) inhere in the nature of reality, are discerned by reason, and are revealed in the religious law. God wills the good and wants to realize what is for the better. This means that humans have free will and are responsible for their actions.

The Ash'ari school of *kalam* refused to impose separate rational criteria upon God's actions. His will is inscrutable, and whatever God determines is good and just. This theistic subjectivism in ethics went along with a theory of atomism and occasionalism in physics. God's sovereign will is the true cause of all occurrences. The particular natural causes we see are merely occasional or incidental. There exists no permanent world order, no laws of nature, no limitation of divine freedom.

The Ash'ariyya rejected Mu'tazili *tanzih* as emptying the notion of God of meaning (*ta'til*) and thus being tantamount to atheism. They claimed that anthropomorphisms could be ascribed to God "without asking how and without comparison" (*bi-la kayfa wa-la tashbih*). In due course, however, even Ash'ari theologians relaxed their hermeneutic fundamentalism and interpreted Qur'anic anthropomorphisms metaphorically. The Ash'ari theory ultimately prevailed in the Islamic environment.

With al-Ghazali the Ash'arites delved more into the teachings of the philosophers, though at a critical distance. Al-Ghazali's *Maqasid al-falasifa* (*Intentions of the Philosophers*), an analytical exposition of the systems of al-Farabi and Avicenna, was widely read (in Arabic, Hebrew, and Latin) as an introduction to philosophy. Al-Ghazali's

writings had the (unintended) effect of initiating philosophy into a
Sunni milieu. In his *Tahafut al-falasifa* al-Ghazali dwells on the inconsistencies of the *falasifa* and argues that they do not succeed in
supplying demonstrative arguments for their metaphysical claims.[55]
He accuses them of unbelief for upholding the world's eternity, for
denying God's omniscience (his knowledge of particulars), and for
rejecting resurrection.

REASON AND REVELATION

In a remarkable conspectus of humankind's intellectual history, al-
Farabi traces the historical evolution of modes of discourse, showing
how human societies have progressed from a primitive level of poetry
and rhetoric, myth and fable (Homer?), to a stage of dialectic (Plato?)
and sophistical reasoning (Sophists?). Finally humans advance to the
stage of science and philosophy, the peak of human development
(Aristotle?). Not all humans, however, can evolve to this pinnacle.
Hence, the founders of national religions portray the truths of philosophy in parabolic form. In the perfect religion the instrumentalism
of rhetoric, poetry, sophistry, and dialectic will be laid bare. Insofar
as proponents of jurisprudence and theology reason from religious
premises that imitate philosophical verities, they are thereby twice
removed from the truth. If, as in the case of Islam, a national religion
comes to a national community (*umma*), like the Arab nation, before
the appearance of philosophy, it may occur that the religion, though
a parabolic version of philosophy, will discard the philosophy from
which it evolves.

Realizing that this religion is a parabolic version of philosophy,
the philosophers will not oppose it. But, alas, the theologians and
other religionists will resist the philosophers and try to exclude them
from their governing and educating role. Religion will then not receive much support from philosophy, while great harm may accrue
to philosophy and philosophers from the religion and its followers. In
the face of this threat philosophers may be forced to combat theologians and religionists, though not the religion itself. From al-Farabi's
perspective, religion was a great achievement of the human spirit.[56]

Al-Farabi and his successors identify the supreme philosopher
with the supreme lawgiver, Imam, and ruler, thereby making Plato's
philosopher-king the head of the Muslim community. The best

polis, or political community (*al-madina al-fadila*) (see *Republic* 462d; *Laws* 710d) is ruled by a supreme ruler whom God inspires through the medium of the Agent Intellect. When the supreme ruler's intellect is activated by the Agent Intellect, he becomes a philosopher. If the emanation reaches his imagination, he becomes in addition "a prophet and warner." In al-Farabi's theory of prophecy, the prophets receive theoretical truths from the emanation of the Agent Intellect upon their rational faculty.[57] This emanation, actuating their faculty of imagination, gives rise to parables (*rumuz*), enigmas (*alghaz*), substitutions (*ibdalat*), and similes (*tashbihat*) – symbolic representations of the truth.[58] The symbols convey the identical knowledge displayed in demonstrative or discursive language used by philosophers. The ancient quarrel between poetry and philosophy is thus resolved in favor of philosophy but not by banishing poetry. *Logos* is imparted by *mythos*. As Aristotle said, "even the lover of myth is in a sense a lover of Wisdom" (*Metaphysics* 1, 982b18). Elsewhere, Aristotle speaks (*Metaphysics* 12:8, 1074b1–5) of a tradition conveyed in mythic form "with a view to the persuasion of the multitude and to its legal and utilitarian expediency."[59]

When the emanation reaches the imagination solely, this person becomes a politician capable of addressing the people with rhetorical effectiveness. He is incapable of directing them to true human perfection, for he himself has not attained this perfection, nor was this ever his aim. The philosopher-king is capable of leading humans to a knowledge of true happiness and the way of attaining it.

The *falasifa* wanted a peaceful coexistence between philosophy and religion. They urged the freedom to philosophize by portraying religion itself as having summoned human beings to contemplate the universe. Averroes contends in his *Decisive Treatise* that the religious law commands us to philosophize, citing Qur'anic verses (e.g. 59:2 and 7:184) inviting humankind to reflect on creation, invoking Abraham as a philosopher who probed the heavens. Philosophy and religion are not at cross-purposes in this respect but identical in their intent. There is no need to enlighten the masses. They are abandoned to the plain meaning of the scriptural text. Philosophers, however, must be free to go beyond the surface meaning of Scripture and explain it in a tropic sense (*ta'wil*).[60]

The philosophers distinguished between *zahir* and *batin*, the external and the internal (deep structure) sense of texts and the inner truth and outer aspect of the religious law. This *zahir–batin* dichotomy was prominent in the milieu of Shiʿism and Sufism. It was not simply a hermeneutic mode but a total *mentalité*, a way of observing the world and of constructing it. Ibn ʿArabi and fellow Sufis visualized the entire cosmos as an array of symbols, similar to the verbal symbols of revelation, requiring hermeneutic exposition. Some humans can comprehend the deep meaning of these cosmic symbols by unveiling mysteries (*kashf, mukashafa*), while others perceive only surface meaning. The cosmos cascades with signs and meanings, with numerical and verbal symbols and divine names. Everything in the world is a figure and a sign of an inner reality. The world is a *speculum* of God.

Intellectuals in the Islamic milieu had a "symbolist mentality."[61] They were convinced that natural and historical reality signified something beyond plain actuality, and that a symbolic dimension of that reality was discernible by the human mind. The meaning of historical events is revealed in prophecy. Sacred texts have a hidden, figurative, mysterious sense lifting them from their historical parameters to an eternal significance. The modern conception of a universe blind and indifferent to human life, history, ideals, and strivings – a vastness of darkness and terror – was remote from their consciousness.

NOTES

1. Taqi al-Din ibn Taymiyya (d. 1328), exemplifying this attitude, says that only science inherited from the prophet [Muhammad] deserves to be called science; the rest is either useless or not science at all; see *Majmuʿat al-rasaʾil al-kubra* (Cairo, 1324/1908), 1:238, cited by I. Goldziher, *Stellung der alten islamischen Orthodoxie zu den antiken Wissenschaften* (Berlin: Verlag der Akademie, 1916), 6.

2. This is not to overlook the school of Isfahan and important figures such as Mir-i Damad (d. 1630), Mulla Sadra Shirazi (d. 1640), or Ibn Khaldun in the Maghreb and Egypt (d. 1406). The study of the sciences was in steady decline from the thirteenth to the fifteenth centuries.

3. L. Strauss, *Persecution and the Art of Writing* (Chicago: University of Chicago Press, 1988), 21 (originally published Glencoe: The Free Press, 1952); and "How to Begin to Study Medieval Philosophy," in his *The Rebirth of Classical Political Rationalism* (Chicago: University of Chicago Press, 1989), 221–4.

4. Abu l-Hasan al-ʿAmiri, *Kitab al-Amad ʿala l-abad*, ed. E. K. Rowson, *A Muslim Philosopher on the Soul and its Fate* (New Haven: American Oriental Society, 1988), 70, 205–9; Abu Sulayman al-Sijistani, *Muntakhab Siwan al-Hikmah*, ed. D. M. Dunlop (The Hague: Mouton, 1979), 3–6.

5. Al-Shahrastani's expression "Islamic philosophers" (*falasifat al-islami*) includes non-Muslim philosophers in an Islamic milieu; see *al-Milal wal-nihal*, ed. M. Badran, 2nd ed. (Cairo: n.p., 1956), II: 168. The word *falasifa* is the plural of *faylasuf* (Gr. *philosophos*). By "Islamic" I mean the overarching civilization that harbored a mosaic of ethnic and religious groups, including Christian and Jewish communities, the way M. G. S. Hodgson intends "Islamicate" in *The Venture of Islam*, 3 vols. (Chicago: University of Chicago Press, 1974).

6. See A. I. Sabra, "The Appropriation and Subsequent Naturalization of Greek Science in Medieval Islam: A Preliminary Statement," *History of Science* 25 (1987), 223–43.

7. R. Walzer, *Greek into Arabic: Essays on Islamic Philosophy* (Cambridge, Mass.: Harvard University Press, 1962); F. Rosenthal (ed.), *The Classical Heritage in Islam*, translated from the German (*Das Fortleben der Antike im Islam*) by E. and J. Marmorstein (London and New York: Routledge, 1975); D. Gutas, *Greek Thought, Arabic Culture: The Graeco–Arabic Translation Movement in Baghdad and Early ʿAbbasid Society (2nd–4th/8th–10th Centuries)* (London and New York: Routledge, 1998).

8. Medieval Hebrew translators generally rendered *shariʿa* as *torah* even when it represented secular law (*nomos*), and modern translators and commentators in their wake invariably take *torah* to be the religious law (Torah), thereby distorting the text's original intent.

9. *Averroes' Commentary on Plato's Republic*, ed. and trans. E. I. J. Rosenthal (Cambridge: Cambridge University Press, 1969); *Averroes on Plato's Republic*, translated, with an introduction and notes, by R. Lerner (Ithaca: Cornell University Press, 1974).

10. *Kitab falsafat Aflatun*, ed. F. Rosenthal and R. Walzer (London: Warburg Institute, 1943); *Kitab falsafat Aristutalis*, ed. M. Mahdi (Beirut: Dar Majallat Shiʿr, 1961); *On the Philosophy of Plato and Aristotle*, trans. M. Mahdi (Ithaca: Cornell University Press, 1969).

11. L. Strauss, "Farabi's Plato," in *Louis Ginzberg Jubilee Volume* (New York: American Academy for Jewish Research, 1945), 357–93. Similarly, in the philosophy of Aristotle, al-Farabi avoided discussing metaphysics save for brief, cryptic remarks such as: "We do not possess a metaphysical science." See T.-A. Druart, "Al-Farabi, Emanation and Metaphysics," in *Neoplatonism and Islamic Thought*, ed.

P. Morewedge (Albany: State University of New York Press, 1992), 127–48, at 131.

12. See L. Strauss, *Philosophy and Law: Contributions to the Understanding of Maimonides and his Predecessors*, trans. E. Adler (Albany: State University of New York Press, 1995), 76, 125, and 152, n. 65; "How Farabi Read Plato's Laws," in his *What is Political Philosophy?* (New York: The Free Press, 1959), 134–54; and see J. Parens, *Metaphysics as Rhetoric: Alfarabi's Summary of Plato's "Laws"* (Albany: State University of New York Press, 1995).

13. See *Ihsa's al-'ulum*, ed. 'U. Amin (Cairo: n.p., 1948), 102–13; trans. F. M. Najjar, *Enumeration of the Sciences*, in *Medieval Political Philosophy: A Sourcebook* (Ithaca: Cornell University Press, 1993), 24–8; see M. Mahdi, "Science, Philosophy, and Religion in Alfarabi's *Enumeration of the Sciences*," in *The Cultural Context of Medieval Learning*, ed. J. E. Murdoch and E. D. Sylla (Dordrecht: Reidel, 1975), 113–47, esp. 140ff.

14. Avicenna, *Aqsam al-'ulum*, in *Majmu'at al-rasa'il* (Cairo: n.p., 1908), 107–8; trans. M. Mahdi, in *Medieval Political Philosophy*, 96–7; trans. J. W. Morris, "The Philosopher-Prophet in Avicenna's Political Philosophy," in *The Political Aspects of Islamic Philosophy: Essays in Honor of Muhsin Mahdi*, ed. C. E. Butterworth (Cambridge, Mass.: Harvard University Press, 1992), 152–98, at 168–70; G. C. Anawati, "Les divisions des sciences intellectuelles d's Avicenne," *Mélanges de l's Institut Dominicain d'Etudes Orientales* 13 (1977), 323–6.

15. *Pseudo-Aristotle in the Middle Ages*: *The Theology and Other Texts*, ed. J. Kraye, W. F. Ryan, and C. B. Schmitt (London: The Warburg Institute, 1986); see especially the articles by F. W. Zimmermann, "The Origins of the So-called *Theology of Aristotle*," 110–240, and P. B. Fenton, "The Arabic and Hebrew Versions of the *Theology of Aristotle*," 241–64.

16. Zimmermann, "Origins," 117–19, 143; and see 148 for an explanation of how Plotinus became "Aristotle."

17. See Zimmermann, "Origins," 177.

18. The *Liber de Causis* was translated by Gerard of Cremona as *Liber de Expositione Bonitatis Purae*. Aquinas commented upon it; see *Commentary on the Book of Causes [Super Librum De Causis Expositio]*, trans. V. A. Guargliardo, C. R. Hess, and R. C. Taylor (Washington, D.C.: The Catholic University of America Press, 1996). Aquinas did not believe it was a work of Aristotle, noting its dependence on Proclus' *Elements* and its resemblance to the views of Dionysius the Areopagite. See R. C. Taylor, "*Kalam fi mahd al-khair (Liber de causis)* in the Islamic Philosophical Milieu," in Kraye, Ryan, and Schmitt (eds.), *Pseudo-Aristotle in the Middle Ages*, 37–52; and see C. d'Ancona Costa,

Recherches sur le Liber de causis (Paris: J. Vrin, 1995). A number of propositions from the *Elements of Theology* have been recovered in Arabic; see G. Endress (ed.), *Proclus Arabus* (Beirut and Wiesbaden: Franz Steiner Verlag, 1973).

19. Proclus, *The Elements of Theology*, ed. and trans. E. R. Dodds (Oxford: Clarendon Press, 1963), Prop. 103, 92–3.

20. Or "the True One," *al-wahid al-haqq*. The epithets are both philosophical and Qur'anic (see 37:4, *wahid*) and see 18:44 and 20:114 for God as the Real, or the Truth (*al-haqq*).

21. U. Rudolph, *Die Doxographie des Pseudo-Ammonius* (Stuttgart: Franz Steiner Verlag, 1989), 34 (trans. 80). For similar ideas in Arabic Plotinus texts and in the al-Kindi milieu, see 120; and see A. Altmann and S. M. Stern (ed. and trans.), *Isaac Israeli: A Neoplatonic Philosopher of the Early Tenth Century* (London: Oxford University Press, 1958), 70–71.

22. Rudolph, *Pseudo-Ammonius* (*Ara' al-falasifa*), 34 (trans. 80); see Kommentar, 121, on the *Textgruppe* (*Theology of Aristotle*, *Liber de Causis*) to which this notion belongs and the affiliation with al-Kindi; and see Altmann and Stern, *Isaac Israeli*, 70–4.

23. See Pseudo-Ammonius, *Ara' al-falasifa*, 37–8. The Empedocles texts are cited by al-ʿAmiri, al-Sijistani, Saʿid al-Andalusi, al-Shahrastani, and al-Shahrazuri.

24. This foreshadows Avicenna's treatment of possible and necessary existence. Avicenna used the library where al-ʿAmiri probably wrote and deposited his *Amad*; see Rowson (ed.), *A Muslim Philosopher*, text and translation on 78–9, 170–1; and see 5, 37, 232–4; D. Gutas, *Avicenna and the Aristotelian Tradition* (Leiden: Brill, 1988), 250.

25. *Theologia* 1:21ff. (trans. G. Lewis, in *Plotini Opera*, ed. P. Henry and H.-R. Schwyzer, 2 vols. [Paris: Desclée de Brouwer, 1959], II: 225). See Fenton, "The Arabic and Hebrew *Theology*," 260 n. 2.

26. J. Pelikan, *What Has Athens to Do with Jerusalem?* (Ann Arbor: University of Michigan Press, 1997), 13.

27. P. Walker, "The Ismaili Vocabulary of Creation," *Studia Islamica* 40 (1974), 74–85.

28. A. C. Lloyd, *The Anatomy of Neoplatonism* (Oxford: Oxford University Press, 1990).

29. *Kitab al-jamʿ bayn ra'yay al-hakimayn Aflatun al-ilahi wa-Aristutalis*, ed. A. N. Nader (Beirut: Imprimerie Catholique, 1959); D. Mallet (trans.), *Deux traités philosophiques: L'harmonie entre les opinions des deux sages, le divin Platon et Aristote* (Damascus: Institut Français de Damas, 1989), 64–5. Some doubt its ascription to al-Farabi.

30. *Kitab al-jamʿ bayn ra'yay al-hakimayn*, 100–4; trans. Mallet, 84–9.

31. *Kitab al-jamʿ bayn ra'yay al-hakimayn*, 84–5; trans. Mallet, 64–5.

32. For Plato, see, e.g., *Phaedrus* 276a–277a. See also al-Farabi's introduction to his *Compendium of Plato's Laws*, ed. Fr. Gabrieli, *Alfarabius Compendium Legum Platonis (Talkhis Nawamis Aflatun)* (London: Warburg Institute, 1952), 3–4.

33. The difference between Plato and Aristotle on style is set forth in a dialogue between them in the biography of Aristotle by al-Mubashshir b. Fatik, *Mukhtar al-hikam*, ed. A. Badawi (Madrid: Instituto Egipcio de Estudios Islámicos, 1958), 184; trans. I. Düring, *Aristotle in the Ancient Biographical Tradition* (Göteborg: Almqvist & Wiksell, 1957), 201 (and see his comment, 432–3). See also the reference to the same correspondence by Avicenna, *Fi ithbat al-nubuwwa*, in *Tisʿ rasaʾil fil-hikma wal-tabʿiyyat* (Istanbul, 1880), 85; trans. M. E. Marmura, in *Medieval Political Philosophy*, 116. See also Galen, *Compendium Timaei Platonis*, ed. P. Kraus and R. Walzer (London: Warburg Institute, 1951), 3, on Aristotle's terse, obscure style. On the terse, compressed style of Aristotle's acroamatic works, as opposed to the more popular style of his dialogues, see W. D. Ross, *The Works of Aristotle.* XII. *Select Fragments* (Oxford: Oxford University Press, 1952), 5.

34. Al-Sijistani, *Muntakhab Siwan al-Hikmah*, 10.

35. F. E. Peters, *Aristoteles Arabus* (Leiden: Brill, 1968); F. E. Peters, *Aristotle and the Arabs* (New York: New York University Press, 1968).

36. See C. H. Lohr, "The Medieval Interpretation of Aristotle," in *The Cambridge History of Later Medieval Philosophy*, ed. N. Kretzmann, A. Kenny, and J. Pinborg (Cambridge: Cambridge University Press, 1982), 91.

37. The matter is treated exhaustively by D. L. Black in *Logic in Aristotle's Rhetoric and Poetics in Medieval Arabic Philosophy* (Leiden: Brill, 1990). The translation of the *Poetics* was a major *tour de force*, as fundamental concepts like comedy and tragedy were foreign to Arabic culture. Jorge Luis Borges refers to this in "Averroes' Search," in *Labyrinths*, ed. D. A. Yates and J. E. Irby (New York: New Directions, 1964), 148–55.

38. The Qurʾan is not explicit about *creatio ex nihilo*, which became doctrinal for Muslim theologians.

39. B. S. Kogan, *Averroes and the Metaphysics of Causation* (Albany: State University of New York Press, 1985), 209–22.

40. *Averroes' Tahafut al-Tahafut (The Incoherence of the Incoherence)*, trans. S. van den Bergh, 2 vols. (London: Oxford University Press, 1954).

41. See al-Farabi, *Kitab al-jadal*, ed. R. al-ʿAjam, in *al-Mantiq ʿinda al-Farabi* (Beirut: Dar El-Machreq, 1986), III: 80–2. See G. Vajda, "A propos d'une citation non identifiée d'Alfarabi dans le 'Guide des égarés'," *Journal asiatique* 258 (1965), 43–50.

42. A.-M. Goichon, *La distinction de l'essence et de l'existence d'après Ibn Sina* (Paris: Desclée de Brouwer, 1937).

43. The idea that the universe may be other than it is or that it may not be at all opens the way for miracles and divine interventions. The notion of the ontological contingency of the world on God is expressed in the Qur'anic verse: "All things shall perish save His countenance" (28:88). The belief that the created world is one of fleeting impermanence evokes the Sufi idea of self-annihilation (*fana'*) in the Being that perdures (*baqa'*).

44. See L. Goodman, *Avicenna* (London and New York: Routledge, 1992), 63–5.

45. The Necessary Being and Allah are not in the strict sense equivalent, as the meaning of God for Islam goes beyond the sense of necessity of being.

46. Al-Ghazali criticizes the Avicennan account of procession of successive intellects and spheres. The philosophers judge on the basis of supposition (*zann*) and surmise (*takhmin*), without verification and certainty; *Tahafut al-falasifa*, trans. M. E. Marmura, *The Incoherence of the Philosophers* (Provo, Ut.: Brigham Young University Press, 1997), 4 and 65–7. Maimonides, in a chapter that has other earmarks of al-Ghazali (*Guide* 2:22), also criticizes Avicennan procession as no more than guess (*hads*) and conjecture (*takhmin*).

47. See his *Letter to al-Kiya*, ed. A. Badawi, *Aristu 'inda l-'arab*, 2nd ed. (Kuwait: Wikalat al-Matbu'at, 1978), 120–2. Avicenna is commenting there on *Metaphysics* 12:6 1071b5–31.

48. See H. A. Davidson, *Alfarabi, Avicenna, and Averroes, on Intellect: Their Cosmologies, Theories of Active Intellect, and Theories of Human Intellect* (New York and Oxford: Oxford University Press, 1992).

49. Averroes, *Commentarium Magnum in Aristotelis de Anima Libros*, ed. F. S. Crawford (Cambridge, Mass.: The Medieval Academy of America, 1953), 406; and see *Averroès l'intelligence et la pensée, grand commentaire du De anima, Livre III*, trans. A. de Libera (Paris: GF-Flammarion, 1998), 111ff. See also O. Leaman, *Averroes and his Philosophy*, 2nd ed. (Richmond: Curzon, 1997), 84–103.

50. Thomas d'Aquin, *L'unité de l'intellect contre les Averroïstes*, trans. A. de Libera (Paris: GF-Flammarion, 1994); R. McInerny, *Aquinas against the Averroists: On there Being only One Intellect* (West Lafayette: Purdue University Press, 1993).

51. P. Merlan uses the term "rationalistic mysticism" to signify that the divine source with which the individual is united is not the God beyond thinking and being but thought thinking itself; see his *Monopsychism, Mysticism, Metaconsciousness: Problems of the Soul*

in the Neoaristotelian and Neoplatonic Tradition (The Hague: Martinus Nijhoff, 1963), 20.

52. For an introduction, see G. F. Hourani, *Reason and Tradition in Islamic Ethics* (Cambridge: Cambridge University Press, 1985).

53. For *kalam*, see H. A. Wolfson, *The Philosophy of the Kalam* (Cambridge, Mass.: Harvard University Press, 1976); J. van Ess, *Theologie und Gesellschaft im 2. und 3. Jahrhundert Hidschra*, 4 vols. (Berlin and New York: Walter de Gruyter, 1991).

54. S. Stroumsa, *Freethinkers of Medieval Islam: Ibn al-Rawandi, Abu Bakr al-Razi and their Impact on Islamic Thought* (Leiden: Brill, 1999). For al-Razi, see especially L. E. Goodman, s.v., *Encyclopaedia of Islam* (Leiden: Brill, 1960–).

55. See al-Ghazali, *The Incoherence of the Philosophers*.

56. F. W. Zimmermann, *Alfarabi's Commentary and Short Treatise on Aristotle's De Interpretatione* (Oxford: Oxford University Press, 1981), cxiv n. 1, from al-Farabi's *Book of Letters (Kitab al-huruf)*, ed. M. Mahdi (Beirut: Dar El-Machreq, 1969), paras. 108–13, 129, 140–53; and see L.V. Berman, "Maimonides, the Disciple of Alfarabi," *Israel Oriental Studies* 4 (1974), 154–78, at 156.

57. See al-Farabi's *Mabadi' ara' ahl al-madina al-fadila*, ed. and trans. R. Walzer, *Al-Farabi on the Perfect State* (Oxford: Clarendon Press, 1985), chs. 14–15, 211–57; see also R. Walzer, "Alfarabi's Theory of Prophecy and Divination," in *Greek into Arabic*, 206–19.

58. *Rumuz* often renders *parabolai* or *mythoi* in translation literature. In *Kitab al-alfaz al-musta'mala fil-mantiq* (*Utterances Employed in Logic*), ed. M. Mahdi (Beirut: Dar El-Machreq, 1968), 90–1, al-Farabi absolves himself from the need to investigate statements resembling lies (or "fables"), lit. "adornments," "embellishments" (*zakharif*) in such a philosophic work. He adds, however, that while such fables may be repugnant in the various kinds of philosophical disciplines, they are perhaps indispensable in rhetoric and in the statements employed in political affairs.

59. The passage is: "Our forefathers in the most remote ages have handed down to us their posterity a tradition, in the form of a myth, that these substances [the heavens] are gods and that the divine encloses the whole of nature. The rest of the tradition has been added later in mythical form with a view to the persuasion of the multitude and to its legal and utilitarian expediency" (trans. W. D. Ross). See Averroes, *Tafsir Ma ba'd at-tabi'at*, ed. M. Bouyges, S.J. (Beirut: Imprimerie Catholique, 1948), VII: 1686.

60. See *Kitab fasl al-maqal*, ed. G. F. Hourani (Leiden: Brill, 1959), 1–2; trans. G. F. Hourani, *Averroes on the Harmony of Philosophy and Religion*

(London: Luzac, 1967), 44–5 (with pagination of the text in the margin). And see the excellent bilingual edition of M. Geoffroy, with introduction by A. de Libera, *Averroès discours décisif* (Paris: GF-Flammarion, 1996), 104–5.

61. M.-D. Chenu, *Nature, Man, and Society in the Twelfth Century*, ed. and trans. J. Taylor and L. K. Little (Toronto: University of Toronto Press, 1997), 119–21.

Part II
Ideas, Works, and Writers

4   Saadya and Jewish *kalam*

In an oft-quoted dictum the twelfth-century Spanish polymath Abraham ibn Ezra describes Saadya as "first and foremost among speakers everywhere." This seemingly simple sentence praises Saadya on more than one level, playing as it does on the multivalence of the word "speakers" (*medabberim*). The context of Ibn Ezra's phrase (in his book on Hebrew grammar) suggests that this word refers here primarily to linguists; yet it can also mean "spokesmen" in a general way, and it is also a literal translation of the Arabic *mutakallimun*, that is, practitioners of dialectic theology. In all likelihood, Ibn Ezra intended all these meanings together. Indeed, Saadya's towering figure dominates the emergence of medieval Jewish scholarship in all fields: linguistics and poetics, philosophy and exegesis, polemics and law, and he is also generally considered to be the most prominent representative of Jewish *kalam*. An inquiry into Saadya's thought, his background, and his influence can thus serve as a convenient introduction to Jewish *kalam*.

Kalam (literally "speech") is a generic name for Islamic dialectical theology. Common to all *kalam* schools is the formulation of a system based on the dual basis of rationality and Scripture, and on the assumption that the two complement, rather than contradict, each other. Also typical of all *kalam* schools is the specific discourse that uses dialectical techniques for the analysis of religious and philosophic problems. Whether it is presented as a strictly theological compendium or in a different kind of literary composition (exegetical, polemical, or a monograph on a specific theological question), a *kalam* work is often recognizable as such even before a thorough acquaintance with its content. Structure and style characterize *kalam* works no less than contents. In terms of the general structure, comprehensive *kalam* works (theological summae) follow a set pattern of discussion, which starts from universal issues (epistemology, the creation of the world, God's unity and justice), and moves on to issues that are more narrowly tied to the specific religion of the author (prophetology, eschatology, and the afterlife). In terms of style, the polemical nature of *kalam* is reflected in arguments ad hominem (*ilzam*), and its dialectical thought is expressed in conventional formulas of dialogue ("If he says:..., he should be told:..."; or: "He said:...; I answered:..."). These stylistic traits constitute the backbone of *kalam* texts. They are common to all schools of *kalam*, and they distinguish *kalam* from other philosophical, rationalistic trends.

Some concern for theological questions (such as free will and predestination) can already be discerned in early, pre-*kalam* Muslim works, but the development of a systematic Muslim theology came only later. Although the theological drive could be said to have come from within Islam, its systematic formulation and the form it took suggest an external influence. This influence was not anchored in the transmission of a specific body of texts (as in the case of the transmission of Greek philosophy and science). Nevertheless, we may assume that the first Muslim theologians were somehow exposed to Hellenistic philosophy, perhaps through the encounter with the Christian academies in Syria and Persia. The first structured school of *kalam*, the Mu'tazila, was established in the mid-eighth (third Islamic) century. The Mu'tazilites, known as "the proponents of God's unity and justice," developed a comprehensive theology, revolving around five basic principles: God's unity; his justice; the intermediate position of a Muslim sinner, as neither a believer nor an infidel; reward and punishment in the afterlife; and the obligation to enjoin virtue and forbid sin. Alongside their theological writings, the Mu'tazilites also developed an extensive complementary exegetical, scientific, and linguistic literature based on the same principles. During the ninth and tenth centuries the Mu'tazila thrived, and its sub-schools developed in two major centers, in Baghdad and in Basra. Aristotelian philosophers berated the *mutakallimun* as mere religious propagandists, but many Muslims regarded the positions held by the Mu'tazila as unrelenting rationalism that compromises religious doctrines. Other schools of *kalam* attempted to strike a different balance between the two basic sources of knowledge, rationality and Scripture. From the tenth century on these schools, and particularly the Ash'ariyya, gained dominance in Muslim theology.

The development of Jewish systematic theology takes place under Islam and mostly in Arabic. Prior to the Islamic conquests, with the exception of Philo's thought, no systematic rationalistic theology was developed by Jews. Philo had no direct continuation in Jewish thought, and Jews in late antiquity used other literary genres to express their theological concerns. Jewish systematic rationalistic thought developed only later, as part of the wholesale Jewish immersion into Arabic culture. As Arabic came to replace both Hebrew and Aramaic as the main cultural language of the Jews, the intellectual activity of eastern Jews became an integral part of the intellectual Islamic scene.

On the whole, works of Jewish *kalam* are constructed along the same lines as works of Muslim *kalam*. They employ the same dialectical techniques and formulas and explore the same conventional topics. The epistemology of the Jewish *mutakallimun* is built upon a firm belief in human rationality as a tool for obtaining a true picture of the world and a sound interpretation of Scripture. The intellectual endeavor is perceived as both a natural human drive and a religious duty. The basic sources of knowledge for each individual are sense perception and rational thought. The knowledge accumulated over the years by generations of scholars is added to these, in the form of transmitted interpretive information ("the veridical tradition").

It is on the basis of these epistemological assumptions that the Jewish *mutakallimun* build their theological system. They argue that contemplation of the world reveals its created nature, and hence the existence of a creator. It also shows that the world must have been created *ex nihilo* (rather than from a preexistent matter). The creator must be of an intrinsically different nature than its creation. And as the world contains plurality, the creator must be a perfect unity. The proof of God's unity is usually combined with the discussion of his attributes. The Jewish *mutakallimun* usually reject the existence of separate divine attributes, and adopt *kalam* formulas that insist on the perfect unity of God with his knowledge, wisdom, life, and so on. The creator must also be benevolent, and Jewish *mutakallimun* insist on the applicability of human moral criteria to God. Although some of God's actions may not be understood by human beings, the basic assumption must remain that he is good in the same sense that we are good.

From God's goodness follows the principle of divine revelation. God endowed human beings with reason to guide them to salvation. Because of his benevolence, God complemented this gift by sending prophets to spell out the best ways of serving him. The prophet, who is a normal, accomplished human being, can be recognized by the miracles he performs, by his moral and intellectual perfection, and by the concord of his message with the content of the revelation received by previous prophets. In works of Jewish *kalam* the true prophet is primarily Moses. Obedience or disobedience to the precepts brought by him will be requited by God in the hereafter as well as in the Messianic age.

This general scheme is so closely akin to Muslim *kalam* that, at first sight, only the prooftexts appear to be different. But Jewish *kalam* developed also some specific concerns, which are not found in the same way in Muslim works.

In some cases, the differences with Muslim *kalam* have nothing to do with religious differences. Whereas some Jewish *mutakallimun* adopted the atomistic physics of the *kalam*, others did not. Their rejection of atomism may be explained by their exposure to the influence of Christian philosophy, to Aristotelian teachings, or to non-atomistic *kalam*. At any rate, it does not stem from a preconceived religious doctrine, nor does it reflect a basic religious disagreement with Islam.

In other cases, however, the differences with Muslim *kalam* are related to the special religious doctrines of both religions. Certain questions that became central to Muslim theology remained of rather marginal interest in Jewish *kalam*. By way of an example we can mention the question of the created or uncreated speech of God, which became a cause célèbre in the debate between traditionalists and rationalists during the heyday of the Mu'tazila. Although the discussions of Jewish *mutakallimun*, and even the solutions they offer, reflect their awareness of the centrality of the question in Muslim *kalam*, it is evident that they do not participate in the heated debate. Jewish theologians agree that the various prophetic revelations were all temporal, and they attempt to reconcile the temporal revelation with God's eternal, unchanging nature. Another example is the question of the status of the sinner who is formally a believer.

In Jewish *kalam*, the discussions of the relative weight of human acts in general and sins in particular are often couched in the Jewish legal tradition, and are not part of the historical disagreement within Muslim theological circles.

The Islamic notion of the abrogation of the law, on the other hand, received much attention, due to its importance in interreligious polemics. In the attempt to rebut their opponents' claims that Mosaic law had been replaced by Christianity or by Islam, Jewish theologians insisted on the immutability of God's revelation, entailed by his own immutability.

As in Muslim *kalam*, Jewish *mutakallimun* devoted much time and energy to polemics. They were engaged in public debates on religious, scientific, and philosophical issues, and polemics is a predominant feature of their writings. They polemicized with other religions, with various philosophical schools (both historical and fictitious), and with each other. Their polemical drive resulted in the development of heresiographical interest: Jewish theologians (e.g. al-Muqammas, Saadya, Qirqisani, Judah Hadassi) attempted to map and classify contemporary opinions and to trace their origin to ancient schools and sects.

A brief outline of the emergence of Jewish *kalam* is given by Moses Maimonides (d. 1204) in his *Guide of the Perplexed* 1:71. According to Maimonides, the meeting of the early Christians with the pagan philosophers had forced the Church Fathers to develop philosophical tools for the defence of their religion. In the same way, centuries later, the encounter of the early Muslims with Christian philosophers had forced the Muslims to develop Islamic theology. Maimonides (whose historical account and evaluation of the *kalam* was influenced by the tenth-century Muslim philosopher al-Farabi) presented the *kalam* as an aberration of truth. In his view, the *mutakallimun* were not true philosophers, but rather people who harnessed philosophical techniques and elements to the defence of their religion. Quoting Themistius, Maimonides hints that, instead of forming their beliefs on the basis of a scientific examination of reality, as philosophers should, the *mutakallimun* tried to bend the facts to fit their convictions. He also implies that the Jewish *mutakallimun* follow the same deplorable practice. According to Maimonides, when the Jews came under the aegis of Islam, they chanced upon the first school of *kalam*, the Mu'tazila, and were deeply influenced by it. As representatives of Jewish *kalam*, Maimonides mentions the geonim (the heads of the talmudic academies in Iraq) and the Karaites (Jewish sectarians who rejected the authority of rabbinic oral law).

Most modern scholars agree with Maimonides that Saadya Gaon, like other geonim, was a *mutakallim*, and that his main source of influence was the Mu'tazila. The question arises, however, how to reconcile Maimonides' devastating evaluation of the *kalam* with the stature of Saadya and the magnitude of his contribution to Jewish thought. Other difficulties contribute to a certain unease concerning Saadya's classification as a *mutakallim*. There are some significant differences between his thought and standard Muslim *kalam*, and his writings contain some elements that seem Aristotelian or Neoplatonic rather than kalamic. One possible solution to these difficulties was suggested by Michael Schwarz, whose analysis of Maimonides' sources offers some explanation for the differences between Maimonides' *mutakallimun* and those contemporary with Saadya. Another solution endeavors to put some distance between Saadya and the *kalam*. Lenn Goodman thus argues that "if Saadya was a mutakallim, he was of quite a different sort from the old type catalogued by his mutakallim contemporary al-Ash'ari."[1]

Saadya's affinities with the *kalam* must therefore be examined with care, and the nature of his *kalam* defined more precisely. In terms of the discipline, Saadya certainly regarded himself as a philosopher in the sense that he was earnestly seeking truth. His commitment to the search for scientific truth can be fully appreciated when we compare Maimonides' above-mentioned sarcastic quotation from Themistius about the true method of the philosopher with Saadya's description of the correct scientific method. Saadya, just like the philosopher Maimonides, believes that "the praiseworthy wise person is he who makes reality his guiding principle and bases his belief thereon" and that "the reprehensible fool...is he who sets up his personal conviction as his guiding principle, assuming that reality is patterned after his beliefs."[2]

In terms of belonging to a school, however, Saadya did not belong to *falsafa*. Occasionally he does refer to the philosophers,[3] but he clearly intends by it the generic name of the discipline, not the school. On the other hand, he never identifies himself as a *mutakallim*, nor does he quote *mutakallimun* by name (but then, Saadya hardly ever quotes anyone by name).

Most modern scholars refer to Saadya as "the first Jewish medieval philosopher," thus overlooking the fact that both Isaac Israeli
(d. c. 932) and the ninth-century al-Muqammas had ventured into
this field before him. Medieval students of Jewish thought often appreciated this fact correctly: Daniel ibn Mashita, for example, in his *Taqwim al-adyan* (composed in 1223), begins his
account of Jewish philosophy with al-Muqammas.[4] The modern mis-
presentation stems from a combination of the paucity of our knowledge of pre-Saadyanic thought on the one hand and from the wish
to insist on Saadya's importance on the other. But in order to evaluate Saadya's role correctly, the fact that he was not the first Jewish
philosopher should in no way be overlooked. Indeed, more often than
not, to be "first" entails a certain lack of sophistication, whereas
Saadya, as a representative of a second generation of Jewish philosophers, presents a relatively mature Jewish *kalam*.

A text that is often mentioned as an example of early Jewish
kalam is an anonymous epistle attributed by its first publisher, Jacob
Mann, to the ninth-century Karaite thinker Daniel al-Qumisi.[5] Although the *Pseudo-Qumisi* is strongly opposed to the use of "foreign
wisdom," it reflects the influence of precisely this wisdom. The epistle, written in Hebrew, contains some Arabic *kalam* concepts, such
as "indicatory sign" (*dalil*), the *kalam* term for a proof. It attempts a
theological formulation of religious doctrines, such as divine unity
and justice and the religious obligation to use reason, and it supports
these doctrines with biblical prooftexts. Nevertheless, the *Pseudo-
Qumisi* is not a *kalam* text in the sense that it does not partake in the
kalam discourse. It does not attempt to offer a systematic analysis of
theological questions, and it does not adopt the typical kalamic analytical discourse. The importance of the *Pseudo-Qumisi* lies perhaps
precisely in the fact that it allows us a glimpse into a transitional period, in which Jewish thinkers were not yet engulfed in the Arabic
intellectual world, but its growing influence was already encroach-
ing on Jewish thought. Although Jewish thinkers were still resisting
the influence of Arabic theology, they were already speaking the language of *kalam*, and under its pressure they were already developing
a theology.

In both Jewish and Islamic theology, most of the early texts are not
extant. We are, however, fortunate to possess about three quarters
of what is probably the first Judeo-Arabic theological summa, which

happens to be also the first extant Arabic summa, earlier than extant Muslim specimens of the same genre. The text, al-Muqammas'
Twenty Chapters, offers a thorough, systematic exposition of Jewish
theology. Al-Muqammas had converted to Christianity and had studied with a teacher named Nana (probably the Jacobite Nonnus of
Nisibis). As we can learn from an Arabic *Life of St. Stephen*, al-
Muqammas' very name seems to stem from Christian-Arab vocabulary, where the word "Muqammas" designates an Arab, perhaps a
person dressed in a tunic (*qamis*) like an Arab. The sobriquet thus
reflects al-Muqammas' position as an Arabic-speaking Jew between
two cultures, the Syriac Christian and the Arabic Muslim. He knew
Syriac and he translated from Syriac two commentaries, on Ecclesiastes and on Genesis.[6] He also wrote some polemical works, and
a work on Aristotelian logic. His literary activity thus reflects a
conscious intellectual effort to establish a comprehensive rational
Jewish theology. But the somewhat rough integration of the various elements in his work reflects the difficulties typical to the
trailblazer.

Al-Muqammas' books were written after he returned to Judaism,
but in his attempt to present universal truths he usually avoids dis-
closing specific Jewish doctrines or using Jewish sources. Moreover,
his extant written work bears clear marks of his Christian schooling.
This is evident not only in the case of his anti-Christian polemics,
which plays an important part in the discussion, but in his whole theology. His theological work closely resembles, in both presentation
and content, works of Muslim *kalam*. But on several plans the
content of his work deviates considerably from the familiar *kalam*
pattern. His writings contains some material, mostly in logic, that
is derived explicitly from Aristotelian philosophy. Unlike most
Muslim *mutakallimun*, al-Muqammas' physics is not atomistic.
And although he is aware of debates and positions current among
contemporary Muslim *mutakallimun*, his final position sometimes
differs from theirs (as in the case of the divine attributes, where the
negative theology he adopts seems closer to the position we usually
identify with Islamic Neoplatonists). Al-Muqammas' discussion of
all these points reflects (and sometimes follows) the common practice in the Christian schools, and some of the deviations from *kalam*
in his system are the same deviations from Muslim *kalam* that we
find later in Saadya's work.

Saadya's predecessors, al-Muqammas and Isaac Israeli, delineate the spectrum of influences to which an educated Jew would be exposed: Christianity and Islam, Christian *kalam* (which includes some Aristotelian philosophy), Muslim *kalam*, and Neoplatonic thought. The role of pioneer belongs to these predecessors, who legitimize these influences and show the way for their integration into Judaism. It was then Saadya who, creatively and systematically, shaped, smoothed the rough ends, and consolidated the foundations laid by his predecessors, and presented the outcome as "Jewish philosophy," with an authority that his predecessors lacked. Precisely because he was not the first, Saadya was free from the chore of pathbreaking, and he could thus use the raw materials in a richer and more mature way.

The twelfth-century Judah ben Barzillai of Barcelona reports a rumor that Saadya had studied with al-Muqammas. We have no proof of that. Saadya, as is his wont, does not identify his sources, and he often thoroughly reworks the material he drew from them. There are nevertheless some paragraphs in Saadya's work that closely resemble al-Muqammas' *Twenty Chapters*, and since al-Muqammas' summa was well known in Saadya's time, our assumption should be that, among the many things Saadya read, he probably read al-Muqammas too.

Saadya, however, goes at least one step further: on the one hand, he seems more familiar with the fruits of Muslim *kalam* than al-Muqammas. On the other hand, his work is thoroughly and overtly Jewish. All of Saadya's literary output is directed toward the establishment of a system that demonstrates the agreement between rationally based knowledge and biblical revelation as interpreted by talmudic tradition.

Saadya was born in 882 in Egypt, which he left in 915. The reasons for his departure are unknown to us, but his subsequent tumultuous career, strewn with heated confrontational episodes involving leading authorities of the Jewish community, suggests that a similar confrontation may have forced him to leave Egypt. He spent the next decade in Palestine, with excursions to Iraq and to Syria. In 928 he moved to Iraq, where he was appointed head of the academy in Sura, a position he held, with interruptions, until his death in 942. The intellectual climate at the end of the ninth century in Egypt, where Saadya passed his formative years, is not very clear to us. While both the Christian intellectual tradition and the memory of the proud philosophical past of late antiquity must have been present, there is little evidence of that, still less of any significant Muslim theological circles. Saadya's literary activity began already in Egypt: there he wrote his first book against the Karaites, and his correspondence with Isaac Israeli suggests that he was exposed to some kind of Neoplatonic influence. According to the Muslim historian al-Mas'udi (d. 957), during Saadya's Palestinian period he studied with a certain Abu Kathir Yahya al-Tabarani, who may or may not have been a Karaite. We have no information concerning Saadya's intellectual contacts with non-Jews, but the common language (Arabic) would have facilitated such contacts. In Syria the Christians had a strong intellectual presence, and the affinity of Jewish Aramaic to Syriac suggests the possibility that Christian writings could have been accessible to Saadya. In Syria Saadya could also have encountered representatives of the various schools of Islamic thought: Sufism, *kalam*, and *falsafa*. Saadya's immersion in this Islamic culture must have become a still more dominant factor after his move to Baghdad. Thus, although we have no definite landmarks of Saadya's education, we can be quite certain that, by the time he wrote his theological summa, he must have had access to practically everything on the intellectual market.

There is no question that Muslim thought in general and Muslim *kalam* in particular grew during Saadya's lifetime to become a major intellectual force. But as a non-Muslim, Saadya was not obliged to choose a school with which to align himself, nor was he committed to follow Muslim rather than Christian patterns of theological activity. Like al-Muqammas before him, Saadya was not committed to any particular philosophical school. Existing philosophical schools were the heritage of a non-Jewish culture, the rich influence of which Saadya did not try to reject. But being a Jew, he felt free to collect material gleaned from various sources: from Mu'tazilite *kalam*, from Christian *kalam*, from *falsafa*, or Neoplatonism, and to combine it as suited his purpose. Henry Malter, who noted the eclectic nature of Saadya's thought, attributed it to his polemical goals. According to Malter, since Saadya needed to offer a Jewish response to Aristotelian and Neoplatonic thoughts, he refuted these thoughts using various elements from them.[7] This explanation, however, does not account for the fact that the eclectic method is not used on a similar scale by Muslim polemicists, for instance. Saadya's flexibility and originality must be attributed primarily to his daring personality. But beyond that, it seems that his position as a Jewish thinker also allowed him a certain freedom of choice. This freedom results from his being an outsider to Muslim *kalam*.

As in the case of the Muslim Mu'tazila, the literary output of the first generations of Jewish medieval thinkers extended beyond philosophical activity. Already al-Muqammas had applied himself to biblical exegesis, logic, and polemics. With Saadya, the expansion of Jewish interests became a full-fledged intellectual project, imprinted by the versatility of Saadya's personality. Through his vision he rewrote the map of Jewish interests: poetics and liturgy, exegesis and grammar, history and law, polemics and applied science. He applied his systematizing drive to all these new fields. And all his literary activity was informed by the *kalam* principle of the conformity of religious revelation with the decrees of the intellect. In its details, this new map often follows the map of Muslim literary activity. Thus from the fact that the Bible is written in Hebrew followed the demand to establish a rationally based theory of language, and this linguistic theory closely resembles the one developed by Muslim grammarians. But the approach as a whole, with its "Scripture-centeredness," also closely follows the Christian apologetic tradition.

SAADYA'S PHILOSOPHY AND ITS PHILOSOPHICAL CONTEXT

Although all of Saadya's oeuvre is inspired by his philosophical convictions, two of his books are properly philosophical: the commentary on the *Book of Creation* (*Sefer Yetzira*), written in 931, and his theological summa, *The Book of Beliefs and Opinions*, composed in 933. While there are some crucial differences between his approach in these two works, the evaluation of Saadya's philosophy must include them both, as well as his other works.

In terms of structure and of style, there is no difficulty in identifying Saadya as a *mutakallim*. The ten chapters of his theological summa are arranged according to the classical *kalam* order of discussion: an introductory chapter on epistemology; the created nature of the world, which proves the existence of a creator (chapter one); the unity and incorporeality of God and the correct understanding of his attributes (chapter two); prophecy and revelation (chapter three);

command and prohibition and the question of free will (chapter four). The remaining six chapters deal with various aspects of reward and punishment, the afterlife, and eschatology. This clearly tilts the balance of this compendium in favor of the more specifically Jewish subjects, the chapters discussing universal issues serving more as an introduction.

Characteristic components of *kalam* that concern the smaller literary units, such as the dialogue formulas, are ubiquitous in all Saadya's works. The *kalam* polemical tendency and logical (argumentative) methodology are developed by Saadya to an art that is unparalleled even in Muslim *kalam* works. A classical *kalam* proof is based on an analytical mapping of the various possible arguments, preparing the ground for a systematic examination and elimination of the wrong ones. Saadya perfected the technique so as to make the logical structure patently clear, by presenting numbered lists of the possibilities and sub-possibilities. Indeed, his obsessive fondness for numbered lists has become his trademark. He develops and refines it in two directions: modular construction and linear accumulation. Saadya's method begins with an analysis that resolves every question into its smallest components. He compares the ideal process of learning to the extraction of cream from milk, or to purifying silver from dross. After reducing each problem systematically to its smallest components, the next stage is to outline all their possible combinations. As Saadya himself tells us, one must gradually and patiently eliminate the wrong solutions, sifting and reducing the possibilities from ten to nine, from nine to eight, and then to seven. He also compares the establishment of knowledge to the construction of meaningful statements first from sounds, then from syllables and words.[8] In his analysis of the process of learning, Saadya assigns the delineation of the various possible arguments to a specific mental faculty. A complete and correct analysis of all the possibilities is an essential precondition for the process of elimination. A faulty analysis is at the origin of most incorrect opinions.[9]

The possibilities are then built into his lists. When refuting the first opinion on the list, he counts several arguments against it. The refutation of the next false opinion will include these arguments and add others, and so on, to the end of the list. Every system in the list contains the characteristics of the previous system and adds to it a new distinctive trait. From the smallest, modular units Saadya gradually constructs various systems, accumulating arguments against them. Thus, for example, his refutation of dualism includes twenty-eight arguments, thirteen of which are accumulated from previous discussions, and the fifteen others are gradually added on, following discussions of epistemology and ontology.

Another example of Saadya's "modular" construction of his lists can be seen in the sixth chapter of *The Book of Beliefs and Opinions*, where Saadya mentions seven theories concerning the soul.[10] A shorter list appears already in Aristotle, but the ultimate origin of Saadya's list is in the Arabic translation of the doxography known as *Pseudo-Plutarch*.[11] These seven theories, however, are preceded by four others, which, although concerned mostly with the question of the creation of the world, also have implications concerning the soul. In the second chapter these four theories were discussed and refuted in the context of creation, where Saadya constructed them as part of a gradual, accumulative refutation of wrong creational systems.[12] The arguments against these four theories, which Saadya had accumulated in the second chapter, are harnessed in the sixth chapter to the discussion of the soul. The "modular" unit is here integrated in a different context, where it serves as the basis for the construction of a new discussion.

A similar analytical deconstruction and recomposition was used by Saadya in his legal work. In the *Book of Testimony and Legal Documents* he presents first the standard clauses that are common to all types of legal document. He then proceeds to construct the individual types of documents, recalling briefly the necessary standard formulas and adding to them the required additional formulas.[13] The theological opinions are constructed by Saadya in the same modular way, *mutatis mutandis*, as the legal documents are constructed from standard and specific clauses.

A correct understanding of the role of this method for Saadya allows us a fuller appreciation of the nature of his polemical activity. Quite often, scholars have found it difficult to identify the various systems he chose to refute. Saadya's descriptions of these systems differ slightly from the ones given by Muslim heresiographers, and as he describes them, they do not seem to agree completely with any known system of thought. This is the case with some of the systems in his list of opinions regarding the creation of the world, the opinions regarding the essence of the soul, and even his taxonomy of

Christianity. But Saadya's intention is not to document and refute existing opinions he may have encountered, nor to preserve the refutation of false opinions he found recorded in books. Saadya's lists do not reflect only his heresiographical interest. After dissecting a problem to its basic components, he reconstructs the possible answers by adding up the components, the modular units, eliminating false answers as he goes. The opinions he attacks may sometimes correspond to existing beliefs, but essentially they are mappings of the logical terrain.

Saadya thus builds his philosophy on a *kalam* technique of analysis of (possible) arguments. He combines it with the *kalam* fascination with heresiography, and incorporates it within a conventional *kalam* structure of theological discussion. His innovation is in the calculated upgrading of the technique into a comprehensive methodology, which dictates the framework of the discussion and informs it with an almost obsessively controlled search for the one, perfectly constructed truth.

Occasionally, Saadya demonstrates familiarity with basic concepts of Aristotelian logic and Aristotelian psychology.[14] His theory of language reflects the Aristotelian view that human language is conventional. Following Aristotle, Saadya distinguishes between the abstract universal notions and their specific expressions in various languages.[15] Saadya could have found this idea in al-Muqammas, who introduces a similar analysis into Jewish thought. Saadya, however, integrates the analysis into a complete linguistic project, the first attempt to build a linguistic theory of the Hebrew language.

Neoplatonic influence is apparent in Saadya's *Commentary on the Book of Creation*. Basic concepts of Arabic Neoplatonism, such as the divine will, appear in this commentary in a way that is usually identified with the longer version of the *Theology of Aristotle*. In fact, Shlomo Pines has suggested that this concept, which is so typical of the system of Gabirol (d. 1054/8), may have reached him through Saadya's commentary on the *Book of Creation*.[16] When reading the chapters on creation in the *Book of Beliefs and Opinions* and comparing it to the commentary on the *Book of Creation*, one gets the impression that these two books reflect different philosophical schools. It may be that the two books were written with a different public in mind, and for different pedagogical purposes. Nevertheless, together they faithfully reflect the wide spectrum of Saadya's philosophical activity. Saadya's philosophy thus includes elements drawn from various sources and various philosophical systems. His handling of these elements is exemplified in two key topics: physics and psychology.

Saadya rejects the *Timaeus* account of prime matter as well as the Aristotelian theory of the world's preexistence. For him, the world is created in time by the creator and according to his will. Saadya's proofs that the world is created are the typical *kalam* proofs, including a classical one, that infers the created nature of the world from the fact that it is never free of constantly changing phenomena. As Herbert Davidson has shown, the origin of this proof (and of the whole body of Saadya's proofs) is the work of John Philoponus, and it is in Saadya's writing that the Philoponan origin of these proofs is best exemplified. But in Saadya's formulation the Aristotelian concepts of matter and form are replaced by the terms "substance" and "accident." These latter terms were used by the *mutakallimun* within an atomistic system. In their system the accidents reside in the substance, but neither one has an independent continuous existence. Substances and accidents exist for a fraction of time and are created each moment anew. Saadya, however, is not an atomist. For him, substance is self-subsistent, and has a durable, continuous existence. The accidents, on the other hand, have only a contingent existence, and they continuously change. The very same use of these terms is found in al-Muqammas, and it is this use that Muslim heresiographers identify as characteristic of Christian theology.

Saadya rejects the Platonic theory of the preexistent soul. According to him, the soul, like everything else in the world, is created in time. But whereas all other things are destined to perdition, the soul, once created, is eternal. The soul is a "pure substance," and its matter is brighter than the spheres, since it is endowed with intellect. For Saadya, intellect is an essential attribute of the soul. He sometimes uses the word "intellect" to denote common sense. He thus employs the word in a way that Maimonides and al-Farabi condemned as a typical *kalam* usage. Saadya does not regard the celestial spheres as endowed with intellect, nor does he see the intellect as having an existence separate from the soul.

In his discussion of the afterlife, Saadya asserts that reward and punishment are given to both soul and body. All human souls suffer from the destruction of the body, but the sinner's soul, which wanders eternally, suffers more than the soul of the righteous, which reaches heaven. Malter has pointed out that Saadya's discussion of death is not philosophical, and that he repeats opinions current among Jews and Muslims.[17] Saadya's attitude to death, however, is an integral part of his understanding of the soul, and this understanding is not just "not philosophical," but in fact strikingly distinguishable from that of the *falasifa*. In the *falasifa*'s system the intellect is of prime importance. Separate intellects control the movement of the spheres, and the notions of redemption, reward, and punishment are centered on the role of the human intellect. The Intellect is of paramount importance also in Neoplatonic theories, where it is identified as the first hypostasis after the One, and redemption is described as the return to it. None of these notions is apparent in Saadya's psychology or eschatology. It is not likely that his ignoring them stems from either ignorance or simple oversight. The negligibility of the Intellect in Saadya's thought demonstrates that he is neither Neoplatonist nor Aristotelian. One may say that Saadya's theory of the soul and the intellect identifies him as a *mutakallim*.

Saadya's bitter opponents were the Karaites. The Karaite movement crystallized in Palestine during the ninth and the tenth centuries, and it soon gained prominence in Jewish communities. As Scripturalists, for whom the Bible is the sole religious authority, the Karaites put the Bible at the center of their whole intellectual activity. The goal of following solely the dicta of the Bible confronts the daily experience of having to decide on matters not specified in Scripture. As the Karaites tried to minimize the place of tradition in the interpretation of the Bible, independent rational reasoning (*qiyas, ijtihad*) became of paramount importance in their thought.

It is thus not surprising that from the tenth century on the Karaites wholeheartedly adopted the rational theology of the *kalam* in its Mu'tazilite version. This development involved a construction of a systematic Mu'tazilite Karaite theology, exemplified in the summa of the tenth-century Yusuf al-Basir, *The Book of Rational Discernment* (*Kitab al-Tamyiz*). Al-Basir adopted the Mu'tazilite theology openly, and he quite often quotes masters of the Basrian school of Muslim *kalam*. The Karaite adoption of the *kalam* involved a major exegetical effort, in which the Bible was interpreted according to the principles of the Mu'tazila. Foremost among the Karaite commentators was Saadya's contemporary Ya'qub al-Qirqisani, whose Bible commentary includes lengthy discussions of *kalam* problems, and who shares the *kalam* fondness for heresiography. The voluminous commentaries of the tenth-century Yefet ben Eli and of the eleventh-century Yeshu'a ben Yehuda ostensibly restrict their discussions to the text of the Bible, but their approach is decidedly that of the *kalam*, and their analysis of the biblical text is thoroughly imbued with the theology of the *kalam*.

The internal conflict within the Jewish community between Rabbanites and Karaites contributed to a heightening of the importance of certain theological issues. Rabbanite and Karaite authors used the same dialectical arguments to prove their respective positions. Both parties agreed on the epistemological value of the true tradition. But the Karaites rejected the validity of the talmudic tradition, which the Rabbanites regarded as "the oral Law," the only authoritative interpretation of Scripture. Consequently, the discussion of tradition in Jewish *kalam* has a special edge. It no longer seeks simply to prove the authenticity of the prophet or to vindicate the Scripture he brought, but also seeks to establish the authority of the correct, unadulterated interpretation of these writings.

It has been suggested that the Karaites were the link that allowed Saadya to introduce new genres into the Jewish literary vocabulary. According to Rina Drory, the Karaites, as sectarians who broke away from rabbinic tradition, were not constrained by loyalty to previous traditional genres. The literary vacuum from which they suffered allowed them the necessary flexibility to be receptive to new genres, such as systematic exegetical literature and theology. According to this suggestion, it was the confrontation with the Karaites that forced the Rabbanites to venture into new fields. Saadya, himself an outsider to the world of the geonate, was flexible enough to shoulder this task.[18]

There is, however, no evidence for the existence of this comprehensive Karaite literary activity prior to the end of the ninth century. There is thus no reason to assume that the Karaites were the bridge between Islamic *kalam* and Saadya. It is more likely that the exposure of Jews to "external wisdom" happened gradually through the spread of the Arabic language and culture, which facilitated contacts between Jews and their gentile neighbors. It seems that both Karaite and Rabbanite intellectuals were exposed to Christian and Muslim influences more or less at the same time. The predominance of Mu'tazilite *kalam* in this formative period, as well as the still central role played by Christian intellectuals, dictated the tenor of Jewish thought.

In the debate between Muslim orthodoxy and Muslim rationalist theologians, the latter were on the defensive. Apart from relatively short periods when it gained the upper hand (as during the reign of al-Ma'mun), rational theology was strongly curbed by the prevalent traditionalist orthodox tendencies. In terms of Islamic religious thought, the Mu'tazila is perceived as extremist and therefore liminal.

The setting of medieval Jewish thought is quite different. Both Saadya and Qirqisani hint at some argument with people who reject rationalistic readings of Scripture. But the accounts of this argument are quite cursory, and no writing of the supposed traditionalists is extant. Their very existence as a significant phenomenon is questionable. Their mention may be only a relic from Islamic literature. Even if we assume that such people did exist, by the tenth century the rationalists had the upper hand. Among Rabbanites, the adoption of *kalam* by Saadya was probably of decisive importance in this respect. Unlike al-Muqammas, who was a marginal figure in the Jewish community, Saadya was, from an early age, a dominant one. His charismatic personality contributed to his reputation as a religious and intellectual authority, and although he did not belong to one of the aristocratic Babylonian families, he soon penetrated their stronghold in the academies. Saadya introduced *kalam* into the world of talmudic scholarship, and endowed it with his authority. After Saadya, hardly anyone questioned the legitimacy of the rationalistic approach, and for a while *kalam* is identified with the theology of mainstream Judaism.

This is patently clear when we examine the literary output of the geonim after Saadya, and in particular Samuel ben Hofni (d. 1013), who followed closely the Basra school of Mu'tazilite *kalam*, and adhered to Saadya's approach to the biblical text. Moreover, some *kalam* doctrines left their mark on Jewish theology even beyond the circles of the *mutakallimun*. In the Iberian Peninsula *kalam* in general and Mu'tazilite *kalam* in particular, were not able to gain a firm foothold. Nevertheless, Spanish Jewish authors, like Judah Halevi (d. 1141) and Joseph ibn Zaddiq (d. 1149) incorporate much kalamic material in their discussions. Another case in point is Maimonides, who, notwithstanding his scathing criticism of the *kalam*, read

Saadya's work and was influenced by it. Like the *mutakallimun*, Maimonides navigated between what he perceived to be the content of the revealed text and his independent philosophical outlook. In this respect one can justify Leo Strauss' scathing remark that, despite Maimonides' aversion to the *kalam*, he in fact practiced "an intelligent, or enlightened kalam."[19] With the shift of the center of the Jewish world to the West (and, to some extent, perhaps also as a result of Maimonides' influence), the interest of Rabbanite Jews in *kalam* waned. This decline of interest is reflected in the choice of texts for translation: Saadya's theological summa was translated into Hebrew, but his Bible commentaries, as well as the commentaries of Samuel ben Hofni and of other *mutakallimun*, were not. They thus remained outside the reach of European Jews.

The one exception to this rule among Rabbanite Jews was the Jewish community of Yemen, where Maimonides' authority did not eclipse Saadya, and the works of these two great rationalists continued to be widely studied down to modern times. In the Jewish Karaite community, on the other hand, *kalam* never lost its authority. Its theses were heralded as the true doctrine of the prophets, and even when Arabic was no longer the vernacular, *kalam* continued to exert its influence through translations and original works in Hebrew, composed in Byzantium as well as in Europe.

NOTES

1. L. E. Goodman, "Maimonides' Responses to Saadya Gaon's Theodicy and their Islamic Backgrounds," in *Studies in Islamic and Judaic Traditions II*, ed. W. M. Brinner and S. D. Ricks (Atlanta: Scholars Press, 1989), 4–7.

2. Saadya, *Kitab al-Amanat wa'l-I'tiqadat*, ed. J. Qafih (Jerusalem: Sura, 1960), 12; Saadya Gaon, *The Book of Beliefs and Opinions*, trans. S. Rosenblatt (New Haven and London: Yale University Press, 1948), 15.

3. As in the introduction to his *Commentary on the Book of Creation; Sefer Yetzira (Kitab al-mabadi)*, ed. J. Qafih (Jerusalem: n.p., 1972), 17–18.

4. P. B. Fenton, "Daniel Ibn al-Mashita's Taqwim al-Adyan: New Light on the Oriental Phase of the Maimonidean Controversy," in *Genizah Research after Ninety Years: The Case of Judaeo-Arabic*, ed. J. Blau and S. C. Reif (Cambridge: Cambridge University Press, 1992), 74–81.

5. L. Nemoy (trans.), "The Pseudo-Qumisian Sermon to the Karaites," *Proceedings of the American Academy for Jewish Research* 43 (1976), 49–105.

6. Cf. S. Stroumsa, "From the Earliest Known Judaeo-Arabic Commentary on Genesis," *Jerusalem Studies in Arabic and Islam* 27 (2002), 375–95.

7. H. Malter, *Saadia Gaon, his Life and Works* (Philadelphia: Jewish Publication Society, 1921), 119, 198.

8. Saadya, *Amanat*, 4–10; Saadya, *Beliefs and Opinions*, 5–12.

9. Saadya, *Amanat*, 10; Saadya, *Beliefs and Opinions*, 13; Saadya, *Commentary on Ecclesiastes*, ed. J. Qafih (Jerusalem: Sura, 1976), 17–18.

10. Saadya, *Amanat*, 193–4; Saadya, *Beliefs and Opinions*, 236–9.

11. H. Davidson, "Saadia's List of Theories of the Soul," in *Jewish Medieval and Renaissance Studies*, ed. A. Altmann (Cambridge, Mass.: Harvard University Press, 1967), 75–94.

12. Saadya, *Amanat*, 44–58; Saadya, *Beliefs and Opinions*, 50–66.

13. R. Brody, *The Geonim of Babylonia and the Shaping of Medieval Jewish Culture* (New Haven and London: Yale University Press, 1998), 257–8

14. For instance, Saadya, *Amanat*, 97–110; Saadya, *Beliefs and Opinions*, 112–16.

15. A. Dotan, *The Dawn of Hebrew Linguistics: The Book of Elegance of the Language of the Hebrews by Saadia Gaon* [Hebrew] (Jerusalem: World Union of Jewish Studies, 1997), 1: 96–104.

16. S. Pines, "Points of Similarity between the Exposition of the Doctrine of the Sefirot in the *Sefer Yetzira* and a Text of the Pseudo-Clementine Homilies: The Implications of this Resemblance; Appendix II: Quotations from Saadya's Commentary on the *Sefer Yetzira* in a Poem by Ibn Gabirol and in the *Fons Vitae*," *Proceedings of the Israel Academy of Sciences and Humanities* 7.3 (1989), 122–6; reprinted in W. Z. Harvey and M. Idel (eds.), *The Collected Works of Shlomo Pines*. v. *Studies in the History of Jewish Thought* (Jerusalem: Magnes Press, 1997), 153–7.

17. Malter, *Saadia*, 228.

18. R. Drory, *The Emergence of Jewish–Arabic Literary Contacts at the Beginning of the Tenth Century* [Hebrew], *Literature, Meaning, Culture* 17 (Tel Aviv, 1988); Drory, *Models and Contacts – Arabic Literature and its Impact on Medieval Jewish Culture* (Leiden: Brill, 2000), ch. 5.

19. L. Strauss, "The Literary Character of the *Guide of the Perplexed*," in his *Persecution and the Art of Writing* (Glencoe: The Free Press, 1952; reprinted, Chicago: University of Chicago Press, 1988), 41. But see W. Z. Harvey, "Why Maimonides was not a Mutakallim," in *Perspectives on Maimonides*, ed. J. L. Kraemer (Oxford: Littman Library, 1991), 105–14.

5 Jewish Neoplatonism: Being above Being and divine emanation in Solomon ibn Gabirol and Isaac Israeli*

INTRODUCTION AND METHODOLOGICAL OVERVIEW

Defining Jewish Neoplatonism is no easy task, due in no small part to the difficulty of defining "Neoplatonism." In an effort to best understand these categories, I will isolate two conceptual issues – the nature of the Godhead, and its relation to the cosmos – in Plotinus (the pagan third-century founder of Neoplatonism), and then, with recourse to Solomon ibn Gabirol in the first case and Isaac Israeli in the second, I will examine the extent to which these issues can be seen to exist – unmodified – within the corpus of Jewish Neoplatonism. By suggesting, first, ways in which each of these Plotinian issues seems, prima facie, at odds with the parallel Jewish Neoplatonic views, but then by emphasizing how in fact they are reconcilable with the Jewish versions, I will challenge oversimplified estimations not only of the nature of Plotinus' own philosophy, but of what real differences exist between it and Jewish Neoplatonism. In this way I will have indirectly been examining what exactly counts as "Neoplatonism," Jewish or otherwise. By proceeding in this way,

* I would like to thank Stephen Gersh for instruction and inspiration in my studies of Neoplatonism, as well as Tamar Rudavsky, Peter King, and the Melton Center for Jewish Studies at The Ohio State University for giving me the opportunity to conduct research on Jewish Neoplatonism. I am especially indebted to Tzvi Langermann and George Pappas for their comments on an earlier draft of this paper, and I would also like to express gratitude to the American Academy for Jewish Research for the post-doctoral fellowship during 2000–2002 that allowed me to further my research, and to Joel Kraemer in particular for giving me so much of his time. Finally, I am grateful to the deans at The Divinity School at The University of Chicago for making a number of research opportunities available to me during the tenure of my fellowship.

I hope to do justice to the elusive connections that exist between various Neoplatonic textual traditions. By focusing on the works of two early Jewish Neoplatonists, this chapter, rather than attempting to be comprehensive, suggests conceptual starting points from which one might address and evaluate the degree, implications, and development of Neoplatonism in any number of other Jewish texts.

Before proceeding, a further clarification of my methodology is in order. In what follows, I aim to analyze Gabirol and Israeli along Plotinian lines. Of course, neither Gabirol nor Israeli was directly influenced by Greek texts of Neoplatonism, and the Arabic versions of Plotinian and Proclean materials by which they were influenced contain many changes from Plotinus' *Enneads*. While mindful of this fact, I am here interested in questioning the extent to which textual changes between Arabic and Greek Neoplatonic texts need be taken as representing deep philosophical differences between the two traditions. I suggest that they need not be seen as representing such differences. While it is certainly possible that, for example, the replacement of Plotinus' notion of a One "above Being" with a God identical to Being, and a similar textual replacement of "emanation" with "creation *ex nihilo*" might represent major departures from Plotinus' worldview, in what follows I aim to examine the extent to which such changes might nonetheless be seen in genuinely Plotinian terms. As long as I can reconcile terminological changes in the Arabic Neoplatonic traditions (and in the Jewish texts that are rooted in those traditions) with Plotinus' own views, there is no prima facie reason to take those changes as reflecting deep conceptual upheavals of Plotinus' own views. In presenting below what I denominate as the "Neoplatonic Naming Principle" and the "Neoplatonic Causal Principle," as well as in addressing the different senses of "*nihil*" in "creation *ex nihilo*," I attempt to provide some means by which the reader might more readily entertain conceptual reconciliations between Arabic (and Jewish) texts and Plotinian Neoplatonism.

JEWISH NEOPLATONISM IN CONTEXT

Among the earliest Neoplatonic Jewish thinkers are Isaac Israeli (850–c. 932/55) and Solomon ibn Gabirol (1021–1054/8). Because of the rootedness of early Jewish Neoplatonists within a host of Arabic textual traditions (Islamic Spain and North Africa being the home of the Jewish Neoplatonists), we might meaningfully categorize them under the broader heading "Arabic Neoplatonists." In fact, Jewish Neoplatonism reveals traces of a huge mix of oftentimes conceptually disparate philosophical and theological Arabic materials, including the vulgate and "longer" versions of the *Theology of Aristotle*, the *Liber de Causis* (or, *Kalam fi mahd al-khayr*), the pseudo-Empedoclean *Book of Five Substances*, *Ibn Hasday's Neoplatonist*, the encyclopedic works of the Ikhwan al-Safa' (the Brethren of Purity), and the writings of al-Kindi, al-Farabi, and Ibn Sina. Additionally we find reverberations of more esoteric Jewish and Islamic materials such as the *Sefer Yetzira* (and its commentaries), the *Ghayat al-Hakim*,[1] and Gnostic Isma'ili materials.[2] Add to this mix Arabic translations of works of Plato, Aristotle, and Neopythagorean treatises and it becomes clear just how many conceptual possibilities must be weighed before interpreting even a single claim within a text of Jewish Neoplatonism.

Apart from the specific background philosophical sources, I might also note that an investigation into a number of literary forms, philosophical as well as non-philosophical, is often helpful, even necessary on occasion,[3] toward the goal of retrieving as complete a picture as possible of a given Jewish Neoplatonist's philosophical doctrine. In addition to philosophical treatises, many of our authors also composed Bible and/or *Sefer Yetzira* (*Book of Creation*) commentaries, as well as devotional and secular poems, many of which are replete with philosophically revealing details. The complicated philosophical system of Gabirol, for example, is presented not only in his famous *Mekor Hayyim* (Lat. *Fons Vitae*), but also in a commentary on Genesis attributed to him by Abraham ibn Ezra, and is certainly evidenced in many of his poems.

Finally, many Jewish Neoplatonic ideas might additionally be found amidst the rich tapestry of kabbalistic materials, though one must caution against anachronistically reading back later ideas into the earliest Jewish Neoplatonic thinkers.[4]

IN THE FOOTSTEPS OF PLOTINUS: TOWARDS A SUBTLER
APPRECIATION OF JEWISH NEOPLATONISM

Turning to an analysis of Jewish Neoplatonism, I will proceed as follows: I commence with Plotinus' views on (1) the nature of the Godhead, and (2) the nature of the Godhead's relationship to the cosmos, along with parallel Jewish Neoplatonic discussions of these issues. In each case, I first examine the ways in which the Jewish Neoplatonic thesis seems to be a rejection – or at least a significant modification – of Plotinus. I then show, in each case, that the Jewish Neoplatonic thesis in question need not be seen in fact as representing any philosophical departure from Plotinus' own.

On the Nature of the Godhead: The Godhead as Being, the Godhead as "Above Being"

GABIROL AND PLOTINUS IN CONFLICT? Neoplatonic texts reveal in general an interest in various grades of reality, a great "chain of being," with one level nested in the next, leading, through a gradual series of ascending layers, to the Godhead itself, the highest level in the hierarchy. In this regard, consider some of the systemizations shown in Figure 1:

Plotinus
1. One (= above Being)
2. Universal Intellect (= Being)
3. World Soul
4. Nature

Proclus
1. One (= above Being)
2. *Henads*
3. Limit and Unlimited
4. One-Being
5. Life
6. Intellect
7. Soul
8. Nature

Liber de Causis
1. Pure Being (*Anniyya mahda*); Being Only (*Anniyya faqat*)
2. Intellect (First Created Being)
3. Soul
4. Nature

Gabirol
1. First Essence, Creator, Being Only (*Esse Tantum*)
2. Will[5]
3. Universal Matter, Universal Form
4. Universal Intellect (First Created Being)
5. [World] Rational Soul
6. [World] Animal / Sensitive Soul
7. [World] Nutritive Soul
8. Sphere / Nature

Figure 1. Neoplatonic Hierarchies of Being

Turning for our purposes to one main difference between these two pagan and two monotheistic cosmologies, one finds that whereas Plotinus and Proclus are committed to a Godhead that is a One above Being, our two monotheistic Neoplatonic systems have in common the apparent rejection of any such description of the Godhead. Instead of placing God "above Being," these systems *identify* God with Being (Arabic, *anniyya*[6]), Being Only (*Esse Tantum*). (In addition, in the case of Gabirol himself, one should note his descriptions of God as the "Primum Esse"[7] and "Esse Verum,"[8] as well as his demarcating an infinite principle of Active Being [*Esse Agens*].[9])

For the Jewish Neoplatonic identification of God with Being Only, consider the following: At a point in the *Fons Vitae* (*FV*) where Gabirol addresses the relevance to God of the four questions that can prima facie be asked of any being, "whether?" "what?" "how?" and "why?", he suggests that only the existential "whether?" question (*"an est?"*, i.e. "whether [something exists]") can be properly asked of God. This latter question is based on Aristotle's classification at *Posterior Analytics* 2:1, and it is in Gabirol's granting to God only an existential "thatness" that he may be seen as identifying God with Being Only. In context, Gabirol's identification of this existential question is presented in the following exchange in the *FV*:

Master: . . . I say that existence (*esse*) from the highest to the lowest extremes is distinguished by four orders, viz.,
   a.   "whether it is" (*an est*),
   b.   "what it is" (*quid est*),
   c.   "how it is" (*quale est*) [i.e. what sort of qualities X has],
   d.   "why it is" (*quare est*).
Moreover, of these, the most worthy is the one concerning which it is asked *only* "whether it is," not "what it is" or "how it is" and not "why it is," as in the case of [sicut] the Exalted and Blessed Unity; and after this is the one concerning which it is asked "what it is," not "how it is" or "why it is," as in the case of Intellect; after this is the one concerning which it is asked "what it is" and "how it is," not "why it is," as in the case of Soul; after this is the one concerning which it is asked "what it is" and "how it is" and "why it is," just as in the case of Nature and the things generated from it; and each one of these is ordered according to the order of number.
Disciple: In what sense?
Master: Since the question "whether it is" is posited according to the order of "one," since it is being only [*quia est esse tantum*] . . .[10]

From the fact that Shem Tov ibn Falaquera, in his Hebrew translation of this passage, employs the term *metziut* for *esse*, Munk suggested that the Arabic term used by Gabirol here would have been *anniyya*.[11] I might add that the language of "Being Only" in the

above passage quite clearly recalls *anniyya faqat* (lit. "Being Only")
which we find in both the *Liber de Causis* and the Arabic Plotinian
materials to describe the Godhead. This notion of God as a pure
Being devoid of any complexity or limitation may be linked to the
Mu'tazilite doctrine of the absolute unity of God (himself seen, as
is the case for Gabirol, as a pure essence), and it might also be related to the identification of God with pure and simple Being in Sufi
theosophy.[12]

In the above remarks in *FV*, then, we find that one can only ascertain *that* God exists (and not *what* his essence is). From this suggestion, together with Gabirol's clear description of this Being as
the First Essence (*al-dhat al-ula*, as evidenced in some of the extant
Arabic fragments of the *Fons Vitae*),[13] God emerges as the essence
which is one with pure Being.[14] In this way, God is essentially unlike
any other existent.

God thus construed as Being Only, then, would certainly seem to
differ from the Plotinian One that is, on the contrary, "above Being."

GABIROL AND PLOTINUS RECONCILED. In what follows, however,
I offer considerations that would lead us to question whether the
Jewish Neoplatonic "God who is Being" must in fact be taken as
conceptually distinct from the Plotinian One "above Being."

One must first note that in both the Arabic (incl. Jewish) Neoplatonic textual milieu, as well as in Plotinus' corpus, God is certainly
"above *limited* (finite) Being." On this, all of our thinkers agree.
Thus, one finds within the Arabic Neoplatonic tradition a bifurcation of *anniyya* into *anniyya faqat* ("Being Only") or *anniyya mahda*
("Pure Being")[15] on the one hand, and "created being" on the other,
with the claim that the former is above the latter.

In this regard Gabirol treats Intellect, the first occurrence of "form
in matter,"[16] as the first created, or limited, being.[17] But, this being
(Intellect) is additionally said to be the cause of "*esse*" in all lower
things,[18] and as such additionally emerges as a brand of generic Being
per se in which all other composite entities subsist. It is clear that
God is "above Being" in at least the sense of transcending the limited
grade of Being associated with Intellect, as well as transcending, by
extension, all lower composite entities that partake of the Being of
Intellect.

Any suggestion, then, that this God is nonetheless not identical with Plotinus' Godhead "above Being" seems to rest on the assumption that, in fact, Plotinus' description is meant as something more extreme than merely "above limited Being."

However, consider the extent to which one might take Plotinus' own description as simply meaning "above limited Being." At *Enneads* 5:5.6, remarking on the access we have to knowing the One, Plotinus says: "the one wanting to contemplate that which is above the intelligible will contemplate the whole of the intelligible having been removed, since one learns 'that it is' in this way, with the 'what it is' having been removed."[19] Following Altmann and Stern,[20] one might see Plotinus' claim here as suggesting that the One is subject only to the existential "whether" question, and not to the "what" question. But, if so, this is no different from Gabirol's above treatment of God's "thatness." So in this regard, Plotinus' treatment of the Godhead is identical to the monotheistic Neoplatonist's account of "God as [identical with] Being."

Consider the sense in which Plotinus places his One "above Being":

Since the substance which is generated [from the One] is form – one could not say that what is generated from that source is anything else – and not the form of some one thing but of everything, so that no other form is left outside it, the One must be without form. But if it is without form it is not a substance; for a substance must be some one particular thing, something, that is, defined and limited; but it is impossible to apprehend the One as a particular thing: for then it would not be the principle, but only that particular thing which you said it was. But if all things are in that which is generated [from the One], which of the things in it are you going to say that the One is? Since it is none of them, it can only be said to be beyond them. But these things are beings, and being: so it is "beyond being."[21]

The One emerges in Plotinus as the principle, origin, and cause of all Being and beings, but is itself devoid of any limitation, and hence is itself "above Being" (*epekeina ontos*, lit. "beyond being"). But given this gloss on the Plotinian description of the Godhead as "above Being," there seems to be no reason to deny the equation of Plotinus' One with the Arabic tradition's *anniyya faqat/mahda*, and hence, with Gabirol's God as Being Only.

So far, then, we have seen that Plotinus identifies the Godhead as the cause of all Being, and also as "above Being." Yet there is Neoplatonic support for affixing the name "Being" to something which is "the cause of" as well as itself *above* Being. In both Plotinus and Proclus we find what we might call the "Neoplatonic Naming Principle" (NNP) at play.[22] This principle says that the cause of some formal reality, while itself lacking that reality, is nonetheless named by that reality. NNP gives us grounds on which to see Plotinus' Godhead under the name "Being," in spite of his not in fact having thus named the One. If such a principle is operative, then one can readily see that Plotinus' One and the "God that is Being" of Gabirol's *Fons Vitae* (and of Arabic texts more generally) are not conceptually distinct.

To this end, consider Gabirol's identification of God with Being, in light of the following Neoplatonic notion, which we might call the "Neoplatonic Causal Principle" (NCP). This principle states that the cause of some formal reality itself lacks – or, is "above" – that formal reality.[23]

To root this principle in Gabirol, one might note his claim that all effects are in their causes (*FV* 3.30, 151, 3), but that they are in their causes only as potencies (*FV* 3.18, 118, 24). As such, causes lack in actuality the formal realities of their effects.

Applying NCP to Gabirol's claim that God is the cause of Being,[24] we might easily conclude that God is, indeed, above Being; we might say he is the "potency to Be," or a principle of preexistence. The mere fact of Gabirol's identifying God as "Being" (*esse, anniyya*), then, does not on its own rule out – and Gabirol's general commitment to NCP in fact supports – a clear sense in which God is "above Being."

In addition to the above sense of "Being" denoting the composite entity of Intellect, there is an additional use of "being" in the *Fons Vitae* to denote the "act of being" that – together with a "potency to Be" – comprises each composite entity. The "act of being" is associated by Gabirol with form,[25] and the "potency to be" with matter, and hence we have here at least one possible sense of his "universal hylomorphic" claim that all substances – even Intellect and intellects – possess both form and matter.[26]

As I suggest at length elsewhere,[27] the status of this "act of being" (form) is unclear in the *Fons Vitae*, since it sometimes emerges as superior to the "pre-*esse*" matter, but sometimes as inferior. To render plausible the possibility of privileging the "pre-*esse*" state of matter over that of formal being, one may here note Gabirol's association of formal being with limitation, finitude,[28] and difference,[29] with matter (or pre-*esse*) on the contrary emerging as a pure, unlimited (formless), and infinite potency associated with unity and sameness.[30] It is this sort of structure (together with a number of detailed claims about matter which I treat of elsewhere)[31] that enables us to see in matter a superiority over the "act of being" associated with the formal. We might summarize this unexpected victory of matter over form as the emergence of potency over act, of "pre-*esse*" over "esse."

Consider the implications of these results for our description of the Godhead in light of Gabirol's own analogical methodology in which the order of things in the microcosm is used to reveal the order of heavenly things (itself rooted in his Neoplatonic belief that the order of things in the microcosm reflects the order of heavenly things).[32] In light of the "microcosmic" priority of "pre-*esse*" to "*esse*" that we have just noted, an analogy between pre-*esse* and God seems to suggest itself quite readily, in that both are infinite, predetermined potencies that precede any formal limitation. Material pre-*esse* – as infinite, pre-limited potency – is to the formal act of *esse*, just as God as infinite, pre-limited potency is to Being (to the formal act of *esse*). While God is not the same as matter, on this analogy he certainly seems to have more in common with the matter of composite existents than with their formal act of being.[33] Gabirol's own principle of analogy seems to suggest, then, that God is more akin to "pre-*esse*" than to *esse*, or that he can be accurately construed as "above Being."

A third approach to reconciling Gabirol's description of God as [only] Being with Plotinus' description of a God who is "above Being" is not so much a reconciliation as it is an acknowledgment of the centrality of paradox within Neoplatonic texts. Gabirol's description of God as "Being" need not rule out attributing to him a description of God as "above Being," even if we take "Being" in both cases as referring to a single reality, unlimited Being only. In fact, that God is actually both identical with and "above" some reality is not only a possibility for Gabirol, but one that would follow closely in the spirit of Neoplatonic apophasis, in which the utter transcendence of the divinity demands that one speaks of him in paradoxical terms.

I might note that this spirit of paradox leads in general to a fluid ontology of the divine realm in Gabirol's *Fons Vitae*, in which God, Will, First Matter, and First Form each seem to be treated under prima facie conflicting descriptions. While these conflicting descriptions need not be seen as paradoxes, the general point seems to reveal a heightened appreciation of the relatively intractable nature of the object in question. Consider just some of the descriptions that arise in the *Fons Vitae* (Figure 2):

God	Transcendent	Immanent, Creator
	Above Being	Pure Being, True Being, First Being;
	Above Substance	[i.e. Being Only]
		First Substance
Will	infinite, unlimited[34]	finite and limited
		(in relation to Form;[35]
		or, with respect to Intellect)[36]
Matter	infinite, unlimited	finite and differentiated
	(here symbolically	(here in the sense of a composite,
	linked with the	"Matter + Form substance")[37]
	"Divine Throne"	
	image,[38] and perhaps	
	with the "'ayin" or,	
	"Nothingness" of	
	Keter Malkhut[39])	
Form	*esse* and source of unity	*esse* and source of diversity
	(here as Second Unity,	(here in opposition to unity of
	manifestation of Will,	matter, in association with Limit)
	impression of the	
	True First Unity [God])	

Figure 2. Descriptions of Reality in Gabirol

When describing a realm that is beyond knowing or definition, one must employ a fluid discourse, by whose opposing affirmations and negations one comes closest to uncovering that which cannot be uncovered.[40]

I have so far addressed the extent to which the relationship between the Jewish Neoplatonic conception of God as Being can consistently and meaningfully be described in Plotinus' own terms as a One "above Being." I turn now to considering the reconcilability of Plotinian emanation with Israeli's prima facie doctrine of creation *ex nihilo*.

On the Nature of God's Relation to the Cosmos:
Emanation and Creation

ISRAELI AND PLOTINUS IN CONFLICT? It may well seem that Isaac Israeli's invocation of "creation" to describe the originative relation between God and the cosmos puts him directly in opposition to Plotinus. Further, it seems that any monotheist thinker would have no choice but to reject Plotinus' description of an "emanating" divinity, on the grounds that such a description of the Godhead (1) seems to rob God of a freely willed creative relationship to the cosmos, problematically submitting him instead to forces of insurmountable necessity, whereby his relationship to the cosmos is entirely beyond his control; and (2) blurs the line between creator and creation, by describing the cosmos as flowing forth from the essence of the divinity himself.

In what follows, I will respond to (1) by showing why Plotinus' God is not in fact robbed of freedom and will, and is certainly not subject to necessity in a problematic way. And in responding to (2), I will emphasize the extent to which the blurring of lines between creator and creation has not generally been seen as problematic from the monotheistic (religious) perspective. After removing the critical force from the above two anti-emanation observations, I conclude that behind the language of creation in Israeli emerges none other than Plotinus' emanating Godhead.

ISRAELI AND PLOTINUS RECONCILED. To respond to the theist's charge that a Plotinian Godhead is not free, but rather is problematically bound by necessity, I offer the following considerations about necessity and freedom:

As long as it is God's own essential goodness that accounts for his emanating, the Neoplatonist need not admit to any "necessitation," or to the presence in the Godhead of the sort of necessitation that brings with it negative overtones, those ordinary cases of necessitation where there is compulsion by some force from without, a compulsion related to the negativity of the material and irrational in the cosmos. On the contrary, when Plotinus speaks of the Godhead's activity as arising "out of necessity," this does not fall under ordinary necessitation (compulsion from without), the kind of necessity that the monotheist critic wishes to identify Plotinian necessity with.

In effect, I suggest that the critic has unjustifiably attached to the unique necessitation of the Godhead's overflow a set of negative associations inappropriately drawn from considerations of ordinary cases of necessitation. As such, the critic's attack on Plotinus' world-view here fails to strike home.

As for the denial of bona fide freedom in Plotinus, if one turns to Plotinus' discussion at *Enneads* 6:8, one finds an explicit description of the One's having willed itself *freely*.[41] More importantly, though, are the reasons we are given by Plotinus for why the One is neither free nor willing, none of which seems to rob the Godhead of anything such as suggested by the monotheist critic of Plotinus.

In light of the Neoplatonic Causal Principle (NCP above) – that, as the cause of freedom in all things,[42] God is himself above freedom – and by applying the Neoplatonic Naming Principle (NNP above), we could well say that God is freedom itself! In effect, his being said to be not "free" is not, as the above monotheist criticism seems to suggest, an attribution to God of some lack; rather it is as an ac-knowledgment of God's role as the cause of all freedom and as free-dom itself. Understanding the matter in this way lends plausibility to seeing Plotinus' worldview as amenable to monotheistic values (and vice versa). Prima facie, one has no reason to insist that Arabic and Jewish Neoplatonic texts reflect a deep opposition to Plotinus and his views.

Freedom and necessity are invariably intertwined in the Neopla-tonic tradition concerning creation, and I now turn to cosmology with a view to ascertaining the possibility of reconciling, of bridging the gap between, Israeli with Plotinus, if possible.

Creation *ex nihilo* is standardly rooted in Genesis 1:1 ("In the be-ginning, God created [*bara*]...") and in the Qur'anic description of God as the *Badi*ʿ (absolute creator). Straightaway, we should note that the biblical notion of creation *ex nihilo* can be taken in at least two different ways, an "orthodox" way and an emanationist way.

According to the former ("orthodox") way of taking creation *ex nihilo*, one stipulates at least two things: (1) The world is created by God "from nothing," in the sense of "not from something/anything"; and (2) the creative act is not a flowing forth of things from the essence of God. On this view, taking creation *ex nihilo* as "creation not from something" not only blocks any suggestion of emanation, but additionally ensures no mistaken identification of *nihil* with the "something" which is matter (the "something" which is a "no-thing"). (This sensitivity is reflected in the use in many contexts of the Arabic expression *la min shay'* ["not from a thing"] as opposed to the expression *min la shay'* ["from no thing"]).[43]

However, a second account of creation *ex nihilo*, one that points in the direction of a Plotinian emanationist view, may be found as well. On this account, the *nihil* of creation *ex nihilo* is identified with God himself. This identification of God with *nihil* is based either on treating "nothing" as a name for God[44] or, more generally, on seeing God as "he who is beyond all predication," and hence, as essentially "no-thing" as far as human cognizing is concerned. Taken this way, creation *ex nihilo* reveals nothing different from Plotinus' own emanationist account of the divinity's relation to the cosmos.

Turning to Israeli, there is debate over which of the above two creation *ex nihilo* accounts best describes his own talk of *ikhtira‘* ("invention," "origination," or "making anew") and *ibda‘* ("absolute creation," or "innovation")[45] in such claims as "the first created things (*mukhtara‘at*) are two simple substances..."[46] While Altmann defends a reading according to which this "absolute creation" is taken by Israeli in the "orthodox" sense,[47] Wolfson suggests the possibility of taking this creation in an emanationist sense.[48] That Israeli is committed to Plotinian emanation as it concerns those things arising from Intellect (including the emergence of the natural realm) is beyond doubt (we find his likening that process to the sun's natural radiation in such claims as "the light which emanates from intellect is essential [*dhati jawhari*], like the light and shining of the sun, which emanates from its essence and substantiality [*dhatiha wa-jawhariyyatiha*]"[49]). The question is only whether it is simply this sort of emanation or a genuinely "orthodox" sense of creation *ex nihilo* that Israeli means to denote in his talk of the "absolute creation" of the first two substances. In the remainder of this chapter, I turn to considerations for and against seeing in Israeli a genuinely orthodox sense of creation *ex nihilo*.

In initial support of seeing in Israeli a commitment to orthodox creation *ex nihilo*, recall his description of the first creations in terms of "innovation" and "making anew" (*al-ibda‘ wa'l-ikhtira‘*), terms that he defines as "making existent existences from the non-existent" (*ta'yis al-aysat min lays*).[50] However, as we have seen in the above account, creation "from nothing" (or, from the non-existent) might indeed be taken in an emanationist sense. So we need more information to support a genuinely orthodox creation *ex nihilo* reading in Israeli. To this end, we may turn to Altmann, who draws our attention to Israeli's demarcation (in *The Book of Substances*) of two causal mechanisms: (1) causality by action, which is creation by the power and by the will (*min al-qudra wa-l-irada*) by way of influence and action ('*ala sabil al-ta'thir wa-l-fi'l*); and (2) essential causality, which is an "essential and substantial" (*dhati jawhari*) emanation, one which, as we have seen, is "like the light and shining of the sun, which emanates from its essence and substantiality."

Since (according to Altmann) the second of these clearly corresponds to emanation, it follows that the first denotes something different, viz., orthodox creation *ex nihilo*. However, does this really follow? As Wolfson has argued, one might just as readily conclude that these two causal mechanisms pick out two varieties of emanation: one kind of emanation that is not entirely "unconscious," and that describes the relationship between God and the first creation(s), and one regular Plotinian variety of emanation that describes the relation between all lower cosmic stages. While Wolfson's remarks suggest that the kind of emanation that Israeli predicates of God is not straightforwardly Plotinian, one might go even further to suggest that there is here no need to see any real departure from Plotinus at all. Even Plotinus can be read as distinguishing the relevance and na-ture of the first emanation from all other emanations (an emanation that, given his description of the One's having "willed itself freely," might even be described as the sort of "not entirely unconscious emanation" to which Wolfson adverts).

Turning back to Altmann, one finds a second argument for see-ing Israeli's creation *ex nihilo* as non-emanative, a second argument that he himself describes as "the most potent argument against any attempt of interpreting his [Israeli's] use of the term creation ex ni-hilo in an emanationist sense."[51] Altmann here reasons as follows: We know that Israeli is committed to the presence of not one, but two "first creations" (viz., First Matter and First Form).[52] But as such, Israeli cannot have held an emanative account of God's cre-ative act without violating the Neoplatonic rule that, in the arena of emanation, "from one comes only one." To successfully avoid breaching the "from one comes only one" rule of emanation, Israeli clearly must not have taken these first two creations as products emanated from (the one) God, but as the effects of an orthodox creation *ex nihilo*. Altmann thus suggests that Wolfson's emanationist reading of Israeli only seems appealing because Wolfson ignores the two first substances,[53] First Form and First Matter.

I must note, though, that, even if Altmann were correct in his suggestion that only orthodox creation *ex nihilo* could save Israeli from violating Neoplatonic doctrine, one cannot rule out the possibility that Israeli was indeed guilty of just such a violation. As such, one cannot simply conclude that Israeli's understanding of God's creative act was non-emanationist. More importantly, one might undercut Altmann's above strategy by questioning his own assumption that Israeli's two simultaneous first creations, First Form and First Matter, would, if emanated, stand in genuine conflict with the "from one comes only one" rule. For, what if the two were really, in some important sense, one? Then there would be no problem in reconciling their emanation from God with the "from one comes only one" dictum. Turning to Israeli, we find that he does indeed describe the two first creations as comprising the single Intellect. Since there is a real sense in which for Israeli the two in question are also a single one (viz., Intellect), a suggestion on Israeli's part that these "two" emanate from the Godhead would not amount to a violation of the Neoplatonic "from one comes only one" rule. Once again, Altmann's argument that only orthodox creation *ex nihilo* is amenable to Israeli's Neoplatonic cosmology is undermined, and one is left with the genuine possibility of seeing in even Israeli's talk of "absolute creation," the Plotinian doctrine of emanation.

CONCLUSION

I have suggested ways of blurring the lines between "Being" and "above Being," as well as between creation *ex nihilo* and divine emanation. I have done this in order to encourage a greater sensitivity to the possibility of discovering sameness (between seemingly disparate traditions), even in apparent difference. I hope in this way to have provided both a sense of the sorts of issues at play in Jewish Neoplatonism, as well as a useful lens through which one might begin to reconceptualize the relationship between monotheist and pagan traditions.

NOTES

1. See discussions in A. Altmann and S. Stern (eds.), *Isaac Israeli: A Neoplatonic Philosopher of the Early Tenth Century* (London: Oxford University Press, 1958); see also D. Pingree, "Some of the Sources of the Ghayat al-Hakim," *Journal of the Warburg and Courtauld Institutes* 43 (1980), 1–15.

2. See S. Pines, "Points of Similarity between the Exposition of the Doctrine of the Sefirot in the *Sefer Yetzira* and a Text of the Pseudo-Clementine Homilies: The Implications of this Resemblance," *Proceedings of the Israel Academy of Sciences and Humanities* 7/3 (1989), 63–141.

3. For example, Gabirol privileges Will over Wisdom in his *Fons Vitae*, but Wisdom over Will in his poetic corpus; see n. 5 below.

4. For a treatment and overview of Jewish Neoplatonic themes in kabbalistic writings, see G. Scholem, "Iqvatav shel Gevirol ba-Qabbalah," in *Measef Sofrei Eretz Yisroel*, ed. E. Steiman and A. A. Kovak (Tel Aviv: n.p., 1939), 160–78. See also M. Idel, "Jewish Kabbalah and Platonism in the Middle Ages and Renaissance," in *Neoplatonism and Jewish Thought*, ed. L. E. Goodman (Albany: State University of New York Press, 1992), 319–51.

5. Though, in his poetic corpus, Wisdom precedes Will; for discussion, see Scholem, "Iqvatav shel Gevirol," and Y. Liebes, "*Sefer Yezirah* ezel R. Shlomo ibn Gevirol u-perush ha-shir Ahavtikha," in *The Beginnings of Jewish Mysticism in Medieval Europe*, ed. J. Dan (*Jerusalem Studies in Jewish Thought* 6 [1987], 73–123). It might additionally be noted that sometimes Will appears in the text to be a self-standing hypostasis, but sometimes it seems to be one with the Godhead.

6. Much scholarship has been devoted to parsing apart the various meanings of such philosophical terms as *anniyya*, *mahiyya*, and *huwiyya*. See S. van den Bergh, s.v. *anniyya*, in *The Encyclopaedia of Islam*, new ed., ed. H. A. R. Gibb et al. (Leiden: Brill, 1960), 1: 33–4; and M.-T. d'Alverny, "Anniyya – Anitas," in *Mélanges offerts à Etienne Gilson* (Toronto: Pontifical Institute of Mediaeval Studies, 1959), 59–91.

7. *FV* 5.32, 316, 23 & 26; 317, 21 & 25. As Gabirol's original Arabic text is non-extant, references are to the twelfth-century Latin translation of the *Fons Vitae* (*FV*), which is earlier and more complete than Falaquera's Hebrew translation; cf. Baeumker's edition, *Avencebrolis [Ibn Gabirol]*

Fons Vitae, ex Arabico in Latinum Translatus ab Johanne Hispano et Domenico Gundissalino, in *Beiträge zur Geschichte der Philosophie des Mittelalters*, ed. C. Baeumker (Münster: Aschendorf, 1892). The translation and emphases are my own.

8. *FV* 5.42, 335, 15.

9. Infinite *esse agens* is demarcated from finite *esse patiens*. See, e.g., *FV* 5.25, 303, 25 ff.

10. *FV* 5.24, 301, 16 ff.

11. S. Munk, *Mélanges de philosophie juive et arabe* (Paris: Ch. Franck, 1859), 111 n. 1.

12. F. Rahman, "Dhat", in *Encyclopaedia of Islam*, new ed. (Leiden: Brill, 1965), II: 220.

13. For Arabic fragments corresponding to *FV* 1.7, 9 and 1.7, 10, see S. Pines, "Sefer Arugat ha-Bosem: ha qetaim mi-tokh Sefer Meqor Hayyim," *Tarbiz* 27 (1957–58), 218–33; reprinted in S. Pines, *Beyn mahshevet Yisrael li-mahshevet ha-amim* (Jerusalem: Mosad Bialik, 1977), 44–60; cf. 52.

   That *essentia* in general (and not just in the case of the proper name "First Essence") corresponds to the Arabic *al-dhat* can be seen in a number of the Pines fragments (see Pines, "Sefer Arugat"), as well as in additional fragments in P. Fenton, "Gleanings from Mosheh ibn Ezra's 'Maqalat al-Hadiqa'," *Sefarad* 36–7, fasc. 2 (1976), 294–6.

14. This idea that God, in his essence, is existence is, of course, a well-rehearsed theme in the history of philosophy. For its extensive development in Avicenna, see A.-M. Goichon, *La distinction de l'essence et de l'existence d'après Ibn Sina* (Paris: Desclée de Brouwer, 1937).

15. See, e.g., *Liber de Causis*: O. Bardenhewer, *Die Pseudo-Aristotelische Schrift, über das reine Gute* (Freiburg im Breisgau: Herdersche Verlagshandlung, 1882), 79, line 1 for *anniyya faqat* and 65, line 7 for *anniyya mahda*.

16. *FV* 5.10, 274, 19; 5.11, 277, 4.

17. That God creates *esse* in this composite way may be seen at *FV* 5.40, 329, 4.

18. *FV* 5.15, 286, 10–17. I discuss this theme in greater detail in my "Solomon ibn Gabirol: Universal Hylomorphism and the Psychic Imagination," Ph.D. dissertation, The Ohio State University, 2000.

19. My translation is here informed by Altmann and Stern's rendering, but sticks to the Greek a bit more closely (Altmann and Stern, *Isaac Israeli*, 21). Armstrong's translation is a bit more confusing, and it is less clear with respect to the point I am trying to emphasize here (cf. *Enneads*, Loeb edition [Cambridge: Harvard University Press, 1966], v: 173–5).

20. Altmann and Stern, *Isaac Israeli*, 21.
21. Plotinus, *Enneads* 5:5.6, lines 2–11, trans. Armstrong, in Loeb Classical Library, v: 173.
22. While not stated as a "naming principle" per se, Proclus' remarks at, e.g., *Elements of Theology*, Proposition 101 clearly evidence this phenomenon. For this principle in Plotinus, see *Enneads* 6.8 on God as "freedom" because he is the cause of freedom; see my treatment of this below.
23. For a circumscribed application of this principle within even the *Liber de Causis*, see Proposition 2, and the claim that the First Cause is above eternity because eternity is caused by it.
24. See, e.g., *FV* 5.42, 335, 16.
25. In support of the association of Being and Form, cf. *FV* 1.13, 16, and *FV* 4.10, 237; 5–7.
26. Gabirol's point taken in this way would not be conceptually dissimilar from Avicenna's analysis of composites into "essence" and "existence." For possible influence of this Avicennian idea on Gabirol, see S. Pines, "Ve-qara el ha-ayin ve-nivqa, lahqor *Keter Malkhut* le-Shlomo ibn Gevirol," *Tarbiz* 50 (1980–81), 339–47.
27. Pessin, "Solomon ibn Gabirol."
28. See, e.g., *FV* 5.28, 308, 7–12, where Form is distinguished from Will in terms of the former's being finite.
29. *FV* 4.9, 231, 13–15.
30. *FV* 4.1, 212, 2–3, and 4.1, 212, 7–8.
31. Pessin, "Solomon ibn Gabirol".
32. For a general introduction to this methodology in Gabirol (including an enumeration of four different applications of this method in the *Fons Vitae*), see J. Schlanger, *La philosophie de Salomon Ibn Gabirol* (Leiden: Brill, 1968), 141–57, and on the "macrocosm/microcosm" in general, 313–16.
33. This theme in Gabirol would additionally seem to suggest that materiality is the clearest mark of the divinity, a theme that, while not consistently reflected throughout the *Fons Vitae*, nonetheless finds support in the claim that "Matter is created from Essence, and Form is from the property of that Essence, i.e., from Wisdom and Unity" (*FV* 5.42, 333, 4–5). While the principle of materiality follows immediately from the First Essence, the principle of form emerges from Wisdom, a modification of that First Essence.
34. As I have already noted (see n. 5), Gabirol's notion of Will – taken under this exalted description – is sometimes seen as identical to the divinity himself.
35. *FV* 5.28, 308, 7–12.

36. Will in its finite and limited actuality is also described as "Word;" see Pines, "Points of Similarity" on the relation of this idea to Saadya.

37. Gabirol sometimes uses "Matter" and "Substance" interchangeably; see his claim to this effect, e.g., at *FV* 1.12.

38. For the depiction of Matter as the Divine Throne in Gabirol, cf. *FV* 5.42. Gabirol also talks of the Throne in his celebrated poem *Keter Malkhut* (The Royal Crown) (for Hebrew text, see *Shirei Shlomo ben Yehudah Ibn Gevirol, II [Shirei qodesh]*, ed. C. Bialik and Y. Ravnitsky [Tel Aviv and Berlin: Dwir-Verlags-Gesellschaft, 1925], poem number 62, 62–78; for an English translation, see B. Lewis, *Solomon ibn Gabirol, The Kingly Crown* [London: Vallentine, Mitchell, 1961]). In this poem, the Throne, while not specifically called "Matter," is described as "higher than all height" (Lewis, *Kingly Crown*, 28).

39. See Lewis, *Kingly Crown*, 33 ("That Will called to the void and it was cleft asunder"). For related analysis of this line (though with the suggestion that this "void" – or "nothingness" – refers to Avicennian pre-existent essence), see Pines, "Ve-qara el ha-ayin."

40. On the fluidity of language and its instrumentality in apophatic discourse, see M. Sells, *Mystical Languages of Unsaying* (Chicago: University of Chicago Press, 1994). For a detailed analysis of this phenomenon in Jewish esoteric texts, see E. Wolfson, *Through a Speculum that Shines: Vision and Imagination in Medieval Jewish Mysticism* (Princeton: Princeton University Press, 1994).

41. See *Enneads* 6:8.12, 13, 21.

42. See *Enneads* 6:8.15, where human freedom is presented in terms of striving towards the Goodness of the Godhead.

43. See H. A. Wolfson, "The Meaning of Ex Nihilo in the Church Fathers, Arabic and Hebrew Philosophy, and St. Thomas," in his *Studies in the History of Philosophy and Religion*, 2 vols., ed. I. Twersky and G. Williams (Cambridge, Mass.: Harvard University Press, 1973), I: 207–21, esp. 212ff.

44. In support of seeing "*nihil*" as literally naming God, note Armstrong's translation of *Enneads* 6:9.5, which has Plotinus naming the One "nothing" (*ouden*). Altmann and Stern, however, point out that Armstrong's rendering of Plotinus is here incorrect (Altmann and Stern, *Isaac Israeli*, 156, with n. 2).

45. This "creation"/"innovation" terminology in Israeli may be traced to al-Kindi, himself preceded in this regard by pseudo-Ammonius, "On the Opinions of the Philosophers." It might also be noted that it is under the influence of this notion in Israeli that Joseph ibn Zaddiq draws the distinction between *khalq* (creation *ex aliquo*, or generation) and *ibda'*

(creation *ex nihilo*, or innovation); see Altmann and Stern, *Isaac Israeli*, 68ff.

46. *The Book of Substances (Kitab al-Jawahir)*, fr. III, in Altmann and Stern, *Isaac Israeli*, 83. For the Judeo-Arabic text, see "The Fragments of Isaac Israeli's 'Book of Substances'," in S. M. Stern, *Medieval Arabic and Hebrew Thought*, ed. F. Zimmermann (London: Variorum, 1983), 24 (line 4).

47. A. Altmann, "Creation and Emanation in Isaac Israeli, a Reappraisal," in *Essays in Jewish Intellectual History*, ed. A. Altmann (Hanover: University Press of New England, 1981), 1–15.

48. H. A. Wolfson, "The Meaning of Ex Nihilo in Isaac Israeli," in his *Studies in the History of Philosophy and Religion*, I: 222–33.

49. *Book of Substances*, 84; S. M. Stern, "Isaac Israeli's Book of Substances," in his *Medieval Arabic and Hebrew Thought*, 139 (followed by the Judeo-Arabic text).

50. *Book of Definitions*, in Altmann and Stern, *Isaac Israeli*, 66 (sec. 42).

51. Altmann, "Creation," 4.

52. For a proposal regarding the roots of this tradition, as well as its reverberations in the *Longer Theology of Aristotle* and in Ibn Hasday's corpus, see S. M. Stern, "Ibn Hasday's Neoplatonist," in his *Medieval Arabic and Hebrew Thought*, 58–120.

53. Altmann, "Creation," 5.

6 Judah Halevi and his use of philosophy in the *Kuzari*

The Book of Refutation and Proof on Behalf of the Despised Religion,[1] better known as *The Kuzari*, is one of the last and most popular works of medieval Judaism's premier poet, Judah Halevi (c. 1075–1141). While originally undertaken to respond to the queries of a Karaite scholar,[2] it was reworked and expanded over nearly two decades into the artful and multifaceted dialogue we now possess. Halevi crafted it to address a broad array of religious, philosophical, and cultural issues that concerned him and his contemporaries in the wake of bloody conflicts generated by the *Reconquista* and the First Crusade. These reflected ongoing quarrels between belief and unbelief and between belief and belief, both within and among the cultures and communities of Andalusia, which continue in important ways to this day. While the work is generally regarded as apologetic in character,[3] it is no mere polemic. Rather, its theological defense of Judaism is deeply informed by philosophy and respectful of both its integrity and methods.[4] In what follows, my goal is to analyze and explain a number of Halevi's key ideas and arguments, to show how he uses them and also revises them, to raise a number of salient questions about them, and to identify the trajectory of their reappearance later in the dialogue.

The *Kuzari* begins with an unnamed narrator mentioning how he was asked about any argumentation he had against those who differ with the Jews, such as the philosophers, the adherents of other religions, and sectarian dissenters. This reminded him of the arguments of the Jewish sage who had persuaded the king of the Khazars to convert centuries before.[5] As is well known, the story behind the narrator's recollection tells of a Khazar king who had a recurrent dream, "as though an angel were addressing him." Its message was that his intentions were pleasing to God, but his actions were not. His initial response was to make a more zealous effort to observe the rites of his pagan religion than before, but to no avail; for each time he did so, "the angel came to him at night" with the same message. Eventually he realized while asleep what he did not realize while awake, that God was commanding him to seek out those actions that would be pleasing. With this he begins to invite the various interlocutors who participate in the dialogue, although not always with the same request. But before he receives the first reply, the narrator tells us that some of the Jewish sage's arguments seemed persuasive because they accorded with his own belief. After deciding to record it "just as it took place," he cites Daniel 12:10: "The intelligent will understand."

This unusual and dramatic introduction not only captures the reader's attention, but also provides useful clues about the king and why he responds as he does to his interlocutors. Indeed, it can also help us understand what kind of reader is likely to do likewise or differently. But the king is not merely a type, certainly not a simple one. His behavior and that of others may also raise important questions that are answered by later developments in the dialogue.[6] Thus, for example, a king is a man of action concerned with providing for his people's long-term survival and prosperity. Whether the Khazar's actions are pleasing to God or not will likely matter to him. So, too, with others concerned with similar tasks and questions. That he is a pagan may make him as impartial a judge as possible, but it may also make him deeply skeptical about anyone's claim to possess a divine revelation. Does his officiating at the sacrifices attest to his piety or to his zeal in exercising independent judgment? When the narrator initially says it was "as though" the angel were addressing the king, but later says unqualifiedly that "the angel came to him at night," what is the significance of this disparity? On what basis is the shift justified? Does any other speaker do likewise? In sum, we will want to study with equal interest the characters, arguments, actions, and ambiguities we encounter.

Strictly speaking, the dialogue begins with the words of "the philosopher," an unnamed thinker who, it would appear, is meant to represent the views and commitments of philosophy as such. He speaks twice (K 1:1 and 3) and in each case negates key elements implicit in the king's thinking. In his opening remarks, he emphatically denies the presuppositions underlying both the king's dream and his quest, and then identifies others to replace them. His purpose is to depict the highest type of life, one that might be called pleasing in itself or pleasing by nature. Thus, we are told that God is simply not the kind of being who can "be pleased with" or "feel hatred towards" others, or even know about particular persons and actions, for these are all examples of deficiency and mutability, whereas God – a perfect being – is beyond both. Similarly, God is not a "creator" who acts in order to realize aims and intentions. "Creator" is merely a metaphor for God as the eternal cause of causes. These causes pour forth from him eternally as a hierarchy of beings, which comprises the world as we know it, namely, an eternal system of necessarily connected causes and effects.

Within this eternal but mutable world, human beings are influenced and perfected by many factors, but most decisively by their genetic inheritance, geographic environment,[7] and education. The perfect human being is one in whom the best possible combination of these factors arises, enabling him to realize his capacities to the fullest. Because of his superior knowledge of the causal system, it is allegedly the philosopher who has the best claim to reaching this level. Indeed, his intellect will be illumined by the Active Intellect, the last in the hierarchy of celestial Intelligences, which is both the intelligible form of the sublunar world and the source of all intellectual knowledge about it, so that he will think he has become one with it.

The practical results of this union are that his limbs will henceforth behave in the most perfect and rational way. Also, he will not experience the fear of extinction – ever; and he will enter into the company of the great savants, like Socrates, Plato, Aristotle, Hermes Trismegistus, and Aesculapius, and become one with them in knowing the truth. Accordingly, the philosopher urges the king, in general terms, to purify his soul of doubts and pursue knowledge of the true realities, while keeping to the path of justice and cultivating the other virtues, so that he may become like the Active Intellect. In that case, he will not be concerned about what law he follows or precisely what actions he performs; and if he still wishes, he may either create a religion for himself or follow one of the intellectual *nomoi* of the philosophers.[8] Only his goal must always be attachment to the Active Intellect, for if anything can be characterized symbolically as "God's being pleased," it is union with that Intellect. Once achieved, it might even provide him with knowledge of hidden things and commands by way of veridical dreams and apposite images.[9]

The king's reply is both revealing and unexpected. He calls the philosopher's statement persuasive, but not in keeping with his request. What is revealing about his response is that it shows the king to be inwardly divided. Intellectually, he is drawn to much, if not most, of what the philosopher says and especially to pursuing the truth through his own efforts. But this cannot be at the price of dismissing his own experience, whether private or public, religious or secular. His reservation becomes clear from the two reasons he offers to explain why the philosopher's statement is inadequate. In the first place, he already knows that his soul is pure and his intentions pleasing, but the recurring dream has told him that this is not enough – his actions are not pleasing. Beyond this, the history of conflict between Christians and Muslims reinforces the point. Each has pure intent in seeking to please God, and each is ready to stake his life and take the lives of others on the belief that intentions are not sufficient, that what ultimately pleases God is performance of the specific actions he commands. Obviously, when they differ about what those actions are, both cannot be right. As for what is unexpected about his reply, surely it is that a non-philosopher claiming to be persuaded by the philosopher's remarks can still confidently question their adequacy both here and in what follows. Clearly, he is not the kind of person who could be described as inferior, unintelligent, excitable, or mentally vacant, and thus passively carried along by whatever moves him. To that extent he is quite unlike the typical recipient of veridical dreams described by Aristotle and may even have been so depicted with Aristotle's account in mind.[10]

Having already discussed the dream and its claims, the philosopher says nothing more about them. Instead, he focuses on what the king regards as evidence of pure intention in his reference to the history of religious conflict. "In the religion of the philosophers," he says, "there is no killing of even one of these people, since they follow the intellect" (K 1:3). The practical import of this terse but emphatic negation could hardly be lost on anyone familiar with the effects of religious fanaticism, but the king, already preoccupied with the difficulties raised by the philosopher, now identifies an important difficulty for the philosopher. On his account, the philosophers' superior qualifications should have made prophecy and even the performance of miracles a common occurrence among them, but in fact we find that philosophers lack these gifts, while non-philosophers sometimes display them. This proves to the Khazar that the "divine order" (which the philosopher would have understood as the hierarchy of separate Intelligences) and at least certain souls have a secret character that differs from what the philosopher claims. It also suggests that, however persuasive the philosopher may have been, his theories have not been consistent with actual experience. When they conflict, experience trumps theory, which must either be rejected or revised.

What is clear from this introductory interchange is that for the philosopher intellectual understanding of the whole of reality, preferably through some kind of causal analysis, is of paramount importance. The realm of praxis is largely a matter of indifference, or at most endowed with instrumental value in helping to attain the primary goal. What is unclear is whether the philosopher's claims represent genuine knowledge or only reasoned opinion or a melange of both. Resolving this question would require a careful examination of the arguments he has to support his claims, but his speech is long on pronouncement and short on argumentation. It also speaks in generalities rather than specifics. And even at this preliminary stage we can see that the philosopher moves all too easily from describing a hypothetical perfect man who *thinks* he is one with the Active Intellect, to someone who has actually *attained union* with it. How is this transition any more justified than the one already noted regarding the king's dream, when we are told first that it came to him repeatedly *as though* an angel were addressing him and later that the angel *came* to him at night? Accordingly, we would do well to inquire into the probable sources on which the exposition is based. Is the philosopher more likely a composite Neoplatonic Aristotelian or a particular thinker in that tradition, discernible through certain characteristic positions or formulations? In what sense can he speak for philosophy as such, if he is rooted in only one tradition of philosophy? This problem becomes particularly acute when we try to make sense of the claim that, upon achieving union with the Active Intellect, the philosopher enters into the company of Socrates, Plato, Aristotle, Hermes Trismegistus, and Aesculapius and *becomes one with them*. Do all of these disparate thinkers really have a common identity? Do they teach the same things or agree on what the truth is? Do they all endorse the same virtues and behave in the same way, when faced with similar circumstances. Given what we know of them, it would seem unlikely. What, then, is the philosopher trying to say?

After concluding that the philosopher knows less about the divine order of things than he supposes, the king turns to a Christian and then to a Muslim scholar for information about each one's knowledge and practice. Their respective expositions address his practical concerns and even allude to Israel's prophetic traditions to support particular claims, but they prove faulty on either logical or empirical grounds. Nevertheless, these exchanges help the king to clarify what he is looking for in order to prove that a specific way of acting pleases God. He wants the kind of incontrovertible empirical evidence that would prompt even skeptics to revise their opinions and develop new and ingenious ways to show how what seemed improbable is probable, as natural scientists do when faced with startling new findings that cannot be rejected.[11] We soon learn that the king himself is a skeptic of this kind, since he truly doubts that God enters into direct contact with flesh and blood. Hence, he adds that the required evidence would have to be: (1) witnessed publicly; (2) apprehended by the external senses, especially sight; (3) conveyed through miraculous transformations of the essences of things that only the creator could produce; and (4) scrutinized repeatedly, lest anyone think imagining and magic are involved. And even if all this were furnished, people would still find it hard to accept (K 1:4–8). If they did so anyway, it would presumably be because such evidence became utterly decisive *for them*. It would also delineate the difference between skepticism and invincible ignorance. No explanation is provided about why just these requirements are chosen or exactly how they might be probative, although a part of the answer emerges in the ensuing exchanges. What is clear is that such criteria are not easily satisfied, and none of his three interlocutors thus far have satisfied them. But sensing, ironically, that the one thing the Christian and the Muslim agree on is the reality of God's interactions with biblical Israel, the king eventually asks a Jewish sage about his belief.

The sage responds not with a statement of his belief (*i'tiqad*), but of his faith (*iman*), a distinction corresponding to the difference between articulating and defending beliefs in theological disputation and adhering to the law by natural inclination in order to draw close to God (K 5:16). Moreover, the faith he expresses is not in the creator of the universe, but the God of the Patriarchs, who miraculously redeemed Israel from Egyptian bondage, parted the sea, sustained them in the wilderness, sent Moses with the law, gave them Syro-Palestine after parting the Jordan, and sent thousands of prophets to support the law (K 1:11). Such a statement is hardly the expression of reasoned conviction that the king had expected, but rather an appeal to lived experience and the unique relationships that inspire trust and loyalty. However, it does point to certain events and developments as public, empirical, and miraculous evidence of God's interactions with human beings, in keeping with the king's requirements, except for the study and testing he mentioned last. The need for skeptical scrutiny therefore remains. Moreover, it directly addresses the king's practical concern with action and governance by its reference to the law and, more broadly, to things as political as they are religious when he speaks of the liberation of slaves, the establishment of a legal system, and the overthrow of a tyranny.[12]

Unimpressed by this introductory statement, the king asks why there is no reference to the creator, who orders, governs, and provides for the world and its inhabitants; for descriptions of this kind are recognized by all religious people as proof of God's wisdom and justice and are beneficial in encouraging the pursuit of truth and justice through imitation of these same divine attributes. The king's unexpected disappointment here reflects his inner division. Insofar as he responds to the dream, he is prepared to take seriously the notion of a God who creates literally, intentionally, and *ex nihilo*; to accept as divine the judgment that his particular actions are displeasing; to embark upon a genuine quest for what pleases God; and to make the radical transformation of familiar things in nature a criterion for believing that God enters into direct contact with human beings. But insofar as he is persuaded by the philosopher, he is primarily interested in the pursuit of truth and justice, in what is probative to the greatest number of people, and in the instrumental value of a metaphorical creator/ruler who can be rationally imitated by ruler and ruled alike. Because the term "creator" is common to both perspectives, it seems likely that at this early stage the king assumes the two perspectives have more in common than they actually do, and is not yet fully aware of the ramifications associated with each one. That is why the sage, seizing upon the king's justification for his query, moves quickly to clarify just what the king's rejoinder assumes (K 1:12–18).

He indicates that the kind of religion the king presupposes is a "syllogistic, governmental religion to which speculation leads" – "syllogistic" in the sense of being based on reasoning and argument and "governmental" in the sense of being designed to aid in governing the passions of both individuals and the community. But apparently because it is rooted in human reflection about divine things, it contains many doubtful points, as the philosophers themselves acknowledge, and generates unending disagreements about both belief and practice. With so many conflicting claims, it comes as no surprise that they can demonstrate only some of them, while others are merely persuasive, not conclusive; and still others do not reach even that level. Except for the reference to demonstration, no specific typology of arguments or nomenclature is provided, probably to dissuade the king from returning to philosophy. But the philosophical reader will surely recognize that behind the explicit reference to conclusive, demonstrative claims lies the well-known classification scheme of dialectical, rhetorical, poetic, and sophistical premises and arguments, in descending order of plausibility, discussed by Aristotle and eagerly studied in the medieval Islamic world.[13] By indicating that the arguments of the philosophers fall variously into all of these categories, the sage implies that the king ought not to be unduly deferential to their claims or their self-confidence. But this also means that his own arguments can and should be appraised by the same standards.

Finding himself far more open to these critical observations than to the sage's opening remarks, the king asks for additional proof. Yet his renewed interest proves to be misguided when the sage notes that his opening remarks were, in fact, the desired demonstration. While he does not tell the king that the demonstration lay in his appeal to direct experience, which is always more evident than even the best logical argument, he does help him to see this for himself by posing two hypothetical cases that elicit contrasting and highly illuminating responses (K 1:19–22). In the first, he asks whether the king would be obligated to acknowledge and recount the virtues of India's ruler and even revere him, were he to learn of the excellent character and just conduct of the Indian people. The king replies with reserve, asking how this information could obligate him, when it is unclear whether the Indian people behave justly on their own account and have no ruler, or on account of their ruler, or because of both together. Without comment or analysis the sage presents the second hypothetical. He asks whether the king would be obligated to obey the ruler of India, if the latter's envoy came to him with gifts that were undoubtedly from the royal palace, a signed letter identifying who sent them, medicines to cure his illnesses and preserve his health, and poisons with which to overcome his enemies. Now, the king responds unhesitatingly in the affirmative, for his previous doubts would have vanished, and he would believe that the dominion and decree (*amr*) of India's ruler would extend to him.

While the king takes each hypothetical at face value and responds in kind, it is clear that each one is ultimately parabolical. In the first, the Indian ruler represents God; India, God's dominion; and the justice of the people, the good order that prevails there. What is unclear is whether this dominion really has a king, what its true extent is, and, if it has a ruler, whether his rule is exclusive or shared with others. If the dominion signifies the entire cosmos, then there are indeed many doubts about whether or not it should be explained by reference to a creator, ruler, or first cause and many conflicting opinions about the merits of the explanations offered. Even without philosophic erudition, the king sees this for himself and therefore comes to appreciate the basic soundness of the sage's remarks about syllogistic, governmental religions. Philosophical readers will recognize that the key issue in such disagreements is whether the cosmos is best explained by its own internal features or by recourse to a transcendent external cause or causes. They would naturally wish to determine which thinkers known to Halevi (e.g. materialists, Socrates, Plato, Aristotle, Stoics, Epicureans, Neoplatonists, and Islamic Aristotelians) would have supported the particular alternatives named by the king and even evaluate which thinker or tradition, if any, presented the most convincing case and why. But in the likely event that different readers will end up supporting different positions, they too would have reason to take seriously not only the sage's preceding comments but also the second hypothetical and its implications.

In this altered framework, India and its ruler retain their previous meanings; but now the ruler initiates contact with the king by sending a messenger from his dominion in accordance with recognized diplomatic procedures. It seems likely that the messenger represents Moses; the signed letter, the Torah; and the efficacious medicines, the commandments prescribed by the Law. It is harder to identify analogues for the unique gifts procured from the palace and the unusually potent poisons, except for the fact that they are very special and betoken a special relationship. The new scenario largely disposes of previous doubts about whether India has a ruler and whether he knows about particular people, like the Khazar. It also helps to explain the king's response to the new query. For accepting and benefiting from gifts creates an obligation for the recipient to respond positively to the giver. Usually, this entails an acknowledgment of indebtedness, an expression of appreciation, and a tacit or explicit promise to use them for the purpose intended. But when such gifts contribute substantially to one's fundamental goals, such as life and well being, acknowledgment of a changed relationship and pledges of enduring loyalty often follow, as we find with vassals and suzerains, or clients and patrons. In the parable, the messenger's arrival with the letter, medicines, and other gifts clearly implies that they all crossed the great metaphysical distance between the divine and human realms. But if they also crossed a great temporal distance, such that the king is the beneficiary of gifts given long ago, then his acceptance of them creates an obligation of loyalty and proper use that is highly reminiscent of the one Socrates says he has to the city and its laws in "the speech of the laws" in Plato's *Crito*.[14]

When asked how he would describe his royal benefactor, the king answers in terms of attributes based on direct observation, supplemented by others that are generally accepted, but implied by the former. This accords well with the king's earlier reference to how natural scientists respond to strange phenomena, that is by according primacy to incontrovertible evidence in shaping their broader explanations and descriptions (K 1:5). By underscoring the importance of direct experience, he also enables the sage to clarify why he addressed the king's questions as he did and why others before him did likewise. For Moses addressed Pharaoh on behalf of the God of the Hebrews, based on his own experience and what was well known from the time of the Patriarchs; and even God addressed the Israelites at Sinai as the God they already worshiped, highlighting both the people's prior and recent experience. By thus linking present experience with prior experience as preserved in and made intelligible by received tradition, the sage is able to claim precisely what philosophers are inclined to deny, namely, that tradition is trustworthy because it is like or equivalent to experience. What makes this plausible, if indeed it is, is that tradition signifies a collective achievement in preserving experience, not just a melange of individual claims haphazardly reported through time.

Still, the sage recognizes that experience, however compelling it might be, is person-specific and limited by particular circumstances. It is not equally applicable in all its entailments. Thus, while all people are equal in being created by God, it does not follow that all people are equal in being obligated to fulfill the law God gave to Israel. The law, rather, is a legacy for Israel, because it was they who collectively experienced liberation from bondage and God's attachment to them. That attachment, in turn, is now attributed to the Jews being the choicest (*safwah*) of Adam's descendants. While converts may join them and even share in their good fortune, they will not be equal to the native-born, apparently because of their different lineage and possibly experience as well. Noting the king's dismay at this response, however, the sage asks for the chance to explain himself further, implying that first appearances can be deceiving and that experience, especially limited experience, does not always speak for itself. Notwithstanding the primacy of experience, explanation and interpretation must also be given their due, if the reliable tradition of the past is to be understood in its fullness. Once the king invites him to proceed, the frame story and introductory exchanges are concluded. But we are left with a key interpretive question. What exactly was the purpose of the hypotheticals concerning the king of India? To contrast and evaluate different ways of proving God's existence? To lay the groundwork for showing that God enters into contact with flesh and blood? To show that a revealed religion with a divine law is superior to syllogistic, governmental religions based on man-made law? Finally, if more than one alternative seems plausible in the immediate context, which is most important for the dialogue as a whole?

To counter the king's skepticism about both divine–human contact and the alleged preeminence of the Jews, the sage calls his attention to the familiar hierarchical structure of reality, with its ascending orders of plants, animals, and human beings endowed with intelligence. While the king accepts the reality of each order and the practical activities that distinguish it, he denies that there is any order of sensuously perceivable beings beyond the intellectual order. Because its activities are also practical, necessitating the improvement of individual character, the household, and the city by means of political regimes and man-made laws, reason's theoretical capacity to understand the ultimate causes of things seems to have no special status. This raises the possibility that intellectual, that is, theoretical, speculation is either not practical, not knowledge, or not what distinguishes human beings as such. By contrast, the king allows that if a man with truly amazing powers of endurance, self-mastery, and knowledge of the past and the future were found, he would belong to a higher level, essentially different from the intellectual order, namely, God's unseen spiritual kingdom. The aforementioned characteristics turn out to be the distinguishing marks of a true prophet, such as Moses, who teaches the people of God's attachment to them and explains the nature of divine governance in terms of God's will and the people's deserts.

Here, the sage enlists the king's skepticism about God's speaking with ordinary human beings to persuade him that such communication might be possible with superhuman beings,[15] who would not only qualify for such contact but also enjoy membership within the divine order itself (al-amr al-ilahi). Such membership, in turn, reduces the metaphysical distance to be crossed in revelation and attests to lineage so high and so noble that those with the strongest claim to having received revelation occupy an essentially different level (rutbah) on the hierarchy (cf. K 1:1, 21). This would explain Israel's preeminence, which even the king dimly and grudgingly recognized by summoning the sage. Still, the plausibility of the account depends largely on what Halevi means by al-amr al-ilahi.

The term has been used variously in Qur'anic, Shi'ite, and Isma'ili sources, and has also generated a wide variety of interpretations when it appears in the Kuzari. In general, it signifies the experienced aspects of divinity in nature and history. But if we are to clarify the multiple meanings it has for Halevi in an organized way, it is helpful to distinguish between three distinct yet related senses of "divine order" originally suggested by Shlomo Pines. The first signifies a dispensation, arrangement, or ordering of things which governs the affairs of all who participate in it, such as angels, prophets, and pious friends of God. This corresponds to the supreme level of reality discussed above, which God, its supreme member, has willed to be as it is. Today, philosophers and social scientists might identify it with the sphere of the sacred or sacred order, as contrasted with the realm of the ordinary. The second sense of "divine order" is derived from the first and signifies the gift or influx of prophecy, either as an experience of the divine or as the power, faculty, or internal principle that makes such experience possible. It is typically bestowed on those belonging to the divine dispensation as a sign of favor and noble rank in a special audience that confers access, information, and special powers to act on the sovereign's behalf, much as a patron might award an "order of merit" to his client or the British monarch present the Order of the British Empire to a distinguished subject. The third and final sense of "divine order" signifies orders in the literal sense of commands or instructions about what pleases or displeases God, and, more broadly, the power or authority that supports such commands.[16]

With regard to knowledge of the past, the king shows consistent interest in the question of creation and especially in God's status as creator (K 1:4, 8, 12, 44ff., 60–2). It comes as no surprise, then, that he eventually asks how the sage would respond to the philosophers' claim that the world is preeternal, given their reputation for careful investigation and accuracy. The sage not only dismisses their claim, but also excuses them for their error in making it. Alas, they were poorly equipped to grasp the truth, as even their own criteria for knowledge of the whole truth attests. Their lineage was deficient because the Greeks were descended from Noah's son, Yafet, rather than Shem, the choicest one. Climate and geography were unfavorable because they lived in the north, outside the temperate zone. Finally, meteorological and other natural catastrophes interfered with the transmission of their traditions, so that, in addition to lacking divine knowledge, their education and training in science and religion were further impaired. Indeed, their disadvantaged condition reflects what an aged Egyptian priest, addressing Solon in Plato's *Timaeus*, says about the Greeks: They are always children, young in soul, because their souls, lacking any ancient learning, are devoid of beliefs about antiquity transmitted by ancient tradition. In essence, they are forever beginning anew because they have little connection to or regard for what is old.[17]

Accordingly, the king learns that what Aristotle imparted as knowledge on this question need not be accepted as true. For in lacking reliable information transmitted by tradition, he relied on himself alone to resolve the problem, preferring arguments supporting the world's preeternity, based on abstract thinking, to any alternative. By doing so, he overtaxed himself and failed to be entirely objective, much less exhaustive, in his investigation. For however much Aristotle may have tried to be scientific, his methods were often arbitrary and his conclusions culture-specific. The sage may even be suggesting that these considerations apply to all thinkers who attempt to resolve difficult questions; they cannot avoid falling back upon the assumptions and perspectives they take from the cities, peoples, and cultures to which they belong.

By contrast, the sage holds that if Aristotle had lived in a nation with widely held, inherited beliefs that could not be rejected, he would have tried to establish the possibility of creation, notwithstanding its difficulties, *just as* he had done regarding past eternity, which is harder to accept (K 1:65; cf. 1:5, 23–5). Here, we might ask if the result would be any less culture-specific and non-objective. Apparently not, as the sage seems to say with his reference to "just as." Still, opting for creation would have provided more detailed information than otherwise available. It would also have withheld the philosopher from directly challenging widely held beliefs and traditions of his society that are linked to the sphere of the sacred and divine. For philosophers living within nations that match the sage's description, and perhaps all philosophers, would presumably not wish to undermine the opinions or laws that have benefited them from birth. Nor need this compromise the philosopher's integrity, absent a decisive demonstration. To underscore the point, the sage invokes God in an informal oath, affirming that the law teaches nothing that repudiates direct sense experience or a demonstration. If so, then it is not in conflict with the ultimate sources of knowledge. This implies that both sources must be accepted, when both are present, and one only, when the other is not. Still, we lack direct empirical evidence of creation, just as we lack a demonstration for it, while the available arguments pro and con counterbalance each other.[18] What we do have is the tradition deriving from Adam, Noah, and Moses, preserved in the law. Because it teaches both the disruption of the customary course of events and the creation of new realities based on prophetic revelation, which is more trustworthy than reasoning, it tips the scales in favor of creation. As such it attests to the power and freedom of the creator to do whatever he wishes, whenever he wishes, from working miracles to enforcing oaths, which undergird all social relations.

If we ask why Halevi deems prophecy more trustworthy than reasoning, three reasons suggest themselves. Prophecy is the self-disclosure of God's wisdom and will, and God alone is in the best position to know the truth about all recondite matters. Furthermore, reliable tradition, which conveys the contents of prophecy with great care, is far more detailed and specific than the tenuous and typically generalized conclusions of philosophical argument. Finally, tradition does not speculate about the evidence it transmits or its causes, but philosophy inevitably does both, usually with disputed results. Therefore, without better evidence or conclusive argumentation, the traditional teaching should be accepted on practical grounds. However, if new and compelling grounds emerge, requiring an adherent of the law to acknowledge the existence of eternal matter and many worlds before this one, his belief that this world had a beginning and that Adam and Eve were its first human inhabitants would remain intact (K 1:67).

This openness to new developments and readiness to consider an acceptable "fall back" position indicates both genuine respect for what science and philosophy might accomplish and an awareness of the interim and dialectical status of the sage's position. It also points to what, for him, is the sine qua non of adherence to the law – belief in the veracity of traditions transmitted from earliest antiquity. If this were undermined, the credibility of more recent traditions, including the divine origin of the written and oral law, would likewise be in doubt. While the king ultimately characterizes the sage's arguments for creation as "persuasive," that is, dialectically, and thus on a par with the philosopher's case for preeternity, it is clear that more will have to be said for the trustworthiness of prophecy and the revealed law than has been said thus far.

The anticipated discussion follows a brief inquiry into what can be known about nature, causality, and divine agency, which prompts the king to ask about the origin of Judaism (K 1:68–80). His preliminary assumptions on the subject are thoroughly naturalistic and suggest that he is still preoccupied with syllogistic, governmental religion. The sage, however, maintains that Judaism arose suddenly, in response to being commanded to exist, like the creation of the world. This duly impresses the king, although it is unclear whether the miraculous suddenness of its emergence or the emphasis on obedience impresses him most. What is entirely clear and perhaps more impressive is the extraordinary loyalty, cohesiveness, and endurance of the Israelites, who, despite the misery of their bondage in Egypt, willingly followed the "two divine sheikhs," Moses and Aaron, through all the dangers and deliverances associated with their liberation and trek through the wilderness. Indeed, the king exclaims that all this represents the divine order at work (K 1:84; cf. 1:10). But while these experiences confirmed their belief in a God who does whatever he wishes, whenever he wishes it, it did not remove their doubt – or the king's – that God enters into contact with flesh and blood.

The theophany at Sinai was intended to remove this doubt once and for all.[19] While the story is admittedly familiar, the philosophical reader will want to read Halevi's presentation of it with considerable care, for it is no mere summary, but rather an unusually artful fusion, displaying both philosophical clarity and rhetorical skill. It unfolds in three phases. The first phase (K 1:87) shows that the Israelites' difficulty arose from the incongruity between speech being a corporeal phenomenon, produced by corporeal organs, and the belief that God is beyond both. If left unresolved, the people would have to conclude that any allegedly divine law was actually a product of human thought and opinion. Hence, the theophany.

The sage describes first what they witnessed: (1) lightning, thunder, earthquakes, and fires enveloping the mountain; (2) Moses entering and later leaving the flames alive; (3) the clear and audible presentation of the Ten Commandments; and (4) two stone tablets with divine writing as a token of the event. He describes next how the multitude reported these events. They held that God spoke directly to them, not to a prophet. Subsequently, once Moses had been designated as intermediary, they believed that they were addressed through speech that "had its origin in God," yet without prior thought on Moses' part. This qualification and the sage's denial that what the prophets call "the Holy Spirit" or the angel "Gabriel" is really the Active Intellect are meant to dismiss the philosophers' account of prophecy as the natural, imaginative mimesis of intellectual perfection. The only attention given to the imagination's role in prophecy is a brief consideration of the view that Moses only imagined, in a dream or a trance, that someone was addressing him. All this is dismissed as a mere conjecturing, because it ignores the multitude's collective, wakeful apprehension of the Ten Commandments, which "they heard as divine speech," and the evidence of the written tablets, which "they saw as divine writing." Moreover, these remained with the people throughout the nine hundred-year-long dispensation of prophecy.

By this point it is clear that the sage has told the story in such a way that all four of the king's evidentiary requirements are satisfied. He has also highlighted the people's transition from disbelief to acceptance of revelation in order to help the king make the same transition. Finally, by repeatedly noting the people's unanimity about what they experienced and about accepting the law as divine, he responds fully to the king's quest for the God-pleasing way of life and to any ruler's desire for consensus, cohesiveness, and conformity to law as a basis for political stability, as readers of Plato's *Laws* will surely recognize.[20]

Phase two of the discussion (K 1:88–90) presents a common misunderstanding about what revelation presupposes and identifies two ways of resolving it. The king's response to the exposition is twofold: he says first that one might be excused for supposing that Jews believe God is corporeal (which reason rejects) but adds that the Jews might be excused for rejecting reason because what they witnessed was undeniable. In effect, by accepting the same evidence, a turning point for the king, he allows experience to trump reason with a vengeance. But the sage refuses to do likewise. Instead, he appeals to God in an oath once more to forbid his accepting anything the intellect deems absurd or impossible. While not a demonstration, this is more than mere rhetoric. For as a performative utterance, it plainly acknowledges the divine order, probably in all of its aforementioned senses, and reminds us that oaths are taken, in part, to establish truth in an inquiry, which in turn necessitates rejecting absurdity and impossibility. Accordingly, the purpose of *this* oath would be to ground all inquiries into truth in the authority of the law and respect for its mandates. Not surprisingly, we soon learn that corporealizing God is forbidden by the second of the Ten Commandments. Only after resolving the problem in reason's favor on a religio-legal basis does he offer a speculative argument to support it. Thus, if we claim that many of God's creations are beyond corporeality, "like the rational soul, which is what man is in reality," how shall we not declare God to be above corporeality? Building upon this clearly Platonic conception of the soul and using Moses as an example, he shows how Moses must be identical with the practical activities of his discerning rational soul rather than his bodily organs, which leads us to describe it in divine, spiritual terms. He adds, tellingly, that no place is too narrow for the soul to enter, nor is it too narrow for the forms of all created things to enter it. Both observations appear to qualify the hard distinction between the intellectual and divine orders discussed earlier and illustrated by the prophet. They also offer much wider scope for intellectual understanding, both theoretical and practical, than previously suggested. Finally, the sage exhorts him not to reject what tradition has reported about the theophany, citing specific examples meant to refute the philosopher's initial remarks, while listing what we, nevertheless, do not know about it. Thus, reason is defended, but discouraged from constructing comprehensive explanations on the basis of limited evidence, lest it mislead. Significantly, the king pronounces all of this to be "persuasive," that is dialectically sufficient, which represents another turning point in his thinking.

Phase three (K 1:91) offers a coda to the sage's exposition. He does not claim categorically that the matter occurred exactly as he described. It may have occurred in a more profound way than he "imagined." Still, whoever witnessed those events became convinced that they came directly from the creator, like the first creation itself. Their doubts were thus dispelled. The first statement represents a qualified "fall back" from his original description and gives the imagination a role in it that is altogether unexpected. It also raises several important questions: What does this development imply for the reliability of tradition? If telling and retelling begins with the witnesses themselves, what is the role of imagination in their experience and reporting of it? Does skepticism follow or does the imagination perhaps have important mimetic functions not yet discussed? Halevi does not tell us outright. The most he says here is that the novel and unprecedented character of the events they witnessed ultimately overcame the people's skepticism and led them to associate the theophany with God's direct and miraculous role in creation, a teaching they could have known only from tradition. For now we can only observe that if the creation was believed to be sui generis, yet unseen by any human witnesses, it would be difficult indeed to understand any description of it, whether divine or human, without recourse to familiar images, metaphors, and analogies of human making that the imagination generates or helps to integrate.

With all four of the king's criteria for divine–human contact largely satisfied and his deepest skepticism overcome, the sage's focus shifts to establishing the nobility of his people, the preeminence of the land of Israel, and the superiority of the law in educating the pious and ultimately the prophets. In broad outline, this agenda parallels and is surely meant to supersede the philosopher's description of what goes into the formation of the perfect man who attains union with the Active Intellect. Here, we can do little more than sketch the trajectory of the individual discussions, recognizing that each one calls for careful analysis in its own right, in its immediate context, and in the larger context of the dialogue.

To answer the charge that Israel's rebelliousness is well known, the sage argues for their inherent nobility (K 1:95). Insofar as God took them from among all other religious communities, and they reached the level of being addressed by God, even God recognizes their unique worth. What is more, they alone retained collectively the gifts that made Adam the noblest creature on earth: a perfect physical constitution, soul, character traits, and intellect, and also a "divine capacity," beyond intellect, identified as "the level at which one may have contact with God and the spiritual beings and also know truths without their being taught." Because of this, Adam and his choicest offspring, culminating in Israel, came to be called "sons of God." Thus, despite being treated as the lowest of the low, Jews can trace their lineage to the highest of the high. Little more is said about this "divine capacity" here except for the fact that, while it is part of their "innate character" and "their natures," it may skip a generation in transmission.

Subsequently and in a different context (K 1:103), we learn that they differ from other human beings by virtue of "a special divine distinctiveness, which made them as though they were a different species and a different, even angelic substance." This very much resembles the sage's earlier characterization of the divine order, except that the essential difference between the intellectual and divine orders is now presented in terms of "as though" and not in terms of "is." Is this a distinction without a difference or a shift away from a much stronger, apparently, biological view of the distinctiveness of the Jews? However important it may be to determine this, it may still be too early to try, for the passage goes on to say that someone who meets a prophet "separates himself from his kind through the purity of his soul and its longing for those [prophetic] levels." Beyond this, "what is desired from [the hereafter] is only that a man's soul might become divine by disengaging itself from its senses, witnessing the highest world for itself, delighting in seeing the light of the divine kingdom, and in hearing the divine speech." Here the sage speaks of a universal human desire for the hereafter; but is one not born into the divine order or born outside it? Can those born outside it become divine, and those born inside it yet not be divine? These passages are certainly relevant to the sage's goal of establishing his people's nobility and distinctiveness, but is he establishing the same kind of nobility and distinctiveness later that he claimed at the beginning?

This puzzling divine capacity is eventually described as "the eye of prophecy" (K 2:24). Later still, long after the king's conversion, the sage offers what appears to be a definition of "the inner eye" in connection with a well-known passage about a near-sighted man who successfully locates the missing camel of a clear-sighted man (K 4:3). After proposing that it is the means by which a genuine prophet apprehends the true nature of things, he says that whoever possesses this eye is truly clear sighted, while all others are like the blind. But he adds, "One might almost [say] that that eye is the imaginative faculty as long as it serves the intellectual faculty." This statement goes far beyond the sage's previous comments in explaining prophecy, but it also raises new difficulties. Can prophecy be unique to the Jews, when all human beings possess both imagination and intellect? Does the sage now support the philosophers' view of prophecy as the imaginative rendering of conceptual truths already discovered? Why then the qualification "almost"? Or is the imagination itself the faculty of prophecy and the intellect at most a salutary restraint? Is there a difference between being "clear sighted" and "truly clear sighted"? While the sage makes no concessions about the nobility of his people, it seems that he does come very close to naturalizing prophecy.

Turning to the trajectory of discussions on Syro-Palestine's preeminence, we recall the land's natural advantages for preserving and transmitting knowledge and reliable tradition from the exchanges on creation and eternity (K 1:63). The sage makes this even more explicit later when he notes that Shem inherited the temperate climes, of which Syro-Palestine is the central and most distinguished part. Indeed, it was specifically set aside for the divine order. Therefore, once the choicest came to dwell there, the divine order began to dwell within an entire community (K 1:95). For as lands are distinguished by the minerals, plants, and animals they produce, so too this land is distinguished by the forms and character traits of the people it produces as revealed in their temperament (K 2:10). This is why Abraham was brought to Syro-Palestine; he was like a choice vine or root, meant to be cultivated in the most perfect soil and surroundings to produce the best possible fruit (K 1:95; 2:12, 14).

Subsequent arguments retain this quasi-ecological foundation, but focus on religious and historical considerations. Thus, Adam was fashioned from its dust and was also buried there. The rivalries between Cain and Abel, Isaac and Ishmael, Jacob and Esau all center on the right of succession and inheriting the land. Accordingly, Jacob did not ascribe his prophetic dream to the purity of his soul, or his religiosity, or superior certainty, but to the land, because the gates of heaven were located there (K 2:14). We also learn that it rests on the dividing line between East and West, such that both nature and the law make it the starting point for reckoning the onset of the Sabbath, the festivals, and the days of the week for the entire inhabited world (K 2:20). Consequently, if the choicest group, "the people of YHVH," the special land, or "inheritance of YHVH," the special occasions appointed by God, known as "the fixed times of YHVH," and the actions, rites, and declamations he requires, called "the service of YHVH," all conjoin in one system, then "the glory of YHVH" ought to appear (K 2:16, cf. 4:3, 17). In the end, both the language and mandates of the law show that the land of Israel is special to the Lord, and actions become complete only within it. Intentions are sincere, and the heart is pure only in places that one believes are special to God, even if this were a phantasy and a metaphor; but all the more so, when it is true (K 5:23). Thus, we find that general geographic and ecological arguments for the land's preeminence make way for specific religio-historical ones that ultimately stress the utility of the land for the life of the law.

Presumably, the superiority of the divine law would lie in its claim to divine origin. But because this is questioned from the outset, Halevi introduces a different and unanticipated consideration. The Jews, as the enduring remnant of the children of Israel, are themselves the proof that God has a law on earth. How this is so, however, remains to be seen (K 1:10). To be sure, both the Muslim and the Christian attest to the divine origin of the law, but not to its continued validity. Hence, it is the sage who first endorses both claims without reservation (K 1:11). He swears that it teaches nothing that repudiates sense experience or demonstrative proof, or countenances anything impossible or absurd (K 1:67, 89). While he usually refers to it by the term *Shari'a*, signifying its divine status, he sometimes employs the more generic term for law, *namus*, human and non-human, but specifies that it has its origin in God, or is the "true *nomos*" (K 1:81; 2:20; 4:17). We have already noted how the assembled multitude at Sinai heard the presentation of the Ten Commandments as divine speech and saw the written words as divine writing (K 1:87). This opens the way for faith in and acceptance of the eternally binding law and the providence it offers, which includes the immortality of souls after the destruction of bodies (K 1:91, 103, 109).

Approximately midway through the dialogue we encounter three successive discussions of the law (K 2:48; 3:7, 11), which both compare and contrast it with the intellectual laws mentioned earlier (K 1:1, 81) and also offer several classifications of its own laws.[21] In the first of these, which takes place after the king's conversion, the sage acknowledges the indispensability of the intellectual and governmental laws as a moral minimum for any group to endure, even the lowest. The divine laws, essentially ceremonial in nature, distinguish Israel and constitute an addition to the former. Still, if the moral minimum is not met, the ceremonial maximum hardly avails (K 2:48). What, then, can plausibly assure that the minimum will be met? Not reason, which recognizes that what is fitting varies from situation to situation. Characteristically, its rules of governance are not legally binding and always allow for exceptions with a view to prudence. Not surprisingly, it reveres a deity who neither knows or cares about human behavior (K 4:19). Rather, the assurance lies in divine laws, mysteriously revealed in great detail to the religious community of a living God, who governs it. Insofar as they are entirely outside the scope of our intellects, they will be adhered to, just as the sick follow the physician's prescriptions (K 3:7). After the king notes that God has a secret in preserving the Jews through observance of Sabbaths and festivals, the sage classifies the laws in accordance with the three highest orders in the hierarchy of being – the divine, the governmental, and the psychic – and shows how each class perfects the corresponding level of the personality, elevating the whole. It would appear, then, that only the God of Abraham, Isaac, and Jacob could plausibly be thought to provide unconditional rules that always apply, but in such copious detail that they address all situations. In comparison with such a law, human legislation is always defective and in need of correction. Near the end of the dialogue, in a recapitulation of the hierarchy, we find that what is most important about the law is its effects. It imparts to its adherents "a divine way of life" that ennobles them by raising them to the level of the angels and even revelation, "the human level closest to the divine" (K 5:20, pr. 4).

The final encounter with philosophy, however, takes the form of a broad exposition and critique (K 5:2–14), which attempts to show the king that he ought not to be persuaded by many of its principal claims because they are untenable. Apparently influenced by al-Ghazali's *The Incoherence of the Philosophers*, the sage now maintains that what the philosophers have genuinely demonstrated is confined mainly to mathematics and logic. In physics, however, their account of the four elements is empirically unsubstantiated. In psychology, their theory of the Active Intellect entails numerous absurdities and lacunae, and in metaphysics their views on divine causation are riddled with inconsistency (K 5:14). The most we can know here is that God governs material things by determining their natural forms (K 5:21; cf. 1:77; 3:11). Even so, let them be excused for their errors and thanked for their achievements.[22] Still, because philosophy offers little wisdom about matters of great importance in living, a return to the divine wisdom embodied in Israel's ancestral tradition is called for. But, as the sage recognizes, a wholehearted turn toward the ancestral tradition can be completed only by a wholehearted return to the ancestral land. Accordingly, as the dialogue concludes, he acts on the logic of his position, as did Halevi himself, and departs for the Holy Land.

NOTES

1. All references to the *Kuzari* (abbreviated by "K" followed by the treatise number, a colon, and the section number) are based on the critical edition of the Judeo-Arabic text: Judah Halevi, *Kitab al-Radd wa-'l-Dalil fi'l-Din al-Dhalil*, ed. D. Z. Baneth, prepared for publication by H. Ben-Shammai (Jerusalem: Magnes Press, 1977). The translations are my own.

2. S. D. Goitein, "Judeo-Arabic Letters from Spain (Early Twelfth Century)," *Orientalia Hispanica* 1 (1974), 337–9.

3. Y. Baer, *A History of the Jews in Christian Spain*, 1 (Philadelphia: Jewish Publication Society, 1978), 74ff.; M. R. Cohen, *Under Crescent and Cross: The Jews in the Middle Ages* (Princeton: Princeton University Press, 1994), 157, 160.

4. See in this connection J. Kraemer, "Maimonides' Use of (Aristotelian) Dialectic," in *Maimonides and the Sciences*, ed. R. S. Cohen and H. Levine (Dordrecht: Kluwer, 2000), 111–30.

5. Cf. D. M. Dunlop, *The History of the Jewish Khazars* (New York: Schocken Books, 1954), 89–170; K. Brook, *The Jews of Khazaria* (Northvale, N.J.: Jason Aronson, 1999), 113–56.

6. See E. Schweid, "The Artistry of the Dialogue in the *Kuzari* and its Theoretical Meaning" [Hebrew], in *Ta'am V'Haqqashah* (Ramat Gan: Masada, 1970), 37–79; L. Strauss, "The Law of Reason in the *Kuzari*," in his *Persecution and the Art of Writing* (Glencoe: The Free Press, 1952; reprinted Chicago: University of Chicago Press, 1988), 98–112; A. Ivry, "Philosophic and Religious Arguments in R. Judah Halevi's Thought" [Hebrew], in *Thought and Action: Essays in Memory of Simon Rawidowicz*, ed. A. Greenberg and A. Ivry (Tel Aviv: Tscherikover Publishers, 1983), 23–33; M. S. Berger, "Toward a New Understanding of Judah Halevi's *Kuzari*," *Journal of Religion* 72 (1992), 210–28; Y. Silman, "The Literary Aspect of the *Kuzari*" [Hebrew], *Da'at* 32–3 (1994), 53–65.

7. Hippocrates, "Airs, Waters, Places," in *Hippocratic Writings*, ed. G. E. R. Lloyd (New York: Penguin Books, 1983), 148–69; A. Altmann, "The Climatological Factor in Judah Halevi's Theory of Prophecy" [Hebrew], *Melilah* 1 (1944), 1–17.

8. Strauss, "Law of Reason," 101 n. 17.

9. H. Davidson, "The Active Intellect in the *Cuzari* and Hallevi's Theory of Causality," *Revue des Etudes Juives* 131 (1973), 351–96, and H. Davidson, *Alfarabi, Avicenna, and Averroes, on Intellect: Their Cosmologies, Theories of the Active Intellect, and Theories of Human Intellect* (New York and Oxford: Oxford University Press, 1992), 181–95, 207, 218–19.

10. Aristotle, *On Prophesying by Dreams* 1, 462b 21–23; 2, 463b 15–23, 464a 19–27.

11. D. Schwartz, "R. Yehudah Halevi on Christianity and Empirical Science" [Hebrew], *AJS Review* 19 (1994), 1–24; T. Langermann, "Science and the *Kuzari*," *Science in Context* 10.3 (1997), 495–522.

12. On the continuing political significance of this narrative, see M. Walzer, *Exodus and Revolution* (New York: Basic Books, 1984).

13. See Aristotle, *Topics* 1: 1, 100a 25–101a 16; 1: 14, 105b 19–31; *Sophistical Refutations* 11, 171b 25–34; *Rhetoric* 1: 1, 1354a 1ff.; I. Madkour, *L'Organon d'Aristote dans le monde Arabe*, 2nd ed. (Paris: Vrin, 1969), 221–39; Kraemer, "Maimonides' Use," 115–17.

14. Plato, *Crito* 50a–54c.

15. S. Pines, "Shi'ite Terms and Conceptions in Judah Halevi's *Kuzari*," *Jerusalem Studies in Arabic and Islam* 2 (1980), 165–251, especially 178–92; W. Z. Harvey, "How to Teach Judah Ha-Levi as a Jamesean, a Nietzschean, or as a Rosenzweigian," in *Paradigms in Jewish Philosophy*, ed. R. Jospe (Madison, N.J.: Farleigh Dickenson University Press, 1997), 129–35.

16. Pines, "Shi'ite Terms," 172–8.

17. Plato, *Timaeus* 22b–c; Schweid, "Artistry of the Dialogue," 48–50.

18. J. L. Kraemer, *Humanism in the Renaissance of Islam: The Cultural Revival during the Buyid Age* (Leiden: Brill, 1986), 15, 24, 73, 181, 187; cf. L. Goodman, *Ibn Tufayl's Hayy ibn Yaqzan* (New York: Twayne Publishers, 1972), 130–1; and Moses Maimonides, *The Guide of the Perplexed*, trans. S. Pines (Chicago: University of Chicago Press, 1963), 2:22–3 (319–22), 2:25 (327–30).

19. On the theophany at Sinai and prophecy generally, see D. Lobel, *Between Mysticism and Philosophy: Sufi Language of Religious Experience in Judah Ha-Levi's Kuzari* (Albany: State University of New York Press, 2000), 92–5, 139–44; H. Kreisel, *Prophecy: The History of an Idea in Medieval Jewish Philosophy* (Dordrecht: Kluwer, 2001), 94–147, especially 100–1, 111–12.

20. Plato, *Laws* 3, 691c–692c, especially 692b–c.

21. Strauss, "Law of Reason," 112–41; cf. A. Sagi and D. Statman, *Religion and Morality* (Amsterdam: Rodopi, 1995).

22. B. Kogan, "Al-Ghazali and Halevi on Philosophy and the Philosophers," in *Medieval Philosophy and the Classic Tradition in Islam, Judaism and Christianity*, ed. J. Inglis (Richmond, UK: Curzon, 2002), 77–8.

7 Maimonides and medieval Jewish Aristotelianism

Moshe ben Maimon, better known in the West as Maimonides, falls temporally at the midpoint of the six-hundred-year history of medieval Jewish philosophy. But from the vantage point of the present he is a central figure in a much more significant way. Maimonides is a Janus-faced figure, looking both forward and backward. He is the culmination of the Judeo-Arabic philosophical tradition, which includes Saadya, Solomon ibn Gabirol, and Judah Halevi. But Maimonides also establishes the Jewish philosophical agenda in Christian lands from the thirteenth century on with the (posthumous) translation of his controversial *Guide of the Perplexed* into Hebrew. His influence in fact extends beyond Jewish philosophy, for his effect upon Christian thinkers such as Aquinas and Meister Eckhart is palpable. Even beyond the medieval period Maimonides is a pivotal figure, who provides a starting point for philosophical speculation. Spinoza has Maimonides in mind throughout his *Tractatus Theologico-Politicus*, published anonymously in 1670. And it is Maimonides to whom Hermann Cohen in the twentieth century turned in developing his own conception of Judaism as ethical monotheism. More than any other Jewish thinker before or after, Maimonides, known among his own people by the acronym Rambam, can reasonably lay claim to a place on any short list of great philosophers. This chapter will attempt to ground this bald claim.

LIFE AND TIMES

Maimonides was born in 1135 (or perhaps 1138, according to some recent scholarship) in Cordova, the court city first of the Umayyad and then of the Almoravid caliphate, in Muslim Spain (Andalusia). His father Maimon, after whom he is named, made his living as a rabbinic judge. Like father, like son. Were it not for the circumstances of history, to which we shall briefly turn, there can be little doubt that Maimonides would have followed in his father's footsteps. And in a sense he did in spite of historical circumstances, insofar as the greatest part of his oeuvre has to do with interpreting and codifying the law. We should note that the father's interests extended beyond the law, to include mathematics and astronomy. Secular studies and scientific investigation were apparently not viewed as antithetical to full membership in the Jewish community. Indeed, the father's interests are indicative of the rich cultural life of Muslim Spain, in which Jews played a role for centuries. This is the culture that produced the philosophy and poetry of Gabirol and Halevi, as well as the philosophical writings of Ibn Bajja (Avempace), Ibn Tufayl, and Maimonides' near contemporary, whom he never knew personally, Ibn Rushd (Averroes). Muslim and Judeo-Arabic Andalusia were living religious cultures, proving by virtue of their literary, artistic, and architectural activities that secular wisdom is commensurate with revelation and a revealed legislation. As we shall see, Maimonides' entire oeuvre, in rabbinic legislation, medicine, and philosophy, is explicable only if contextualized against this "enlightened" background. Perhaps his greatness will be seen to lie not so much in particular turns of argument, but rather in the power of his conviction that his own religious tradition could well participate in the wider, general culture.

This general cultural outlook was shattered just when Maimonides was entering his teenage years in 1148 with the fierce arrival of the Almohads, Berber tribesmen from North Africa. They conquered Cordova, forcing all non-Muslims to convert on pain of death. Maimon and his family fled, and after a period of wandering throughout Spain settled in Fez in Morocco. Their stay there was short lived since North Africa was also under Almohad rule, and their continuing exile drove them eastwards, first to Palestine and finally to Egypt, where the family settled in 1165 in al-Fustat, a suburb of Cairo. In Egypt Maimonides was to remain for the rest of his life, and from 1185 served as court physician to the vizier of Saladin. Maimonides died on 13 December 1204. He is buried in Tiberias, near the Sea of Galilee, where his tomb may still be seen. Upon it is inscribed: "From Moses [the prophet] to Moses [Maimonides] there had arisen no one like him."

Such in brief is the life of Maimonides, a life characterized by insecurity and flight, and the consequent need for stability and order. Letters written in response to queries from fellow Jews and Jewish communities throughout the world from Morocco to Yemen attest to his sensitivity to their own calamities and the felt need to respond in a calm and sympathetic way. Throughout his life Maimonides never seems to have forgotten the frailty and the limits of the human condition and the contingencies inherent in human life. In time he was appointed head of the Egyptian Jewish community as his fame as a rabbinic and legal authority spread. He was consulted on issues that arose out of the forced conversion of Jews under Islam and on issues of proselytization.[1]

WORKS AND INTERPRETIVE STRATEGIES

The Maimonidean corpus is voluminous. There are numerous treatises devoted to medical practice and the treatment of various ailments, as are befitting a practicing physician. Much legal counsel and sage advice is to be found in the many epistles that Maimonides wrote to his co-religionists. He may have written at a young age a treatise on logic, although recent scholarship has called this into question. For present purposes, however, we may single out three works: a commentary on the Mishnah (1168), the Jewish legal code; the *Mishneh Torah* (1180), a codification of the aforementioned Mishnah; and the *Guide of the Perplexed* (1190), the greatest of all Jewish philosophical works. With respect to his legal and philosophical writings, scholars have divided over the years, indeed over the centuries, as to whether Maimonides' writings can be understood in a unified way, if not committed to a single set of doctrines, then at least grounded in, and giving full play to, both Torah and philosophy, *or* whether they must be bifurcated into theological works, on the one hand, and philosophical works, on the other. One Maimonides or two? Put another way, to what extent did Maimonides believe in a dialogue between Athens and Jerusalem, philosophy and revealed law? For the dualist interpreter, denying the commensurability of philosophy and revealed law, the commentary on the Mishnah and the *Mishneh Torah* are regarded as (simply) theological, better legal, treatises, written for the benefit of the Jewish community as a whole and, therefore, lacking in conclusions resultant upon such philosophical speculation that only a small minority could comprehend. By contrast, the *Guide of the Perplexed* is, according to the dualist position, a strictly philosophical treatise, written for the benefit of a neophyte in philosophy (and those like him), presenting conclusions, indeed Maimonides' real views, derived from philosophical premises.

Historically, this dualist position regarding Maimonides' legal and philosophical writings has been the most prominent, ever since the translation of the *Guide* from its original Judeo-Arabic into Hebrew in 1204 (the very year of Maimonides' death) by Samuel ibn Tibbon. Within three decades of its translation, the *Guide* was embroiled in controversy on account of its presumed commitment to a host of seemingly anti-biblical positions about, inter alia, creation of the world, immortality, and the nature of prophecy. Whether or not Maimonides' real views are at odds with a literal interpretation of Scripture, something to which we shall return, the controversy that the work engendered is indicative of the dualist position noted. Again, that very position presupposes a sharp dichotomy between Athens and Jerusalem, between philosophy and revelation, and on the basis of this dichotomy brands the *Guide* as philosophical and *hence* contrary to biblical teaching. Among recent scholars, Leo Strauss may be singled out as the spokesman for the dualist position.[2]

On the other side of the debate are those who tend to see Maimonides' legal and philosophical works as of a piece, forming a coherent whole. Part of the argument for this latter, "coherentist," view comes from the existence *within* the commentary on the Mishnah and the *Mishneh Torah* themselves of *philosophically* rich discussions of the nature of the human soul, the genesis and structure of human character, and the fundamental principles of Jewish belief and the foundations of the Torah. Given the appearance of such philosophical discussions within, ex hypothesi, non-philosophical works, the coherentist argument goes, the dualist position cannot be sustained. This point resonates historically as well, for at the same time as the *Guide* was condemned by the religious authorities in the 1230s, so too was his *Book of Knowledge* (*Sefer ha-Madda*), the very first treatise of the *Mishneh Torah*, the codification the law. This latter work seemed dangerous enough to require incineration, and such a response seems to the coherentist to dissipate the dualist bifurcation of the Maimonidean corpus.

Further, even though the *Guide* is explicitly addressed to a neophyte in philosophical speculation, it is not thereby understood by the coherentist as expressive of but one side of the reason/revelation dichotomy, but rather as committed to demonstrating the harmony or compatibility of the two, to overcoming the presumed dualism. Even if the *Guide* proceeds at a higher level of philosophical sophistication than his other works, an unarguable point, the issue for the coherentist is that Maimonides is intent upon displaying in the *Guide* the deep philosophical nature and structure of Judaism. For the coherentist, then, the presumed dichotomy of reason and revelation is undercut both by the appearance of philosophy in the legal works and by the prima facie endeavor of the *Guide* itself, to explicate Judaism philosophically. Among recent scholars, Julius Guttmann may be singled out as a preeminent coherentist. For the interested reader, the Guttmann–Strauss debate in the 1930s and 1940s concerning the nature of the *Guide* in particular and Jewish philosophy in general repays close study.[3]

Before turning to Maimonides' philosophical views in the *Guide*, one must first try to adjudicate the dualist–coherentist debate outlined above. The very presentation and nature of Maimonides' philosophical views is at issue, depending upon whether one adopts a dualist or a coherentist position. If the former, Maimonides' philosophical views must stand quite opposed to canonical biblical positions, whatever those might be, as well as those presented in his own non-philosophical works such as the commentary on the Mishnah and the *Mishneh Torah*. In this case, Maimonides may well be understood to hold, for example, an Aristotelian (non-biblical) belief in the eternity of the world. If, however, one holds a coherentist position, in which Maimonides' philosophical views are not ipso facto at odds with canonical biblical ones, whatever those might be, then one will expect Maimonides to be less dismissive of traditional views and rather more concerned with teasing out the inherent "philosophicality" of them, if possible. For the coherentist, unlike the dualist, there would be no prima facie reason to withhold support for the biblical belief in the createdness of the world, however this latter is to be construed. Alas, this cosmological issue has historically not been easy to resolve, for Maimonides' *explicit* commitment to the createdness of the world in the *Guide* (2:25) is held by the dualist interpreter of Maimonides to be disingenuous, hiding his *real* belief in the eternity of the world.

This apparent esoteric–exoteric distinction cannot easily be dismissed. Maimonides is quite explicit about the need to hide the truth from those incapable of receiving it (*Guide*, introduction). This point, as old as Plato, is taken globally by the dualist not merely as a pedagogical and rhetorical point about matching the mode of presentation to the intended audience, but rather as a politically charged directive to obscure the truth from non-philosophers. To reveal the truth, to reveal a belief in, say, the eternity of the world, would be to confuse the unwary reader and to court antinomianism, to undercut belief in the law and drive the non-philosopher from the community of believers.

The major problem besetting the dualist position and its commitment to an esoteric–exoteric distinction is its seeming arbitrariness. Without denying the Platonically inspired caution against the unadorned presentation of truth to those not ready to receive it, one may be troubled by the dualist position that takes such a caution as license to understand Maimonides' various philosophical positions in ways diametrically opposed to their explicit presentations. So, for instance, the dualist holds that Maimonides' *real* view concerning the eternity or createdness of the world is, as noted, the Aristotelian belief in the eternity of the world, even though Maimonides insists that this cannot be proved.

Given such arbitrariness, serious consideration should be given to the coherentist position, but with this caution: The coherentist position, which sees Maimonides' project as one of harmonizing reason and revelation, of illuminating the inherent "philosophicality" of the religious tradition, is anachronistically (mis-)conceived if interpreted from the vantage point of the modern (Enlightenment) project of showing, proving, the rationality of revelation (religion). This latter project, Kantian and Mendelssohnian, presupposes the very dichotomy between Athens and Jerusalem, between reason and revelation, that Maimonides (and, for that matter, his contemporary Averroes) denied. For them, reason and revelation are not so *unrelated* to each other that an argument had to be produced to bring them, like Humpty Dumpty, back together again. Rather, the presumption is in favor of the philosophical intelligibility of Scripture, and given this, the project is one of interpreting the latter in light of such a philosophical presumption. If you will, Maimonides is engaged in biblical exegesis *more philosophico*, not in the Kantian project of delimiting the nature and scope of human understanding to make room for faith. As we shall see, Maimonides is second to no one in pointing out the limits of human understanding relative to divine wisdom, but his project, unlike Kant's, presupposes the philosophical intelligibility of revealed truth.

MAIMONIDES' ARISTOTELIANISM

In the history of medieval Jewish philosophy one usually sees Maimonides described as an Aristotelian, and Julius Guttmann speaks for the traditional historiography of Jewish philosophy when he writes, "In the middle of the twelfth century Aristotelianism displaced Neoplatonism as the dominating influence in Jewish philosophy of religion."[4] A quick look at the Contents to this volume would certainly seem to support this claim, but of late Alfred Ivry has suggested that "It is not the least of the paradoxes of the *Guide* that Maimonides' underlying philosophical base is one he was loath to acknowledge."[5] The "philosophical base" to which Ivry is referring is Neoplatonism. We should immediately note the rather rigid dichotomization presupposed by both positions – Aristotelianism vs. Neoplatonism. But such dichotomization is manifestly unhistorical, as both Guttmann and Ivry are aware. Much Neoplatonic doctrine went under Aristotle's name in the late antique attempt to harmonize Plato and Aristotle; further, as Porphyry tells us straightforwardly in his *Vita Plotini* (ch. 14), his teacher's writings include both Stoic and Peripatetic doctrines, and that in particular Aristotle's *Metaphysics* are to be found condensed (somehow) in them. Finally, we might note that the brilliant (and generally respectful) commentators on Aristotle of the early centuries of the Common Era were almost all Neoplatonists, developing their own positions within manifestly Aristotelian categories, even as they sometimes foisted their own views upon Aristotle. And within Islamic and Jewish philosophical circles, as Guttmann notes, "Islamic and Jewish Neoplatonism had absorbed many Aristotelian elements in addition to those already present in the original Neoplatonic system; conversely, Aristotelianism had undergone a Neoplatonic

transformation in the hands of its Islamic adherents."[6] Indeed, it is
no easy task to disentangle Aristotelian from Neoplatonic strands
in Maimonides, or in other medieval thinkers. Too often we gloss
as "un-Aristotelian," alternatively as "Neoplatonic," Maimonides'
anti-materialist remarks in the *Guide*, but a close inspection of some
of those passages, particularly ones dealing with prophecy (*Guide*
2:36, 40), reveals that Maimonides is grounding his remarks with
explicit reference to passages in Aristotle's *Ethics* denigrating the
sense of touch (*Nicomachean Ethics* 3:10).

   In the final analysis I believe it makes good sense to consider Maimonides an Aristotelian, and I shall ground this claim momentarily.
But prima facie a problem immediately arises, if one adopts, as I am
inclined to, the aforementioned coherentist position. That position,
it will be recalled, understands Maimonides' philosophical program
as one of philosophically explicating, and in this sense justifying, traditional scriptural beliefs on creation, miracles, prophecy, and so on.
Such beliefs are manifestly un-Aristotelian, and so a real question
arises as to the applicability of "Aristotelianism" to Maimonides.
Two options are available for one wishing to retain the attribution:
(1) drop the commitment to coherentism, and in its place adopt the
dualist position, which sees an esoteric Aristotelianism at play. Alternatively, (2) if one wishes to retain a commitment to the coherentist position, one must reinterpret Maimonides' Aristotelianism in
such a way that it is compatible with a correlative commitment to
such *un-Aristotelian* views as the creation of the world, miracles, and
the like. The latter seems a tall order, for it requires one to defend the
Aristotelianism of one who holds manifestly un-Aristotelian views.
Can such a position as this be maintained? I believe it can.

   Consider the following claim by Ralph McInerny about Aquinas
and the latter's relationship to Aristotle:

[W]e find many references to Aristotle in Thomas, we find the invocation
of doctrines, the quoting of phrases. Confronted with these, we should not
consult Aristotle for guidance on what Thomas is saying. Far better to see
what Thomas means, *how he is using the doctrines or language of Aristotle
for his own purposes. It is almost as if Aristotle were a language Thomas
used to make independent points of his own.*[7]

I can find no better way than McInerny's to defend my claim
about Maimonides' Aristotelianism. Contra the (Straussian) dualist,

Maimonides is not a closet Aristotelian, who for political reasons hides his real (Aristotelian) views on the eternity of the world, the impossibility of miracles, and so on. Rather, as Aquinas is with respect to Aristotle, so Maimonides may best be understood philosophically as engaged in a critical dialogue with Aristotle, almost invariably, as we shall see, disagreeing with him, but indebted to Aristotle for his mode of discourse, argument forms, and philosophical vocabulary. I suggest that it is in precisely these latter senses that Maimonides may well be accounted an Aristotelian. As Aquinas uses Aristotle "for his own purposes," so too does Maimonides.

It is thus not on account of any of the specific *conclusions* Maimonides reaches that we should consider him an Aristotelian. Contra Aristotle, Maimonides does not think the world is beginningless, though he may think it has no end (*Guide* 2:27), nor does he think that the *summum bonum* resides in contemplative activity (alone) (*Guide* 3:54), or that the mean is normative in moral matters in quite as general a way as does Aristotle (*Mishneh Torah: Hilkhot De'ot*, chs. 1–2). Further, although Maimonides accepts the distinction that Aristotle makes between the moral and the intellectual virtues (commentary on the Mishnah: *Shemonah Peraqim* [*Eight Chapters*], ch. 2; *Guide* 1:1–2; 3:54), unlike Aristotle, Maimonides is clear that the former are necessary, even if not sufficient, conditions for attainment of the most exalted of the latter (*Guide* 2:32; 3:54). At one stage of his career Maimonides' view of the human psyche is opposed to Aristotle's in understanding it as constituted of parts utterly idiosyncratic to the human species (*Shemonah Peraqim*, ch. 1). It is clear that Maimonides has a considerably more libertarian view of human freedom than does Aristotle, who believes that after a certain point in human development character is fate (*Shemonah Peraqim*, ch. 8). Maimonides believes that the prophet, paradigmatic in both character and intellectual attainment, is insulated from contingency, a view seemingly opposed to the ineliminability of luck in the Aristotelian moral scheme (*Guide* 3:22–3). Perhaps, most startlingly, Maimonides, an empiricist like Aristotle, believes that human knowledge is severely limited on account of our finite nature. The most important (metaphysical) matters are beyond our ken and linguistic capacities, and a yawning chasm separates human from divine wisdom (*Guide* 1:52, 54, 58). I do not think it can be reasonably maintained that Aristotle was an epistemological finitist. Nor is humility an Aristotelian virtue, as it certainly is for Maimonides (*Hilkhot De'ot*, chs. 1–2).

Given all these prima facie un-Aristotelianisms in Maimonides' thought, we have before us a choice regarding Maimonides' purported Aristotelianism: either we can accept his explicit views at face value and reinterpret Maimonides' Aristotelianism accordingly, *or* we may conclude that Maimonides is being pretty consistently disingenuous, even duplicitous, with a view to hiding his doctrinaire Aristotelianism. I hope my preference is clear. Maimonides is not an Aristotelian on account of any agreement with Aristotle on substantive issues, but rather on account of his creative use, and adaptation, of Aristotelian categories and argument forms "for his own purposes," the main purpose being of course the explication of his own religious tradition. One can be an Aristotelian simply by taking the question of whether the world is eternal or not seriously, something Maimonides certainly does in the second part of the *Guide*, as he argues against Aristotle. Maimonides' philosophical starting point is Aristotle, and it is from Aristotle that he develops his own philosophical positions.

THE GUIDE OF THE PERPLEXED

The Guide of the Perplexed, written in Judeo-Arabic and completed by 1190, has had an unparalleled influence within the Jewish world, while also influencing Christian scholastics such as Aquinas, William of Auvergne, and Giles of Rome. As we have noted, within Jewish circles it is Maimonides against whom Spinoza, the first modern Jewish thinker, is primarily reacting in his critique of revealed religion, the *Tractatus Theologico-Politicus* (1670). And it is Maimonides to whom Hermann Cohen in the twentieth century turns in developing his own conception of Judaism as ethical monotheism.

What is it about Maimonides that accounts for his influence? Wherein lies his greatness as a thinker? It is too simple to suppose that the philosophical rigor he displays or the arguments he produces in his work are unsurpassed. A good argument can be made that Gersonides and Crescas, two of Maimonides' successors in Jewish philosophy, present in their major philosophical works positions as rigorously argued for and as ingenious as Maimonides'. Further, the fact that these latter thinkers disagree with Maimonides on crucial issues such as creation and divine providence should caution one against supposing that Maimonides' positions are normative and decisive in these areas. They are not. So, again, wherein lies his greatness as a thinker? Perhaps it is in the fact that he best *defined*, gave shape to, a variety of classical problems, problems that *subsequent* to his presentation became subjects of dispute, both within and outside of Jewish philosophical circles. Within the context of monotheistic religion, issues concerning the limits of human understanding, divine language, the createdness or eternity of the world order, the nature of prophecy, divine providence, the intelligibility of divine law, and the nature of the *summum bonum* (the highest human good) had been discussed for centuries, with a variety of positions canvassed. In Jewish philosophical circles Philo commenced the tradition in Alexandria, and then from the tenth century the tradition of philosophical speculation in Judaism moved to Arabic-speaking lands. So Maimonides had his predecessors, but none had the wit to so vivify and interrelate the aforementioned subjects of discussion by means of employment of the regnant philosophical categories. In the previous section we have seen that in the main Maimonides uses Aristotelian categories and arguments for his own purposes. No one before Maimonides so clearly understood and interpreted Judaism, the biblical and rabbinic tradition, as at root expressive of *philosophical* truth. No one before Maimonides gave a set of canonical problems besetting Judaism such a definite philosophical shape. After him, and because of him, Jewish philosophers would argue interminably about the nature of divine language and divine providence, and about the nature and scope of prophecy and the human good. In sum, perhaps Maimonides' true greatness as a philosopher lies not in the answers he gave to specific problems, but rather in the form in which he set the questions and the interrelations he revealed between seemingly disparate subjects.

Maimonides' specific answers to the host of philosophical questions and problems he sets himself in the *Guide* are as controversial as they are influential. I have noted that scholars are divided as to what his real beliefs are, and I can only present my considered views, based upon the interpretive strategy outlined previously. Before we turn to his particular views it is important to understand the overarching *practical* thrust of the *Guide*.[8] It is addressed to an erstwhile student perplexed about the intelligibility of Scripture. As a result of his perplexity, born of a youthful impetuosity, his very life, a life lived according to halakhic (traditional) norms, is rendered problematic. Maimonides thus is called upon not merely to provide answers to specific "theoretical" worries, but also, indeed with greater urgency, to provide a perspicuous justification for the life in question. One must never overlook this practical-pedagogical dimension of the *Guide*, and the way(s) in which theory subserves practice. Indeed, this practical-pedagogical motivation reveals itself in the *Guide* in the very order in which philosophical topics are presented over the course of its tripartite division. As we shall see, Maimonides moves from logic and language to physics (and cosmology) to metaphysics and philosophical psychology to, finally, legal, moral, and political philosophy. This progression, which maps on to the ancient ordering of the Aristotelian corpus, is to be seen as culminating in the practical sciences. And, as suggested, the telos of Maimonides' philosophical masterpiece (like Spinoza's *Ethics*) is the good life. The *Guide* moves a smart young interlocutor, perplexed by the prima facie philosophical unintelligibility of his religious tradition and way of life, from a state of aporia to one in which the intelligibility of the tradition is revealed and a potential alienation from the community is overcome.

The *Guide* is an enormous work, over six hundred pages in the standard English translation by Shlomo Pines,[9] and this practical impetus is often overlooked when one focuses piecemeal on one or another "theoretical" issue. For Maimonides, negative theology, a finitist epistemology, the difficulty of metaphysics, and even an understanding of the createdness of the world order are issues deeply intertwined with axiological ones. To give but one example of a practical dimension embedded in a "theoretical" discussion: Maimonides' semantic theory, presented in his celebrated discussion of divine attributes (*Guide* 1:50–60), is offered, in large part I would suggest, to deflate the young interlocutor's impetuosity concerning the (unlimited) scope and powers of human knowledge, the very *cause* of his initial perplexity and estrangement. In teaching, via the ("theoretical") discussion of divine attributes, that human knowledge is perforce limited, Maimonides hopes pari passu to curb the young man's impetuosity, his naive epistemological optimism. And this latter desideratum is a practical point, requiring a change in *character*. In sum, for Maimonides the doctrine of divine attributes entails humility as its desired outcome. As Menachem Kellner has suggested, "Maimonides' book [the *Guide*] is transformative and not simply expository, subsuming throughout a practical aim."[10]

I turn now to a brief overview of some of the main themes of the *Guide*, following the order in which they are presented over the three parts of the text. I trust that readers new to Maimonides and the *Guide* will turn to the relevant portions of the text itself to make up their own minds about the positions attributed to him. Maimonides is an epistemological finitist, but contrary to some recent scholarship, not a skeptic (*Guide* 1:31–4). He believes that the scope of human understanding about divine, including celestial, matters is severely circumscribed. He is adamant about the chasm that separates human from divine knowledge. Divine wisdom and human wisdom have nothing in common, save the name. Correlative to this epistemological finitism is Maimonides' so-called negative theology, his most famous (and notorious) philosophical doctrine, which was criticized in Jewish philosophical circles by Gersonides and outside those circles by Aquinas (*Guide* 1:50–60). Given that God is utterly transcendent, irreducible to anything material on pain of idolatrous anthropomorphism, Maimonides offers a critique of divine language, that is human discourse about God. Such discourse cannot describe God in any straightforward and direct manner, and hence a variety of periphrases are required to render divine language logically perspicuous. All purported essential predications about God, that It is one, eternal, etc., must be understood, and hence reparsed, as denials of imperfections of It. God's unity must be understood as denying multiplicity and multiformity of It; and in so understanding God's unity as a denial of multiplicity and multiformity we ipso facto point to God's transcendent nature as being utterly other than, and irreducible to, human form and the corporeality of the material realm. Further, all purported non-essential predications of God, that It is angry, merciful, and so on, must be understood as attributes of divine action, analogous to human actions springing from the relevant dispositions. So, in asserting that "God is angry," what we really intend is that God acts in a manner analogous to such actions that are expressive of the human feeling of anger. But, of course, in so attributing anger to God, we do not thereby attribute to It any feelings whatsoever. In so reconceptualizing and reparsing all divine attributes, Maimonides is above all concerned to safeguard God's simple nature from any tincture of divisibility and corporeality. In this regard he is concerned to guard against the too-human need for understanding the divine in human terms. Indeed, on a general level Maimonides wishes to understand monotheistic religion as above all committed to weaning humankind from idolatry. The overarching purpose of the commandments is to expunge idolatry, and the Maimonidean teaching concerning divine attributes must be understood in the light of this ultimate goal.

Maimonides' position on the creation or eternity of the world has, as previously noted, aroused considerable controversy. He presents three views, creation *ex nihilo* (the biblical view), creation from pre-existing matter (the Platonic view), and the Aristotelian view that is committed to the eternity of the world (*Guide* 2:13). His discussion on this issue is the best example in the Maimonidean corpus of a creative mind working within and between two traditions, the religious and the philosophical, using the regnant philosophical norms to explicate the religious tradition, whatever the latter may be. Maimonides is clear that none of the views presented, not even the Aristotelian one, is to be ruled out on the basis of what Scripture says. Maimonides may be guilty of the charge that Spinoza brings against him of reading philosophy into Scripture – though, for his part, Maimonides would describe his project as one of eliciting ("teasing out") from the text its deepest truth – but he cannot be convicted of the charge of defending, in *kalam* fashion, a *particular* view on the issue at hand. Maimonides' wish is (simply) to defend the use of philosophy in explicating Scripture, wherever the argument may lead. So committed is he to the philosophical foundations of Scripture that even the Aristotelian position concerning the eternity of the world must be evaluated dispassionately and philosophically. And were it to turn out that the Aristotelian belief in the eternity of the world is philosophically demonstrable, then Maimonides is quite clear that he would perforce believe it. Maimonides is not being disingenuous here. He is firmly committed to evaluating all arguments on their philosophical merits alone, and then corroborating the truth, whatever it may be, by reference to Scripture.[11]

Maimonides finds both the Aristotelian and the Platonic positions inconclusive, though he suggests that the latter view, creation from preexistent matter, is consistent with divine omnipotence over nature (*Guide* 2:25). Neither the Aristotelian nor the Platonic position being worthy of acceptance, Maimonides presents a kind of transcendental argument on behalf of the biblical account, creation *ex nihilo*. Given the existence of revelation, revealed law, one must presuppose the existence of a God who is free to do as It pleases, when It pleases. This entails an absolute lack of constraint on the creator, thus paving the way for belief in creation *ex nihilo*, though it should be noted that the Platonic view, creation from preexistent matter, is likewise consistent with revelation and divine freedom. In developing his own position here Maimonides is not begging the question on behalf of the biblical account of creation. He is not presuming in advance the latter's veracity. What he is taking as a given is the historicity of revelation and then deducing from this the nature of God and the appropriate account of creation. It is upon this presumption that Spinoza (and others) found their critique of Maimonides and revealed religion.

Maimonides' view of prophecy in the *Guide* follows hard on his account of creation (*Guide* 2:32–48). Prophecy is understood as the epitome of intellectual excellence. Further, there is a political aspect to prophecy, namely the prophet as lawgiver, a view Maimonides took over from his great Muslim predecessor, al-Farabi (tenth century). In the person of Moses, the paradigmatic prophet and lawgiver, the prophet emerges as the Maimonidean analogue to the Platonic philosopher-king. For Maimonides, prophecy is both a natural as well as a supernatural phenomenon. The prophet comes to be through one's own efforts as well as on account of divine imprimatur. Maimonides denies the naturalistic (Aristotelian?) view of prophecy that makes it a wholly human intellectual achievement. But he also denies the possibility that just anyone can become a prophet through God's will alone and through no effort of one's own. For Maimonides, effort and merit are rewarded and God makes prophets of (virtually all) those who by themselves have achieved the moral and intellectual capacity for it. That God cannot make anyone a prophet should not be understood as a limiting condition upon the divine. Given that prophecy requires intellectual excellence as a necessary condition for its existence, an ignoramus cannot, by definition, be a prophet. God is not, and cannot be, constrained by what is an impossibility.

For Maimonides, divine providential knowledge and care extends to the level of particulars, but, importantly, only to particular human beings, and not in a way that precludes human freedom (*Guide* 3:8–24). In his discussion, Maimonides is especially concerned to counter the Aristotelian view that holds that, since knowledge is of the universal, divine providence (and care) does not extend to the realm of particular human beings. He is also concerned to counter the Ash'arite (voluntaristic) view that sees, contra Aristotle, the divine hand everywhere and in everything, with the result that all is predetermined or, at least, overdetermined. In countering these views, Maimonides wishes to safeguard both human freedom and responsibility *and* a notion of divine providential care, reward and punishment. A canonical problem throughout the medieval period was the apparent incompatibility of divine knowledge and human freedom.[12] If God knows all, what was, is, and shall be, then what becomes of human freedom, which presupposes an open, indeterminate future? Maimonides' response is that human beings are free and hence responsible for their actions on account of their very humanity, a state of being and cognizing utterly distinct from that of the divine.[13]

Reminiscent of his earlier discussion in the *Guide* concerning divine attributes and the human incapacity to comprehend and hence describe the divine, Maimonides in the present context safeguards human freedom by virtue of the absolute equivocity that obtains between human and divine wisdom (and being). As humans, we are (really) free to choose good or evil. And for Maimonides, we shall reap what we sow. But, surprisingly, by choosing goodness and being morally upright we are not thereby guaranteed providential care and insulation from suffering. Maimonides' brilliant gloss on the book of Job clarifies his position on divine justice (*Guide* 3:22–3). As he memorably puts it of Job's righteousness and concomitant suffering:

> The most marvelous and extraordinary thing about [Job] is the fact that knowledge is not attributed to him. He is not said to be a "wise" or a "comprehending" or an "intelligent" man. Only moral virtue and righteousness in action are ascribed to him. For if he had been wise, his situation would not have been obscure to him . . . (*Guide* 3:22; Pines' translation).

Job's (undeniable) righteousness is no safeguard from the contingencies and reversals of fortune that literally define the world order. Indeed, Job's "innocence" (lack) of *intellectual* insight into the true nature of the world is the very cause of his suffering. He suffers precisely on account of his "innocence" (ignorance), and his incomprehension and consequent indignation are indicative of his traditional (and commonsensical) belief that the good prosper and the evil suffer. For Maimonides, Job's suffering forces us to reconceptualize this commonsensical belief about the apparent connection between righteousness and human well being and to become aware that the divine intentions for the created order are beyond our capacity to understand, or at least considerably different than we too readily assume (*Guide* 3:13). Providential care and insulation from the vagaries of fortune are for Maimonides a function of intellectual insight and knowledge of God, not of wealth, health, or even moral virtue. Short of such (prophetic) insight, even the righteous person, like Job himself, may suffer misfortune. For Maimonides, God does not love the sinner, nor the fool.

The final part of the *Guide* is given over in large measure to legal, moral, and political philosophy (*Guide* 3:25–54). This is as it should be, if one recalls the overarching practical thrust of the work as a whole. Though God's infinite wisdom is beyond human ken, It gave humans a law by which they could perfect themselves. With a view to elaborating true human felicity, Maimonides offers an extended discussion concerning the meaning and purpose of divine law (*Guide* 3:25–49). Its purpose is twofold: perfection of the body and perfection of the soul. The law has both a social and a spiritual function, and upon these twin bases Maimonides explicates the reasons for the commandments (*ta'amei ha-mitzvot*). What stands out in the discussion is its psychohistorical sensitivity, for Maimonides understands the nature and structure of the law, indeed its very existence, in the light of the psychohistorical circumstances of those initially bound by it (*Guide* 3:32). Maimonides of course is not suggesting that as circumstances change, so does the law. The law is forever binding, but its particular form, especially as manifest in the ritual laws (*huqqim*), is due to the psychohistorical circumstances in which it was promulgated. So, for example, the laws pertaining to sacrifice (*qorbanot*), now in disuse, were originally instituted for the purpose of weaning idol worshipers from belief in the divinity of material objects. Maimonides' point is that sacrifice, the mode whereby the ancient idol worshipers paid homage to their gods, had to be retained if ever the object of *their* worship was to be altered. Maimonides, unlike modern scholars and theologians, does not worry overmuch about the binding nature of the law, its eternity. But its manifest historicity should not be read as any sort of commitment to a reductionist historicism on Maimonides' part. Law has, as noted, a dual function, social and spiritual, and, given this, the commandments must be understood both historically *and* with reference to the ultimate goals of human life.

The last chapters of Maimonides' masterwork present his final thoughts about the *summum bonum*, the goal of human existence (*Guide* 3:51–4). One should not be surprised that the telos is an intellectualist one, knowledge of God (and Its creation) and an *imitatio Dei* consequent upon such knowledge. Correlative to the degrees of divine providential care consequent upon intellectual insight is a graded hierarchy of human perfection and happiness. Human happiness is a function of knowledge of God and imitation of Its ways. In this intellectualist and elitist vision Maimonides seems to join hands with Aristotle, who likewise presents an intellectualist portrait of the human good and consequently holds the belief that true human felicity is attainable only by a very few. But while one cannot gainsay Maimonides' elitism, he does temper or reconceptualize the intellectualist vision of the human good, for the *imitatio Dei* consequent upon knowledge of God entails moral and political action for the benefit of humankind.[14] Contrary to Aristotelian *imitatio Dei*, which is apolitical, evincing divine unconcern for the material world, Maimonidean *imitatio Dei*, paradigmatically illustrated by Mosaic prophecy, mirrors God's providential care for Its creation. For Maimonides, human beings achieve their true end and best express their knowledge and love of God by ennobling the created order.

INFLUENCE

Of Aquinas, McInerny says,

There is an old maxim, passed on by Pico della Mirandola: *Sine Thoma, Aristoteles mutus esset*: without Thomas, Aristotle would be silent. The phrase is a signal tribute to the [Thomistic] commentaries [on Aristotle]. But the reverse of the claim is also true, and true throughout Thomas's career: *Sine Aristotele, Thomas non esset* [without Aristotle, Thomas would not be].[15]

This latter claim is as applicable to Maimonides as it is to Aquinas, and we have seen previously the immense indebtedness of Maimonides to Aristotle. It is quite impossible to imagine Maimonides without Aristotle. It is equally impossible to imagine Jewish philosophy without Maimonides. Without Maimonides,

Jewish philosophy would not be. This is a very grand claim, but as you continue (I hope) to read through this history of Jewish philosophy, it is impossible to overlook the impact that the translation of Maimonides' philosophical work into Hebrew had on the intellectual public. From the early thirteenth century on Maimonides' views became the starting point for all the relevant theoretical discussions on creation, divine language, prophecy, divine providence, and so on. His positions were agreed upon, disagreed upon, interpreted, and misinterpreted. For some, he was the final word; for others, a singularly dangerous influence. Maimonides' influence is ubiquitous. Perhaps this is best explained by a unique combination of a deep religious sensibility and an unwavering loyalty to the general philosophical and scientific culture of his time. The two are not unrelated for Maimonides. For him, love of God is a function of intellectual activity (only). As a general religious claim, this one is hardly uncontroversial, but I believe it best encapsulates the trajectory of his religious philosophy. Even his greatest critic, Spinoza, fell under its sway.[16]

NOTES

1. A. Halkin (trans.) and D. Hartman, *Crisis and Leadership: Epistles of Maimonides* (Philadelphia: Jewish Publication Society, 1985).
2. L. Strauss, "How to Begin to Study *The Guide of the Perplexed*," in *The Guide of the Perplexed*, trans. S. Pines (Chicago: University of Chicago Press, 1963), xi–lvi; L. Strauss, "The Literary Character of *The Guide of the Perplexed*," in *Essays on Maimonides: An Octocentennial Volume*, ed. S. W. Baron (New York: Columbia University Press, 1941), 37–91.
3. J. Guttmann, *Philosophies of Judaism*, trans. D. Silverman (New York: Schocken Books, 1973 [1933]), 172–207, 503–4 n.125; L. Strauss, *Philosophy and the Law: Contributions to the Understanding of Maimonides and his Predecessors*, trans. E. Adler (Albany: State University of New York Press, 1994 [1935]); J. Guttmann, "Philosophie der Religion oder Philosophie des Gesetzes?," *Proceedings of the Israel Academy of Sciences and Humanities* 5 (1974), 148–73 (written 1940–45); see also E. Schweid, "Religion and Philosophy: The Scholarly-Theological Debate between Julius Guttmann and Leo Strauss," *Maimonidean Studies* 1 (1990), 163–95; K. H. Green, *Jew and Philosopher: The Return to Maimonides in the Jewish Thought of Leo Strauss* (Albany: State University of New York Press, 1993).
4. Guttmann, *Philosophies of Judaism*, 152.

5. A. Ivry, "Neoplatonic Currents in Maimonides' Thought," in *Perspectives on Maimonides: Philosophical and Historical Studies*, ed. J. L. Kraemer (Oxford: Littman Library, 1991), 138.

6. Guttmann, *Philosophies of Judaism*, 152.

7. R. McInerny (ed. and trans.), *Thomas Aquinas: Selected Writings* (Harmondsworth: Penguin, 1998), xxxi; my emphasis.

8. D. H. Frank, "Reason in Action: The 'Practicality' of Maimonides' *Guide*," in *Commandment and Community: New Essays in Jewish Legal and Political Philosophy*, ed. D. H. Frank (Albany: State University of New York Press, 1995), 69–84; J. Stern, "Maimonides' Demonstrations: Principles and Practice," *Medieval Philosophy and Theology* 10 (2001), 47–84.

9. S. Pines (trans.), *The Guide of the Perplexed*, 2 vols. (Chicago: University of Chicago Press, 1963). A revised edition of a classic abridgment in English of the *Guide* was published by Hackett in 1995: C. Rabin (trans.), *The Guide of the Perplexed*, with introduction and commentary by J. Guttmann and new introduction by D. H. Frank (Indianapolis: Hackett, 1995).

10. M. Kellner, *Maimonides on Human Perfection* (Atlanta: Scholars Press, 1990), 64.

11. From the beginning of his intellectual career to the end Maimonides is committed to such philosophical openness. In the forward to the early *Shemonah Peraqim* (*Eight Chapters*), the introduction to his commentary on *Pirqei Avot*, Maimonides writes, "Know . . . that the ideas presented in these chapters and in the following commentary are not of my own invention; neither did I think out the explanations contained therein, but I have gleaned them from the words of the wise occurring in the midrashim, in the Talmud, and in other of their works, as well as from the words of the philosophers, ancient and recent, and also from the works of various authors, *as one should accept the truth from whatever source it proceeds*" (trans. J. Gorfinkle; my emphasis). Maimonides is as good as his word, for the emphasized last sentiment is itself derived from an Arab source, al-Kindi! (*On First Philosophy*, 103 [= 58, in A. Ivry [ed.], *Al-Kindi's Metaphysics* [Albany: State University of New York Press, 1974]).

12. T. M. Rudavsky (ed.), *Divine Omniscience and Omnipotence in Medieval Philosophy* (Dordrecht: Reidel, 1984).

13. The classic Maimonidean defense of human free will is found in *Shemonah Peraqim*, ch. 8. For the equivocity of human and divine knowledge, see *Guide* 3:20.

14. *Guide* 3:54. Maimonides develops his views here about *imitatio Dei* with reference to Jeremiah 9:22–3: "Let not the wise man glory in his wisdom; let not the strong man glory in his strength; let not the rich

man glory in his riches. But only in this should one glory: in his earnest devotion to Me. For I the Lord act with kindness, justice, and equity in the world; for in these I delight." Of this verse, Maimonides comments: "Thus the end that he [Jeremiah] sets forth in this verse may be stated as follows: It is clear that the perfection of man that may truly be gloried in is the one acquired by him who has achieved, in a measure corresponding to his capacity, apprehension of Him, may He be exalted, and who knows His providence extending over His creatures as manifested in the act of bringing them into being and in their governance as it is. The way of life of such an individual, after he has achieved this apprehension, will always have in view loving-kindness, righteousness, and judgment, through assimilation to His actions, may He be exalted, just as we have explained several times in this treatise."

15. McInerny (ed. and trans.), *Thomas Aquinas*, xxxiv.
16. *Ethics* V, Props. 32–3, 42 (cf. *Guide* 3:51); and see W. Z. Harvey, "A Portrait of Spinoza as a Maimonidean," *Journal of the History of Philosophy* 19 (1981), 151–72.

8   Maimonides and the sciences

No single person had as great an impact on Jewish thought as did Moses Maimonides (1138–1204). In addition to his tremendous accomplishments in the fields of philosophy and law, Maimonides was thoroughly versed in the sciences of his day, and the sciences were fully integrated into his view of Judaism; indeed, Maimonides' outlook was guided in large part by the scientific opinion of his day.[1] His philosophy asserts the unity of all truth, that the deity, in keeping with Arabic usage, is in fact The Truth (al-haqq), and that the religious imperative to know God is essentially the same as the philosophical imperative to determine the truth. Many statements issuing from the different branches of knowledge claim to be true. However, Maimonides affirms, the strongest and securest claims to truth are made by the sciences, most especially the mathematical sciences, whose statements are demonstrated with logical rigor. Moreover, of all the components of the cosmos, it is the heavenly bodies, with their regular motion and subtle physics, that disclose something approaching the nature of the divine. Furthermore, the human body is marvelously constructed, and its study is also useful for the religious quest. The science of medicine, which conducts this investigation, is also important as a guide for the conduct of a healthy life – a life as free as possible from the physical and emotional disturbances that interfere with the religious quest.

These three points – science's ability to formulate true statements, and the special roles assigned to astronomy and medicine – are the most telling causes for Maimonides' decision to assign a very prominent role to the sciences in his religious philosophy. In this chapter I shall attempt to cover the most important areas where this decision came into play. After briefly describing Maimonides' education and contributions to the scientific literature, I shall discuss a complex of issues related to astronomy, arguably the most important science for Maimonides. Next I shall turn to medicine, discussing, in turn, medical, philosophical, and religious regimens for health; teleology; and the definitions of humanity and the fixity of the species. In the third section I shall discuss mathematics, numerology, and Pythagoreanism. Finally, in the fourth section, I shall describe Maimonides' evolving views on the question of miracles.

SCIENTIFIC EDUCATION AND CAREER

Maimonides' formative years were spent in Spain and North Africa. With the exception of some very revealing remarks concerning his extreme grief at the loss of his brother, Maimonides never discusses his personal biography. However, there are some scattered references in the *Guide* to his education in astronomy, and one finds some remarks in his medical writings on his training in that field. All of the recorded episodes took place before Maimonides' emigration to the East, and all of the scholars named – Ibn Bajja, Jabir ibn Aflah, Abu Marwan ibn Zuhr – with whom Maimonides had direct or indirect contact (via students or relations) were Andalusians as well. According to the Arabic bibliographers, Maimonides edited texts in the exact sciences by Ibn Aflah and Ibn Hud, both of them Andalusians. The problem of epicycles and eccenters, a source of much consternation for Maimonides, vexed Andalusian astronomers in particular, though the problem was raised in the East as well. Finally, the majority of medical authorities whom Maimonides cites hailed from the Muslim West. Maimonides was a Maghrebian working in Egypt.

Almost all of Maimonides' extant scientific writings are in the field of medicine. These include two large compendia, *Fusul Musa* (*Pirqei Moshe*) and his epitomes of the works of Galen, which he wrote for his own use, and about half a dozen monographs on a variety of medical issues (hygiene and regimen, asthma, hemorrhoids, toxicology, sexual medicine) that were written at the behest of patrons. In addition, he wrote a commentary on Hippocrates' *Aphorisms*, a work that, as Maimonides himself tells us, was widely studied, and not just by physicians.

As far as the exact sciences are concerned, Maimonides has left us a method for solving the rather complicated problem of the possibility of sighting the lunar crescent. Unlike his other scientific writings, this work is in Hebrew, integrated into Maimonides' comprehensive legal encyclopaedia, *Mishneh Torah*. He is reported to have written a number of treatises in mathematics. All that remains, however, are some notes to the *Conics* of Apollonius.

ASTRONOMY

Maimonides' most telling pronouncements on the scientific enterprise and its place in his thought are related to astronomy. Issues connected with the science of the heavens are raised at several junctures in the *Guide*, and several chapters are devoted to the subject. Maimonides clearly is of the opinion that a thorough mastery of astronomy is a prerequisite for the religious quest and that knowledge of the heavens must necessarily precede any knowledge of God. Just how much one can know of God, or how much secure knowledge of the heavens is available, remain difficult problems for Maimonides and his interpreters.

Before examining some of the astronomical passages from the *Guide*, however, let us first look at the discussion in Maimonides' legal code, *Mishneh Torah*. The latter is a legal code directed toward the widest possible Jewish audience. By contrast, the *Guide* – if we may take the dedicatory epistle at face value – contains information that Maimonides chose to reveal to his prize student only after the latter had completed his studies in astronomy, mathematics, and logic. Moreover, some twenty difficult years separate the two works, and Maimonides surely underwent some changes of heart, of greater or lesser significance. The first four chapters of the first section of *Mishneh Torah*, *The Basic Principles of the Torah*, contain a straightforward and concise account of metaphysics and natural science. Maimonides himself tells us (4:10) that the subject of the first two is "Ma'aseh Merkavah" – theology and metaphysics – and that of the second two "Ma'aseh Bereshit" – physics. Chapter 1 concerns the deity. The beginning of chapter 2 outlines humanity's quest for the deity, to know, fear, and ultimately to love God; the rest of the chapter describes the "creatures that are form without matter at all, that is to say, the angels." The first paragraphs are meant to indicate that the bridge between the lower world and its most noble creature, the human being, is knowledge of God, which can only be obtained by

means of a thorough study of the created world: this notion is a
key element in Maimonides' philosophy and one toward which his
commitment is constant, whatever deliberations, doubts, and shifts
in attitude he may have undergone over the years.

Maimonides endorses the standard medieval cosmology: an earth-
centered, finite, and spherical cosmos, within which there is a sharp
distinction between the celestial and terrestrial realms. The former
reaches from the outermost orb to the orb of the moon; the latter
comprises the remaining space, which is occupied by the earth and its
atmosphere.[2] Both realms contain bodies that are made up of matter
and form and are in unceasing motion; but here the similarity ends.
The composition of the heavenly bodies is fixed and unchanging,
and their circular motions are unending. By contrast, bodies in the
terrestrial realm are in constant flux; they undergo growth, diminu-
tion, generation, corruption, and other forms of motion, constantly
exchanging one form for another. Terrestrial processes are all ultimately driven by the motion of the heavenly sphere; this dynamic,
unidirectional connection gives a unity of sorts to the cosmos.
Moreover, the heavenly beings are living and intelligent. On earth,
however, only individuals belonging to one species – the human
species – have the potential to become intelligent.

Let us look at this picture in somewhat more detail. Chapter 3
describes "creatures that are compounded of form and matter, but
which do not change from body to body or from form to form...
but rather their form is forever fixed within their matter"; these
are the celestial bodies. The heavens are made up of colorless orbs,
superimposed upon each other "like the layers of an onion." There
are eighteen orbs that encompass the earth and another eight that do
not; the latter are the epicycles. No geometrical models are described,
and very few quantities are displayed. The "slow motion" of the fixed
stars, that is precession, is said to approximate in seventy years the
motion of the sun in one day. The volume of the earth is 40 times
that of the moon, and that of the sun 170 times that of the earth, so
that the sun is some 6,800 times as large as the moon.

Most astronomical texts deal at great length with the motions of
the stars in longitude and latitude; discussions of their sizes, when
included at all, are usually quite brief. Maimonides' relative allot-
ment of space to these topics in *Mishneh Torah* thus seems to reflect the purposes of his exposition, which in this case are to enthral

a mathematically uneducated audience with some hints about the cosmic dimensions. The data as he presents them are correct by the standards of medieval astronomy. Maimonides has not distorted anything; he has rather selected certain facts out of many and presented them in a way that suits his purpose. Does this observation hold true for other features of his account? As we shall see, Maimonides was aware of serious doubts that beset some features of the picture he presents, for example epicycles; and he certainly knew of these problems at the time he wrote *Mishneh Torah*. Why does he include epicycles in his account? Is he deliberately misleading the audience of the *Mishneh Torah*, the great majority of whom would not wish to entertain any doubts at all concerning sublime matters? Or is it rather the readers of the *Guide* whom he is misdirecting by exaggerating the implications of his doubts on this matter? We shall take up these critical questions a bit later.

Let us first look at an important point that is stressed both in the *Mishneh Torah* and in the *Guide*. In the former (*Basic Principles* 3:1) Maimonides states: "The ninth orb is the one which completes a cycle each day from east to west. It is that which encompasses everything, and it is that which sets everything in [circular] motion."[3] The outermost orb is identified as the cause of all motion in the cosmos. The immediate context of the passage may suggest that the outermost orb is the cause only of the circular motion of all the other celestial orbs. However, in the next chapter (*Basic Principles* 4:6), the revolution of the orb is named as the cause of all physical alteration in the terrestrial sphere. This is a key axiom in Maimonides' cosmology, suggesting that all change or motion can be traced ultimately to a single source, namely, the outermost orb, whose motion (one circuit every twenty-four hours) is swift and powerful; it is an important unifying principle for the cosmos with telling theological implications.

His vacillations with regard to several important issues notwithstanding, Maimonides is certain about what he says about the outermost orb. Its truth is never questioned in the *Guide*; quite the contrary, the special role of the outermost orb is treated there as one of the bedrocks of belief. One key exposition of this theme is found in *Guide* 2:30, where Maimonides indicates some hints about the special status of the outermost orb in biblical and aggadic texts relating to the "making of the firmament" described in Genesis 1:6–8.[4]

Interpretations of this passage have differed greatly.[5] This much, however, is clear: Maimonides takes the biblical "water" to refer to some undifferentiated primeval stuff. On the second day, parts of this "water" were given different forms, resulting in a fundamental division in the material components of the universe. But what was differentiated into what? And, presuming that the biblical story will, in Maimonides' interpretation, refer to some basic natural processes, which processes are hinted at in the biblical narrative? Shem Tov ibn Falaquera is representative of the consensus of commentators on the *Guide* in finding in Maimonides a reference to the threefold division of the earth's atmosphere: the "upper waters" are Aristotle's hot exhalation, the "firmament" (*raqiʿa*) is the lower stratum occupied by the cold exhalation, and the "oceans" refer to the elemental waters found on earth. Ibn Falaquera refers to another commentator, Moses Narboni, who adds that the natural process involved here is that of rainfall, once again according to Aristotle's theory.

To be sure, some Jewish rationalists, most notably Abraham ibn Ezra (twelfth century), had interpreted the biblical "firmament" as the atmosphere. There is a strong tendency among Jewish thinkers, which peaked in the fourteenth century, to conflate the views of Maimonides and Ibn Ezra; and it is possible that many readers of the *Guide* expected Maimonides to interpret the biblical story just as Ibn Ezra had done. Indeed, Maimonides refers to just this interpretation when he observes, "For if the matter is considered according to its external meaning and with a recourse only to superficial speculation, it [the firmament and the thing above it] does not exist at all. For between us and the lowest heaven, there exists no body except the elements..."[6] However, Maimonides immediately draws a sharp distinction between this approach and the Bible's "inner meaning and...what was truly intended" – and Maimonides is eager to find the inner meaning and true intention of the biblical verse.

It seems to me that Maimonides' discussion was misconstrued by the medieval translators and most of the commentators, who, misled by a seemingly ambiguous Arabic word, thought Maimonides to be describing processes within the earth's atmosphere, in a manner similar to that described by Aristotelian meteorology. In fact, Maimonides is talking about something else entirely. He is returning to an important theme to which he had earlier devoted an entire chapter (*Guide* 2:26), namely that the material component of the heavens is utterly different from that of the earth; this, he stresses, is one of the fundamental principles of cosmology. In the passage under scrutiny Maimonides suggests that the further differentiation, within the celestial realm, between the all-encompassing highest sphere and the rest of the heavens is so significant as to warrant inclusion in the biblical creation story; indeed, it is the second differentiation to have occurred, preceded only by the differentiation between darkness and light. Hence it is true to say that the biblical "water," which signifies the primordial stuff of the universe, was divided not into two, but into three basic components: the highest orb, the rest of the heavens, and the terrestrial realm. The distinction between the highest orb and the heavens had been adumbrated before, at the beginning of *Guide* 2:9. In the passage from *Guide* 2:30, it appears that Maimonides wishes to go one step further, implying that the distinction between the two is every bit as significant as that between the heavens and the earth.

In contrast to the exposition of *Guide* 2:30, the special status of the outermost orb is spelled out rather plainly in *Guide* 1:70, where Maimonides discloses the basic features of his worldview, discussing both the physical workings of the cosmos and the manner in which God is the cause of it all. This scheme was held by Maimonides to be correct, whatever doubts or unsolved problems beset the details of its operation. The key tenets of Maimonides' cosmology are that "the deity ... is the mover of the highest heaven, by whose motion everything that is in motion within this heaven is moved; at the same time, he, may he be exalted, is separate from this [that is, the highest] heaven and not a force subsisting within it." (*Guide* 1:70).

In sum, then, according to our interpretation, Maimonides asserts that the cosmos has three main components: the outermost orb, set in motion directly by God; the heavens, which transmit downward the motion imparted to them by the outermost orb; and the terrestrial sphere, whose complex motions and processes are ultimately caused by the heavenly motions. This fundamental differentiation of the material world is conveyed by the biblical account of the second day of the creation. However, the great majority of readers of the *Guide* understood Maimonides to be referring in his explication of the text from Genesis to a different process of differentiation, namely the stratification of the atmosphere, in line with the doctrines of Aristotle's *Meteorology*.

By either account, the Bible narrates the differentiation in mythic fashion, so as to hide a great secret from the masses. Maimonides remains firm in wishing not to uncover matters that are best left hidden; indeed, his exposition is cryptic enough to allow the widely divergent interpretations mentioned in the preceding paragraph. Yet both of these "secrets" are revealed in the *Mishneh Torah*. I have already cited the passage that clarifies the special function of the highest orb. The atmospheric events, which belong to the general class of processes of change and alteration, are mentioned several times, for example in *Basic Principles* 4:5:

These four elements change into one another constantly, every day and every hour; but only part of them, not their entire body. How [does it happen]? The part of the earth that is adjacent to water changes, disintegrates, and becomes water. Similarly, the part of the water that is adjacent to the air changes, evaporates, and becomes air... and so also the part of the air that is adjacent to water changes, precipitates, and becomes water...

How are we to explain this? How can Maimonides freely disclose scientific information that, by his own account, was occluded by the Bible, and later by the rabbis? In the years that intervene between the writing of the *Mishneh Torah* and the *Guide* Maimonides' thought certainly did evolve, but not in such a radical form that he would try to cover up information he himself had freely shared earlier on. I suggest a combination of explanations that will flesh out not only the differences between the two texts, but some important facets of Maimonides' attitude toward the scientific enterprise as well.[7]

We must first bring into the picture Maimonides' views on the history of science. Maimonides adheres to a rather simple picture of the steady progress of science over time. Later generations possess more and better knowledge than did earlier generations. The Israelites to whom the creation story, along with the rest of the Torah, was revealed constituted a community of emancipated slaves, who, perhaps, had not fully shaken off their spiritual bondage. Moreover, at that moment in history – well before the time of Aristotle – the level of scientific knowledge that was available was not very high. The Bible, therefore, had good reason to narrate the creation as a story. By the time of the rabbis, science had progressed considerably. Nevertheless, the intellectual level of the masses remained low, and many details, especially in the field of astronomy, remained obscure

even to the best of scholars. Thus the rabbis too had to speak in parables. By Maimonides' own time, however, the situation had changed
radically. Astronomy had advanced well beyond what even Aristotle
had known. Moreover, a plethora of rich texts, written for the
most part in Arabic, made scientific knowledge widely available.
There was thus no reason why Maimonides, in his *Mishneh Torah*,
could not offer the same type of summary account that could be
found in a large number of works that were in circulation at the
time.

The *Guide*, however, has a special purpose: to inform the intelligent and perplexed Jew that the very truths that he could now freely
access are found in the traditional sources. For the reasons just outlined, these ancient sources could relay their message only figuratively. Maimonides took it upon himself to show how, when read
properly, the traditional texts contain a true account. But this is still
not a full answer to our questions: Why is Maimonides' interpretation no less cryptic than the text he is explicating? If science is no
longer a secret, why must Maimonides be so cautious and elusive in
suggesting the correct interpretation?

The answer to these questions lies in the fact that Maimonides
had to deal not only with the texts but with a considerable body
of interpretation that had built up around them. Maimonides knows
full well that many Jews who have assimilated other approaches will
not be sympathetic to his reading. Although he is generally careful
not to engage earlier exegetes in polemics, his feelings come out
clearly in this passage from the introduction to the *Guide*:

But those who are confused and whose brains have been polluted by false
opinions and misleading ways deemed by them to be true sciences, and who
hold themselves to be men of speculation without having any knowledge of
anything that can truly be called science, those will flee from many of its
[the *Guide*'s] chapters (*Guide* 1: introduction).

S. Munk was certain that Maimonides was here targeting the *mutakallimun*, the Muslim thinkers who advocated an atomistic occasionalism and whose views found considerable appeal among some
Jewish thinkers.[8] However, in view of the wide range of approaches
that are criticized ever so obliquely in the *Guide*, it is more likely that
Maimonides is here lumping together the variety of interpretations
of Jewish doctrine known to him, and which, in his estimation, had

made significant enough inroads among Jewish literati that it would be best for him only to hint at his own interpretation.

Having said all of this, we must acknowledge the existence of some differences in the facts as they are presented in the two works, particularly in matters of astronomy. To recapitulate: according to the *Mishneh Torah*, there are eighteen geocentric orbs and another eight epicycles; and the ninth orb is the highest, all-encompassing sphere. Is this account acceptable to the Maimonides of the *Guide*? The correct reply, in my view, is yes, but not precisely.

Let us first look at the count of the spheres. Concerning the geocentric orbs, Maimonides writes in *Guide* 1:72, "It is not possible . . . that the number of the spheres encompassing the world should be less than eighteen. It is, however, possible that their number should be greater than eighteen." The number of spheres presented straightforwardly in the *Mishneh Torah* is, in truth, only the *minimum* number of spheres required to account for the observed motions. The rabbis counted the highest sphere, *aravot*, as the seventh. In this connection Maimonides comments, "Do not think it blameworthy that according to their reckoning there were seven heavens, whereas there are more than that. For sometimes . . . a sphere is counted as one though there be several heavens contained in it" (*Guide* 1:70). Taken in conjunction with the preceding citation, we may add that Maimonides is not to be held accountable for counting the highest sphere as the ninth, even though that too may not be precise.

It appears to be the case, then, that the information provided in the *Mishneh Torah* is not false or misleading. It is, however, less precise than the plain style of its exposition may imply. It is important to have this point in mind when turning to the third and most difficult issue, namely the existence of epicycles, and, more generally, the truth of Ptolemaic astronomy. A number of Islamic astronomers had raised serious doubts about some of Ptolemy's devices, especially epicycles and eccenters. Andalusian scholars evinced a particular sensitivity to these problems, and, as he informs us in the *Guide*, Maimonides in his youth had inquired about them directly from some leading Andalusian scholars. An entire chapter of the *Guide* (2:24) is devoted to these issues. Maimonides reviews some solutions that had come to his attention – he is in fact our only source for some of this material – none of which he finds to be satisfying. He ends the chapter with two seemingly contradictory pronouncements, first declaring it to be wrong "to fatigue the minds with notions that cannot be grasped by them" but then, in his final musing, allowing for the possibility that someone else may find a solution.

The precise nature of Maimonides' position on this question, and the implications for his ideas on the task of astronomy and the limits of human knowledge, have exercised scholars for several decades.[9] Maimonides realized that geocentric spheres alone could not suffice to account for the observed phenomena. He overemphasized the depths of the dilemma in order to score an important point against Aristotle's doctrine of the eternity of the universe, which rests principally on the unending, regular, and circular motions of the heavens. He was confident enough about the necessity of the epicycles that he could present them in the *Mishneh Torah* as part of the true cosmography. However, the precise configuration that would account for the transmission of the swift, daily motion of the encompassing orb downward was unknown to him.

The differences between the *Mishneh Torah* and the *Guide* are those that one finds between an elementary and an advanced course in the sciences. Information that, at the introductory level, is dryly presented as "the simple facts," turns out to be less simple and less certain the more one advances in one's studies. The *Guide* was written for an advanced student, one who could and should know how to handle the doubts that inevitably arise in any serious inquiry. Maimonides (*Guide* 1:32) warns his readers:

When points appearing as dubious appear to him [the serious student] or the thing does not seem to him to be demonstrated, he should not deny or reject it, hastening to pronounce it false, but rather should persevere and thereby have regard for the honour of his Creator. He should refrain and hold back.

MEDICINE AND THE LIFE SCIENCES

Maimonides achieved great fame for his expertise in medicine. Despite the interest that has been shown in his medical career, little can be said at present concerning Maimonides' achievements in medicine, beyond summarizing the contents of his treatises. Moreover, his interest in the life sciences connects strongly to some key issues of his philosophy, and these connections remain for the most part unexplored. In the following I shall point to some key issues and attempt to indicate their significance.[10]

Perhaps the most critical problem from the point of view of Maimonides' religious philosophy concerns the definition of "species," specifically, does humanity constitute a species?[11] Though Maimonides does speak of the human species, he intimates that in the case of humans the concept is not exact. Instead, he appears to hold that those people who succeed in actualizing their humanity form a collection of individuals so different from the other that the term "species" must be stretched considerably in order to apply to all. Allusions to this position are found in the chapter of the *Guide* (2:40) where Maimonides speaks of man as a political animal:

[T]here are many differences between the individuals belonging to it [the human species], so that you can hardly find two individuals who are in accord with respect to one of the species of moral habits . . . Nothing like this great difference between the various individuals is found among the other species of animals, in which the difference between the individuals belonging to the same species is small, man being in this respect an exception.

That chapter is concerned with politics, and Maimonides points to the wide divergence between individuals in order to make the point that human societies require wise governance. Here, as elsewhere in the *Guide*, however, a point that is raised ostensibly as a preamble to a particular argument is, in fact, of importance in its own right.

The reader of the *Guide* is informed about the full implications of these remarks only after Maimonides has spoken about prophecy and providence. The central text is the beginning of *Guide* 3:18, where Maimonides writes:

I say that it is known that no species exists outside the mind . . . and that every existent outside the mind is an individual or a group of individuals. This being known, it is also known that the divine overflow that exists united to the human species, I mean the human intellect, is merely what exists as individual intellects . . .

Species is a mental concept, useful for organizing knowledge, and medicine would be hard pressed to do without it. However, according to Maimonides, species have no independent existence detached from the objects they classify. Therefore, we are free to classify individuals bearing all the outward, physical forms of humans as either human or beast, with all that this classification implies. Individuals who have achieved some measure of (intellectual) perfection, so as to warrant divine governance, have thereby achieved the key distinguishing trait of humans: linkage of their intellect with the divine. The "ignorant and disobedient," by contrast, "have been relegated to the rank of the individuals of all the other species of animal" (*Guide* 3:18).

This approach jibes well with some remarks found in Maimonides' medical writings, where the individual's body is called an "animal," which must be trained and disciplined, just as one trains a beast of burden. For example, a person should not become dependent on laxatives, since this will cause his personal "beast" to be lazy with regard to digestion and excretion. Beyond situations relating to specific medical problems, however, the notion of discipline or regimen is a central concept of the medicine of the period, and one in which the tasks of medicine, philosophy, and religion overlap and, occasionally, come into conflict. Maimonides emphasizes the preventive role of a medical regimen in preserving health. He considered the topic important enough to be included in his law code, *Mishneh Torah*, where several chapters are devoted to advice on proper diet, sleep, bathing, and sexual activity, culminating in a promise that whoever follows these guidelines rigorously will, barring any major natural catastrophe, enjoy a full and healthy life (*Laws of Ethics* [*Hilkhot De'ot*] chs. 3–4).

In principle, there should be no conflict between the various regimes. Rules governing personal hygiene (medicine), regulations concerning societal and family relationships (politics), and injunctions and prohibitions that serve to limit involvement in worldly pursuits, thereby freeing energy for intellectual and spiritual attainments (religion and philosophy), should and most often do complement each other. Occasionally, however, the rules conflict, for example in the case of wine. For certain afflictions medical opinion recommended wine. Maimonides, however, knows that that beverage is forbidden to Muslims. Hence, after offering his professional advice that wine is appropriate, he leaves the decision whether or not to follow it to the patient's conscience. It must be added, however, that in his writings directed at Jews, Maimonides betrays some sympathy for that particular Islamic prohibition. Thus, at the end of *Guide* 3:48, he points out that the Nazirite is called holy solely on account of his abstention from drink. Some important facets of Maimonides' biography and scientific activities are connected to his medical career. During his formative years in Spain and North Africa, Maimonides actively sought out teachers and savants in a variety of fields. However, during his long residence at Fustat – the pinnacle of his career, as we might view it – he seems to have deliberately avoided meeting anyone, whether Jew or non-Jew. The one facet of his activity that forced him to come into contact with other scholars was his position as physician at the court of the vizier. His medical monographs were all written as a result of his connections with the upper echelons of Egyptian society.

Unlike the exact sciences, where it suffices to have at one's command some general rules and basic skills, medicine demands of its practitioners a large storehouse of empirical data. To be sure, medicine has a logic of its own; Maimonides writes in one of his letters that he demands of himself to be able to reproduce the "manner of reasoning" (*wajh al-qiyas*) underlying any medical opinion that he may offer. Nonetheless, the rules of inference are obviously not as stringent as they are in the mathematical sciences; in particular, repeated observations of the efficacy of a certain treatment, even if there is (as yet) no theoretical explanation as to why it should work, are sufficient. All of this argues in favor of the institution of a committee of doctors, whose combined expertise should overcome any difficulties. Maimonides endorses the institution in principle but is wary of it in practice, given the fact that pride and other non-professional considerations may intervene. Moreover, he records such a failed joint effort of the best doctors at Marrakesh as one of the formative experiences of his education.

MATHEMATICS

Arabic histories report that Maimonides wrote and edited a number of works on mathematics. However, the only such writing to be uncovered so far are some notes to Apollonius' *Conics*, which cover as well Ibn al-Haytham's reconstruction of Book 8 of that work.[12] Further evidence for his aptitude in mathematics is found in his method for computing the visibility of the lunar crescent, which includes, by his own admission, some approximations that cancel each other out, thus not affecting the overall accuracy of the method; some scattered remarks in the *Guide*, including a reference to the property of the asymptotes to the hyperbola; and the note, at the very beginning of the *Guide*, that he had studied mathematics with his prize pupil, Yosef ben Yehudah.

As we have already seen, Maimonides values astronomy – mathematical astronomy – highly. Moreover, throughout the *Guide* he repeatedly studies the relation or proportion (*nisba*) between things, a clear indication of his mathematical leanings.[13] On the other hand, he does not seem to identify with the (mystical) type of religious philosophy which sees in number the deepest secrets of creation. He studiously ignores *Sefer Yetzira*, whose Pythagoreanism had a strong impact on Jewish thought. Indeed, Maimonides openly declares (*Guide* 2:8) that some cosmological doctrines endorsed by the rabbis – the theory that the stars move freely through the heavens, or the notion that the heavenly bodies emit sounds – are those of Pythagoras and his school, and that they have been repudiated by Aristotle. Maimonides rejects them as well.

Nonetheless, there are some hints that Maimonides may not have been as unsympathetic to Pythagoreanism as he would like us to believe.[14] In *Guide* 1:34, he plainly states, "How very many are the premises thus taken from the nature of numbers and the properties of geometrical figures from which we draw inferences concerning things that we should deny with respect to God, may he be exalted." Ostensibly, when he refers to the nature of numbers (*tabi'at al-a'dad*), Maimonides has in mind nothing other than correct notions concerning one (unity and uniformity) and other numbers, which are indispensable for denying any multiplicity to God.

Yet Maimonides' numerous references to tetrads and, to a lesser extent, his preference for the number fourteen, betray a deeper interest in the "nature of numbers."[15] Tetrads are invoked in a variety of contexts, some of them of telling importance. Maimonides takes some trouble to prove that the biblical "chariot" (*merkavah*), whose cosmic symbolism is of such importance for the rabbis, is drawn by four horses. According to Maimonides, an array of astronomical, psychic, and other forces group themselves into foursomes. These are discussed in *Guide* 2:10, where Maimonides states: "This number four is wondrous (*'ajib*) and an object of reflection (*mawdiʿ taʾammul*)." Elsewhere in the *Guide* (1:72) four types of astral forces are matched to four classes of terrestrial beings. Moreover, Maimonides concludes the *Guide* with remarks on the four classes of watchmen recognized by Jewish law, the four species that are taken on the Sukkoth festival, and humanity's four perfections (*Guide* 3:54). The number fourteen figures in the plan of some of Maimonides' writings: he lists fourteen rules at the beginning of his *Book of Commandments*, and he divides the *Mishneh Torah* into fourteen sections.

MIRACLES AND THE NATURAL ORDER

Miracles present the most vexing issue for the religious thinker who is committed to the scientific enterprise. By their very nature, miracles seem to be a denial of the laws of nature whose clarification is the chief task of the scientist. On the other hand, a denial of any form of miracle leads to the exclusion of any religiously meaningful role for God in the happenings of the cosmos and, especially, in human affairs.

Maimonides' view of miracles, more than his stance on any other issue related to the sciences, appears to have undergone a clear shift over the years. Broadly speaking – and the generalizations that I am about to make certainly need to be qualified – it is my view that the youthful Maimonides, impressed by the success of the scientific enterprise, favored naturalistic explanations of the events considered to be miraculous by Jewish tradition. According to that tradition, miracles were, so to speak, programmed into the universe at the very start, and thus do not in any serious way challenge the scientific approach. In the last chapter of his prefatory essay to the Mishnaic tractate *Avot* (known as the *Eight Chapters*), Maimonides writes that the divine will had, during the process of creation, "placed in the natures of those [natural] things whatever new thing would happen. When that new thing did happen, at the required time, people mistakenly thought that it had just happened to be right now, but that is not the case."[16] In his usual manner, Maimonides shows that his own interpretation – namely, that natural phenomena which the common folk take to be miracles only appear to be miraculous on account of their synchronicity with other events of historical import – is identical with the views of the rabbis, though the latter are usually couched in midrashic allusion.

As he matured, however, Maimonides became more receptive to the need for miracles as well as their possibility. Doubts and uncertainties, some of which have been mentioned above, dampened his enthusiasm for the unlimited explanatory power of natural philosophy. In addition, as he refined his own religious philosophy, he became increasingly aware of the necessity for miracles, that is, for some expressions of the omnipotence of the divine will. No chapter in the *Guide* is set aside specifically for the topic of miracles – a decision noteworthy in its own right – and the discussions that the reader encounters at various junctures in the book are neither complete nor consistent.

Maimonides' final position is that miracles consist of events that in themselves are entirely "possible" within the natural order; it is the persistence of events, each of which is by itself natural, over a period of time and in a particular context that makes them (each event individually and the set as a whole) miraculous. This point is stated in *Guide* 3:50 where he writes: "Now one of the miracles of the law, and one of the greatest among them, is the sojourn of Israel for forty years in the desert and the finding of the manna there every day." However, the fullest treatment is to be found in one of Maimonides' last compositions, the *Letter on Resurrection*. Maimonides appends to that treatise, which is in the main a defense against the accusation that he denies bodily resurrection, a disquisition on miracles. We find the same general rule as that in the *Guide*, but the example is different:

Now, as the miracle in things that are possible is concerned: the longer it endures and persists, the more likely it is to be a miracle. Therefore, we are convinced about the endurance of blessings at times of obedience, and curses at times of disobedience, throughout the bygone ages (*fi ghabir al-dahr*), in connection with this nation [Israel]. In that way they become "a sign and a miracle," as we have explained.[17]

In sum, then, Maimonides never abandoned his belief in an orderly universe, whose regular and complex workings – described quite accurately by Aristotle, despite some shortcomings – offer the surest evidence for the existence of the deity. However, there are some deviations from the fixed rules which can be discerned only over a long period of time. When these deviations are synchronized with human (especially Jewish) history, they are recorded as miracles; other deviations, for example the uneven distribution of stars in the heavenly vault, are permanent features of the cosmos. Taken together, these facts call into question the claim that the deity does not intervene; they attest to creation, indicating that the natural order as described by Aristotle is the product of divine will, not mere necessity.

NOTES

1. Two volumes of studies devoted to Maimonides' interest in the sciences are: R. Cohen and H. Levine (eds.), *Maimonides and the Sciences* (Dordrecht: Kluwer, 2000); and T. Lévy and R. Rashed (eds.), *Maïmonide et les traditions scientifiques et philosophiques médiévales (arabe, hébreu, latin)* (Paris and Louvain: Peeters, forthcoming).

2. I use the term "atmosphere" anachronistically and imprecisely to refer to the orbs of air and fire, which, according to the medieval conception, reach to the lower limit of the moon's orbit.

3. There is a nice double entendre in the Hebrew, which can be vocalized either *mesobeb* (set in circular motion) or *mesabeb* (cause).

4. See the translation of S. Pines, *The Guide of the Perplexed* (Chicago: University of Chicago Press, 1963), 2:352–4 (hereafter: *Guide*).

5. Y. T. Langermann, " 'The Making of the Firmament': R. Hayyim Israeli, R. Isaac Israeli and Maimonides" [Hebrew], in *Shlomo Pines Jubilee Volume*, ed. M. Idel, W. Z. Harvey, and E. Schweid (Jerusalem: Magnes Press, 1988), 1: 461–76.

6. *Guide* 2:353. Note that Ibn Ezra generally presents the plain interpretation (*peshat*).

7. The following expands upon some earlier publications of mine, with some revision: "The 'True Perplexity': The *Guide of the Perplexed*, Part II, Chapter 24," in *Perspectives on Maimonides: Philosophical and Historical Studies*, ed. J. L. Kraemer (Oxford: Littman Library, 1991), 159–74; "Maimonides and Astronomy: Some Further Reflections," in Y. T. Langermann, *The Jews and the Sciences in the Middle Ages* (Aldershot: Variorum, 1999), study IV.

8. S. Munk, *Le guide des égarés* (Paris, 1856; reprinted Lagrasse: Verdier, 1979), 1: 25 n. 1.

9. The surge of interest can be traced to the landmark article of S. Pines, "The Limitations of Human Knowledge according to al-Farabi, ibn Bajja, and Maimonides," in *Studies in Medieval Jewish History and Literature*, ed. I. Twersky (Cambridge, Mass.: Harvard University Press, 1979), 82–109; reprinted, W. Z. Harvey and M. Idel (eds.), *The Collected Works of Shlomo Pines. v. Studies in the History of Jewish Thought* (Jerusalem: Magnes Press, 1997). Some recent contributions include H. Davidson,

"Maimonides on Metaphysical Knowledge," *Maimonidean Studies* 3 (1995), 49–103; J. Stern, "Maimonides on the Growth of Knowledge and the Limitations of the Intellect," in Lévy and Rashed (eds.), *Maïmonide et les traditions scientifiques*.

10. The discussion here is based in large measure upon my study, "L'oeuvre médicale de Maïmonide: Un aperçu général," in Lévy and Rashed (eds.), *Maïmonide et les traditions scientifiques*, to which the reader is referred for full citations and bibliography.

11. My remarks on this subject seem to be pertinent for the formulation of a Jewish response to Darwinism.

12. Y. T. Langermann, "The Mathematical Writings of Maimonides," *Jewish Quarterly Review* 75 (1984), 57–65.

13. Clearly much of this stems from the importance of "proportion" in the Hellenistic philosophical tradition; still I believe that Maimonides evinces a deeper mathematical approach; cf. the contribution of R. Rashed, "Mathématiques et philosophie selon Maïmonide," in Lévy and Rashed (eds.), *Maïmonide et les traditions scientifiques*.

14. It is appropriate here to recall the very strong remarks of D. Kaufmann ("Die Spuren al-Bataljusi in der jüdischen Religions-Philosophie," in *Jahresbericht der Landes-Rabbinerschule in Budapest* [Budapest, 1880], 36–40) concerning Maimonides' debt to Ibn al-Sayyid al-Batalyawsi, in whose thinking the Pythagorean strain is prominent. As far as I know, Kaufmann's suggestions, though they are well documented, have been totally ignored.

15. Y. T. Langermann, "Maimonides' Repudiation of Astrology," *Maimonidean Studies* 2 (1992), 123–58, esp. 145–6; cf. G. Freudenthal, "Maimonides' Stance on Astrology in Context: Cosmology, Physics, Medicine, and Providence," in *Moses Maimonides: Physician, Scientist, and Philosopher*, ed. F. Rosner and S. Kottek (Northvale, N.J.: Jason Aronson, 1993), 77–90.

16. My translation from the Arabic text published by Y. Qafih, *Maimonides' Commentary on the Mishnah, Seder Nezikim* (Jerusalem: n.p., 1967), 399.

17. My translation from the Arabic text published by Y. Qafih, *Iggerot Moshe ben Maimon* (Jerusalem: n.p., 1984), 99–100.

9 Medieval Jewish political thought

Politics is the art (*techne*) of human government. Political science, in its classical sense, is the body of knowledge informing the practice of this art. According to Maimonides, in his *Treatise on the Art of Logic*, political science "falls into four parts: first, the individual's governance of himself; second, the governance of the household; third, the governance of the city; and fourth, the governance of the large nation or of the nations."[1] Governance of the city has traditionally been the axial political activity. It is from the city, the *polis*, that the art receives its name: politics. Indeed, "governance of the city is a science that imparts to its citizens knowledge of true happiness and imparts to them the [way of] striving to achieve it." The science of the governance of the city furthermore prescribes for the citizens "the rules of justice that order their associations properly." The comprehensive quality of the city determines the specific shape of individual ethics and household management. The government of an empire is an amplification of the basic comprehensive unit, the city.

Maimonides' definition of political science raises important questions. Medieval Jews did not have a city (or state) of their own, and although the Jews are a nation, they were dispersed among many nations; they lacked sovereignty and a specific territory of their own. Is there any significance to a discussion of politics for a people in exile?

Provisionally we might say that exile is a political condition. Identifying politics with sovereignty is a prejudice deriving from a world dominated by nation-states. On this view, sovereignty is the mark of political individuation. It determines both the legal and territorial boundaries of the polity, and is the legitimate political expression of a nation. Medieval empires were structured differently, however.

They were less cohesive in their internal structure, tolerating a plurality of legal systems and autonomous modes of political organization within them. The medieval Jewish communities, whether in the world of Islam or in Christendom, enjoyed a wide range of autonomy of governance and law.[2] Going beyond institutional arrangements, exile in the Jewish self-perception is but a chapter in a longer religio-political history. It is a temporary hiatus between a glorious past of land, kingdom, and Temple and a redemptive messianic future. Exile however, is not a suspension of the political. The typical Jewish political structure of the exile is the *kehillah* or *kahal*, the Jewish community. Exilic politics is the governance of Jewish communal life in its internal domestic aspect. It also extends to the forging of an external policy of survival in a dark chapter of a historical drama whose theological-political significance resonates throughout the cultures of Islam and of Christendom.[3]

Reconsidering the concepts of politics and of exile leads however to a second question. Does the ancient science of politics have any significance for a nation guided by revealed divine law? Hasn't political science been superseded by revealed law?

Maimonides is well aware of the question. The wise men of ancient "religious communities" and the philosophers of ancient times, he says, had formulated regimens and rules for their communities, and written books expounding these subjects. Yet he ends his discussion of political science by stating that "In these times . . . the regimes and the *nomoi* have been dispensed with, and men are being governed by divine commands."[4]

Even a cursory glance at Maimonides' works reveals that he believed there is much guidance to be culled from the wisdom of the ancient philosophers. The concepts and terminology of political science echo throughout Maimonides' writings. His *Commentary on the Mishnah*, includes an introductory essay to tractate *Avot*, *The Eight Chapters*, a short treatise on ethics and political leadership modeled on al-Farabi's *Aphorisms of the Statesman*.[5] And in *The Guide of the Perplexed*, Maimonides begins his account of divine law by citing the Aristotelian conception of human political nature: "It has been explained with utmost clarity that man is political by nature and that it is in his nature to live in a society."[6]

Considering Maimonides' exposition of Aristotle's statement in further detail provides the key to his appropriation of classic political science. The human political situation is characterized by a plurality of individual traits and inclinations on one hand, and by a natural propensity for society to fulfill basic human needs, on the other. Therefore,

> it is by no means possible that his society should be perfected except – and this is necessarily so – through a ruler who gauges the actions of individuals, perfecting that which is deficient and reducing that which is excessive, and who prescribes actions and moral habits that all of them must always practice in the same way, so that the natural diversity is hidden through the multiple points of conventional accord and so that the community becomes well ordered. Therefore I say that the law, although it is not natural, enters into what is natural (*Guide* 2:40, 382).

Although divine law is not natural, it is nevertheless political; it is situated in man's natural political condition. Its divine character is expressed in the fact that it not only orders the human polity but attends "also to the soundness of belief," taking pains "to inculcate correct opinions with regard to God" (*Guide* 2:40, 384). Divine law, although politically situated, ultimately aims to cultivate human rational excellence.

If Maimonides' code, the *Mishneh Torah*, is to be viewed as the recasting of the positive tradition of rabbinic law according to this ideal of divine law conceived in terms of traditional political science, then we may conclude that the *Mishneh Torah* itself is nothing short of a constitution for the Jewish polis. The particular laws of ancient rulers, and their regimes, were superseded by the positive law of revelation, but the teleology of the divine law is articulated through the theory and discourse of classical political science.[7]

Maimonides' political philosophy of divine law has important ramifications for his conception of the Jewish collective, his understanding of the constitutional structure of a Jewish polity, and for his vision of messianic redemption. But before presenting the Maimonidean paradigm, it is important to consider the single most important counterexample to it. Maimonides' project of restructuring the traditional rabbinic legal code, infusing it with the spirit of philosophical political science, can be understood as a carrying out in a Jewish context a program previously outlined by Muslim philosophers in an Islamic context. The interpretive potential of this approach for Judaism had already been critiqued a generation before Maimonides, by Judah Halevi in his *Kuzari*.

The *Kuzari*'s critique of philosophy breaks new ground in medieval Jewish thought. Saadya's programmatic question at the beginning of *The Book of Beliefs and Opinions* is urbane, almost subdued: What is the relation between revealed knowledge and rational knowledge?[8] Halevi's point of departure in the *Kuzari* is of greater urgency: What is the true religion? Judaism is here measured against its competition, Christianity and Islam, both of which claim to have inherited the prophetic word, superseding Judaism, and which now divide the world between them. Living in Toledo, on the border between Christianity and Islam, who had turned Spain into a western frontier of their war for religious domination, Halevi acutely experienced this battle and Judaism's indignity in its midst.[9] Testimony of his sentiment is the *Kuzari*'s subtitle, "The Book of Refutation and Proof on Behalf of the Despised Religion."[10]

The question of the true religion shapes Halevi's treatment of philosophy, and determines his attitude toward it. Philosophy in his view is not a neutral science. It is no less compelling a spiritual adversary than Christianity or Islam. In fact it is a more serious and tenacious one. Philosophy identifies human excellence with the cultivation of substantive rationality, locating human perfection within a comprehensive cosmology. The problem faced by religion is not (the Saadyanic) one of revelation and rationality as sources of knowledge; the real issue is the nature of human excellence.

Halevi's articulation of the challenge faced by Judaism lends depth to his discussion. Jewish philosophy must begin by attending to Jewish existence, to the meaning of Judaism as a religion confronting history. And in his challenge to Aristotelianism, Halevi is the first to raise the question of whether religion makes unique metaphysical and epistemological claims that would render Aristotelianism inadequate in accounting at least for religious, if not for human, experience.[11]

The two opposing ideal-type philosophies of Judaism[12] developed by Halevi and then Maimonides, in the early and later decades of the twelfth century respectively, mark a maturation of Jewish philosophical discourse. It is less naive in its understanding of Aristotelian rationalism, more sophisticated in its self-reflection, and yet at the same time more ambitious in scope than its predecessors.

Regarding their respective attitudes to political philosophy, the basic controversy may be formulated with regard to collective identity. A community in exile is characterized by the fact that it is not territory but *identity* that marks the boundaries of its jurisdiction. According to Halevi's *haver*, the charismatic identity of the collective precedes its political institutionalization.[13] In contradistinction, for Maimonides, the collective is conceived in political-legal terms, and this institutionalization is constitutive of it. The respective articulations of Halevi and Maimonides continue to resonate in all subsequent discussions of political philosophy in (and beyond) Hispano-Jewish culture.

THE ANTI-POLITICS OF THE *KUZARI*

The memorable initial exchange between the Khazar king and the *haver* succinctly presents the principles of the latter's political theology. Already in this opening encounter, and against the backdrop of his earnest search for religious truth, the king of the Khazars comes up against the brute force of the fact of (divine) election. The *haver's* particularistic casting of the Sinaitic revelation elicits the king's exasperated conclusion that "your religious law is a legacy for yourselves only!" (1:26). This exclamation receives a swift rejoinder by the *haver* who states that this is indeed the case "because we are the choicest of the descendents of Adam" (1:27). Insult is thus added to frustrated desire. The king, who has seen the solution to his quest for religious certainty dangled before him within arm's reach (1:13), now has it snatched away by exclusion (1:26). (In fact, the tenor of metaphysical desire and near fulfillment remain central to the dramatic tension of the book. Ultimately both the king and the *haver* live in exile. In an unredeemed world our deepest desires cannot be fulfilled. Neither the king nor the *haver* can achieve prophecy. But both make the gesture toward attainment, the king by converting to Judaism and the *haver* by undertaking the conversion-like journey to *Eretz Yisrael*.)[14]

The *haver* assuages the king's dismay by expounding his theory of the five ontological orders of the universe. The distinction drawn between rational perfection and religious perfection is crucial to the present discussion:

The sage said: [it is] by [virtue of] intellectual order [that] the rational [animal] is distinguished from all [other] animals. Moreover, the improvement of [people's] character traits, and then the improvement of the household, and then [finally] the improvement of the city necessarily follows from it. Therefore, political regime and political *nomoi* [i.e. laws] come into being (1:35).

The *haver* here attributes to politics the comprehensive quality we noted above in Maimonides' definition. Politics encompasses all human activity from the individual to the household and on to the city. Ontologically speaking, it is located in the "intellectual order" characterized by human rationality.

The *haver*, however, proceeds to lead the Khazar to the realization that a higher order of being, the prophetic, exists, as exemplified by Moses:

If we should find a man who enters fire without harming him, who goes without food for a long period...whose face has a radiance...who does not fall ill or become senile or worn out, so that when he reaches his [allotted] life span, he dies a death freely chosen...in addition to knowing things about what has been and what will be...(1:41)

The king agrees that "this level would be truly divine [and] heavenly, if it exists; and this [kind of individual] would belong to the dominion of the divine order and not [to that] of the intellectual, the psychic, or the physical [order]" (1:42). The *haver* triumphantly concludes the discussion by declaring that these are indeed the attributes of Moses who is considered a genuine prophet by Christianity and Islam too. It is through his unique calling that "the multitude became aware of the divinity's attachment to them, as well as [the fact] that they have a Lord who governs them as he wishes" (1:43).

The *haver*'s theory of orders constructs a hierarchy in which the human order marked by rationality and politics is outranked by a divine order marked by prophecy and providence. The former are lower and limited, the latter are certain and without constraints. The religious transcends the political, here identified with the rational.

This model allows for a racial interpretation of Jewish peoplehood. The historical narrative of the biblical book of Genesis is reconstructed as a recounting of the genetic lineage of the "divine order," the human potential for prophecy:

Its details can be explained by [taking into account] the life span of Adam, Seth, and Enosh up to Noah, then [from] Shem and Eber to Abraham, then [from] Isaac and Jacob to Moses, peace be upon them. By virtue of their attachment [to the divine order], these men were the very best part and choicest [offspring] of Adam, [although] each of them had children like [worthless] husks, who did not resemble their fathers so that [the] divine order did not attach itself to them. The chronology, then, was determined by those who [were] divine. Now they were [only] individuals, not groups, until Jacob begot the [ancestors of] the twelve tribes, who were all well-suited for the divine order. Thus, divinity came to exist within a [whole] group . . . (1:47)

The seemingly despised and deprived "Jews"[15] are discovered to be in reality the authentic carriers of the "divine order" in human existence. In fact, the children of Israel mark a qualitative step in human religious development, for it is in them that "divinity came to exist within a [whole] group." A society as a whole, a collective, is the bearer of a prophetic potential, and in the Sinaitic revelation it was momentarily realized.

Jewish peoplehood is understood in genetic terms as the propensity for carrying prophetic potential.[16] The identity of the collective precedes in its significance any institutional expression it may take on in the course of ordinary existence. It thus precedes the giving of the law at Sinai. Revelation does not create peoplehood; it is rather its most sublime expression. This genetic quality also determines the impermeability of the group boundaries. Therefore, argues the *haver*, "the person who enters the religion of Israel [from the outside] is not equal to the person who is pure, since those who are pure are specifically qualified for prophecy" (1:115). Conversion to Judaism cannot effect an ontological transformation. Ruth's classic declaration "your people shall be my people, and your God my God" (Ruth 1:16) can only attain partial realization. A conversion to Judaism cannot effect a conversion to Jewishness. "The aim of others [should be] to learn from them and to become learned saints, not prophets" (1:115).

Biblical history, as the *haver* interprets it, reflects a conception of divinity that overrides the rational and political:

We have been promised that we are to be attached to the divine order through prophecy . . . and that the divine order will be attached to us through acts of providence, marvels, and miracles. [God therefore promises Israel:] My angels will also move about freely in whatever takes place among you on earth . . . protecting you and fighting for you . . . The world will conduct its affairs according to the natural course except for you . . . You will conquer your enemies without preparation, by which you will understand that your affairs do not proceed according to a natural norm, but rather [according to] one that is willed (1:109).

God's sovereign will is vindicated when breaking through the strictures of nature, thereby creating real history.

Central to the *haver*'s account of biblical history is the contrast
between nature and natural constraint, on the one hand, and divine will, on the other. Notice, however, that the contrast itself is
not biblical, but rather an interpretation of the significance of biblical history cast in philosophical terms. Biblical historical narrative
is non-philosophical in character. Paradoxically, it is precisely the
haver's internalization of philosophical discourse that leads to his
novel formulation of religious history. Moreover, the more rigidly
scientific the conceptualization of nature, the better it serves as a
foil to God's sovereign will. On this construction, rational philosophy and political history (the fourth order) serve to articulate a backdrop whose miraculous negation creates religious history (the fifth
and highest order).

So although the *Kuzari* embarks on a thorough critique of philosophy, the dialogue paradoxically turns out to be deeply imbued by a
philosophical world picture. The fundamental concerns of the book,
such as the true religion and the major themes of the *haver*'s theology, are articulated by means of an internalization of philosophical
discourse that leads to a reconstruction of biblical theology. This
comes out in the theory of political obligation.

Although the theory of orders establishes the ontological foundation of collective identity and determines its precedence over legal-
political institutionalization, the *haver* provides a separate moral
argument to establish political obligation. The ontological theory
serves to explain why this people is worthy of revelation, but is
apparently insufficient to justify their obligation to its norms. The
argument of obligation is explicated by the *haver* in the form of a
parable of the king of India:

If his messenger came to you with [typically] Indian gifts...accompanied
by medicines that cure you of your illnesses and preserve your health, as
well as poisons for your enemies and those who wage war against you, with
which you may confront them and kill them without [either] preparation or
[superior] numbers, would you be obligated to obey him? (1:21)

Obligation is a function of indebtedness. The king also subscribes to
this premise and concludes: "Yes, of course...I would believe that
his dominion and command extend to me" (1:22).

Two antecedent formulations should be mentioned, that of the rabbis and that of Saadya. Here is one such rabbinic formulation:

"I the Lord am your God" (Exod. 20:2). Why were the Ten Commandments not proclaimed at the beginning of the Torah? A parable: what is this like? Like a human king who entered a province [*medina*] and said to the people: Shall I reign over you? They replied: Have you conferred upon us any benefit that you should reign over us? What did he do [then]? He built the city wall for them, he brought in the water supply for them, and he fought their battles. [Then] he said to them: Shall I reign over you? They replied: Yes, yes.[17]

While this rabbinic formulation recognizes the power of indebtedness, it views consent as an important component of political legitimacy. This type of rabbinic interpretation seeks to retain a fidelity to the biblical form of the covenant. In contrast, medieval Jewish philosophers by and large neglect the covenant as a legitimating instrument. Halevi's formulation is more imperative in the obligatory entailment it expects of indebtedness and is thus closer to the following arguments by Saadya. The duty to adhere to this religion, argues Saadya, is a dictate of reason:

Logic [*al-'aql*] demands that whoever does something good be compensated either by means of a favor shown to him, if he is in need of it, or by means of thanks, if he does not require any reward. Since, therefore, this is one of the general demands of reason, it would not have been seemly for the creator, exalted and magnified be he, to neglect it in his own case. It was on the contrary necessary for him to command his creatures to serve him and thank him for having created them.[18]

The obligatory entailments of indebtedness are the first imperatives of reason. Obligation is a form of gratitude conceived of as a rational imperative, not as a sentiment. But whereas the scope of Saadya's argument is universal – human beings incur a debt of gratitude by their very creatureliness – Halevi's parable captures the particular indebtedness incurred by the people of Israel to God by his unique providential grace.

The indebtedness model of political obligation assumes the independence of rational morality from revelation and the priority of the former in establishing the obligatory character of the latter. This assumption fits well Saadya's conception of revelation as a functional complement to reason. It fits less well the *haver's* overall effort to establish the religious inadequacy of reason. The *haver* doubtless insists on moral rectitude as a necessary preamble to religious excellence:

The intellectual *nomoi*...are the preparation and preamble to the divine religious law and precede it [both] in nature and in time. They are indispensable for governing any group of human beings, no matter what [it may be], so that even a band of robbers cannot avoid adhering to justice in what is [simply] between them. Otherwise, their association would not last (2:48).

The bindingness of the basic rules of justice is taken for granted: "they are indispensible for...any group." Upon closer scrutiny, however, this very quality allows the *haver* to deny to these rules a constitutive role in understanding the nature of the collective. Morality is as indispensable as eating and drinking, and is not definatory of Jewish uniqueness:

Now, when Israel's rebelliousness got to the point that they disregarded [even] the intellectual [and] governmental laws – which are [as] indispensable for [the existence of] every group as certain natural things are indispensable for every individual, like eating and drinking, moving and resting, and sleeping and being awake – but nevertheless held fast to the [various] acts of worship pertaining to the sacrifices and other divine commandments, which are based on hearing [i.e., revelation alone], he [God] became satisfied with less from them (2:48).

The force of the moral argument is further diluted when we consider the *haver*'s critique of the adequacy of human moral judgment:

The governmental actions and the intellectual *nomoi* are the things that are known. But the divine [ones], which are added to these in order to be realized within [the] religious community of [the] living God who governs it, are not known until they come from him in a clear [and] detailed manner. Indeed, even if the essential characteristics of those governmental and intellectual ones were known, their precise determination is not known...However, defining [all] that and determining it [in detail] so that it is appropriate for everyone belongs only to God, exalted be he (3:7).[19]

Although Saadya provides a similar argument,[20] its force is to display the utility of the shortcut afforded by revelation to human reason. The *haver* is however bolstering the Archimedean role of revelation for his entire theology:

As for the divine actions, they are outside the scope of our intellects; but they are also not rejected by the intellect. Rather, the intellect will follow them unquestioningly, just as a person who is sick will follow the physician unquestioningly with regard to his medicines and prescriptions. Don't you see how far circumcision is from syllogistic reasoning and [how] it has no connection with governance? (3:7)

The *haver* concedes that morality and justice are indispensable for the continued existence of the collective, but the force of his argument is to deny their encroachment upon the ceremonial laws that in his view are the key to realizing the unique religious potential of the Jewish collective.

If political science is expected to supply a theory of governance, then Halevi does not provide such a theory. Yet, although not explicit, a particular conception of politics, or rather anti-politics, does arise from the book. The guiding themes of the philosophy of Judaism expounded by the *haver* bear directly upon key political concerns. The *haver* defines the collective as prepolitical, and his notion of providence transcends human political agency. There is no independent sphere of politics left between peoplehood and providence. Implicit then in the critique of rationalism is a rejection of politics too.

MAIMONIDES' POLITICAL PHILOSOPHY OF LAW

Maimonides counters the rejection of politics by stressing the centrality of law to Judaism. Law is his tool for carving out the space of the political. Viewed from the Maimonidean perspective, the Torah presumes the political nature of human beings. This is precisely why revelation takes the form of law. Maimonides subordinates peoplehood to the law on the one hand, and redefines biblical theology to bring it into line with his rationalism on the other. The God of nature and the God of law must be one, with the result that the negation of nature cannot be the guiding principle of history.[21] History is not a theological category but a politically based religious one.

Saadya's declaration that "our nation [*ummatna*] of the children of Israel is a nation [*umma*] only by virtue of its laws"[22] coheres well with Maimonides. The Jewish collective is guided by divine law and all of Maimonides' works are devoted to its explication. The *Commentary on the Mishnah* focuses on Judah the Prince's model codification. The *Book of Commandments* is a treatise on the jurisprudence of Halakhah, while the *Mishneh Torah* is its grand codification. Finally *The Guide of the Perplexed* is described by Maimonides as a treatise in "the science of law in its true sense" (*Guide* 1 Intro. 5).

"The law as a whole" argues Maimonides, "aims at two things: the welfare of the soul [rational perfection] and the welfare of the body [social stability and moral virtue]" (*Guide* 3:27, 510). Divine law, as we have already seen, is politically situated. The project of the Torah is to form a human society aimed at rational perfection, the noblest achievement of which is knowledge of God.

In the "Laws concerning Idolatry" (*Mishneh Torah*), Maimonides constructs a historical narrative of the formation of the Jewish collective. Maimonides describes the creation of a religious movement by Abraham who "went from city to city and from kingdom to kingdom, calling and gathering together the inhabitants till he arrived in the land of Canaan" (1:3).[23] One should note that Halevi's reconstruction of the Genesis narrative attributes no special role to Abraham. For Maimonides, in contradistinction, Abraham plays a foundational role as a teacher creating an international religious movement by spreading his philosophical monotheism: "When the people flocked to him and questioned him regarding his assertions, he would instruct each one according to his capacity till he had brought him to the way of truth, and thus thousands and tens of thousands joined him." Abraham "implanted in their hearts this great doctrine" of monotheism and "composed books on it, and taught and morally strengthened all who joined him." His sons continued his charge, and it is this multi-ethnic religious movement that forms the kernel of what was later to become the Jewish nation:

The patriarch Jacob instructed all his sons, set apart Levi, appointed him head (teacher), and placed him in a college to teach the way of God and keep the charge of Abraham. He charged his sons to appoint from the tribe of Levi one instructor after another, in uninterrupted succession, so that the doctrine might never be forgotten. And so it went on with ever increasing vigor among Jacob's children and their adherents till they became a people [*umma*] that knew God.

In contrast to the Abrahamic movement, the Mosaic project is that of giving legal and political form to the ideal of creating a people that knows God.[24] Maimonides reiterates this commitment in the *Guide* where he describes the criterion informing the commandments of the law, namely "the man who is perfect among the people. For it is the aim of this law that everyone should be such a man. Only that law is called by us divine law." And such a law is contrasted to "other political regimens, such as the *nomoi* of the Greeks" (*Guide* 2:39, 381).

Whereas Halevi's reconstruction of the Genesis narrative is cast in the form of tracing the lineage of an ethnically grounded "divine order," Maimonides interprets this narrative in terms of a dramatic struggle to overcome idolatry. Central to the struggle is the effort to educate an entire society to appreciate knowledge of the one true God as the highest human good. Initiated as a movement by Abraham, it reaches fruition as a transformative political agenda in the Mosaic law. Maimonides proceeds to recast the Halakhah of rabbinic Judaism to fit this interpretation of the Mosaic enterprise. One of the most important halakhic ramifications of this agenda is his revolutionary project of laying out dogmas of belief. Maimonides devised a systematic doctrine of required beliefs, the thirteen principles of faith. This project serves to create a religious educational agenda expressive of religious values such as knowledge and fear and love of God. Anchored in the legal categories of apostasy and heresy, it furthermore serves to delineate the boundaries of the Jewish collective as a community of faith.[25] On this conception, converts are warmly embraced as those who relive the Abrahamic journey to the one true God in their personal spiritual quest.

Maimonides' account of law is as committed to its political foundations as to its rational aspirations. He therefore postulates the following relation between the two:

Know that as between these two aims, one is indubitably greater in nobility, namely the welfare of the soul – I mean the procuring of correct opinions – while the second aim – I mean the welfare of the body – is prior in nature and time. The latter aim consists in the governance of the city and the well-being of the states of all its people according to their capacity. This second aim is the more certain one, and it is the one regarding which every effort has been made precisely to expound it and all its particulars. For the first aim can only be achieved after achieving this second one (*Guide* 3:27, 510).

Although Halevi too spoke of a precedence of laws of justice necessary for the maintenance of any human association, his point was a moral one about priorities of values. For Maimonides, however, the principle of precedence has important institutional implications, and it guides his interpretation of the law. One reason for this difference is Maimonides' rejection of the theory of indebtedness as a theory of political obligation. That theory assumes the prior existence of rational moral imperatives that Maimonides rejects for epistemological reasons coupled with political ones.[26]

Maimonides takes moral injunctions to be conventional. This explains the proto-Hobbesian flavor of his depiction of the human political condition that we noted above, and the role of the ruler in it. "It is by no means possible," argues Maimonides, that human "society should be perfected except – and this is necessarily so – through a ruler who gauges the actions of individuals" (*Guide* 2:40, 382). It is this ruler who "prescribes actions and moral habits that all of them must always practice in the same way, so that the natural diversity is hidden through the multiple points of conventional accord and so that the community becomes well ordered." The ruler defines the norms of "conventional accord."[27]

Even after Israel receives the divine law the precedence of the political remains a guiding principle of its constitutional theory of monarchy. The discussion of a "ruler" in the *Guide* gives way to a discussion of the king in the *Mishneh Torah*. As a committed monarchist, Maimonides views the king as the indispensable cohesive force of the body-politic. The king's role is well anchored in his broad range of extra-legal prerogatives:

The king is empowered to put to death anyone who rebels against him. Even if any of his subjects is ordered by him to go to a certain place and he does not go, or is ordered to stay home and fails to do so, he is culpable, and the king may, if he so decides, put him to death ... If a person kills another and there is no clear evidence, or if no warning has been given him, or there is only one witness, or if one kills accidentally a person whom he hated, the king may, if the exigency of the hour demands it, put him to death in order to insure the stability of the social order [*le-takken ha-olam*]. He may put to death many offenders in one day, hang them, and suffer them to be hanging for a long time so as to put fear in the hearts of others and break the power of the wicked.[28]

The politically pivotal role of the king is established by his power
to command on pain of death. In the passage preceding the one just
cited, Maimonides makes clear that such power is allotted to Israelite
kings who are not God fearing too, although they cannot be held
accountable for their actions:

> We have already stated that the kings of the House of David may be judged
> and testified against. But with respect to the kings of Israel, the Rabbis en-
> acted that they neither judge nor be judged, neither testify nor be testified
> against, because they are arrogant, and (if they be treated as commoners) the
> cause of religion would suffer.[29]

Echoing the arguments of the biblical monarchic tradition as expounded in the books of Judges and Samuel, and in the talmudic
tractate *Sanhedrin*, Maimonides views political stability to be en-
sured by the presence of a king. Anarchy is judged to be a greater evil
than tyranny.

Thus, if we take Maimonides' principle of the priority of the political and interpret it institutionally, the result would be the following
grading of kings in terms of their legitimacy, from lowest to highest:

1. An Israelite king who does not adhere to Halakhah.[30]
2. Davidic kings who are pious and accept halakhic guidance.
3. A Davidic king who is not only pious, but a philosopher too.

Maimonides' discussion of messianism at the end of the "Laws of
Kings" (*Mishneh Torah*) is concerned mostly with the messianic status of option 2. "King Messiah will arise and restore the kingdom of
David to its former state and original sovereignty. He will rebuild the
sanctuary and gather the dispersed of Israel. All the ancient laws will
be reinstituted in his days."[31] The reconciliation of monarchic politics and divine law in the person of the king is a major achievement
of this era. If therefore there arises such a king,

> who meditates on the Torah, occupies himself with the commandments, as
> did his ancestor David, observes the precepts prescribed in the written and
> the oral Law, prevails upon Israel to walk in the ways of the Torah and to
> repair its breaches, and fights the battles of the Lord, it may be assumed that
> he is the Messiah.[32]

The ultimate test is the degree of the king's actual success in his endeavors: "If he does these things and succeeds, rebuilds the sanctuary

on its site, and gathers the dispersed of Israel, he is beyond all doubt the Messiah." If he does "not meet with full success, or [is] slain, it is obvious that he is not the Messiah promised in the Torah."[33]

Maimonides' hopes reach even higher, for a king who would resemble not only David, the original king, in his political achievements, but Moses, the original lawgiver, in his prophetic status: "The king who will arise from the seed of David will possess more wisdom than Solomon and will be a great prophet, approaching Moses our teacher." His pedagogical capacities are reminiscent of Abraham's: "He will teach the whole of the Jewish people and instruct them in the way of God; and all nations will come to hear him."[34]

Whether or how such a king would exercise his living wisdom remains a matter of speculation.[35] At least in the *Mishneh Torah*, Maimonides consistently stresses the continuing constraints of the political and the legal:

The general principle is: this law of ours with its statutes and ordinances . . . is for ever and all eternity; it is not to be added to or to be taken away from . . . Said the Rabbis: The sole difference between the present [this world] and the messianic days is delivery from servitude to foreign powers.[36]

BEYOND MEDIEVAL PHILOSOPHY

The basic paradigms of Halevi and Maimonides are elaborated, and their disparate elements synthesized, by the many writers of the three centuries following their original formulations. While a radical philosopher like Samuel ibn Tibbon, translator of Maimonides' *Guide*, focused on the esoteric teachings imparted by Judaism, figures like Menahem Meiri attempted to continue the Maimonidean project of synthesizing Halakhah and philosophy. Meiri espoused one of the more radically tolerant conceptions of other monotheistic religions. The Catalonian school of halakhists who followed Nahmanides, such as Solomon ibn Adret (Rashba) and Nissim Gerondi (Ran), combined Halevian notions of the inalienability of Jewish identity with Maimonidean-like constitutional politics. Recounting the history of medieval Jewish philosophy from the point of view of political thought is a project yet to be undertaken. I will end the present discussion by pointing to the postmedieval amplifications of the basic paradigms by the two most important heirs to the Hispano-Jewish tradition, Isaac Abravanel and Baruch Spinoza. Both thinkers can be read as model responses to the profound crisis emerging from the demise of Jewish culture in Spain and its final destruction with the expulsion of the Jews in 1492.

The catastrophe of the expulsion called for new theological-political models for Jewish self-understanding. The sense of crisis was dramatically articulated in the works of Isaac Abravanel, leader of the Hispano-Jewish community, and member of Queen Isabella's court, who chose expulsion rather than conversion to Catholicism. In his commentary to the covenant at Moab (Deuteronomy 29), Abravanel addresses the problems of the ongoing validity of the covenant in great detail:

> The first and greatest of them all, which has occasioned an intense struggle among contemporary scholars in the Kingdom of Aragon, concerns the issue of the covenant ... Who gave authority to the desert generation whose feet stood at Sinai to obligate those succeeding them ... causing them to be liable for punishment?[37]

My present interest is not in the important issue of the obligation of future generations, but in Abravanel's vivid depiction of the reigning mood of crisis in the Kingdom of Aragon. The responsibility for upholding of the covenant, and enduring the price thereof, is no longer self-evident to many Jews. The importance of their collective identity and of the obligatory nature of their law is no longer clear to a sufficient number of them and occasions "an intense struggle."

Abravanel ultimately adopts a Halevi-like anti-politics in his effort to provide hope and meaning to his stricken community. He develops a theocratic and messianic political doctrine as the only solution to the political and historical cul-de-sac of Jewish history.

> Delivering them through war, laying down laws and commandments, and determining occasional punishment outside the law – are all performed by God for his people. Therefore, God is their king, and they have no need for a [human] king for anything.[38]

And although he was aware of republicanism as a budding alternative to the monarchic politics reigning in Europe, he could not discern in it an alternative to better the Jewish lot in exile.[39]

Spinoza's *Theological-Political Treatise* is heir to the Hispano-Jewish philosophical tradition and at the same time one of its severest critiques. The theological-political problem assumed by its very title encapsulates Spinoza's conflicting approaches to this tradition. Spinoza delivers a bitter critique of all the central themes of medieval Jewish political theology, rejecting the major tenets of its various paradigms. He argues that the (divine) election is no more than a promise of material good fortune, the law is no longer binding after the destruction of the Judean state, and biblical prophecy has little to do with philosophical excellence.[40] At the same time, and despite this critique, Spinoza recognizes that no sovereign can afford to remain indifferent to religion and that therefore no sovereign can do without a theology to buttress the legitimacy of his reign. And so his book not only destroys, but it attempts to salvage some theological constructions, in order to rebuild a political theology to provide legitimacy for his sovereign, the modern republic. Spinoza embraces modern republicanism as the regime best suited to accept him as an individual and best suited for the cultivation of the philosophic life.[41]

Interpreters of Maimonides have been troubled by Spinoza's intimate entanglement with Maimonides in the course of his project.[42] Like Maimonides, Spinoza views the knowledge of God, and the love of God, as the highest human good. Like Maimonides, he seeks a polity that would be congenial to the philosopher, and develops a political theology, including principles of faith, for his polity. To what degree is Spinoza providing an authentic interpretation of Maimonides? Spinoza makes an effort to distance himself from Maimonides, whom he views as a dogmatist, but he nevertheless adopts many of his interpretive strategies.[43] Indeed, Leo Strauss has argued that a basic continuity of purpose exists in Maimonides' and Spinoza's attempts to safeguard the philosopher from persecution by the reigning clergy.[44] The question forces the issue of the credibility of the Maimonidean project in a manner analogous to its medieval critique at the hands of the rejecters of philosophical rationalism. This theological-political agenda was initiated by Plato in the *Republic* and in the *Laws*: Is the Maimonidean adoption of Platonic political philosophy a thinly veiled harbinger of the Spinozistic attack on religion, or is Maimonides providing an authentic philosophical exposition of the foundations of Halakhah?

The latter is the case: Maimonides endorses the Mosaic law as the framework for his enterprise, while Spinoza unequivocally rejects it.

The Maimonidean projects of recasting the legal tradition of rabbinic Judaism and of reinterpreting the basic religious values of the Mosaic law are undertaken with the purpose of revolutionizing the role of philosophy in attaining religious excellence. It is no doubt a revolutionary undertaking, but one that is undertaken from within, with a basic fidelity to the institutional structures of Judaism. Maimonides and Halevi both engaged in religious and social criticism. Maimonides lashes out against the idolatrous tendencies of popular religion, whereas Halevi engaged in social criticism that is surprisingly candid in its treatment of instances of Jewish hypocrisy.[45] Both, however, aim to strengthen religious commitment. In contrast, the theological-political project of Spinoza, like that of Hobbes before him, includes a critique of religion that aims to eradicate its institutional structure. Ultimately, Maimonides accepted the responsibility of Jewish communal leadership, while Spinoza left the Jewish community.

Although they point to the limits of medieval philosophy, Abravanel's and Spinoza's active engagements with its basic paradigms serve to link Halevi and Maimonides to modernity. In this way the works of Halevi and Maimonides have continued to influence the shaping of Jewish self-understanding long after their initial appearance.

NOTES

1. R. Lerner and M. Mahdi (eds.), *Medieval Political Philosophy: A Sourcebook* (Ithaca: Cornell University Press, 1972), 189. For an analysis, see L. Strauss, "Maimonides' Statement on Political Science," in his *What is Political Philosophy?* (Westport, Conn.: Greenwood Press, 1973), 155–69, and L. V. Berman, "A Reexamination of Maimonides' 'Statement on Political Science'," *Journal of the American Oriental Society* 89 (1969), 106–11.

2. On medieval legal pluralism, see H. Berman, *Law and Revolution* (Cambridge, Mass.: Harvard University Press, 1983). On Jewish legal autonomy, see M. Elon, *Jewish Law: History, Sources and Principles*, trans. B. Auerbach and M. Sykes (Philadelphia and Jerusalem: Jewish Publication Society, 1994), ii: 678–779. See too the description of Jewish

communal life and organization in S. D. Goitein, *A Mediterranean Society: The Jewish Communities of the Arab World as Portrayed in the Documents of the Cairo Geniza*. II. *The Community* (Berkeley: University of California Press, 1971).

3.	See I. Schorsch, "On the History of the Political Judgment of the Jew," in his *From Text to Context: The Turn to History in Modern Judaism* (Hanover, N.H. and London: Brandeis University Press, 1994), 118–32; A. Funkenstein, "The Passivity of Diaspora Jewry: Myth and Reality" [Hebrew], in his *Perceptions of Jewish History from the Antiquity to the Present* (Tel Aviv: Am Oved, 1991), 232–42; D. Biale, *Power and Powerlessness in Jewish History* (New York: Schocken Books, 1986), 5–9, 34–86.

4.	Lerner and Mahdi (eds.), *Medieval Political Philosophy*, 190.

5.	Al-Farabi, *Fusul al-Madani (Aphorisms of the Statesman)*, ed. D. M. Dunlop (Cambridge: Cambridge University Press, 1961). See J. Macy, "The Theological-Political Teaching of *Shemonah Peraqim*: A Reappraisal of the Text and of its Arabic Sources," in *Proceedings of the Eighth World Congress of Jewish Studies, 1981* (Jerusalem: World Union of Jewish Studies, 1982), Division C: 31–40, and, more generally, L. V. Berman, "Maimonides, the Disciple of Alfarabi," in *Maimonides: A Collection of Critical Essays*, ed. J. Buijs (Notre Dame: University of Notre Dame Press, 1988), 195–214.

6.	Moses Maimonides, *The Guide of the Perplexed*, trans. with an introduction by S. Pines (Chicago: The University of Chicago Press, 1963), 2:40, 381. For Aristotle, see R. G. Mulgan, "Aristotle's Doctrine that Man is a Political Animal," *Hermes* 102 (1974), 438–45.

7.	"The ideal state is understood according to Plato's guidance: the prophet is the founder of the Platonic state" (L. Strauss, *Philosophy and Law: Contributions to the Understanding of Maimonides and his Predecessors*, trans. E. Adler [Albany: State University of New York Press, 1995 (1935)], 127).

8.	"Inasmuch as all matters of religious belief, as imparted by our master, can be attained by means of research and correct speculation, what was the reason that prompted [divine] wisdom to transmit them to us by way of prophecy and support them by means of visible proofs and miracles rather than intellectual demonstrations?" (Saadya Gaon, *The Book of Beliefs and Opinions*, trans. S. Rosenblatt [New Haven and London: Yale University Press, 1976], Introduction: 6, 31); see too B. Septimus, *Hispano-Jewish Culture in Transition: The Career and Controversies of Ramah* (Cambridge, Mass.: Harvard University Press, 1982), 61–3. Consider in this respect Saadya's critique of abstinence in book 10, in contrast to Bahya ibn Paquda's radical embracing of Sufism a century later in the final two chapters of his *Duties of the Heart*, or in contrast to Gabirol's Neoplatonism.

9. See Y. Baer, "Ha-Matzav ha-Politi shel Yehudei Sefard be-Doro shel R. Yehudah Halevi," *Zion* 1 (1936), 6–23, reprinted in his *Studies in the History of the Jewish People* (Jerusalem: The Historical Society of Israel, 1985), 251–68.

10. Judah Halevi, *The Kuzari*, trans. L. V. Berman and B. S. Kogan, Yale Judaica Series (New Haven: Yale University Press, forthcoming); used with the permission of B. S. Kogan.

11. The irreducible character of religious experience is a central theme of Julius Guttmann's interpretation of Halevi, "Ha-Yahas bein ha-Dat uvein ha-Filosofyah lefi Yehudah Halevi," in *Religion and Knowledge*, trans. S. Esh and ed. S. H. Bergman and N. Rotenstreich (Jerusalem: Magnes Press, 1979), 66–85. Notice that it is the king who first introduces the key notion of *amr al-ilahi*, divine order, in *Kuzari* 1:4, while rejecting the philosopher's account of human excellence. This point is intentionally obscured by Judah ibn Tibbon, who in his Hebrew translation has translated this as *davar elohi*, rather than his usual *inyan elohi* when it is employed by the *haver*. I interpret Ibn Tibbon's translation as a harmonizing one aimed at crediting the *haver* with the theology focused on the irreducibility of the divine order. For the Judeo-Arabic text, see *The Book of Refutation and Proof of the Despised Faith (the Book of the Khazars) known as the Kuzari*, ed. D. H. Baneth (Jerusalem: Magnes Press, 1977), 6; for the Hebrew translation, see *Sefer ha-Kuzari, be-ha'Atakato shel Rabbi Yehudah ibn Tibbon*, ed. A. Zifroni (Jerusalem and Tel Aviv: Schocken Books, 1971), 12.

12. See D. Hartman, *Israelis and the Jewish Tradition: An Ancient People Debating its Future* (New Haven: Yale University Press, 2000). The term "ideal-type" conveys the fact that even though they aspire to provide systematic presentations of a Judaism loyal to the rabbinic normative tradition, the very success of the presentation comes at the price of distortion of detail. Their paradigms are plagued by constant gaps, reconstructions, and even distortions when compared to the inner dynamics of halakhic development. (See M. Lorberbaum, "Maimonides' Letter to Ovadyah," *S'vara* 3 [1993], 57–64.) Whether Maimonides actually read the *Kuzari* is unclear; see H. Kreisel, "Judah Halevi's Influence on Maimonides: A Preliminary Appraisal," *Maimonidean Studies* 2 (1992), 95–121. Even if it were established that Maimonides never read the book (something I believe, along with Kreisel, to be unlikely), the value of describing Halevi and Maimonides as alternative paradigms would not be diminished.

13. *Haver* is normally translated "rabbi" or "sage." These translations obscure the unique connection to the rabbinic development of the priestly

holiness tradition implied by the term *haver* as a possible source of inspiration of the *Kuzari*'s theory of ritual. In Mishnah, *Demai* 2:3, *haver* is
a member initiated into Pharisee purity norms. Furthermore, it is by no
means self-evident that Halevi should be identified with the *haver*. The
dialogical character of the work is too subtle for a cursory treatment. See
L. Strauss, "The Law of Reason in the *Kuzari*," in his *Persecution and
the Art of Writing* (Chicago: Chicago University Press, 1988), 95–141,
and A. Motzkin, "On Yehuda Halevi's *Kuzari* as a Platonic Dialogue"
[Hebrew], *Iyyun* 28 (1978), 209–19. Y. Silman, *Philosopher and Prophet:
Judah Halevi, the Kuzari, and the Evolution of his Thought* (Albany:
State University of New York Press, 1995), is the most thorough reconstruction of Halevi's course of philosophical development. However,
like all documentary-hypothesis analyses, here too the redactor's intentions remain elusive (see the critical review of Silman by D. H. Frank
in *AJS Review* 22 [1997]).

14. On Halevi's own prophetic experiences, see A. Komem, "Bein Shirah
    li-Nevuah," *Molad* 25 (1969), 676–97.
15. Cf. the Khazar's characterization in 1:4.
16. For a different account of the course of Halevi's argument, see Silman,
    Philosopher and Prophet, 285–8.
17. *Mekhilta de'Rabbi Ishmael*, Bahodesh 5, in *The Jewish Political
    Tradition. I. Authority*, ed. M. Walzer, M. Lorberbaum, and N. Zohar,
    and co-ed. Y. Lorberbaum (New Haven and London: Yale University
    Press, 2000), 27–8. There is also a powerful countertradition in rabbinic
    Judaism denying any role to consent; see *Jewish Political Tradition*,
    28–34. The point of the citation below is to display the interpretive
    choice involved in the medieval tradition.
18. Saadya, *Beliefs and Opinions* III: 1, 139. For the Judeo-Arabic, see
    *Sefer ha-Nivhar be-Emunot uva-De'ot le-Rabbeinu Sa'adiah ben
    Joseph Fayyumi*, ed. and Hebrew trans. J. Kafih (Jerusalem: Sura,
    1970).
19. Halevi gives the following examples: "for we know that giving charity
    and sharing [what we have] are obligatory, and that training the soul by
    means of fasting and obedience is obligatory. [We also know that] deceit
    is disgraceful, and promiscuous behavior with women is disgraceful too;
    as is having intercourse with some [of one's] relatives, whereas honoring
    [one's] parents is obligatory and whatever [else] resembles that" (3:7); see
    too Guttmann, "Ha-Yahas bein ha-Dat," 69.
20. *Beliefs and Opinions* III: 3, 145–7.
21. Maimonides' discussion of history in the context of theodicy in the
    Guide shows how intricate a problem he viewed it to be; see *Guide*
    3:10–13, 32.
22. *Beliefs and Opinions* III: 7, 158 (Hebrew, 132).

23. *The Code of Maimonides: Book of Knowledge*, trans. B. Septimus, Yale Judaica Series (New Haven: Yale University Press, forthcoming); used with the permission of B. Septimus; see too M. Kellner, *Maimonides on Judaism and the Jewish People* (Albany: State University of New York Press, 1991), and his "Chosenness, not Chauvinism: Maimonides on the Chosen People," in *A People Apart: Chosenness and Ritual in Jewish Philosophical Thought*, ed. D. H. Frank (Albany: State University of New York Press, 1993), 51–75.

24. See I. Twersky, *Introduction to the Code of Maimonides (Mishneh Torah)* (New Haven and London: Yale University Press, 1980), 485–6; D. Hartman, "Philosophy and Halakhah as Two Ways of Challenging Idolatry in Maimonides' Thought" [Hebrew], *Jerusalem Studies in Jewish Thought* 7 (1988), 319–33; and D. H. Frank, "Idolatry and the Love of Appearances: Maimonides and Plato on False Wisdom," in *Proceedings of the Academy for Jewish Philosophy*, ed. D. Novak and N. Samuelson (Lanham, London, and New York: University Press of America, 1992), III: 162–4.

25. "If a man doubts any of these foundations, he leaves the community [of Israel], denies the fundamental, and is called a sectarian, *epikoros*, and one who 'cuts among the plantings'," *Commentary to the Mishnah*, Sanhedrin 10:1, in M. Kellner, *Dogma in Medieval Jewish Thought: From Maimonides to Abravanel* (Oxford: Littman Library, 1986), 16.

26. This theme has been much discussed in the literature, and I refer to a few representative works: S. Pines, "Truth and Falsehood versus Good and Evil," in *Studies in Maimonides*, ed. I. Twersky (Cambridge, Mass.: Harvard University Press, 1991), 95–157; M. Fox, *Interpreting Maimonides: Studies in Methodology, Metaphysics, and Moral Philosophy* (Chicago: University of Chicago Press, 1990), 124–226; H. Kreisel, *Maimonides' Political Thought: Studies in Ethics, Law, and the Human Ideal* (Albany: State University of New York Press, 1999), 93–188.

27. Hence the importance Maimonides attributes to the ethics of leadership; see L. V. Berman, "Maimonides on Political Leadership," in *Kinship and Consent*, ed. D. J. Elazar (Ramat Gan: Turtledove, 1987), 113–25; A. Funkenstein, "The Image of the Ruler in Jewish Sources," in his *Perceptions of Jewish History* (Berkeley: University of California Press, 1993), 155–68.

28. *The Code of Maimonides, Book Fourteen: The Book of Judges*, trans. A. M. Hershman (New Haven and London: Yale University Press, 1963), "Laws Concerning Kings and Wars," 1:8, 10, 213–14. See M. Lorberbaum, *Politics and the Limits of Law: Secularizing the Political in Medieval Jewish Thought* (Stanford: Stanford University Press, 2001), 43–69.

29. "Laws of Kings," 3:7, 213.

30. In cases, however, where the king's "coins do not circulate in the localities" under his rule the king should be "regarded as a robber who uses force, and as a troop of armed bandits, whose laws are not binding." "Such a king and all his servants," he argues, "are deemed robbers in every respect." (*The Code of Maimonides, Book Eleven: The Book of Torts*, trans. H. Klein [New Haven and London: Yale University Press, 1954], "Laws of Robbery and Lost Property," 5:18, 110.)

31. "Laws of Kings," 11:1, 238.

32. "Laws of Kings," 11:4, 240.

33. *A Maimonides Reader*, ed. I. Twersky (West Orange, N.J.: Behrman House, 1972), "Laws of Kings," 11:4, 226.

34. Twersky, *Maimonides Reader*, "Laws of Repentance," 9:2, 83.

35. See J. Macy, "The Rule of Law and the Rule of Wisdom in Plato, al-Farabi, and Maimonides," in *Studies in Islamic and Judaic Traditions*, ed. W. M. Brinner and S. D. Ricks (Atlanta: Scholars Press, 1986), 205–32.

36. "Laws of Kings," 11:3, 12:2, 239–41. Maimonides' messianic vision and its attendant antinomian undertones are the subject of great scholarly debate. See G. Scholem, *The Messianic Idea in Judaism and Other Essays on Jewish Spirituality* (New York: Schocken Books, 1971) 1–36; A. Funkenstein, "Maimonides: Political Theory and Realistic Messianism," in *Perceptions*, 131–51; A. Ravitzky, " 'To the Utmost of Human Capacity': Maimonides on the Days of the Messiah," in *Perspectives on Maimonides: Philosophical and Historical Studies*, ed. J. L. Kraemer (Oxford: Littman Library, 1991), 221–56; Lorberbaum, *Politics*, 77–89.

37. Isaac Abravanel, "Commentary to the Pentateuch, Deuteronomy 29," in Walzer, Lorberbaum, and Zohar (eds.), *The Jewish Political Tradition*, 37.

38. Isaac Abravanel, "Commentary to the Pentateuch, Deuteronomy 17," in Walzer, Lorberbaum, and Zohar (eds.), *The Jewish Political Tradition*, 153.

39. See L. Strauss, "On Abravanel's Philosophical Tendency and Political Teachings," in *Isaac Abravanel: Six Lectures*, ed. J. B. Trend and H. Loewe (Cambridge: Cambridge University Press, 1937), 95–129; B. Netanyahu, *Don Isaac Abravanel: Statesman and Philosopher* (Philadelphia: Jewish Publication Society, 1982), 150ff. See also G. Weiler, *Jewish Theocracy* (Leiden: Brill, 1988), 69–85.

40. See Spinoza, *Political Treatise* and *Theologico-Political Treatise*, in *The Chief Works of Spinoza*, trans. R. H. M. Elwes (New York: Dover 1955), II: chs. 1–5.

41. See the recent discussion in S. B. Smith, *Spinoza, Liberalism, and the Question of Jewish Identity* (New Haven and London: Yale University Press, 1997).

42. See H. Cohen, "Charakteristik der Ethik Maimunis," in *Moses ben Maimon*, ed. W. Bacher et al. (Leipzig: G. Fock, 1908), 1: 63–134.

43. See S. Pines, "Spinoza's *Tractatus Theologico-Politicus*, Maimonides, and Kant," in *The Collected Works of Shlomo Pines. v. Studies in the History of Jewish Thought*, ed. W. Harvey and M. Idel (Jerusalem: Magnes Press, 1997), 687–711.

44. Cf. Strauss, *Persecution*, 7–21.

45. Cf. *Guide* 1:35–6; *Kuzari* 1:112–15, 2:23–4.

10 Judaism and Sufism

INTRODUCTION

Upon catching sight today in the synagogues of Safed or Jerusalem of the white-clad, bearded kabbalists, engrossed in their meditations, one is unavoidably struck by the similarity in appearance with the swaying, white-capped Sufis performing the *dhikr* ritual. In point of fact, the similarity is not only external; of all forms of mysticism, perhaps an unsuspected and yet remarkable parallelism exists between Islamic and Jewish mysticism. Though the two tendencies appear to have developed quite independently, there have been significant points of intersection between them. Within the wider framework of the influence of Islamic thought and spirituality, the study of the interaction between Israel and Ishmael in the domain of mysticism is one of the most fascinating chapters of comparative religion. Even in the broad lines of their respective historical evolutions, Jewish and Islamic esotericism betray a remarkable resemblance. Both went through formative periods characterized by ecstatic experiences and followed by periods of consolidation in which mystical tendencies were tempered by legalism and philosophy. Both underwent profound transformations and were entirely renewed in the late Middle Ages by novel cosmological and speculative systems, sometimes imbued with "prophetic" aspirations, and both finally developed into institutionalized brotherhoods.

The Provençal kabbalists and even the Ashkenazi pietists saw as their spiritual forbears the sages of the geonic period in Baghdad, whose mystical speculations form the ancient sources of kabbalistic literature. Their early writings, such as the contemplation of the heavenly chariot (*sofei ha-merkavah*) bear a striking resemblance to

the Sufi accounts of spiritual ascension such as that of al-Bistami.
The mystics of Islam too see Baghdad as their spiritual cradle and
it is there that Sufism's formative period evolved in the shadow of
the thriving Eastern well-springs of Jewish spirituality. The subsequent efforts of Sufism to shed itself of the suspicion of heresy by
espousing strictly orthodox norms, as exemplified in the works of al-
Ghazali (d. 1111), also bear parallels in the undertakings of R. Abraham Maimonides (d. 1237). Just as Sufism integrated philosophical
elements from the Neoplatonic and Aristotelian systems, so too the
thirteenth- and fourteenth-century Spanish kabbalists in particular
undertook to reconcile the doctrines of kabbalah and philosophy.
The "science of letters" plays a central role in the speculative and
contemplative methods of many Sufis, such as al-Tustari and Ibn
'Arabi (d. 1240), just as its Hebrew equivalent permeated the works
of kabbalists, such as R. Abraham Abu'l-'Afiyah/Abulafia (d. after
1291). Indeed, the latter's meditative technique, called *hazkarah*, recalls both by its name and method the Sufi *dhikr* ritual. The speculative and cosmological system embodied in Muhyi al-Din ibn 'Arabi's
"Meccan Revelations" (*al-Futuhat* – the Hebrew mystical equivalent *petah*, as for example in the title of R. Moses Luzzatto's *Pithei
Hokmah* – has a similar meaning) completely revolutionized Islamic
mysticism, as did the teachings of R. Isaac Luria (d. 1572), which
reached maturity in the Muslim East. Just as all previous Sufi theory was *reinterpreted* through the prism of Ibn 'Arabi's system, so
too in Judaism the Spanish kabbalah and even its crowning work,
the *Zohar*, was reconstrued in the light of Lurianism. It is noteworthy that even in the literary domain there are remarkable analogies.
A necessary part of the writings of Ibn 'Arabi's school was devoted
to the listing and clarification of *istilahat* or the technical terms involved in his teachings. Similarly, the kabbalists engaged in the composition of technical lexicons (*kinnuyim*) in the expounding of their
doctrine. The flowering of Sufi brotherhoods around their *shaykh*
(master) affords yet again an instructive analogy to the various
Hasidic groups centered around the charismatic *zaddiq*. Finally, the
politicization in the modern era of Sufi fraternities and the involvement of their spiritual leaders in secular areas, such as politics and
academia (such as the Khalwati in Egypt), parallel the activities in
prewar Poland and contemporary Israel of Hasidic dynasties, whose
ranks have furnished not a few public figures and academic scholars.

BEGINNINGS IN THE EAST

From a strictly chronological point of view, it was Judaism that initially influenced Sufism in its formative period in Baghdad. Surprisingly, while scholars have recognized the influence of Neoplatonism and Christian pietism on the evolution of Muslim asceticism at this time, they have failed to point out the profound mark imprinted on Sufism by the ambient Jewish milieu. Indeed, Mesopotamia, cradle of the Babylonian Talmud, was at the focal center of the world of Jewish learning, which, moreover, readily underwent the process of Arabization after the Muslim conquest. Among the great personalities attached to the talmudic academies of Baghdad were to be found certain charismatic figures who embodied the ancient rabbinic pietistic ideals of simplicity and saintliness, virtues cherished by nascent Sufism. Moreover, Sufi hagiography has preserved a number of edifying tales of "the pious men from among the children of Israel," known as *isra'iliyyat*. Many of these tales are traceable to rabbinic sources such as the *Pirkei Avot* (*Chapters of the Fathers*), one of the foundations of Jewish pietism.

One particularly important concept undoubtedly originating in talmudic literature, which was assimilated at this time and which was to play a fundamental role in Islamic mysticism, was the belief in a hidden hierarchy of saints, whose blessings sustained the world. Supposedly these elements had been transmitted through interreligious contacts or Jewish converts to Islam. However, once Sufism had asserted itself as a spiritual force, it began to exert a compelling attraction for Jews. A certain number of conversions took place precisely in Sufi circles in Baghdad, where we find Jews attending the lectures of the first mystical masters. Indeed, Sufi historiographers like to relate accounts of the miraculous conversion of Jews to Islam through the action of Muslim mystics, such as Ibrahim al-Khawwas. These kinds of contact were no doubt facilitated by the relative openness of certain Sufi masters toward members of other religious persuasions. Though traces of Sufi beliefs concerning the ascetic ideal and the vanity of the lower world may be detected in the works of tenth-century Jewish authors in Baghdad, such as Saadya Gaon (d. 942), it is, however, only during the Judeo-Arabic cultural symbiosis in Spain in the following century that definite evidence of literary influence can be pinpointed.

THE GOLDEN AGE OF SPAIN

It is well known that the Iberian peninsula was a fertile terrain of intercultural exchange between Jew, Christian, and Muslim. From a much later period we have evidence of theological discussions between the great Muslim mystic Muhyi al-Din ibn ʿArabi (d. 1240) and a Jewish rabbi on the nature of the letters of the Holy Scriptures. It can be assumed that such contacts also took place in previous times. There had been an early flowering of Sufism in Andalusia, mainly owing to the teachings of the Muslim mystical master Ibn Masarrah (886–931). While overestimating the latter's influence on Muslim and Jewish Neoplatonism in Andalusia, scholars have overlooked the significant fact that Ibn Masarrah, as well as his spiritual heir, Sahl al-Tustari, laid significant emphasis on the mystical role of the Arabic alphabet. This discipline is also a fundamental aspect of the theosophical system of Ibn ʿArabi, and a subject that, as just pointed out, he would discuss with Jews. From talmudic times (third to fourth centuries CE), and later in the kabbalah, these numerical speculations, known as *gematria*, were a central part of Jewish exegesis and esotericism. The striking similarities between the development of these mystical conceptions in both religions leaves no doubt as to an initial Jewish influence on the Muslim "science of letters" and their later interaction.

Although definite literary traces of Islamic mysticism are already present in the religious poetry of the prominent Andalusian Hebrew poets such as Solomon ibn Gabirol (d. 1054/8) and Judah Halevi (1075–1141), the first Jewish medieval prose work to exhibit a profound appreciation of Sufi doctrine was the *Faraʾid al-qulub* (*Duties of the Heart*), a treatise on ascetic theology composed in Arabic by R. Bahya ibn Paquda (c. 1080). In an effort to remedy the ritual formalism and religious desiccation of his fellow Jews, Bahya devised an individualistic, inward itinerary, guiding the soul through contemplation and love to union with the "supernal light," based on the progressive spiritual stages of the path as set out in Sufi pietistic manuals. Bahya's use of Sufi sources was not altogether indiscriminate; he notably rejects forms of extreme asceticism and self-mortification preached by certain contemplative Sufis and he adopts a reserved line on the question of union with God. Despite the pains he takes to camouflage material of a too ostensibly Islamic character by replacing the Qur'anic quotations of his sources with biblical ones, his words in the introduction to the book betray his apprehension at introducing a novel kind of devotion into the Jewish fold. He preempts the disapproval of his coreligionists by justifying himself with the talmudic adage "Whoso pronounces a word of wisdom, even a Gentile, is to be called a wise man." The *Duties of the Heart* was one of the first classics of Judeo-Arabic literature to be translated into the holy tongue. The Hebrew version, which greatly attenuated its Islamic stamp, was to wield an abiding influence on Jewish spirituality right down to present times, infusing generations of Jewish readers with Sufi notions. After having influenced the Spanish and thereafter the Palestinian kabbalists, who were particularly interested in Bahya's reflections on solitary meditation, the *Duties of the Heart* was avidly read in the eighteenth century by the Polish Hasidim, who borrowed from it some of their basic ethical concepts, such as quietism, the distinction between external and internal solitude, and that between physical and spiritual warfare. Thus we find in the writings of one of the first Hasidic proponents, Jacob Joseph of Polonnoy, the famous quotation: "You have returned from the lesser war, now prepare for the greater war [with one's nature]." Bahya cites this saying in the name of the "Sage," but in reality the Muslim sources upon which he drew attribute it to the Prophet Muhammad! The works of some later Andalusian authors likewise betray familiarity with Muslim mystical writings. The allegorical commentary on the Song of Songs composed in Arabic by Joseph ibn 'Aqnin (twelfth century) takes on the character of a Sufi treatise on divine love. Even more remarkable is the fact that in this book the author provides definitions of love that are culled from al-Qushayri's *Risalah* ("Epistle"), one of Sufism's basic textbooks. Furthermore in his *Tibb al-nufus* (*Hygiene of the Souls*), Ibn 'Aqnin does not hesitate to quote the Sufi mystics such as al-Junayd (d. 910) and Ibn Adham, referring to them by their Sufi epithets: *shaykh at-ta'ifah*, "the elder of the community," and *al-ruhani al-akmal*, "the perfect spirit."

These examples, of great interest for the historian of Andalusian Sufism, remained, however, isolated and sporadic, no doubt on account of the waning influence of Sufism itself, relentlessly persecuted on Spanish soil by Malikite intolerance. There is no evidence that even Bahya's book, notwithstanding its popularity, gave rise to a sizeable movement of a Sufi brand of Jewish pietists. However, elsewhere, the following centuries were to witness the growth and spread of Sufism in other lands and its sustained influence on Jewish spirituality.

THE JEWISH PIETIST MOVEMENT IN EGYPT

Egypt had long been a hotbed of mysticism. Long after the Therapeuts and the Christian anchorites, the country produced some of the foremost Muslim mystics, such as Dhu al-Nun al-Misri (796–861) and the foremost Sufi poet, 'Umar ibn al-Farid (d. 1235). Here flourished the great charismatic figures such as Abu'l-Hasan al-Shadhili (d. 1258), Muhammad al-Badawi (d. 1276), Abu'l-'Abbas al-Mursi (d. 1287), and Ibn 'Ata' Allah (d. 1309), whose influence certainly extended beyond the Islamic community. Under their sway Sufism became progressively institutionalized, giving rise to the establishment of flourishing brotherhoods in the urban centers. No doubt their infectious spiritual fervor had repercussions on the local Jewish populations. Moreover, Egypt had become a haven for Jewish refugees fleeing Almohad persecution in the West and Crusader wars in the East. Such social upheavals probably encouraged mystical yearnings, heightened by messianic expectations. Dissatisfied with the excessive rationalism of Peripatetic philosophy, certain individual Jews in search of deeper religious expression looked toward their immediate spiritual model, the Sufis.

Though the exact period and the personalities involved in the emergence of this tendency remain uncertain, it seems that at the time of the eminent scholar and leader Moses Maimonides (1138–1204) a number of Jews had already begun to adopt the Sufi way of life. Indeed several documents have survived from this period bearing personal names qualified by the epithet *he-hasid*, "the pious." This was no mere honorific title, but designated an individual who followed a spiritual regime akin to that of the Sufis. The interest Sufi literature held for Jews during this period is well attested by the multiple documents brought to light in the Cairo Geniza. The latter, a lumber-room attached to an ancient synagogue, has preserved thousands of sacred writings dating from the medieval period, which were discovered at the end of the nineteenth century. They included numerous texts of a Sufi character, testifying to the popularity of this kind of literature among Jewish readers. These manuscripts are basically of two sorts: on the one hand, Muslim Sufi writings either in Arabic characters or copied into Hebrew letters for the convenience of Jewish readers, or, on the other, pietist writings of Sufi inspiration written by Jewish authors.

Among the first category all the tendencies of Sufi literature are represented, from the early masters of Baghdad right down to the Illuminationist Ishraqi school founded by Suhrawardi in the twelfth century. There are texts by al-Junayd, pages from al-Qushayri's *Risalah*, poems by al-Hallaj, the *Mahasin al-majalis* by the Andalusian mystic Ibn al-ʿArif, the *Munqidh min al-dalal* (al-Ghazali's spiritual autobiography), al-Shaydhalah's *Treatise on Divine Love*, Suhrawardi's *Kalimat al-tasawwuf* and his *Hayakil al-nur*, to name just a few. In addition to these are to be found various texts containing quotations, tales, anecdotes, and even songs by Sufi masters.

The second category is made up of the Jewish pietists' own compositions. These include ethical manuals and theological treatises, descriptions of mystical states as well as exegetical works. Though these writings are based on traditional rabbinic themes, they show an attempt to reinterpret the scriptural narrative in harmony with Sufi doctrine, often portraying biblical figures as masters of the Sufi path. They are not, however, simple Judaized adaptations of Muslim texts, but original compositions, dexterously transposed in the biblical and rabbinic texture.

The most outstanding author about whom anything substantial is known was none other than R. Abraham (1186–1237), son of the great rationalist Jewish philosopher Moses Maimonides. At the death of his father (1204) Abraham became the spiritual leader of Egyptian Jewry and later acceded to a position of political eminence as *nagid*, "head of the Jews." Not only was he virtually the supreme religious and political figure of his time, but he was also an ardent protagonist of the Sufi form of Jewish pietism henceforth known as *hasidut*. It is unknown when he embraced this tendency but it is thought that he was already dedicated to the pietist way of life when he succeeded his illustrious father in 1205. Abraham Maimonides composed a commentary on the Pentateuch wherein he often depicts the ancient biblical characters as pietists in the same way as Sufi literature adorns the Prophet and his companions in the garb of the early Sufis. However Abraham's magnum opus was the *Kifayat* al- ʿAbidin (*Compendium for the Servants of God*), a monumental legal and ethical treatise, which, though in many respects similar to his father's *Mishneh Torah*, is distinctive in the strong propensity he displays therein for mysticism of a manifestly Muslim type. Indeed, far from sharing Bahya's misgivings about using Muslim sources, Abraham Maimonides overtly expresses his admiration for the Sufis in whom he sees the heirs of ancient Israelite traditions. At one point, after having claimed that the true dress of the ancient prophets of Israel was similar to the ragged garments (*muraqqaʿat*) worn by the Sufis, he declares: "Do not regard as unseemly our comparison of that [the true dress of the prophets] to the conduct of the Sufis, for the latter imitate the prophets [of Israel] and walk in their footsteps, not the prophets in theirs."[1]

Similarly, the Sufi initiation ritual, consisting in the investiture of the master's cloak (*khirqah*), was originally practiced by the prophets of Israel, according to the author of the *Kifayah*:

By casting his cloak over [Elisha], Elijah hinted to him, as if in joyful annunciation, that his garments and dress as well as the rest of his conduct would be like his. Thus he announced to him the fact that Elijah's spiritual perfection would be transferred to him and that he [Elisha] would attain the degree which he himself had attained. Thou art aware of the ways of the ancient saints [*awliyaʾ*] of Israel, which are not or but little practised among our contemporaries, that have now become the practice of the Sufis of Islam, "on account of the iniquities of Israel," namely that the master invests the novice [*murid*] with a cloak [*khirqah*] as the latter is about to enter upon the mystical path [*tariq*]. "They have taken up thine own words" (Deuteronomy 33:3). This is why we moreover take over from them and emulate them in the wearing of sleeveless tunics and the like.[2]

The idea that Sufi practices are of Jewish origin is repeated by Abraham elsewhere when he deals with the Sufi ascetic discipline:

We see also the Sufis of Islam practice self-mortification by combating sleep and perhaps that practice is derived from the words of [king] David... Observe then these wonderful traditions and sigh with regret over how they have been transferred from us and appeared amongst a nation other than ours whereas they have disappeared in our midst. My soul shall weep in secret... because of the pride of Israel that was taken from them and bestowed upon the nations of the world.[3]

Unlike his father who had written a purely legal code, Abraham Maimonides emphasized the spiritual significance of the precepts and discussed the "mysteries" they conceal, in a manner similar to the Muslim mystics, such as al-Ghazali in his *Ihya' 'ulum al-din*. The author of the *Kifayah* believed that he had rediscovered some of these mysteries in the traditions preserved by the Sufis, which had been forgotten by the Jews on account of the multiple tribulations of the Exile. This belief provides a key as to the reason why the pietists adopted manifestly Muslim customs. Furthermore, it seems that the pietists, who called themselves "the disciples of the prophets," were profoundly convinced of the imminent renewal of prophecy in Israel. They believed that the Sufi practices were not only originally ancient Jewish traditions, but also an integral part of a "prophetic discipline." Thus their restoration to the Jewish fold was meant to accelerate the prophetic process.

These "reforms" included a number of devotional practices, clearly inspired by Muslim models, whose purpose was to enhance the decorum and purport of synagogue worship. As a preliminary to prayer, the *nagid* insisted on the ritual ablution of hands and feet, though not strictly required by Jewish law. On the other hand, this rite was obligatory in Muslim custom and considered especially meritorious by Sufi authors. Abraham instituted the arrangement of worshipers in rows, as in mosques, facing Jerusalem at all times during the synagogue services. He prescribed various postures during certain prayers, such as standing, kneeling, and frequent bowing, as well as the spreading of the hands and weeping in supplication. In addition to canonical prayers, nightly vigils and daily fasts were recommended. However, the most telling ritual adopted by the pietists was that of solitary meditation, a characteristic Sufi practice known as *khalwah*. Here the devotee would retire from society for protracted periods in an isolated and dark place in order to devote himself to worship and meditation. Abraham Maimonides also considered this practice of Jewish origin:

Also do the Sufis of Islam practice solitude in dark places and isolate themselves in them until the sensitive part of the soul becomes atrophied so that it is not even able to see the light. This however requires strong inner illumination wherewith the soul will be preoccupied so as not to be pained over the external darkness. Now Rabbi Abraham he-Hasid used to be of the opinion that solitude in darkness was the thing alluded to in the statement of Isaiah: "Who is among you that feareth the Lord that obeyeth the voice of His servant, who walketh in darkness and hath no light? Let him trust in the name of the Lord, and stay upon his God" (Isaiah 50:10).[4]

As is known, one of the most typical aspects of the Sufi path is the necessity of spiritual development under the guidance of a master. Abraham Maimonides sees the origin of this principle in the discipline of the ancient prophets:

Know that generally in order for the Way to attain successfully its true goal [wusul], it must be pursued under the guidance [taslik] of a person who has already attained this goal, as it is said in the tradition: "Acquire a master" [Avot 1:6]. The biblical accounts concerning masters and their disciples are well known: Joshua the servant of Moses was one of his disciples, who, having attained the goal, succeeded him. The prophets adopted the same conduct. Samuel's guide [musallik] was Eli, Elijah was that of Elisha, and Jeremiah that of Barukh son of Neriah. Moreover the "disciples of the prophets" were thus called because the prophets were their spiritual guides. This practice was adopted by other nations [the Sufis], who instituted in imitation of Jewish custom the relation between shaykh and servant, master and disciple . . . If the wayfarer is capable and remains faithful to instructions, he will attain his goal through the guidance of an accomplished master.[5]

Certain Jewish pietist texts also mention the typical Sufi practice of *dhikr*, or "spiritual recollection," but so far no details have been discovered on how this specific ritual was carried out in Jewish circles, as it most probably was. Because of their protracted devotions, the pietists established special prayer-halls; it is known, for instance, that Abraham Maimonides possessed his own private synagogue. In addition to the foregoing practices, other aspects of the pietist discipline of an ascetic nature are to be found in the writings of other members of the pietist circle. Notably, contrary to traditional Jewish ethics, the Jewish pietists, like certain Sufis, advocated celibacy and considered marriage and family responsibilities an impediment to spiritual fulfillment. Obadyah Maimonides, Abraham's son, says the following about marriage: "Know that the true mystics of this path strived to perfect their souls before marriage in the knowledge that after begetting spouse and offspring there would be little opportunity for spiritual achievement."[6] The same author also shunned all material superfluities and taught a regime of extreme austerity:

Cover thy head, let fall thy tears, and let purity follow in thy wake, spend thy days in fasting throughout the day. Delight not in the joys of the vulgar and be not dismayed at that which grieves them. In a word be not sad with their sadness and rejoice not with their merriment. Despise frivolity and laughter, rather observe silence and speak not except out of necessity. Eat not except out of compulsion and sleep not unless overcome, and all the while thy heart should contemplate this pursuit and thy thoughts be engaged therein.[7]

The figure of Abraham Maimonides inaugurates a long association of the celebrated Maimonides family with pietism of a Sufi type, lasting, no doubt with some interruptions, for nearly two centuries. Indeed, Abraham's own son, just mentioned, Obadyah Maimonides (1228–1265), had strong leanings towards Sufism, as can be gathered from his composition *al-Maqala al-Hawdiyyah* (*The Treatise of the Pool*). The latter is an ethical vade mecum and a mystical manual for the spiritual wayfarer upon the path leading to God through union with the intelligible realm. It is based on the typically Sufi comparison of the heart to a pool that must be cleansed before it can be filled with the vivifying waters of gnosis. Couched in an allusive style, the treatise is replete with Sufi technical terms. Also worthy of note is Obadyah's tendency to project Sufi stereotypes into the patriarchal past. Thus Abraham, Isaac, and Jacob become wandering hermits practicing solitary meditation in the wilderness.

David ben Joshua (c. 1335–1415), the last of the Maimonideans recorded by history, was also interested in Sufism. His work *al-Murshid ila t-tafarrud* (*The Guide to Detachment*), one of the last creations of neoclassical Judeo-Arabic literature, represents the most far-reaching synthesis between traditional rabbinical ethics and the spiritual states of the Sufi path. Following the tradition of Sufi manuals, which begin with a definition of Sufism, the author first proposes a definition of *hasidut*. The body of the work is based on an ethical formula taught by the rabbis, which David develops as the central motif of a spiritual program largely construed in the light of the mystical stations of the Sufi path and the Illuminationist philosophy of Suhrawardi. Thus he derives the initial virtue, *zehirut*, normally signifying "precaution," from the root *zhr* "to shine," associating it with the Illuminationist notion of *ishraq*, since the first step on the path to perfection is motivated by the quest for light.

The centrality of the Maimonidean family is further indicated by the fact that a certain number of personalities associated with the pietist circle were also related to this prestigious dynasty. Abraham Abu Rabiʿa he-Hasid was one of the leaders of the Jewish Sufis in Egypt. He was the author of a mystical commentary on the Song of Songs, which is conceived of as an allegorical dialogue between the mystic intoxicated with divine love and the object of his desire, the beatific vision. Another noteworthy adept of the pietist circle was R. Hananʾel ben Samuel al-Amshati, who was not only a member of Abraham Maimonides' rabbinical court but also his father-in-law. Several Geniza documents refer to him as "he-Hasid," the "pietist." He is now known to have been the author of a considerable exegetical work that reflects his stature not only as a philosopher, but also as a mystic insofar as his explanations resound with Sufi technical terms. Moreover, R. Hananʾel was a committed pietist activist, for a certain document portrays him alongside his son-in-law defending the movement. Indeed the introduction of their novel practices did not go unchallenged, and the pietists, like many revivalist movements in religious history, met with virulent opposition. Despite Abraham Maimonides' political and religious prestige, which immensely contributed to the furtherance of the pietist movement, he had to face fierce opponents, who even went so far as to denounce him to the Muslim authorities, accusing the pietists of introducing "false ideas," "unlawful changes," and "gentile (Sufi) customs" into the synagogue. Opposition continued during the office as *nagid* of Abraham's son David Maimonides (1222–1300), whose synagogue was closed down, and who, at one point, was compelled to leave Egypt, seeking refuge in Acre. This opposition, coupled with the fact that access to the "pietist way" was reserved from its very inception for the select few, may explain why the movement did not gain universal approval but, with the general decline of Oriental Jewry, gradually disappeared into total oblivion.

LATER INFLUENCES

Sufism continued sporadically to be a source of fascination for individual Jews in ensuing centuries. Mention has already been made of the fact that R. David II Maimonides (c. 1335–1415) showed interest in Sufism. A complaint addressed to him by a Jewish housewife has been preserved in the Geniza, informing him that her husband, infatuated with Sufism, had abandoned her in order to go and live in a Sufi convent under the guidance of the famous Sufi al-Kurani in the Muqattam mountains outside Cairo. According to information provided by the Arab biographer al-Kutubi, the Jews of Damascus would assemble in the house of the Sufi al-Hasan ibn Hud (thirteenth century) in order to study Maimonides' *Guide of the Perplexed* under his supervision. Did this mean that they sought to interpret the *Guide* in the light of Sufism? As late as the sixteenth century the great Egyptian Muslim mystic al-Sha'arani relates in his autobiography the reputation he enjoyed amongst his Jewish admirers who would attend his lectures and request him to write amulets to protect their children. Jews also maintained contacts with Sufis in other localities. Karaite Jews showed an interest in Sufi writings, which they were still copying in the seventeenth century. Perhaps they felt a kinship between Sufi asceticism and their own rather austere brand of ethics.

Traces of Sufism are also to be found in the writings of fifteenth-century Yemenite Jews who freely use Sufi concepts and quote verses from the mystical poetry of the Sufi martyr al-Hallaj. In Spain and Provence, during the great movement of translation in the thirteenth century, many Sufi concepts percolated into Jewish literature through the intermediary of Hebrew translations, especially those of the works of al-Ghazali.

Similarly, but in a completely different part of the Islamic world, the copying into Hebrew characters of Persian Sufi poetry, such as that of Rumi and Sa'di, no doubt contributed to the diffusion of Sufi ideas among Persian Jews. It is worthwhile recalling in this context the exquisite *rub'ayyat* of Sarmad (d. 1661), a remarkable Persian Jew who became a wandering Sufi dervish in India.

THE EARLY KABBALISTS

Yet another area where contacts took place between Jews and Sufis was the Holy Land, where thriving centers of Muslim culture such as Jerusalem and even Safed flowered in the thirteenth century. Contemporary Palestinian kabbalists close to the circle of

R. Abraham Abu'l-ʿAfiyah/Abulafia (d. after 1291) not only betray a
certain number of Sufi practices in their esoteric discipline but also
testify to their having directly observed the Sufi *dhikr* ritual. Abu'l-
ʿAfiyah may himself have encountered Sufis during his brief visit
to Acre around 1260 or elsewhere in the course of his wide travels.
The focal point of his ecstatic method is the practice of *hazkarah*, a
term itself strikingly reminiscent of the Arabic *dhikr*. Independently
of canonical prayer, the purpose of this activity was to prepare the
devotee for prophetic inspiration. The meditative ritual, practiced
in an isolated and dark place, as set out in Abu'l-ʿAfiyah's writings,
obviously involves Sufi techniques. After preliminary preparations,
the devotee, arrayed in white, adopts a special posture and proceeds
to pronounce the divine name accompanied with respiratory control
and movements of the head.

Abu'l-ʿAfiyah's doctrines were propagated in the East. The kabbalists of the Holy Land, such as Isaac of Acco, Shem Tov ibn Gaon,
and the anonymous author of *Shaʿarey Zedeq*, adopted the meditative method of his prophetic kabbalah, further enriching it with
elements of Sufi provenance. Isaac of Acco (c. 1270–1340) in particular seemed to have had direct knowledge of Sufi techniques,
including solitary meditation (*khalwah* in Arabic, *hitbodedut* in
Hebrew) and the visualization of letters. Isaac is also an important
link in the transmission of these methods to the later kabbalists of
Safed. He himself may have had personal contacts with Sufis, for he
had a good knowledge of Arabic. Alternatively, he may have made
the acquaintance of David Maimonides and his pietist companions
during the latter's exile in Acco (Acre) which lasted until 1289.

THE KABBALISTS OF SAFED

The historians of the extraordinary kabbalistic school of Safed have
insufficiently taken into account the influence of the Islamic environment when dealing with the novel practices introduced by the
disciples of R. Isaac Luria (1534–1572), himself a native of Egypt. The
Turkish traveler Evliya Chelebi testifies that in the sixteenth century, that is during the very heyday of Lurianic kabbalah, Safed was a
vibrant Sufi center which possessed its *tekkiye*, or Sufi convent, and
spiritual retreats. It is not unreasonable therefore to suppose that
behind some of the mystical rituals initiated by the kabbalists lie

Sufi models. Among the most significant, mention can be made of saint worship and visitation of the tombs of saints and their invocation, which are similar to Muslim practices connected with the *ziyarah* rite, the gathering of spiritual brotherhoods (*havurot*) around the person of the saint, and spiritual concerts (*baqashshot*), vigils consisting in the singing of devotional poems, similar to the Sufi *sama'* ceremony.

However, the most important ritual was that of *hitbodedut*, "solitary meditation." After a hiatus of more than a century, contemplative elements of a Sufi character resurge in the writings of the sixteenth-century Spanish exiles established in the Holy Land. Though this phenomenon can be seen as a continuation of Abu'l-'Afiyah's school, the possibility cannot be excluded that it is a survival from the doctrine of the Jewish Sufis. Among the first authors to evoke anew this discipline were Judah al-Butini (d. 1519) in his *Sullam ha-'aliyah* (*Ladder of Ascension*, a title in itself redolent of Sufism) and Moses Cordovero (d. 1570) in his *Pardes rimmonim* (*Orchard of Pomegranates*). Meditation and breath control continued to be practiced in dark places in order to bring about an internal illumination of the soul. Other techniques observed during the periodic retreats also betray Sufi influence: ritual purity, complete silence, fasting, restriction of sleep and food, confidence in God, and, above all, the repetition of divine names as a path to ecstasy.

THE SHABBATIANS

The last significant contact between Jewish and Muslim mystics took place during the religious turmoil brought about by the mystical messiah Shabbetai Zevi (d. 1676), whose tragic destiny led him to conversion to Islam. During his confinement in Adrianople, while still inwardly practicing Judaism, Shabbetai Zevi would attend *dhikr* seances in the Bektashi convent at Hizirlik and, it seems, established contacts with the famous khalwati mystic, Muhammad al-Niyazi (d. 1694). His apostate followers, known as the Dönmeh, continued to maintain close relations with the mystical brotherhoods in Turkey and in particular with the syncretistic Bektashis, from whom they borrowed a certain number of rituals and Turkish liturgical poems and melodies which were included in their ceremonies.

It is well known that the eighteenth-century East European Hasidic movement took root and first grew in the southern Polish province of Podolia, which had once been under Ottoman control and was a hotbed of Shabbatian activism. The sectarians in this area continued to maintain close ties with their brethren under Muslim rule in Salonika. It is interesting to speculate to what extent Sufi ideas percolated into Podolia and influenced the nascent Hasidic movement. The veneration of the *zaddiq* (Hasidic saint), visiting the tombs of saints, the importance of music and dance as forms of worship provide very striking and thought-provoking analogies to Sufi models. Finally, the phenomenon of *hitbodedut*, sometimes also accompanied with the visualization of letters composing the divine name, also occupied an important place in certain Hasidic courts, such as that of Braslav. Although, as we have seen, this practice was probably of Islamic origin, its presence in Hasidism can be traced back through Jewish channels to kabbalistic circles, which had in their time been influenced by Sufi practices.

CONCLUSION

The bilateral influence of Jewish and Muslim mysticism entails one of the most striking chapters of the intimate interaction between Judaism and Islam. As such it provides a precious testimony of their reciprocal receptivity in the esoteric domain, even though in the exoteric one they remained mutually exclusive. Furthermore, with what concerns the Jewish pietist movement in Egypt and the kabbalistic school in the Holy Land, it is noteworthy that this cross-fertilization came about during one of the most fecund and intense periods in the formation of Jewish spirituality. These crossroads, of singular significance for the history of religion, undoubtedly open up new and far-reaching perspectives of interfaith exchange, whose contours are yet to be explored.

NOTES

1. S. Rosenblatt (ed.), *The High Ways to Perfection of Abraham Maimonides* (New York: Columbia University Press, 1927), II: 320.
2. Rosenblatt (ed.), *The High Ways*, I: 153.
3. Rosenblatt (ed.), *The High Ways*, II: 266.

4. Rosenblatt (ed.), *The High Ways*, II: 418.
5. Rosenblatt (ed.), *The High Ways*, II: 422.
6. P. Fenton, *The Treatise of the Pool, al-Maqala al-Hawdiyya by ‘Obadyah Maimonides* (London: Octagon, 1995 [revised ed.]), 94.
7. Fenton, *The Treatise of the Pool*, 116.

11 Philosophy and kabbalah: 1200–1600

Philosophy and kabbalah were highly variegated programs for the interpretation of rabbinic Judaism. Although kabbalah was rooted in the esoteric traditions of late antiquity, it became a self-conscious program for the interpretation of Judaism at the end of the twelfth century, to counter Maimonidean intellectualism. Nonetheless, kabbalists addressed the theoretical issues of concern to the rationalist philosophers and theorized within the conceptual framework of contemporary philosophy. In the second half of the thirteenth century, two types of kabbalah were consolidated: theosophic kabbalah mythologized philosophical categories while articulating a comprehensive alternative to rationalist philosophy. Prophetic (or ecstatic) kabbalah, by contrast, developed a full-fledged intellectual mysticism on the basis of Maimonides' theory of knowledge and gave kabbalistic doctrines a philosophical reading. During the fourteenth century a few Jewish philosophers, especially those who cultivated the study of astrology and astral magic, viewed kabbalah and philosophy as compatible schemas that give different names to the same entities. In the fifteenth and sixteenth centuries, the philosophic reading of kabbalah was prevalent in Italy where kabbalah was viewed by Jews, and even by some Christian humanists, as ancient speculative lore necessary for intellectual perfection. In Spain and in the Spanish diaspora the mythical aspects of kabbalah were more prominent. While some kabbalists had a very negative view of philosophy, the dominant attitude toward kabbalah among Iberian philosophers was quite positive. They considered that kabbalah revealed knowledge that completes and perfects human reason and went on to recast medieval Aristotelianism in accord with the teachings of kabbalah. The absorption of kabbalah into philosophy, on the one hand, and the dissolution of medieval Aristotelianism, on the other hand, led to the rise of kabbalah as the dominant Jewish theology in the seventeenth century. In Jewish intellectual history, kabbalah and philosophy were closely intertwined.

THE RISE AND SPREAD OF KABBALAH

Medieval Jewish rationalism emerged in the early tenth century as a reinterpretation of rabbinic theism. The personal, highly anthropomorphic and anthropopathic depictions of God in rabbinic midrash and in the esoteric, ecstatic literature of the *hekhalot* and *merkavah* literature were problematized by Islamic rationalism and by Karaite sectarianism. In particular, the detailed descriptions of God's body in the *Shiur Qomah* (Measure of the [Divine] Body) corpus, in which each limb of God was given fantastic measurements and linked to the primordial Torah, were regarded as an intellectual embarrassment. If rabbinic Judaism is true, as Jews claimed in their debates with Muslim and Christian theologians, then Jewish philosophers must explain away what they considered to be intellectually unacceptable. Saadya Gaon defended the rationality of Judaism by subjecting the main beliefs of rabbinic Judaism to a thorough philosophical analysis and by showing how they are compatible with philosophic knowledge. In the case of *Shiur Qomah*, for example, Saadya claimed that the text was not rabbinic and that the figure described is not God but a "Created Glory," namely, an entity created by God.

Following Saadya Gaon, Jewish philosophers during the eleventh century continued to intellectualize Judaism, believing that they in fact provided a deeper, more sophisticated justification for allegiance to the revealed tradition. Reason, the mark of being human, provided philosophers with a clear knowledge of truth, thereby enabling them to come closer to God. The philosophers conceptualized God in impersonal, abstract terms, privileged the intellect as the vehicle for interaction with God, and equated the worship of God with the knowledge of God. For the philosophers, the attainment of intellectual perfection through the study of philosophy was a religious obligation.

The intellectualization of rabbinic Judaism reached its zenith in Moses Maimonides. Yet, for Maimonides, philosophic truths were not identical with Neoplatonic metaphysics and cosmology, but with the teachings of Aristotle, which Maimonides had absorbed primarily from the writings of al-Farabi. Maimonides' intellectualization of Judaism was problematic not merely because on crucial issues, such as the origin of the universe, Aristotle's philosophy conflicted with rabbinic beliefs, but because Maimonides posited Aristotelian philosophy as the inner, hidden meaning of divinely revealed Scripture. Moreover, in his *Mishneh Torah*, Maimonides made his philosophic rendering of rabbinic Judaism obligatory for all Jews. The rapid acceptance of Maimonides' code of Jewish law in Mediterranean communities entailed the dissemination of Maimonides' negative theology, his intellectualist conception of God, and his historical and anthropological rationalization of the commandments (*ta'amei ha-mitzvot*). Kabbalah emerged in the late twelfth century in Provence in order to curb the spread of Maimonides' intellectualist rendering of rabbinic Judaism.

That kabbalah emerged in Provence at that time was no accident. During the eleventh and twelfth centuries, the Jewish community in Provence witnessed unusual creativity in Halakhah, midrash, and Aggadah, but after the destruction of Andalusian Jewry in 1148, Provençal Jewry was also exposed to Judeo-Arabic philosophy. Refugees from Andalusia, such as the Ibn Tibbon and Ibn Kimhi families, settled in Provence, translated philosophical texts into Hebrew, and promoted the philosophic curriculum. The first critique of Maimonides' *Mishneh Torah* came from R. Abraham ben David of Posquières (known as Rabad), who spoke as a defender of the received tradition, from which Maimonides allegedly deviated. R. Abraham ben David and members of his circle were Jewish mystics who regarded themselves as preservers of the received tradition (i.e. the literal meaning of kabbalah). They claimed to have received communications from the prophet Elijah – the symbol of the Jewish tradition – about the mysteries of God, prayers, and the meaning of Scripture.[1] These esoteric teachings were received and transmitted orally from master to disciple (allegedly going back to Sinai) and were to be divulged only to those who are religiously and intellectually fit to receive them. The historian can reconstruct this orally transmitted tradition only from references to it in later kabbalistic texts.

Provençal kabbalah had two main sources: the theological speculations of Hasidei Ashkenaz (German Pietists), which elaborated the teachings of *hekhalot* and *merkavah* texts,[2] and *Sefer ha-Bahir* (*Book of Brightness*), a midrash ascribed to a second-century rabbi, R. Nehunya ben ha-Qanah, one of the heroes of rabbinic esotericism.[3] Despite the differences between these two traditions, they both presented a view of God that differed markedly from Maimonides' God, or at least the revealed aspect of God, was no longer a simple unity, but a unity within a plurality of forces. This conception of a multi-layered deity (i.e. theosophy) had deep sexual overtones, elaborating the anthropomorphism of *Shiur Qomah* into a dynamic view of a bipolar sexual being. The interplay between the masculine and feminine aspects of the Godhead was said to be affected by extra-deical reality, especially by the deeds of Israel (i.e. theurgy). Their sins activate Evil whereas their observance of divine commandments empowers the forces of holiness. By the turn of the thirteenth century, then, what Maimonides rejected as unacceptable interpretation of Judaism asserted itself as the correct, esoteric meaning of the received tradition.

Both Maimonides and the kabbalists claimed to have fathomed the inner meaning of divine revelation, designated in rabbinic Judaism as *ma'aseh bereshit* (account of creation) and *ma'aseh merkavah* (account of the chariot). Maimonides perpetuated rabbinic esotericism when he couched his *Guide of the Perplexed* in a form of a personal letter to his beloved student, Joseph ben Judah ibn Sham'un. But Maimonides also departed from the rabbinic tradition when he identified *ma'aseh bereshit* and *ma'aseh merkavah* with the sciences of physics and metaphysics respectively. That meant that the esoteric meaning of the received tradition is identical with the truths of philosophy, and that, in principle, the hidden meaning of divine revelation was accessible to human reason. Any philosopher, Jew or non-Jew, could know it by virtue of natural human reason. By contrast, the kabbalists claimed that the esoteric dimension of rabbinic Judaism cannot be known except through divine revelation to those chosen by God, and that the philosophy of Aristotle, or any other non-Jew, has nothing to say about it. Moreover, the mysteries of God, the universe, and the holy life embedded in the revealed Torah were all disclosed through a unique medium: the Hebrew language.

Hebrew, the kabbalists maintained contrary to Maimonides, was not a product of human convention, but rather a unique language chosen by God to be the very medium of creation. This view was articulated in the anonymous *Sefer Yetzira* (*The Book of Creation*), a composition from the early rabbinic period, although, ironically, it too manifested the impact of Hellenistic Neopythagoreanism and perhaps even of Indian philosophy.[4] On the basis of *Sefer Yetzira* and further elaborations by the German pietists, kabbalists developed a linguistic theory according to which the Hebrew alphabet itself has a mystical import: the goal of religious life – clinging to God (*devequt*) – is to be attained through knowledge of the Tetragrammaton, the divine name whose endless permutations constitute the revealed Torah. Since the Torah is also the blueprint of the cosmos, knowledge of divine names was believed to empower the knower to master natural processes. Kabbalah was closely aligned with magic.

From Provence, kabbalah spread to Spain during the thirteenth century, where kabbalistic fraternities in various urban centers in Catalonia (e.g. Gerona, Barcelona) and in Castile (e.g. Toledo, Burgos, Soria, and Guadalajara) claimed to present "the kabbalah." Kabbalistic speculations differed in accord with the personal orientation of a given kabbalist, the exposure to philosophy, and the geo-cultural context. Thus the kabbalists of Gerona – R. Ezra ben Solomon, R. Azriel, and R. Jacob ben Sheshet – revealed a Neoplatonic bent of mind and delved into the dialectics of singularity and multiplicity by articulating the theosophic meaning of the received tradition and its theurgic implications.[5] The kabbalists active in Barcelona (such as R. Moses ben Nahman and his disciples R. Meir ibn Sahula, R. Isaac Todros, and R. Solomon ibn Adret) augmented theosophical speculations with the theory about recurrent cosmic cycles and developed the theurgic meaning of Jewish rituals.[6] The kabbalists in Toledo and Burgos – R. Isaac and R. Jacob ha-Cohen and their disciple, R. Moses of Burgos, and Todros ben Joseph Abulafia – were deeply interested in the problem of evil, and their speculations suggested affinity with Gnostic dualism that flourished among Christian heretical movements in the early thirteenth century. Another kabbalistic circle – the anonymous author of *Sefer ha-Iyyun* (*The Book of Contemplation*) and its cognate literature – was primarily concerned with the mysticism of light, most likely under the influence of certain Ismaili or Sufi traditions.[7] And finally there were kabbalists, such as Joseph Gikatilah, who elaborated mysticism of language on the basis of *hekhalot* and *merkavah* literature.

All these diverse theological interests were manifested in distinct literary genres. Spanish kabbalists composed commentaries on the Bible, commentaries on talmudic homilies, commentaries on ancient mystical texts of the *hekhalot* and *merkavah* corpus and *Sefer Yetzira*, lists of symbolic codes, systematic expositions of the commandments, speculations on the Hebrew alphabet and Torah cantillation, and a manual for the attainment of ecstatic and mystical experiences. By means of exegetical activity, Spanish kabbalah consolidated a distinctive worldview that elaborated and expanded the motifs and ideas of rabbinic Judaism. Undoubtedly, the kabbalistic hermeneutical activity was meant to rebut the philosophic readings of Scripture and Aggadah that proliferated during the thirteenth century as Maimonides' hermeneutical principles were put into practice.

The kabbalists developed their response to Maimonidean rationalism while the Jewish community worldwide, especially in Provence and Spain, was engulfed in a heated debate about the legacy of Maimonides. The kabbalists tended to side with the anti-Maimonist camp, even though all kabbalists had deep respect for Maimonides, and some were intimately familiar with his *Guide of the Perplexed*. In the 1280s and 1290s, during the third phase of the Maimonidean controversy, two main types of Spanish kabbalah were consolidated: the theosophic kabbalah of *Sefer ha-Zohar* (*The Book of Splendor*), whose main author was Moses de Leon, and the prophetic (or ecstatic) kabbalah of Abraham Abulafia.

Modern scholarship has treated these two strands of kabbalah as two religious orientations:[8] whereas the former delved into the inner life of the deity, the latter focused on the psychological processes within the human soul and its striving for intellectual perfection; whereas the former insisted on the human ability to affect God, the latter was interested in the mystical union of the human intellect and God; whereas the former elaborated the mythic, anthropomorphic, and ethnocentric dimensions of Judaism, the latter was more open to conversation with non-Jewish modes of thought, and made kabbalah amenable to philosophic exposition. Whereas the *Zohar* saw itself as an alternative to Maimonides' philosophy, Abulafia developed his prophetic kabbalah on the basis of Maimonides' philosophy and claimed to have accomplished its ideal. The distinction between theosophic and prophetic kabbalah, however, is useful so

long as it is not taken too rigidly,[9] and it will structure my reconstruction of the interface between philosophy and kabbalah in the
post-Maimonidean period.

THEOSOPHIC KABBALAH AS A RESPONSE
TO MAIMONIDES

Sefer ha-Zohar began to circulate in Spain in the late 1280s and the
person most responsible for it was R. Moses de Leon, the author
of several Hebrew kabbalistic works. The *Zohar*, however, was most
likely the product of a kabbalistic fraternity in Castile,[10] and its originality lies not in the novelty of its doctrine (almost all of which could
be traced to previous kabbalistic texts), but in its literary structure.
The *Zohar* presented itself as an ancient, rabbinic midrash on the
Pentateuch, authored by R. Simon bar Yohai, a rabbi of the second
century, who is the main protagonist of the *Zohar*. Imitating the
spoken speech of ancient rabbis, the *Zohar* is written in a peculiar
Aramaic, even though it is studded with many idiosyncratic words
and phrases that betray its medieval provenance. Although it is arranged in accordance with the sequence of the Torah's weekly portions, the *Zohar* is not a linear commentary on the Pentateuch, but a
series of elaborate and intricate homilies that merely take their point
of departure from the verses of the given Torah portion. With unparalleled spiritual energy, creative imagination, and subtle artistry, the
Zohar interwove biblical, rabbinic, pietistic, philosophic, and kabbalistic motifs into a colorful fabric, which it presents as the true,
hidden meaning of the divinely revealed, authoritative tradition. In
other words, the *Zohar* saw itself as *the* authentic, inner, esoteric
wisdom of Judaism (*hokhmat ha-nistar*). A comparison of theosophic
kabbalah with Maimonides' philosophy will clarify how theosophic
kabbalah responded to Maimonides' philosophy.

The Concealed and Revealed God

Maimonides insisted on the unbridgeable ontological gap between
God and all other existents and, therefore, on the unknowability
of God. Theosophic kabbalah struggled with the same theoretical
problems but it was convinced that some positive knowledge of God
was possible. With Maimonides, theosophic kabbalists held that the

essence of God is unknowable. This is the Eyn Sof (literally, "without limit" or "the infinite") that could not be defined, characterized, or comprehended conceptually. The Eyn Sof is Nothingness ('ayin), or better still, No-Thingness. The Eyn Sof is neither a this nor a that, neither a thing nor the opposite of any particular thing. The Eyn Sof, however, is not a static entity but a living reality that is the source of all existents (one of the meanings of 'ayin in Hebrew is "spring," or "source"; many kabbalistic concepts developed on the basis of Hebrew wordplays). Whatever exists ultimately emanates from the Eyn Sof but the process of emanation (in Hebrew atzilut) begins not with spiritual extra-deical entities, such as the Separate Intellects of medieval Aristotelianism, but with the emanation of God's own powers, the ten sefirot.

The term sefirot originated in Sefer Yetzira where it referred to ten ideal numbers that functioned, along with the twenty-two letters of the Hebrew alphabet, as the "building blocks" of the universe. Jewish philosophers prior to Maimonides – Shabbtai Donnolo, Judah Barzilai of Barcelona, Dunash ibn Tamim, Solomon ibn Gabirol, Abraham ibn Ezra, and Judah Halevi commented on Sefer Yetzira – understood the term sefirot mathematically, and their commentaries focused on the cosmological implications of the ancient text.[11] In theosophic kabbalah, however, the term sefirot was associated either with the divine light (accordingly, the term was linked to the word sappir, namely, "sapphire"), or with the disclosure of God's personal character traits (in which case the term sefirot was linked to the word le-sapper [meaning, "to tell"]). The ten dynamic sefirot are the deus revelatus and the Eyn Sof is the deus obsconditus.

The ontological status of the sefirot and their relationship to the Eyn Sof was a hotly debated issue among the kabbalists, analogous to the philosophic debates about the relationship between God and the Separate Intellects. Generally speaking there were two main approaches to the ontological status of the sefirot: one viewed the sefirot as the essence of God ('atzmut) and the other regarded them as instruments of God's activity (kelim).[12] The former and dominant position of theosophic kabbalah was represented in the Zohar and it manifested the mythical and pantheistic tendencies of kabbalah. The ten sefirot were viewed as a dynamic reality, each with its own distinctive characteristics, whose constant interaction was affected by non-divine reality, especially by the deeds of human beings. The dynamism of the sefirotic world was expressed in organic symbolism, mainly the symbolism of the inverted tree and the symbolism of the primordial human (adam qadmon).[13] Kabbalistic theosophy is mainly the hermeneutical development of sefirotic symbolism on the basis of Scripture and rabbinic Aggadot.[14] Kabbalistic symbolism provided the infrastructure, so to speak, of Jewish ritual life. Each prescribed act was linked symbolically to a particular sefirah, so that the performance of the act with the proper intention was understood to sanctify the religious practitioner and facilitate attachment with God.[15] Kabbalistic symbolic hermeneutics was intended to counter the rationalization of the mitzvot by the philosophers.

By contrast, the view that the sefirot are the instruments of divine activity was articulated by kabbalists who had a more philosophic frame of mind, and who, therefore, were more reticent about the pantheistic and mythical implications of kabbalistic theosophy. The sefirot were understood either as divine attributes of action, as did R. Menahem Rencanati,[16] or identified with the Separate Intellects, as did Abraham Abulafia, to whom we shall return below. This approach went hand in hand with the demythologization of kabbalistic readings of rabbinic Aggadot carried out by the anonymous Sefer Ma'arekhet Elohut (The Constellation of the Godhead), a kabbalistic text from the fourteenth century. The instrumentalist interpretation made possible the attempts to coordinate the kabbalistic and philosophic schemas.

The confidence of the theosophic kabbalists that some positive knowledge of God was possible was rooted in their understanding of Torah. For theosophic kabbalists, the Torah is not a divine law simply because it could be demonstrated that the Torah secures the well being of the body and soul on account of the intellectual perfection of its recipient, the prophet Moses. Nor is the Torah divine because it is a perfect expression of philosophic-scientific truths in human language. Rather, the Torah is a symbolic revelation of God's inner life whose surface, literal meaning pertains to the mundane world (i.e. to the world of nature and of human history), but whose inner, esoteric meaning pertains to the infinite processes within the Godhead.[17] For the kabbalists, then, creation and revelation were two sides of the same process: God's self-disclosure. While the exoteric aspect of the Torah pertains to events in the physical world and in human history, the esoteric meaning of these events points to events within the Godhead. If Maimonides identified the mysteries of the Torah with the laws that govern the universe, theosophic kabbalists equated them with events within the Godhead, which Maimonides claimed are, in principle, beyond the ken of human knowledge. Kabbalistic theosophy, then, viewed itself to be epistemically superior to rationalist philosophy because it pertained to God and not just to the world created by God.

From the One to the Many: The Great Chain of Being

The Jewish tradition affirms the belief that God created the world, although the precise meaning of the creative act remains open to interpretation. In the twelfth century thinkers such as Solomon ibn Gabirol explained the creative act within the Neoplatonic doctrine of emanation in an attempt to clarify the relationship between matter and form and between divine wisdom and will. The theosophic kabbalists, especially the kabbalists of Gerona, struggled with the same problem when they delved into the process by which the *sefirot* came into being out of the singularity of the Eyn Sof without disturbing its unity and simplicity.[18] The kabbalists designated the *sefirot*'s coming into being as "emanation," in contradistinction with the "creation" of everything else. This was no more than a semantic difference to differentiate between the unity of the Godhead and the multiplicity of extra-deical reality. On the basis of Neoplatonic metaphysics, the theosophic kabbalists envisioned all existents as part of a hierarchical Great Chain of Being that emanates from the divine source. All levels of reality are linked to each other, but the lower a thing is on the ontological ladder, the more remote it is from the divine source, and, therefore, the more corporeal.

The cosmology of theosophic kabbalah blended medieval Neoplatonized Aristotelianism with the language and imagery of *hekhalot* and *merkavah* literature. By the fourteenth century, kabbalists spoke of four distinct cosmic realms: the realm of the *sefirot* (*atzilut*), the realm of the Separate Intellects (*beriah*), the realm of the celestial bodies (*yetzira*), and the terrestrial, sublunar world (*asiyah*). With Maimonides and his followers, kabbalists identified the ten Separate Intellects, the souls and movers of the celestial spheres, with the angels of the Jewish tradition. But unlike the philosophers, the kabbalists personified the Separate Intellects in accord with Jewish

angelology and gave them a distinct identity. Similarly, the kabbalists depicted the celestial spheres not only in accord with medieval
astronomy and astrology, but also in line with the descriptions of
the heavens in ancient rabbinic sources. Finally, kabbalists gave the
main focus of medieval cosmology and epistemology – the Active Intellect – a new meaning when they incorporated it into the sefirotic
doctrine. Some kabbalists, such as Jacob ben Sheshet, identified it
with the second *sefirah*, *hokhmah* (wisdom),[19] thereby regarding the
intellect as the abstract paradigm of all existence. Other kabbalists
identified the Active Intellect either with the tenth *sefirah*, *malkhut*
or with the angelic being Metatron of ancient Jewish esotericism.[20]
How a given kabbalist interpreted the Active Intellect depended on
the philosophic sources (Aristotelian or Neoplatonic) at the disposal
of the kabbalist and on his general orientation. Be this as it may,
kabbalistic speculations about the structure of the universe were
embedded in the prevalent cosmological theories.

The terrestrial, sublunar realm too was arranged hierarchically.
Made of various blends of four elements (air, water, earth, and fire),
the various beings in the terrestrial world (minerals, plants, and animals) also formed a hierarchy whose zenith was the human being.
For the theosophic kabbalists, nature could be known not through
empirical observation, but through the proper decoding of the sefirotic symbolism, since the *sefirot* constitute the paradigm of all
things. In other words, nature mirrors the essence of God. The best
way to fathom God and nature is to understand the human being,
the microcosmic reflection of the macrocosm. Therefore, theosophic
kabbalah could be said to be simultaneously anthropocentric and
theocentric.

Humans are particularly susceptible to one aspect of reality –
the existence of evil. Here, too, theosophic kabbalists addressed a
philosophical question while giving it a mythical answer. Whereas
Maimonides denied the metaphysical reality of evil, theosophic kabbalah, especially the kabbalists of Castile and the *Zohar*, reified evil
into a full-fledged realm – the *sitrah ahrah* (the "Other Side"). They
went on to describe its population, an assortment of demons ruled by
Samael and his female consort Lilith, and detail their mischievous activities in accordance with ancient and medieval Jewish demonology
and folklore.[21] The kabbalists were fully aware that a stark dualism
of good and evil challenges Jewish monotheism and made efforts to

tone it down by saying that the *sitrah ahrah* lacks vitality and depends on the "negative energy" of external sources. This is provided by human sins that empower Evil, on the one hand, while diminishing the powers of the Good, on the other hand. The paradigmatic sin was Adam's sin in the Garden of Eden.

The Fall of Adam was not an epistemic change from theoretical to practical reasoning, as Maimonides had explained, but the activation of the roots of evil that existed potentially in the deity itself. The first sin was interpreted either as isolation of the masculine and feminine aspects of the divine, and hence the introduction of fragmentation into the divine unity, or as an unbalanced relationship between lovingkindness (the fourth *sefirah, hesed*) and judgment (the fifth *sefirah, gevurah*) within the deity. The result was the reification of the *sitrah ahrah* into a separate domain. In the corporeal world, humans are the main battleground between the forces of Good and Evil, and the responsibility for overpowering evil lies with humans. The task is enormous but not futile, since for kabbalists the revealed Torah itself is the antidote against evil. In the drama between good and evil, Israel played the leading role.

Israel and the Holy Life: From the Many to the One

As much as kabbalistic cosmology reflected the philosophic assumptions of the day, so kabbalistic anthropology and psychology were inseparable from prevalent theories, even though the kabbalists developed their views in response to Maimonidean philosophy. Like the philosophers, the kabbalists understood the human mental-physical complex as a composition of a corporeal body and an incorporeal soul. In theosophic kabbalah as well as in medieval philosophy the term "soul" is ambiguous. It is used to refer both to the soul in contradistinction to the body, as well as to the highest functions of the human soul, the cognitive/spiritual power by which humans can interact with God, as opposed to the lower functions of the soul which are related more closely to the corporeal body. The highest function of the soul captures what is most distinctive about humans. The main difference between Maimonides and the *Zohar* on this score is that when the latter speaks of the human soul it has in mind the soul of one group of people – Israel. For kabbalists, the souls of non-Jews originate from the realm of the Separate Intellects, whereas the souls of Israel are divine particles that originate from the sefirotic realm as a result of the reproductive processes within the Godhead.

The *Zohar* elaborates the myth of the soul in a manner that resembles the narrative in Plato's *Republic* (614c–620d), even though the description moves within the motifs of rabbinic midrash and Jewish esotericism. Contrary to Maimonides who, along with Aristotle, defined the soul as the form of the body, in theosophic kabbalah the soul is an incorporeal, eternal substance that preexists the body and that is, in principle, capable of surviving the death of the body, provided the embodied person manages his or her affairs correctly throughout life. In great detail and with considerable psychological insight, the *Zohar* depicts the coming to be of the soul in terms of conception, impregnation, and birth, and its sad departure from the supernal world as it descends into the human body. The various functions of the soul – the nutritive, appetitive, and rational – are referred to as *nefesh*, *ruah*, and *neshamah* respectively and are correlated with specific *sefirot*. In this way the human being is indeed a reflection of the primordial man.

While the soul resides in the body it is influenced by its own innate proclivity to sin, and therefore the soul's task is to control the corporeal body. If the body has the upper hand over the holy soul, the person is doomed to fall prey to the forces of evil, but if the body is properly managed by the soul, through the performance of the *mitzvot*, the commandments, the human being cannot only suppress the proclivities of the body but also perfect the soul. The purification of the soul through the performance of the commandments is the primary, and most difficult, task of human life. Human life is thus viewed as an arduous, intentional attempt to attain perfection, very much as Maimonides and his followers maintained. But, unlike them, the vehicle for religious perfection was to be found not in intellectual cognition, through the study of philosophy and its related sciences, but in the very performance of the holy sacraments of the Torah. The holiness of the soul could be protected and enhanced through the performance of the commandments, the prescriptions that God gave to Israel, the chosen people.

The difference between theosophic kabbalah and Maimonidean philosophy is most evident in regard to the rationale of the commandments (*ta'amei ha-mitzvot*). Maimonides believed that the specific reasons for the commandments could be known rationally in reference to the particular state of intellectual development of Israel at a given time in history. The theosophic kabbalists, by contrast, viewed the commandments as mysteries whose meaning could be reduced to a rational explanation. How the *mitzvot* are to be performed and how they sanctify Israel by linking the religious practitioner to God could be known only through received tradition. Moreover, the primary purpose of the commandments is not the betterment of human social order, as the philosophers held, but the restoration of the imbalance within the Godhead. This metaphysical imbalance is manifested historically in the exile of the Jewish people and their subordination to the gentiles. Therefore, when Israel performs the commandments correctly, linking each one to the sefirotic world, Israel could correct the imbalance in the life of the individual, the community, the cosmos, and the Godhead. According to kabbalah, then, the observance of God's prescribed commandments is a redemptive activity.

Kabbalistic eschatology manifests similarity to and differences from the Maimonidean approach. Maimonides naturalized the messianic age and diminished the apocalyptic elements of rabbinic speculations about the end of time. Maimonides, instead, focused on the world-to-come that he interpreted to mean a perfect cognitive state that consists in immortal life by the perfected intellect. In principle, those who live in the parameters of the divine law and devote their lives to the cultivation of philosophy have a chance of experiencing the immortality of the intellect. Like Maimonides, the theosophic kabbalists were interested in the salvation of the individual soul and believed that it could be achieved by those who possess the knowledge of kabbalah. But if Maimonides, in principle, could not provide a description of the bliss of immortal life, the *Zohar* was replete with descriptions of the blissful, postmortem world, presumably encountered by the author (or his protagonist) through ecstatic, mystical experiences. Likewise, whereas in most of the *Zohar* there is little overt interest in messianism, in the most obtuse sections of the *Zohar*, as Yehuda Liebes has shown,[22] R. Shimon bar Yohai is depicted as a mystic whose religious perfection at the moment of death heralds the coming of the messianic age. The messianic import of the *Zohar* was fully understood by an anonymous author who imitated the style of the *Zohar* in two compositions *Tiqquney Zohar (The Elaborations of the Zohar)* and the *Ra'aya Mehmna*

(*The Faithful Shepherd*), even though his own views about the *sefirot* varied markedly from the *Zohar*'s. The imitation was sufficiently successful that these texts were considered part of the Zoharic anthology and were printed together.

Soon after its circulation, the *Zohar* itself quickly attracted the respect of other kabbalists, who composed dictionaries to it, imitated its style, and attempted to fathom its meaning. While the *Zohar* was gaining acceptance among a small group of kabbalists, the kabbalah of Abraham Abulafia, by contrast, was rejected as nonauthoritative. The halakhic leader of Aragonese Jewry, R. Solomon ben Adret (known as Rashba), who was himself a theosophic kabbalist and a student of R. Moses ben Nahman, banned the study of Abulafia's work. Not coincidentally, this is the same person who in 1305 imposed a ban on the study of philosophy for students under twenty-five years of age, and who opposed the use of astral magic for medical purposes. The opposition to Abulafia and the reservations about philosophy were closely related, since Abulafia developed his own interpretation of kabbalah on the basis of Maimonides' philosophy, thereby deviating from what Rashba considered the authentic, esoteric tradition.

PHILOSOPHIC APPROACHES TO KABBALAH

Abraham Abulafia's Prophetic Kabbalah

Abraham Abulafia's "prophetic kabbalah" was a creative blend of ancient Jewish esotericism, German Pietism, theosophic kabbalah, and Maimonides' rationalist philosophy. For Abulafia, kabbalah meant first and foremost an uninterrupted transmission of the innermost truths of Judaism from ancient times.[23] Along with Maimonides he believed that the Jews on account of their exile have forgotten these ancient truths and therefore their redemption tarries. Therefore, to bring about redemption, it was necessary to disclose the hidden truths of the Torah so as to enlighten the Jewish people, an urgency shared by rationalist philosophers and theosophic kabbalists as well. Abulafia understood mystical enlightenment precisely as did Maimonides: it is a state of cognitive perfection in which the human intellect unites with the Active Intellect and receives from it divine overflow. This was intellectual mysticism par excellence, which the prophet Moses has attained, and apparently Abulafia believed that he too had reached the exalted state, thus giving his opponents good reason to suspect him.

Within the received tradition, Abulafia distinguished between two sets of teachings: the kabbalah of the *sefirot* and the kabbalah of divine names. In several works Abulafia spoke quite harshly and critically against those who believed that the *sefirot* are hypostatic potencies that do not compromise the unity of God.[24] Abulafia adhered to the philosophic conception of divine simplicity and regarded the theosophic position as tantamount to heresy and analogous to the Christian doctrine of the Trinity. Nonetheless, Abulafia studied the works of the theosophic kabbalists "and in some cases appropriated their symbolism and mode of disclosure."[25] But if the *sefirot* are not the essence of God, what are they? Abulafia held that the *sefirot* are identical with the Separate Intellects and contain the ideal, intelligible forms. The ten *sefirot* are the "conduits that channel the divine overflow and thus act as the forces that unify God's energy in the universe."[26] In accord with the cosmological doctrine of Maimonides, in which a lower intellect contains the knowledge of the intellect above it, Abulafia could reasonably claim that the Active Intellect contains all ten *sefirot* (similarly, the theosophic kabbalists held that *malkhut*, the last, tenth *sefirah*, contains all the *sefirot* above it). Accordingly, Abulafia found the word *kol* (meaning "all") the most appropriate symbol of the Active Intellect, the Intellect in charge of all processes in the sublunar world and the source of all knowledge. This identification would play a role in the attempts to coordinate philosophy and kabbalah during the fourteenth century.

The identification of the *sefirot* with the Separate Intellects, all contained within the Active Intellect, was the key to Abulafia's anthropocentric interpretation of the doctrine, on the one hand, and to his intellectual mysticism, on the other hand. For the Aristotelian philosophers, the Separate Intellects were the rational souls of the living, celestial bodies. They presumably explained the perfect circular motion of celestial spheres as well as motion and change in the terrestrial, sublunar world. Abulafia took this cosmological doctrine and gave it an anthropological or psychological interpretation.[27] For Abulafia, the *sefirot* are internal states of human experiences, they are part of the human psyche, since the human is a microcosm of the macrocosm. Knowledge of the *sefirot* is a form of self-knowledge, a process that requires the acquisition of moral and intellectual virtues and that culminates in the conjunction between the human intellect and the Active Intellect. This cognitive union is prophecy, a reception of divine efflux from God through the Active Intellect, precisely as Maimonides and his Muslim sources explained. The kabbalah of the *sefirot*, anthropologically or psychologically interpreted, is thus the highest example of the philosophic maxim "Know Thyself."

The main obstacle to self-knowledge is the corporeal body itself, especially the power of imagination. However, the Jewish tradition itself, according to Abulafia, also reveals the way to break through human embodiment and to free oneself from the errors of human imagination. This is the highest form of kabbalah, "the path of the [divine] names" (*derekh ha-shemot*), which is religiously superior to knowledge of the *sefirot*. Building on the linguistic theory of *Sefer Yetzira* and the mystical practices of the German Pietists, Abulafia articulated exegetical, meditative and contemplative techniques that purportedly result in a mystical union with God. However, with the theosophic kabbalists Abulafia rooted the mystical path in the Hebrew language itself, which he regarded as the "mother of all languages" because it is "in accord with nature."[28] God chose Hebrew to be the language for the creation of the universe because of the unique, perfect properties of Hebrew.

To know how Hebrew serves as the medium of creation the practitioner of kabbalah had to break down the sacred language into its atomic components – the Hebrew letters – and recombine their numerical value according to a particular code, a code that Abulafia derived from the principles of Maimonides' philosophy. This contemplative human activity, one can surmise, was probably one of the reasons why Ibn Adret opposed Abulafia's kabbalah, because Abulafia gave the human exegete an activist role in the exegetical process. For Abulafia, however, there was no contradiction between reception of tradition and the creative, intellectual activity. In fact, the contemplative activity of letter combination (in Hebrew, *harkavah*) was the deepest meaning of *ma'aseh merkavah*, as far as Abulafia was concerned. Abulafia was deeply convinced that his letter combination as well as the visualization of letters was the practice that broke through the limits of human embodiment and brought about the liberation of the rational soul from the shackles of the body. Abulafia defined this cognitive state as prophecy.

Abulafia's kabbalah was not merely a theoretical endeavor but a full-fledged, experiential program to achieve paranormal psychic states that culminate in a mystical union with the Active Intellect. As a result, the human intellect attains immortality, precisely as Maimonides taught. In addition to the performance of the commandments and rigorous learning of philosophy and its sciences, Abulafia's program included seclusion, breathing, physical postures, recitation of the divine names, visualization of letters, and letter combination.[29] Most of these techniques were developed on the basis of existing Jewish practices, but some have analogues in other mystical systems, mainly Sufism, and perhaps were influenced by the contact Abulafia had with Sufis during his travels in Palestine and in the Balkans.

Following Maimonides, Abulafia understood prophecy as a mystical union between the human intellect and the Active Intellect. At that moment of union the intellectually perfect human receives the "Word of God" that contains the ten *sefirot*, which are, in turn, contained in the Active Intellect.[30] Knowledge of the Active Intellect thus amounts to knowledge of the mysteries of the Torah, the primordial paradigm that God consulted in the creation of the world. It follows that the prophet, who is the intellectually perfect man, also possesses the knowledge of the created world. Though Abulafia himself was not interested in the operation of the natural world, his philosophy could lead one to a keen interest in nature as well as to the desire to manipulate nature, that is to engage in magic. This was made clear during the fourteenth century among philosophers who engaged in astrology and in astral magic and who interpreted the Torah as a scientific-astrological text, even though they developed their views independently of Abulafia.

Since Abulafia believed that he actually attained ultimate cognitive perfection and possessed the inner meaning of the Torah, it is no surprise that he viewed himself both as a prophet (along the lines of Maimonides' theory of prophecy) and as a messiah (also in accord with Maimonides' naturalist and intellectualist understanding of messianism). In Sicily during the early 1290s Abulafia was actively engaged in messianic propaganda. With Maimonides, however, he interpreted redemption in radical spiritual terms: he shifted

redemption from the historical to the psychological realm, minimized the catastrophic elements of popular Jewish eschatology, and
did not advocate the departure of the Jews from the diaspora. Although his messianism was highly individual, his political activism
was rebuffed by the papal authority.[31] While Ibn Adret's opposition to
Abulafia limited the dissemination of his works in Spain, Abulafia's
works were preserved in Sicily and southern Italy and would be the
main source for knowledge of kabbalah during the fifteenth century.
Moreover, Abulafia's notion that the *sefirot* are identical with the
Separate Intellect became the basis of attempts to coordinate philosophy and kabbalah in Spain and Provence during the fourteenth
century. These attempts were fused with a renewed interest in the
philosophy of Abraham ibn Ezra and the cultivation of astrology and
astral magic.

Coordinating Philosophy and Kabbalah

During the fourteenth century, Jewish philosophy in Spain and
Provence was dominated by the legacy of Maimonides; all Jewish
philosophers saw themselves as interpreters of Maimonides. However, by this time Aristotle's philosophy was better understood,
because Aristotle was now studied through the commentaries of
Averroes. Averroes' metaphysics differed from Maimonides' in that
Averroes explicitly identified God with the First Intellect and thus
softened the radical Otherness of God. In the *Long Commentary on
Metaphysics* and in the *Tahafut al-Tahafut (The Incoherence of the
Incoherence)* Averroes explained that each of the Separate Intellects
cognizes God and that by thinking himself God thinks all existents
in the most perfect and noblest way. God could thus be viewed as the
principle and cause of the hierarchy of existents and the intelligible
order of the universe.

The Averroean position became the standard exposition of Aristotle in the fourteenth century and it facilitated the attempts to
coordinate kabbalah and philosophy. If the Active Intellect is the
intelligible order of the universe (*siddur ha-nimtza'ot*), knowledge
of the Active Intellect, namely, scientific knowledge, consisted of
knowledge of the sublunar world. Hence it was appropriate to speak
about the Active Intellect as the "All," the abstract paradigm of the
sublunar world. This understanding of the word "All," however,

could be found already in the twelfth century in the writings of Abraham ibn Ezra, the biblical exegete, grammarian, Neoplatonic philosopher, mathematician, astronomer, astrologer, and poet.[32] His terse and cryptic commentaries on the Torah became the focus of intense scrutiny during the fourteenth century by Jewish philosophers who considered him a superb metaphysician. Thirty supercommentaries on Ibn Ezra's biblical commentaries were composed in the fourteenth century,[33] illustrating how Ibn Ezra's religious naturalism and interest in astrology is compatible with Averroes' philosophy.[34]

One cryptic comment in Ibn Ezra's biblical commentary became crucial to the attempts to read kabbalah into Aristotelian philosophy. In his commentary on Numbers 20:8 Ibn Ezra said: "Know that when the 'part' knows the All [kol], it conjoins with the All, and through the All it creates signs and wonders." This comment, cited as a support of the notion of conjunction between the human intellect and the Active Intellect, enables the human to know the natural order and to manipulate it. If humans can know the pattern of the sublunar world, as it is known to the Active Intellect, humans can know how nature works and they can intervene or manipulate natural processes by virtue of the spiritual power they possess. This view went hand in hand with Ibn Ezra's claim that the intellectually perfect man, that is the prophet, can perform miracles as much as it was in accord with Ibn Ezra's keen interest in astrology.[35] Unlike Maimonides, who rejected the scientific validity of astrology,[36] Ibn Ezra saw it as a valid science that has practical benefits if the spiritual efflux that originates from the celestial sphere can be harnessed. One way to harness the spiritual energy of the stars was to create icons that presumably captured the energy and applied it to healing inflicted people. This practice became disputed in the last phase of the Maimonidean controversy, and Abba Mari, who asked Ibn Adret to place philosophy and science under a ban, agitated primarily against the use of astral magic in medicine.[37]

Among the Jewish philosophers who composed supercommentaries on Abraham ibn Ezra the attitude toward kabbalah was not uniform. Some of them – such as Solomon al-Kostantini, Samuel ibn Zarza, and Shem Tov ibn Shaprut – were either indifferent to kabbalah or even opposed it. Al-Kostantini, for example, regarded kabbalah as a form of fideism antithetical to rational inquiry. Likewise, Ibn Zarza rarely mentioned kabbalists and definitely did not take their teachings seriously.[38] But others – such as Joseph ibn Waqar, Moses Narboni, and Samuel ibn Motot (or ibn Matut), who were influenced by Judah ben Nissim ibn Malka,[39] were much more open to kabbalah and attempted to reconcile philosophy and kabbalah within a hierarchy of being and a hierarchy of knowledge. Thus, according to Ibn Waqar, astrology pertains to the events in the sublunar world, philosophy (i.e. physics and metaphysics) provides information about the supralunar world of the Separate Intellects, and kabbalah consists of gnosis of the divine world that could not be known without divine assistance.[40]

A typical example of someone who attempts to fit kabbalistic terminology into the philosophic schema is Moses ben Joshua Narboni (d. 1362). He illustrates how an Aristotelian philosopher, steeped in Averroes' commentaries on Aristotle, could coordinate philosophy and kabbalah on the basis of the cryptic comments of Abraham ibn Ezra.[41] Narboni wrote a commentary on Averroes' *Epistle on the Possibility of Conjunction between the Human and the Divine Intellect*, in which he detailed the theory that intellectual perfection is possible in this life. This is precisely the view of Abulafia, except that Narboni proceeded to prove it within the contours of Averroes' theory of knowledge.[42] Narboni's optimism about the capacity of the human intellect is also evident in his commentary on Ibn Tufayl's *Hayy ibn Yaqzan*, a philosophical novel that illustrated how intellectual perfection could be attained even by a person who grows up in total isolation from human society or by a person who lives in an imperfect political regime. In that commentary Narboni coordinated the ten *sefirot* and the ten Separate Intellects, following Ibn Waqar, even though the details of Narboni are quite idiosyncratic.[43] The *sefirot* are correlated to the celestial spheres as follows: the first *sefirah*, *keter*, is correlated to the all-encompassing, starless sphere; the second *sefirah*, *hokhmah*, is correlated with the sphere of the fixed stars; and the third *sefirah*, *binah*, is correlated with Saturn. It is not clear whether *keter* is identified with Eyn Sof or not, but since at one point Narboni does refer to God as *keter* it stands to reason that he was a consistent Averroean and understood God (or Eyn Sof) to be identical with the First Intellect, and hence the First Mover. The lower seven *sefirot* do not correspond exactly to the terminology of theosophic kabbalah, but it is obvious that they are based on some version of it. The fourth *sefirah, hesed,* is also called *tiferet* and corresponds to Jupiter; *netzah* corresponds to Mars; *hod* to the sun; *malkhut* to Venus; and *me'on zedek* to Mercury. *Yesod* corresponds to the moon, and the tenth *sefirah* is called *kallah* or *knesset Israel,* the collective symbol of Israel, which Narboni identifies with the Active Intellect, the intelligible order of the sublunar world. This correlation of the Separate Intellect with the *sefirot* indicates that for Narboni philosophy and kabbalah were two systems that had different names for the same spiritual entities.

Similarly Narboni advanced a philosophical reading of the *Shiur Qomah,* grafting Averroean metaphysics onto Ibn Ezra's comment about *Shiur Qomah* in Exodus 22:13 and in *Yesod Mora.* According to Narboni, *Shiur Qomah* is but a figurative expression for Averroes' idea that God is the "Form of the World," in which all things exist in a perfect and noble way. In other words, whereas the theosophic kabbalists understood the *Shiur Qomah* to refer to the sefirotic structure within the Godhead, Narboni understood it to refer to the intelligible order of the world that includes both corporeal and spiritual dimensions. Since most philosophers agreed that the human being is a microcosm of the macrocosm, the anthropomorphism of the *Shiur Qomah* was not problematic theologically. The human being is but a prism in which the structure of reality is reflected. For Narboni, kabbalah and philosophy were parallel speculative systems that gave different names to the same cosmic or metaphysical entities.

The return to pre-Maimonidean philosophers involved not only Abraham ibn Ezra but also Judah Halevi, whose *Kuzari* included a long discussion of *Sefer Yetzira.* In Provence at the turn of the fifteenth century a group of scholars – Isaac de Lates, Prat Maimon (Solomon ben Menahem), and his students Jacob Farisol, Nethanel Kaspi, and Solomon ben Judah of Lunel – composed commentaries on Halevi's *Kuzari* and advanced a new Jewish theology that was deeply steeped in astrology. The Provençal scholars were all admirers of Levi ben Abraham of Villefranche, the cause célèbre of the final phase of the Maimonidean controversy. That scholar advocated the scientific validity of astrology, the effectiveness of drawing spiritual energy for human needs, and the permissibility of astral magic on halakhic grounds. For him, the stars do influence human physical well being as manifested in human health and sickness, and they even determine the forms for corporeal things. Hence the use of talismans and other icons of the stars to draw spiritual energy downward is beneficial and halakhically permissible.[44]

Following Levi ben Abraham, Prat Maimon, for example, regarded the spiritual energy of the sun to be the source of religious and intellectual virtues, including the attainment of prophecy. To absorb the spiritual energy, proper preparation is necessary; a special place and an icon should be used for the purpose of attaining prophetic overflow. Thus the sacrifices of ancient Israel were explained as mediums that enabled Israel's priests to focus their imagination as they engaged in the prognostication of the future, in their attempts to draw spiritual energy from the supernal world for the benefit of Israel. This view was shared by Moses Narboni and Nissim of Marseilles as well as by Prat Maimon and his student Nethanel Kaspi. The latter two scholars regarded the ancient Temple as an elaborate talisman to draw the heavenly energy to earth, and they believed that certain locations were more apt to receive the supernal overflow than others. This notion, however, was not endorsed by Levi ben Abraham, for whom the Temple was not a talisman, but strictly a symbol of eternal truths about the heavenly spheres that should be contemplated rather than used for any benefit.

Interpreting the biblical past in light of astrology and astrological magic was just another expression of the rationalist assumption that Scripture is a scientific text, an assumption that was shared both by followers of Maimonides and by Abulafia. Since Scripture is necessarily true and astrology is a true science, the Torah must be read in light of the science of astrology. Writing super-commentaries on Abraham ibn Ezra's biblical commentaries was the most effective way to prove that congruence. Out of this astrological reading of the Torah a full-fledged astral theology emerged, whose main tenets are the following themes: the Torah was given at Sinai on the basis of astrological calculations; biblical events reflect the influences of the stars, and biblical personalities and rabbinic sages were expert astrologers; prophecy is predicated on knowledge of astrology; miracles are understood to be the results of the prophet's intellectual perfection. Further, Moses was able to overcome the Egyptian magicians, because he was a superior astrologer. His intellectual perfection included the knowledge of astrology, culminating in the conjunction between his intellect and the Active Intellect. He was a practicing magician who correctly understood the causal link between earthly and celestial powers. The knowledge of astrology enables the intellectually perfect to extricate themselves from astral causality. Moreover, the uniqueness of the people of Israel is explained by its ability to transcend the impact of astral causality through mastery of the astrological sciences. Most importantly, the commandments themselves function as tools in the manipulation of astral forces. The commandments either manifest the influence of a given celestial body or are given as techniques to draw spiritual energy from the celestial spheres into the corporeal world. In this regard the commandments mitigate the destructive forces of the corporeal world that are regulated by the celestial bodies. Observance of the commandments thus has an instrumental value, for the more consistently one performs them, the more one can extricate oneself from the impact of the stars.

In short, by the turn of the fifteenth century philosopher-scientists proposed a strictly naturalistic interpretation for the Torah on the basis of astral determinism. Given this theology, it is easy to understand how philosopher-scientists could also be interested in kabbalah not only as a speculative system, but also as a praxis that included use of talismans, amulets, incantations, and divinations. The best example of such a thinker is Yohanan Alemanno in Italy.

Intellectual Perfection, Kabbalah, and Magic

The philosophic approach to kabbalah was most characteristic of Jewish intellectual activity in Italy during the late fifteenth century and throughout the sixteenth century. The best example is Yohanan Alemanno, who fused Halakhah, biblical exegesis, philosophy, science, kabbalah, and magic into a coherent system, illustrating the Renaissance ideal of comprehensive learning. Alemanno was a student of Judah ben Yehiel Messer Leon, an outstanding Aristotelian Jewish philosopher, whose philosophic and medical expertise was recognized by Christian society. He was awarded a medical degree by Emperor Frederick III in the 1450s, along with the unusual privilege to grant degrees to Jewish students. Alemanno received the honorary degree from his Jewish teacher, though Alemanno's own social standing derived not from it but from the patronage of the wealthiest Jewish banker in Florence, R. Yehiel Nissim of Pisa.

Alemanno also departed from his revered teacher in regard to the study of kabbalah.

In the 1470s kabbalah was beginning to attract the interest of Christian humanists, who revived the Platonic tradition in their search for the ancient *prisca theologica* that they believed culminated in the truths of Christianity. Because Christian humanists maintained that kabbalah was part of this knowledge, they treated kabbalah with deep respect, regarded it as the only true insight of Judaism, and had kabbalistic texts translated into Latin. Flavius Mithridates, the most prolific translator of kabbalistic texts into Latin, also added his own forgeries of kabbalistic texts and finally converted to Christianity. The translated texts included primarily the works of Abulafia and of the Italian kabbalist R. Menahem Rencanati.[45] The *Zohar*, by contrast, was relatively unknown in Italy until the last decade of the fifteenth century, when copies of it were brought to Italy with refugees of the expulsion.[46] Judah Messer Leon was very concerned about the interest of non-Jews in kabbalah and their missionizing successes, and attempted to ban the study of kabbalah in Italy, but to no avail. Judah Messer Leon's own son, David, and the father's best students, Yohanan Alemanno and Abraham de Balmes, were all interested in kabbalah and studied it despite their master's disapproval.

In Italy, kabbalah was viewed as a type of speculative lore. It was studied auto-didactically from extant texts without the supervision of authoritative mentors. The absence of authoritative traditions, and the limited knowledge of the *Zohar*, facilitated a degree of hermeneutical freedom that was not common in Spain. A scholar interested in kabbalah could rely on his own intellectual powers in the interpretation of kabbalistic texts and articulate his own peculiar reading of kabbalah on the basis of his philosophic knowledge, precisely as Abraham Abulafia had done. This, in turn, further enhanced the image of kabbalah as an ancient, theoretical science with a universal appeal, rather than as a set of practices for the proper observance of Jewish law. It is no surprise that in Italy Christian humanists could view kabbalah as an integral part of universal, ancient wisdom and would desire to learn it from Jewish masters. Yohanan Alemanno and David Messer Leon are examples of philosophic approaches to kabbalah common among Jewish intellectuals in Italy. About the *sefirot*, however, there was no agreement among them.

Whereas Alemanno held that the *sefirot* were the instruments of divine activity, David Messer Leon viewed them as the essence of God that exists in God in the most perfect manner, as Thomas Aquinas understood divine perfections.[47] During the sixteenth century Alemanno's fusion of philosophy, kabbalah, and magic prevailed in Italy, whereas David Messer Leon fled Italy to the Ottoman Empire in 1494. Although his view of the *sefirot* as the essence of God was in accord with the prevalent Zoharic position, his philosophic exposition of the doctrine was rejected by Iberian kabbalists.

Alemanno mastered the entire scope of Jewish biblical, halakhic, and philosophic learning. In addition he also studied alchemy, astrology, astral medicine, physiognomy, dream interpretation, and talismanic magic from a vast array of sources including the recently published Hermetic corpus, the works of Arabic Neoplatonic philosophers (e.g. Batalyawsi), the Jewish Neoplatonic philosophers (e.g. Ibn Ezra, Ibn Zarza, Ibn Motot), medieval magical and astrological manuals (e.g. the *Ghayat al-Hakim* and *Book of the Palm-Date*), and kabbalah. From these highly diverse sources, Alemanno developed an organic view of nature in which there is no meaningful distinction between the animate and the inanimate, and in which bodies exert influences on each other through sympathies and antipathies. Projecting mind into nature, Alemanno endowed all existing things with spirit, which served as the locus and carrier of active life and perception. In this organically ordered universe the spiritual could penetrate the physical or, more precisely, a spiritual energy assumed material forms.

Alemanno's interest in the manipulation of nature was related to the views of his fourteenth-century philosophic sources and Abulafia's mysticism of language. For Alemanno (who was an ardent student of Abulafia's writings), the mastery of nature and the mystical union with God were possible through the manipulation of the Hebrew letters, the "building blocks" of the universe. Whoever breaks the limits of human embodiment through various contemplative and meditative techniques and proper exegesis of the exoteric Torah can "tap into" the spiritual energy of the Godhead and channel the divine efflux into the corporeal world, either into his own body or into material objects. Through self-spiritualization, the magician-philosopher may control natural substances, prognosticate future events, heal the physically and mentally afflicted, attain a temporary union with God in this life, and enjoy the bliss of immortality in the afterlife. The prototype of the perfect man was King Solomon. To his *Commentary on Song of Songs*, entitled *Heshek Shlomo* (*The Desire of Solomon*), which Alemanno had composed in 1488 for his student Pico della Mirandola, Alemanno appended a biography of King Solomon, entitled *Shir ha-Ma'alot* (*The Song of Solomon's Virtues*).[48]

King Solomon was the highest example of the Renaissance magus: a person who acquired all the virtues and apprehended all the arts and the sciences that Alemanno presented in an architectonic order. Like Abulafia, Alemanno composed his book as a practical manual for religio-intellectual perfection to be attained *in this life*, culminating in the conjunction of the human intellect with God, or, more precisely, with *tiferet*, the sixth *sefirah* and center of the serifotic realm. Presumably the one who follows the detailed recipe for perfection provided by Alemanno would experience perfection in this life, as did Solomon. The perfect man, as Idel has put it, is "an accomplished philosopher, a magician and theurgian, and finally a mystic."[49] Alemanno's view that the perfect man was indeed an intermediary between the corporeal and the spiritual levels of reality became a prominent theme of Renaissance philosophy when it was adopted by his disciple, Pico della Mirandola. And Alemanno's linguistic approach to nature would influence Pico's nephew, Alberto Pio, as well as Yohannes Reuchlin.

Whereas Christian humanists were impressed by Alemanno, his fusion of philosophy and kabbalah raised the ire of his own Jewish contemporaries. Aristotelian philosophers, such as Elijah del Medigo, found it intellectually unacceptable, and the recent refugees from Spain who accepted the authority of the *Zohar* and its theosophic-theurgic doctrines did not regard Alemanno's fusion of philosophy and kabbalah as authoritative. In the first half of the sixteenth century, Jewish intellectuals such as Jacob Mantino, Obadia Sforno, Moses Provenzzalo, and Azariah Figo continued to perpetuate the Aristotelian tradition in Italy's universities and were instrumental in the printing of Averroes' commentaries on the Aristotelian corpus. Yet, the involvement of Jewish scholars with Renaissance Aristotelianism was overshadowed by the popularity of Platonism, which also found a responsive chord among Jewish thinkers. For example, Judah Moscato composed a commentary on Yehuda Halevi's

Kuzari, entitled *Qol Yehudah* (*The Voice of Judah*) that treated the long discourse on *Sefer Yetzira* in light of the non-Aristotelian philosophies of nature prevalent in the sixteenth century. Displaying an impressive command of Aristotelian and Neoplatonic philosophy, kabbalah, Renaissance humanism, and Hermeticism, Moscato posed a hierarchical relationship between human knowledge and divinely revealed knowledge.[50] All branches of natural philosophy are now deemed to be but finite, imperfect approximations of the infinite, divine wisdom revealed in the Torah and interpreted by the authoritative tradition. The same mindset is evident also in Abraham Yagel, who followed in the footsteps of Alemanno. Going beyond the parameters of Aristotle's natural philosophy, he was immersed in the new scientific discoveries in astronomy, human physiology, botany, zoology, and mineralogy, while also wishing to capture the occult powers of nature through the study of kabbalah, alchemy, astrology, and magic.[51]

KABBALAH AS AUTHORITATIVE JEWISH THEOLOGY

Whereas in Italy the fusion of philosophy and kabbalah reflected the distinctive intellectual climate of the Renaissance, in Spain the interplay of the two programs was shaped by the tragic events of 1391. The year-long persecution destroyed thousands of Jewish communities and brought about the unprecedented event of collective apostasy to Christianity. These events led the Jewish intelligentsia to a thorough self-examination of their cultural orientation. Since philosophy was the hallmark of Judeo-Hispanic culture, philosophy, the philosophic paideia, and the philosophers were all placed on the defensive as the cause of the failure of Jews to uphold the ancestral faith. These accusations were advanced by moralists such as Solomon Al'ami, who railed against the moral breakdown of Hispano-Jewish society in general, as well as by Shem Tov ibn Shem Tov, a trained philosopher who despaired of Jewish Aristotelianism and was to embrace kabbalah as the correct interpretation of rabbinic Judaism. His *Sefer ha-Emunot* (*Book of Beliefs*) is a summary of kabbalistic teachings that were culled from extant texts rather than from a living teacher. The influence of kabbalah on philosophy was also evident in the case of Hasdai Crescas (d. 1410/11), the most severe critic of Maimonidean philosophy. Crescas' own analysis of divine attributes as essential attributes was directly indebted to the kabbalistic doctrine of *sefirot* and the kabbalistic conception of infinity.[52]

Despite growing skepticism about philosophy, educated Jews continued to cultivate the study of philosophy and regard it as necessary for the attainment of religious perfection. Furthermore, philosophy entered the curriculum of certain yeshivot in Castile and helped to shape halakhic discourse. Aristotelian logic was employed to understand God's revealed word with scientific precision. It is very plausible that the penetration of philosophy into the very heart of rabbinic training in academies of higher Jewish learning prompted the demonization of philosophy by a group of anonymous kabbalists in Castile who composed *Sefer ha-Meshiv* (*The Book of the Answering Angel*).[53] They regarded philosophy not only as alien to Judaism, but also as inherently evil, a manifestation of the *sitrah ahrah*. According to *Sefer ha-Meshiv*, the mysteries of the infinite Torah could not be known through the inquiries of the philosophers and their astrological manipulations, but from direct revelations by an angelic being. Using specific techniques for conjuring angels or through methods of dream interpretation, these anonymous kabbalists claimed to have disclosed the eschatological meaning of Scripture, promising imminent redemption.

Among the intellectual elite in Iberian Jewry there was no sharp dichotomy between philosophy and kabbalah. The same scholars who preserved the Aristotelian tradition also had a positive attitude toward kabbalah and regarded the *Zohar* as an authentic, ancient midrash. Kabbalah was now regarded an integral part of the authoritative, revealed tradition that transcends the limits of natural human reason. In fact, the philosophers themselves accentuated the inability of philosophy alone to bring about human salvation, a view that was developed in the context of the intense polemics with Christianity. As Jewish philosophers became more familiar with Christian Scholasticism, they realized that Christianity could no longer be dismissed as intellectually inferior to Judaism. Under the influence of Scholasticism, Jewish thinkers adopted the formal distinction between philosophy and theology as articulated by Thomas Aquinas.

During the second half of the fifteenth century Jewish philosophers differentiated between rationalist, empirical philosophy (*derekh ha-haqirah; derekh ha-hipus*) and traditional, received faith (*derekh ha-emunah ve-ha-qabbalah*), which parallels the distinction between philosophy (or natural theology) and theology (or sacred doctrine) respectively. Philosophy and theology differed from each other in terms of origin, scope, and aim. Whereas philosophy consists of truths that natural human reason can demonstrate without divine assistance, theology contains true propositions that exceed the ken of natural human reason. Whereas philosophy proceeds from knowledge of the effect to knowledge of the cause, theology proceeds from knowledge of the cause to knowledge of the effects. Whereas philosophy encompasses knowledge extracted from sensible, created things, theology contains revealed knowledge about the supernatural realm of divine things. Whereas philosophy is prone to errors, mistakes, and uncertainty, theology is certain, reliable, and complete. Whereas philosophical wisdom is a cognitive activity of the intellect, theology involves the assent of the will through faith. Whereas philosophy alone falls short of securing personal immortality and can at best guarantee earthly happiness, the sacred doctrines of theology are salvific, securing transcendent happiness in the world to come.

The distinction between "the path of investigation" and "the path of faith" paralleled the distinction between the natural and supernatural orders of reality. According to Isaac Abravanel, Abraham Bibago, Abraham Shalom, and Isaac Arama, Israel (both collectively and individually) belongs simultaneously to the natural and supernatural orders. As created human beings, the affairs of Israel fall under the laws of nature, whose regularity and stability manifest God's wisdom and general, providential care for the created universe. On this level, all events can be known scientifically, especially by employing the science of astrology. Yet Israel also benefits from special, direct, and particular providence that transcends natural determinism and is not transparent to human reason. God's revelation at Sinai was a miraculous event, expressing God's free will and divine intervention in nature. As such the revelation from God was not predicated on perfection of the natural human intellect and therefore encompassed all of Israel, regardless of its degree of intellectual perfection. With the giving of the Torah, Israel was governed directly by the will of God. Israel's affairs therefore manifested the believers' faith in God and willingness to observe the Torah's commandments.

Within this schema Jewish philosophers viewed the specific doctrines of kabbalah as an integral part of Jewish sacred doctrine, or theology, even though their knowledge of kabbalah was quite limited.

The gradual acceptance of kabbalah as authoritative interpretation went hand in hand with the gradual veneration of the *Zohar* among Sephardic intellectuals and the portrayal of R. Shimon bar Yohai, the presumed author of the *Zohar*, as an example of the perfect human being. The antiquity of the *Zohar* was cited as evidence for the antiquity and authority of kabbalah, for example by Judah Abravanel, himself an Aristotelian thinker who was also fully immersed in Renaissance humanism.[54]

The expulsion from Spain and the horrendous suffering it inflicted on Iberian Jews further contributed to the gradual acceptance of kabbalah as the authoritative interpretation of the revealed tradition. After the expulsion there was both growing opposition to philosophy and even a renewal of the debate about Maimonides, as well as the consolidation and systematization of five centuries of philosophical activity. Criticism of philosophy was voiced by Joseph Ya'abetz, one of the exiles, who found his way to Italy. Ya'abetz was schooled in Aristotelianism and continued to reflect on Judaism in the framework of Maimonidean rationalism. But Ya'abetz opposed a certain (possible) interpretation of Maimonides according to which philosophy alone is salvific and the Torah is but the socio-political context in which one could attain philosophical perfection. Instead, Ya'abetz highlighted the qualitative difference between philosophic, discursive knowledge and prophetic knowledge, and demanded the subordination of philosophy to the revealed tradition. So long as philosophy was properly employed to articulate the meaning of divine revealed propositions, it was permissible for Jews to engage in philosophy. This view was common even among Sephardic exiles, who expressly asserted the superiority of kabbalah over philosophy and who were creative kabbalists, such as Solomon Alkabetz and Moses Cordovero.

Whether or not the expulsion from Spain was the direct cause of the proliferation of kabbalah in the sixteenth century is still debated. Idel has argued that there was no causal connection between the expulsion and the rise of sixteenth-century messianism or the dissemination of kabbalah. Other factors, such as the impulse to preserve kabbalistic oral traditions and the encounter between the Sephardic kabbalists and kabbalists in Italy and in Greece, were no less important. However, it seems that expulsion itself did inspire the need for consolidation and systematization of kabbalistic traditions, giving rise to systematic "summa kabbalistica," so to speak, by Meir ibn Gabbai and by Moses Cordovero. Although both presenters of kabbalah were steeped in philosophy, their consolidation of kabbalah actually elaborated the mythical dimensions of the received tradition. The very exposure of Sephardic kabbalists to other forms of kabbalah itself necessitated rethinking and reformulating kabbalah.

One feature of the postexpulsion period was the rise of the *Zohar* as a canonic, sacred text in certain Jewish communities.[55] An important impetus to the dissemination of kabbalah in the sixteenth century was the printing of the *Zohar* in Italy by two Christian publishing houses in Mantua and in Cremona (1558 and 1559). Although this event was accompanied by a heated public controversy about the propriety of publicizing secret, oral traditions, there was no doubt that the interest of Christian scholars in the *Zohar* and its publication, five years after the burning of the Talmud, added to its prestige. In some communities, especially in North Africa, the *Zohar* was also regarded as a holy book that had to be treated as a sacred object because it contains occult powers that can heal or bring other concrete benefits. And in Safed the study of the *Zohar* was the main activity of the kabbalistic fraternity that modeled itself after the kabbalistic fraternity depicted in the *Zohar*. Under the leadership of Isaac Luria, the kabbalists of Safed elaborated the mythical and anthropomorphic aspects of Zoharic theosophy and its concomitant sacramental understanding of Jewish rituals. In Safed, the *Zohar* was also regarded as an authoritative source in terms of Jewish law, and several rituals entered Jewish practice solely on the authority of the *Zohar* when Joseph Karo codified them into his code of Jewish law, the *Shulhan Arukh (Prepared Table)*.[56]

The acceptance of the *Zohar* as a canonic text influenced Jewish philosophy in the Ottoman Empire during the sixteenth century. The Sephardic exiles recovered from their trauma by devoting their energies to consolidating their Judeo-Hispanic cultural legacy, including philosophy. The exiles and their descendants composed philosophical encyclopaedias and digests, continued to comment on Aristotle, and treated Maimonides with utmost respect. However, especially in Salonica, philosophic knowledge was viewed as the handmaiden of the hermeneutics of sacred texts. Creatively weaving philosophy with midrash and kabbalah, thinkers such as Meir Arama, Joseph Taitatzak, Meir Aderbi, Isaac Arroyo, Moses Almosnino, and Moses

Alsheikh elaborated their exegetical and homiletical activities in their pursuit of holiness.[57]

The impact of kabbalah on philosophy is most evident in the conception of Torah. Philosophers identified the Torah with the essence of God, and accordingly viewed the revealed Torah as the manifestation of the transcendent, supernal, primordial Torah, which they then identified with the infinite wisdom of God. Under the influence of kabbalah, those who cultivated philosophy now asserted that the Torah comprised the name of God. Still loyal to an Aristotelian hierarchical cosmology, the philosophers located the supernal Torah above the realm of immaterial beings that are not governed by the laws of motion and temporal change. Identified with God's wisdom, the supernal Torah is the intelligible order of the universe, the paradigm that God consulted when he brought the universe into existence. By cleaving to the revealed Torah (through Torah study and the performance of the commandments), the religious devotee could attain a spiritual perfection, overcome the limits of human corporeality and particularity, and enjoy the spiritual reward of the world to come, a mystical union with God.

This view led to paradoxical results. On the one hand, the autonomy of philosophy was curtailed as the philosopher became primarily an interpreter of sacred texts, whose infinite meaning was never fully exhausted. On the other hand, philosophical vocabulary and reasoning became more widely known among the educated classes, and philosophical esotericism reached its end. Philosophy was now viewed as a useful method for the exposition of the exoteric meaning of the sacred tradition; the esoteric dimension was reserved to kabbalah. The fact that the very people who studied philosophy also recognized the limitations of philosophy and subordinated it to kabbalah went hand in hand with the gradual dissolution of Aristotelianism. With the rise of new observational data and new physical theories, the Neoplatonized Aristotelianism that characterized Jewish rationalism reached an end by the turn of the seventeenth century.

The interface between philosophy and kabbalah continued in the early seventeenth century, especially among former *conversos*. For Abraham Cohen Herrera, for example, the elaborate myths of Lurianic kabbalah were totally compatible with Renaissance Platonism, even though kabbalah was not reducible to Platonism.[58]

Exposed to Lurianic kabbalah through the teachings of Israel Sarug, Herrera diminished the messianic orientation of Luria as he interprets the stark anthropomorphism of Lurianic kabbalah philosophically. By the mid-seventeenth century, however, Spinoza, the child of former *conversos*, dealt the most serious blow to the interface between philosophy and kabbalah, when he debunked the foundational Jewish belief that the Torah teaches scientific truths in the language of humans. Viewing the Torah only as a political-moral text, Spinoza regarded it as the product of prophetic imagination rather than as a revelation from God, thus undermining the entire medieval exegetical endeavor, shared by both philosophers and kabbalists. Spinoza paved the path for modern Jewish secularism, for which science is the exclusive domain of truth.

CONCLUSION

The interplay of philosophy and kabbalah characterized Jewish thought in the post-Maimonidean era. Although kabbalah emerged to curb Maimonideanism, rationalist philosophy and kabbalah had much in common. Both were theoretical inquiries about God, the origin and structure of the universe, and the place of humans in the order of things. Both wrestled with the same questions within the same conceptual framework of medieval Neoplatonized Aristotelianism. As metaphysicians, both groups of thinkers dealt with the paradoxes of singularity and multiplicity and approached them either ontologically and cosmologically or psychologically and epistemologically. Because both philosophers and kabbalists presupposed the existence of non-corporeal reality, they were deeply aware of the inherent limitations of the embodied human mind and maintained that humans require divine assistance in the form of revelation in order to know that which is beyond the ken of natural human reason. The disputed questions between philosophers and kabbalists, and within each camp, pertained to the boundary of human knowledge, the nature of revelatory experience, and the precise meaning of the received tradition.

As Jewish theologians who lived within the strictures of Halakhah, philosophers and kabbalists took for granted that Scripture was divinely revealed, and their primary intellectual task was hermeneutical – to penetrate the deep, hidden meaning of the sacred text. Both philosophy and kabbalah were esoteric endeavors whose privileged knowledge was accessible only to the select few who were intellectually and spiritually suitable. The difference between them concerned the precise content of the esoteric meaning of the revealed tradition and the proper way of transmitting it. As esoteric and elitist programs, both philosophy and kabbalah were determined to protect their privileged knowledge from misinterpretation or misapplication. Hence they employed complex rhetorical devices to conceal the very secrets they set out to reveal. Finally, both programs regarded their privileged knowledge to be the exclusive path toward religious perfection, culminating in the bliss of immortality in the afterlife. Thus both philosophy and kabbalah contributed to the interiorization of Jewish religious life by shifting the focus of Jewish messianism from collective, political redemption to personal salvation of the individual soul.

NOTES

1. See G. Scholem, *Origins of the Kabbalah*, trans. A. Arkush, ed. R. J. Z. Werblowsky (Philadelphia: Jewish Publication Society, 1987), 199–364.
2. On the esoteric doctrines of German Pietism and their impact on Provençal kabbalah, see E. Wolfson, *Through the Speculum that Shines: Vision and Imagination in Medieval Jewish Mysticism* (Princeton: Princeton University Press, 1994), 188–269.
3. On *Sefer ha-Bahir*, see Scholem, *Origins*, 35–198; E. Wolfson, "The Tree that is All: Jewish-Christian Roots of a Kabbalistic Symbol in *Sefer ha-Bahir*," *Jewish Thought and Philosophy* 3 (1993), 31–76.
4. On *Sefer Yetzira*'s conception of language, see M. Idel, *Golem: Jewish Magical and Mystical Tradition on the Artificial Anthropoid* (Albany: State University of New York Press, 1990), 9–26. On the possible Indian sources, see Y. Liebes, *Ars Poetica in Sefer Yetzira* [Hebrew] (Tel Aviv: Schocken Books, 2000). Liebes proposes Northern Mesopotamia as the possible location for the composition of this text, which he dates to the first century BCE, while the Jerusalem Temple was still in existence. Even if such early dating is accepted for the composition of the text, the edited version of the text is no earlier than the eighth century.
5. See M. Idel, "Jewish Kabbalah and Platonism in the Middle Ages and the Renaissance," in *Neoplatonism and Jewish Thought*, ed. L. E. Goodman (Albany: State University of New York Press, 1992), 319–51; Scholem, *Origins*, 365–475.

6. See M. Idel, "'We have No Kabbalistic Tradition on This'," in *Rabbi Moses Nahmanides (Ramban): Explorations in his Religious and Literary Virtuosity*, ed. I. Twersky (Cambridge, Mass.: Harvard University Press, 1983), 51–73.

7. See M. Verman, *The Books of Contemplation: Medieval Jewish Mystical Sources* (Albany: State University of New York Press, 1992).

8. See G. Scholem, *Major Trends in Jewish Mysticism* (New York: Schocken Books, 1941); M. Idel, *Kabbalah: New Perspectives* (New Haven: Yale University Press, 1994); H. Tirosh-Rothschild, "Continuity and Revision in the Study of Kabbalah," *AJS Review* 16 (1991), 161–92.

9. See E. Wolfson, *Abraham Abulafia – Kabbalist and Prophet: Hermeneutics, Theosophy and Theurgy* (Los Angeles: Cherub Press, 2000); E. Wolfson, "Letter Symbolism and Merkavah Imagery," in *'Alei Shefer: Studies in the Literature of Jewish Thought Presented to Rabbi Dr. Alexander Safran*, ed. M. Hallamish (Ramat-Gan: Bar-Ilan University Press, 1990), 195–236. Wolfson has shown that Abulafia's linguistic mysticism was shared by the *Zohar*, and, conversely, that Abulafia did not reject the kabbalistic doctrine of *sefirot* but only a certain interpretation of it. By the same token, Abulafia's kabbalah is not devoid of ethnocentrism, as much as the *Zohar* manifests strong ecstatic and mystical impulses.

10. Y. Liebes, "How was the Zohar Written?," in his *Studies in the Zohar*, trans. A. Schwartz, S. Nakache, and P. Peli (Albany: State University of New York Press, 1992), 85–138.

11. See R. Jospe, "Early Philosophical Commentaries on the *Sefer Yezirah*: Some Comments," *Revue des Etudes Juives* 149 (1990), 369–415; E. Wolfson, "The Theosophy of Shabbetai Donnolo, with Special Emphasis on the Doctrine of *Sefirot* in *Sefer Hakhmoni*," *Jewish History* 6 (1992), 281–316; Wolfson, *Abraham Abulafia*, 135.

12. See M. Idel, "Between the Views of Sefirot as Essence and Instruments in the Renaissance Period" [Hebrew], *Italia* 3 (1982), 89–111.

13. See G. Scholem, "The Meaning of Torah in Jewish Mysticism," in his *On the Kabbalah and its Symbolism* (New York: Schocken Books, 1965), 32–86.

14. The most detailed exposition of kabbalistic symbolism is I. Tishby, *The Wisdom of the Zohar: An Anthology of Texts*, 3 vols., trans. D. Goldstein (London: Littman Library, 1989).

15. See D. Matt, "The Mystic and the Mizvot," in *Jewish Spirituality: From the Bible through the Middle Ages*, ed. A. Green (New York: Crossroad, 1986), 367–404.

16. See M. Idel, *R. Menahem Rencanati the Kabbalist* [Hebrew] (Tel Aviv: Schocken Books, 1998), 175–231.

17. See M. Idel, "The Infinities of Torah," in *Midrash and Literature*, ed. G. Hartman and S. Budik (New Haven: Yale University Press, 1986), 141–57.

18. Isaac ibn Latif is an example of a thirteenth-century thinker who attempted to coordinate the Neoplatonic metaphysics of Gabirol with the doctrine of *sefirot* espoused by the kabbalists of Gerona. See S. O. Heller Wilensky, "Isaac ibn Latif: Philosopher or Kabbalist," in *Jewish Medieval and Renaissance Studies*, ed. A. Altmann (Cambridge, Mass.: Harvard University Press, 1967), 185–223.

19. See Yaacov ben Sheshet, *Sefer Meshiv Devarim Nekhohim*, ed. G. Vajda and E. Gottlieb (Jerusalem: Israel Academy of Sciences and Humanities, 1968), 101.

20. Wolfson, "Letter Symbolism," 196–7 n. 5.

21. See Tishby, *Wisdom of the Zohar*, ii: 447–546.

22. See Y. Liebes, "The Messiah of the Zohar," in his *Studies in the Zohar*, 1–84.

23. Wolfson, *Abraham Abulafia*, 53

24. Ibid., 102.

25. Ibid., 116.

26. Ibid., 139.

27. See M. Idel, "Abraham Abulafia and Unio Mystica," in his *Studies in Ecstatic Kabbalah* (Albany: State University of New York Press, 1988), 1–31.

28. M. Idel, *Language, Torah, and Hermeneutics in Abraham Abulafia*, trans. M. Kallus (Albany: State University of New York Press, 1989), 15.

29. See M. Idel, "*Hitbodedut* as Concentration in Ecstatic Kabbalah," in *Jewish Spirituality*, 405–38.

30. See Wolfson, *Abraham Abulafia*, 141; Idel, *Language, Torah, and Hermeneutics*, 33–5.

31. For a full discussion of Abulafia's messianic activities, see M. Idel, *Messianic Mystics* (New Haven: Yale University Press, 1998), 58–100.

32. See E. Wolfson, "God, the Demiurge and the Intellect: On the Usage of the Word Kol in Abraham ibn Ezra," *Revue des Etudes Juives* 149 (1990), 77–111.

33. See D. Schwartz, "Concerning the Philosophical Super-Commentaries on R. Abraham ibn Ezra's Commentaries" [Hebrew] '*Alei Sefer* 18 (1995–96), 71–114; U. Simon, "Interpreting the Interpreter: Supercommentaries on Ibn Ezra's Commentaries," in *Rabbi Abraham ibn Ezra: Studies in the Writings of a Twelfth-Century Jewish Polymath*, ed. I. Twersky and J. Harris (Cambridge, Mass.: Harvard University Press, 1993), 86–128.

34. For a detailed exposition of Ibn Ezra's use of astrology, see S. Sela, *Astrology and Biblical Exegesis in Abraham ibn Ezra's Jewish Thought* [Hebrew] (Ramat-Gan: Bar-Ilan University Press, 1999). On the application of Ibn Ezra's astrological doctrines during the fourteenth century, see D. Schwartz, *Astral Magic in Medieval Jewish Thought* [Hebrew] (Ramat-Gan: Bar-Ilan University Press, 1999).

35. This view is discussed in detail by H. Kreisel, "Miracles in Medieval Jewish Philosophy," *Jewish Quarterly Review* 75 (2) (1984), 99–133.

36. See Y. Langermann, "Maimonides' Repudiation of Astrology," *Maimonidean Studies* 2 (1992), 123–58.

37. See D. Schwartz, "The Debate on Astral Magic in Provence in the Fourteenth Century" [Hebrew], *Zion* 58(2) (1993), 141–74.

38. See D. Schwartz, "Astrology and Astral Magic in *Megaleh Amoqut* by R. Solomon al-Constantini" [Hebrew], *Jerusalem Studies in Jewish Folklore* 15 (1993), 40–41.

39. See M. Idel, "The Beginnings of the Kabbalah in North Africa? The Forgotten Document of R. Yehuda ben Nissim ibn Malka" [Hebrew], *Pe'amim* 43 (1990), 8–12; C. Sirat, *A History of Jewish Philosophy in the Middle Ages* (Cambridge: Cambridge University Press, 1985), 259–62.

40. See G. Vajda, *Recherches sur la philosophie et la kabbale dans la pensée juive du Moyen-Age* (Paris and La Haye: Mouton, 1962), 115–297, 385–91; G. Scholem, "Joseph ibn Waqar's Arabic Work on Kabbalah and Philosophy," *Kiryat Sepher* 20 (1943), 153–62.

41. See A. Altmann, "Moses Narboni's 'Epistle on *Shiur Qoma*'," in Altmann (ed.), *Jewish Medieval and Renaissance Studies*, 180–209. This essay was incorporated into Altmann, "Moses Narboni's 'Epistle on *Shiur Qoma*': A Critical Edition of the Hebrew Text with an Introduction and an Annotated English Translation," in his *Studies in Religious Philosophy and Mysticism* (Plainview, N.Y.: Libraries Press, 1975), 225–88. The citations are from the earlier publication.

42. See A. Ivry, "Moses of Narbonne 'Treatise on the Perfection of the Soul': A Methodological and Conceptual Analysis," *Jewish Quarterly Review* 57 (1966), 271–97; K. Bland (ed. and trans.), *The Epistle on the Possibility of Conjunction with the Active Intellect by Ibn Rushd with the Commentary of Moses Narboni* (New York: Jewish Theological Seminary, 1982), 1–19.

43. The relevant text was published by M. Hayoun, "Moise de Narbonne: Sur les sefirot, les sphères, et les intellects séparés. Edition critique d'un passage de son commentaire sur le *Hayy ibn Yaqzan*," *Jewish Quarterly Review* 76 (1985), 97–147; Altmann, "Moses Narboni," 199–200.

44. See Schwartz, *Astral Magic*, 237–62.

45. On the translations by Flavius Mithridates, see C. Wirszubski, *Pico della Mirandola's Encounter with Jewish Mysticism* (Cambridge, Mass.: Harvard University Press, 1989), 69–76 and passim.

46. See M. Idel, "Major Currents in Italian Kabbalah Between 1560–1660," in *Essential Papers on Jewish Culture in Renaissance and Baroque Italy*, ed. D. B. Ruderman (New York: New York University Press, 1992), 345–72; M. Idel "Encounters between Spanish and Italian Kabbalists in the Generation of the Expulsion," in *Crisis and Creativity in the Sephardic World 1391–1648*, ed. B. Gampel (New York: Columbia University Press, 1997), 189–222.

47. See H. Tirosh-Rothschild, "Sefirot as the Essence of God in the Writings of R. David Messer Leon," *AJS Review* 7–8 (1982), 409–25.

48. See A. Lesley, "'The Song of Solomon's Ascents' by Yohanan Alemanno: Love and Human Perfection according to a Jewish Colleague of Giovanni Pico," Ph.D. dissertation, University of California, Berkeley, 1976.

49. See M. Idel, "The Anthropology of Yohanan Alemanno: Sources and Influences," *Annali di Storia dell'Esegesi* 7/1 (1990), 103. For a fuller treatment of Alemanno's kabbalah, see M. Idel, "The Magical and Neoplatonic Interpretations of Kabbalah in the Renaissance," in *Jewish Thought in the Sixteenth Century*, ed. B. Cooperman (Cambridge, Mass.: Harvard University Press, 1983), 186–242.

50. See H. Tirosh-Samuelson, "Theology of Nature in Sixteenth-Century Italian Jewish Philosophy," *Science in Context* 10 (1997), 529–70.

51. See D. Ruderman, *Kabbalah, Magic, and Science: The Cultural Universe of a Sixteenth-Century Jewish Physician* (Cambridge, Mass.: Harvard University Press, 1988).

52. See W. Harvey, "Kabbalistic Elements in *Or Adonai* by R. Hasdai Crescas" [Hebrew], *Jerusalem Studies in Jewish Thought* 2 (1) (1982–83), 75–109.

53. See M. Idel, "Inquiries in the Doctrine of *Sefer Ha-Meshiv*" [Hebrew], *Sefunot* 17 (1983), 185–266.

54. See M. Idel, "Kabbalah and Philosophy in R. Isaac and Judah Abravanel" [Hebrew], in *The Philosophy of Leone Ebreo: Four Lectures*, ed. M. Dorman and Z. Levy (Haifa: Ha-Kibbutz Ha-Meuchad, 1985), 73–112.

55. On the rise of the *Zohar* to a canonic, authoritative, and holy text, see B. Huss, "*Sefer ha-Zohar* as a Canonical, Sacred and Holy Text: Changing Perspectives of the Book of Splendor between the Thirteenth and Eighteenth Century," *Journal of Jewish Thought and Philosophy* 7 (1998), 257–307.

56. On the *Zohar* as a source of Jewish normative rituals, see J. Katz, *Halakha and Kabbalah: Studies in the History of Jewish Religion, its*

Various Faces and Social Relevance [Hebrew] (Jerusalem: Magnes Press, 1984), 52–69, 102–24.

57. For a fuller treatment of these thinkers, see H. Tirosh-Rothschild, "Jewish Philosophy on the Eve of Modernity," in *History of Jewish Philosophy*, ed. D. H. Frank and O. Leaman (London and New York: Routledge, 1997), 529–49.

58. A. Altmann, "Lurianic Kabbalah in a Platonic Key: Abraham Cohen Herrera's *Puerta del Cielo*," *Hebrew Union College Annual* 53 (1982), 326.

12 Arabic into Hebrew: The Hebrew translation movement and the influence of Averroes upon medieval Jewish thought

THE FIRST HEBREW TRANSLATIONS OF SCIENTIFIC WORKS

The translation into Hebrew of Arabic scientific and philosophic works in the thirteenth century and the first third of the fourteenth century made possible the flowering of science and philosophy among Jews in Western Europe in the late Middle Ages. The first scientific work to be translated from Arabic into Hebrew was an Arabic version of Aristotle's *Meteorology*. Samuel ibn Tibbon, the translator of Maimonides' *Guide of the Perplexed*, translated this work in 1210.[1] This translation would be one of only three works of Aristotle to be translated into Hebrew directly from the Arabic translations, but it did not get the translation movement of scientific texts off to a running start.[2] Ibn Tibbon himself, whose son Moses would become one of the most prolific and proficient of the Arabic-to-Hebrew translators of scientific texts,[3] showed surprisingly little interest in the translation of scientific texts.[4] In fact, he claimed that he consented to translate the *Meteorology* only after the persistent entreaties of a learned scholar and dear friend, who had originally asked him to translate all Aristotle's physical works, and when Ibn Tibbon refused, begged him to translate at least the *Meteorology*.[5] But this was a poor choice. Unlike many of the Arabic translations of Aristotle's works of the time, which could be found in fine copies of competent or even impressive translations, this text was available in seemingly corrupt copies of a poor Arabic paraphrase. To make sense of it Ibn Tibbon had to translate creatively, constantly comparing and relying on testimonia such as the commentaries of Alexander of Aphrodisias and Averroes. More problematic was the fact,

258

acknowledged by ancients and medievals alike, that Aristotle's four physical writings ought to be read in their proper order, beginning with the *Physics* and concluding with the *Meteorology*. Ibn Tibbon himself acknowledged that "someone who has not previously acquired knowledge and learning from books that precede this one (sc. the *Meteorology*) will understand very little of this introduction" (i.e. Aristotle's introductory remarks at the beginning of the book "that are useful for what he wants to explain in it").[6] But his readers who could not read Arabic had no access to the *Physics* and the other physical writings, and unfortunately it would be some forty years before those works or epitomes of them would be translated into Hebrew.

One can imagine the frustration of the scientifically inclined Jews of Western Europe in the first half century following Maimonides' death. Not only were the basic texts of Aristotelian natural science inaccessible to them, but – because they did not know Aristotelian science – so virtually was the great book of Jewish thought that Ibn Tibbon had translated into Hebrew, Maimonides' *Guide of the Perplexed*. Maimonides had written in the introduction to the *Guide* that that work was written for those who have studied the "science of the philosophers" and have "knowledge of the true sciences." Levi ben Abraham of Villefranche explained that Maimonides "did not compose his enlightening book except for one who has studied all the books of the sciences." Levi wrote his rhymed encyclopedia, *Battei ha-Nefesh ve-ha-Lehashim*, in 1276 in order to make available the scientific knowledge needed for understanding the *Guide*. The same, it seems, was his motivation for subsequently writing *Livyat Hen*, his lengthier prose encyclopedia.[7] The need for a familiarity with physics and metaphysics for understanding the *Guide* is expressed clearly by Levi's contemporary, the learned talmudist Menahem ha-Meiri:

I am aware that [the scholars of Barcelona] permit all books, whether of Jewish or non-Jewish authorship, save the books of physics and metaphysics ... How shall we understand ... the *Guide of the Perplexed* ... without the books of physics and metaphysics?[8]

Actually by the time Levi wrote *Battei ha-Nefesh*, numerous works on Aristotelian science had already been translated into Hebrew. The systematic translation of Aristotelian science and philosophy may be traced to Samuel ibn Tibbon's son-in-law Jacob Anatoli. Anatoli realized that Aristotelian science begins with logic, "which serves the philosopher as a tool serves the artisan." Pressed by his friends and intimates, "the scholarly and educated men of Narbonne and Béziers, who were eager to approach this subject," he translated Averroes' middle commentaries on the first four books of Aristotle's *Organon* in 1232 in Naples.[9] Kalonymus ben Kalonymus translated the middle commentaries on the following two books in Provence in 1313; and Todros Todrosi translated the concluding two books in Trinquetaille in 1337. Anatoli also opened up the scientific study of astronomy for Hebrew readers through his translations of Ptolemy's *Almagest* and the epitomes of it by al-Farghani and Averroes.

The first translation of a work of Aristotelian science, apart from Aristotle's *Meteorology*, was made by Moses ibn Tibbon. In 1244 in Provence he translated Averroes' *Epitome of On the Soul*. Around 1250 he translated Averroes' epitomes of the *Physics* and of the other three books of Aristotelian physical science, in 1254 Averroes' *Epitome of Parva Naturalia*, and in 1258 the *Epitome of the Metaphysics*. These epitomes finally provided Hebrew readers with a taste of Aristotelian science and a knowledge of its contents, but they did not provide them with the requisite knowledge of the subject matter. This was accomplished through Averroes' middle commentaries.[10] The first Hebrew translation of a middle commentary was of *On the Soul*. Moses ibn Tibbon translated it, curiously the only middle commentary he translated, in 1261, but Shem Tov ben Isaac of Tortosa had already translated the same text some years before.[11] Solomon ibn Ayyub translated the *Middle Commentary on On the Heavens* in Béziers in 1259. Ibn Tibbon also translated several important works on astronomy, as well as Euclid's *Elements* and several commentaries on it. The translation of Aristotelian science continued with Zerahyah ben Isaac Hen's translations of the two works by Aristotle noted above, and his translations of the middle commentaries on the *Physics* and the *Metaphysics* in Rome in 1284.[12] The process of translating the scientific middle commentaries of Averroes on Aristotle was completed by the prolific translator Kalonymus ben Kalonymus in 1316–17. Kalonymus translated the middle commentaries on the *Physics*, *On Generation and Corruption*, *Meteorology*, and *Metaphysics*. Earlier Jacob ben Makhir had finished the Hebrew translation of Averroes' epitomes on Aristotle with a translation of the *Epitome of the Logic* in 1289 and the *Epitome of the Book of Animals* in 1302. Kalonymus began translating Averroes' five long commentaries, with his translation in 1314 of the *Long Commentary on the Posterior Analytics*, and seems to have undertaken translations of the long commentaries on the *Physics* and *Metaphysics* at that time. These Hebrew translations of the long commentaries did not achieve great popularity, and it is not known if the other two long commentaries were ever translated directly from the Arabic.

The next stage in the transmission of Aristotelian science to the Hebrew world was the series of super-commentaries on Averroes' commentaries undertaken by Gersonides in the years 1321–4 and by his students and colleagues in subsequent years.[13] H. A. Wolfson has in fact argued that Averroes' commentaries cannot be properly studied without them.[14] These super-commentaries explicated the commentaries of Averroes as Averroes had explicated the texts of Aristotle. As Gersonides explains in his introduction to the epitomes on the physical writings, "for even though most of what Averroes says is very clear, there remain some profound things that he does not sufficiently explain."[15] His stated aim is more ambitious in his introduction to the middle commentaries on the physical writings, and herein lies the greatest import of these super-commentaries:

In the places where our opinion does not agree with that of Aristotle, we will mention our opinions and refute those of Aristotle. This is what has aroused us to write these commentaries. This is in addition to the benefit which follows from such a commentary for the students in helping them understand some difficult things.[16]

Through the success of the Arabic-to-Hebrew translation movement of scientific and philosophic texts – both in terms of the sheer quantity of material translated and the impressive accuracy of most of the translations – and through the commentaries they engendered, it became possible for Jews to master Aristotelian science and to contribute to scientific progress.[17]

I have focused on the translation of texts of Aristotelian science because for some time this was *the* science of the Hebrew scholars and the primary concern of the leading translators.[18] But the translation movement of scientific texts was far more encompassing than this.

The breadth and depth of the output of this movement may be gauged from Moritz Steinschneider's monumental work, *Die hebräischen Übersetzungen des Mittelalters* (Berlin, 1893).[19] Ernest Renan's (and Adolf Neubauer's) *Les rabbins français du commencement du XIVe siècle* (Paris, 1877) and *Les écrivains juifs français du XIVe siècle* (Paris, 1893) still provide valuable information on the French translators and their literary activity. The extent of the translation movement may also be seen in recent studies such as Mauro Zonta's *La filosofia antica nel medioevo ebraico* and Gad Freudenthal's, "Les sciences dans les communautés juives médiévales de Provence: Leur appropriation, leur rôle."[20]

WHAT DETERMINED WHICH TEXTS WOULD BE TRANSLATED?

What determined which texts would be translated and how accurate were these translations? About ten years ago I suggested that Maimonides' recommendation in his well-known letter to Samuel ibn Tibbon of which philosophers to study and which to avoid "to a remarkable extent determined the philosophers and the philosophic texts that were to be translated from Arabic into Hebrew."[21] This still seems true to me, and is evidenced by the following five features of the translation activity:

1. It seems as if the translators sought to make available the complete works of Aristotelian science, at least as they were presented by the leading commentators. This qualification is significant and immediately distinguishes the Arabic-to-Hebrew translation activity from the Greek-to-Arabic and Greek-to-Latin ones, for, unlike the latter where translations were prepared of virtually all the available Aristotelian texts, only three texts of Aristotle were translated directly from Arabic to Hebrew, while all but one or two of Averroes' commentaries on them were so translated.

2. There is an almost total absence of translations of ancient philosophers other than Aristotle (or Pseudo-Aristotle) and his commentators Alexander of Aphrodisias and Themistius. Even Plato and the Arabic summaries and translations of epitomes of his dialogues were untranslated, with the sole exception of Averroes' *Commentary on the Republic.*

3. There appears to have been minimal interest in translating the many Neoplatonic books written or translated into Arabic.

4. There is a marked and early interest in translating the logical and propaedeutic writings of al-Farabi.

5. There is a surprising disinterest in translating the writings of Avicenna, especially *al-Shifa'* (*The Cure*), so popular in later Arabic and Latin thought.

All these features follow Maimonides' letter to Ibn Tibbon wherein (1) Aristotle's writings are singled out as the "foundations of all works on the sciences," but as works that can only be understood fully with the help of the commentators Alexander of Aphrodisias, Themistius, and Averroes; (2) the reader is told that Aristotle's works "suffice" and "there is no need to study the other ancient philosophers, including Plato"; (3) no Neoplatonic work is recommended; (4) al-Farabi is particularly praised for his works on logic; and (5) Avicenna's works are described as not as good as those of al-Farabi, but still useful.[22] This does not mean, of course, that the translators did not part from Maimonides' advice, nor that he somehow determined precisely what titles a particular translator would translate, for each translator had his own motivations and interests. It does suggest, however, that Maimonides' letter helped determine, either directly or indirectly, the philosophers and the philosophic texts that would be translated from Arabic to Hebrew and hence studied by non-Arabic reading medieval Jewish thinkers.

Apart from their efforts to translate Aristotelian science and the logical writings of Aristotle and his Islamic followers, the translators – and again special mention must be made of the most proficient and prolific among them, Moses ibn Tibbon and Kalonymus ben Kalonymus – sought to make available the leading works of mathematics, astronomy, and the art of medicine. Here Maimonides' letter was of little help, but a host of informed translators succeeded in translating from Arabic many of the important books in these fields, including works by Euclid, Archimedes, Nicomachus, Ptolemy, Hippocrates, Galen, al-Hajjaj, al-Kindi, Thabit ibn Qurrah, al-Farghani, Ibn Jabir al-Battani, Ibn al-Haytham, Jabir ibn Aflah, and al-Bitruji.[23]

THE ACCURACY OF THE ARABIC-TO-HEBREW TRANSLATORS

The Hebrew translators aimed at great accuracy in their translations and succeeded to a great extent. Of course, when they translated Arabic translations of Greek texts, their translations were dependent on the accuracy of those translations. Many of these, particularly those of Hunayn ibn Ishaq and his school, were remarkably accurate. The method of translation of this school was contrasted with that of Yahya ibn al-Bitriq – the author of the unsatisfactory Arabic translation of Aristotle's *Meteorology* mentioned above – and others. The latter method seeks to translate literally, studying each Greek word and choosing a suitable Arabic equivalent. This method did not work so well given the great syntactical differences between Arabic and Greek, and the fact that there were not always suitable Arabic terms for the underlying Greek ones. The former method was far more successful. It translates sentence by sentence, translating the meaning of the sentence without concern for the order of the words.[24]

In principle many of the medievals held that the word-for-word method of translation should be avoided in Arabic-to-Hebrew translations as well. Thus Moses ibn Ezra advised in the twelfth century, "If you wish to translate anything from Arabic into Hebrew, adhere to the intended meaning and do not translate word for word."[25] Similarly, Maimonides cautioned Samuel ibn Tibbon:

Whoever wishes to translate from language to language and intends to translate one word with another and preserve also the order of the words and sentences will run into trouble and his translation will be dubious and exceedingly confused ... It is not proper to do it this way. Rather the one who translates from language to language must first understand the sense, and then express what is understood of the sense in the target language.[26]

This advice was hardly new for Ibn Tibbon. His father Judah, often called the father of the medieval Hebrew translation movement, explicitly emphasized the problems and shortcomings of literal translations, while acknowledging one possible benefit. Judah wrote in his preface to his translation of Bahya ibn Paquda's *Duties of the Heart*:

And if it were possible for a translator to translate word for word, without adding or omitting, this danger [of perverting the contents] could be avoided, although admittedly such a literal translation would be hard to understand – except for the great scholars who know the ways of the holy tongue. The language would be neither pleasant nor conform to the general usage, and would completely obscure the subject.[27]

Samuel was certainly familiar with his father's views on the art of translation and in fact cites his preface and refers approvingly to the views on translation stated there in his own preface to his translation

of Maimonides' *Guide of the Perplexed*.[28] Yet this does not mean
that he or his father eschewed the literal method. Thus Irene Zwiep,
who has touched upon the attitudes toward translation of the medieval Arabic-to-Hebrew translators, may be correct but is misleading when she writes that the "testimonies [of the Ibn Tibbons] prove
that they themselves did not aim at providing slavish, word for word
translations. Like the majority of their Muslim colleagues, they were
concerned about the contents of the work under translation rather
than its language."[29] They were certainly concerned above all with
the meaning of the text they were translating, but they were also
concerned with the language. Indeed the best of the translators took
special care to translate Arabic technical terms always with the same
Hebrew technical term. While in theory they may not have aimed at
the literal method with all its shortcomings, in practice their translations were often slavishly word for word.[30] This is true to such
an extent that it is often possible – and not particularly difficult –
to reconstruct with some accuracy the Arabic source text from its
medieval Hebrew translation. These translations are thus in general
reliable and so accurate that they are valuable testimonia for editing
the Arabic originals.

PARAPHRASES AND SELECTIVE TRANSLATIONS

Not all the translators, however, aimed at faithfulness in their
translations. Unlike the great thirteenth- and fourteenth-century
Arabic-to-Hebrew translators, Shem Tov ibn Joseph Falaquera (c.
1225–1295) rarely simply translated books, but rather developed his
own style of selective and paraphrastic translation. Indicative of this
style are large sections of his *Reshit Hokhmah* (*Beginning of Wisdom*), the first book of a philosophic trilogy, promised at the end
of his *Iggeret ha-Vikkuah* (*Epistle of the Debate*).[31] Falaquera wrote
Reshit Hokhmah in order to provide the seeker of wisdom with those
things that he needs to grasp at the beginning of his study.[32] He divided the work into three parts. The first part is on the moral virtues
that this seeker of wisdom will need. The second part is on the enumeration of the sciences, and is essentially an abridged translation
of al-Farabi's *Ihsa'al-ʿulum* (*Enumeration of the Sciences*), incon-
spicuously interspersed with two lengthy, but very much abridged,
passages from his *Kitab al-huruf* (*Book of Letters*), some passages

from Avicenna's *Fi aqsam al-'ulum* (*On the Division of the Sciences*), and a selection, as Mauro Zonta has recently shown, from Averroes' *Epitome of the Isagoge*. The third part purports to show that philosophy is necessary for the attainment of happiness, and is an abridged translation of the Farabian trilogy that Muhsin Mahdi has translated into English under the title *Alfarabi's Philosophy of Plato and Aristotle*. Despite Falaquera's ponderous reliance on Islamic sources, not a single Islamic author is mentioned by name in *Reshit Hokhmah*. Instead Falaquera writes that "most of my words [in this book] concerning the sciences are those of the leading philosophers and the experts among them. I have not written anything new of my own, but have collected [these words] from the books that are dispersed."[33] Falaquera, who was as familiar with the works of the Islamic *falasifa* as any Jew in the Middle Ages, did not translate or paraphrase their writings in order to make known their opinions as *their* opinions, but rather to guide and teach true science and philosophy to the seeker of wisdom. He thus saw no need to attribute these writings to their authors. Moreover, he had no compunctions in *Reshit Hokhmah* about adapting some of al-Farabi's most important philosophic works to his own needs and purposes through judicious omission of words or passages and combination of various texts.[34] Falaquera's abridged, at times paraphrastic, rendering of *Alfarabi's Philosophy of Plato and Aristotle* was the only Hebrew version of the three books that comprise this trilogy, and yet none of the medievals who studied Falaquera's text would have known that they were reading al-Farabi.

More important for the history of the transmission of science and philosophy is Falaquera's *De'ot ha-Filosofim* (*Opinions of the Philosophers*), the third book of his philosophic trilogy. If *Reshit Hokhmah* was intended as an introductory work, *De'ot ha-Filosofim* comes to teach the reader true science and instruct him in the opinions of the true philosophers about what is. This is Falaquera's major work and yet he writes in his introduction that "there is not a thing in this entire composition that I say of my own; rather all that I write are the words of Aristotle as explained in the commentaries of the scholar Averroes, for he was the last of the commentators and he incorporated what was best from the [earlier] commentaries."[35] While Falaquera did borrow from other authors, it is true that his main source is Averroes and in particular his middle commentaries and to a lesser extent epitomes. These texts are often translated accurately, but with no hesitation on the part of Falaquera to abridge the translation and to blend it in his own style with other sources, usually other commentaries by Averroes, for the sake of clarification or comprehensiveness. Short passages from other works and other authors are inserted when it suits Falaquera's purposes, at times attributed to the author and at times not. Falaquera's *De'ot* thus varies from complete and literal translation of a passage to abridged paraphrastic translation to selective translation interspersed with other texts.

This approach fits in with Falaquera's stated intention in writing the *De'ot*:

I endeavored to translate these opinions [of the philosophers] from Arabic to Hebrew, and to compile them from the books that are scattered there, so that whoever wishes to grasp these [opinions] will find them in one book, and will not need to weary himself by reading all the books [on these subjects], for all the opinions [of the philosophers], general and particular, on natural science and divine science are included in this composition.[36]

In other words, Falaquera's goal was to offer in a single volume a complete text curriculum for the study of natural science and metaphysics through translation of the best available texts, which for him meant the commentaries of Averroes on Aristotle, so that the student who wished to learn natural science and divine science – that is, physics and metaphysics – would need to consult only this book. His goal explicitly was *not* to write something new and original, nor was it simply to translate an important text. Neither was his goal to teach us something about al-Farabi, Avicenna, Averroes, or any other thinker. His goal was to teach wisdom and science, and this meant for him, as we have seen, Aristotelian science as it was explained by Averroes. The value of this scientific work, rooted in Averroes' middle commentaries, will be appreciated if it is recalled that at the time of its writing the only middle commentaries to have been translated were those on *On the Heavens* and *On the Soul*. This work offered the Hebrew reader for the first time comprehensive access to the full range of Aristotelian science.[37]

While the encyclopedic *De'ot ha-Filosofim* presented the first full treatment of Aristotelian science, it was not the first systematic attempt to put forward Aristotelian science in a single volume. This honor goes to Judah ben Solomon ha-Kohen of Toledo's *Midrash ha-Hokhmah*, which was compiled in Hebrew in Italy in 1247. The *Midrash ha-Hokhmah* is considered the first of the great medieval encyclopedias of science and philosophy; Falaquera's *De'ot* is the second. Yet although Judah ben Solomon, like Falaquera, also relied most heavily on Averroes' middle commentaries, his treatment is much briefer and more concise, contenting himself with the main points of the sciences. The result is a very difficult text. Resianne Fontaine, who has written several important studies on the *Midrash ha-Hokhmah*, has concluded that it "remains doubtful to what extent the epitomized pieces of information could actually have enabled a reader without previous scientific knowledge to get a clear picture of Aristotelian philosophy...It cannot be denied that the fragmentary character of the text must have made high demands on the interested lay-reader."[38] Nonetheless, however terse and obscure, this encyclopedia provided the first Hebrew account of Aristotelian natural science and metaphysics, predating Moses ibn Tibbon's translations of Averroes' epitomes by several years. One can only imagine – and there is surprisingly little evidence of this – the excitement with which this encyclopedia must have been received by the science-starved Hebrew reader of the mid-thirteenth century. In this light the importance of the thirteenth-century Hebrew encyclopedias of science and philosophy becomes clear. While interest in them likely diminished once the actual and full translations of the scientific texts of Aristotle and Averroes became available, in their day they served as precious vehicles for the acquisition of scientific knowledge.[39]

THE CENTRALITY OF AVERROES

As we have seen, the hundred plus years of translation activity from Arabic to Hebrew in the fields of the sciences had succeeded in making available accurate versions of a wide and impressive range of scientific works of ancient Greek and medieval Islamic thinkers. At the heart of this translation movement was not, as one might have expected, the works of Aristotle, *the* philosopher, but rather the many commentaries of Averroes on the Aristotelian corpus.[40] These commentaries, particularly the middle commentaries, were very popular in the fourteenth and fifteenth centuries and became at that time the authoritative sources for learning natural science in Hebrew. I have already suggested, following Ernest Renan, how it is that Jews came to learn science from Averroes, and how he became the most widely translated and widely read philosopher in the Hebrew middle ages.[41] Renan has written that the Jews were Averroes' true philosophic heirs, and it was thanks to the "high recommendation of Maimonides [that his] name became almost instantaneously the foremost philosophic authority among the Jews."[42] While it is a mistake to think that Averroes' works "were preserved and promoted after his death only by the Jews" or that the "philosophical works of Averroes were not read in the Islamic world after Averroes' fall from grace in 1195, and until the early twentieth century,"[43] it is certainly true that he had a stature among the Jews that overshadowed even his position as *the* commentator in the Latin West. Among the Jews, Averroes not only supplanted al-Farabi and Avicenna, he also supplanted Aristotle. What is most significant for the history of Jewish philosophy is that Averroes' influence upon the Jews extended beyond his dominant role as commentator and into the province of religious philosophy. Moreover, as Isadore Twersky has shown, his influence was not limited to philosophers, but extended over writers of all literary genres. To these authors, as a result of the "translating, paraphrasing, commentatorial and critical work" of dozens of thirteenth- and fourteenth-century scholars, Averroes became a "household name."[44] What was the nature of Averroes' influence upon the Jews and how did he become so influential?

AVERROES' INFLUENCE UPON THE JEWS

Averroes' commentaries among the Jews – at first via the paraphrastic translations and other accounts of them in the thirteenth-century Hebrew encyclopedias, and then via the accurate translations of them – were the authoritative sources of scientific learning. Leading translators such as the Ibn Tibbon family and Kalonymus ben Kalonymus showed no interest in translating into Hebrew the science of Avicenna or al-Ghazali's reformulation of it. The reason for this may be discerned in Kalonymus' open letter to Joseph ibn Kaspi, wherein he distinguishes Avicenna and al-Ghazali from the "important philosophers" (*hashuvei ha-filosofim*) Alexander of Aphrodisias, al-Farabi, Ibn Bajja, and Averroes.[45] These views were shared by learned Aristotelians such as Gersonides and Joseph ibn Kaspi, who also had no use for the scientific writings of Avicenna and al-Ghazali. Indeed when Aristotelian philosophers such as Isaac Albalag, Moses Narboni, and Moses ben Judah did turn to al-Ghazali's account of Avicennian science, they did so as a springboard for teaching essentially Averroean science. The best science in their eyes was simply Aristotelian as explicated by Averroes. There was no reason for serious students of natural science to look elsewhere.

Yet it must be remembered that Jews turned to Averroes to learn and understand Aristotle; they did not turn to him – at least at first – as a source of theology. Indeed Maimonides recommended him in his letter to Samuel ibn Tibbon as a commentator on Aristotle, and not for his religious philosophy or for his theology. But it was not so easy to separate the two, particularly as Averroes hinted at his own heterodox teachings on particular issues in religious philosophy most boldly in the relatively safe confines of a lengthy commentary. It made sense that the scholar who understood and could explain science the best would also be of help in understanding the complexities of those difficult questions of religious philosophy such as the creation or eternity of the world, God's knowledge of particulars, and the possibility of individual immortality. Perhaps beginning with Ibn Tibbon, Averroes gradually began to have an impact on the understanding of philosophically inclined Jews on precisely these issues. It was inevitable, and while Maimonides may have underestimated the dangers to orthodoxy lurking in these commentaries, others were well attuned to them.

Judah ben Solomon, who, as we have seen, was the first to spread the knowledge of Averroean natural science in Hebrew through his encyclopedia *Midrash ha-Hokhmah*, exhibits a critical attitude to both Aristotle and Averroes, particularly regarding their teachings, such as those on creation/eternity, that directly bear on religion.[46] It has been suggested that Judah's manifest un-Tibbonid terminology may have been motivated by his critical attitude towards Aristotelian philosophy.[47] In particular it seems that his terminology may have been an expression of his disapproval of Ibn Tibbon's wholehearted acceptance of Aristotelian teachings, including those that counter those of orthodoxy, and his desire "to direct the reader away from Ibn Tibbon's interpretation of that philosophy."[48] Judah's concerns about the inroads of Aristotelian/Averroean theology into

Jewish thinking, shared by his philosophically learned Spanish antirationalist coreligionists, were well founded. Bernard Septimus has
observed that, by the time the great Maimonidean controversy of the
1230s erupted in Provence, "radical tendencies had received still further impetus through the influence of Averroës."[49] To the extent that
this influence was significant already in the 1230s – at a time when
few writings of Averroes were available to the Hebrew reader – it was
as a result of the emerging stature and influence of Ibn Tibbon –
himself directly influenced by Averroes – and his theological-
philosophical writings.[50]

With the translation of Averroes' commentaries into Hebrew, the
impact of his personal theological-philosophical views upon Jewish
thought grew stronger and stronger. This is true despite the fact that
his commentaries on Aristotle were for the most part explications of
the texts, and in those places where he did wish to reveal to fellow
philosophers his own not so orthodox views, he usually intimated
them via hint and allusion. Jewish thinkers who defended their study
of Averroes readily admitted that he said things that went counter
to their religion, but emphasized that they accepted only the truth
and certainly not anything that contradicts the Torah.[51] In this vein,
Jacob ben Makhir wrote in 1304, in the midst of the conflict that was
raging over the study of philosophy and that would result in 1305 in
Solomon ibn Adret's ban against the study of Greek philosophy and
science by anyone under twenty-five years old:

I admit that there are some detestable ideas expressed in the philosophical
writings, but this does not justify your refusal to make ourselves acquainted
with the good ideas they contain...The convictions of a people are by no
means weakened, and their faith is nowhere and never undermined, at least
not ours, for the truth of which we possess the best of proofs...I myself know
very well the borderline which philosophy must not cross in its criticism of
the Bible.[52]

While the ban of 1305 for various reasons would have little
effect on the future study of philosophy, the worries expressed by
its supporters were legitimate. Jacob ben Makhir's faith and convictions may not have been weakened by his translation and study of
Averroean science, but many others were not as firm in their beliefs.
It has thus been argued that the dominant influence of Averroes to
a great extent explains the unprecedented mass forced conversions

of the Jews to Christianity during the massacres of 1391.[53] How could Jewish adherents to Averroes' views that the world is eternal, that God does not really know particulars, and that there is no personal immortality (but that these and other such beliefs are concessions to the ignorant masses) be expected to sacrifice their lives for the sanctification of the name of a God who does not know them or their actions? Hasdai Crescas, in his efforts to rebuild and strengthen the decimated Jewish communities of Spain, thus sought to counter Averroean heterodoxy at its root by questioning and refuting the bases of Aristotelian-Averroean science.[54] While he emerged as "one of the outstanding men in a philosophical current which brought about the disintegration of mediaeval Aristotelianism and paved the way for the new philosophy and physics,"[55] his own interest in seeking other ways of understanding Aristotle led him to take seriously the hitherto mostly ignored scientific writings of other Islamic thinkers such as Avicenna and al-Ghazali. Avicenna's physics and metaphysics had been directly accessible to Hebrew readers since about 1340 through Todros Todrosi's translation of al-Najah (The Salvation). At that time two or three translations of al-Ghazali's reworking of Avicennian Aristotelian science, Maqasid al-falasifa (Intentions of the Philosophers), were also in circulation (the first stemming from the end of the thirteenth century). Nonetheless, prior to Crescas, Avicenna and al-Ghazali seem to have had little impact on those Hebrew readers who wished to study and understand Aristotelian science.[56] In the fifteenth century, following Crescas, al-Ghazali's Maqasid al-falasifa emerged as the single most popular work of Aristotelian science among Jews. It was also in this century that one finds what Mauro Zonta has called a "sort of highly sophisticated Hebrew Scholasticism." More and more Jewish philosophers, particularly in Spain, were being influenced by Christian Scholastic thought.[57] In short, as one modern historian sums up, "Averroes lost his status as the most authoritative commentator on Aristotle and instead, Jewish philosophers consulted alternative readings of Aristotle by Hellenistic, Muslim, and Christian philosophers."[58] Averroes' commentaries, of course, continued to be studied and valued throughout the medieval period, but there was less interest among Jews in his theological-philosophical views. By the middle of the sixteenth century, serious study of Averroes was again undertaken only by the few.[59]

NOTES

1. On the nature of this translation, see R. Fontaine, *Otot ha-Shamayim: Samuel ibn Tibbon's Hebrew Version of Aristotle's "Meteorology"* (Leiden: Brill, 1995), introduction, ix–lxxi. Hebrew translations of certain logical works by al-Farabi possibly date from the end of the twelfth century.

2. The other two were the late thirteenth-century Hebrew translations by Zerahyah ben Isaac Shealtiel Hen of *On Generation and Corruption* and *On the Soul*. Full Hebrew translations of Aristotle's *Posterior Analytics*, *Physics*, and *Metaphysics* could be found in the Hebrew translations of Averroes' long commentaries on these works. There may also have been a Hebrew translation of the *Long Commentary on On the Heavens*.

3. His father Judah had translated into Hebrew classic works of Jewish thought such as Saadya Gaon's *Beliefs and Opinions*, Bahya ibn Paquda's *Duties of the Heart*, and Judah Halevi's *Kuzari*.

4. This is not to say that Samuel did not translate many works that were of interest to the philosophically inclined Jews of his time. In addition to his translation of the *Guide*, Samuel translated several important treatises and letters by Maimonides. Among other works attributed to him are translations of an Arabic commentary on Galen's *Ars Parva* and three treatises on the intellect by Averroes and his son.

5. Fontaine, *Otot ha-Shamayim*, 2–3. On Ibn Tibbon's own interest in the *Meteorology*, see ibid., xi–xii.

6. Fontaine, *Otot ha-Shamayim*, 26–9. Cf. Aristotle, *Meteorology* 1:1 338a20–339a9.

7. On Levi's motivations in writing his encyclopedias, see W. Harvey, "Levi ben Abraham of Villefranche's Controversial Encyclopedia," in *The Medieval Hebrew Encyclopedias of Science and Philosophy*, ed. S. Harvey (Dordrecht: Kluwer, 2000), esp. 172 and 179. See, similarly, the statement of aim of the author of the anonymous mid-thirteenth century *Ruah Hen* (Warsaw, 1826), 1a.

8. Cited by G. Stern, "What Divided the Moderate Maimonidean Scholars of Southern France in 1305," in *Studies in Jewish History and Thought in Memory of Isadore Twersky*, ed. J. Harris (Cambridge, Mass.: Harvard University Press, forthcoming).

9. See Anatoli's introduction to his translations, *Averroes' Middle Commentaries on Porphyry's Isagoge and on Aristotle's Categories*, trans. H. Davidson (Cambridge, Mass.: The Mediaeval Academy of America, 1969), 3–5. On the various motivations of the translators, see J.-P. Rothschild, "Motivations et méthodes des traductions en hébreu du

milieu du XIIe à la fin du XVe siècle," in *Traduction et traducteurs au moyen âge*, ed. G. Contamine (Paris: Editions du CNRS, 1989), 279–302, and M. Zonta, *La filosofia antica nel medioevo ebraico* (Brescia: Paideia, 1996), 65–88.

10. That Averroes himself would have agreed with this assessment is suggested by the following words from the colophon to his *Middle Commentary on the Physics*: "I already have among the multitude a commentary that I made in my youth, and it is short. I saw fit now to do this more complete commentary." Translated from the Hebrew translation of the *Middle Commentary on the Physics* by Kalonymus ben Kalonymus, Paris, Bibliothèque Nationale, MS héb. 938 (Oratoire 125), fol. 156v.

11. One may wonder why Moses ibn Tibbon translated the *Epitome of On the Soul* before, and so many years before, he translated the other epitomes, and why the only middle commentary he translated was the *Middle Commentary on On the Soul*. The answer probably derives from Aristotle's high praise for psychology at the very beginning of *On the Soul*. On Averroes' views on the significance of *On the Soul* for the other sciences, see A. L. Ivry, "La logique de la science de l'âme: Etude sur la méthode dans le *Commentaire* d'Averroès," in *Penser avec Aristote*, ed. M. A. Sinaceur (Toulouse: Erès, 1991), 697–8, and A. L. Ivry, "Averroes' *Short Commentary* on Aristotle's *De Anima*," *Documenti e studi sulla tradizione filosofica medievale* 8 (1997), 520–3. Still this answer is not very satisfactory. Averroes himself wrote the *Middle Commentary on On the Soul* after the other middle commentaries on natural science (his other two commentaries on *On the Soul* are not dated), and Gersonides wrote his commentary on the *Epitome of On the Soul* after he had completed his commentaries on Averroes' epitomes of the books of natural science. This is the proper and expected order.

12. Zerahyah is a good example of a translator who sought to translate the most useful texts of Aristotelian science that had not yet been translated. Thus he was the first to translate Averroes' middle commentaries on the *Physics* and the *Metaphysics*. Since there were already translations of the middle commentaries on *On the Heavens* and *On the Soul*, he translated Themistius' commentary on the former and Aristotle's own text of the latter. None of these translations appears to have been particularly popular. The translations of the middle commentaries were virtually unknown in Provence and Spain and in any event were overshadowed by those made by Kalonymus ben Kalonymus some thirty years later. Among Zerahyah's other translations are six medical works, three by Maimonides, two by Galen, and part of Avicenna's *Canon*.

13. See R. Glasner, "Levi ben Gershom and the Study of Ibn Rushd in the Fourteenth Century," *Jewish Quarterly Review* 86 (1995), 51–90. Glasner has shown that Gersonides not only composed the first super-commentary on Averroes, but that the other known supercommentaries from the fourteenth century, not written by him, were composed by his students, who studied Averroes' commentaries under his direction.

14. See H. A. Wolfson, "Plan for the Publication of a *Corpus Commentari-orum Averrois in Aristotelem*," in his *Studies in the History of Philosophy and Religion*, ed. I. Twersky and G. Williams (Cambridge, Mass.: Harvard University Press, 1973), 1:441.

15. Gersonides, *Commentary on Averroes' Epitome of the Physics*, London, Jews' College MS Bet Hamidrash 43, fol. 126r.

16. Gersonides, *Commentary on Averroes' Middle Commentary on the Physics*, Paris, Bibliothèque Nationale, MS héb. 964, fol. 1v. The extent of Gersonides' critique of Aristotelian science in his supercommentaries is just now coming to light. For a clear illustration, see R. Glasner, "Gersonides' Theory of Natural Motion," *Early Science and Medicine* 1 (1996), 151–203, and R. Glasner, "Gersonides on Simple and Composite Movements," *Studies in History and Philosophy of Science* 28 (1997), 545–84.

17. On the "limits of the appropriation of science and philosophy by the medieval Jews," see G. Freudenthal, "Science in the Medieval Jewish Culture of Southern France," *History of Science* 33 (1995), 23–58, and the article by Freudenthal cited below, n. 20. As for the statement concerning the medieval Jewish contributions to scientific progress, this requires some qualification. Freudenthal writes ("Science in Jewish Culture", 30) that Jews writing in Hebrew, with the exception of Gersonides and Crescas, "scarcely went beyond what they had received through translations; they did not venture to make contributions of their own . . . Some scientific disciplines were not at all appropriated, and to those that were appropriated, astronomy excepted, the Hebrew-writing scholars made few original contributions."

18. For an impressively full inventory of the medieval Hebrew translations of texts of Aristotelian science, including commentaries by Alexander of Aphrodisias, Themistius, al-Farabi, Avicenna, Ibn Bajja, and Latin authors, see G. Tamani and M. Zonta, *Aristoteles Hebraicus* (Venice: Supernova, 1997), 31–49.

19. C. Manekin has begun to update and translate this immense text; see his "Steinschneider's *Die hebräischen Übersetzungen des Mittelalters*: From Reference Work to Digitalized Database," *Jewish Studies Quarterly* 7 (2000), 141–59.

20. See Zonta, *La filosofia antica*, and G. Freudenthal, "Les sciences dans les communautés juives médiévales de Provence: Leur appropriation, leur rôle," *Revue des Etudes Juives* 152 (1993), 29–136.

21. S. Harvey, "Did Maimonides' Letter to Samuel ibn Tibbon Determine Which Philosophers Would be Studied by Later Jewish Thinkers?," *Jewish Quarterly Review* 83 (1992), 51–70.

22. See ibid.

23. On the limits of the translation movement, see Freudenthal, "Science in Jewish Culture" and "Les sciences." I say Maimonides' letter was of little help to the translators in determining what scientific texts to translate in the fields of mathematics, astronomy, and medicine. Freudenthal goes beyond this and attributes to Maimonides the subsequent lack of serious interest in mathematics and other non-Aristotelian sciences. His claim is that Maimonides "set a low value on science *per se*, channeling talent and originality elsewhere" ("Science in Jewish Culture", 50; cf. ibid., 32–4, and "Les sciences," 104–6). While I have benefitted greatly from both studies by Freudenthal and while it does seem that Maimonides did not inspire original contributions in the sciences, I do not agree that he "set a low value on science *per se*."

24. On these two methods of translation from Greek to Arabic, see Khalil al-Safadi (d. 1363), *Al-Ghayth al-musajjam*, trans. in F. Rosenthal, *The Classical Heritage in Islam* (London and New York: Routledge, 1975), 17. Al-Safadi attributes the former method to Hunayn ibn Ishaq, al-Jawhari, and others, and the latter method to Ibn al-Bitriq, Ibn Na'imah al-Himsi, and others. See similarly the passage by Maimonides cited below, n. 26, where he attributes the former method to Hunayn ibn Ishaq and his son Ishaq ibn Hunayn, and the latter method to Ibn al-Bitriq. For a critical evaluation al-Safadi's remarks, see D. Gutas, *Greek Thought, Arabic Culture: The Graeco–Arabic Translation Movement in Baghdad and Early 'Abbasid Society* (London: Routledge, 1998), 142–3. See further F. E. Peters, *Aristotle and the Arabs* (New York: New York University Press, 1968), 57–67.

25. *Al-Muhadarah wa'l-mudhakarah*, trans. in Rosenthal, *Classical Heritage*, 18.

26. I. Shailat, *Iggerot ha-Rambam* (Jerusalem: Shailat Publishing [Maaliyot], 1988), 532–3.

27. This passage is cited in translation in I. Zwiep, *Mother of Reason and Revelation: A Short History of Medieval Jewish Linguistic Thought* (Amsterdam: J. C. Gieben, 1997), 71. On Judah's views on translation, see ibid., 69–75, and Zonta, *La filosofia antica*, 99–104. For views of other medieval Hebrew translators on the methods of translation, see

the discussion and analysis in Zonta *La filosofia antica*, 96–116, and Rothschild, "Motivations et méthodes", 297–301.

28. Samuel's preface is found in Maimonides, *Moreh ha-Nevukhim*, ed. Y. ibn Shmuel (Jerusalem: Mosad Harav Kook, 1981), cxvii–cxxii. For the reference to Judah's preface, see cxvii–cxviii. Samuel here (cxix) is one of the first to refer to his father as the "father of the translators" (*avi ha-ma'tiqim*).

29. See Zwiep, *Mother of Reason*, 71. I have benefitted from Zwiep's discussion, supported with apt quotations, of the medieval views on Arabic-to-Hebrew translation (63–76). Nonetheless, one must judge the extent of literalness of the translations on the basis of the translations themselves, and not on the authors' stated aims. Thus I would want to qualify her claim (73) that the "very ideal of changing words without affecting their meaning was utterly contradictory to the prevalent monadic view on signification, which had been fostered by the notion of the – conventional – incongruity between languages." The leading Arabic-to-Hebrew translators no doubt endowed technical Hebrew terms they coined or borrowed from their predecessors with the same range of technical meanings that the underlying Arabic term had. Often these technical terms were formed from Hebrew roots identical to the Arabic roots or with the same non-technical meanings as the Arabic roots.

30. A. Ivry calls "literalism…the hallmark of [the Ibn Tibbon] school [of translation]"; see his "Philosophical Translations from the Arabic in Hebrew during the Middle Ages," in *Rencontres de cultures dans la philosophie médiévale*, ed. J. Hamesse and M. Fattori (Louvain-la-Neuve and Cassino: Publications de l'Institut d'Etudes Médiévales, 1990), 181. Zonta, *La filosofia antica*, 107, writes that, for many of the medieval translators, only the literal translation can "bestow doctrinal validity upon the words of an author."

31. See the passage in the *Iggeret ha-Vikkuah*, ed. and trans. in S. Harvey, *Falaquera's "Epistle of the Debate": An Introduction to Jewish Philosophy* (Cambridge, Mass.: Harvard University Press, 1987), 79–80 (English, 51). Falaquera was a prolific writer. For a list and description of eighteen of his works, see R. Jospe, *Torah and Sophia: The Life and Thought of Shem Tov ibn Falaquera* (Cincinnati: Hebrew Union College Press, 1988), 31–76.

32. See *Reshit Hokhmah*, ed. M. David (Berlin, 1902), 9.

33. Ibid. On the sources of *Reshit Hokhmah*, see Jospe, *Torah and Sophia*, 39–42. On Averroes' *Epitome of the Isagoge* as a source of Falaquera's in *Reshit Hokhmah*, see M. Zonta, *Un dizionario filosofico ebraico del*

XIII secolo: L'introduzione al "Sefer De'ot ha-Filosofim" di Shem Tob ibn Falaquera (Turin: Silvio Zamorani Editore, 1992), 141–4.

34. For a striking example of this and an explanation for it, see my "A Note on the Paraphrases of Alfarabi's Political Writing in *Reshit Hokhmah*" [Hebrew], *Tarbiz* 65 (1996), 729–41.

35. This passage from the introduction is cited from S. Harvey, "Shem-Tov Falaquera's *De'ot ha-Filosofim*: Its Sources and Use of Sources," in Harvey (ed.), *Medieval Hebrew Encyclopedias*, 214.

36. Cited from ibid., 216.

37. On the structure and sources of the *De'ot*, see ibid., 211–37.

38. See R. Fontaine, "Judah ben Solomon ha-Cohen's *Midrash ha-Hokhmah*: Its Sources and Use of Sources," in Harvey (ed.), *Medieval Hebrew Encyclopedias*, 191–210. The quotation is from 201.

39. On the thirteenth-century Hebrew encyclopedias of science and philosophy, see Harvey (ed.), *Medieval Hebrew Encyclopedias*, esp. introduction and chs. 8–18.

40. As we have seen, during this period, in contrast to the only three independent Arabic-to-Hebrew translations of Aristotle's works (see above, n. 2), at least thirty-four of Averroes' thirty-six commentaries on Aristotle were translated from Arabic into Hebrew. See the list of Hebrew translations of books of Aristotelian science, referred to above, n. 18.

41. See above, n. 21.

42. E. Renan, *Averroès et l'averroïsme*, 2nd ed. (Paris: Michel Lévy, 1861), 180.

43. C. Burnett argues against these views in his "The 'Sons of Averroes with the Emperor Frederick' and the transmission of the philosophical works by Ibn Rushd," in *Averroes and the Aristotelian Tradition*, ed. G. Endress and J. A. Aertsen (Leiden: Brill, 1999), 259–76; the former view is cited on 259, the latter on 275. Both views are untenable and not nearly as widespread and popular in recent scholarship as Burnett makes them out to be.

44. I. Twersky, "Aspects of the Social and Cultural History of Provençal Jewry," in *Jewish Society through the Ages*, ed. H. H. Ben-Sasson and S. Ettinger (New York: Schocken Books, 1971), 202.

45. *Kalonymus ben Kalonymus' Sendschreiben an Joseph Kaspi*, ed. J. Perles (Munich, 1879), 9.

46. On Judah's attitude toward his sources, see Fontaine, "Judah ben Solomon ha-Cohen's *Midrash ha-Hokhmah*," 202–7. Note Judah's statement about Averroes, cited on 204.

47. See Zonta, *La filosofia antica*, 122–3, and R. Fontaine, "Arabic Terms in Judah ben Solomon ha-Cohen's *Midrash ha-Hokhmah*," *DS-NELL* 1–2 (1997), 128–31.

48. Fontaine, "Arabic Terms," 129.

49. B. Septimus, *Hispano-Jewish Culture in Transition: The Career and Controversies of Ramah* (Cambridge, Mass.: Harvard University Press, 1982), 148, n. 17; see further 62–3.

50. Despite the important and eye-opening studies on Ibn Tibbon's esotericism of the past four decades, particularly by G. Vajda and A. Ravitzky, the full extent of Averroes' influence on Ibn Tibbon still needs to be spelled out. This influence was already suggested in Vajda's pioneering study, "An Analysis of the *Ma'amar Yiqqawu ha-Mayim* by Samuel Ibn Tibbon," *Journal of Jewish Studies* 10 (1959), 137–49. Vajda wrote of the possible influence of Averroes' apologetic *Decisive Treatise* upon him, and of the "clear indications of the influence" of Averroes' heterodox teachings upon him, and alluded to his radical Averroism (see esp. 141 n. 11, 147 n. 29, and 149). Later studies by Ravitzky showed Ibn Tibbon to be even more radical than Vajda suspected. G. Freudenthal thus saw radical Averroism "exemplified in the thought of Samuel ibn Tibbon"; see his "Science in Jewish Culture," 43.

51. Harvey, *Falaquera's "Epistle"*, 15 n. 4, 18 n. 11, 19 n. 13. See, further, the passage from Falaquera's *De'ot ha-Filosofim*, quoted in Jospe, *Torah and Sophia*, 52. Ironically, this attitude in part derives directly from Averroes. See his *Decisive Treatise*, trans. G. Hourani (London: Luzac, 1967), 47–50.

52. Jacob ben Makhir's letter to Solomon ibn Adret, trans. in F. Kobler, *Letters of Jews through the Ages*, 2 vols. (London: East and West Library, 1953), 1: 252–3.

53. See W. Harvey, "Hasdai Crescas's Critique of the Theory of the Acquired Intellect," Ph.D. dissertation, Columbia University, 1973, esp. 84–103; for discussion of the view propounded by Y. Baer in his *A History of the Jews in Christian Spain*, 2 vols. (Philadelphia: Jewish Publication Society, 1978) that "Averroist philosophy was a major cause of communal disaster," see 85–7 n. 117. For a different perspective that questions some of Baer's conclusions and points to the value of philosophy in preserving Jewish identity, see M. Saperstein, "The Social and Cultural Context: Thirteenth to Fifteenth Centuries," in *History of Jewish Philosophy*, ed. D. H. Frank and O. Leaman (London and New York: Routledge, 1997), 294–330, esp. 295–6 and 312–13 and the notes thereto.

54. See Harvey, "Crescas's Critique." On Crescas' critique of Aristotelian science, see H. A. Wolfson, *Crescas' Critique of Aristotle* (Cambridge, Mass.: Harvard University Press, 1929).

55. S. Pines, *Scholasticism after Thomas Aquinas and the Teachings of Hasdai Crescas and his Predecessors* (Jerusalem: Israel Academy of Sciences and Humanities, 1967), 22–3.

56. The influence of Avicenna in Hebrew translation in the fourteenth and fifteenth centuries has recently been studied by M. Zonta; see his "The Relationship of European Jewish Philosophy to Islamic and Christian Philosophies in the Late Middle Ages," *Jewish Studies Quarterly* 7 (2000), 127–40, and his two studies referred to in his n. 2. On al-Ghazali's influence during this same period, see my "Why did Fourteenth-Century Jews Turn to Alghazali's Account of Natural Science?" *Jewish Quarterly Review* 91 (2001), 359–76.

57. See Zonta's discussion of "Hebrew-Latin Philosophy" in Zonta, "Relationship," and the studies noted there. On the relation of anti-Christian polemics to the impact of Christian Scholastic philosophy on Jewish thought in Spain, see D. Lasker, "The Impact of Christianity on Late Iberian Jewish Philosophy," in *In Iberia and Beyond: Hispanic Jews between Cultures*, ed. B. Cooperman (Newark: University of Delaware Press, 1998), 175–90.

58. H. Tirosh-Rothschild, "Jewish Philosophy on the Eve of Modernity," in Frank and Leaman (eds.), *History of Jewish Philosophy*, 545. I would delete the word "most." Averroes was *the* authoritative commentator on Aristotle, and it was this authority that he gradually lost in the fifteenth and sixteenth centuries.

59. On the study of Averroes in the sixteenth century, see ibid., 499–563, and A. L. Ivry, "Remnants of Jewish Averroism in the Renaissance," in *Jewish Thought in the Sixteenth Century*, ed. B. Cooperman (Cambridge, Mass.: Harvard University Press, 1983), 243–65.

13 Philosophy in southern France: Controversy over philosophic study and the influence of Averroes upon Jewish thought*

In the summer of 1305, Rabbi Solomon ibn Adret and his court in Barcelona prohibited the study of Greco-Arabic philosophy and science to Catalonian Jews below the age of twenty-five.[1] In order to protect their community from any potential effects of this decree, a group of prominent Jewish scholars in the city of Montpellier prohibited the placement of any obstacle in the way of southern French Jews, of any age, wishing to pursue Greco-Arabic learning. The transgression of either injunction by Jews within its jurisdiction carried the severe penalty of excommunication or communal banishment. The leader of a more conservative philosophic group in Montpellier, frustrated by the brazen action of his southern French adversaries, declared their proclamation on behalf of Greco-Arabic learning "illegitimate" and excommunicated its promulgators. At the time of this flurry of conflicting excommunications, philosophic perspectives were well incorporated into southern French Jewish culture; yet some more conservative Jewish thinkers felt that the character of philosophic interpretation in the South of France had become so extreme that it endangered the historical and normative fabric of Judaism. Abba Mari of Montpellier, the philosophically oriented thinker who sounded the alarm, cited the influence of the Muslim philosopher Averroes as critical to this treacherous exegetical turn that he hoped to reverse by encouraging the scholars of neighboring Catalonia to prohibit access to Greco-Arabic learning until an age at

---

* The following essay is intended primarily for the English-speaking reader. Endnotes are simply directive rather than exhaustive. More detailed documentation will be found in my *Like a Rose among Thorns: Southern French Jewry and the Philosophic Tradition* (forthcoming).

which aspiring philosophers generally would have achieved a traditional religious commitment. Abba Mari ultimately failed to achieve his goal of steering Jewish culture in the South of France along safer paths, but his efforts opened the window wide upon a whole world of Jewish intellectual and spiritual ferment.[2] This chapter will tell the story of the intense controversy over philosophic study in the South of France at the beginning of the fourteenth century, and lay bare the issues raised by the pursuit of Greco-Arabic learning for southern French Jewish culture.

SPANISH PHILOSOPHIC FERTILIZATION

At the time of the excommunications in Montpellier, the South of France was divided between three kingdoms, Aragon, France, and Burgundy. In spite of these political divisions, common descent and shared cultural patrimony gave the Jews of southern France the sense of belonging to one place, which they often referred to simply as "this land" (ha'aretz ha-zot). By 1300, the Jews of southern France could look back on more than a century and a half of diversified cultural achievement: in Jewish legal scholarship, in the study of Hebrew language and biblical interpretation, in preaching, in polemics, and in poetry. The growth of scientific and philosophic study among southern French Jews during this period affected all of these fields, and contributed to the distinct self-perception of the community.[3] The catalyst for the growth of Jewish philosophic culture in the South of France came from Andalusia, in southern Spain. In 1147, the Jews of Andalusia were forced to leave their homes as Berber tribes that would tolerate no other faith but Islam took power there. On account of this Berber invasion out of North Africa, the Andalusian Jewish community – the most sophisticated in the world in terms of its rich, deep, and lengthy interaction with Greco-Arabic learning – was forced beyond its original borders. Some of the Andalusian Jews decided to move elsewhere in the Islamic world, others relocated northward to Christian Spain. A small but significant group reached southern France. The arrival of these scholars initiated the transformation of southern French Jewish culture. Unlike the Andalusians, the southern French scholars had focused their learning almost exclusively upon rabbinic scholarship. Of course, southern French Jews had no knowledge of the Arabic language in which the learning of

Andalusia was contained. The questions, categories, and modes of discussion found in a philosophically and scientifically engaged culture like that of Andalusia were therefore quite foreign to southern French Jews. Nevertheless, the intellectual elite of southern French Jewry welcomed their newly arrived colleagues and was receptive to their learning.

Following a period of oral transmission, curious southern French scholars commissioned the new arrivals to begin translating philosophic and scientific works from Arabic into Hebrew. As a result of this fortuitous emigration of scholars from Spain to France, a translation movement developed. From its beginning, one family was central to the translation movement: the family of translators and commentators named Tibbon. Judah ibn Tibbon, an émigré from Granada, established the family in the South of France, and in his wake, we know of at least five generations of Tibbonide scholarly activity there. Through their many translations, members of the Tibbon family, including Judah, his son Samuel, and grandson Moses, among others, taught the Jews of southern France about the learning of the Arabic world. In addition, many other scholars joined the Tibbon family by learning Arabic and contributing Hebrew translations – to the great enrichment of southern French Jewish culture. Southern French Jewry sustained this movement of translation from Arabic into Hebrew for a period of over 150 years. At first, the translation of more basic works from within Jewish tradition was undertaken. Subsequently, the translators expanded the scope of their work to produce Hebrew versions of weighty and sophisticated works belonging to the Arabic philosophic tradition. The corpus of translations into Hebrew of Greek, Arabic, and Judeo-Arabic learning in mathematics, astronomy, medicine, ethics, physics, and metaphysics is nothing less than staggering.[4]

THE MATURATION OF JEWISH PHILOSOPHIC CULTURE IN THE SOUTH OF FRANCE

This newly translated knowledge brought deep tensions and uneasiness to southern French Jewry. In 1204, Samuel ibn Tibbon translated *The Guide of the Perplexed* of Maimonides. In studying Maimonides' great philosophic work, as well as his code of Jewish law *Mishneh Torah*, at least a few local scholars began to appreciate how Maimonides' serious engagement with Greco-Arabic learning had led him to interpret Jewish teachings in ways that were quite foreign to traditional rabbinic understandings. In the 1230s, a group of southern French scholars banned Maimonides' works. An intense controversy ensued that involved the entire southern French Jewish community as well as the Jewish scholars of northern France, Catalonia, and Castile.[5] This attempt to forcefully expel the new Judeo-Arabic perspectives from the South of France failed and, in the following decades, the works of Maimonides influenced southern French Jewish culture profoundly. Southern French Jews embraced the newly translated Judeo-Arabic texts and continued to support translation from the Arabic. In addition, the mere study of philosophic and scientific writings translated from the Arabic began to shift to the production of original work in Hebrew as well. Over the course of the thirteenth century, the works of the esteemed translator and biblical commentator Samuel ibn Tibbon – along with those of his students and followers – came to symbolize the growing philosophic sophistication of southern French Jewish culture and of the growth in the South of France of a Jewish community whose thought and writing incorporated philosophic and scientific learning.

Yet Ibn Tibbon himself believed that the moderate understanding of Maimonides prevalent in the South of France during the first half of the century was based upon a misreading of *The Guide of the Perplexed*.[6] Deeply entrenched in the Greco-Arabic philosophic corpus, Ibn Tibbon gave great weight to philosophy in his understanding of Jewish tradition. In his *Ecclesiastes Commentary*, for example, he seems less concerned to mediate between the Jewish tradition and philosophy, than to reveal the inner philosophic meaning of Scripture. "Those [philosophic] truths which had been concealed [within Jewish tradition] ever since the time of our prophets and sages are today all known to the nations of the world."[7] As southern French Jewish philosophic culture matured, however, the views of Ibn Tibbon became more popular. At the turn the fourteenth century, a significant number of southern French Jewish scholars could appreciate, for example, the subtleties of the philosophic debate as to whether the world had been created out of nothing by the will of God or, as seemed increasingly likely, had come into being by more naturalistic means. Frequently, trained philosophers were of the opinion that they had encountered decisive arguments against the creation of the world *ex nihilo*, and therefore felt compelled to live with the welter of theological and exegetical problems that this typically entailed. Models for the survival of the soul after death that emphasized the role of the properly developed intellect took greater hold and raised doubts about the nature of the relationship between the observance of the commandments and immortality. The use of philosophic allegory in biblical interpretation flourished, both in order to satisfy the need to have Scripture speak philosophically, as well as to resolve philosophic problems that a simple reading of Scripture sometimes raised.

A CONSERVATIVE MAIMONIDEAN RESPONSE

The ways in which the students of Ibn Tibbon sought to widen the scope of allegorical interpretation, and make it more public, seemed to other more traditional southern French scholars to endanger the historicity of biblical narrative and, at times, even threaten the literal meaning of the commandments. For this reason, the efflorescence of philosophic allegory in the South of France deeply troubled the conservative Jewish rationalists of the region. Abba Mari ben Moses of Montpellier, for example, describes the situation in the most urgent terms: "They have nearly stripped the Torah of its literal meanings and left it naked!"[8] In response to such alarming cultural developments, Abba Mari hopes to restore philosophic interpretation to the esoteric state implied by Maimonides' prescription that philosophic education proceed gradually and in stages from basic to more advanced subjects.[9] In Abba Mari's vision, the study of science and philosophy in the South of France would be restricted to the community's senior members, while the stream of philosophic translation and innovative commentary inspired by the Tibbons would dry up. Over the course of his struggle, Abba Mari is forced to change his strategy. Initially, he attempts to attack the writings of the southern French philosopher-translators themselves, while expressing great esteem for the Greco-Arabic philosophic works that they had translated. The translated philosophic works of non-Jews, he argues, pose no danger to Jews because they can be identified by all as foreign and studied with the appropriate skepticism.[10] According to Abba Mari, non-Jews might reason philosophically that the world is eternal, as they had no revelation to obligate them to believe in the creation. They had not experienced the miracles of the Exodus nor did they benefit from hearing God at Sinai. In Abba Mari's initial argument, Maimonides had removed any intellectual threat to the Jewish community from the non-Jewish philosophy by demonstrating that the eternity of the world cannot be proven.[11] At this point in his struggle, Abba Mari still hopes for success in attacking the Tibbonide stream in southern French Jewish culture directly. He argues that the danger to the community lurks only in Jewish philosophic works, as the simple believer might read them with uncritical acceptance.[12] The new works of Jewish philosophic interpretation, Abba Mari argues, might infect the innocent and credulous mind of the casual reader who stood open to and unguarded against their heresy. Even a thick veil of esotericism would not offer sufficient protection. Thus, the very presence of such works within the Jewish community is intolerable. In Abba Mari's view, southern French Jewish scholars who adopt the positions of the Arabic philosophers and reinterpret the Torah in their light may not be excused, and their works must be destroyed.[13] Abba Mari never informs us precisely to which works he refers, but his audience, of course, would have understood the writings of Samuel ibn Tibbon and his followers.

THE TURN TO BARCELONA

To his dismay, Abba Mari finds insufficient support for his views in the South of France.[14] Therefore, he turns outside of his immediate geographic and cultural context to the leader of the neighboring Catalonian community, Solomon ben Abraham ibn Adret (Rashba) of Barcelona. Rashba's support could be invaluable, as he was widely regarded as the greatest Jewish legal scholar of the day. And Abba Mari had every reason to believe that Rashba would support his cause, as Catalonian Jewry, and Rashba himself, did not share southern French Jewry's distinctive relationship to the philosophic tradition. In fact, Rashba angrily condemns the adoption by southern French scholars of the Maimonidean identification of Aristotelian physics and metaphysics with the esoteric teaching of Torah of Israel, with the disciplines that the Mishnah calls "the account of creation" and "the account of the chariot."[15] In response to this fundamental rationalist identification, Rashba demurs: To maintain that Aristotle lectured publicly on "hidden teaching," while the ancient Jewish sages and their students remained largely ignorant is patently absurd.[16] Thus Abba Mari could write to Rashba to censure the philosophic allegorists of southern France with confidence that his request would be well received.[17] According to Abba Mari, the devotion of a certain group of southern French scholars to Averroes' *Commentaries* inspires their reckless interpretation.[18] In the South of France, Aristotle's writings were not available for study directly, but only as they are found embedded in Averroes' *Commentaries*.[19] Translated, in large part, by Samuel ibn Tibbon's son Moses in the mid-thirteenth century, Averroes' *Commentaries* on the Aristotelian corpus were among the most sophisticated philosophic works in circulation.[20] Although the precise identity of the scholars whom Abba Mari condemns is unclear, enthusiasm for the Hebrew translations of Averroes' *Commentaries* places this condemned group squarely within the cultural orbit of the philosopher-translators of southern France. Abba Mari fears that their "Christian-like" reading of the commandments endangers religious observance and that their public discussion of the Torah's inner philosophic meaning violates talmudic law.[21] With a gravity and formality appropriate to the circumstances, he publicly calls upon Rashba to exercise his far-reaching prestige as a legal scholar to lead southern French Jewish authorities in action against those who systematically reinterpret Jewish tradition with far-reaching philosophic allegory.[22] With this call to arms, Abba Mari initiates an intensive open correspondence between himself and Rashba as well as between himself and scholars from all over the South of France about the nature of southern French Jewish culture and the proper place of allegorical interpretation and Greco-Arabic philosophy in the curriculum of southern French Jewry. Abba Mari's electrifying literary exchanges compel other southern French scholars to write open letters to Rashba on these very same matters, and Rashba feels obligated to respond publicly to them as well. The prose of this extensive correspondence evinces considerable emotive force and literary craft. The felicitous, and often entertaining, reuse of phrases from biblical and rabbinic texts and the frequent introduction of rhymed prose are among the literary devices that these writers are able to exploit with expertise and apparent ease. In his selective anthology of this correspondence, which he entitles *An Offering of Zeal*, Abba Mari does indeed include the correspondence of his adversaries, although not fully. Abba Mari may have intended to include additional material in a companion volume that he promised to edit of the more lengthy southern French letters.[23] However that may be, Abba Mari's decision to exclude (or suppress) material from circulation through his *Offering of Zeal* generally resulted in its loss to posterity. Nevertheless, fragments of additional valuable material survive due to a variety of circumstances. In one extraordinary case, Simeon ben Joseph, a protégé of Abba Mari, wrote a lengthy point-by-point response to an exceedingly important letter by the great southern French talmudist Menahem ha-Meiri of Perpignan.[24] As Meiri's letter does not survive independently, it would have been lost to us were it not for Simeon's extensive citation of it in his rebuttal *Hoshen Mishpat*, which itself only survives in a unique copy contained within the folios of one late manuscript.[25]

RASHBA REFUSES TO INTERVENE

In his reply to Abba Mari, Rashba implies that the philosophic allegory of the accused southern French interpreters involves a heretical departure from a religious tradition held in common with Christians and Muslims,[26] and that Jews should not tolerate such heresy any more than would gentiles. Underlying Rashba's critique is his belief that the southern French interpreters seek to destroy the normative character of Judaism through allegory.[27] Despite these forceful condemnations, Rashba publicly rejects Abba Mari's invitation to intervene. The Catalonian scholar asserts that, although Abba Mari's intentions please him, he can do nothing to help; his involvement in southern French affairs would be perceived as an unwarranted intrusion.[28] Rashba instead encourages Abba Mari to find like-minded southern French scholars who will take his concerns to heart. Nevertheless, in an unsigned private note inserted into the manuscript quire of his *responsum*,[29] Rashba reveals his intense antipathy toward the most popular and esteemed Torah commentary in southern France, the *Malmad ha-Talmidim* of the philosophic translator and son-in-law of Samuel ibn Tibbon, Jacob Anatoli.[30] In this work, Anatoli – whom Rashba here derides as the "elderly king" – makes plain how "the Torah conceals that which Existence has

revealed to the philosophers."[31] After publicly refusing to acknowledge any justification for his intervention, Rashba concludes under
the cover of private, unofficial communication: We here in Catalonia
take the strongest possible exception to southern French philosophic
interpretation as represented by the "elderly king,"[32] but we can
take no action against your leaders who expound it.[33] When eventually leaked, Rashba's private message creates a furor in the South
of France. While Abba Mari never denies that Rashba penned this
note, he insists, "We do not know to precisely [which scholar the
note] refers."[34] Many others in the South of France, however, had no
doubt that Rashba had denounced Jacob Anatoli and his *Malmad ha-
Talmidim*, and public readings of the Anatoli's work were convened
in protest.[35]

A BAN ON "GREEK BOOKS"

After the receipt of Rashba's private note, Abba Mari put aside his
efforts to attack Jewish philosophic interpretation directly; its support in southern France was overwhelming and Rashba did not
feel empowered to stand against it. Shortly afterward, however,
Rashba writes to Crescas Vidal, a Barcelonan Jew living in Perpignan,
to inquire regarding the character of philosophic interpretation in
southern France.[36] In response, Crescas suggests that Rashba formally prohibit the study of Greco-Arabic scientific and philosophic
works – with the exception of the study of medicine – before the age
of thirty on pain of excommunication. Crescas argues that such a
prohibition would force southern French Jews to delve deeply into
the Talmud as youths, and only later, after they have matured and
their religious commitments have been established, to turn to philosophy. Crescas concludes, "At the moment there is reason to fear
that the philosophically inspired youths, who have not seen the light
of Torah, will – heaven forbid – turn the whole country to heresy."[37]
Despite Crescas' grave concerns, Rashba is unwilling to promulgate an excommunication for southern France on his authority
alone, and continues to exhort Perpignan Jews to remedy their own
situation.[38]

   As his new strategy to redirect the course of Jewish culture in the
South of France, Abba Mari adopts the suggestion of Crescas Vidal.
In a position paper in favor of the prohibition of Greco-Arabic

philosophic works to the young, Abba Mari's argument turns on a passage from the *Guide of the Perplexed* concerning the obstacles that stand in the way of intellectual perfection. In this passage, Maimonides expresses the view that it is not proper to begin philosophic study until an age at which one's sexual drive is diminished (*Guide* 1:34). Abba Mari argues that if an age restriction applies to philosophic works written by Jews, it applies even more so to similar works – full of erroneous and dangerous teachings – written by gentiles.[39] In the context of this argument, he emphasizes that the study of Averroes' *Commentaries* has led to the adoption of heretical views, which, in turn, have been incorporated into Jewish exegesis.[40] Abba Mari makes no attempt to critique Averroes' philosophic argument that the world is eternal. Rather, he insists that Maimonides would not have young Jews study such a dangerous work whose arguments were so difficult to refute. Based on his own study of Averroes, Abba Mari argues that the prerequisites that the Maimonidean tradition had established in regard to who may study Jewish philosophic works should be observed even more scrupulously for Greco-Arabic works, indeed under penalty of excommunication. Abba Mari acknowledges that precious things may be learned from the works of the Arabic philosophers; however, the risk and the potential cost of acquiring them through study of such dangerous works is simply too great for the average person, and should be reserved for great sages. Having failed to impugn the southern French philosopher-translators directly, Abba Mari resolved to attack Greco-Arabic learning as an alternate path to rein in Jewish philosophic culture in the South of France. Despite a rather cool early reception in Perpignan,[41] Abba Mari and Rashba resolve to continue their struggle to implement a prohibition of Greco-Arabic scientific and philosophic writing in the South of France until an age at which individuals generally have achieved a traditional religious commitment.

THE SOUTH OF FRANCE FAILS TO ACT

Operating discreetly, Rashba and Abba Mari set out to stimulate the scholars of southern France to prohibit Greco-Arabic philosophic works. Rashba transmits to Abba Mari and his colleague Todros of Beaucaire a sealed document, signed by the scholars of Barcelona, that formally asks the scholars of Montpellier to prohibit the study of Greco-Arabic works, medical works excepted, until the age of thirty.[42] Rashba instructs the two men to test the climate of opinion in Montpellier before making the letter public. Over a period of a month or two, Todros and Abba Mari vet a few leading scholars and are convinced that they can win approval for the excommunication from the elders of the Jewish community. They plan, therefore, to read the Barcelona request publicly on a Sabbath in Elul, 1304. On the Friday before that Sabbath, the physician, astronomer, and philosophic translator Jacob ben Makhir ibn Tibbon approaches Abba Mari.[43] He expresses his absolute objection to a ban on scientific study and asks Abba Mari to terminate his efforts toward this end. A dispute ensues, and neither man is able to convince the other. For Jacob ben Makhir, it is patent that the Barcelona community was reaching into the jurisdiction of another community and violating its local autonomy. In a report to Rashba, Abba Mari quotes Jacob ben Makhir: "What do they [the Catalonian rabbis] have to do with us? God placed a boundary between them and us. We shall not obey or submit to them."[44] Abba Mari claims that Jacob initially supported his efforts, until Judah ben Moses ibn Tibbon persuaded him to oppose them.[45] On the following Sabbath, Abba Mari reads the Barcelona letter to the community, hoping that its authority might lead to a consensus in favor of a ban. Jacob ben Makhir comes forward and raises his voice against the excommunication that the letter proposes. The gathering ends in confusion, and no community action is taken.[46]

Upon hearing the news, Rashba temporarily retreats. To the protests of the group in Montpellier against a ban he responds, "Great ones of judgment and council! Act as your intellect sees fit. We have no more involvement in this matter."[47] Abba Mari, on the other hand, asks Rashba to increase his involvement.[48] In addition to the formal request already sent to the elders of Montpellier to proclaim a ban, Abba Mari asks Rashba to actually pronounce a ban in Barcelona to serve as a model for the communities of southern France. In this fashion, Abba Mari hopes to put further pressure on his own community to enact a ban. Rashba declines to grant these requests, at least for the time being. However, he encourages Abba Mari to continue the struggle toward the proclamation of a ban in the Midi without the help of an excommunication in Barcelona.[49] Rather than accept defeat, Abba Mari is spurred to action. He urges the leaders of several communities to write to Rashba, to indicate their support for the ban that the Barcelona leaders had advised at Montpellier, and to request Rashba's leadership in its pronouncement.[50] Abba Mari's colleague, Jacob of Beaucaire travels east of the Rhône, throughout Provence and Comtat Venaissin, to inform Jews of Abba Mari's struggle and to enlist their support.[51] Rashba remains unmoved and responds to the requests of the elders of Aix,[52] Argentière,[53] and Lunel,[54] as he did to Abba Mari: The initiative for an excommunication must come from the South of France.

THE EXCOMMUNICATION AT BARCELONA

The involvement of the nasi (leader) of Narbonne,[55] Kalonymus ben Todros, turns out to be decisive. Abba Mari sends his position paper on the controversy to Rashba with the nasi's approbation.[56] After eight months of silence – in part due to illness – Rashba writes to Abba Mari and to Kalonymus ha-Nasi that he has reconsidered and is willing to promulgate a model Spanish excommunication.[57] Nevertheless, Rashba insists that the initiative for the ban must begin, at least formally, in southern France.[58] After numerous expressions of reluctance and irritation, Abba Mari and Kalonymus ben Todros send their formal request to Barcelona, and promise to follow suit with a southern French ban after the Catalonian version is promulgated.[59] On the Ninth of Av, 1305, the elders of Barcelona proclaim a ban – for their community and for a fifty-year period – on the study of Greco-Arabic works on physics and metaphysics before the age of twenty-five.[60] In two sections of Rashba's promulgation, he asks the scholars of southern France to enact a parallel decree in the most forceful and urgent terms.[61] However, southern French documents in support of the Catalonian ban are never sent. Even the excommunication of Barcelona fails to create the support necessary for a similar proclamation in the South of France.

THE REACTION FROM PERPIGNAN

The great talmudist Menahem ha-Meiri of Perpignan views Abba Mari's call to Barcelona as contributing not only to the slander of prominent southern French Jewish scholars, but also to the defamation of their generations-old cultural ideal of commitment to traditional Jewish and Greco-Arabic learning.[62] While Meiri reveres Rashba as a talmudist,[63] he believes that Ibn Adret's hostility toward philosophy and kabbalistic orientation render his opinion regarding the course of Jewish culture in the South of France of little relevance.[64] Unlike Abba Mari, Meiri trusts the Tibbonide elite, as integral members of a larger philosophically sophisticated and God-fearing community, to handle the *Commentaries* of Averroes in a fashion that is ultimately compatible with Jewish tradition.[65] In his argument against the example set by the Catalonian ban, Meiri counters that the works of Averroes, while so critical to the sophistication of Jewish philosophic discourse in the South of France, have had little to do with the spread of philosophic allegory there. According to Meiri, those who misuse philosophic allegory are thoroughly unaware of Averroes' *Commentaries*, and the problematic public interpretation of Scripture does not draw upon such highly technical works. To the contrary, the inspiration for the dangerous interpretation comes, as Abba Mari himself had argued, from Jewish authors within the philosophic tradition, including Maimonides and the esteemed philosopher-translators of southern France.[66] Meiri supports Abba Mari's original claim that locally venerated Jewish works encourage the dangerous proliferation of allegorical interpretation in the South of France, but he proposes a rather different solution to this problem. He advises that allegorical interpreters be directed toward those sections of Scripture that are neither legal nor historical in nature, and hence may be subjected to philosophic allegoresis without ill effect.[67]

THE EXCOMMUNICATIONS AT MONTPELLIER

Upon hearing of the Barcelona excommunications, Abba Mari's adversaries in Montpellier issue an angry communiqué to Rashba stating that the Catalonian attempt to influence Jewish culture in southern France constitutes a violation of local rabbinical sovereignty.[68] "One kingdom should not infringe upon its neighbor even so much as a hair's breadth," they exclaim.[69] Rashba should never have entertained such "treachery," in their evaluation.[70] Abba Mari's adversaries brazenly equate Rashba's prohibition of the study of physics and metaphysics with a prohibition of the activity through which immortality is achieved. In their view, it is not only the validity of the Maimonidean legacy that is at stake – as Meiri would have it – but also access to immortality itself.[71] According to these scholars, only the intellect "acquired" as a result of philosophic comprehension survives death. Hence, one may unite with God in love and attain immortality only through the study of physics and metaphysics;[72] and the potentially invaluable benefits of philosophic study must doubtless remain accessible to all. Such an unequivocal public affirmation of the teaching that immortality is directly dependent upon philosophic comprehension – and by implication dependent only instrumentally upon the observance of the commandments – indicates how thoroughly the philosophic interpretation of Judaism has enveloped an important segment of southern French Jewry.

As befits their understanding of the immeasurable importance of philosophic study, Abba Mari's adversaries act expeditiously to counter any potential effect of the Barcelona ban in southern France. So as to obtain the royal permission necessary in order to promulgate an excommunication in France, they discreetly bribe the local *seigneur*; and, despite Abba Mari's best efforts, they successfully pronounce a ban upon anyone who would prevent any pupil, regardless of age, from the study of philosophy.[73] "Quite to the contrary!" Abba Mari retorts, excommunicating his adversaries by formally invoking the rule, "Anyone who excommunicates unjustly, himself stands under the ban."[74] Abba Mari hopes to ensure that his adversaries' excommunication would be considered invalid, and that his counterexcommunication would stand. To that end he writes to Rashba,[75] scholars throughout southern France, and even to Asher ben Yehiel of Toledo[76] for their legal opinions as to which excommunication is in force.

Rashba rules the pro-philosophic excommunication erroneous and without precedent, but asks Abba Mari to put an end to the fighting by revoking his counterexcommunication that is, as a result, in force.[77] Menahem ha-Meiri, on the other hand, rules both the ban of Abba Mari and that of his adversaries equally valid and equally inappropriate. In matters touching upon cultural commitments, Meiri argues, each coherent community must legislate for itself and, without anger or offense, restrain itself from interfering in the affairs of others.[78] One's attitude toward philosophic study, in

Meiri's view, is a result of one's education and personal inclination. The permissibility of such study, therefore, should not be the subject of legislation, as its inevitable violation involves the disgrace of rabbinic authority.[79] Abba Mari, nevertheless, refuses to give up his struggle and continues to seek southern French supporters for his excommunication.[80]

The controversy is disrupted when, in distant Paris, Philip the Fair, the king of France, decrees an expulsion of all the Jews of his realm – which includes most of southern France – and seizes their property.[81] At the royal court, the circumstances of the expulsion relate to the expanding political and economic powers of the French crown. Abba Mari, however, attributes the expulsion to divine retribution for the sins of his adversaries.[82] About ten weeks after the promulgation in Paris, the Jews of Montpellier are exiled. The Jews of Perpignan are not subject to the decrees of the king of France, as James II of Majorca holds title to Roussillon and Perpignan is his capital. Many Montpellierian Jews journey to Perpignan, but Abba Mari is exiled to Arles in Provence. Four months later, he attempts to resettle in Perpignan, but the agents of the James II, at the behest of local Jews, refuse him entry.[83] As there is no evidence that Abba Mari revoked the excommunication of his adversaries, perhaps they too retained their stance against him.

CONCLUSION

Throughout the controversy over philosophic study, Abba Mari and his circle evince great clarity of purpose, persistent energy, and significant skill in a variety of ways: in their efforts to persuade their colleagues that philosophic interpretation in the South of France indeed had broken all bounds; in obtaining the consent of Rashba and his court to take significant risks on their behalf; and in gathering, editing, and publishing much of the controversy's correspondence in their *Offering of Zeal*. The activity of the Tibbons and their followers, including the extensive use of philosophic allegory as an interpretive lens, as well as their strong commitment to the Hebrew translation of Greco-Arabic learning, deeply discomfited Abba Mari. To his mind, Maimonides had wrestled successfully and conclusively with the great philosophic dilemmas affecting Judaism, and the *Guide of the Perplexed* was therefore a monumental work. The continued inquiry into fundamental questions by lesser minds as well as widening the scope of philosophic interpretation could breed only confusion and heresy in his view. Indeed, thought Abba Mari, had Maimonides himself not warned of the grave dangers involved in the careless transmission of philosophic teaching? Beyond his concern for the requirements of esotericism, Abba Mari also seems to have sensed something new and extraordinarily powerful in the works of Averroes that added greatly to his unease. Upon reading Averroes' *Commentary* to Aristotle's *De Caelo*, Abba Mari almost wonders aloud: Were Maimonides' demonstrations reconciling Judaism with the philosophic tradition, in fact, all conclusive? Might anyone return to these ponderous and arcane matters to adjudicate them? The way simply must be closed off.

When local support was not forthcoming, Abba Mari wisely found a strong ally in Rashba and the scholars of Barcelona who – unlike the southern French – were deeply ambivalent about the religious value of the philosophic tradition. Without doubt, the Catalonian scholars would have been pleased to see Abba Mari succeed against those southern French scholars who sought such an expansive role for philosophy within Judaism. To Rashba, the southern French notions that there was a religious imperative to study physics and metaphysics and that immortality depended directly upon intellectual comprehension were patently absurd. Over the course of the controversy, Abba Mari and his supporters managed to convince Rashba to provide ever-greater backing for their cause, culminating with his promulgation of a model prohibition of Greco-Arabic learning in Catalonia. When even this dramatic action failed to produce the desired results, the possibilities for Rashba's involvement clearly had been exhausted. Rashba made it patent that, despite his intense concern for Abba Mari's struggle, he would not attempt to impose his will directly upon the leaders of southern French Jewry. In any case, such an action almost certainly would have done no good. Abba Mari's powerful adversaries deemed even the promulgation of Rashba's model decree as a hostile overreaching of Catalonian jurisdiction, and they made it quite clear how strongly they disapproved of Rashba's consort with Abba Mari.

The controversy over philosophic study does not appear to have changed the course of Jewish culture in the South of France. In

the wake of the expulsion, southern French Jewish culture continued to develop with growing philosophic sophistication; no longer,
of course, in the ancient centers of Languedoc where the French
king would invite Jews to return periodically throughout the fourteenth century only to expel them again a few years later; nor in
Perpignan and its county of Roussillon, which came increasingly
under the influence of the crown of Aragon and by the second half
of the fourteenth century largely lost its southern French character; but, especially, in Provence, in the regions of Avignon, Orange,
and Comtat Venaissin, where Jews were the subjects of either the
pope or the king of Burgundy. In this region, one has little sense
that the French expulsions were disruptive to Jewish life. One might
even speculate that the Languedocian immigration to Provence led
to an intensification of Jewish philosophic culture there, where it
flourished to an extent greater than before until the turn of the fourteenth century. For example, Gersonides (d. 1344), one of the greatest
philosophers, mathematicians, and astronomers of the medieval
period lived and worked in Orange, almost completely within the
context of Jewish culture and the Hebrew translations of Greco-
Arabic learning. Yedayah ha-Penini, who in his twenties had sent a
Ketav ha-Hitnatzlut to Rashba in defense of the local Jewish culture, was Gersonides' student as well as an author of important
scientific works in his own right. A Provençal circle devoted to
the study of Arabic philosophy discussed and wrote commentaries
upon important Greco-Arabic philosophic works.[84] Its senior member, Samuel ben Judah of Marseilles, translated Averroes' commentaries to Plato's *Republic* and to Aristotle's *Nicomachean Ethics* into
Hebrew for the first time. Joseph ibn Kaspi of Argentière composed
significant philosophic commentaries to many books of the Bible as
well as to Maimonides' *Guide of the Perplexed*. Nissim ben Moses
of Marseilles wrote a *Torah Commentary* with a philosophically
inspired political interpretation of Judaism. Another contemporary
Provençal group, gathered around Solomon Prat Maimon, devoted
itself to the interpretation of the *Kuzari* of Judah Halevi with substantial philosophic creativity and sophistication. All this fourteenth-
century southern French philosophic study and writing occurred
in the county of Provence, where philosophic activity heretofore
had been limited. Other important examples might be adduced
as well.

NOTES

1. Various aspects of this controversy have been addressed by historical research; see, for example, J. Sarachek, *Faith and Reason: The Conflict over the Rationalism of Maimonides* (Williamsport: The Bayard Press, 1935), 73–127; Y. Baer, *A History of the Jews in Christian Spain*, 2 vols. (Philadelphia: Jewish Publication Society of America, 1978), 1: 289–305; A. Halkin, "Yedaiah Bedershi's Apology," in *Jewish Medieval and Renaissance Studies*, ed. A. Altmann (Cambridge, Mass.: Harvard University Press, 1967), 165–84; A. Halkin, "Why was Levi ben Hayyim Hounded?," *Proceedings of the American Academy for Jewish Research* 34 (1966), 65–76; J. Shatzmiller, "Rationalisme et orthodoxie religieuse chez les juifs provençaux au commencement du XIVe siècle," *Provence historique* 22 (1972), 261–86; J. Shatzmiller, "Ben Abba Mari la-Rashba: ha-masa u-matan she-qadam le-herem be-Bartzelona," *Mehqarim be-Toledot ʿAm Yisrael ve-Eretz Yisrael* 3 (1974), 121–37; M. Saperstein, "The Conflict over the Rashba's Herem on Philosophical Study: A Political Perspective," *Jewish History* 1 (1986), 27–38; D. Schwartz, "'Hokhma Yevanit' – Behina Mehudeshet bi-Tequfat ha-Pulmus ʿal Limud ha-Filosofia," *Sinai* 104 (1989), 148–53; D. Schwartz, "Changing Fronts in the Controversies over Philosophy in Medieval Spain and Provence," *Journal of Jewish Thought and Philosophy* 7 (1997), 61–82; D. Schwartz, "Birurim Rʿayoniyim be-Suggyat ha-Pulmusim ʿal ha-Filosofia bi-Yeme ha-Benayim," *Kobetz ʿal Yad* 14 (1998), 299–348; and M. Halbertal, *People of the Book: Canon, Meaning, and Authority* (Cambridge, Mass.: Harvard University Press, 1997), 109–19.

2. To my knowledge, the documents that survive from this affair are the following: *Minhat Qenaʾot*, ed. Abba Mari ben Moses, in *Teshuvot ha-Rashba*, ed. H. Dimitrovsky, 2 vols. (Jerusalem: Mosad ha-Rav Kook, 1990); a few of these letters are found also in *Sheʾelot u-Teshuvot ha-Rashbah*, 7 vols. (Jerusalem: Mekhon Tiferet ha-Torah, 1988), II nos. 414–17; Simeon ben Joseph, *Hoshen Mishpat*, in D. Kaufmann, "Simeon b. Josefs Sendschreiben an Menachem b. Salomo," in *Jubelschrift zum neunzigsten Geburtstag des Dr. L. Zunz* (Berlin: L. Gershel, 1884), Hebrew section, 142–74; D. Kaufmann, "Deux lettres de Siméon ben Joseph," *Revue des Etudes Juives* 29 (1894), 214–28; and Yedayah ha-Penini, *Ketav ha-Hitnatzlut*, in *Sheʾelot u-Teshuvot ha-Rashbah*, 1, no. 418.

3. See I. Twersky, "Aspects of the Social and Cultural History of Provençal Jewry," *Journal of World History* 11 (1968), 185–207; G. Freudenthal, "Les sciences dans les communautés juives médiévales de Provence: Leur appropriation, leur rôle," *Revue des Etudes Juives* 152

(1993), 29–136; G. Freudenthal, "Science in Medieval Jewish Culture," *History of Science* 33 (1995), 23–58.

4. The bulk of the translations described in Steinschneider's awesome *Die hebräischen Übersetzungen des Mittelalters und die Juden als Dolmetscher* (Berlin, 1893) was produced by and for the Jews of southern France.

5. See B. Septimus, *Hispano-Jewish Culture in Transition: The Career and Controversies of Ramah* (Cambridge, Mass.: Harvard University Press, 1982).

6. Samuel ibn Tibbon, *Commentary on Ecclesiastes*, MS Parma 2182, 7v–8r as cited and translated in A. Ravitzky, "Samuel ibn Tibbon and the Esoteric Character of the *Guide of the Perplexed*," *AJS Review* 6 (1981), 89–90.

7. See A. Ravitzky, "The Secrets of the *Guide to the Perplexed*: Between the Thirteenth and Twentieth Centuries," in *Studies in Maimonides*, ed. I. Twersky (Cambridge, Mass.: Harvard University Press, 1990), 179.

8. *Minhat Qena'ot*, 408.

9. *Minhat Qena'ot*, 652; cf. *Guide* 1:34, and 3:51, 54.

10. *Minhat Qena'ot*, 317.

11. *Minhat Qena'ot*, 257.

12. *Minhat Qena'ot*, 317.

13. *Minhat Qena'ot*, 258.

14. *Hoshen Mishpat*, 150.

15. Maimonides, *Mishnah Commentary, Hagigah* 2:1, and *Guide* 1:71.

16. *Minhat Qena'ot*, 277–8.

17. *Minhat Qena'ot*, 272.

18. The twelfth-century Andalusian Muslim philosopher Averroes had succeeded in peeling away from Aristotle much of the Neoplatonic interpretive accretion that was often much more conducive to many religious thinkers. On the importance of Averroes in the history of philosophy, see J. Jolivet (ed.), *Multiple Averroes: Actes du Colloque international organisé à l'occasion du 850e anniversaire de la naissance d'Averroes* (Paris: Belles Lettres, 1978); and G. Endress and J. Aertsen (eds.), *Averroes and the Aristotelian Tradition: Sources, Constitution, and Reception of the Philosophy of Ibn Rushd (1126–1198)* (Leiden: Brill, 1999).

19. The Hebrew version of Aristotle's *Meteorology* is an exception, although significantly indebted to Averroes' commentaries; see A. Ravitzky, "Sefer ha-Metorologica le-Aristo u-Darke ha-Parshanut ha-Maimonit le-Ma'ase Bereshit," *Mehqere Yerushalayim be-Mahshevet Yisrael* 9 (1990), 225–50.

20. R. Glasner, "Levi ben Gershom and the Study of Ibn Rushd in the Fourteenth Century," *Jewish Quarterly Review* 86 (1995), 51–90, has taken great care to demonstrate that the Hebrew super-commentarial tradition to Averroes' works does not begin before the 1320s. The keen interest for the works of Averroes described here by Abba Mari therefore represents an earlier, more preliminary stage in the European Jewish encounter with this important Muslim philosopher.

21. *Minhat Qena'ot*, 316.

22. *Minhat Qena'ot*, 273; cf. *Minhat Qena'ot*, 316–18.

23. *Minhat Qena'ot*, 824–5.

24. On Meiri, see M. Halbertal, *Ben Torah le-Hokhmah: Rabi Menahem ha-Meiri u-Ba'ale he-Halakhah ha-Maimonim be-Provence* (Jerusalem: Magnes Press, 2000).

25. See n. 2.

26. *Minhat Qena'ot*, 412.

27. *Minhat Qena'ot*, 345.

28. *Minhat Qena'ot*, 280.

29. See *Minhat Qena'ot*, 358.

30. Anatoli's translations of Averroes' *Middle Commentary to Porphyry's Isagoge* and *Aristotle's Categories and Analytics*, completed in Naples in 1232, are dedicated to Frederick II. On Anatoli at the court of Frederick II, see E. H. Kantorowicz, *Frederick the Second* (New York: F. Ungar, 1957), 343–6; G. Sermoneta, "Federico II e il pensiero ebraico nell'Italia del suo tempo," in *Federico II e l'arte del duecento italiano* (Gulatina: Congedo, 1980), 183–97; D. Abulafia, *A Medieval Emperor* (London: Penguin Press, 1988), 244–8, 255–8. On the *Malmad* as a source for Christian–Jewish contacts in southern France, see M. Saperstein, "Christians and Christianity in the Sermons of Jacob Anatoli," *Jewish History* 6 (1992), 225–42.

31. Jacob Anatoli, *Malmad ha-Talmidim* (Lyck: Meqitze Nirdamim, 1866), 32b.

32. Cf. Ecclesiastes 4:13.

33. *Minhat Qena'ot*, 358–9.

34. *Minhat Qena'ot*, 358. Abba Mari protects Rashba and refuses to identify the "elderly king"; see *Minhat Qena'ot*, 692. Simeon ben Joseph states that the accusation that Rashba denounced Anatoli is a fabrication; see Kaufmann, "Deux lettres de Siméon ben Joseph," 221.

35. See Solomon ben Isaac of Lunel's letter to Rashba, *Minhat Qena'ot*, 472, and Abba Mari's report, *Minhat Qena'ot*, 692.

36. *Minhat Qena'ot*, 359.

37. *Minhat Qena'ot*, 372.

38. Rashba wrote four more letters to Perpignan: *Minhat Qena'ot*, 374–85, 385–90, 390–5, 395–9.

39. *Minhat Qena'ot*, 652–3.
40. *Minhat Qena'ot*, 655, but cf. Maimonides' letter to Samuel ibn Tibbon, *'Iggrot ha-Rambam*, ed. Y. Shilat (Jerusalem: Yeshivat Ma'aleh Adumim, 1989), II: 552.
41. See *Minhat Qena'ot*, 399–404 and 407–8.
42. See *Minhat Qena'ot*, 409–14.
43. On the scientific activity of Jacob ben Makhir, see J. Shatzmiller, "Contacts et échanges entre savants juifs et chrétiens à Montpellier vers 1300," in *Juifs et judaïsme de Languedoc* (Toulouse: E. Privat, 1977), 337–44; J. Shatzmiller, "In Search of the 'Book of Figures': Medicine and Astrology in Montpellier at the Turn of the Fourteenth Century," *AJS Review* 7–8 (1982–83), 383–407.
44. *Minhat Qena'ot*, 418.
45. *Minhat Qena'ot*, 416 and 445.
46. *Minhat Qena'ot*, 414–19.
47. *Minhat Qena'ot*, 452.
48. *Minhat Qena'ot*, 442.
49. *Minhat Qena'ot*, 461.
50. *Minhat Qena'ot*, 489.
51. *Minhat Qena'ot*, 599–616. Jacob is the brother of Todros of Beaucaire, another partner in Abba Mari's struggle; see *Minhat Qena'ot*, 409–14.
52. *Minhat Qena'ot*, 551–63.
53. *Minhat Qena'ot*, 564–75.
54. *Minhat Qena'ot*, 616–32.
55. The authority and influence of the nasi during this period is uncertain. For a brief history of the office of the nasi of Narbonne, and documentation of its stature in the twelfth century, see Shatzmiller, "Ben Abba Mari le-Rashba," 135–6.
56. *Minhat Qena'ot*, 637–62 (*Sefer ha-Yareah*). For the nasi's approbation, see *Minhat Qena'ot*, 662.
57. *Minhat Qena'ot*, 665, 667, and 673.
58. Upon receipt of Rashba's letter, Abba Mari writes to him to request that the Catalonian ban prohibit philosophic study until the age of twenty-five only, five years less than originally proposed. Abba Mari suggests that this reduction will reduce the objections to a similar ban in southern France; see *Minhat Qena'ot*, 674–6.
59. *Minhat Qena'ot*, 696–7.
60. *Minhat Qena'ot*, ch. 99.
61. *Minhat Qena'ot*, 722 and 730.
62. *Hoshen Mishpat*, 163. For an alternative view of the southern French Jewish community, see the report of the German-born anti-rationalist talmudist Asher ben Yehiel, *Minhat Qena'ot*, 596–7; and see

I. Ta-Shema, "Shiqqulim Filosofiyyim be-Hakhra'at ha-Halakhah bi-Sefarad," *Tzefunot* 3 (1985), 99–110.

63. See, e.g., *Bet ha-Behirah, Avot,* Introduction, ed. S. Z. Havlin (Jerusalem: Ofeq, 1991), 142.

64. *Hoshen Mishpat,* 150–1. Meiri's statement about Rashba's kabbalistic orientation, although perhaps generally known, astonished numerous contemporaries with its frankness; see Simeon's comment at this point, *Hoshen Mishpat,* 152.

65. *Hoshen Mishpat,* 157–8.

66. *Hoshen Mishpat,* 166.

67. *Hoshen Mishpat,* 167.

68. *Minhat Qena'ot,* 845–53; cf. the letters of Solomon of Lunel, *Minhat Qena'ot,* 470–5, and of Yedayah ha-Penini, *Ketav ha-Hitnatzlut.* The letter of Jacob ben Makhir ibn Tibbon, who died before the excommunications, also shares much with these letters of protest; see *Minhat Qena'ot,* 506–13.

69. *Minhat Qena'ot,* 849; cf. *Minhat Qena'ot,* 856.

70. Yedayah ha-Penini is most disturbed by the correspondence that Rashba had sent throughout Aragon, Castile, and Navarre for support (*Minhat Qena'ot,* 687–9), thereby tarnishing the reputation of southern French Jewry internationally; see *Ketav ha-Hitnatzlut,* 157b.

71. *Minhat Qena'ot,* 852; cf. Maimonides, *Mishneh Torah, Yesode ha-Torah* 2:1; *Teshuvah* 10:2–6.

72. Meiri, however, separates himself from those who make philosophic study a prerequisite for immortality; see *Hoshen Mishpat,* 155.

73. Concerning this transaction, no document survives from the pro-philosophic group (or from Christian authorities); see J. Shatzmiller, "L'excommunication, la communauté juive et les autorités tem-porelles au Moyen-Age," in *Les juifs dans l'histoire de France* (Leiden: Brill, 1980), 61–9; J. Shatzmiller, *Recherches sur la com-munauté juive de Manosque au Moyen Age* (Paris: Mouton, 1973), 52–3 n. 1.

74. *Minhat Qena'ot,* 701–2.

75. *Minhat Qena'ot,* 702–3.

76. *Minhat Qena'ot,* ch. 119. Asher had arrived from Germany just a year before. For his journey, see *Minhat Qena'ot,* 596.

77. *Minhat Qena'ot,* ch. 104. This instruction fulfills Yedayah ha-Penini's call to Rashba to seek the reconciliation of conflicting factions in Mont-pellier; see *Ketav ha-Hitnatzlut,* 174a.

78. *Hoshen Mishpat,* 171–2.

79. *Hoshen Mishpat,* 166.

80. *Minhat Qena'ot,* chs. 111–19.

81. See W. C. Jordan, *The French Monarchy and the Jews: From Philip Augustus to the Last of the Capetians* (Philadelphia: University of Pennsylvania Press, 1989), 214–15. Abba Mari gives the 10th of Av, 1306 as the date of the king's decree.

82. *Minhat Qena'ot*, 835.

83. *Minhat Qena'ot*, 836–7.

84. See L. V. Berman, "Ketav Yad ha-Mekune 'Shoshan Limudim' ve-Yahso li-'Kehal ha-Me'ayanim' ha-Provansali," *Kiryat Sefer* 53 (1978), 368–72; Glasner, "Levi ben Gershom and the Study of Ibn Rushd," 51–90.

14   Conservative tendencies in Gersonides' religious philosophy

Levi ben Gershom (Gersonides, 1288–1344), philosopher, scientist, and rabbinical authority,[1] has often been portrayed in the scholarly literature as a faithful follower of Aristotle and an unorthodox, even radical, theologian: "The boldest of all Jewish philosophers"[2] Gersonides "may be the truest disciple of Aristotle whom medieval Jewish philosophy produced" and hence is "essentially alien to those biblical doctrines which in his formulation he seemed to approach."[3] In Gersonides' system "mosaic dogma [gives] way to the requirements of Aristotelianism" since his intellectual worldview is "Islamic peripateticism in all its purety."[4] One scholar considers his theory of the world's creation to be "almost in the spirit of modern deism" because it "[limits] the direct activity of God to the act of the creation of the world."[5] Another deems his theory of divine knowledge "a theological monstrosity";[6] still another claims that it "radically destroys the whole of history as told in the Bible."[7]

The conception of Gersonides as a religiously radical thinker, which has colored much modern scholarship, has its origins among certain Spanish and Italian rabbis of the fifteenth century, despite (or perhaps because of) the popularity of his writings during that period. To my knowledge it does not appear among the Jewish philosopher-scientists and rabbis of fourteenth-century Provence, Gersonides' native and intellectual environment.[8] He was indeed censured by his contemporaries for his deviations from authorities, but the authorities in question were thinkers like Aristotle and Averroes.[9] His consistently critical attitude toward Averroes, who truly was a faithful Aristotelian, finds expression in many of his writings, especially in the *Wars of the Lord*, where Averroes' views are repeatedly rejected.

Our topic here, however, is not Gersonides' philosophical and scientific unorthodoxy, but rather his conservative religious tendencies, although the two are related, as we shall see. In the first part of the chapter I shall consider briefly his views on personal immortality, divine providence (including miracles and the resurrection of the dead), the allegorization of Scripture, and the creation of the world. I shall argue that, in each case, Gersonides moves away from the regnant Jewish philosophical positions of his day in the direction of more traditional conceptions.[10] In the second part I shall analyze at greater length his views on God's knowledge of human actions and events, which have been viewed as theologically bold even by the few scholars who recognize Gersonides' conservative tendencies.[11] I shall present an interpretation of these views that brings them in line with the conservative thrust of his other doctrines.

A word of caution: although Gersonides' views are more conservative than those of his philosophical contemporaries, they are still sufficiently philosophical to disturb the traditionalists. Gersonides was quite aware that his interpretations of religious doctrine, which he stated openly and explicitly, would be unacceptable to the philosophically uninitiated, an audience for whom he never wrote a single word. For such people, he held, it was sufficent to believe in the dogmas of religions rather than to understand them. Rather he addressed his solutions to those who are "deeply perplexed" by the questions under consideration, who are not satisfied by merely professing true beliefs, but who want clear conceptions of them.[12] In this he did not differ from more orthodox Jewish Aristotelians like Isaac Albalag, Levi ben Abraham, Isaac Pollegar, Joseph ibn Kaspi, and Moses of Narbonne. But unlike these thinkers, who were influenced in varying degrees by the Averroist position that made philosophy independent of Scripture, Gersonides believed that Scripture aided in the philosopher's quest. Not only must Scripture be interpreted in accord with philosophical truth, but the former often provides guidance (*haysharah*) for the latter.[13] As we shall see, Gersonides was willing to use scriptural reports as "empirical data" for his philosophical theories, and in this he differs from his contemporaries.

Gersonides differs from them in another respect as well: whereas the others were known primarily as experts in philosophy, only he among them was known as a scholar of Jewish law.[14] This no doubt enhanced his reputation among subsequent generations of

Jewish thinkers and guaranteed that his philosophical views would be widely considered – and criticized. Gersonides' biblical commentaries were among the earliest Jewish books printed, and his commentaries on the prophetic writings were included in many editions of rabbinic Bibles. By contrast, none of the aforementioned thinkers achieved as widespread a readership; indeed, the few works of theirs that were printed did not appear until modern times.

THE SURVIVAL OF THE SOUL[15]

The tradition of philosophy to which Gersonides was heir was predominantly Islamic and Aristotelian; the doctrines of the Islamic philosophers had been transmitted both directly, through Hebrew translations of the relevant texts, or indirectly, through Hebrew translations of the Jewish philosophers in Islamic lands. Islamic Aristotelian psychology, which consisted in the main of various interpretations of Aristotle's doctrine of the soul, provided the conceptual framework for discussions of the soul's survival after death. Since Aristotle viewed the soul as "the actuality of a natural body having life potentially within it,"[16] it followed for him that when a body ceased to exist, so did its soul. But he also suggested, in a notoriously cryptic passage, that one faculty or function of the human soul, namely, intellect when it is actively thinking, is both "present in the soul" and separate (or separable) from the body, immortal, and eternal.[17] So it became the task of his commentators to explain the nature of intellect, especially the nature of the "actively thinking intellect" and its relationship to the passive intellect, and to see whether this theory provided the basis for the belief in the immortality of the soul.

The Islamic Aristotelians, following some of their Greek predecessors, viewed the Active Intellect as an eternal incorporeal intelligence that played a causative role in human intellection, and in the generation and destruction of sublunar entities.[18] Although this interpretation of the Active Intellect seemed to condemn the human intellect to oblivion upon death (since the Active Intellect alone was described as eternal), it actually provided a way for its survival. For the question became how can the human intellect somehow participate in the Active Intellect's eternality. Averroes' answer, in at least some of his writings, was that the human intellect can have the Active Intellect as the object of its thought, thereby conjoining in some manner with it,[19] and shedding the human intellect's personality.[20] The interpretation of the immortality of the soul as the general immortality of the intellect was popular among Gersonides' philosophical predecessors and contemporaries in Provence and Northern Spain.[21] Even Maimonides was interpreted by some medieval commentators as holding that the intellects that survive death are numerically one,[22] although he did not apparently believe in the possibility of the human intellect's conjoining with the Active Intellect. As is the case with most of Maimonides' doctrines, there is considerable disagreement of interpretation, with at least one scholar suggesting that Maimoinides allows for gradations of surviving intellects according to their degree of attaining intellectual perfection.[23] Since Maimonides' views do not figure in Gersonides' discussion of the subject, it is impossible to determine how he was interpreted by the latter. The one view discussed by Gersonides that clearly allows for a differentiation and gradation of souls after death is that of Avicenna, who argues for the substantiality of the intellect and its contents. Gersonides rejects this view on philosophical grounds.[24]

Gersonides' own position is as follows: human intellects survive death, and their immortality (and concomitant pleasure and happiness) is directly proportionate to the number and nature of the eternally true concepts and propositions – the technical word he uses for them is "intelligibles" – that have been acquired during their lifetime. The intelligibles are acquired through experience of the world around us, but they ultimately derive from the set of intelligibles that is contained within (i.e. constitutes) the Active Intellect. Although the sets belonging to the "acquired intellect" and the Active Intellect are identical in a certain way, they are also distinct, just as, say, your knowledge of Euclidean geometry and Euclid's knowledge is in one sense the same and in another sense different. According to Gersonides, the intelligibles are acquired in succession during one's lifetime and do not cohere with each other, but upon death they form a unified conceptual entity that thinks continually and experiences intellectual pleasure.[25] Since the sensory apparatus decays with the body, no new intelligibles are added after death. So the acquired intellect of Reuben upon death differs from the acquired intellect of Simeon upon death, and both are immortal.[26] By means of this doctrine of differentiated acquired intellects, which is much more explicit than anything in Maimonides, and diverges sharply from the philosophers of Provence and Northern Spain, Gersonides provides a philosophical interpretation of the soul's survival after death, a fundamental religious concept.

Does Gersonides' position on the intellect's survival imply personal immortality? That depends on the meaning of "personal immortality." If it means the survival of one's memories, self-perception, phenomenal awareness, and so on, then the answer is no. All these are linked to bodily functions and faculties, so that when the body dies, they pass out of existence. If the phrase is taken to mean the survival after death of the individual, then the answer is still no. For, strictly speaking, it is improper to speak of incorporeal acquired intellects as individuals. Matter is the principle of individuation according to Gersonides, and disembodied intellects are immaterial. Nevertheless, they are differentiated from each other because each set of intelligibles comprising the acquired intellects forms a different, unified concept. Acquired intellects after death appear to be like the movers of the celestial spheres, differing from each other not as individuals of the same species, but rather as different species with unique members. So one can say that by modifying the Aristotelian framework Gersonides is able to provide for a measure of personal immortality, a feat that even Maimonides does not (explicitly) perform.

The philosophical difficulty lies not in the question of the acquired intellect's survival, but in its continuity with the human intellect. After all, "personal immortality" generally implies that the entity that exists before death is in some sense identical with the one that survives death, and that there is some sort of mental continuity. What is the relation between the acquired intellect and the intellect that precedes it? Crescas argued that there can be no identity; the acquired intellect, were it to exist, would be an entirely different substance from the human soul.[27] If he is correct, then it is difficult to understand Gersonides' theory as one of personal *survival*. The prospect that upon death my intellect will be replaced by something entirely different and permanent may give me joy and comfort, but I can hardly see it as my own survival, since one identity is shedded and another acquired. But we can point to at least two elements within Gersonides' theory that make for mental continuity and that enable him to argue that the acquired intellects that survive the deaths of our bodies are identical with who we are beforehand.

First, the sublunar intelligibles that are acquired by a human intellect are acquired with the aid of the soul's sensory faculties through a process of abstraction.[28] They are not received as full-blown, spiritual emanations from the Active Intellect. True, they derive from the order of intelligibles that is in the mind of the Active Intellect, which plays a causal role in their generation within the human, material intellect, and in a *certain sense* the sublunar intelligibles are that order. But their number and concatenation is a function of an individual's experience, although they are not ontologically dependent upon material objects. In claiming that the acquired intellect is a generated, eternal, spiritual substance, Gersonides knowingly deviates from the Aristotelian principles that only material entities are generated, and that whatever is generated is destroyed. But these deviations allow him to posit an origin and development of the acquired intellect before the death of the body that *continues* upon the death of the body. The acquired intellect is constituted incrementally while the embodied soul is alive. With the removal of material impediments upon death, the acquired intellect is not substantially altered but rather united or, to use a computer metaphor, "defragmented."

Second, Gersonides claims that when we discover some new truth we experience intellectual joy or pleasure that is a foretaste of the joy or pleasure that will be experienced after death, only that the latter will be immeasurably greater and eternal.[29] This implies that whatever "consciousness" survives the death of the body, it includes the activity of thinking and the experience of "intellectual pleasure" of which the human mind is conscious during one's lifetime.

Gersonides does not provide in the *Wars of the Lord* a detailed philosophical interpretation of the rabbinic doctrines of the afterlife and so on; he merely cites rabbinic sources that can be interpreted to conform with his doctrine. This omission left him open to later criticisms, especially those of Crescas. But the issue here is not whether Gersonides' intellectualist interpretation of traditional doctrines such as "All Israel has a portion in the world-to-come" is religiously adequate or intellectually satisfying, but whether it represents a radical stance vis-à-vis his Jewish philosophical predecessors and contemporaries. On the contrary, his deviations from the prevailing Jewish philosophical view, which posited only the most general sort of immortality, enabled him to offer a philosophical interpretation of personal immortality that can be more easily squared with traditional themes.

DIVINE PROVIDENCE[30]

The medieval Jewish philosophical discussion of divine providence is often portrayed as an attempt to synthesize two competing conceptions of divine activity: the biblical conception of a personal God who supervises his creation, and the Greek philosophical conception of a remote, impersonal deity whose entire activity consists of self-intellection. Yet this does not do justice to either the implicit naturalism of the biblical account (the biblical God often lets history run its course) or to the various interpretations of divine providence within Greek philosophy itself. Moreover, it conflates the issue of the *extent* of divine providence, that is what phenomena fall under the range of providentiary activities, and its *nature*, that is how providence works. These two issues are conceptually distinct. One could claim that every single sublunar phenomenon is a result of divine providence (or an expression of divine will) and at the same time be a thoroughgoing naturalist with respect to divine activity – provided that natural processes become the vehicle for divine providence.

The Jewish philosophers of the twelfth through early fourteenth centuries all agreed that God's activity is eternal and his will immutable, and that he does not begin or cease to will or to act at a certain time in history. They also agreed that God supervises the world via intermediaries, for example the celestial spheres, intellects, and, in general, the natures of things. And they all agreed that biblical descriptions that characterize God as a person are to be interpreted metaphorically. These three assumptions are enough to rule out both literal biblical conceptions of a personal God who intervenes in history and deist conceptions of a God whose activity is limited to the creation of an autonomous, mechanistic system of nature.

Where these philosophers differed is over the extent of divine providence or, better, what providential significance, if any, should be accorded to various phenomena. To make everything the result of direct divine causal activity, or to overly restrict its sphere, were both unacceptable options. Jewish philosophers generally tried to stake out a middle position that would reflect the biblical conception of a God who provides in some way for all of creation, but who also takes special care of some individuals and peoples. For the former they adopted the Aristotelian interpretation of general providence as the preservation of the species that resulted from the continuous movement of the celestial spheres. For the latter they adopted (and altered) the Aristotelian theory of intellect, which made individual providence consist in, or consequent upon, the acquisition of knowledge. Since there are varying degrees of intellectual achievement, there will be varying degrees of individual providence. This may mean simply that the wise man will generally have a longer, healthier, and more productive life than a fool; his knowledge (whose source is divine) protects him from material evils. Or it may mean that since a person's ultimate good consists of the perfection of the intellect and what that entails, the wise man ipso facto achieves a higher reward than the fool no matter what his material fortunes. In either case, the more perfect the intellect, the greater the individual providence. Thus both general and individual providence are given naturalistic interpretations of a sort. *All* of the Jewish philosophers I have mentioned, including Maimonides, accepted some version of this naturalistic picture of providence.

But there is a very large gap left by this naturalistic picture. Neither general providence (via the preservation of the species) nor individual providence (via the theory of intellection) accords providential significance to the vast range of *non-essential properties* that distinguish individuals of each species. These include such "accidents" as physical characteristics, temperaments, psychic dispositions, and even the events that befall an individual. And when these events are bad and the people they befall good, then the problem of evil becomes acute. Consider the case brought by Maimonides of the "excellent and superior men" who drown when a hurricane sinks their ship.[31] According to Aristotle, Maimonides informs us, the sinking of the ship is a chance event (and hence not pertinent to the question of divine providence). Yet even if we grant that it is a chance event, he continues, "the fact that the people in the ship went on board...is not in our opinion due to chance, but to divine will in accordance with the deserts of those people as determined in His judgements, *the rule of which cannot be attained by our intellects*."[32] The simple reading of this is that divine will metes out justice according to unfathomable criteria. But it is also possible to read Maimonides as hinting that events like the drowning of humans at sea are not brought about by a specific divine volition, but by natural, voluntary, and accidental causes of which we are ignorant.[33] This reading, which abolishes the distinction between the positions of Maimonides and Aristotle, is found in some of the commentaries on the *Guide* by Gersonides' more Aristotelian contemporaries.[34] Yet whether events fail to have providential meaning (Aristotle), or whether their meaning is inaccessible to humans for whatever reason (Maimonides), they are inexplicable.

Gersonides closes the explanatory gap by claiming that *all* natural sublunar phenomena pertaining to humans, essential and non-essential, are ordered according to a divine plan (*siddur*, order) that is contained in the Active Intellect, and implemented by influences of the heavenly bodies. The Active Intellect produces, with the aid of the heavenly bodies, the "general natures" of things, that is their essential properties, as well as the "particular natures," that is their non-essential properties, such as shape, size, temperament, and other accidents (including events) that befall them.[35] The role of the heavenly bodies is to prepare the composition of the material substratum to receive the influence from the Active Intellect. Hence they are the instruments whereby the Active Intellect's causal activity in the material realm is realized.[36] Even what we consider to be chance and fortuitous events occur according to the divine plan: a chance event has determinate causes, which include the planetary influences that determine the fortunes of humans.[37] This is a striking claim, and what impels Gersonides to make it is the overwhelming "empirical" evidence that such chance events can be predicted. The fact that certain individuals receive information about future events, even chance and fortuitous ones, through veridical dreams, divination, and prophecy implies that such events are ordered.[38]

The aforementioned distinction between general and individual providence is interpreted by Gersonides as a distinction between astral-based and intellect-based providence, respectively. The former includes not only the basic properties, instincts, physical organs, and so on that allow the species to survive and flourish, but also the variegated natural dispositions and inclinations found in humans, whose matter is more refined in composition and hence more susceptible to astral influence. This variety enables humans to form larger cooperatives and societies for their mutual protection and well being. True, because of the nature of sublunar matter, especially the instability of the sublunar elements, corruption must follow generation, and on an individual and societal level, evils (e.g. illness, death, wars, natural disasters) will occur. But God has provided humans with another providential instrument, the intellect, by means of which they can escape the evils that are destined to befall them because of the astral order. Insofar as people employ their intellect and acquire knowledge, they are protected to a large extent from material evils. In claiming that humans are able to choose and act according to intellect in opposition to their astrally based native temperament, Gersonides injects into an otherwise deterministic system a modicum of contingency, enough for him to affirm human accountability and to justify obedience to the law, reward and punishment, and so on. We shall see the implications of this contingency for God's knowledge of human actions below.

Because Gersonides, unlike Maimonides and the other Jewish philosophers, views non-essential properties as ordered, that is as occurring as part of a fathomable divine plan, he is able to give a much richer account of divine providence than any of them, and a much closer reading of God's providential activity as described by the Bible. In many cases God is said to "bring about" (le-sabev) events even when they are not explicitly attributed to him in the text. For example, each link in the chain of events that results in the successful revolt of General Jehu against King Joram described in 2 Kings 9 – the wounding of King Joram by the Arameans in Ramot Gilead, which forces the removal of the king to another town, which then clears the way for the prophet Elisha to approach Jehu, who then revolts against Joram – is interpreted by Gersonides as brought about by God.[39] And yet the importance of human initiative and endeavor is constantly emphasized. The prophet is able to understand the historical events that are occurring about him and their implications for the future, and, armed with that knowledge, to seize the opportunity. Gersonides praises repeatedly the biblical personages for not relying passively on God's promised protection, but endeavoring to receive it in the most appropriate manner.[40]

Often when Gersonides claims that God causes an event "providentially" he does not spell out what sort of providence is at work, and at times he even confesses his ignorance. Thus the commentator ponders whether Sichon's obstinacy (Deuteronomy 2:31) was the result of a divine miracle (individual providence) or his astral destiny (general providence).[41] Sometimes, Scripture itself provides the answer, as when it reports that God hardened Pharaoh's heart so that "I might show these signs of mine before him: and that you may tell in the ears of your son, and your son's son, what things I have done in Egypt...that you may know that I am the Lord" (Exodus 10:1–2). The hardening of Pharaoh's heart, according to Gersonides, was a miracle intended to teach the Israelites a lesson in divine omnipotence, thereby raising their intellectual/spiritual level in preparation for the receiving of the law.[42] Gersonides' appeal to the miraculous here should be contrasted with the naturalistic exegesis of his contemporary Joseph ibn Kaspi, who claims that God "hardens Pharaoh's heart" only in the remote sense that he creates humans with the power of choice. Kaspi appeals to the Maimonidean principle that Scripture often attributes natural events and accidents to divine causal agency.[43] Gersonides accepts the principle, but adds that accidents may also occur miraculously because of divine individual providence. Even an unintended homicide may be the result of a providential miracle.[44]

Gersonides' frequent appeals to miracles to explain providential phenomena may seem inconsistent with his naturalism. They are indeed inconsistent with the claim that all phenomena result from, and are explicable with reference to, the stable natures of things. But they are not inconsistent with the claim that the divine plan, according to which all phenomena, even miracles, occur, is instantiated in a regular, "lawlike" fashion. Gersonides does not believe that miracles are produced through the agency of a personal God who responds in time to a need "down on earth." He also dismisses the rabbinic view that specific miraculous events are "programmed" at creation to occur at the appropriate time, partly on the grounds that such a view eliminates contingency.[45] Miraculous *events* are not "programmed" but the *orders* governing them are, because they are part of the divine plan that governs the sublunar universe. When the right historical conditions obtain, the miraculous event will occur.[46] Although Gersonides is more willing to consider certain events as miracles than his philosophical contemporaries, he shares their desire to minimize the irregularities and deviations of nature, often citing the principle that God endeavors to bring things about with the least amount of divergence from the natural order. [47]

The most extraordinary miracle has yet to occur, namely, the bodily resurrection of the dead. Few if any of Gersonides' philosophical contemporaries advocated the doctrine of bodily resurrection, and none, including Maimonides, accorded to it a significant eschatological function.[48] According to Gersonides' novel interpretation, this miracle will be performed by King Messiah in order to convince the nations of the world to recognize and to worship God and to strengthen Israel's faith in him.[49] It will also provide the opportunity for the acquired intellects to return to bodies and to acquire more intelligibles. The righteous will achieve a higher degree of perfection and hence a greater immortality of the soul.[50] The importance of the doctrine of bodily resurrection in Gersonides' eschatology indicates, once again, the conservative thrust of his thinking.

THE TESTIMONY OF SCRIPTURE

Gersonides also differs from his philosophical contemporaries in his almost total acceptance of the historicity of scriptural accounts and his disinclination to interpret them exclusively as allegories. Not only does he criticize "recent philosophers" for allegorizing biblical figures such as Cain, Abel, and Seth, but he disagrees with Maimonides over allegorizing Eve, and for considering the visitation of the three angels to have taken place in Abraham's dream.[51] He may be implicitly criticizing Maimonides when he emphasizes that the garden of Eden was an actual place, around which Scripture wisely constructed a philosophical allegory so as to conceal its philosophical import.[52] Only when the biblical story conflicts with established philosophical truth is one forced to interpret it allegorically. Since it is "despicable" that God would create the snake as a rational creature and later reduce him to an inferior state, it is "very evident" that the snake is to be taken as an allegory and not literally.[53]

Because of his confidence in scriptural testimony, Gersonides is much more willing than his contemporaries to affirm biblical doctrines whose philosophical basis is somewhat tenuous or far-fetched. For example, he employs the intellectualist theory of individual providence not only to explain Abraham's well being, but to account for the prosperity of Abraham's family and even the indestructibility of the Jewish people. But if individual providence consists of the knowledge communicated to Abraham, how can this extend beyond him to his family or to his descendants? Gersonides' answer is that

Abraham's own well being requires his knowledge of his descendants' survival, otherwise he would be pained and troubled by the knowledge of their extinction. But this fails to explain why long after Abraham's death the Jewish people benefit from his special providence to the extent that their indestructibility is guaranteed.[54] Similarly, Gersonides accepts at face value the biblical view that the prophet's prayer on behalf of another person can be efficacious. But it is hard to see how this works on his model of petitional prayer, where the petitioner, through the experience of prayer, elevates herself to a spiritual level at which she receives the providential overflow. How can that overflow extend to another who is not spiritually worthy?[55] Here, as elsewhere, Gersonides is content to appeal to the biblical narrative as testimony for the truth of certain doctrines.

This failure to work out the details is often frustrating for readers who would like to be able to understand Gersonides' acceptance of certain biblical doctrines in light of his philosophical principles. But it is of a piece with his general empiricist methodology: when experience (or reliable reports about it) present us with incontrovertible data, we must accept them as genuine even if our theories seem unable to provide a detailed or adequate explanation; examples given by Gersonides are the sun's ability to heat sublunar things[56] and astral influence on human affairs.[57] Incontrovertible experience convinces him that the stars influence the lives of humans, and that the sun warms things on earth, even though accepted physical theories cannot account for these phenomena adequately. He appears likewise convinced that there are certain "phenomena" that are well attested by the Bible and other sources that must be accepted as true, and which, if possible, we can explain. Since the miracle-reports contained in Scripture are confirmed by the authority of the prophets and the men of their day, the acceptance of these reports is no less founded than Aristotle's and Ptolemy's acceptance of the observations of their predecessors.[58]

CREATION OF THE WORLD[59]

The thirteenth- and fourteenth-century Jewish philosophers in Provence and northern Spain were familiar with three positions on the world's origin: temporal creation of the world out of nothing (Maimonides, al-Ghazali), eternal emanation of the world out of God (al-Farabi, Avicenna), and the eternal production of the world by God (Averroes). From Maimonides and Averroes they learned of the Aristotelian theory of the eternity of the universe, which they tended to identify with the theory of eternal production, as well as the Platonic theory of creation from preexistent matter, which they understood as temporal creation. Most of them accepted some form of an eternity thesis which ruled out creation at an instant of time.[60] So when Gersonides maintains that God created the world at an instant, he deviates once again from the regnant philosophical position in the direction of tradition, this time in the direction of Maimonides.

Why, then, has Gersonides often been portrayed as a heterodox thinker on the subject of creation? Aside from the general tendency to view Gersonides as a radical theologian, there seem to be two reasons: first, he explicitly rejects the theory of creation out of absolute nothing, which, because of Maimonides' influence, emerged as the orthodox doctrine; and second, he claimed that he had proved his theory of creation conclusively, whereas Maimonides, as well as some of Gersonides' contemporaries, held the doctrine of temporal creation to be unprovable conclusively but useful for religion. If orthodoxy is as much a sociological category as a doctrinal one, then Gersonides' attempt to "demystify" temporal creation by demonstrating it rationally could indeed be interpreted as unorthodox.

Ironically, Maimonides is much more impressed by the philosophical coherence of Aristotle's eternity thesis than is Gersonides. He rejects it in the *Guide* because it implies that the world is produced through the necessity of God's nature and not voluntarily, whereas he believes that there is clear, albeit not conclusive, evidence that the world is produced voluntarily. Moreover, the eternity thesis, he claims, destroys the law in its entirety, drains the biblical miracles of their meaning, and makes a mockery out of divinely promised reward and punishment.[61] But having emphasized the importance of volitional creation, and having adduced evidence of divine will to buttress his position philosophically, Maimonides is content to maintain an Aristotelian world of natural necessity, at least with respect to the sublunar sphere – the very sphere where many of the biblical miracles take place. For all his earnestness in pleading the case of volitional creation, because of the undesirable theological and religious implications of the eternity thesis, Maimonides is too much the Aristotelian to embrace whole-heartedly divine voluntarism. His ambiguous pronouncements on the subject of creation led some of his thirteenth- and fourteenth-century commentators, as well as some twentieth-century scholars, to claim that he secretly held the eternity thesis.

Gersonides argues that the thesis of volitional creation at an instant is not only true but also philosophically demonstrable. His general strategy is to argue from what he considers to be the teleological features of the heavens – their goal-directedness, possession of non-essential properties, and existence for the sake of something else, the sublunar world – to their being the product of an intelligent agent.[62] This, in itself, does not prove volitional creation at an instant, because the Averroists claimed that God is also an efficient cause and therefore eternally produces the heavens, for it would be absurd for an efficient cause to be idle. To this Gersonides responds by distinguishing between two aspects of the divine efficient causal activity, what we may call the production of forms and their bestowal in matter. God produces the forms eternally through his eternal act of self-intellection; these constitute the intelligible order of the universe. But he bestows the forms at an instant, and this is the creation of the world. This bestowal does not arise necessarily, but rather as the result of divine beneficence and grace. To use an imprecise, but helpful, analogy, God is like an architect who designs in his mind the ideal house for its inhabitants and then actually brings the house into being. The plan is eternal; its instantiation occurs at an instant.[63] All the orders within the divine plan of the world, including those orders that govern the miraculous and realm of special providence, are for the well being and protection of creatures, whether material or spiritual.

Once the world is created, God no longer appears as an efficient cause in bestowing the forms, but rather serves as their final cause in the following manner: inasmuch as the movers of the sphere desire and love God, they desire that the various activities emanate from them upon the world in accordance with what their apprehension of the law of the first cause required. It is this picture that has been claimed to approximate deism, the view that God creates the world in accordance with rational laws discoverable by humans and that later God withdraws and refrains from interfering in the processes of nature and the ways of man. Now, inasmuch as Gersonides interprets metaphorically God's interferences in the world as recorded by Scripture, he shares some of the naturalistic tendencies of the deists (as do many other medieval Jewish philosophers, including Maimonides). But his theory nowhere implies that God ceases to be an agent after creation, only that he ceases to be a creator. On the contrary, he is "continuously active with respect to all creatures, and all knowers desire [to emulate him]; for each one of them longs for its perfection to accrue to it, and this perfection is no other than the law [allotted] to it in the soul of the first cause."[64] Hence, "God is more properly described as 'active' than anything else."[65] Despite some superficial similarities, modern deism and Gersonides' views are quite different, which relate ultimately to the differences in their underlying scientific and philosophical worldviews.

As we noted, Gersonides disagrees with Maimonides over whether the world was created from absolute nothing. His own view, that the world was created out of a body devoid of form, is sometimes presented as a modification of the Platonic theory of creation from preexistent matter.[66] Gersonides himself viewed it as a completely new position, which shares elements of the Platonic and the Maimonidean ones: "The world is created from something insofar as it is generated from [some kind] of body; it is created from nothing insofar as this body is devoid of form."[67] As a philosopher and as an empiricist he cannot make sense of the world being created out of absolute nothing, but it should be pointed out that his own theory of volitional creation at an instant appears to be close in spirit to that of Maimonides. Maimonides and Gersonides share much more in common on the question of creation of the world than is generally thought, and certainly much more in common than Gersonides shares with his philosophical contemporaries, who believed in eternal production of the world. Gersonides' task, it appears, is to make Maimonides' theory of volitional, temporal creation philosophically respectable. In any event, his view on creation is no more, and perhaps less, religiously problematic than the Platonic view, which Maimonides himself did not find religiously problematic.

To sum up the discussion until this point: we have seen that in some of the key doctrines of medieval Jewish philosophy – the survival of the soul, general and individual providence, miracles, the allegorization of biblical histories, the resurrection of the dead, and the creation of the world – Gersonides adopts more religiously conservative positions than those of his philosophical contemporaries, and, in the case of the soul's survival and providence, arguably than those of Maimonides. These conservative tendencies go hand-in-hand with his philosophical boldness insofar as they necessitated deviations from the regnant Aristotelian/Averroist positions. In many cases it appears that Aristotelianism gives way to the requirements of "mosaic dogma." In any event, his intellectual worldview is hardly "Islamic peripateticism in all its purety."[68]

There is still the matter of God's knowledge of particulars, which many scholars, even those who recognize conservative tendencies in Gersonides, view as theologically problematic. His doctrine was taken by his medieval critics to imply that God possesses only general knowledge of material particulars and only probable knowledge of future contingents.[69] He was said to have denied divine foreknowledge in order to affirm human free choice,[70] and to have excluded from the scope of divine knowledge all human actions and events that originate in choice.[71] This is puzzling because Gersonides himself claims that God is omniscient, and, specifically, that he knows particulars; that there is no phenomenon (particular thing, event, etc.) that escapes his knowledge, and that not only does his knowledge provide humans for every eventuality, but also that through it he comes into direct contact with them. We shall see that there is really no difference in *Tendenz* between Gersonides' views on divine knowledge of "sublunar things" and his views on the other subjects considered above. In the context of post-Maimonidean philosophy in Provence through the mid-fourteenth century, they all represent moves away from Aristotle in the direction of tradition.

GOD'S KNOWLEDGE OF "POSSIBLE
PARTICULAR THINGS"[72]

The question that Gersonides discusses in *Wars of the Lord* 3 is "Whether the Lord knows the possible particular things in the sublunar realm and whether he does not; and if he knows them, in what manner does he know them." He appears to understand "particular things" or "particulars" as concrete substances and accidents, that is instantiations in time and space of the intelligible plan of sublunar reality. Particular things possess "general natures" (essences, essential properties) and "particular natures" (non-essential properties, accidental features that derive from their material composition).

Reuben, for example, is a particular substance who possesses a general nature (rational animality) and a particular nature (short, indolent, with a taste for corned beef, etc.). Particular events and character traits are viewed as concrete accidents, that is cases of non-essential properties.

What are *"possible* particular things"? Here Gersonides is ambiguous. In *Wars of the Lord* 2 he argues that sublunar possibility is connected to the "accidents that befall human individuals" – not all accidents, it appears, but those that relate to human intellect and choice. So possible particular things would include, on this reading, events like Reuben's eating corned beef, or character traits like his indolence. All things being equal, Reuben can choose to eat or not to eat the corned beef and can choose to rid himself or not to rid himself of this character trait. Possible particular things would not include, on this reading, events like Fido's burying a bone or physical characteristics like Dinah's ruddy complexion. These are particulars to be sure, but they are not related to intellect and choice.[73] Let us call this the narrow sense of "possible particular things."

But when Gersonides lists his predecessors' views on God's knowledge of particulars, he uses formulations that do not depend upon this understanding of possibility. First he cites an interpretation of Aristotle to the effect that God does not know any thing in the sublunar realm. He then cites another interpretation to the effect that God knows sublunar things "from the aspect of the general nature which they possess, which are the essential things, and not by virtue of what they possess qua particulars, which are the possible things." And finally he brings the opinion of "our great Torah sages like Maimonides," which claims that God knows these possible particulars, all of them, "from the aspect of their being particular." The first interpretation, later attributed to Averroes, rules out any sort of knowledge of particulars; according to the second, probably that of Themistius,[74] God knows particulars via their essential properties, but not via their non-essential properties; and Maimonides says that God knows particulars as individuals. Nowhere in the opening discussion is the problem of knowing possible particulars limited to the problem of knowing matters that relate to human intellect and choice. The same is true of most of the arguments for and against God's knowledge of particulars, until Gersonides offers his own solution in *Wars of the Lord* 3:4.

It appears, then, that Gersonides intends by "possible particular things" to include all non-essential properties that particularize sublunar phenomena, that is properties that may or may not obtain in an individual of a given species. Let us call this the broad sense of "possible particular things." These include not only instances of accidental properties such as "white" and "tall," but of events like "eating corned beef" and character traits like "indolent," all of which are constitutive of the "particular nature" of a sublunar thing.[75] On this reading, the initial question can be rephrased as: "Whether the Lord knows the non-essential properties that particularize things in the sublunar realm or whether he does not; and if he knows them, in what manner does he know them?" Aristotle, according to either the first or second interpretation, answers that he does not. Maimonides answers that he does, but with a *unique* kind of knowledge that knows particulars in their particularity.[76] Having set up the question in this manner, Gersonides can claim that none of his philosophical predecessors provides an adequate account of God's knowledge of "possible particular things."

Gersonides' project in *Wars of the Lord* 3 is to supply that account. As we shall see below, his main strategy is to enlarge the scope of knowledge to include objects that are non-essential, particularizing properties. That he feels confident enough to deviate from Aristotle should come as no surprise; we saw earlier that Gersonides rejects certain Aristotelian principles in his discussion on creation, and that Maimonides, who is philosophically inclined to accept these principles, can only provide skeptical arguments to undermine the force of Aristotle's proofs for the world's eternity. Something similar happens to the two philosophers in the case of divine knowledge. Maimonides argues that God knows particulars, that there is no way of explaining this using the standard, that is Aristotelian, account of knowledge (which Maimonides apparently accepts), and hence that God knows particulars in a unique way.[77] Gersonides, by contrast, argues that God knows particulars, that the standard account of knowledge can be modified to allow for knowledge of particulars, and hence that there is no need to posit an essential difference between the way God knows and the way humans know.

The sort of knowledge Gersonides has in mind is what Aristotle calls *episteme*, and what he himself calls *yedi'ah amitit* ("true knowledge") – the knowledge of why something is what it is, and why it cannot be otherwise. *Episteme* is the knowledge of a phenomenon through its cause/explanation; hence it is sometimes translated as "understanding."[78] *Episteme* is contrasted by Aristotle with sense-knowledge, which may show us that something is, but not why it is what it is and why it cannot be otherwise.[79] For example, we can observe that Reuben speaks, but we do not know it, that is, understand it, unless we know by virtue of what Reuben speaks, his rational animality. Now, if God's knowledge is of the "epistemic" variety (all agree that it is not of the sense–knowledge variety), then it seems that he cannot understand particular natures, for particular natures are composed of accidents, and accidents, according to Aristotle, cannot fall within the scope of *episteme*.[80] So it follows that, if God can understand anything about sublunar things, he understands them only from the aspect of their *general* natures. This is precisely Aristotle's view according to the second interpretation mentioned above. As Gersonides writes in his commentary to the *Posterior Analytics*, "True knowledge (*yedi'ah amitit*)...although it applies to the particular thing, applies to it...from the aspect of the general nature existing within it" – from the aspect of the general nature, and not from the aspect of the particular nature, the non-essential, particularizing properties.[81]

To include particularizing accidents within the scope of *episteme*, Gersonides appeals to his view in *Wars of the Lord* 2:2, that the accidents that particularize a sublunar thing are ordered by the Active Intellect, through the influence of the heavenly bodies on its material composition. Non-essential properties, as well as essential properties, are therefore ordered according to the plan of the Active Intellect, a plan that ultimately derives from the plan within the mind of God. That accidents are ordered by the Active Intellect implies that they are knowable with *episteme* by scientists, prophets, prognosticators – and by God. As Gersonides puts it: "It is clear that the aspect from which the Lord knows these 'possible particulars' is the aspect of their being ordered and determined 'by the heavenly bodies,' as is the case with active intellect, as was explained. For from this aspect they are knowable..."[82] In *Wars of the Lord* 2 we learn that the Active Intellect knows sublunar phenomena by knowing the plan by which they are determined. In *Wars of the Lord* 3 we learn that God knows all phenomena, including the particular natures of sublunar things, by knowing truly the plan of reality by which they are determined. By expanding the scope of "true knowledge" Gersonides enables particulars to be truly known. So, unlike the Aristotelians, he provides for God's knowledge of particulars. But, unlike Maimonides, he does not have to abandon philosophy to do so.

But is this really knowledge of particulars? Some have objected that knowing the plan by which a particular is ordered is not the same as knowing the particular. For example, Sarah may know the rules of a computer adventure game because she is the master programmer, but that does not mean, or even imply, that she knows a particular game that I shall play on January 1, 2001. But one should recall that Gersonides interprets "knows" as "truly knows" and to "truly know" a thing is to understand it. If Sarah is the creator of the game, then is there anything about the particular game I shall play on January 1, 2001 that she fails to understand? Let us assume that all my moves will be made in accordance with the rules, and let us assume further that one of those moves results in the "death" of my computer alter ego. Is that move inexplicable to the inventor of the game? But if there are no inexplicable moves, then there is nothing that is not understood. (Whether Gersonides allows for "inexplicable moves" will be taken up below.)

Let us take the computer-game analogy one step further. Say that a particularly stupid move of mine results in the "death" of my computer alter ego. I can anthropomorphize and say that the computer, after "seeing" my stupid move, "punishes" me by causing my alter ego's death. Or I can say that Sarah designed the game in such a way that in the situation in which I found myself, were anybody to make a move similar to the one I shall make, that person would "die." This is how the inventor of the game "punishes" me and anybody like me in the same situation. Similarly, by creating the world according to the divine plan, God provides for individual humans, rewards and punishes them, and even influences their history, without apprehending the particulars as materially instantiated individuals.

Another objection to Gersonides' theory is that particulars are ontologically different from the plan governing them, and so Gersonides can claim at best that by understanding the plan, God has general knowledge *about* particulars, but not that he actually knows particulars. This argument assumes a certain type of ontological distinction between the plan and its particular instantiations in order to justify the claim that, when one understands the former, one does not understand the latter. Now, Gersonides does hold that such a distinction exists between particulars and universals, because the latter are mental concepts that exist potentially in material particulars and actually in the mind. But he also holds that the intelligibles that compose the plan do *not* signify universals but rather arbitrary individuals of a certain type. So instead of claiming that God knows universals, Gersonides claims that he knows particulars from the aspect of their universal (and particular) *natures*. Unlike universals, these natures are not found in the particulars potentially, but rather they are said to *actually exist* as *aspects* of the particular.[83] If one subtracts from particulars their universal and particular natures, there is simply nothing left to understand about them. To know the intelligible plan of sublunar reality with "true knowledge" is to understand the particulars because the latter are nothing more than instantiations of the former.[84]

So far we have been understanding "possible particular things" in the broad sense as referring to the non-essential properties that constitute the particular nature of a sublunar thing. But when Gersonides offers his own solution to the question of whether God knows possible particular things in the sublunar realm, he takes the phrase in its narrow sense as referring to those non-essential properties that relate to an individual's intellect and choice. We recall that God provides humans with intellect and choice so that they can avoid the evils that are destined to befall them by virtue of their astral destiny. The question is whether God knows particular accidents that are related to intellect and choice, and if he does, how? For example, can God know the choice that Reuben makes, and what follows from that choice?

Say, for example, that Dinah offers Reuben a sandwich of corned beef and Swiss cheese, which he is astrally predisposed to eat (because of his natural propensity to eat whatever corned beef is placed before him). As he is about to take a bite, he recalls that he is forbidden by Jewish law to eat cheese and meat together, and because of his adherence to Jewish law he refrains from eating the sandwich. Let us assume that Reuben has acted in opposition to his astrally determined predisposition. Now, can his choice and action be "truly known"? The question here is not whether and how his choice can be known in advance, but rather *whether and how his choice can be understood at all*? For if "true knowledge" of particular actions is via the intelligible plan that governs them, and if that intelligible plan with respect to human action is to be identified with the astral order, then events that are *not* ordered by the astral order – such as Reuben's refraining from eating his sandwich – cannot be "truly known" either by God or, for that matter, by any knower.

At first glance, this appears to be Gersonides' conclusion when he writes (in the continuation of the passage quoted above): "The aspect from which [the Lord] does not know them is the aspect of their being unordered 'by the heavenly bodies,' which is the aspect through which they are possible, for from this aspect knowledge cannot apply to them." Gersonides' point is generally understood as follows: because certain events involve choice between various courses of actions, and these choices are undetermined by astral influence, then their occurrence is only possible, and hence they cannot be known *in advance* by God. Humans are given the power of free choice, whose outcome even God cannot *foreknow*. But this interpretation is untenable for two reasons: First, it implies that the objects of God's knowledge are possible individuals that come into and pass out of existence, and that such things cannot be known until they come to exist. But, as we have seen, the objects of knowledge for *any* knower are not particulars in their particular aspect (i.e. materially instantiated individuals), which come into and pass out of existence, but the universal and particular natures of things, which are eternal. And given the Aristotelian view of knowledge as understanding, this makes sense. I do not *understand* anything further about Reuben's natural propensity to eat corned beef if I see him take another bite out of his sandwich, just as I do not understand anything further about a stone's downward motion when released if I see it released for the tenth time. Moreover, the interpretation assumes that humans are endowed with a power to choose arbitrarily, that is through no "ordering" principle, and hence God cannot know choices of this sort. But Gersonides nowhere says that; rather he says that humans can use rationally motivated choice in order to avoid astrally fated evils. So our question is whether a choice, motivated by reason, and hence opposed to the astral order, can be understood? And from the passage above, it appears that it cannot.

But can this interpretation really be what Gersonides intends? Let us return to Reuben, who has decided not to eat the corned beef and cheese sandwich because of his obedience to Jewish law. His choice is not arbitrary; it is ordered and determined by (his adherence to) the law.[85] Now is Jewish law unknowable "epistemically"? Certainly not – for Gersonides, it is the paradigm of the rational law; all of its rules are directed for its adherents' well being. The intelligible order of sublunar reality incorporates not only the astral order but also the rational order or, more precisely, the intelligible order is instantiated both indirectly, through the instrumentality of the celestial bodies, and directly, through the unmediated agency of the Active Intellect to the human intellect. Insofar as Reuben chooses to refrain from eating his sandwich, his choice and subsequent action are eternally understood by God or by any knower. So Gersonides is technically correct when he writes that "possible particulars," that is those sublunar things that involve intellect and choice, are unknowable from the aspect of their being unordered (by the heavenly bodies). What he omits to say, however, is that choices and actions according to reason are also ordered by the Active Intellect and hence they are "epistemically" knowable, that is understandable. The only thing that is inexplicable is whether humans *actually* choose according to their astrally disposed disposition or according to reason. Human choice is motivated by two principles that often are in conflict: native temperament and intellect; therein lies its contingency. But whatever humans choose, their choice is "truly knowable." In the game of life there are no inexplicable moves.

As evidence for this interpretation, consider Gersonides' claim that prophets can have foreknowledge of *non*-astrally ordered events. It is part of his general theory of prophecy in *Wars of the Lord* 2 that the prophet is able to predict the future because the Active Intellect communicates to him the plan of sublunar reality, which he then applies to his particular situation. Now most of Gersonides' examples involve the prophet's knowledge of events ordered by the astral plan, but there are cases when he speaks of the prophet's ability to foreknow events not ordered by the astral plan, such as the miraculous events that follow from individual providence. In fact, this ability is one of the things that distinguishes prophets from other prognosticators according to Gersonides' *Commentary on the Numbers* 22–5, Lesson 8:

Divination and magic lack the power to communicate future matters of someone to whom providence is attached. For those matters are unordered by the astral overflow ... but prophecy communicates this because it is ordered and flows from the [Active] Intellect ... Thus you find that God (may he be blessed) informed Abraham of the miracles and wonders that would be created via particular providence during the period of the exodus of Egypt in order to attract [the Israelites] to his service.[86]

God "truly knows" events that befall humans that are *not* ordered by the heavenly bodies. In this case the reference is to miracles rather than decisions motivated by reason, but the former is as unordered by the heavenly bodies as the latter.

More pertinent is the notion of God's "particular knowledge" which one finds in Gersonides' scriptural commentaries. When the Bible speaks of God's "seeing" or "knowing" humans, Gersonides interprets such language in light of his theory of individual providence. Thus when God says of Abraham, "For I knew him" (Genesis 18:19), Gersonides writes that "God (may he be blessed) will know that nation that will branch out from Abraham, and his providence will join with it, like the meaning of [the verse], "For God knows the way of the righteous."[87] Similarly, the verse, "For you [Noah] have I seen righteous before me in this generation" (Genesis 7:1) means that "the righteous is watched over by God (may he be blessed) with a marvelous providence to save him from the evils that are prepared to befall him, as is proved from the salvation of Noah."[88] It does not mean that God has a direct cognitive relation with Noah in all his particularity as a material individual, but that he has a providential relationship with Noah, *and anybody righteous like Noah*, from the aspect of his being righteous. Now "being righteous" is not a state that results from the astral order, or at least the astral order alone, and yet God is said to "know" Noah. But how does "particular knowledge" work?

Gersonides does not give a philosophical account of the providential knowledge he finds in the Bible, but I offer the following speculation on his behalf: God knows himself immediately in an eternal act of self-intellection, and because he is the intelligible plan of existence, the object of his knowledge is the intelligible plan. Now insofar as humans choose and act according to their astrally ordered disposition, they are known (with "true knowledge") via the astrally ordered plan that is a part of the intelligible plan. In other words, to explain ultimately the human actions and events that constitute people's particular natures, one ultimately has recourse to that plan. This is the clear message of *Wars of the Lord* 3. But insofar as humans choose and act according to right reason, based on their knowledge of the true and the good, they enter into a providential relationship with God, which Gersonides calls God's "particular knowledge," rather than knowledge of particulars. Scripture distinguishes between these two types of knowledge by portraying God's knowledge of particulars as hearsay and his "particular knowledge" as observational. Thus when the Bible says that God has heard reports of the evil actions of the Sodomites, this alludes to knowledge of particulars via the astral plan: "For he knows people's actions according to what has been prepared for them from the date of their being created by heavenly bodies assigned by God to watch over human individuals with a general providence."[89] But if the Sodomites do not sin then God knows them directly ("If not, I shall know it") in the sense that his providence will be attached to them. The choice is up to the Sodomites, but no matter what they choose, their actions are explicable. God knows/understands all.

All well and good, reply Gersonides' critics, but the fact remains that God does not actually *see* the individual Sodomites and what they choose, so how can his providence attach itself to them? Let us return to our computer-game analogy. When I first begin to play the game, I make all sorts of mistakes, for which I am "punished" by losing points, and perhaps by "dying." The consequences of my mistakes follow from the rules of the game and the design of the program; the programmer/inventor does not "see" me at the computer and decide to punish me. Now, as I gain knowledge of the game, my game improves. I learn from my mistakes; if I am fortunate, I am given a book about the game written by a master gamester. The more I play, the more I understand the mind of Sarah, the programmer; in fact, my mind becomes a lot like her mind, and, in a certain sense, we are of the same mind. She understands *me* because she understands players like me, players with my mindset. In fact, she may even be said to understand players like me better than worse players, because she understands her own mind, and mine more closely approximates hers than do theirs.

True, Sarah does not know me in all my concrete particularity, as a material individual. But – and here is the question that is rarely

asked – is my "concrete particularity" really who I am? Or is it accidental in the sense that it is neither part of my universal nor my
particular *nature*? Such questions return us to the problem of self-
identity, which we examined with reference to the survival of the
acquired intellect; how can I identify myself with a set of eternal
verities that "I" have acquired? Whether such an identification is
plausible or not, Gersonides accepts it and uses it to explain his
concept of the soul's survival, and God's "particular knowledge" of
humans. Indeed, the notion of the acquired intellect's conjunction
"in some manner" with God is the flip side of individual providence;
both emphasize the *connection* between God and humans when they
become of a similar mindset.

The emphasis on the connection between God and humans is
a significant feature that distinguishes Gersonides' theology from
deism. A deist can hold that God creates a world in which reward
and punishment for human actions are built into the system, as it
were, but not that he enters into a relationship with humans. God,
on that view, may be likened to a parent who goes away on vacation
leaving her children with a detailed series of instructions, money for
food, baby-sitter, and so on, but without the phone number where she
can be reached. Even if she is able to provide for total supervision of
their activities, with the appropriate rewards and punishments, the
children will lack the contact that, some say, is essential for their
well being. Gersonides' theory of "particular," that is providential,
knowledge supplies the element of contact that is essential to the
biblical conception of God knowing humans. Not only are reward
and punishment built into the world, as it were, but so is a direct
connection with its author.

Gersonides does not discuss his doctrine of "particular knowledge" as extensively as his doctrine of divine knowledge of particulars. But perhaps this is because the former is not as original
as the latter. The idea that humans entered a providential bond
with the deity through intellection is found in the Islamic philosophers, Maimonides, and his Jewish successors in the thirteenth
and fourteenth centuries. But the explanation of how God knows/
understands the *non*-essential characters, dispositions, actions, and
events of ordinary humans, all within the rigorous demands of
Aristotelian science, while preserving contingency, could justifi-
ably be described by Gersonides as "something wondrous ... that was

hidden from all the earlier thinkers whose words have reached us."[90] That he found his theory taught by Scripture is not surprising; perhaps this is one of the cases where Scripture guided him to philosophical truth.

To sum up: Gersonides' treatment of God's knowledge of particulars, far from constituting a departure from his interpretations of other religious doctrines, is closely related in style and substance to them. Whether writing about God's knowledge, divine providence, personal immortality, the creation of the world, and the allegorization of Scripture, he is ready and willing to deviate from the more faithful Aristotelianism of his Jewish contemporaries, in the direction of a more biblical conception of God.[91] Like Maimonides, he argues that God knows particulars, but he provides a philosophical analysis of *how* particulars are known which Maimonides does not.[92]

In closing, we may entertain four brief speculations as to how Gersonides, despite these conservative tendencies, acquired the reputation of a theologically unorthodox thinker:

First, Gersonides' reputation on these matters was determined by his Spanish and Italian rabbinical critics, who lived in a more conservative philosophical and theological atmosphere than did the Jewish philosophers of thirteenth- and fourteenth-century Provence. This conservatism appears to have deepened in subsequent periods, when Aristotelianism went into decline.

Second, Gersonides' theory of divine knowledge of particulars was interpreted by these critics as claiming that God's omniscience is limited in order to make room for human freedom. I have argued elsewhere that this interpretation does not do justice to the complexity of Gersonides' account of divine knowledge or human choice.[93] But if it were correct, then there would obviously be good reason to view his theory as unorthodox.

Third, only recently have Gersonides' commentaries, philosophical and scriptural, become the object of scholarly research. The scriptural commentaries are pertinent to our inquiry for several reasons: they provide us with many examples of how Gersonides applies his philosophical principles to the biblical conceptions and doctrines; they are the sources of doctrines like God's "particular knowledge" that do not appear in the *Wars of the Lord*; and they demonstrate his expertise in Jewish law and his conservative position on the allegorization of the historical passages I mentioned above.

Fourth, Gersonides' attempts to provide unambiguous philosophical solutions to the problems of religious philosophy were bound to
annoy those theologians who thought that such matters were insol-
uble, a fact of which he was aware.[94] Here Maimonides had a certain
"advantage," for he claimed that the creation of the world cannot
be demonstrated and that God's knowledge of particulars cannot be
explained. It is not that Gersonides had less of a commitment to the
fundamental principles of religion than Maimonides. On the contrary, he posits the rule that, where philosophy clashes with such
principles, the former must be abandoned. But one searches in vain
for an example of that rule in his writings! Gersonides is always ready
to harmonize Scripture to accord with philosophy or to deviate from
strict Aristotelianism to accommodate religious dogma.[95] The likes
of his philosophical optimism, born of a "dogmatic rationalism,"[96]
would not be seen again in Jewish philosophy, at least not until Moses
Mendelssohn.

BIBLIOGRAPHICAL NOTE

The last thirty years have witnessed growing interest in Gersonides'
multi-faceted oeuvre. For recent overviews of his life and thought,
see S. Feldman, "Levi ben Gershom (Gersonides)," in *History of Jewish Philosophy*, ed. D. H. Frank and O. Leaman (London and New
York: Routledge, 1997), 379–98, and G. Freudenthal, "Gersonides,"
in *History of Islamic Philosophy*, ed. S. Nasr and O. Leaman
(London and New York: Routledge, 1995), 739–54. The comprehensive monograph on his philosophy and theology is C. Touati,
La pensée philosophique et théologique de Gersonide (Paris: Editions de Minuit, 1973). The septicentennial of Gersonides' birth in
1988 produced two collections of scholarly essays: G. Dahan (ed.),
Gersonide en son temps (Louvain: Peeters, 1991) and G. Freudenthal (ed.), *Studies on Gersonides: A Fourteenth-Century Jewish
Philosopher-Scientist* (Leiden: Brill, 1992). The latter volume includes M. Kellner's, "Bibliographia Gersonideana: An Annotated
List of Writings by and about R. Levi ben Gershom," 367–414. A
periodically updated version of this bibliography is available on the
web at: http://research.haifa.ac.il/~kellner/
    Gersonides' philosophical *magnum opus* is the *Sefer Mil-
hamot Adonai*, an English translation of which has recently been

completed: *Levi ben Gershom (Gersonides): The Wars of the Lord*, trans. with notes, S. Feldman, 3 vols. (Philadelphia and New York: Jewish Publication Society and Jewish Theological Seminary of America, 1984–99). There is no critical edition of the Hebrew text. References in the present essay are to the edition published in Leipzig, 1866 and reprinted in Berlin, 1923.

Several ongoing projects involving the publication of Gersonides' writings should be noted: The Hebrew text of Gersonides' *Commentary on the Torah* is appearing in three separate editions, that of I. Levi (Jerusalem: Mosad Harav Kook, 1992–2000), of B. Braner et al. (Maaleh Edumim: Maaliyot, 1993–), and of M. Cohen (Ramat-Gan: Bar-Ilan University Press, 1997–). Cohen has already published editions of Gersonides' commentaries on Joshua, Judges, 1 and 2 Samuel, and 1 and 2 Kings as part of the *Miqraot Gedolot Ha-Keter* (Ramat-Gan: Bar-Ilan University Press, 1992–). These, together with the commentaries on Proverbs and Job, are available on CD-ROM as part of the Bar-Ilan Responsa Project. The same commentaries, together with the Leipzig edition of the *Milhamot Adonai*, are available on the DBS Software's Judaica Scholar CD-ROM. It is to be hoped that more editions and translations of his philosophical and scientific works will see the light of day soon.

NOTES

1. For details, see the bibliographical note at the end of this chapter.
2. S. Munk, *Mélanges de philosophie juive et arabe* (Paris: A. Franck, 1857), 497.
3. J. Guttmann, *Philosophies of Judaism*, trans. D. Silverman (New York: Holt, Rinehart & Winston, 1964), 224.
4. E. Renan, *Averroès et l'averroïsme*, 4th ed. (Paris: Calmann Lévy, 1882), 193–4.
5. Guttmann, *Philosophies of Judaism*, 215.
6. I. Husik, *A History of Mediaeval Jewish Philosophy* (New York: Macmillan, 1916), 346.
7. C. Sirat, *A History of Jewish Philosophy in the Middle Ages* (Cambridge: Cambridge University Press, 1985), 296.
8. More work needs to be done on the early reception of Gersonides. For the influence of Gersonides on R. Nissim ben Reuben Gerondi (Ran), see S. Klein-Braslavy, "R. Nissim ben Réuben de Gérone devant la philosophie de son temps," Thèse de Doctorat de 3ᵉ cycle, Ecole Pratique des

Hautes Etudes, Section des Sciences Religieuses, Paris, 1972. See C. Touati, *La pensée philosophique et théologique de Gersonide* (Paris: Editions de Minuit, 1973), 542.

9. Among the early critics of Gersonides we find Samuel b. Judah of Marseilles, his student Judah Kohen, Moses of Narbonne, and Yedayah ha-Penini. For the first three, see C. Manekin, "Preliminary Observations on Gersonides' Logical Writings," *Proceedings of the American Academy for Jewish Research* 52 (1985), 85–113, esp. 101–4. (The commentary on Averroes' *Epitome of the Organon* attributed to Moses b. Joshua of Narbonne [102] should be attributed, in light of subsequent research, to Mordecai Nathan.) For Yedayah ha-Penini, see R. Glasner, *A Fourteenth Century Scientific Philosophical Controversy: Jedaiah Ha-Penini's Treatise on Opposite Motions and Book of Confutations* [Hebrew] (Jerusalem: World Union of Jewish Studies, 1998), 13–106.

10. I do not wish to imply that Gersonides' conservative tendencies, or his deviations from Aristotle, are *motivated* by religious concerns. The question of motivation is unanswerable.

11. See, for example, Touati, *La pensée*, 562, and M. Nehorai, "Maimonides and Gersonides: Two Approaches to the Nature of Providence" [Hebrew] *Da'at* 20 (1988), 51–64.

12. *Wars of the Lord* Introduction, 4. (This and subsequent references to the Hebrew text are to the edition published in Leipzig, 1866 and reprinted in Berlin, 1923.) Cf. S. Feldman (trans.), *Levi ben Gershom (Gersonides): The Wars of the Lord*, 3 vols. (Philadelphia and New York: Jewish Publication Society and the Jewish Theological Seminary of America, 1984–99), I: 94.

13. *Wars of the Lord* Introduction, 7; trans. Feldman, I: 98. Cf. Touati, *La pensée*, 94–7, for the central role that *haysharah* (direction, guidance) plays in Gersonides' understanding of Torah, and its relation to philosophical truth.

14. Touati, *La pensée*, 60–3, 542–3.

15. In addition to the studies mentioned in the notes below, the reader may consult: S. Feldman, "Gersonides on the Possibility of Conjunction with the Agent Intellect," *AJS Review* 3 (1978), 99–120, and A. Ivry, "Gersonides and Averroes on the Intellect: The Evidence of the Supercommentary on the *De Anima*," in *Gersonide en son temps: Science et philosophie médiévales*, ed. G. Dahan (Louvain: Peeters, 1991), 235–51.

16. *De Anima* 2:1, 412a22.

17. *De Anima* 3:5, 430a18–23.

18. Whether Aristotle himself viewed this faculty or function as immanent to the human soul or as a transcendent substance has been debated. For

references, see H. Davidson, "Gersonides on the Material and Active Intellects," in *Studies on Gersonides: A Fourteenth-Century Jewish Philosopher-Scientist*, ed. G. Freudenthal (Leiden: Brill, 1992), 205–6, esp. n. 30.

19. Whether this conjunction occurs at the beginning of human intellectual development or after death was debated in the middle ages. See H. Davidson, *Alfarabi, Avicenna, and Averroes on Intellect: Their Cosmologies, Theories of the Active Intellect, and Theories of Human Intellect* (New York and Oxford: Oxford University Press, 1992), 321–5, which summarizes the views of philosophers before Averroes, and analyzes the development of Averroes' views on conjunction.

20. See ibid., 335–8, for Averroes' views on the immortality of the intellect.

21. See Falaquera, *Opinions of the Philosophers* VI:B:3, cited in R. Jospe, *Torah and Sophia: The Life and Thought of Shem Tov ibn Falaquera* (Cincinnati: Hebrew Union College Press, 1988), 261, which is a citation from Averroes' *Middle Commentary*; Pollegar, *The Support of Religion*, ed. J. Levinger (Tel Aviv: Tel Aviv University Press, 1984), 49–51, 175–6; Kaspi, *Filigrees of Silver (Commentary on the "Guide of the Perplexed")*, ed. S. Werbluner (Frankfurt am Main, 1848), 72, 83 (my thanks to Hannah Kasher for referring me to these and subsequent passages in Kaspi); Narboni, *Commentary to Hayy ibn Yaqzan*, Paris-BN héb. 915, fol. 11b, cited in M. Hayoun, *La philosophie et la théologie de Moïse de Narbonne (1300–1362)* (Tübingen: J. C. B. Mohr, 1989), 211; cf. references cited in nn. 46 and 47. See also G. Holzman, "The Theory of the Intellect and Soul in the Thought of Rabbi Moshe Narboni Based on his Commentaries on the Writings of Ibn Rushd, Ibn Tufayl, Ibn Bajja, and al-Ghazali," Ph.D. dissertation, Hebrew University, Jerusalem, 1996. According to A. Ivry ("Moses of Narbonne's 'Treatise on the Perfection of the Soul': A Methodological and Conceptual Analysis," *Jewish Quarterly Review* 57 [1966–67], 271–97, esp. 278 and 295), Narboni denies the personal immortality of the intellect (following Averroes), but affirms some sort of immortality of the soul.

   Interestingly, on this issue Isaac Albalag parts company with Averroes and prefers the Avicennan view that intellects remain differentiated after separation from the body. See Albalag, *Emendation of the Opinions*, 21, 22; G. Vajda, *Isaac Albalag: Averroïste juif, traducteur et annotateur d'al-Ghazali* (Paris: J. Vrin, 1960), 249, finds this deviation difficult to reconcile with Albalag's commentary on the biblical creation narrative.

22. On the basis of *Guide* 1:74; trans. S. Pines, *The Guide of the Perplexed* (Chicago: University of Chicago Press), 221. See Efodi's *Commentary on the "Guide"* (Lemberg, 1866), 60b, 61a; Kaspi, *Filigrees of Silver*,

132; and Narboni's *Commentary on the "Guide"*, ed. J. Goldenthal (Vienna, 1852), 19b–20a.

23. See A. Altmann, "Maimonides on the Intellect and the Scope of Metaphysics," in his *Von der mittelalterlichen zur modernen Aufklärung* (Tübingen: J. C. B. Mohr, 1987), 89–90.

24. *Wars of the Lord* 1:10, 80; trans. Feldman, II: 209–10.

25. For a different interpretation of acquired intellects postmortem, see M. Kellner, "Gersonides on the Role of the Active Intellect in Human Cognition," *Hebrew Union College Annual* 65 (1994), 233–59, esp. 258.

26. *Wars of the Lord* 1:13, 89–91; trans. Feldman, I: 223–5.

27. See W. Z. Harvey, "Hasdai Crescas' Critique of the Theory of the Acquired Intellect," Ph.D. dissertation, Columbia University, 1973, 125–43.

28. On this see Davidson, "Gersonides on the Material and Active Intellects," 195–265, esp. 247–8; cf. Kellner, "Gersonides on the Role of the Active Intellect in Human Cognition," 247.

29. *Wars of the Lord* 1:13, 90; trans. Feldman, I: 224–5.

30. In addition to the studies mentioned in the notes below, the reader may consult: D. Burrell, "Maimonides, Aquinas, and Gersonides on Providence and Evil," *Religious Studies* 20 (1984), 335–51; I. Dobbs-Weinstein, "The Existential Dimension of Providence in the Thought of Maimonides," in Dahan (ed.), *Gersonide en son temps*, 159–78; M. Kellner, "Gersonides, Providence, and the Rabbinic Tradition," *Journal of the American Academy of Religion* 42 (1974), 673–85.

31. *Guide* 3:17; trans. Pines, 465–6. The example is especially poignant when we recall that Maimonides' beloved brother David drowned at sea.

32. *Guide* 3:17; trans. Pines, 472.

33. Cf. *Guide* 2:48; trans. Pines, 409–12.

34. See Narboni on *Guide* 3:17, 54b. Both Falaquera (*Moreh ha-Moreh* [*Guide to the Guide*], ed. Y. Shiffman [Jerusalem: World Union of Jewish Studies, 2001], 311–13) and Kaspi (*Filigrees of Silver*, 126–8) ad loc. cite Averroes' *Kitab al-Kashf* 3, wherein it is implied that the divine decree should be interpreted in a naturalistic, Aristotelian manner.

35. *Wars of the Lord* 2:3, 98–9; trans. Feldman, II: 39.

36. *Wars of the Lord* 1:7, 50; trans. Feldman, I: 38.

37. Accidents occurring to other animals besides man are not ordered by the heavenly bodies except insofar as they are related to man (*Wars of the Lord* 2:2, 97; trans. Feldman, II: 37).

38. Gersonides conceives of an event as a non-essential property of substance; in this he is aided by the ambiguity of the Hebrew term

miqreh (lit.: "happening"), which he uses for properties (snub-nosed) and events (winning the lottery on Tuesday). Both happen to an individual in some sense of "happen," and both are ordered by the heavens. Actually, the word "event" is not adequate for this second sense of *miqreh*. For Gersonides does not call an event that occurs by virtue of reason (e.g. Reuben's decision at t_1 to refrain from eating a corned beef and Swiss cheese sandwich) a *miqreh*, and it would be odd to use a word meaning "accident" to designate an event ordered by a non-accidental feature of humanity. Still, in what follows I shall use the language of "events."

39. *Commentary to II Kings* 12:8, Lesson 1, ed. M. Cohen (Ramat-Gan: Bar-Ilan University Press, 1996), 215b.

40. For Abraham, see Gersonides' *Commentary on Genesis* 12:10, Lesson 1, ed. B. Braner and E. Freiman (Maaleh Edumim: Maaliyot, 1993), 202. (Subsequent page references to the *Commentary on Genesis* are to this edition.) For Isaac, see on 26:1, Lesson 1:343; for Jacob, see on 31:18, Lesson 33:99; on 31:19–21, Lesson 34:400; and on 43:11–14, Lesson 16:505–6. (Note that this last passage is called a "doctrinal" lesson rather than an "ethical" one.) For Noah, see on 6:14–22, Lesson 4:169–70; for Joseph see on 40:14, Lesson 7:472.

41. *Wars of the Lord* 2:6, 183–4; trans. Feldman, II: 202–3. See R. Eisen, *Gersonides on Providence, Covenant, and the Chosen People: A Study in Medieval Jewish Philosophy and Biblical Commentary* (Albany: State University of New York Press, 1995), 25, where the author points out that there is no empirical way of distinguishing such miracles from natural events.

42. Eisen, *Gersonides on Providence*, 25. God only brings evils upon people who deserve them, but any such evils must be for some good, since God is their author.

43. See *A Refining Pot for Silver*, ed. I. Last (Cracow: J. Fisher, 1906), 144 (Exodus 4:21), trans. C. Manekin in *The Jewish Philosophy Reader*, ed. D. H. Frank, O. Leaman, and C. H. Manekin (London and New York: Routledge, 2000), 251–2; cf. *The Silver is Finished*, ed. I. Last (London, 1913), 19–23.

44. See *Commentary on Exodus* 21:13, ed. Y. Levy (Jerusalem, 1994), 208. Here, too, Gersonides claims that there may be no way to discern a natural event from a miraculous one.

45. *Wars of the Lord* 6:2.10; trans. Feldman, III: 479–80.

46. E.g., had Pharaoh not pursued the Israelites, the waters of the Red Sea would not have divided.

47. He does not follow Moses Narboni's lead in viewing some of the biblical reports of miracles as philosophical allegories; see Hayoun, *La philosophie*, 72.

48. See Touati, *La pensée*, 533 and the reference to other philosophers in n. 27.
49. See *Commentary on the Torah* (Venice, 1547), 198b, 213d, 247a.
50. See *Commentary on Daniel*, in *Otzar ha-Perushim*, ii (Tel Aviv: n.p., 1966), 8c, 9a.
51. See Touati, *La pensée*, 484; according to Touati, the phrase "recent philosophers" refers to Levi ben Abraham of Villefranche.
52. See *Commentary on Genesis* 2:10–14, Explanation of the Terms, ed. B. Braner and E. Freiman (Jerusalem: Maaliyyot Institute, 1993), 92,
53. Ibid., 114–15.
54. See Eisen, *Gersonides on Providence*, 177.
55. Inasmuch as individual providence is said to consist of beneficial knowledge (*Wars of the Lord* 4:5, 167; trans. Feldman, ii: 178), certainly such knowledge can benefit others who are not worthy of receiving it themselves. But this does not seem to go far enough.
56. *Wars of the Lord* 5:1.43, cited in D. Schwartz, *Astral Magic in Medieval Jewish Thought* [Hebrew] (Ramat-Gan: Bar-Ilan University Press, 1999), 49. My thanks to Gad Freudenthal, who is working on a critical edition of this chapter, for this reference.
57. See *Wars of the Lord* 2:2, 95; trans. Feldman, ii: 33. Although astrologers frequently make successful predictions, they often fail because of the "inadequate procedures of verification characteristic of this discipline."
58. *Wars of the Lord* 6:2.6, 441–2; trans. Feldman, iii: 470.
59. In addition to the studies mentioned in the notes below, the reader may consult: H. Davidson, *Proofs for Eternity, Creation and the Existence of God in Medieval Islamic and Jewish Philosophy* (New York and Oxford: Oxford University Press, 1987); G. Freudenthal, "Cosmogonie et physique chez Gersonides," *Revue des Etudes Juives* 145 (1986), 294–314; M. Kellner, "Gersonides on the Problem of Volitional Creation," *Hebrew Union College Annual* 51 (1980), 111–28; T. Rudavsky, "Creation, Time and Infinity in Gersonides," *Journal of the History of Philosophy* 26 (1988), 25–44.
60. Isaac Abravanel in *The Works of God* 2:1 (ed. B. Genut-Dror [Jerusalem: Reuben Mass, 1988], 32) lists Kaspi, Falaquera, Abner (of Burgos?), Narboni, and Albalag as members of the "accursed sect" that believed in eternity. See Kaspi, *Filigrees of Silver*, 100, where creation *ex nihilo* is interpreted as eternal production of the world. Passages in Falaquera bearing on the question of creation are cited by Jospe in *Torah and Sophia*, 156–62; according to Jospe, it is not clear that Falaquera held an eternity thesis; Albalag, *Emendation of the Opinions* 30, 30–1; Narboni, Commentary to Ibn Tufayl's *Hayy ibn Yaqzan*,

fol. 42b, cited in Hayoun, *La philosophie*, 147; cf. the passage cited on 139.

61. See *Guide* 2:19–25; trans. Pines, 302–30, esp. 328.

62. *Wars of the Lord* 6:1.6–9, 308–28; trans. Feldman, III: 239–69.

63. *Wars of the Lord* 6:1.18, 377; trans. Feldman, III: 343.

64. *Wars of the Lord* 5:3.11, 278; trans. Feldman, III: 170.

65. *Wars of the Lord* 5:3.12, 283; trans. Feldman, III: 182.

66. See, e.g., Feldman's remarks in his translation of the *Wars of the Lord*, III: 220–1.

67. *Wars of the Lord* 6:1.17, 367; trans. Feldman, III: 330.

68. Cf. S. Feldman, "Platonic Themes in Gersonides' Cosmology," in *Salo W. Baron Jubilee Volume*, ed. S. Lieberman and A. Hyman (Jerusalem: American Academy for Jewish Research, 1975), I: 383–405, and S. Feldman, "Platonic Motifs in Gersonides' Theory of the Agent Intellect," in *Neoplatonism and Jewish Thought*, ed. L. E. Goodman (Albany: State University of New York Press, 1992), 240–61. In some ways Gersonides appears to be closer philosophically and temperamentally to Avicenna than to Averroes.

69. Hasdai Crescas, *The Light of the Lord* 2:1.3, ed. S. Fisher (Jerusalem: Sifrei Ramot, 1990), 138; Abraham Shalom, *Dwelling of Peace* 3:3 (Venice, 1575), 45a. Isaac Arama, *The Binding of Isaac* 19 (Pressburg: V. Kittseer, 1849), 136a; Isaac Abravanel, *Commentary on the Torah* (Warsaw, 1862), I: 46c.

70. *The Binding of Isaac*, 16, 1:116a; cf. Isaac Arama, *Abshalom's Memorial* (Leipzig, 1859), 96.

71. *The Light of the Lord* 2:1.3, 138; *Dwelling of Peace* 12:1.2, 199b–200a; *The Binding of Isaac* 19, 1:136a.

72. In addition to the studies mentioned in the notes below, the reader may consult: S. Feldman, "The Binding of Isaac: A Test-Case of Divine Foreknowledge," in *Divine Omniscience and Omnipotence in Medieval Philosophy*, ed. T. Rudavsky (Dordrecht: Reidel, 1985), 105–33; S. Klein-Braslavy, "Gersonides on Determinism, Possibility, Choice, and Foreknowledge" [Hebrew], *Da'at* 22 (1989), 5–53; T. Rudavsky, "Divine Omniscience and Future Contingents in Gersonides," *Journal of the History of Philosophy* 21 (1983), 513–36; N. Samuelson, "Gersonides' Account of God's Knowledge of Particulars," *Journal of the History of Philosophy* 10 (1972), 399–416. Some of the points mentioned cursorily in this section are amplified in C. Manekin, "On the Limited-Omniscience Interpretation of Gersonides' Theory of Divine Knowledge," in *Perspectives on Jewish Thought and Mysticism*, ed. A. Ivry, E. Wolfson, and A. Arkush (Reading: Harwood Academic Publishers, 1998), 135–70; and C. Manekin, "Freedom

Within Reason? Gersonides on Human Choice," in *Freedom and Moral Responsibility: General and Jewish Perspectives*, ed. C. Manekin and M. Kellner (College Park: University of Maryland Press, 1997), 165–204.

73. According to the Aristotelians, Fido desires to bury the bone, but he does not choose to, because choice requires reason, which dogs lack.

74. Gersonides refers to the discussion in *Wars of the Lord* 5:3.3, where he mentions two interpretations of Aristotle regarding the question of God's knowledge of the world proposed by Averroes and Themistius, respectively. Averroes' interpretation clearly matches the first interpretation here, but what is cited in the name of Themistius does not match the second interpretation here. Other statements of Themistius, however, in the *Commentary on the Metaphysics*, and as reported by Averroes in the latter's *Long Commentary on the Metaphysics*, both of which were known to Gersonides, suggest the identification. Feldman associates the second interpretation with Avicenna, whose theory is mentioned (without attribution) in the *Long Commentary* as a development of Themistius' position. For the history of that position, see S. Pines, "Some Distinctive Metaphysical Conceptions in Themistius' Commentary on Book Lambda, and their Place in the History of Philosophy," in *Aristoteles Werk und Wirkung*, ed. J. Wiesner (Berlin: de Gruyter, 1987), II: 177–204.

75. It is not apparent to me that Gersonides consistently distinguishes between event-types and event-tokens, e.g. between "finding a treasure" and "finding a treasure at t_1". For the purposes of this chapter I shall consider them both as accidents.

76. I.e. if "knowledge" is predicated of God and humans with absolute equivocation, then God does not know particulars according to the standard account of knowledge. This, at least, follows from the commonly held interpretation of "absolute equivocation."

77. At one point in his discussion of God's knowledge of particulars Maimonides writes: "As for knowledge of the infinite, there is a difficulty about it. Some of the people of speculation came to profess the opinion that knowledge has for its object the species, but, in a certain sense, extends to all the individuals of the species. This is the opinion of all those who adhere to a Law in view of what is required by the necessities of speculation. The philosophers, however, affirm decidedly that His knowledge may not have for its object a non-existent thing, etc." (*Guide* 3:20; trans. Pines, 481). The first sentence is cited by Gersonides in *Wars of the Lord* 3 as evidence that his theory is in accord with the Torah (law). But Maimonides implies that the theory of "some of the people of speculation," while religiously satisfactory, is not shared by the philosophers. Once again, it appears that, as a philosopher, he

prefers the Aristotelian position, with all its attendant difficulties, to the more religiously palatable one of the "men of speculation." Gersonides does not follow suit.

78. On the translation of *episteme* as "understanding," see J. Barnes, *Aristotle's Posterior Analytics*, 2nd ed., Clarendon Aristotle Series (Oxford: Oxford University Press, 1994), 82. There has been some debate over the merits of "understanding" in its ordinary English usage to capture Aristotelian *episteme*; see C. C. W. Taylor, "Aristotle's Epistemology," in *Epistemology: Companions to Ancient Thought* 1, ed. S. Everson (Cambridge: Cambridge University Press, 1990), 116–41.

79. *Posterior Analytics* 1:31

80. *Metaphysics* 1:1, 6:2.

81. Oxford, Bodleian Mich. Heb. Ms. 486 <Ol. 84> [Neubauer 1362], fol. 39b.

82. *Wars of the Lord* 3:4, 138; trans. Feldman, II: 117 (slightly altered).

83. *Wars of the Lord* 1:10, 69; trans. Feldman, I: 195.

84. Hence Gersonides does not hold that God knows universals rather than particulars, nor that God can only know particulars universally, whereas humans can know them universally and particularly. These opinions are erroneously ascribed to him in some of the scholarly literature.

85. But does not Reuben freely choose to adhere to Jewish law? Only insofar as his reason *compels* him to; see Manekin, "Freedom Within Reason?," 193–4.

86. Ed. I. Levy, vol. IV: 139.

87. *Commentary on Genesis* 18:19, Explanation of the Terms, ed. Braner and Freiman, 252. The reference is to Psalms 1:6.

88. *Commentary on Genesis* 7:1, Lesson 1, ed. Braner and Freiman, 168.

89. *Commentary on Genesis* 18:21, Lesson 16, ed. Braner and Freiman, 272.

90. Ibid.

91. Cf. Touati, *La pensée*, 563: "*Au fond, rien de véritablement fondamental dans les données de la Tradition n'est éliminé par Gersonide; mais tout est transposé sur un plan philosophique*" (italics his). This is the theme of the present chapter, but I also believe, pace Touati, that one can find in Gersonides' thought "la présence immanente de Dieu dans l'histoire individuelle" – at least "in a certain manner."

92. In *Wars of the Lord* 3:1 Gersonides considers the views of Aristotle and Maimonides as the only ones worthy of investigation on the issue of divine knowledge of sublunar things. But in *Wars of the Lord* 6:1.29 he writes that none of his predecessors had anything partially or wholly correct to say save Maimonides, "and yet it is not fitting that God's knowledge should be posited in this manner." It is entirely appropriate

that Gersonides should give higher marks to Maimonides than to Aristotle since he agrees with the former that God knows particulars.

93. See the articles cited in n. 72.

94. See *Wars of the Lord*, Introduction, 4; trans. Feldman, I: 94.

95. One can mention in this regard Gersonides' affirmation of the chosenness of Israel, its special providence, its superiority over other nations, the preeminence of its land as a place for prophecy and conjunction with God, and other particularist doctrines.

96. See A. Funkenstein, "Gersonides' Biblical Commentary: Science, History and Providence," in Freudenthal (ed.), *Studies on Gersonides*, 305–16, esp. 314, where the author claims that "of all medieval Jewish philosophers of the first rank, Gersonides came closest to being a dogmatic rationalist." The similarities between the philosophical temperaments of Gersonides and Leibniz are striking in this regard.

Part III
The Later Years

15 The impact of Scholasticism upon Jewish philosophy in the fourteenth and fifteenth centuries

In a classic article, Shlomo Pines argued that post-Thomistic Scholasticism, most notably Duns Scotus and the school of Parisian physics (e.g., Jean Buridan, Nicole Oresme), had a strong impact upon fourteenth- and fifteenth-century Jewish philosophy.[1] Pines pointed in this article to the "interest displayed by contemporary Jewish thinkers in the new problems under discussion, or in the old problems in a new formulation unfamiliar to the Arabic-Jewish tradition."[2] In what follows I shall explore Pines' thesis against the backdrop of specific issues in Jewish philosophy. More specifically, I shall claim that Scholastic influences upon fourteenth- and fifteenth-century Jewish philosophy can be seen in the increased attention paid to Scholastic logic, in increased analysis of the logical and theological status of future contingents, in metaphysical concerns having to do with identity and individuation, and in the development of non-Aristotelian physics. Before turning to the issues themselves, however, I would like to situate this study by briefly examining important developments within the world of Christian Scholasticism.

INTRODUCTION: FAITH, BELIEF, AND HERESY IN SCHOLASTIC AND JEWISH PHILOSOPHY

In order to appreciate the content of Scholastic discussions during this period, we must say more about the importance of the condemnation of philosophy of 1277. The condemnation of 1277 represents the culmination of a series of earlier condemnations in the Christian universities, and raised the thorny issue of heresy. In the thirteenth century, academic censure involved university-trained scholars who were accused of heresy. The word "heresy" was used among thirteenth- and fourteenth-century Scholastics to refer to false teachings and erroneous views, as well as to clear-cut heresies. Many Scholastics used the criterion of willful adherence to distinguish a heretical from an erroneous doctrine: errors become heresies when they are "defended with pertinacity."[3]

On December 10, 1270, Bishop Stephen Tempier condemned a series of thirteen propositions, among them the eternity of the world. This condemnation appears to have been largely ignored, as evidenced, for example, by the fact that at least four separate treatises on the eternity of the world were written shortly after 1270.[4] This was followed with a condemnation of 219 propositions in philosophy and theology by Bishop Tempier on March 7, 1277; this condemnation is one of the most studied events in the history of the University of Paris.[5] Many historians have presented this condemnation as a reaction to the radical Aristotelian teachings being disseminated at the University of Paris. Doctrines such as the eternity of the universe were seen to be in conflict with Christian belief, and it was forbidden to hold or defend them on pain of excommunication.[6]

Menachem Kellner compares the proliferation of accusations of heresy and subsequent condemnations in the Scholastic world with the relative absence of schisms, sects, and charges of heresy in the medieval Jewish theological arena.[7] Despite the many differing accounts concerning the basic principles of Judaism in Maimonides, Duran, Crescas, Albo, Arama, Bibago, Abravanel, and others, we find few accusations of heresy. Kellner suggests that in part this can be traced to a traditional Jewish notion of faith as a (non-cognitivist) "trust in God," rather than as a propositional affirmation or denial. In fact, it is Maimonides who introduced into Judaism a propositional or cognitivist notion of belief by defining heresy as the questioning of any of the thirteen principles of faith articulated in his introduction to the tenth chapter of *Tractate Sanhedrin* (*Pereq Heleq*). In this work Maimonides argued that anybody who questions (disbelieves) any one of these thirteen principles excludes himself from the community of Israel, and hence forfeits his share in the world to come.[8] According to Maimonides, adherence to these principles is a necessary condition for assuring immortality of the soul. As Shalom Rosenberg points out, the topic of belief (*emunah*) thus becomes inextricably linked to the view one adopts concerning immortality of the soul.[9]

Maimonides' cognitivist conception of belief, tying immortality to intellectual attainment, defined post-Maimonidean philosophy. Beyond even this, many Jewish philosophers, influenced by Averroes, replaced Maimonides' cognitivist conception with an even more stringent Aristotelian distinction between knowledge and true opinion. Arguing that only knowledge can be truly salvific, philosophers such as Gersonides maintained that non-philosophers who do not attain to rational knowledge (in the robust Aristotelian sense of demonstrated science) cannot achieve immortality; thus rational speculation (not just belief) is a sufficient condition for attaining immortality.[10]

The subject of dogma and belief is revisited with even greater urgency in the fifteenth century. In large part this is due to the intense Christian persecutions experienced by Iberian Jews between 1391 and 1418. Jewish intellectual leaders were drawn into the debate not only to define who is a Jew, and who merits immortality, but also to articulate the doctrinal content of Judaism in contradistinction to Christianity. Jews were forced to respond to a Christian challenge rooted in credal concerns, thus bringing to the fore questions concerning the nature of belief.[11]

When Scholasticism infiltrates Jewish circles in the late fourteenth century, *emunah* (belief or conviction) takes on the additional meaning of "faith" (*fides*).[12] We find Jewish and Christian philosophers vacillating between a volitional and a nonvolitional understanding of belief. Some philosophers collapsed the distinction between true belief and knowledge, and in so doing argued that knowledge is inferior to faith (*fides, emunah*). Other theories emphasized the primacy of will over that of intellect in the acquisition of beliefs. Many examples of the nonrational status of belief abound in fourteenth- and fifteenth-century Jewish literature. In his work *Derekh Emunah* (*The Way of Belief*), Abraham Bibago (d. c. 1489) acknowledges that knowledge can be achieved through rational inquiry, but argues that accepting propositions on faith (the way of *emunah*) is often superior to the first mode. Reflecting Aquinas' characterization of *fides*, Bibago claims that the superiority of *emunah* lies in its volitional character.[13]

Hasdai Crescas (c. 1340–1410/11), however, rejected the volitional view of belief. In his major philosophical work *Light of the Lord* (*Or Adonai*), Crescas argued that, in contradistinction to Maimonides, Jews are not commanded to believe anything, since assent or denial is not subject to choice or will.[14] Arguing that the will has no power over extra-mental existents, Crescas rejects the notion that the will moves the intellect. In *Light* 2:5 Crescas argues that human action is motivated by the agent's own will, but the will is determined by prior causes, both internal and external. Beliefs, however, are imposed upon our minds, leaving no room for will.[15] In this determinist scheme the will affects the emotional response taken to beliefs, that is the "joy and pleasure" we experience, and thus is causally connected to our divine reward and punishment. Many scholars have tried to trace the formative influences upon Crescas' doctrine of will. In his recent study of Crescas' *Sermon on the Passover*, Aviezer Ravitzky has argued that Crescas' discussion of will appears to reflect a connection to Latin Scholasticism in its acceptance of Scotist ideas regarding the moral and religious primacy of the will.[16] After noting important similarities and differences between Aquinas' and Crescas' conceptions of belief, Ravitzky turns to a comparison of Scotus and Crescas. Most importantly, both philosophers reject Aquinas' insistence upon ultimate felicity being attained through intellect, and replace it with a theory of ultimate felicity (beatitude) that is achieved through will.[17]

THE INFLUENCE OF SCHOLASTIC METHOD UPON JEWISH PHILOSOPHY

Turning more specifically to the Scholastic influences upon fourteenth- and fifteenth-century Jewish philosophy, we must note several historiographical issues. First, we must be careful to distinguish by geographical area as well as by temporal period. Charles Manekin and others have argued that the major fourteenth-century Jewish philosophers of northern Spain and Provence (e.g., Gersonides, Isaac Pollegar, Ibn Kaspi, and Narboni) show little sign, if any, of Scholastic influence.[18] On the other hand, we know that the Spanish Jewish philosophers of the late fourteenth and fifteenth centuries (Profiat Duran, Crescas, Albo, Bibago, Arama, and Abravanel) were involved in Christian polemics; this involvement necessitates an engagement with Scholasticism in order to address the challenges posed by Christianity.[19]

But how was this engagement effected? Did Jewish philosophers, for example, know Latin? Daniel Lasker argues that, although the anti-Christian polemicists certainly were familiar with Christian sources, not all had a reading knowledge of Latin. It is not unreasonable to postulate, however, that Jews and Christians communicated with one another in the vernacular. A good example is the apparent interaction between Gersonides (1288–1344) and the Christian clerics who commissioned from him works in astronomy, music (*De Numeris Harmonicis*), and astrology.[20] Furthermore, inasmuch as Jewish philosophers during this period rarely mention Christian writers by name, it is often difficult to trace individual Scholastic influences. Hillel of Verona, for example, used unattributed passages (a not uncommon practice) from the Latin Avicenna and Averroes, interwoven with passages from Aquinas' *Tractatus de Unitate Intellectus contra Averroistas* and Dominico Gundisalvo, in his own work *Tagmulei ha-Nefesh (Retributions of the Soul)*, written in 1291.[21] Even translations can be ambiguous. Although the works of Aristotle, Boethius, Albertus Magnus, Aquinas, Ockham, and Marsilius of Inghen were translated into Hebrew by Elijah Habillo (late fifteenth century), Abraham Shalom (d. 1492), Meir Alguades (d. 1410), and Azariah ben Joseph (late fifteenth century), it is not clear to what extent they actually were incorporated into Jewish philosophy.

By the fourteenth century, we see Scholastic method firmly entrenched among the Schoolmen. The most prominent method used is the *quaestio* method adopted by Aquinas, Scotus, and the later Scholastics.[22] By mid-century, this method appears in Jewish texts as well. Marc Saperstein has documented the use of syllogistic forms of argument, as well as the incorporation of the Scholastic method of *disputatio*, into medieval Jewish sermons. Crescas' celebrated *Sermon on the Passover* is an excellent case study.[23] That Scholastic method influenced Jewish philosophical writings can be seen as well in the works of Gersonides, Crescas, and Isaac Abravanel, among others, who organized their discourses thematically as a set of disputed questions with the same order of exposition as found in Scholastic texts: formulation of the question, citation of supporting arguments, citation of antithetical argument, and resolution of the original question, generally in support of the antithetical arguments.

In part this facility with Scholastic method can be traced to an increased interest in Scholastic logic. As Manekin and Rosenberg have noted, the influence of Scholastic logic upon Jewish thought was extensive.[24] Already in fourteenth-century Provence we find treatises that demonstrate the influence of Scholastic logic. One such work is an extensive gloss commentary upon Peter of Spain's *Tractatus*, written in 1320 by Hezekiah bar Halafta.[25] By the end of the fourteenth and beginning of the fifteenth centuries, we find the *Tractatus* being translated into Hebrew and enjoying increased popularity. One reason for the popularity of Scholastic logic undoubtedly rested on the perception among Jews that logical training would prepare them for the rigors of disputation with Christians; without such training, the Jews saw themselves at a distinct theological disadvantage. Another reason may have had to do with the perceived importance of logic for a sound medical education; inasmuch as Jewish physicians were certified before a mixed tribunal of Jews and Christians, knowledge of Scholastic logic was presumed to be helpful in their preparation.[26]

Scholastic thought is extremely influential upon Hebrew logic in Italy as well. Sermoneta has documented the Thomistic trend among Italian Jews, who translated Aquinas into Hebrew and used his logical analysis for their own purposes.[27] For example, Judah ben Moses Romano in the fourteenth century translated selected works of Aquinas and Giles of Rome into Hebrew. Once Jews were admitted to the faculties of medicine and philosophy in Italian universities, they were in a position to incorporate Christian teachings and specifically logic.[28] A good example of this university status for Jews is Judah ben Yehiel Messer Leon, who studied at the universities of Bologna and Padua in the latter part of the fifteenth century, was awarded a doctorate in philosophy and medicine, and incorporated the Scholastic logic as reflected in the works of Walter Burley and Paul of Venice into his writings. Messer Leon wrote a treatise on Hebrew rhetoric, a history of Hebrew grammar, an introductory textbook on logic entitled *Sefer Mikhlal Yofi* (*The Book of the Perfection of Beauty*), and commentaries on Averroes' middle commentaries on the first five books of Aristotle's *Organon*.[29]

DIVINE OMNISCIENCE AND HUMAN FREEDOM

In the thirteenth and fourteenth centuries the problem of divine omniscience comprises a number of subsidiary problems: the problem of (logical) fatalism as introduced by Aristotle in his *De Interpretatione* and further developed by the Stoics, the problem of God's foreknowledge of human events and the relation of this knowledge to free will, and particular theological difficulties centering around the notions of prophecy, providence, and retribution.[30] Medieval philosophers in general are concerned with the extent and limits of God's knowledge of particulars in the sublunar universe. How to account for divine knowledge while denying, on the one hand, (divine) plurality and, on the other hand, the effects of causal activity upon God becomes a major consideration for Jewish and Scholastic thinkers alike.

Two main solutions to the problem of divine foreknowledge presented themselves: compatibilism and incompatibilism. I will take *compatibilism* to be the view that God's knowledge is compatible with human freedom. Most Jewish philosophers, along with their Scholastic contemporaries, adopted a form of compatibilism, claiming that God's foreknowledge of future contingent events in no way impedes human freedom. The compatibilist, therefore, has no problem with asserting both that God has foreknowledge that I will do a particular action and that I do that action freely. But compatibilism is not immune from logical difficulties, and *incompatibilists* are quick to point to discrepancies between upholding both foreknowledge and human freedom. One form of incompatibilism, which I shall term *indeterminism*, is that God simply does not know future contingent events. Starting with human freedom and the existence of contingency as a given, the indeterminist will deny God's omniscience on the grounds that if an action is truly indeterminate prior to its actualization, then it cannot be known by God. Clearly this position safeguards human freedom at the expense of divine omniscience. Another strand of incompatibilism, *determinism*, claims that if God knows the causal chain of events that unfolds from his knowledge, human actions are ultimately determined by this knowledge. Both indeterminism and determinism had their adherents in Jewish philosophy, albeit in very few numbers.[31]

Jewish analyses exhibit increasing sophistication in the fourteenth and fifteenth centuries. Before the fourteenth century, the question of "freedom of will" (*behira hofshit*) is not discussed among Jewish philosophers. In the thirteenth century, the terms *behira* (choice) and *efshar* (contingency) rather than *ratzon* (will) and *hofshi* (free) were used. Maimonides, for example, argued that God's knowledge is unique and hence we cannot understand the compatibility between divine knowledge and human free will.[32] By the fifteenth century the term *behira hofshit* is utilized, presumably as a sign of the influence of the Scholastic concept of *liberum arbitrium*.[33] Among the Christian Scholastics it was especially Duns Scotus, and William of Ockham after him, who asserted that will in its primary act is free with regard to opposite acts. Consider, for example, the reputed "voluntarism" of Duns Scotus, which consists precisely in his insistence that the free will is capable of choosing other than it does.[34]

Intimated but not fully developed by his predecessor Abraham ibn Daud, indeterminism finds its fullest expression in Gersonides' work *Sefer Milhamot ha-Shem* (*Wars of the Lord*). In the context of an elaborate discussion of astrology, Gersonides claims that human beings can overcome the determining influences of their astrological signs. Although this ability is rare, and real instances of free will are uncommon, intellect and will can move humans to do something other than what has been determined from the standpoint of the heavenly bodies.[35] One implication of this position is that all future contingents are truly open. Inasmuch as an immutable deity cannot be omniscient, if omniscience entails knowing objects that undergo change, Gersonides argues that God does not know future contingents. According to Gersonides, God knows that certain states of affairs may or may not be actualized. But insofar as they are contingent states, God does not know which of the two alternatives will in fact be actualized. God's inability to foreknow future contingents is not a defect in his knowledge. With respect to future contingents, God knows their ordered nature or essence, and he knows that they are contingent, but God does not know which alternative will become actual.[36] For God has placed within humans purposive reason "so as to move (humans) toward something other than that which has been determined from the aspect of the heavenly bodies, insofar as this is possible to make straight that which chance has convoluted."[37]

Shlomo Pines has argued that Gersonides' conception of free action is not found among Muslim Aristotelians or Jews, and it is therefore probable that Gersonides and other Jewish Aristotelians had absorbed it from Christian Scholasticism. Pines then suggests that Gersonides was familiar with the Scholastic debate over the Pelagian controversy.[38] Unfortunately, however, no texts exist to tie the two discussions; as Seymour Feldman and, more recently, Manekin have argued, the similarities between Gersonides and medieval Scholastics on the issue of providence can be just as convincingly explained by parallel attempts to reconcile astrology with Aristotelianism.[39] In fact, Ibn Kaspi may have been more familiar with the Pelagian debate, since he uses the Latin term *contingentia futura* in its Hebrew equivalent (*he-atid ha-efshari*).[40]

The more "conservative" fifteenth-century philosophers rejected Gersonides' indeterminism and denial of divine omniscience. Against Gersonides' indeterminism we have Crescas' theological determinism. Manekin has suggested that these reactionary positions may be seen as "the result of the Scholastic milieu, in which the doctrine of divine knowledge of particulars qua particulars was taken for granted by the fourteenth century."[41]

Abner of Burgos is the first Jewish philosopher to present a strict determinist theory (although by the time he wrote his treatise on free will in the 1320s, Abner had converted to Christianity). In his *Treatise on Free Will*, Narboni describes Abner as follows: "There was a scholar, an older contemporary of mine, one of the singular men of his time, who composed a treatise on Determinism, in which he stated that 'the possible' does not exist, but only 'the inevitable' since everything is predestined."[42] Defining a voluntary agent as one who can equally perform one of two alternatives, Abner introduces the notion of "complete will" to describe the causal chain that combines the motivating stimulus and the imaginative faculty. Human actions are completely determined in so far as the will flows necessarily from a rigid causal chain.[43] Thus Abner upholds strict celestial determinism, arguing that God's eternal knowledge causally necessitates human actions; if human choice were free, God could not have foreknowledge of human actions. Ultimately we have no control over what we do or refrain from doing. Baer notes that Abner's theory of determinism is a curious blend of Pauline and Augustinian doctrines of predestination, interwoven with Muslim fatalism and astrology. According to Abner, the human being has no choice, not even in matters of faith.[44] As Colette Sirat points out, Abner's theory of will justifies in advance forced baptisms and the tortures of the Inquisition. In *Minhat Qena'ot*, Abner argues that an individual who wills something under torture acts voluntarily.[45]

Of the three opponents to Abner – Isaac Pollegar, Moses of Narbonne, and Ibn Kaspi – Pollegar was the first to respond and did so vociferously in his treatise *Ezer ha-Dat* (*The Support of the Faith*).[46] Of Pollegar himself we know very little, except that he was a close friend of Abner's before the latter's conversion to Christianity. While Abner sees himself as a defender of astral determinism, as well as divine knowledge of particulars, Pollegar reiterates Maimonides' arguments against astrology, arguing that astrology is both false and harmful to religion.[47] Presenting his arguments as a dialogue between an astrologer and a wise man (*haver*), Pollegar tries to retain both God's foreknowledge and human freedom. He argues that determinism is incompatible with human agency, and in its stead proposes a theory of "pre-established harmony" according to which God's will and human will are in synchrony: "my will is linked to the will of my creator and both unite at the same instant so that my will is part of his, and thus I am drawn by him; when he wishes and desires to act, then I too wish it."[48]

Determinism is supported most forcefully by Crescas. It is his discussion that most clearly reflects developments in contemporary Latin philosophy, particularly the voluntarist theories advanced by Duns Scotus and his followers. Zev Harvey has noted that the Scotist philosophers Anfredus Gonteri and Peter Thomae (d. 1340) had taught at the Fransciscan *studium generale* in Barcelona in the early fourteenth century. The *studium generale* was situated about five hundred meters from the Jewish Quarter, where Crescas lived and taught until he moved to Saragossa in 1389.[49] In the *Light of the Lord* we find two treatments of the problem of divine omniscience, the second of which is later than the first. While the first is based on Crescas' *Sermon on the Passover*, the second, complementary position on the problem of determinism and choice appears to have been worked out within the framework of the Scotist tradition.[50]

In *Light* Crescas lists three principles that are necessitated by tradition: that God's knowledge encompasses the infinite, that God's knowledge extends over that which does not (now) exist, and that God's knowledge extends over the (disjunctive) parts of the possible, without changing the nature of the possible. Crescas' stated goal in this work is to examine those arguments of the philosophers, and that of Gersonides in particular, which threaten these principles. In standard Scholastic fashion, Crescas lists arguments both for and against the three principles, with the intention of supporting the former. He first claims that our knowledge is derivative, whereas

God's knowledge is active and causal.[51] God knows things not because he knows himself, but *eo ipso*; it is through his knowledge that they exist. It is here that Crescas' determinism is introduced. Does this temporal change from future to past affect God's essence? Crescas responds that, because God knows before the occurrence of an event that it will happen, God's essence does not change when the event actually occurs. But how can we call a thing possible if God knows before its occurrence how it will happen? Crescas attempts to distinguish two senses of contingency, arguing that a thing may be necessary in one way and possible in another.[52] Events known by God, although "possible in themselves," nevertheless are necessary with respect to their causal history. In other words, if God knows p, then the truth value of p is determinate and "is necessary in terms of its causes."[53] On analogy with an individual's knowledge that does not change the nature of the possibility of the thing known, so too does Crescas argue that the knowledge of God does not change the nature of the possibility in question.

In *Light* 2:5.1 Crescas turns more specifically to the problem of free choice (*behira*). Crescas is unequivocal that free choice presupposes possibility, albeit in a narrow sense of possibility. Crescas argues that natural phenomena are "possible in themselves and necessary with respect to their causes."[54] What this means is that from the perspective of its causal history, every event is necessary. Only in light of human epistemological weakness (viz. our inability to know this causal history) can an event be said to be possible. As necessary, events can be foreknown; as possible per se, they are "*qua possibile*."

THEORIES OF INDIVIDUATION

Metaphysical issues concerning the identity and individuation of particulars, a topic of much importance in Christian philosophy, are found only derivatively among Jewish philosophers. Part of the difference in scope between Jewish and Scholastic discussions is due to the fact that until the fourteenth century Jewish writers had little access to the logical writings of Aristotle, and so the specific logical issues related to individuation that arose out of the *Categories* and *De Interpretatione* were of little direct concern to them. Further, inasmuch as Jewish philosophers were obviously not concerned with those ontological issues that arose out of a trinitarian conception of God, they did not feel as obliged as did their Scholastic counterparts to construct elaborate theories of identity and individuation to account for the unity within diversity of the Godhead. In general, I agree with Jorge Gracia and Udo Thiel that we must distinguish a number of issues pertaining to the problem of the individuation of persons:[55] the metaphysical question of what makes an individual the individual it is and distinguishes it from all other individuals of the same kind, the epistemological question of how we know individuals and how they differ from one another, and the specific problem of identity through time – the conditions of an individual remaining the same over time. These issues appear in medieval Jewish texts but primarily within the context of problems associated with the immortality of the soul.

When we turn to the fourteenth century, we see the influence of Scholasticism reflected in the work of Yedayah ben Abraham Bedersi ha-Penini (c. 1270–1340), who lived primarily in southern France (Perpignan and Montpellier). Of his purely philosophical works, his short treatise *A Treatise upon Personal or Individual Forms*, which appears only in manuscript form, examines the issue of individual forms.[56] In upholding the existence of personal and individual forms, Bedersi places himself directly in the Scotist camp. Hence he stands in contradistinction to Judeo-Arabic thinkers who followed the Aristotelian tradition according to which forms by definition are universal and not individual. According to Scotus and in contrast to Aristotle, individual differences are explained in terms of a thing's *haecceitas* ("thisness"). Although Scotus himself did not identify this *haecceitas* with "personal forms," his disciples tended to obscure the distinction.[57] It should be noted that nowhere in this treatise does Bedersi quote Scotus or other Scholastics directly; nevertheless, both Pines and Sirat have emphasized the obvious Scotist element in his discussion.[58] What is not clear is whether Bedersi took his sources from an unknown Scholastic work or whether he was influenced by general Scholastic discussions and then developed the details of his theory on his own.[59] In any event, even a brief examination of Bedersi's treatise reveals a new dimension in Jewish discussions of individuation.

The question posed by Bedersi is one that was popularly discussed in thirteenth-century Scholastic circles, namely, whether individuals have their own individual forms in addition to those that accrue to the species. Bedersi allows for two possibilities: in the first case, each individual has its own personal form that is super-added to the form of the species in question; in the second, individuals belonging to the same species differ only with respect to numerical diversity. Epistemologically, Bedersi suggests that individual members of species can be defined only in terms of the species: "Individuals are not intellected under the rubric of the species, that is, their individual forms; for what is intellected is always general and separate from the material element. Hence individuals are not definable except in terms of the species."[60]

Bedersi's major metaphysical contention is that the difference between members of a species derives in large part from the forms that inhere in the individual species; on this basis he postulates the existence of individual forms.[61] It is here that Bedersi most clearly resembles Scotism. Both Bedersi and Scotus understand individuation not as something derived primarily from matter, but rather as rooted in form. This does not mean that individuation eschews matter entirely. According to Scotus, the individual differs from the universal formally as well as virtually.[62] The principle of individuation contains both a formal and a material element. Although matter plays a role for both Scotus and Bedersi, in both cases the ultimate difference with regard to individuals is formal: it is individual forms that individuate an entity.

ALTERNATIVES TO ARISTOTELIAN SCIENCE: TIME, VOID, AND PLURALITY OF WORLDS

Throughout the fourteenth and fifteenth centuries, the problem of creation continues to occupy philosophers and theologians, both Jewish and Scholastic. The three major positions on creation are temporal creation of the world *ex nihilo*, eternal emanation of the world out of God, and eternal production of the world by God. Maimonides had set the parameters for the discussion, disputing (in *Guide* 2:13–25) the demonstrability of Aristotle's arguments for the eternity of the world and arguing (at least prima facie) for its *ex nihilo* creation.[63] But Maimonides found his critics in Gersonides, Crescas, Albalag, and Narboni, among others, all of whom subjected his theory of time and creation to critical examination. Both Albalag and

Narboni sided with the Averroist thesis that the world is eternally produced by God as First Cause.[64] However, among the Scholastics, Thomas Aquinas cited Maimonides' discussion of creation with approval, and used it as a basis for arguing that the creation of the world cannot be proved demonstratively.[65] By the 1270s numerous Scholastic treatises appeared in support of the eternity thesis; as mentioned earlier, this proliferation was in part responsible for the condemnation of 1277. Of the 219 propositions condemned by Bishop Tempier in 1277, about thirty have to do with the eternity of the soul, of the intelligences, of the heavens, and of matter, in addition to the eternity of the world.

One of the most pervasive results of the condemnation of 1277 was that it encouraged alternatives to Aristotelian natural philosophy.[66] More specifically, the condemned propositions directly affected theories of place, the void, and the plurality of worlds, thus inaugurating a pre-Copernican revolution. The two propositions most important to this new way of thinking are proposition 34 "Quod prima causa non posset plures mundos facere," and proposition 49 "Quod Deus non possit movere celum motu recto. Et ratio est, quia tunc relinqueret vacuum."[67] As John Murdoch and others have argued, these two propositions represented the foundation of the whole edifice of Aristotelian physics. Being declared anathema implicitly demanded the creation of a new physics that would circumvent the condemned propositions.

In exploring the consequences of these condemnations, Scholastic philosophers were encouraged to develop concepts contrary to Aristotelian physics and cosmology. As a result of proposition 49, for example, there arose an emphasis upon God's absolute power (potentia Dei absoluta) to do anything short of a logical contradiction. Proposition 34 led to speculation about the existence of multiple universes. Prior to the condemnations, Scholastic philosophers considered the impossibility of multiple worlds against the backdrop of Aristotelian arguments that outside the world there cannot be any place because there are no bodies; and there cannot be a void, because a void is a place where there could be a body where there is presently no body.[68] Inasmuch as these arguments were linked to the issue of God's omnipotence as well, it became increasingly common to argue that God's creative omnipotence allowed for the creation of multiple worlds. For example, God was said to create multiple worlds, each with its own center. On the supposition that God did make other worlds, it was argued that empty space would intervene between them. So if God could create a vacuum between worlds, certainly God could create vacua within the world.[69]

Already in Gersonides, we find echoes of this concern. In *Wars of the Lord* 6:1.19, Gersonides examines the possibility of a plurality of coexisting universes. Unlike Aristotle, Gersonides has postulated the existence of a primordial body/matter outside the universe, and so for him the question is whether there exists a sufficient quantity of this primordial body to generate other universes.[70] Gersonides argues that the existence of a multiplicity of universes would require postulating a vacuum between the regions of primordial matter, a hypothesis he considers "absurd." It is not unreasonable to suppose that Gersonides' discussion is influenced by the 1277 condemnation.[71]

The most articulate exponent within Jewish philosophy of these new interests is Crescas. Despite Tzvi Langermann's point that Crescas had no interest in science per se, no agenda for harmonizing science and theology,[72] it is clear that Crescas is embroiled in precisely the same set of scientific issues that occupied Scholastic philosophers after the condemnation of 1277. Zev Harvey suggests that Crescas' work is "perhaps connected in some way with the pioneering work in natural science being conducted at the University of Paris."[73] More specifically, Harvey has compared the works of Nicole Oresme and Crescas, arguing that they are the two most important philosophers representing the new physics. Both argue for the existence of many worlds; both claim that many worlds do not imply the existence of more than one God; and both argue that generation and corruption in the sublunary world is evidence for successive worlds. Oresme wrote in the 1340s in Paris, which was then the center of the "new physics." He came to Pamplona in 1338–1342, and Crescas visited Pamplona during this period. Crescas himself describes his analysis and critique of Aristotelian science as having "no small benefit for this science" (*to'elet eyno me'at ba-hokhma ha-zot*).[74]

In an attempt to uphold the basic dogmas of Judaism, Crescas subjects Aristotle's physics and metaphysics to a trenchant critique. His rejection of Aristotle's theories of place and the infinite forms part of an extended attempt to weaken Aristotle's hold upon Jewish philosophy. In Aristotle's *Physics* 4:1, space is identified with place (*topos*) and forms an integral part of Aristotle's theory of motion, which is defined as "change of place."[75] Place is then properly defined by Aristotle as "the boundary of the containing body at which it is in contact with the contained body."[76] On the basis of this characterization, Aristotle proceeds in *Physics* 4:6 to reject the possibility of a vacuum, for in a theory that does not allow for a place not correlated to any body, there can be no "empty space" or void.

One important implication of Crescas' alternative conception of place and infinity has to do with his postulating the existence of the vacuum. According to Crescas, place is prior to bodies: in contradistinction to Aristotle's conception of place, space for Crescas is not a mere relationship of bodies but is the "interval between the limits of that which surrounds."[77] Space is seen by Crescas as an infinite continuum ready to receive matter. Because this place or extension of bodies is identified with space, there is no contradiction in postulating the existence of space not filled with body, that is the vacuum.[78] Crescas, in fact, assumes that place is identical with the void, on the grounds that "place must be equal to the whole of its occupant as well as to [the sum of] its parts."[79]

This conception of place and time allows Crescas to maintain that the infinite universe (*ha-metziut*) contains many worlds (*olamot rabbim*). An extensive discussion of multiple worlds is found in *Light* 4:2. In this section, he adopts the *quaestio* method, starting with the Scholastic opener "whether" (*ha'im = utrum*), and then presents arguments for both the affirmative and negative position. He explores the affirmative position by offering two arguments: the first maintains that there is nothing that precludes creation from occurring in another world or worlds, whereas the second suggests that inasmuch as the "more he increases worlds, the more he increases goodness," it is logically possible from the nature of God that there exists many worlds.[80] Ari Ackerman has noted the similarity of these arguments to those found in William of Auvergne, John Buridan, Albert of Saxony, Nicole Oresme, and Thomas Aquinas.[81] After examining both the positive and negative arguments, Crescas concludes in true Scholastic fashion that "what has been proved from them is only the possibility of a plurality."[82] That is, the arguments have shown that multiple worlds are possible, in contradistinction to Aristotle's claim that the unicity of worlds is necessary, but they do not show that a plurality of worlds actually exists.

The condemnation of 1277 affects theories of time as well. Notwithstanding the condemnation of the eternity of time, the Aristotelian emphasis upon eternity was nevertheless embraced and refined by the Scholastics.[83] The Aristotelian definition of time reappears throughout the fourteenth, fifteenth, and early sixteenth centuries, but with progressive modification. Both Pines and Sirat have argued that Gersonides' discussion of the "now" (atah) is very similar to the *Quaestiones super Libros Physicorum* attributed (apparently wrongly) to Siger of Brabant.[84] Gersonides' critical refutation of Aristotle's eternity thesis introduces the motif of time and its relation to motion. In contradistinction to Aristotle, who postulated the eternity of time and motion, Gersonides insists that both time and motion are finite, thereby hoping to refute Aristotle's eternity of the world thesis by showing that the infinity of time and motion fail as exceptions to Aristotle's own finite universe.[85]

Aristotle's second argument for eternity, as presented by Gersonides in *Wars of the Lord* 6:1.11, is based on his definition of the instant as the middle point between the "before" (ha-qodem) and "after" (ha-mit'acher). The main thrust of Aristotle's argument, as presented by Gersonides, is that, in order to account for the coming into existence of any present instant, there must exist a prior actual instant; but in the case of the first instant, there could be no prior instant, actual or potential. Gersonides' major objection centers on Aristotle's formulation of the notion of the instant. More specifically, Gersonides distinguishes two roles of the instant: an initial instant that does not yet constitute time, and subsequent instants that demarcate "before" from "after." According to Gersonides, these two notions of the instant serve different functions. The first delimits a particular portion of time, namely continuous quantity, and is characterized in terms of duration. The latter, on the other hand, reflects the Aristotelian function of the instant as characterizing division. Gersonides claims that if there were no difference between these two functions of the instant, we could not distinguish between any two sets of fractions of time, for example three hours and three days, because our measure of the two sets would be identical. Since each period of time would be divided by the same kind of instant, there would be no way of distinguishing three days from three hours.[86] Gersonides' point is that Aristotle's original objections to the finitude of time obtain only if the instant is understood in the second sense. When the instant is taken as an initial instant of a temporal span, we see that there can be a "first instant" without contradiction. Hence the instant taken in the sense of duration need not be preceded by a past time.[87] It is here that Pines notes the similarity between Gersonides and the Scholastic text alluded to above: both texts maintain that because the "now" plays two roles in Aristotle, it is possible that in the case of the temporal beginning of the universe, only one of these roles – that of limit – is being utilized.[88]

But Aristotle had additional critics as well, beginning with Plotinus and then much later Crescas, who emphasized that time is the product of the soul and is defined in accordance with duration rather than number. In contradistinction to Aristotle, Crescas wishes to make several points. The first is that time can measure rest as well as motion. Secondly, time can be measured by rest as well as by motion. And finally, time exists only in the soul. The first two points are captured in Crescas' revised definition of time: "the correct definition of time is that it is the measure of the continuity of motion or of rest between two instants."[89] In this definition Crescas retains Aristotle's and Maimonides' notion of time as a "measure" or "number." However, Crescas adds the important qualification that time is the measure not only of motion or change, but of rest as well.

Crescas proceeds to say that the genus most appropriate to time is magnitude. Inasmuch as time belongs to continuous quantity and number to discrete quantity, if we describe time as number, we describe it by a genus that is not essential to it. On this basis Crescas concludes that "the existence of time is only in the soul."[90] It is because humans have a mental conception of this measure that time even exists. The reality of time depends upon a thinking mind, and is indefinite, becoming definite only by being measured by motion. It is in this context that Crescas comes closest to reflecting his near Scholastic contemporaries Peter Aureol and William of Ockham. According to Peter Aureol, for example, time exists only in the mind.[91] And William of Ockham develops an even more subjectivist view, according to which time is a "cosmic clock," which measures the duration of temporal events and things. Like Crescas, who denies the real existence of time as an accident of substance, Ockham claims that time and instants of time are not really existent Aristotelian accidents.[92]

CONCLUSION: PRELUDE TO THE MODERN ERA

In this chapter I have examined a number of topics within fourteenth- and fifteenth-century Jewish philosophy that reflect the influences, either direct or indirect, of Christian Scholasticism as it was shaped by the condemnation of 1277. Although late medieval science and philosophy were indebted to Aristotle and his medieval followers, the underlying intellectual structure of the medieval world was crumbling. Jewish philosophers, as well as their Scholastic peers, pay increased attention to the natural science of their day. Later, in the sixteenth and seventeenth centuries, natural science and philosophy become more clearly distinguished, and their subject matters become subject to different types of methodological investigation. The heliocentrism of Copernicus threatens Aristotle's equation of time with motion in that, as Piero Ariotti has argued, heliocentrism does not provide Copernicus and his successors with directly observable uniform motions or constant intervals of time, so important to Aristotle's theory.[93]

Jewish philosophers in Renaissance Italy were influenced both by the Copernican revolution as well as by the Humanist revival of Platonism and Neoplatonism. The interconnections between philosophy, theology, and science found their way into Jewish philosophical texts from the late fifteenth century. Tracing the impact of the Copernican revolution upon Jewish thought in the fifteenth century, Hillel Levine suggests that European Jewry, although close to the Copernican debates, was "curiously unshaken" by the implications of the Copernican revolution upon metaphysical and epistemological speculation.[94] David Ruderman and others, however, have surveyed the impact of astronomy upon sixteenth-century eastern European Jewish philosophers. Citing the works of Moses Isserles of Cracow, the Maharal of Prague, and David Gans, Isserles' most successful student in the sciences, Ruderman raises the tantalizing question of the extent to which developments in current astronomy affected their works.[95] David Gans, for example, appears to be up-to-date on contemporary work in astronomy and science; in his work *Nehmad ve-Na'im*, he traces recent developments in astronomy and mentions Copernicus as the greatest astronomer since Ptolemy. Nevertheless, as André Neher and Ruderman have both pointed out, in his own astronomical writings Gans adheres to the geocentric models of Brahe

and Kepler.[96] Neher records a supposed conversation between David
Gans and Tycho Brahe in which Gans valiantly upholds the rabbinic
view over current astronomy.[97]

Joseph Solomon del Medigo (1591–1655), on the other hand, recognized the challenge of the new Copernican astronomy. Ruderman
has emphasized del Medigo's tendency, along with that of his mentor Galileo, to understand the natural world outside the framework
of Aristotelian physics; it is this tendency that is aligned with del
Medigo's interest in kabbalah and Neoplatonic thought.[98] In his work
Sefer Elim del Medigo describes the "strange astronomy," as well as
the dangers inherent in this new astronomy, which challenged the
reigning metaphysics.[99] In *Gevurot Hashem*, a work appended to
Sefer Elim, del Medigo is more enthusiastic in his attitude toward
Copernicus, demonstrating his knowledge of the new astronomy:

Happiness and joy were added to me when I heard that they (the researchers)
have begun in our time to think that the entire universe is like a lantern
and is called *"lanterna"*; and the candle burning within it is the solar body,
which stands in the center and whose light spreads out until the sphere of
Saturn which is at the outer limit of this universe.[100]

Del Medigo thus typifies the tendency of Jewish philosophers to look
outward, toward new developments in science and philosophy.

NOTES

1.   S. Pines, *Scholasticism after Thomas Aquinas and the Teachings of
      Hasdai Crescas and his Predecessors*, in *Proceedings of the Israel
      Academy of Sciences and Humanities* 1.10 (1967), 1–101.
2.   Pines, *Scholasticism*, 3.
3.   For a discussion of the different attitudes toward heresy in the Scholas-
      tic world, see J. M. M. H. Thijssen, *Censure and Heresy at the Uni-
      versity of Paris 1200–1400* (Philadelphia: University of Pennsylvania
      Press, 1998), 2.
4.   See R. C. Dales, *Medieval Discussions of the Eternity of the World*
      (Leiden: Brill, 1990), 129.
5.   For a careful study of the condemnation, see Thijssen, *Censure and
      Heresy*, ch. 2.
6.   See Thijssen, *Censure and Heresy*, 40–1.
7.   See M. Kellner, *Dogma in Medieval Jewish Thought: From Maimonides
      to Abravanel* (Oxford: Littman Library, 1986), 207.
8.   Maimonides' text can be found in Kellner, *Dogma*, 16.

9. See S. Rosenberg, "The Concept of *Emunah* in Post-Maimonidean Jewish Philosophy," in *Studies in Medieval Jewish History and Literature*, ed. I. Twersky (Cambridge, Mass.: Harvard University Press, 1984), II: 294.

10. See Levi ben Gershom, *The Wars of the Lord*, trans. S. Feldman, 3 vols. (Philadelphia: Jewish Publication Society, 1984–99), Part 1, chs. 11–12, 212ff.

11. Kellner, *Dogma*, 80–2.

12. See Manekin's discussion of *emunah* in C. Manekin, "Hebrew Philosophy in the Fourteenth and Fifteenth Centuries: An Overview," in *History of Jewish Philosophy*, ed. D. H. Frank and O. Leaman (London and New York: Routledge, 1997), 350–78.

13. See Abraham Bibago, *Derekh Emunah (The Way of Faith)*, ed. C. Frankel (Jerusalem: Bialik Institute, 1978), II.5:227–8. The comparison to Aquinas' *De Veritate* is made by the editor.

14. Hasdai Crescas, *The Light of the Lord (Or Adonai)*, trans. and ed. S. Fisher (Jerusalem: Sifrei Ramot, 1990), 2:5.5.

15. See A. Ravitzky, *Derashat ha-Pesah le-Rab Hasdai Crescas u-Mehqarim be-Mishnato ha-Pilosofit* (Jerusalem: Israel Academy of Sciences and Humanities, 1988), vii.

16. Ravitzky, *Derashat ha-Pesah*, viii. The *Sermon* is undated, and so scholars have disagreed over whether or not it predates *Light of the Lord*. Ravitzky has argued that the *Sermon* is a preliminary study which is then incorporated by Crescas into *Light*.

17. See Ravitzky, *Derashat ha-Pesah*, 54–60. See Scotus, *Reportata Parisiensia* 4:48–9; *Opus Oxoniense* 4:49.3, nos. 5ff.

18. See, e.g., Manekin, "Hebrew Philosophy," 352.

19. H. Tirosh-Rothschild discusses this point in her article "Jewish Philosophy on the Eve of Modernity," in *History of Jewish Philosophy*, ed. D. H. Frank and O. Leaman (London and New York: Routledge, 1997), 504.

20. For further discussion of Gersonides' interaction with Christian clergy, possibly even the Avignonese pope Clement VI, see Feldman's introductory comments in *The Wars of the Lord*, I: 3–54.

21. Hillel ben Samuel of Verona, *Sefer Tagmulei ha-Nefesh le-Hillel ben Shmu'el mi-Verona*, ed. G. Sermoneta (Jerusalem: Magnes Press, 1981).

22. For a brief discussion of the history and development of the *quaestio* method, see J. Marenbon, *Later Medieval Philosophy (1150–1350): An Introduction* (London: Routledge & Kegan Paul, 1987), 10–14.

23. For more detailed discussions of the influence of Scholastic method upon Jewish sermons, see M. Saperstein, *"Your Voice like a Ram's Horn": Themes and Texts in Traditional Jewish Preaching* (Cincinnati: Hebrew Union College Press, 1996), 17, 83ff.

24. See C. Manekin, "Scholastic Logic and the Jews," *Bulletin de Philosophie Médiévale* 41 (1999), 123–47.

25. The original manuscript (called *Be'ur la-Mabo* by Steinschneider) is found in Oxford, Bodley Ms. Mich. 314 [Neubauer 2187] (IMHM 20690, ff. 43–129). In the introduction to this work, the author claims that he "saw among them [i.e. the Christians] a commentary on the comprehensive introduction on all the principles of Logic...[I]t is called *Trakktat* in their language...I yearned for this commentary, I seized it, had it read before me, took my writing materials, moved my pen, and translated it from their language to our own." I take this quotation from Manekin, "Scholastic Logic and the Jews," 126.

26. For further discussion of this point, see C. Manekin, "When the Jews Learned Logic from the Pope: Three Medieval Hebrew Translations of the Tractatus of Peter of Spain," *Science in Context* 10 (1997), 406.

27. See Sermoneta's comments in Hillel ben Samuel of Verona, *Sefer Tagmulei ha-Nefesh le-Hillel ben Shmu'el mi-Verona*, ed. G. Sermoneta (Jerusalem: Magnes Press, 1981).

28. For extensive discussion of the development of medicine among Jews, see D. Ruderman, *Jewish Thought and Scientific Discovery in Early Modern Europe* (New Haven: Yale University Press, 1995).

29. For further discussion of Messer Leon, see Manekin, "Scholastic Logic and the Jews"; H. Tirosh-Rothschild, *Between Worlds: The Life and Thought of Rabbi David ben Judah Messer Leon* (Albany: State University of New York Press, 1991); and I. Husik, *Judah Messer Leon's Commentary on the "Vetus Logica"* (Leiden: Brill, 1901).

30. For an introductory survey to the vast primary and secondary literature dealing with issues connected with God's omniscience, the following works should be consulted: C. Normore, "Future Contingents," in *The Cambridge History of Later Medieval Philosophy*, ed. N. Kretzmann, A. Kenny, and J. Pinborg (Cambridge: Cambridge University Press, 1982), 358–81; T. M. Rudavsky (ed.), *Divine Omniscience and Omnipotence in Medieval Philosophy* (Dordrecht: Reidel, 1984); T. M. Rudavsky, *Time Matters: Time, Creation, and Cosmology in Medieval Jewish Philosophy* (Albany: State University of New York Press, 2000).

31. For a detailed analysis of these solutions in Jewish philosophy, see Rudavsky, *Time Matters*, ch. 4.

32. For Maimonides' discussion of divine omniscience, see *The Guide of the Perplexed*, trans. S. Pines (Chicago: University of Chicago Press, 1963), 3:17–21.

33. C. Manekin, "Freedom Within Reason? Gersonides on Human Choice," in *Freedom and Moral Responsibility: General and Jewish Perspectives*, ed. C. Manekin and M. Kellner (College Park: University of Maryland Press, 1997), 168.

34. For Duns Scotus' theory of the free will, see his *Quaestiones Super Libros Metaphysicorum* 9:15, n. 2. For a discussion of Scotus' indeterminism, see R. Cross, *Duns Scotus* (Oxford: Oxford University Press, 1999), ch. 7.

35. Gersonides, *Milhamot* 2:2, 97; *Wars of the Lord* (trans. Feldman), II:34.

36. Gersonides, *Milhamot* 3:4, 138; *Wars of the Lord*, II: 117.

37. Gersonides, *Milhamot* 2:2, 96; *Wars of the Lord*, II: 33.

38. Pines, "Scholasticism," 8.

39. See Manekin, "Freedom within Reason," 197.

40. Ibn Kaspi's discussion can be found in Ibn Kaspi, *Tam ha-Kesef*, ed I. Last (London, 1913), 20–1. See Pines' discussion in "Scholasticism," which suggests a connection between Ibn Kaspi and the Pelagians, notably Durandus of Saint-Purcain.

41. Manekin, "Hebrew Philosophy," 372.

42. Y. Baer, *A History of the Jews in Christian Spain*, 2 vols. (Philadelphia: Jewish Publication Society, 1978), I: 332.

43. Manekin, "Hebrew Philosophy," 367; see Y. Baer, "*Minhat Qenaot* and its Influence on Hasdai Crescas," *Tarbiz* 11 (1940), 191–2.

44. Baer, "*Minhat*," 192.

45. For discussion of Abner's theory of will, see C. Sirat, *A History of Jewish Philosophy in the Middle Ages* (Cambridge: Cambridge University Press, 1985), 312.

46. Isaac Pollegar, *Ezer ha-Dat*, ed. J. Levinger (Tel Aviv: Tel Aviv University Press, 1984).

47. See Pollegar, *Ezer ha-Dat*, part 3.

48. Pollegar, *Ezer ha-Dat*, 119–20.

49. W. Z. Harvey, *Physics and Metaphysics in Hasdai Crescas* (Amsterdam: J.C. Gieben, 1998), 138.

50. For discussion of the two strata within Crescas, and their relationship to Scholastic philosophy, see Ravitzky, *Derashat ha-Pesah*, 39. Ravitzky argues that Crescas' *Sermon* was written before *Light*, and that the discussion of determinism in *Sermon* was influenced by Duns Scotus, while the parallel passage in *Light* was influenced by Abner. But Harvey, in a review of Ravitzky's work, argues that there is a greater likelihood that the works of Abner were known to Crescas before those of Scotus. (W. Harvey, "First Publication of the Passover Sermon by R. Hasdai Crescas" [Hebrew], *Tarbiz* 58 [1989], 531–5.)

51. Crescas, *Or Adonai* 32b (in Harvey, *Physics and Metaphysics*, 247).

52. Crescas, *Or Adonai* 2:1.4.

53. Feldman, "Crescas' Theological Determinism," *Da'at* 9 (1982), 17; *Or Adonai* 2:1.4.

54. Crescas, *Or Adonai* 2:5.

55. See U. Thiel, "Individuation," in *The Cambridge History of Seventeenth-Century Philosophy*, ed. D. Garber and M. Ayers (Cambridge: Cambridge University Press, 1998), 212–62; and U. Thiel, "Personal Identity," in *The Cambridge History of Seventeenth-Century Philosophy*, 868–912.

56. Y. Bedersi, *A Treatise upon Personal or Individual Forms* is found in Paris, Bibliothèque Nationale Man. 984 héb. fol. 66a-93b. A synopsis of the contents of this treatise can be found in S. Pines, "Individual Forms in the Thought of Yedaya Bedersi" (Hebrew), in *Harry A. Wolfson Jubilee Volume* (Jerusalem: American Academy for Jewish Research, 1965), 187–201.

57. For Scotus' theory of individuation (*haecceitas*) see his *Ordinatio* 2:3.1 passim; see the discussion in Cross, *Duns Scotus*, 148–50; A. B. Wolter, "John Duns Scotus," in *Individuation in Scholasticism: The Later Middle Ages and the Counter-Reformation 1150–1650*, ed. J. J. E. Gracia (Albany: State University of New York Press, 1994), 271–98.

58. Sirat, *History*, 277; Pines, "Individual Forms," 5. Pines states that "the personal forms serving as the subject of [Bedersi's] deliberations are but a variant of the concept accepted by the disciples of Duns Scotus... [H]is stand in this matter is comprehensible only if one assumes that he was decisively influenced on this point by Scotist teachings, for he could not have a hold in any other theory and most decidedly not in the Islamic-Jewish philosophical teachings."

59. See Pines, "Individual Forms," 11–12, 21. Pines suggests that there may have been a literary tradition, possibly due to perceived persecution, according to which late medieval Jewish philosophers did not directly mention their Christian sources.

60. Bedersi, *Treatise*, 66b; see the comment in Pines, "Individual Forms," 3.

61. See the discussion of this point in Pines, "Individual Forms," 9–10.

62. "Similiter forma individualis determinat naturam specificam ut sit haec vere; non tamen illa forma est proprie haec, sive hoc aliquid, quia si sic, tunc sequitur quod differentia esset species" (Duns Scotus, *In Met.* 1:7.213, n. 16).

63. Maimonides' arguments are discussed extensively in Rudavsky, *Time Matters*, ch. 2.

64. See Manekin, "Hebrew Philosophy," 363; Albalag's theory of creation is discussed in Isaac Albalag, *Sefer Tikkun ha-Deot* (Jerusalem: Israel Academy of Sciences and Humanities, 1973). For a discussion of Narboni's theory, see M. Hayoun, *La philosophie et la théologie de Moise de Narbonne* (Tübingen: J. C. B. Mohr, 1989), 139–53.

65. See Dales, *Medieval Discussions*, 97ff. Aquinas mentions Maimonides' *Dux Dubitantium* (*Guide of the Perplexed*) approvingly in his commentary on the *Sentences* 2, dist. 1, quaest. 1, art. 5.

66. For an extensive discussion of the importance of the condemnation of 1277 upon medieval science, see E. Grant, "The Effect of the Condemnation of 1277," in *The Cambridge History of Later Medieval Philosophy*, ed. N. Kretzmann, A. Kenny, and J. Pinborg (Cambridge: Cambridge University Press, 1982), 537–8.

67. J. Murdoch, "Pierre Duhem and the History of Late Medieval Science and Philosophy in the Latin West," in *Gli studi di filosofia medievale fra otto e novecento*, ed. R. Imbach and A. Maierù (Rome: Edizioni di Storia e Letteratura, 1991). Proposition 34 reads: "That the first cause could not make many worlds." Proposition 49 reads: "That God could not move the heavens with rectilinear motion, and the reason is that a vacuum would remain."

68. P. Duhem, *Medieval Cosmology*, trans. R. Ariew (Chicago: University of Chicago Press, 1985), 442.

69. Grant, "The Effect of the Condemnation of 1277," 537–40.

70. For a discussion of Gersonides' theory of the primordial body, see Rudavsky, *Time Matters*, 44.

71. See Feldman's note in *Wars of the Lord*, III: 347 n. 8.

72. Y. Langermann, *The Jews and the Sciences in the Middle Ages* (Aldershot: Variorum, 1999), 46.

73. Harvey, *Physics and Metaphysics*, 23.

74. Crescas, *Or Adonai* 1:2.1 (in H. A. Wolfson, *Crescas' Critique of Aristotle* [Cambridge, Mass.: Harvard University Press, 1929], 180).

75. Aristotle, *Physics* 4:1, 208a 31.

76. Aristotle, *Physics* 4:4, 212a 5–7.

77. Crescas, *Or Adonai* 1:1.2 (in Wolfson, *Crescas' Critique*, 195).

78. For a detailed analysis of Crescas' conception of space, see Wolfson, *Crescas' Critique*, 38–69. See also H. Davidson, *Proofs for Eternity, Creation, and the Existence of God in Medieval Islamic and Jewish Philosophy* (New York and Oxford: Oxford University Press, 1987), 253ff.

79. Crescas, *Or Adonai* 1:1.2 (in Wolfson, *Crescas' Critique*, 199).

80. Harvey, *Physics and Metaphysics*, 36.

81. A. Ackerman, "Hasdai Crescas' Discussions of the Possibility of Multiple Worlds" (unpublished paper, 1999). A comparison of Crescas and Oresme can be found in Pines, *Scholasticism*, 504–6; Harvey, *Physics and Metaphysics*, 23–9. Harvey notes important differences between Oresme's theory of place and that of Crescas.

82. Harvey, *Physics and Metaphysics*, 39.

83. S. Hutton, "Some Renaissance Critiques of Aristotle's Theory of Time," *Annals of Science* 34 (1977), 348.

84. Sirat, *History*, 308; Pines, *Scholasticism*, 11.

85. For an examination of the underlying logical moves implicit in Gersonides' attack, see S. Feldman, "Gersonides' Proofs for the Creation of the Universe," *Proceedings of the American Academy for Jewish Research* 35 (1967), 113–37.

86. Gersonides, *Milhamot* 6:1.21, 387; *Wars of the Lord*, III: 359.

87. Gersonides, *Milhamot* 6:1.21, 387–8; *Wars of the Lord*, III: 360–1.

88. See Pines, *Scholasticism*, 12.

89. Crescas, *Or Adonai* 1:2.15 (in Wolfson, *Crescas' Critique*, 289).

90. Ibid.

91. Peter Aureol's discussion can be found in his *Commentariorum in secundum librum sententiarum pars secundus*, dist. II, quaest. I, art. I, quoted in Duhem, *Le système du monde* (Paris: Hermann, 1913–17), 300ff.

92. For a sustained discussion of William Ockham's theory of time, see M. M. Adams, *William Ockham* (Notre Dame: University of Notre Dame Press, 1987), 853ff.; Duhem, *Le système du monde*, 305ff.

93. P. Ariotti, "Toward Absolute Time: The Undermining and Refutation of the Aristotelian Conception of Time in the Sixteenth and Seventeenth Centuries," *Annals of Science* 30 (1973), 37.

94. H. Levine, "Paradise not Surrendered: Jewish Reactions to Copernicus and the Growth of Modern Science," in *Epistemology, Methodology and the Social Sciences*, ed. R. S. Cohen and M. W. Wartofsky (Dordrecht: Reidel, 1983), 204.

95. See Ruderman, *Jewish Thought and Scientific Discovery*, 68ff.

96. See Gans, *Nehmad*, 9a. For discussions of David Gans, see Levine, "Paradise not Surrendered," 207; A. Neher, *Jewish Thought and the Scientific Revolution of the Sixteenth Century: David Gans (1541–1613) and his Times*, trans. D. Maisel (Oxford: Oxford University Press, 1986), 216ff.; Ruderman, *Jewish Thought and Scientific Discovery*, 83.

97. Neher, *Jewish Thought*, 216–18.

98. See Ruderman, *Jewish Thought and Scientific Discovery*, 134.

99. Joseph del Medigo, *Sefer Elim* (Amsterdam, 1629; repr. Odessa, 1864–7); see Levine, "Paradise not Surrendered," 208–9. For a survey and discussion of del Medigo's work, see I. Barzilay, *Yoseph Shlomo Delmedigo (Yashar of Candia): His Life, Works, and Times* (Leiden: Brill, 1974); Ruderman, *Jewish Thought and Scientific Discovery*, 118–52.

100. Del Medigo, *Sefer Gevurot Hashem*, in *Sefer Elim*, 292.

16 Jewish philosophy and the Jewish–Christian philosophical dialogue in fifteenth-century Spain

Fifteenth-century Hispanic Jewish philosophy has been condemned as lacking originality and creativity. According to many, the last century of Jewish philosophical activity on Iberian soil[1] represents the swan song of the rich and illustrious history of Spanish Jewish philosophy. Scholars generally attribute this supposed intellectual sterility to the persecution that Jews suffered during this period. Speaking for many, Julius Guttmann argues, "The frightful pressure under which Spanish Jewry, the foremost bearers of Jewish philosophy, lived during the fifteenth century precluded any productive or original philosophical work."[2]

Although this criticism of fifteenth-century Hispanic Jewish philosophy does capture an element of its intellectual orientation, in other respects Jewish philosophy in Spain flourished in the final century before the expulsion. Relatively few philosophical works were written by Spanish Jews in the thirteenth century and the first half of the fourteenth century. By contrast, Hispanic Jewish thinkers in the following century composed a host of philosophical commentaries on scriptural and rabbinic texts, commentaries on Islamic and Jewish philosophers, philosophical sermons, and independent philosophical and theological treatises. Moreover, these philosophers used new philosophical sources and developed new literary genres by which to express original philosophical conclusions.

Before we examine more closely the nature and character of fifteenth-century Hispanic Jewish philosophy, I must outline some of the essential features of the historical context in which these philosophers were active. In particular, I will briefly present the changes that

Hispano-Jewish society underwent in this period and the response of Jewish philosophy to these shifting conditions.[3]

THE DECLINE OF SPANISH JEWRY

The decline of Spanish Jewry that began in the middle of the fourteenth century was intensified with the anti-Jewish riots of 1391 that ravished the Jewish communities throughout Castile and Aragon. Many Jews perished at the hands of the rioters and numerous others were baptized, either voluntarily or under duress. The aggressive missionary activity of the Church did not abate – particularly in the three decades following the riots – and was accompanied by the anti-Jewish preaching of, for example, Vicente Ferrer, disputations such as the Tortosa debate, and anti-Jewish legislation. This produced a continuous stream of Jews to the baptismal font (with varying degrees of sincerity), creating within many communities a large number of *conversos*. Those who remained within the Jewish community could not be unaffected by these traumatic events. Apart from their economic, demographic, and social impact, the massacres and the ensuing disasters brought about theological doubt and confusion among Jews who had not converted.

Theological confusion among Spanish Jewry was especially prevalent among the Jewish intellectual elite, where skeptical attitudes had already taken root. Evidence of this trend is Joshua Lorki's letter to the convert Pablo de Santa Maria, formerly R. Solomon Halevi.[4] Lorki there raised numerous objections to the Christian belief in Jesus' resurrection, the virgin birth, and trinitarianism. He was especially critical of the Christian dogma concerning the incarnation of Jesus, characterizing it as irrational and inconceivable. However, Lorki's inquiry to Pablo de Santa Maria, his close friend, should not be read as a Jewish polemic against Christian dogma. Rather, it is an inquisitive and searching plea from a Jew whose faith had been eroded, but who was not yet prepared to embrace Christianity (a step that he took shortly afterwards). Raising questions that hindered his entrance into Christian faith, Lorki requested from Pablo de Santa Maria solutions that "could solve for me a multitude of doubts."[5] Thus, Lorki's letter captures his tenuous theological state between Judaism and Christianity, an attitude shared by many of his fellow Jews.

PHILOSOPHICAL NATURALISM AND ASTROLOGY

Along with its gradual decline in the second half of the fourteenth century, Spanish Jewry experienced the emergence of a radical form of Jewish philosophy, committed to a principled naturalism on many issues. During the thirteenth and the beginning of the fourteenth century, Spanish rabbinic scholars such as Nahmanides and Solomon ben Abraham ibn Adret were generally successful in limiting the impact of radical rationalism in their midst. By contrast, southern France became the home for Jewish philosophers who espoused radical (naturalist and reductionist) views regarding, inter alia, immortality, human perfection, divine knowledge and activity, the reasons for the commandments, and the scope of allegorical exegesis.

The insulation of Spanish Jewry from the full-blown rationalism of southern French Jewry, however, weakened in the middle of the fourteenth century. At that time, a circle of Neoplatonic Jewish philosophers were active in Castile.[6] This philosophical circle included Solomon ben Hanokh al-Kostantini, Solomon Franco, Ezra Gatino, Samuel Sarsa, Shem Tov ibn Meir, Shem Tov ibn Shaprut, Solomon ben Abraham ibn Yaish, and Solomon ben Meir ibn Yaish. Influenced by the philosophy of Abraham ibn Ezra and Maimonides, they combined the rationalism of their southern French colleagues with an interest in astrology and magic. They maintained that immortality is a natural process that entails a state of communion with the Active Intellect. These philosophers also claimed that this act of communion allows one to break free of astral influences that govern all sublunar events. Likewise, their interpretations of the Bible and Aggadah and their approach to the issue of *taʿamei ha-mitzvot* (the reasons for the commandments) were shaped by their dual commitment to rationalism and astral magic. In addition, they rejected a literal understanding of creation *ex nihilo* and at times espoused views that limit the scope of God's knowledge and providence.

Although this group appeared mainly in the second half of the fourteenth century in Castile, its influence can be felt at the beginning of the fifteenth century in Aragon. This is evident from the single extant sermon of Vidal Joseph Caballeria, a Saragossan Jewish philosopher, who eventually converted.[7] There, Vidal presented an astral and naturalistic interpretation of the exodus from Egypt taken wholesale from the work of Solomon al-Kostantini, a prominent member of the

Castilian philosophical circle. In addition, Vidal identified intellectual with human perfection, and posited the former as a prerequisite for the attainment of immortality.

THE ATTACK ON PHILOSOPHICAL RATIONALISM

One response among Jewish intellectuals to the traumatic events of 1391, the ensuing spiritual crisis, and the emergence of radical philosophical trends in their midst was an attack on philosophical rationalism.[8] Many Spanish Jewish scholars in the second half of the fourteenth century blamed the Aristotelian philosophy of Maimonides and his successors for the tragic conditions that plagued Spanish Jewry. Intent on restricting what they perceived as the pernicious influence of philosophy, they combated the rationalism of Jewish philosophers. Their attack was two pronged: they cited traditional prooftexts to show the heretical nature of the innovations of the philosophers and employed philosophical tools in an attempt to disprove the philosophers' conclusions.

The most articulate and sophisticated critique that emerged from this antirationalistic trend was that of Hasdai Crescas, the leader of Aragonese Jewry at the end of the fourteenth century and the first decade of the fifteenth century. Crescas' antirationalism continued a tendency initiated by Nahmanides and reinforced by other representatives of the rabbinic leadership of the kingdom of Aragon in the thirteenth and fourteenth centuries, such as Solomon ibn Adret. In particular, Crescas' philosophy drew upon the works of his teacher and previous spiritual leader of Aragonese Jewry, Nissim Gerondi.[9] Crescas differed from his rabbinic predecessors, however, in the balance between his rabbinic and philosophical writings. Nahmanides, Solomon ibn Adret, and Nissim Gerondi concentrated their intellectual efforts on legal exegesis. In contradistinction, with the increased presence of radical rationalism in Spain, Crescas chose to focus primarily on combating the rationalists.

Crescas composed his philosophical magnum opus, *The Light of the Lord*, in response to the perceived threat of rationalism. This work was completed in 1411, but was largely written in the final decades of the fourteenth century.[10] Crescas sets out to disprove the major tenets of Maimonides' philosophy and its Aristotelian scientific and metaphysical foundations. He begins with arguments against the validity of Aristotelian physics and presents alternative theories regarding space, time, and motion. He also criticized Maimonides' proofs of God's existence and unity and his theory of negative attributes. In its place, he offers a theory that allows for positive essential attributes of the divine.

Crescas also opposed Maimonides' theories of human perfection and immortality. For Crescas, Maimonides' belief that the ultimate perfection cultivated by the Torah is intellectual perfection was especially problematic. Crescas argued that this approach neutralizes the importance of religious rituals and creates an elitism in which only the intellectually gifted can flourish. In opposition to Maimonides' theory that identified intellectual advancement as necessary for attainment of the *summum bonum*, Crescas claimed that the performance of the commandments and the love of God that they engender are the prerequisites for perfection and immortality. Crescas' antagonistic stance to philosophy was adopted by other scholars in the second half of the fourteenth century, such as R. Joseph ibn Shoshan, Profiat Duran (Efodi), and R. Isaac Perfet (Rivash).[11]

The antirationalist trend of Crescas and his colleagues continued in the fifteenth century with the Spanish kabbalists. One of the central features of kabbalistic literature during this period was its antagonism toward philosophy. Kabbalists identified philosophy as the chief cause for the material and spiritual decline of Spanish Jewry. The first kabbalist to castigate philosophy for its supposed contribution to the wave of conversions was Shem Tov ibn Shem Tov.[12] Shem Tov's intimate knowledge of philosophy allowed him to provide a detailed catalogue and analysis of the views of the Jewish philosophers. Marshaling texts from the writings of Maimonides, Abraham ibn Ezra, Albalag, and others, Shem Tov argued that the Jewish philosophers expressed heretical views in the areas of human perfection, immortality, divine providence, and knowledge.[13]

The anonymous author of *Sefer ha-Meshiv* continued and intensified the attack on Jewish philosophy among fifteenth-century Spanish kabbalists.[14] In this and related kabbalistic works, philosophy was depicted as an impure force that originates from the demonic realm (*sitrah ahrah*). Unlike the previous kabbalistic attacks, *Sefer ha-Meshiv* presented no arguments against the views of the philosophers. Instead of debating the philosophers' conclusions and arguments, it vilified philosophy as a corrupting influence that is responsible for the exilic state of the Jews.

A MORE MODERATE POSITION

The hostile attitude toward philosophy was, however, not the dominant approach among the rabbinic leadership and the intellectual elite of fifteenth-century Jewish Spain. In fact, during this period, antirationalism was generally confined to the kabbalists.[15] Most Jewish philosophers of fifteenth-century Spain eschewed the hostile attitude toward philosophy articulated by Hasdai Crescas and his circle that was prevalent at the end of the fourteenth century.[16] Instead, they adopted a moderate stance that defended the value of philosophical speculation while guarding against more radical tendencies. Representatives of this group include Abraham ben Judah, Moses ha-Kohen, Mattetyahu Yitzhari, Zerahia Halevi, Joseph Albo, Joseph ibn Shem Tov, Isaac ibn Shem Tov, Shem Tov ibn Shem Tov, Moses ibn Waqar, Abraham Bibago, Joel ibn Shu'eib, Eli Habilio, and Abraham Shalom.[17]

The philosophical outlook of these Jewish intellectuals produced lines of continuity between them and the Jewish philosophers of the preceding two centuries. Jewish philosophy in the thirteenth, fourteenth, and fifteenth centuries was profoundly influenced by the philosophy of Maimonides and the Islamic Aristotelians. As a result, much of Jewish philosophical literature during this period was expressed in the form of commentaries on the Aristotelian, Averroean, and Maimonidean corpus. Jewish philosophers at this time also shared a predilection toward philosophical exegesis of traditional texts, composing commentaries on biblical texts and rabbinic Aggadah. The issues addressed were familiar: proofs (often with identical arguments and conclusions) for God's existence, divine attributes, divine knowledge and providence, human perfection, and the reasons for the commandments.[18] Yet, despite these similarities, important differences existed between the Jewish philosophical enterprise in fifteenth-century Jewish Spain and that of the two preceding centuries.[19]

Many Jewish philosophers in southern France and Spain during the thirteenth and fourteenth centuries were primarily concerned with quite general philosophical problems, with disseminating philosophical knowledge, and with interpreting the Jewish tradition according to "alien wisdom." Most of these philosophers adopted radical philosophical doctrines, and their exegesis of biblical and rabbinic texts and their analysis of theological doctrine reflected their rationalistic assumptions. Consequently, creation *ex nihilo* and divine omniscience were often reinterpreted – even repudiated – by philosophers such as Samuel ibn Tibbon, Isaac Albalag, Jacob Anatoli, Joseph ibn Kaspi, Gersonides, and Solomon al-Kostantini. These philosophers often equated human, intellectual, and religious perfection, depicted prophecy as an expression of philosophical truths, and adopted elitist political theories.

By contrast, Jewish philosophers of late fourteenth- and fifteenth-century Spain were deeply involved in defending more "conservative," theistic doctrines expressed in the rabbinic tradition.[20] In the wake of the theological confusion that plagued their communities, these philosophers – who were generally also the rabbinic and political leaders – composed defenses of Judaism that attempted to justify and defend traditional doctrines against both the attacks of Christian theologians and the criticism of radical philosophers.

The theistic commitments of these philosophers led them to share the apprehension of their antirationalistic colleagues about the radical views adopted by certain Jewish philosophers and to consider them a danger to the faith of the masses. They therefore argued against the philosophers' rationalist axiology which valued speculative knowledge over faith accepted upon authority. More specifically, they rejected the philosophers' understanding of immortality as contemplation of intelligibilia and their understanding of the commandments (*mitzvot*) as means towards achieving the true human good, actualizing one's intellectual potential. In place of this, they generally held that *performance* of the commandments was itself sufficient for salvation. In addition, echoing Scholastic notions, they emphasized that only faith (*emunah*) can secure ultimate felicity.[21]

These thinkers also opposed the naturalism of the philosophers and its implications for divine creation, providence, and knowledge. Much energy was devoted to disproving previous attempts to explain creation as an eternal process, as well as theories that limited divine omniscience and providence. Rather than limiting providence to select individuals, these fifteenth-century Hispano-Jewish philosophers argued that divine providence extends to *all* individuals. Moreover, by contrast to the indirect governance of other nations through the natural realm and through astrological influence, God *directly* oversees the history and destiny of the Jewish nation.

Such opposition to what was conceived of as excessive rationalism and naturalism among certain of their Jewish philosophical colleagues did not lead them to reject philosophy wholesale, however.[22]
Indeed, anti-rationalism was problematic for theologians whose message was directed at Jews who were wavering between Judaism and
Christianity. Such an anti-philosophical critique would hinder attempts to *argue* for the rationality of Judaism and the irrationality of
Christianity. By arguing against the ability of the human intellect
to ascertain religious truth, an important tool in their polemical
arsenal would be lost. No longer could one argue that a rational
inspection of Jewish and Christian beliefs would demonstrate the
irrationality of Christian dogma.

Thus, apart from their polemic against radical rationalism, most
Hispano-Jewish philosophers of the fifteenth century also critiqued
those Jewish thinkers who opposed the study of philosophy and argued that it was prohibited (even occasionally voicing criticism of
the talmudic scholars who focused exclusively on the study of Jewish
law). They therefore supplied arguments for the positions that philosophical inquiry was permitted and the reading of philosophical texts
was not heretical. Although maintaining that reason cannot uncover
all the truths supplied by revelation, they also asserted that, if rational inquiry is conducted properly, the conclusions gained thereby
will never contradict the Torah. These scholars rebuffed the approach
of the antirationalists by dismissing the charge that philosophy
contributed to the crisis that engulfed Spanish Jewry.

In an age of theological confusion and religious polemics, they
asserted that philosophy was an important means for clarifying religious doctrine, and for defending Judaism against Christian polemics.
Although Torah was viewed as a more reliable source of truth than
philosophy, the study of nature and metaphysical inquiry would
inevitably lead to a deeper understanding of God and thereby contribute to human felicity. Many of these philosophers concluded that
rational investigation of religious principles was obligatory and even
part of the commandment to study the Torah.

PHILOSOPHICAL SOURCES

The polemic-apologetic orientation of the fifteenth-century
Hispano-Jewish philosophers manifested itself in the choice of their

philosophical sources.[23] Like their counterparts in thirteenth- and fourteenth-century Spain and southern France, these later thinkers were influenced by al-Farabi, Avicenna, and Averroes. However, the formative influence of Islamic philosophers was limited. By contrast to the naturalism of the Jewish philosophers of thirteenth- and fourteenth-century Spain, the Jewish philosophers of fifteenth-century Spain more selectively borrowed ideas from the Islamic philosophers. Only ideas that were compatible with – or even supportive of – their conservative philosophical outlook were taken on. They looked especially favorably upon those conclusions that could be employed to polemicize against Christianity.[24]

The disparate uses of philosophical sources is apparent in the influence of Maimonides on these two groups. Among Jewish philosophers of thirteenth- and fourteenth-century Spain and Provence, the greatest single influence was undoubtedly Maimonides. These philosophers were particularly interested in the central role that Maimonides ascribed to intellectual activity in the acquisition of human perfection and in his attempt to minimize God's intervention in the natural order. They often portrayed Maimonides very naturalistically, minimizing or negating elements of his philosophy opposed to their own.[25] By contrast, Hispano-Jewish philosophers of the later period presented a different Maimonides.[26] While equally under the sway of Maimonides' philosophy, they were attracted to Maimonides' critique of the theory of eternity and his argument at the end of the *Guide* that human perfection is not equivalent to intellectual perfection.[27] They viewed Maimonides as a philosopher who was able to defend religious doctrine against a radical onslaught. They therefore opposed those Jewish philosophers who attributed to Maimonides views they judged as heretical and those who attacked Maimonides based on these "misinterpretations" of his philosophy.

The underlying differences between the dominant trends among Jewish philosophers of fifteenth-century Spain and those of Spain and Provence in the two preceding centuries was not only confined to the different employment of similar philosophical sources. It also presented itself in the choice of philosophical sources themselves. The philosophical sources for thirteenth- and fourteenth-century Hispano- and southern French Jewish philosophers were, as noted, Maimonides and the Islamic philosophers. And like Maimonides himself, his thirteenth- and fourteenth-century followers shared a contempt for those philosophers that preceded the master; thus, they rarely cited Saadya Gaon, Judah Halevi, Abraham ibn Daud, and other important early medieval Jewish philosophers, with the exception of Abraham ibn Ezra.[28]

By contrast, the search of Jewish philosophers of fifteenth-century Jewish Spain for philosophical confirmation of their theistic doctrines led them to a more favorable view of pre-Maimonidean thinkers. The less radical conclusions of many early Jewish philosophers attracted them. For example, Saadya's *kalam*, apologetic in its intent, corresponded to their own interests. In particular, they were influenced by his approach to issues of free will and the necessity of revelation and creation. Judah Halevi's *Kuzari* also experienced a revival in the final century of Hispano-Jewish philosophy. While Jewish philosophers were generally reluctant to adopt Halevi's hostile attitude to philosophy, they often looked to his defense of Judaism in their own discussions of divine providence, human perfection, and the reasons for the commandments. Another pre-Maimonidean Jewish philosopher who was resurrected among late fourteenth- and fifteenth-century Hispano-Jewish philosophers was Abraham ibn Daud. His philosophical magnum opus, *Emunah Ramah*, was translated twice at the end of the fourteenth century and became influential.[29]

The most important change regarding philosophical sources, however, relates to Christian philosophical sources. Unlike most of their predecessors, many Jewish philosophers of fifteenth-century Spain were strongly influenced by Christian Scholasticism. Outside of Italy, Christian philosophy had a minimal influence on medieval Jewish philosophy until the late fourteenth century, and Christian philosophers are never explicitly cited before then in the works of non-Italian Jewish philosophers.[30] By contrast, Spanish Jewish philosophers commencing with Hasdai Crescas were substantially influenced by trends in Christian Scholasticism. They were attracted both by Aquinas and other moderate Christian rationalists, as well as by the anti-Aristotelian critique leveled by the *via moderna* of the Christian nominalists.

What accounts for the new-found interest in Christian philosophy in an age of profound tension between Jewish and Christian intellectuals? Prima facie, one would suspect that the heightened enmity between Christianity and Judaism and the threat of conversion to Christianity that was the lot of fifteenth-century Hispanic Jewry would serve as a barrier to the acceptance of notions from Christian philosophers and not as a pretext for the flourishing of Christian–Jewish philosophical dialogue. Further, although one would anticipate a correlation between a commitment to philosophical inquiry and an interest in the regnant philosophical doctrines and debates that occupy the intellectual landscape of the neighboring culture, it is still perplexing why the influence of Scholasticism was so pronounced among thinkers whose commitment to philosophy was (*ex hypothesi*) so reserved.[31]

These various impediments, however, could also be seen as contributing to Jewish interest in Christian philosophy. The heightened tension between Jews and Christians, due to the increased polemical activity between Jewish and Christian scholars, led to Jewish interest in becoming acquainted with Christian philosophical and theological doctrines.[32] In addition, the Jewish philosophers' opposition to some of the conclusions of some of the radical rationalists can also be seen as a contributing factor to a late Jewish interest in Scholasticism. There is evidence that the effective philosophical opposition of Christian philosophers to the radical rationalists attracted those Jewish philosophers who were involved in a similar pursuit. For example, Eli Habillo, in the introduction to his translation of Jean Versoris' commentary on Aristotle's *Physics*, contrasts Jewish philosophers who slavishly followed "the pagan doctrines of Aristotle and his followers" with Christian philosophers who effectively harmonized their philosophical sensibilities with their religious beliefs.[33]

LITERARY GENRES

Another feature of fifteenth-century Hispano-Jewish philosophy, influenced by its polemical orientation, is the choice of literary genres adopted. In the previous two centuries, Jewish philosophical discourse oscillated between technical and esoteric discussions directed to a philosophically sophisticated audience, and more popular discussions geared for a wider readership. Jewish philosophers composed philosophical encyclopedias that introduced philosophical lore to a novice, as well as biblical and aggadic commentaries that served as a means of popularizing philosophical doctrine. However, commentaries on Averroes' works, esoteric biblical commentaries, and technical works on logic – all inaccessible to those uninitiated in philosophical doctrine – were equally popular among Jewish philosophers.

In the following century the balance between genres geared for a limited, philosophically sophisticated audience and those suitable for a more popular audience shifted. Jewish philosophers continued to compose technical philosophical works directed to their fellow philosophers, such as Isaac ibn Shem Tov's numerous supercommentaries on Averroes' commentaries and the philosophical letters of Abraham Shalom, Eli Habillo, and Abraham Bibago.[34] However, Hispano-Jewish philosophers, preoccupied with defending theistic doctrine to a wide audience, were more likely to employ genres that were accessible to the masses. Consequently, fifteenth-century Jewish Spain witnessed a flourishing of the philosophical sermon, a useful means of expressing philosophical doctrine in a popular medium. While previously the only collection of Jewish philosophical sermons was Jacob Anatoli's *Malmad ha-Talmidim*, at least five collections of Jewish philosophical sermons were composed in fifteenth-century Spain. In addition, these sermonic collections introduced important changes into the form of the Jewish sermon, some of them resulting from the impact of elements of the Scholastic *quaestio* method.[35] Likewise, Spanish Jewish philosophers from the end of the fourteenth century wrote popular philosophical works organized around and defending different theological principles. Although this genre possesses certain similarities to Jewish *kalam* works, it is most similar to – and evidently influenced by – the literary structure of Christian philosophical *summae*.

A CASE STUDY: THE SCOPE AND NATURE OF DIVINE KNOWLEDGE

The eclectic, polemical, and theistic nature of fifteenth-century Hispano-Jewish philosophy, its reliance on Christian philosophical sources, and the distinction between it and radical trends in thirteenth- and fourteenth-century Spanish and southern French Jewish philosophy can be best illustrated by an examination of a particular issue that was discussed extensively by these philosophers.

The issue that we shall explore briefly is the scope and nature of divine knowledge.

Many Jewish philosophers of the thirteenth and fourteenth centuries rejected the belief in God's omniscient knowledge of all sublunar events. The most elaborate and influential presentation of this view was that of the fourteenth-century Provençal philosopher Gersonides.[36] He claimed that divine knowledge must be confined to the fixed and the ordered and cannot extend to that which is contingent and undetermined.[37] Gersonides also concluded that the restrictions on divine knowledge can be reconciled with a belief in God's knowledge of particulars and providence over terrestrial affairs. The reconciliation depended on positing causal influence of the Active Intellect and the heavenly bodies on sublunar events. Astral causality is so encompassing, according to Gersonides, that most terrestrial events, including those involving human choice, are determined and ordered, thus allowing for God's knowledge of sublunar events. However, Gersonides was unwilling to place all human affairs within the realm of the fixed and the ordered. Gersonides maintained that intellect allows human beings to choose the good even when it contravenes the decree of the heavenly bodies.[38] Although humans generally do not use their intellect to subvert the divine order,[39] there are rare occurrences when human choice thwarts the heavenly mandate.

Jewish philosophers of the late fourteenth and fifteenth centuries forcefully opposed the position of Gersonides and his Spanish philosophical colleagues who had put forth a limited divine omniscience theory.[40] Gersonides' position, they maintained, attributes to God a certain ignorance, an imperfection unattributable to God. Instead, they argued that God knows all individuals and particulars qua particulars. They marshaled as proof traditional arguments that had appeared among previous Jewish philosophers, particularly Maimonides. They attempted thus to disprove Gersonides' arguments against Maimonides' negative theology, an essential component of Maimonides' compatibilist view.

These thinkers also looked to Scholasticism. For instance, Zerahia Halevi in his defense of a volitional conception of human choice acknowledges his debt to logical notions developed by "the new logicians" (ha-hegyonim ha-hadashim), a reference to the philosophical movement of which William of Ockham was the foremost representative.[41] One of the most interesting of these discussions (and fairly representative) is Abraham Bibago's discussion in his *The Way of Belief*.[42] Bibago begins his treatment of divine knowledge by depicting the views of those who deny God's omniscience as believers in astrological influence and astral magic, perhaps making reference to views expressed by contemporary Spanish Jewish rationalists. He then sets out to refute this approach. In this regard, he offers two proofs for God's omniscience and knowledge of particulars. Following Aquinas, he argues that God must be omniscient, because he possesses all perfections in their most eminent form, and that a creator must have knowledge of all his creations.[43] Bibago also attempts to weaken the arguments of the limited divine omniscience theory by supporting Maimonides' position that divine and human knowledge share nothing in common except the name. Bibago supplies counterarguments for each of Gersonides' arguments against Maimonides.[44] Bibago's defense, however, incorporates many elements that are seemingly inconsistent with Maimonides' negative theology. In particular, he ascribes to Maimonides a view of Crescas that disallows comparison between divine and human knowledge, because God's knowledge is infinite and human knowledge is finite.[45]

In summary, two trends occupy the intellectual landscape of late fourteenth- and fifteenth-century Spanish Jewry. In the second half of the fourteenth century and in the fifteenth century, antirationalism grew in response to the growing influence of Jewish philosophy in Spain and the theological and social crisis that engulfed it. However, the antirationalist trend in Jewish philosophy was dwarfed by a moderate rationalism that dominated Hispano-Jewish intellectual circles. These philosophers opposed the radical trends that had emerged among southern French and Spanish Jewish philosophers, but they were not willing to adopt an antirationalist stance that prohibited the study of philosophy and denied any significant value and efficacy to rational inquiry. The moderate rationalism is, in many ways, similar to and influenced by approaches developed by Christian Scholastics, particularly Aquinas. Paradoxically, at the height of Jewish–Christian animosity and polemical activity, Jewish philosophers saw their Christian philosophical colleagues as models for combating radical rationalism effectively without thereby adopting antirationalistic positions. Thus, fifteenth-century Jewish philosophy must be seen, among other things, as beginning a new chapter in the Jewish–Christian philosophical dialogue.[46]

NOTES

1. It should be noted that by "Spain" (Iberia) I am referring to the kingdoms of Aragon and Castile. In addition, the developments that I am discussing in this chapter begin in the late fourteenth century and continue until the expulsion. Nevertheless, I generally speak here about the fifteenth century. I would like to thank Professor Zev Harvey for his helpful comments on this chapter.

2. J. Guttmann, *Philosophies of Judaism*, trans. D. Silverman (New York: Schocken Books, 1966), 242. One important exception to this trend in scholarship is the approach of H. Tirosh-Rothschild (Samuelson) (see nn. 16 and 17 below), which has greatly informed my understanding of this period.

3. On this period, see Y. Baer, *A History of the Jews in Christian Spain*, 2 vols. (Philadelphia: Jewish Publication Society, 1978), II: 95–423; S. W. Baron, *A Social and Religious History of the Jews* (New York: Columbia University Press, 1965), X: 167–219; E. Gutwirth, "Towards Expulsion: 1391–1492," in *Spain and the Jews*, ed. E. Kedourie (London: Thames & Hudson, 1992), 51–73.

4. *Ketav Divrei Hakhamim*, ed. E. Ashkenazi (Metz, 1849), 41–6.

5. *Ketav Divrei Hakhamim*, 42.

6. On this group, see the many studies and texts published by D. Schwartz: *The Philosophy of a Fourteenth Century Jewish Neoplatonic Circle* [Hebrew] (Jerusalem: Mosad Bialik, 1996), and the works cited there on 31 n. 42.

7. D. Schwartz, "Vidal Joseph Caballeria's Sermon on the Exodus from Egypt" [Hebrew] *Asufot* 7 (1993), 261–80.

8. On anti-rationalism in this period, see D. Schwartz, "The Spiritual-Intellectual Decline of the Jewish Community in Spain at the End of the Fourteenth Century" [Hebrew] *Pe'amim* 46–47 (1991), 92–114; E. Lawee, "The Path to Felicity: Teachings and Tensions in 'Even Shetiyyah of Abraham ben Judah, Disciple of Hasdai Crescas," *Medieval Studies* 59 (1997), 183–223.

9. R. Nissim's critique of philosophy is analyzed in S. Klein-Braslavy, "Vérité prophétique et vérité philosophique chez Nissim de Gérone," *Revue des Etudes Juives* 134 (1975), 72–99. Paradoxically, Crescas was most indebted to R. Nissim for the formulation of his naturalistic account of creation and causality.

10. *Light of the Lord*, ed. S. Fisher (Jerusalem: Sifrei Ramot, 1990). For many of the studies devoted to explicating Crescas' philosophy, see the references in M. Idel, "Jewish Thought in Medieval Spain," in *The Sephardi Legacy*, ed. H. Beinart (Jerusalem: Magnes Press, 1992), 1: 261–81, 270 n. 36; W. Z. Harvey, *Physics and Metaphysics in Hasdai Crescas* (Amsterdam: J. C. Gieben, 1998).

11. Efodi voiced his criticism of Jewish philosophers in the introduction to his *Ma'aseh Efodi* (D. Rapel, "The Introduction to Profiat Duran's *Ma'aseh Efodi*" [Hebrew] *Sinai* 100 [1987], 770–4). Rivash's opposition to philosophy appears in one of his responsa (*She'elot u-Teshuvot le-Rabenu ha-Gadol Marenu ve-Rabenu ha-Rav Yitzhak bar Sheshet*, ed. D. Metzger [Jerusalem: n.p., 1993], nos. 45, 49–51; see also his responsa on the conflict between scientific conclusions and halakhic sources: nos. 251, 447). Ibn Shoshan's criticism of philosophy was expressed in his commentary on *Avot* (*R. Joseph Ibn Shoshan's Commentary on Avot*, ed. S. Kasher and J. Bleichkrovitz [Jerusalem: n.p., 1968], 81–3, 130, 153). Although no explicit evidence of an association between Crescas and Ibn Shoshan exists, the latter was in contact with the Rivash (*She'elot u-Teshuvot le-Rabenu*, no. 157).

12. E. Gottlieb, *Studies in Kabbalastic Literature* [Hebrew] (Tel Aviv: Tel Aviv University Press, 1976), 347–56.

13. Another fifteenth-century kabbalistic, yet philosophically informed, critique of philosophy was the anonymous author of *Sefer Poke'ah Ivrim*. On this work, see B. Huss, "*Sefer Poke'ah Ivrim*: New Information for the History of Kabbalistic Literature," [Hebrew] *Tarbiz* 61 (1992), 489–504. On his attitude toward philosophy, see B. Huss, "On the Status of Kabbalah after the Riots of 1391," [Hebrew] *Pe'amim* 56 (1993), 20–32.

14. On this work, see M. Idel, "Inquiries in the Thought of *Sefer ha-Meshiv*," [Hebrew] *Sefunot* (NS) 2 (17) (1983), 185–266; M. Idel, "The Origin of Alchemy according to Zosimos and a Hebrew Parallel," *Revue des Etudes Juives* 145 (1986), 117–25; M. Idel, "*Sefer ha-Meshiv*'s Attitude to Christianity," [Hebrew] *Zion* 46 (1981), 77–91. On his attitude to philosophy, see Idel, "Thought of *Sefer ha-Meshiv*," 232–43.

15. Note should also be made of the following exceptions: the Spanish ethicist, Solomon Alami, in his *Iggeret Musar* (1415) identified the philosophers as the cause of the unrest that plagued his community and criticized their view of human perfection and their allegorical exegesis (*Iggeret Musar*, ed. A. Haberman [Jerusalem: Meqorot, 1946], 25, 30, 32, 35, 41–3, 46). See also the attack against philosophy leveled by the poet, Solomon Bonafed (E. Gutwirth, "Social Criticism in Bonafed's Invective," *Sefarad* 14 [1985], 28–9).

16. General overviews of fifteenth-century Hispano-Jewish philosophy can be found in: Guttmann, *Philosophies of Judaism*, 242–56; C. Sirat, *A History of Jewish Philosophy in the Middle Ages* (Cambridge: Cambridge University Press, 1985), 345–97; H. Davidson, "Medieval Jewish Philosophy in the Sixteenth Century," in *Jewish Thought in the Sixteenth Century*, ed. B. Cooperman (Cambridge, Mass.: Harvard University Press, 1983), 110–14; H. Tirosh-Rothschild, "Jewish Philosophy on the Eve of Modernity," in *History of Jewish Philosophy*, ed. D. H. Frank and O. Leaman (London and New York: Routledge, 1997), 500–12.

17. See the bibliographic references assembled in Idel, "Jewish Thought in Medieval Spain," 270–1; see also H. Tirosh-Rothschild, "Political Philosophy in the Thought of Abraham Shalom: The Platonic Tradition," [Hebrew] *Jerusalem Studies in Jewish Thought* 9 (1990), 409–40; H. Tirosh-Rothschild, "Human Felicity – Fifteenth Century Sephardic Perspectives on Happiness," in *In Iberia and Beyond: Hispanic Jews between Cultures*, ed. B. Cooperman (Newark: University of Delaware Press, 1998), 191–244; A. Ravitzky, "The Paradoxical Concept of Free Will in Mattathias ha-Yizhari," in *From Rome to Jerusalem: Memorial Volume for Prof. Joseph Sermoneta*, ed. A. Ravitzky (Jerusalem: Hebrew University, 1998), 239–56; J. Schwartzman, "R. Isaac ben Shem Tov's Commentary on *Moreh Nevukim*," *Da'at* 26 (1991), 43–59; A. Nuriel, "The Philosophy of Abraham ben Shem Tov Bibago," Ph.D. dissertation, Hebrew University of Jerusalem, 1975; J. Hacker, "The Role of Abraham Bibago in the Polemic on the Place of Philosophy in Jewish Life in Spain in the Fifteenth Century," [Hebrew] *Proceedings of the Fifth World Congress of Jewish Studies* (Jerusalem: World Union of Jewish Studies, 1969), III: 151–8.

18. On the similar topics discussed and conclusions reached by all medieval Jewish – as well as Islamic and Christian – philosophers, see H. Wolfson, *From Philo to Spinoza* (New York: Behrman House, 1977).

19. On the differences between fifteenth-century Hispano-Jewish philosophy and Jewish philosophy of the two preceding centuries, see M. Kellner, *Dogma in Medieval Jewish Thought: From Maimonides to Abravanel* (Oxford: Littman Library, 1986), 82–6, 66–9.

20. On the defense of theistic doctrine in medieval Jewish philosophy, see H. Tirosh-Rothschild, *Between Worlds: The Life and Thought of Rabbi David ben Judah Messer Leon* (Albany: State University of New York Press, 1991), 184–7. On the conservative orientation of fifteenth-century Hispano-Jewish philosophy, see Davidson, "Medieval Jewish Philosophy," 110–4.

21. On the relationship between conceptions of human perfection of fifteenth-century Hispano-Jewish philosophers and those of Scholastic

philosophers, see Tirosh-Rothschild, "Jewish Philosophy on the Eve of Modernity," 500–12; Tirosh-Rothschild, "Human Felicity."

22. On the defense of philosophy among fifteenth-century Hispano-Jewish philosophers, see S. Regev, "The Problem of Philosophical Study in Fifteenth-Century Jewish Thought: R. Joseph ibn Shem Tov and R. Abraham Bibago," [Hebrew] *Da'at* 16 (1986), 63–88.

23. I will here and in the next section discuss the impact of the polemical-apologetic orientation of fifteenth-century Hispano-Jewish philosophers on the philosophical sources and literary genres that they employ. I have chosen these issues because, despite the large body of research on this group of philosophers, the link between their polemical–apologetic orientation and the philosophical sources and literary genres that they employ is rarely discussed.

24. See, e.g., Albo's use of Averroes documented in D. Lasker, "Averroistic Trends in Jewish–Christian Polemics," *Speculum* 55 (1980), 294–304.

25. A. Ravitzky, "The Secrets of Maimonides: Between the Thirteenth and the Twentieth Centuries," in his *History and Faith: Studies in Jewish Philosophy* (Amsterdam: J. C. Gieben, 1996), 248–56.

26. Ravitzky, "The Secrets of Maimonides," 266 and the sources cited in n. 56; Schwartzman, "R. Isaac ben Shem Tov's Commentary on *Moreh Nevukhim*," 56–8.

27. For instance, see Shem Tov ben Joseph ibn Shem Tov's commentary on *Guide* 3:51: *Sefer Moreh Nevukim im Arbah Perushim* (Warsaw, 1862), 64b.

28. On Maimonides' disparaging attitude to his Jewish philosophical predecessors, see *Guide* 1:71.

29. On the translation of Abraham ibn Daud's philosophical work, see A. Eran, "The Relationship between the Two Translations of Abraham ibn Daud's *al-Akidah al-Rafiah*," [Hebrew] *Tarbiz* (1996), 79–107.

30. This is contrary to the view of Shlomo Pines, who attempted to document the influence of Christian philosophy on southern French and Spanish Jewish philosophy in the thirteenth and fourteenth centuries. Pines thesis is presented in *Scholasticism after Thomas Aquinas and the Teachings of Hasdai Crescas and his Predecessors*, in *The Collected Works of Shlomo Pines: Studies in the History of Jewish Thought*, ed. W. Z. Harvey and M. Idel (Jerusalem: Magnes Press, 1997), v: 489–589, and other studies. Many of the links that Pines draws between the views of Christian Scholastics and medieval Jewish philosophers (with the exception of Crescas) are tenuous. In addition, his explanation that the absence of references to Christian philosophers among the Jewish philosophers of thirteenth- and fourteenth-century Spain and southern France is a literary convention is not convincing. I do not deny that

   further research might well uncover more connections between the
   Jewish philosophers of thirteenth- and fourteenth-century Spain and
   southern France and Scholastic sources, but I doubt that these connections will approximate the scope of the impact of Christian philosophical material that one finds in Hasdai Crescas, Abraham Bibago, and
   Joseph ibn Shem Tov.

31. Another surprising aspect is the fact that most of the radical Jewish
   rationalists such as Gersonides and Joseph ibn Kaspi lived in southern
   France, i.e. closer to the centers of Christian philosophy than the more
   Christian-influenced Jewish philosophers who resided on the southern
   side of the Pyrenees.

32. On the connection between philosophy and polemics in fifteenth-
   century Iberian Jewry, see D. Lasker, "Christianity and Late Iberian
   Jewish Philosophy," in Cooperman (ed.), *In Iberia and Beyond*,
   175–90.

33. This passage is cited and analyzed in J.-P. Rothschild, "Question de
   philosophie soumise par Eli Habillo à Sem Tob Ibn Sem Tov, v. 1472,"
   Archives d'Histoire Doctrinale et Littéraire du Moyen Age 61 (1994),
   111. Note also Arama's recognition of the success of Christian philosophers in their opposition to the influence of philosophical doctrine on
   their theological principles (*Hazut Kasheh* [Jerusalem, n.d.], ch. 8).

34. H. Wolfson, "Isaac ibn Shem-Tob's Unknown Commentaries on the
   Physics and his other Unkown Works," in his *Studies in the History of
   Philosophy and Religion*, ed. I. Twersky and G. H. Williams (Cambridge,
   Mass.: Harvard University Press, 1977), II: 477–90.

35. A. Ravitzky, *Crescas' Sermon on the Passover and Studies in his Philosophy* [Hebrew] (Jerusalem: Israel Academy of Sciences and Humanities,
   1988), 130; M. Saperstein, *"Your Voice like a Ram's Horn": Themes
   and Texts in Traditional Jewish Preaching* (Cincinnati: Hebrew Union
   College Press, 1996), 1983.

36. On Gersonides' treatment of divine knowledge and human choice, see
   S. Klein-Braslavy, "Gersonides on Determinism, Possibility, Choice,
   and Foreknowledge," [Hebrew] *Da'at* 22 (1989), 5–53; C. Manekin,
   "Freedom Within Reason? Gersonides on Human Choice," in *Freedom and Moral Responsibility: General and Jewish Perspectives*, ed.
   C. Manekin and M. Kellner (College Park: University of Maryland Press,
   1997), 165–204.

37. *Milhamot Adonai* (Riva di Trento, 1560), 3:3–4, 21d–25a. A translation
   of these sections is found in *The Wars of the Lord*, trans. S. Feldman
   (Philadelphia: Jewish Publication Society, 1987), II: 107–31.

38. Gersonides' view that the intellect allows a person to escape the causal
   effects of the heavens can be found in *Milhamot Adonai* 17a–b (trans.

Feldman, 34–5). He limited human choice to choosing the good in *Milhamot Adonai* 19b; trans. Feldman, 60.

39. *Milhamot Adonai* 17b; trans. Feldman, 36: "Even though choice, which stems from reason, has the power to upset this order, this occurs rarely."

40. D. Schwartz, "Between Divine and Human Knowledge: The Trajectory of a Medieval Epistemological Conception," [Hebrew] *Iyyun* 39 (1990), 211–22.

41. A. Ackerman, "The Philosophic Sermons of Zerahia ben Isaac Halevi Saladin: Jewish Philosophic and Sermonic Activity in Late 14th and Early 15th Century Aragon," Ph.D. dissertation, Hebrew University of Jerusalem, 2000, 136–9.

42. Bibago, *The Way of Belief* (Constantinople, 1521) (reprinted, Jerusalem: Meqorot, 1970), 8a–14b.

43. Aquinas, *Summa Theologica* Ia 14, 6.

44. Bibago, *The Way of Belief*, 12a–14b.

45. Crescas, *Light of the Lord* 1:3.3.

46. It would be interesting to inspect fifteenth-century Spanish-Christian philosophy to see if the heightened polemical activity between Christians and Jews in fifteenth-century Spain produced only a unidirectional influence of Christian thought on Jewish philosophy or, as I suspect, an impact that was bidirectional.

17 Hasdai Crescas and anti-Aristotelianism

INTRODUCTION: FOURTEENTH-CENTURY PHYSICS

The fourteenth century saw the emergence of a new trend in medieval philosophy and science. While continuing to adhere generally to an Aristotelian understanding of nature, Christian scholars began to question and modify certain premises of Aristotelian physics and to suggest non-Aristotelian alternatives, reviving pre-Socratic or Hellenistic views and developing original ideas based on observation and experience. Such remarkable figures as Thomas Bradwardine and his successors in Oxford, and Jean Buridan and his students in Paris challenged basic Aristotelian tenets about infinity, place, vacuum, motion, and material substance, suggesting the possibility of an infinite cosmos filled by multiple worlds. Although motivated largely by Christian doctrine and the condemnations of Aristotle, this move towards critical inquiry led to a new conception of the universe, which anticipated and contributed to the scientific revolution of the sixteenth and seventeenth centuries.[1]

The outstanding Jewish representative of this critical trend in European philosophy was Hasdai Crescas (c. 1340–1410/11), legal scholar, communal leader, and courtier in Barcelona and Saragossa. Perhaps influenced by the Paris physicists, and motivated by similar theological interests, Crescas in his *Light of the Lord* subjected Maimonides' summary of Aristotelian physics to a searching attack. Unlike his Christian counterparts, however, Crescas was not content merely to speculate about problem areas within a generally coherent natural science. Exploiting divergences within the Aristotelian tradition, and borrowing existing anti-Aristotelian arguments, Crescas sought nothing less than to demolish the system

391

as a whole. Although his immediate Jewish followers and critics expressed reservations about Crescas' innovations, his ideas were taken
up and elaborated by anti-Aristotelians in the Renaissance and Ref-
ormation. The *Light of the Lord* itself was not translated into Latin
or any Romance language, but it was cited and used famously by
Pico della Mirandola and Spinoza. It may have influenced, if only
indirectly, some of Giordano Bruno's theories about the infinite universe and Galileo's novel conceptions of weight and velocity.[2]

Crescas' critique of Aristotelian physics forms the first part of
his *Light of the Lord*. It is the foundation of an elaborate refutation
not only of Aristotle's physical principles, but also of the theological doctrines espoused by Aristotle's Jewish followers. Following
a brief discussion of Crescas' life and works, and an outline of the
Light of the Lord as a whole, the present introduction to Crescas'
anti-Aristotelianism will focus on his arguments concerning motion,
place, infinity, time, and matter.

LIFE AND WRITINGS

Born into a prominent family, Crescas spent his early years in
Barcelona, where he studied in the academy of Nissim b. Reuben
Gerondi. It was under the tutelage of Nissim, the leading representative of a Barcelona tradition going back to Moses Nahmanides,
that Crescas acquired his knowledge of and critical attitude toward
philosophy. Gaining expertise in law, philosophy, and perhaps also
kabbalah, it seems that Crescas was considered a major scholar in his
own right already by 1370. He is cited favorably in legal writings and
participated with his teacher in a literary exchange of poems. After
serving briefly as rabbi in Barcelona, Crescas moved to Saragossa
in 1389, where he was appointed communal rabbi and given royal
power to adjudicate capital cases in all of the kingdom of Aragon.
The move to Saragossa, the capital city of Aragon, brought him into
contact with an urbane Jewish population that included a thriving
circle of poets, translators, and courtiers. It was within this circle that
he taught not only law but also philosophy, and his students became
the leading figures of the following generation. His court position,
moreover, afforded him greater contact with Christian scholars and
statesmen, both in Saragossa and throughout Aragon and Navarre.
In 1401 he was sent as emissary to Pamplona where, it has been

speculated, he could have learned about the natural philosophy of Nicole Oresme.[3]

Crescas was residing in Saragossa during the riots of 1391, which destroyed many of the Jewish communities of Castile and Aragon. Although Saragossa was spared, due to the strong royal presence in the city, Crescas himself suffered the loss of his only son, who was killed as a martyr in Barcelona. The riots, which shaped the remaining years of Jewish life in Spain, had significant impact on Crescas' career as well. As leader of the Jews, he used his royal connections to help restore and reconstruct Jewish communities that had been destroyed by the rioting. He instituted decrees to address the emergency situation and wrote, and encouraged others to write, polemical works aimed at countering Christian missionaries. This interest in refuting Christianity, moreover, is evident in his *Light of the Lord* as well. Several issues discussed in his polemical work, such as the superiority of the prophecy of Moses, that spiritual reward is promised in the Bible, and the status of demons, were taken up again in his philosophical work. More interesting is the fact that Crescas borrowed several ideas from Christian philosophy not only to combat his religious opponent, but to develop a philosophy or theology that could rival the belief system adopted by so many *conversos*. Crescas' peculiar ideas about free will, for instance, seem to derive from the apostate Abner of Burgos (Alfonso of Valladolid) and show some affinity with Duns Scotus. It was Abner, moreover, who announced in Hebrew certain anti-Aristotelian positions that Crescas would later take up and further develop.[4]

The *Light of the Lord*, Crescas' philosophical-theological summa, was conceived as part 1 of a two-part work. But it seems that political turmoil and communal responsibility prevented him from writing the companion volume, a legal work that, he hoped, would supplant Maimonides' *Mishneh Torah*. The difficult historical setting in which Crescas worked, moreover, seems to have affected the *Light of the Lord* as well, for he continued writing and revising his major work over several years, reworking sections and adding chapters in response to his growing knowledge of Christian philosophy. The latest version of the work, which is dated 1410, includes 4 books, 18 parts, 116 chapters, and 13 "investigations." The subject of Book 1 is the root of all belief, namely the existence, unity, and incorporeality of God. Book 2 treats of six necessary dogmas, without which the law could not survive, namely divine knowledge of individuals, providence, divine power, prophecy, free will, and the final aim of the Torah. Book 3 consists of eight beliefs that, while not necessary per se, render anyone who denies them a heretic, namely creation, immortality of the soul, reward and punishment, resurrection of the dead, eternity of the Torah, superiority of the prophecy of Moses, power of the priest to prophesy, and messianic redemption. Book 3 includes an appendix as well, with three additional beliefs: efficacy of prayer and the priestly blessing, repentance, and the holy days. Book 4 consists of separate investigations into the validity of thirteen disputed beliefs, including the question of future eternity, the plurality of worlds, whether celestial bodies are living and rational, astral influence, demons, the power of amulets and incantations, reincarnation, future reward of a minor, the meaning of "heaven" and "hell," the content of the "account of the beginning" and "account of the chariot," whether intellect, intelligible, and intellectually cognizing subject can become one, the prime mover, and the scope of metaphysics.[5]

The first twenty-five chapters of Book 1, Part 1, and the first fourteen chapters of Book 1, Part 2, in which Crescas sets out his main critique of Aristotle's conception of nature, have been edited, translated, and copiously annotated by H. A. Wolfson. Consistent with his approach to Jewish philosophy in general, Wolfson attempted to identify the source of every statement or argument of Crescas in existing Hebrew texts, including the vast corpus of literature translated from Arabic. Focusing attention on Crescas' contributions to the history of science, moreover, Wolfson rearranged the text, placing the critique of each philosophical proposition directly after its explanation, and separating the chapters with scientific interest from the larger theological context. The more recent work of S. Pines and W. Z. Harvey, on the other hand, has pointed to parallels in contemporary Christian philosophy and has even suggested personal connections with Scholastic philosophers. Harvey and H. Davidson, furthermore, have examined the critique of physics together with the refutation of Maimonides' proofs for the existence, unity, and incorporeality of God. Thus, while the following discussion of Crescas' critique will follow the work of Wolfson, parallel developments in Christian philosophy will also be noted and theological implications will be emphasized.

It is only within these larger contexts that Crescas' achievement can be appreciated fully.[6]

A few preliminary remarks about the theological setting of Crescas' work, namely the critique of Maimonides' proofs and propositions, along with a brief explanation of his critical method, will lead into discussion of the arguments themselves. The views of Aristotle presented throughout correspond with Crescas' understanding of them. Examples have been selected with a view to illustrating his method and bringing out the main points and implications. Resemblances to the work of John Philoponus will also be cited, to provide further orientation with respect to the history of anti-Aristotelianism. Finally, the notes at the beginning of each section provide select bibliography related to all issues discussed.[7]

THE CRITIQUE OF ARISTOTELIAN PHYSICS

In the second part of the *Guide of the Perplexed*, Maimonides attempts to prove, on philosophical grounds, the existence, unity, and incorporeality of God. In order to achieve this purpose, he sets forth twenty-six propositions, twenty-five of which, he claims, have been demonstrated, whereas the twenty-sixth, the eternity of motion, he assumes for the sake of argument. From these twenty-six propositions, Maimonides then derives six proofs, according to Crescas' enumeration, for the existence, unity, and incorporeality of God. The first and third of these six proofs are the most important and are briefly stated here. According to the first proof, the circular motion of the outermost sphere is perpetual and requires a mover. But the mover cannot be a body or a force in a body; it must therefore be an incorporeal force outside the body, and this incorporeal force is God. According to the third proof, existence is either necessary or possible. If the existence of everything were only possible, it would be equally possible for everything not to exist. Over infinite time this possibility for nonexistence would have to become actual; but since everything has not passed into nonexistence, there must be an existent that is necessary in itself, and this necessary existent is God.[8]

The first proof set forth by Maimonides, based on motion and the impossibility of an infinite regress, is derived from Aristotle's

Physics and *Metaphysics*. The third proof, on the other hand, based on necessary and possible existence, derives from Avicenna's peculiar reading of Aristotle's *Metaphysics*, and was subsequently rejected by Averroes. While both proofs continued to exercise considerable influence throughout the Middle Ages, with philosophers defending either Avicenna or Averroes, Crescas approached these two arguments in a different way. Although Maimonides' conclusions may or may not follow necessarily from these twenty-six propositions, it is not at all clear that the propositions themselves have been sufficiently demonstrated. An examination of Maimonides' proofs, therefore, requires an examination of his propositions, and this examination, as has been indicated, is the main function of Book 1. All twenty-six propositions and the six proofs derived from them are explained in 1:1; fourteen of the propositions and all six proofs are critiqued in 1:2; and Crescas' own proofs for the existence, unity, and incorporeality of God, based on prophecy rather than reason, are set forth in 1:3. His critique of the twenty-sixth proposition, the eternity of motion, is found mainly in 3:1, in the course of his discussion of creation.

The method used by Crescas throughout his critique is dialectical. The arguments of his opponent are first established in detail, with implications drawn out and difficulties resolved. The very system he has painstakingly built up is then demolished, with both premises and conclusions attacked. The twenty-six propositions used by Maimonides serve as the framework for Crescas' initial presentation of Aristotelian philosophy, which he elaborates based on the commentaries and treatises by al-Ghazali, Ibn Daud, al-Tabrizi, Averroes, Gersonides, and Moses Narboni.[9] His critique of these same propositions is similarly constructed from Aristotelian sources but, as already mentioned, he exploits dissident views within the tradition itself, focuses on basic problems, finds exceptions to general rules, and draws inspiration from anti-Aristotelian and non-Aristotelian traditions. The dialectical character of his work gives the impression of a school exercise, in which Crescas aims at "scoring a point here and a point there," as Wolfson felicitously describes it.[10] But the few positive statements about the "true meaning" of place, motion, and time, and the occasional reference to God as Place and to the existence of multiple worlds, Indicate that something more is at stake than any academic prize. For, as we will see, the God that Crescas worships cannot be limited by the finite world of

Aristotelian physics. He is not a mere cause of motion or of existence, but rather an infinite source of love and goodness, the creator and ruler of an unlimited universe, infinitely extended and filled with a plurality of independent worlds.

Place as Three-Dimensional Extension[11]

The first subject of Crescas' critique of Aristotle is infinity. Following the order of Maimonides' propositions, Aristotle's arguments against the possibility of an infinite magnitude are first explained in detail and then refuted. While Aristotle's arguments, Crescas admits, are impressive, they depend upon further arguments against the possibility of a vacuum, while the arguments against the possibility of a vacuum are based upon Aristotle's peculiar notions about place and motion, which notions are not free from doubt. As with Maimonides' proofs for the existence of God, therefore, Crescas is led to reexamine these basic principles of Aristotelian physics.

That Aristotle's ideas about place and motion were problematic was recognized already in antiquity. It was this existence of sustained examination and criticism in the commentary tradition that allowed Crescas' critique to proceed with surprising ease. An interest in the properties of the vacuum, moreover, had increased in intensity during the fourteenth century. The idea of a completely empty space served as a theoretical laboratory of sorts in which Scholastic philosophers could test their novel ideas about nature. Although Crescas depends upon these existing traditions, as will be seen, he was unique in carrying old and new insights to their logical conclusion. After a brief explanation of the main arguments used by Aristotle to deny the existence of a vacuum, Crescas' refutation of his opponent will be discussed. The full significance of his own conclusions and their relationship to existing sources will also be considered.

Three ideas in Aristotle's conception of motion are most distinct and notoriously flawed. All three are brought to bear on his discussion of vacuum. Locomotion, in his opinion, consists in a change of place, from point of origin to destination. But a vacuum is homogeneous. There are no distinct places or predetermined regions in which motion can take place. Thus any body or element in a vacuum would either move not at all or in all directions at once; but, Aristotle explains, such indiscriminate movement is absurd. Moreover, the absence of any medium in a vacuum made it impossible for Aristotle to conceive of either violent or natural motion. That a javelin continues to move once released from the hand, in Aristotle's opinion, is the result not of some force imported to the javelin itself but to the surrounding air. In a vacuum, however, where there is no air, any projectile would immediately cease to move. The velocity of elements, finally, which have a natural inclination to move either up or down, is in Aristotle's opinion measured by the ratio of weight or levity to resistance. But because in a vacuum there is no resistance, there could be no ratio. Motion in such a state of existence would be instantaneous, but, according to Aristotle, instantaneous motion is impossible.

While the existence of a vacuum led to absurdities when considered in light of Aristotle's theory of motion, the rejection of such an empty space was directly tied to his definition of place. If a vacuum were considered the place of a body, Aristotle argued, then this three-dimensional extension would itself constitute a body. What this means is that if another body were to enter into this empty space, it would enter into an existing three-dimensional body, and if one body could enter another, then all bodies could enter into one; the entire world, that is, "could enter into a grain of mustard seed."[12] Because the existence of two bodies in one place at the same time is impossible, according to Aristotle, there can be no vacuum. Moreover, if there were dimensions existing separate from a material body, these dimensions would themselves have dimensions, and so on, continuing to infinity. But because an infinite regress is impossible, such an empty space cannot exist. It is in light of these considerations that Aristotle set forth his own definition of place as the limit of the surrounding body. Place is not three-dimensional extension but two-dimensional surface. It is an accident of the body it defines, separate but coterminous, not existing in itself.

Returning now from Aristotle to his trenchant critic, Crescas denies the first two arguments even when accepting Aristotle's conception of motion and place. For direction, he maintains, could be oriented with respect to the center of the earth and the lunar sphere, absolute reference points that could guide the movement of anything contained within the vacuum. Crescas does not use an impetus theory to account for violent motion in a vacuum, as had John Philoponus in the sixth century, but his argument against interpenetrability bears a striking resemblance to that used by his anti-Aristotelian forbear. Like Philoponus, Crescas rehabilitates the definition of place as three-dimensional extension, arguing that dimensions can be considered incorporeal; by eliminating the connection between three-dimensional space and material body, Aristotle's absurdities are easily resolved. As for Aristotle's argument from velocity, there was no need for Crescas to search beyond the Aristotelian tradition itself to find a suitable source of inspiration. Borrowing Ibn Bajja's theory of motion, Crescas argues that velocity should be construed not as a ratio of force to resistance (that is, $V = F/R$) but as a subtraction (namely, $V = F - R$). Thus, finite motion is not only possible in a vacuum, but rather it is precisely this motion in a vacuum that expresses an element's true weight. But while Ibn Bajja continued to believe that a real vacuum was impossible, such reservations did not affect Crescas. The true place of a body, he explains emphatically, is a three-dimensional vacuum. This he asserts and more: the universe as a whole is a similarly conceived vacuum, a vast and unlimited space, completely homogeneous and infinitely extended.

Relative Weight and Motion[13]

While the definition of place as three-dimensional extension and the critique of Aristotle's arguments against the possibility of a vacuum opened the way for Crescas to assert the existence of an infinite universe, Crescas' rejection of the theory of natural motion, to which we now turn our attention, served to eliminate Aristotle's rejection of multiple worlds. The refutation of Aristotle's theory, like the arguments concerning vacuum, is set forth in the long critique of Maimonides' first proposition; it is taken up again and elaborated at *Light of the Lord* 1:1, ch. 6.

The main argument against the possibility of multiple worlds, set forth at *De Caelo* 1:8–9, runs as follows. All material existence, according to Aristotle, can be reduced to four basic elements possessing specific characteristics. Fire and air, for example, are light, whereas earth and water are heavy. But weight and levity are defined not in terms of mass but in terms of direction, and direction is determined not by the elements' motion but by a fixed natural state. Thus fire and air incline upward because they seek to return to their natural place in the upper region, while water and earth incline downward, seeking to return to their natural place around the center. If there existed another world, Aristotle continues, that other world would be organized in the same way as ours. But the existence of that other world would introduce an additional natural place for each element. Thus the element earth, for example, would incline both downward toward the center of this world and upward toward the center of the other world, while the element fire, similarly, would incline both upward toward the lunar sphere of this world and downward toward the region of fire in the other world. Because contrary natural motions are impossible, Aristotle concludes, there cannot be multiple worlds. The world in which we live is unique, centered at earth, and bounded by the outer sphere.

Consistent with his conception of nature and final causation, Aristotle's theory of natural motion is construed in absolute terms. The center is absolute down and, by analogy, the lunar sphere is absolute up. Fire is considered to possess absolute lightness, which means that it would not descend even if all air were removed from the region below. The regions of the four elements, moreover, are predetermined and prior to motion with respect to nature and existence. But, Crescas maintains, regardless of Aristotle's assertions to support these claims, none of these principles set forth by him has been proved. By adapting to his own purpose an example that had been used by the philosophers to illustrate the impossibility of a vacuum, Crescas then sets forth an alternative theory. There is no absolute light or heavy, he maintains, and all elements incline toward the center. That air and fire rise is not due to some native inclination and predetermined place, but to the force exerted by the heavier elements, which, in the course of their natural descent downward, push lighter elements upward. Thus if someone were to dig a ditch, air would descend downward into the area formerly filled with earth not because "nature abhors a vacuum," but because the heavier element earth, which had previously impeded air's downward descent, had been removed.

In contrast to Aristotle, in Crescas' view all bodies are heavy. Weight and direction are not absolute, and place is determined not by fixed regions but by the relative jockeying for position of heavy and heavier bodies. As with Crescas' definition of place as extension, here too he was anticipated by Philoponus, while Philoponus himself may have worked with a more ancient Platonic model. Moreover, Crescas' older contemporary Nicole Oresme had similarly applied the theory of relative weight to the problem of multiple worlds. But while Philoponus, good Platonist that he was, continued to affirm the existence of one perfect world, and while Oresme's speculations remained in the realm of thought experiment, Crescas drew actual conclusions. With Aristotle's theory of natural motion eliminated, and with his rejection of a vacuum outside the world refuted, multiple worlds made sense, even when these worlds had similar composition. All of these worlds, whether finite or infinite, would have unique centers around which matter could organize according to weight.

First Matter as Corporeal Form[14]

The rejection of Aristotle's absolute levity and predetermined place led Crescas to reconceive celestial motion as well. In the same way that sublunar elements tend to move downward, he maintains, so too celestial bodies tend to revolve around. Both types of motion are governed not by volition, soul, or intellect, but by a natural property related to the possession or privation of weight: sublunar bodies move down as a result of their relative heaviness, whereas celestial bodies circle around as a result of their weightlessness. Crescas does not present a consistent account of this important idea, even though it would serve his critique of Maimonides' first proof for existence. But while he did not draw out all the implications of this doctrine, he did pursue a more general critique of Aristotle's distinction between the celestial and sublunar realms. The most important move in this direction is his elimination of first matter, which is set out most clearly in his explanation and critique of Maimonides' tenth proposition.

That there is a sharp distinction between the upper and lower worlds is repeated throughout Aristotle's writings; it is a fundamental aspect of his conception of the world. In the lower world, he argues, below the sphere of the moon, material existence is composed of the four elements. Composite existents come to be and pass away as a result of mixture and blending, with organic beings decomposing into their elemental parts. But that these four elements can change into one another and mix, for Aristotle, meant that there must be some underlying substrate, a first matter, a pure potentiality,

capable of receiving all forms. But while the lower world is composite and constantly subject to change, the elements being drawn away
and returning to their natural places, in the upper world there is no
perceived change in substance, and change in place occurs only by
accident, for circular motion is continuous and has no beginning
or end. The celestial bodies, therefore, must be made of a different
substance, a fifth element, what Aristotle calls aether.

But how exactly these matters differ and how they relate to form
is not completely spelled out. Thus Crescas, in order to provide
further explanation, presents the opinions of two opposing schools
of thought. According to Avicenna, he explains, despite the differences between celestial and sublunar matter, bodies in both regions are composed of matter and form. First matter in the lower
world, moreover, takes on corporeal form, a predisposition for three-
dimensionality, before assuming the specific forms of the four elements. According to Averroes, on the other hand, always the critic
of his eastern predecessor, corporeal form is not a predisposition
for three-dimensionality but three-dimensionality pure and simple.
Moreover, bodies in the celestial world could not be composed of
matter and form, for composition implies division, and division implies corruptibility. Rather, it is corporeal form itself, an actualization rather than a potentiality, which serves as substrate in the heavens. Impressed by Averroes' reasoning, Crescas then takes an additional step, adapting Averroes' principle to a very different purpose.
Why not understand first matter in the same way, he asks, not as
an underlying potentiality without real existence, but as a corporeal form, actualized, existing, a pure three-dimensionality capable
of assuming all forms.

As with his non-Aristotelian conception of motion and place, here
too Crescas' corporeal form resembles the three-dimensionality of
Philoponus. But while Philoponus works with earlier Neoplatonic
traditions, it seems that Crescas draws from much later sources
and begins to point away from hylomorphism altogether. While his
idea of a similar corporeal form as substrate in lower and upper
world resembles Gabirol's universal matter, a theory he could have
gleaned from Ibn Daud's critique thereof, his suggestion that specific form be considered not as actualizing the substance, but as
a sort of accident, moves toward a type of atomism that had been
subscribed to by the *mutakallimun*. Corporeal form conceived as

three-dimensionality points toward the existence of an actually existing indivisible body, serving as the smallest building block of all
existence. But whatever Crescas' source or influence, and however
his true belief regarding atomism should be understood, the implication seems clear. If both lower and upper worlds are made of the
same stuff, then it is not only sublunar but also celestial bodies that
are subject to both generation and corruption. Citing the rabbis to
reinforce this conclusion, he asserts that God creates worlds and
destroys them.

Time and Eternity[15]

While Crescas' critique of the Aristotelian arguments against infinity and vacuum, and his rejection of natural motion and first matter,
led to a new conception of the universe, his discussion of time led
from the universe itself to its origin. Moving once again from Aristotle to his critic, not only the theories of time themselves but also
the implications with respect to creation will be considered in the
following discussion.

Time, according to Aristotle, is an accident consequent upon motion. It is the measure of prior and posterior, with the present, a
nonexistent "now," marking the transition from past to future. What
this means is that, if motion were to cease, in particular the daily
motion of the outermost sphere, time too would cease to exist, and
if motion and time ceased to exist, there could be no material existence in the sublunar world. But since circular motion, according to
Aristotle, is perfect and eternal, having no beginning or end, there
always was motion and time, and there always will be motion and
time.

Because Aristotle believed in the eternity of the world, this relation between time and motion posed no problem. On the contrary,
it both derived from and reinforced his belief in both past and future eternity. But this relation between time and motion could not
but affect the medieval Jew who aimed to describe God's creation of
the world. For, while there could be no time before the creation of
motion, the initial motion of creation would itself imply a preexistent time. Any instant, that is, defined by Aristotle as the transition
from past to future, implies the existence of prior time, and prior
time implies the existence of prior motion, and so on, continuing to

infinity. Even if one could escape this infinite regress and conceive of a creation *ex nihilo*, still Aristotle's theory would require a revision of the biblical account. For the luminaries, upon whose motion time depends, could not have been created on the fourth day. It is only with the circular motion of the celestial bodies that the days themselves can be counted and that the generation of plants, animals, and humankind can proceed.

As with other aspects of the Aristotelian system, Crescas approaches the subject of time and eternity not by defending a positive doctrine, but by attacking the underlying principles held true by Aristotle. Although time does measure motion, Crescas admits, it also measures rest. While Aristotle had already recognized this fact, rest is conceived by him not as a real quantity, but as the privation of motion; the measure of time based on rest is simply the measure of a corresponding absence of motion. What Crescas has in mind, in contrast, is not privation of motion, but absolute rest, not an absence of something that could exist, but a state in which motion is completely impossible. Advocating a non-Aristotelian opinion resembling that of Peter Aureol and William of Ockham, Crescas asserts that time ought to be conceived not as an accident of motion or even as a substance, but rather as a duration or extension which exists only in the soul. That time can be measured in any definite sense did, of course, require some motion or change, but real time, absolute time, could exist without, and even before, the existence of motion.

Returning now to the question of creation, Crescas' non-Aristotelian conception of time leads to the following result. Time, like space, is defined as an infinite extension. It can exist before the creation of this world or any other worlds that exist or have existed; these worlds, in other words, can be created in space and in time. In this way does Crescas conceive of the preexistent universe as a space-time continuum. But, despite the similarity between Crescas' God as "Place" and Spinoza's God as infinite extension, the question as to whether this infinite space-time continuum is created by, emanates from, or is an attribute of God remains a subject of dispute.

God of Love and Love of God[16]

Crescas' critique of the Aristotelian conception of nature was devastating. Although Hebrew commentators on Averroes and

Maimonides in the fifteenth century attempted to defend the
Stagirite against his Jewish critic, it is clear, at least in retrospect,
that they had chosen the losing side. More important from Crescas'
perspective was not the demise of Aristotle's physics per se but the
conception of God based upon it. As has been emphasized throughout
the previous discussion, however, although Crescas' method in the
Light of the Lord was critical, his purpose in undertaking this work
was not only the destruction of his opponent's system. His attack
on Aristotle's physical principles depended upon and pointed toward
a new conception of the universe. The purpose of this final section
of the chapter is to consider briefly Crescas' positive conception of
God, and of humanity's relationship to God, as it emerges from his
critique. Here, too, while his ideas stand in sharp contrast to those
of his Jewish predecessors, they anticipate, and lead toward, certain
dominant trends in Renaissance and early modern philosophy.

The two main arguments used by Maimonides to prove the existence, unity, and incorporeality of God, which have been described previously, are easily dismissed once Crescas has refuted the
premises upon which they are based. If celestial motion, like sublunar motion, is natural rather than volitional, there is no need for
any external cause let alone an infinite incorporeal force. If an infinite series of causes and effects is possible, moreover, as is proved in
proposition 3, then there is no need for a necessary existent to secure
the propensity of existence over nonexistence. Although one could
reconfigure Avicenna's metaphysical proof, which Crescas tries to
do, it would point to an unmoved mover but say nothing about
the true God of Israel. Exploiting a skeptical tendency within the
philosophical tradition itself, Crescas argues that no positive knowledge of God can be had through philosophical means. Thus, turning
from philosophy to Scripture, he sets out on a different path. Focusing on a few key biblical texts, and drawing upon his own peculiar
conception of the universe, Crescas conceives of God not as a cause
of motion, but as an infinite source of love. Creator of a beginningless
universe, God fills this vast empty space with nothing but the good
and rules it with nothing but joy. It is through love that God gave the
law to Israel, and it is through love, expressed as obedience to the
law, that Israel can cleave to and conjoin with God. This, Crescas
maintains, is the final purpose and ultimate reward of human
existence.

Although love of God was important for Maimonides as well, God was conceived by him as an object of love rather than lover, and man's love of God was construed primarily in cognitive terms. Love of God is knowledge of God, and knowledge of God is achieved through the philosophical study of nature. Insofar as immortality is possible, so Crescas represents the Aristotelian position, it is achieved by acquiring true knowledge, which true knowledge survives separate from the body after death. But not only is this opinion heretical, Crescas argues, it is also absurd. Even if this were possible, which he denies, it would lead to the immortality of something other than the human being, not of man as rational animal but of a separate intellect. Moreover, this theory of the acquired intellect puts too much stock in human achievement, while refusing to recognize the fixed nature of God's world, which consists, according to Crescas, of an infinite series of causal relations that determine both actions and beliefs. Thus, true love, in Crescas' opinion, is not study but obedience, and obedience is measured not in the action per se but in the will and desire to achieve that act. Reward is the pleasure experienced in pursuing this higher desire, and this pleasure, according to Crescas, which is unique to each individual, survives after death in a self-subsistent soul that is eternal by nature. This, Crescas explains triumphantly, is humankind's final reward. It is not limited to philosophers but rather is achieved even by the minor child who has responded "amen" to the recitation of daily prayers.

It is perhaps here, even more than in his critique of physics, that the influence of Crescas' contemporary situation can be felt. His emphatic rejection of reward through knowledge resembles Abner of Burgos' attack on Isaac Pollegar, a former student or colleague of Abner and devout Maimonidean. The focus on love and determinism, similarly, seems to draw from Christian ideas about divine grace and predestination, whereas the emphasis on will over intellect, as already mentioned, resembles the position set forth by Duns Scotus. A general preoccupation with issues of salvation, moreover, and a willingness to forgive coerced transgression, are very much in line with the contemporary despair faced by Jews and *conversos* in an increasingly hostile world. The preoccupation with humankind's final end, in particular, would continue throughout the fifteenth century, when the debate in Spain revolved around Aristotle's *Nicomachean Ethics*. But in the Renaissance, it was the doctrine of love that would have particular appeal. While Crescas' idea of cosmic love, it has been suggested, was known and used by Leone Ebreo, his ideas in general could have found favor among Christian Platonists such as Ficino and Pico della Mirandola, anti-Aristotelians and the first architects of a fully worked out philosophy of love.

CONCLUSION: RELIGIOUS CRITIQUE AND SCIENTIFIC PROGRESS[17]

Crescas is generally considered to be the last great Jewish philosopher of the Middle Ages. Although the question of his originality with respect to the formulation of individual arguments remains unclear, his critical selection of existing sources and creative use of them for his own purposes puts him on an equal level with the Jewish Aristotelians whom he aimed to topple. His critical insight, sensible argumentation, periodic appeal to observation or experience, and unwillingness to accept any scientific tradition, no matter how noble its source, cannot but find favor in the eyes of a modern reader. Nor can one fail to admire his vision of the universe as an infinite space with multiple worlds. It would be another two hundred years before his good judgment could be confirmed by advances in technology. On account of his influence on Pico and Spinoza, if not others, his *Light of the Lord* marks a real turning point in the history of science. He was part of, and contributed to, the movement away from the Aristotelian system, which, as Wolfson has described it, had "gone off into the wilds of speculation and built up an artificial structure entirely divorced from nature."[18]

While the present introduction to Crescas' philosophy has attempted to reinforce this view, it has also tried to point toward another part of the story. Although Crescas was a man before his time, his attack on Aristotelian physics was not only motivated by a critical spirit of scientific inquiry, an innate intellectual curiosity which drove him to question the received opinions of his day. Unlike his contemporary Christians in Oxford and Paris, Crescas did not write commentaries on Aristotle or Averroes. There are no occasional treatises on difficult problems that remain from his pen or scientific inventions that derive from his philosophical critique. The *Light of the Lord*, as any cursory glance at the table of contents will verify, is primarily a theological work. Thus, no matter how much Crescas might have been driven in his investigations by a love of science, it was this larger project of freeing rabbinic Judaism from Aristotle that motivated his work. But rather than undermining Crescas' philosophical achievement, the highlighting of his religious goals serves to bring out an important factor, both in his work and that of the fourteenth-century physicists. It was allegiance to religion that gave scholars such as Crescas the strength and independence of mind to challenge the traditional philosophy of the day. It was exactly this religious critique of philosophy, not based on an appeal to biblical and rabbinic sources, but through the grappling with philosophy on its own terms, that opened the way to the scientific revolution of the early modern period. Ultimately, this is Crescas' greatest achievement, even if it is something he had not anticipated and would not have desired.

NOTES

1. I wish to thank Professor Alfred Ivry and Dr. Angela Jaffray for helpful comments and advice. For introduction to the fourteenth-century physicists, see E. Grant, *Planets, Stars, and Orbs: The Medieval Cosmos, 1200–1687* (Cambridge: Cambridge University Press, 1996), with full bibliography and brief discussion of the disputes regarding the question of continuity between medieval and modern science.

2. On the influence of and criticism of Crescas, see H. A. Wolfson, *Crescas' Critique of Aristotle* (Cambridge, Mass.: Harvard University Press, 1929), 1–37; H. Davidson, *The Philosophy of Abraham Shalom* (Berkeley: University of California Press, 1964); W. Z. Harvey, "Hasdai Crescas' Critique of the Theory of the Acquired Intellect," Ph.D. dissertation, Columbia University, 1973. For the citations by Pico, and possible influence on Bruno and Galileo, see Wolfson, *Crescas' Critique*, index s.v., and C. B. Schmitt, *Gianfrancesco Pico della Mirandola (1469–1533) and his Critique of Aristotle* (The Hague: Nijhoff, 1967). For the influence on Spinoza, see H. A. Wolfson, *The Philosophy of Spinoza* (Cambridge, Mass.: Harvard University Press, 1934), index, s.v.; W. Z. Harvey, *Physics and Metaphysics in Hasdai Crescas*, Amsterdam Studies in Jewish Thought, 6 (Amsterdam: J. C. Gieben, 1998), index, s.v.

3. For biographical details, and information on the Barcelona tradition as well as Crescas' circle in Saragossa, see in general Y. Baer, *A History of the Jews in Christian Spain* (Philadelphia: Jewish Publication Society, 1978), II, index, s.v. On Crescas and kabbalah, see W. Z. Harvey, "Kabbalistic Elements in Hasdai Crescas' *Light of the Lord*," [Hebrew]

Jerusalem Studies in Jewish Thought 2 (1982–83), 75–109; N. Ophir, "Sod ha-Qadish: A Kabbalistic Text Attributed to Rabbi Hasdai Crescas," [Hebrew] *Da'at* 46 (2001), 13–28. For references in legal writings and the exchange of poems, see, e.g., A. Hershman, *Rabbi Isaac b. Sheshet and his Times* (New York: Jewish Theological Seminary, 1943), index, s.v.; L. Feldman, "An Exchange of Epistles and Poems between Nissim ben Reuben, Abraham bar Isaac Halevi, Don Judah bar Sheshet Crescas, and Don Hasdai Crescas," [Hebrew] *Qobes al Yad* 7 (1968), 125–60. For contact with Christians, see Harvey, *Physics and Metaphysics*, 23–9; W. Z. Harvey, "Hasdai Crescas and Bernat Metge on the Soul," [Hebrew] *Jerusalem Studies in Jewish Thought* 5 (1986), 141–54.

4. For details regarding the riots and efforts at restoration, see in general Baer, *History of the Jews*. Crescas himself records these events in his letter to Avignon, trans. in F. Kobler (ed.), *Letters of Jews through the Ages* (New York: East and West Library, 1952), 1: 272–5. One of Crescas' polemical works survives in medieval Hebrew translation: *Refutation of the Christian Principles*, ed. D. Lasker (Beer Sheva: Ben-Gurion University, 1990), and trans. D. Lasker (Albany: State University of New York Press, 1992). On the relationship of Efodi's polemical work to Crescas, see F. Talmage, *The Polemical Writings of Profiat Duran* [Hebrew] (Jerusalem: Merkaz Shazar, 1981), introduction. On Crescas' determinism and the influence of Abner and Duns Scotus, see Y. Baer, "Abner of Burgos' *Minhat Qena'ot* and its Influence on Hasdai Crescas," [Hebrew] *Tarbiz* 11 (1940), 188–206; A. Ravitzky, *Crescas' Sermon on Passover and Studies in his Philosophy* [Hebrew] (Jerusalem: Israel Academy of Sciences and Humanities, 1988), introduction; W. Z. Harvey, "The First Publication of the Sermon of Rabbi Hasdai Crescas," [Hebrew] *Tarbiz* 58 (1989), 531–5; Harvey, *Physics and Metaphysics*, part 2; S. Feldman, "Crescas' Theological Determinism," *Da'at* 9 (1982), 3–28; S. Feldman, "A Debate Concerning Determinism in Late Medieval Jewish Philosophy," *Proceedings of the American Academy for Jewish Research* 51 (1984), 15–54. Abner's novel scientific views are mentioned by Isaac Pollegar: "[W]hen you expounded in public... that primary matter is substance and possesses form, that there is a vacuum, that the angels are corporeal, and the other heresies and farces which you asserted in your detestable book that you called *The New Philosophizing*" (J. Hecht, "The Polemical Exchange between Isaac Pollegar and Abner of Burgos/Alfonso of Valladolid According to Parma MS 2440," Ph.D. dissertation, New York University, 1993, 113–14). The book that Pollegar refers to is apparently lost, which makes it impossible to evaluate just what influence it might have had on Crescas, but the few remarks preserved here are suggestive.

5. The manuscripts, with various revisions, have been discussed most recently by N. Ophir, "Rabbi Hasdai Crescas as Philosophic Exegete of Rabbinic Sources," [Hebrew] Ph.D. dissertation, Hebrew University, 1993. The first edition, Ferrara (1555), was reprinted as a facsimile in 1970. The new edition by S. Fisher (Jerusalem, 1990) should be read together with the texts edited by Wolfson, *Crescas' Critique*; Harvey, "Hasdai Crescas' Critique"; Y. Eisenberg, *Torat ha-Beriah shel Hasdai Crescas* (Jerusalem: n.p., 1980); Y. Eisenberg, *Ha-Reshut Netunah* (Jerusalem: Haskel, 1982). A critical edition of the entire text is being prepared by Harvey. Although there is no complete translation, large sections have been rendered into English by Wolfson, *Crescas' Critique*; Harvey, "Hasdai Crescas' Critique"; Harvey, *Physics and Metaphysics*; S. Feldman, in *With Perfect Faith*, ed. J. D. Bleich (New York: Ktav, 1983); M. Kellner, *Dogma in Medieval Jewish Thought: From Maimonides to Abravanel* (Oxford: Littman Library, 1986). Short introductions to the book as a whole, with accompanying bibliographies, can be found in most encyclopedias of Judaism or philosophy, and in the standard histories of medieval Jewish philosophy. Several monographs have been written, including, besides those already mentioned, M. Joel, *Don Chasdai Creskas' religionsphilosophische Lehren* (Breslau: Schletter, 1886; translated into Hebrew, Tel Aviv: n.p., 1927); M. Waxman, *The Philosophy of Don Hasdai Crescas* (New York: Columbia University Press, 1920); S. B. Urbach, *The Philosophical Thought of Rabbi Hasdai Crescas* [Hebrew] (Jerusalem: n.p., 1961); E. Schweid, *The Religious Philosophy of Hasdai Crescas* [Hebrew] (Jerusalem: n.p., 1970). On specific topics, in addition to the literature cited throughout the notes, see the recent book by H. Kreisel, *Prophecy: The History of an Idea in Medieval Jewish Philosophy*, Amsterdam Studies in Jewish Thought, 8 (Dordrecht: Kluwer, 2001), 425–85.

6. The basic work is Wolfson, *Crescas' Critique*. For the broader approach, see especially S. Pines, *Scholasticism after Thomas Aquinas and the Teachings of Hasdai Crescas and his Predecessors*, trans. A. Ivry, republished in *The Collected Works of Shlomo Pines: Studies in the History of Jewish Thought* (Jerusalem: Magnes Press, 1997), v: 489–589; H. Davidson, *Proofs for Eternity, Creation, and the Existence of God in Medieval Islamic and Jewish Philosophy* (New York and Oxford: Oxford University Press, 1987); Harvey, *Physics and Metaphysics*.

7. The similarities between Crescas and Philoponus, the sixth-century Christian Neoplatonist and father of anti-Aristotelianism, are striking. They have been noted by Pines and others, and deserve further research. For an introduction to Philoponus' innovations, see R. Sorabji (ed.), *Philoponus and the Rejection of Aristotelian Science* (Ithaca: Cornell

University Press, 1987). For a full bibliography of Philoponus' influence in Arabic, see R. Wisnovsky, "Yahya al-Nahwi," in *Encyclopedia of Islam*, new ed. (Leiden: Brill, 2001), XI: 251–3.

8. See *Guide*, Preface to part 2, 2:1–2. See also Davidson, *Proofs* and Harvey, *Physics and Metaphysics*, for discussion of the proofs and Crescas' critique.

9. For method, see Wolfson, *Crescas' Critique*, 1–37, and index, for references to the authors mentioned here.

10. Wolfson, *Crescas' Critique*, 114.

11. The following discussion focuses on *Light of the Lord* 1:1, ch. 1, and 1:2, ch. 1. It is based on Wolfson, *Crescas' Critique*, 38–69, 114–27, 136–49, 178–91, 327–46, 391–425; Harvey, *Physics and Metaphysics*, ch. 1. For background in Aristotle, and history of the major issues discussed here, see E. Grant, *Much Ado about Nothing: Theories of Space and Vacuum from the Middle Ages to the Scientific Revolution* (Cambridge: Cambridge University Press, 1981), with full bibliography. The similar theories in Philoponus are explained in Sorabji (ed.), *Philoponus*.

12. Wolfson, *Crescas' Critique*, 146–7.

13. The following discussion focuses on *Light of the Lord* 1:1, ch. 1, 1:2, ch. 1, 1:1, ch. 6, and 4:1–2. It is based on Wolfson, *Crescas' Critique*, 70–92, 114–27, 150–7, 184–5, 190–203, 214–17, 346–66, 409–14, 423–63, 471–6; Harvey, *Physics and Metaphysics*, ch. 1. For the question of multiplicity of worlds in general, and in Scholasticism in particular, see Grant, *Planets, Stars, and Orbs*, ch. 8, with full bibliography. For problems related to natural place and motion, in Aristotle and the commentary tradition, see especially R. Glasner, "Gersonides' Theory of Natural Motion," *Early Science and Medicine* 1 (1996), 151–203. For Philoponus' similar view concerning relative weight and direction, see Sorabji (ed.), *Philoponus*.

14. The following discussion focuses on *Light of the Lord* 1:1, ch. 10, and 1:2, ch. 7. It is based on Wolfson, *Crescas' Critique*, 99–113, 114–27, 256–63, 569–602; A. Hyman, "Aristotle's 'First Matter' and Avicenna's and Averroes' 'Corporeal Form'," in *Harry A. Wolfson Jubilee Volume*, ed. S. Lieberman and A. Hyman (Jerusalem: American Academy for Jewish Research, 1965), I: 385–406; Harvey, *Physics and Metaphysics*, ch. 1. For further discussion of the Aristotelian and Neoplatonic background regarding celestial and sublunar matter, and the similar view of Philoponus, see especially F. A. J. de Haas, *John Philoponus' New Definition of Prime Matter: Aspects of its Background in Neoplatonism and the Ancient Commentary Tradition* (Leiden: Brill, 1997), with full bibliography.

15. The following discussion focuses on *Light of the Lord* 1:1, ch. 15, and
    1:2, ch. 11, as well as relevant sections in 3:1. It is based on Wolfson,
    Crescas' Critique, 93–8, 114–27, 282–91, 633–64; H. A. Wolfson,
    "Emanation and Creation ex Nihilo in Crescas," [Hebrew] in *Sefer Assaf*
    (Jerusalem: Mosad Harav Kook, 1953), 230–6; Pines, *Scholasticism*;
    W. Z. Harvey, "Albo's Discussion of Time," *Jewish Quarterly Review*
    70 (1980), 210–38; W. Z. Harvey, "The Term Hitdabbequt in Crescas'
    Definition of Time," *Jewish Quarterly Review* 71 (1981), 44–7; Harvey,
    Physics and Metaphysics, ch. 1; S. Feldman, "The Theory of Eternal
    Creation in Hasdai Crescas and Some of his Predecessors," *Viator* 11
    (1980), 289–320; T. M. Rudavsky, *Time Matters: Time, Creation, and
    Cosmology in Medieval Jewish Thought* (Albany: State University of
    New York Press, 2000), with full bibliography. As for the relationship to
    Spinoza, the negative view is argued, with reference to earlier studies,
    by Harvey, *Physics and Metaphysics*, 29–30.

16. The following discussion focuses on *Light of the Lord* 1:1, chs. 27–32,
    1:2, chs. 15–20, 1:3, chs. 1–6, 2:6, ch. 1. It is based on H. A. Wolfson,
    "Crescas on the Problem of Divine Attributes," *Jewish Quarterly Re-
    view* 7 (1916), 175–221; Harvey, "Hasdai Crescas' Critique"; W. Z.
    Harvey, "Crescas vs. Maimonides on Knowledge and Pleasure," in *A
    Straight Path: Studies in Medieval Philosophy and Culture, Essays
    in Honor of Arthur Hyman*, ed. R. Link-Salinger, R. Long, and
    C. Manekin (Washington, D.C.: The Catholic University of America
    Press, 1988), 113–23; W. Z. Harvey, "Knowledge of God According
    to Thomas Aquinas, Judah Romano, and Hasdai Crescas," [Hebrew]
    Jerusalem Studies in Jewish Thought 14 (1998), 223–38; W. Z. Harvey,
    "Maimonides' First Commandment, Physics, and Doubt," in *Hazon
    Nahum: Studies in Jewish Law, Thought, and History Presented to
    Dr. Norman Lamm*, ed. Y. Elman and J. S. Gurock (New York: Yeshiva
    University Press, 1998), 149–62; Harvey, *Physics and Metaphysics*,
    chs. 2–4. The similarity between Abner and Duns Scotus with respect
    to free will has already been mentioned; the critique of Pollegar is in
    Hecht, "The Polemical Exchange." For disputes about immortality in
    the fifteenth century, see the recent discussion by H. Tirosh-Rothschild,
    "Human Felicity: Fifteenth-Century Sephardic Perspectives on Happi-
    ness," in *In Iberia and Beyond: Hispanic Jews between Cultures*, ed.
    B. Cooperman (Newark: University of Delaware Press, 1998), 191–244.
    For the influence of the contemporary political situation on Crescas'
    philosophy, see Ophir, "Rabbi Hasdai Crescas as Philosophic Exegete of
    Rabbinic Sources"; for Crescas' influence on Leone Ebreo, see Harvey,
    Physics and Metaphysics, 114–17.

17. For the evaluation of Crescas' contribution, see Wolfson, *Crescas'*
    Critique, 114–27; S. Pines, *Scholasticism*; Harvey, *Physics and Meta-*
    physics; Y. T. Langermann, "Science in the Jewish Communities of the
    Iberian Peninsula," in his *The Jews and the Sciences in the Middle*
    Ages (Aldershot: Variorum, 1999). Wolfson, Pines, and Harvey empha-
    size Crescas' scientific achievement; Langermann argues that Crescas
    had no interest in science per se.
18. Wolfson, *Crescas' Critique*, 127.

18 The end and aftereffects of medieval Jewish philosophy

INTRODUCTION

Although the main center of the development and maturation of Jewish philosophy came to an end with the expulsion of the Jews from Spain, Jewish philosophy did not disappear. The exiled Sephardic Jews who were interested in philosophy took with them their philosophical libraries and continued their philosophical pursuits in their new domiciles. Some of these transplanted Spanish émigrés continued to do philosophy in the ways they knew and were used to; some, however, absorbed in various degrees the philosophical environment of their new abodes, which were considerably different from the philosophical culture in which they were educated. This was most notable in Italy, where some of the more prominent Sephardic exiles settled. After all, Italy was the home of the Renaissance, during which philosophy, as well as the arts and literature, underwent some significant transformations.

The very existence of a distinctive Renaissance philosophy has sometimes been questioned, and consequently a distinctive Renaissance Jewish philosophy has been challenged.[1] There is no question that medieval Aristotelianism, in its various forms, continued unabated throughout the fifteenth–seventeenth centuries, especially in the universities. And it found its adherents and advocates amongst Jewish philosophical thinkers, as we shall see. But there is no doubt that the philosophical climate in fifteenth-century Italy was changing and that new or different philosophical books were being read and made part of the philosophical culture of the period. This was most evident, but not exclusively so, in the revival and rediscovery of the Platonic tradition. Throughout the fifteenth century new translations of Plato's writings, especially those unknown in the Middle Ages, were made available. This recovery of Plato reached its culmination with the complete Latin translation of Plato's dialogues by Marsilio Ficino in 1484. In 1492 Ficino published his Latin translation of the *Enneads* of Plotinus, a philosopher who was virtually unknown in the West until Ficino's translation.[2] Translations from other Platonic philosophers, such as Porphyry and Proclus, were also made available. Although Platonism did not become an integral component of the academic study of philosophy, it did attract some of the more intellectually adventurous thinkers of the fifteenth and sixteenth centuries, such as Ficino, Pico della Mirandola, and Francesco Patrizzi. Indeed, some scholars have maintained that there is a strong strain of Platonism in the founder of modern science, Galileo. This return to Plato will be evident among several Jewish philosophers of the period.[3]

An account of philosophical thought during this period should not neglect the world of science. After all, scientific study and speculation were part of the medieval philosophical curriculum, and the scientists of the early modern period considered themselves to be "natural philosophers," or "philosophers of nature." Insofar as these scientific speculations led to the development of new and, in some cases, radical ideas, we can legitimately speak of a "scientific revolution," which began in the sixteenth century and culminated with Newton at the end of the seventeenth century. And in between we have Copernicus, Galileo, Kepler, Descartes, and Leibniz. Although some of the Jewish thinkers of the period were largely oblivious to these newer developments, some were not; after all, Tycho Brahe had as one of his assistants R. David Gans, along with Johannes Kepler. And one of Galileo's more faithful students was R. Joseph Solomon del Medigo. The story of Jewish philosophy during the "long century" of 1450–1650 should then include some discussion of the impact of the new science.

Finally, Renaissance philosophy is permeated with a feature of medieval Jewish thought that in the Middle Ages was for the most part kept distinct from philosophy – mysticism, especially the kabbalah. By the end of the fourteenth century the mystical theosophy of Iberian Jewry had eclipsed philosophy in its influence and by the fifteenth century had begun to infiltrate Christian circles, so much so that one can speak of a "Christian kabbalah" during the

Renaissance.[4] As we shall see, many of the characters in the story I am about to tell were touched by kabbalah in one way or another. Some adopted it wholeheartedly; others rejected it completely; and some paid their respects to it and then went their own way. It is a factor that needs to be considered in any discussion of Jewish philosophical thought during this period.

THE PERSISTENCE OF MEDIEVAL JEWISH ARISTOTELIANISM IN THE ITALIAN RENAISSANCE: ELIJAH DEL MEDIGO

Not only Spain but Italy too provided a home for the pursuit of philosophy by Jews during the late medieval period. Both in Sicily and on the mainland a philosophical literature in Hebrew emerged based primarily upon Maimonides, but with a good dose of Aquinas thrown in, primarily to counter the more radical interpretations of Aristotle and Maimonides suggested by philosophers, both Jewish and Christian, influenced by Averroes. We can therefore speak of an indigenous Italo-Jewish philosophical tradition in the medieval period that was essentially Aristotelian in character.[5] This tradition was perpetuated in a more "radical" form by Elijah del Medigo (c. 1460–1493), who adopted an Averroist reading of Aristotle. A native of Crete, del Medigo came to Italy to study medicine at the University of Padua. Since the medical curriculum at that time consisted of the study of philosophy as well as the sciences, del Medigo was introduced to the study of Aristotle by teachers who were deeply influenced by Averroes' interpretation of Aristotle.[6] Del Medigo perpetuated this tradition. Evidently he lectured in Padua, something quite unusual for a Jew at that time; eventually he became a teacher of Pico della Mirandola. The latter was interested in many things, and among them was Aristotle, as well as Plato, and the key to Aristotle in those days was Averroes. Del Medigo became Pico's tutor in Averroes, and translated into Latin several of Averroes' treatises for Pico's use. Eventually their relationship came to an end, most likely because Pico became less interested in Aristotle and Averroes and turned his attention and loyalty to Plato and the kabbalah, subjects in which del Medigo had minimal or no interest. As we shall see, Pico was to hire another Jewish teacher for instruction in kabbalah.

Del Medigo's Averroism is most apparent in his translations and commentaries on those short treatises Averroes had written on one of the more controversial themes in medieval philosophy – the immortality of the soul, a topic that was to occupy the minds of many Renaissance thinkers as well. Averroes had formulated a radical theory of human immortality that del Medigo taught to Pico, who probably rejected it and thus concluded that he needed a different teacher. Averroes' theory is not easy to state succinctly, for it is quite complicated and he appears to have modified it throughout his career. In two obscure paragraphs in *De Anima* 3:5 Aristotle suggests that the primary efficient cause of human thinking is some eternal, incorporeal intellect that is always thinking. His main commentator in antiquity, Alexander of Aphrodisias, formulated an entire vocabulary for this suggestion, whereby this active cause of human thought became known as the "Active, or Agent, Intellect," whereas the human intellect became the "material intellect." When engaged in thinking the material intellect becomes the "intellect in act"; when perfected it is the "acquired intellect." The Agent Intellect is transcendent and eternal; indeed, for Alexander it is God. Although Alexander was not obsessed with the problem of immortality, he did suggest that we can attain immortality by perfecting our intellect and thereby achieve conjunction with the Agent Intellect. It is not clear whether or not for Alexander the achieved state of immortality is individual.[7]

By the time this doctrine reached Averroes it had undergone several alternative interpretations and modifications. Ultimately Averroes developed his own theory, according to which human immortality is achieved, as Alexander had suggested, by conjunction, indeed union, with the Agent Intellect. But whereas Alexander had been relatively silent or ambivalent on the issue of individual immortality, Averroes was quite clear: there is no individual immortality. He reached this radical and striking conclusion as the result of his view that there really is only *one* material intellect, which all humans share individually while they have corporeal existence. However, when an individual dies, that which individuates them, all their corporeal history, disappears; all that remains is the one material intellect, which at this stage is no longer individuated. Indeed, the material intellect is really just the Agent Intellect as seen from the human point of view; or, the Agent Intellect is the form of the material intellect. No matter how we look at it, our immortality has nothing personal about or in it. In reality there is just one intellect, and ultimately all are one in it.[8]

In his translations and commentaries on Averroes' short essays on this topic del Medigo faithfully reports this theory and offers no criticisms of it. According to Kalman Bland, del Medigo believed that Averroes' reading of Aristotle was correct and that Aristotle had the true psychology. In short, Averroes had the right idea about human immortality. On the other hand, del Medigo realized that Jewish religious tradition teaches individual reward and punishment after death, thus implying a plurality of intellects. Moreover, it emphasizes the doctrine of the resurrection of the dead, a notion difficult to reconcile with intellectual conjunction. Sensing some difficulty here, del Medigo explicitly expresses his loyalty to religious tradition in the following: "Let none of my co-religionists think that the opinion which I firmly believe is this [Aristotelian] one. For my belief is truly the belief of the Jews."[9] This, coupled with his commitment to Averroism, allows one to see in del Medigo the seeds of the so-called "double truth theory," to which we shall turn shortly.

For reasons that are still unclear del Medigo left Italy in 1490 and returned to his native Crete, where he composed his last work *Behinat ha-Dat (The Examination of Religion)*. Whereas the treatises on Averroes have now only historical interest, this latter work raises some interesting issues concerning the relationship between revealed religion and philosophy. And it is in this work that the issue of the "double truth theory" arises with full force. The work appears to be modeled after Averroes' treatise *On the Harmony between Religion and Philosophy (Fasl al-Maqal)*, in which Averroes dealt with a variety of issues, especially the legitimacy of philosophy and its relationship to theology. Not only did Averroes legitimize philosophy, he made its study obligatory for those who are qualified.[10]

Del Medigo's *Behinat ha-Dat* likewise attempts to legitimize philosophy before Jewish law, but he does not stretch the Torah beyond recognition to make it say that philosophy is commanded. The Bible permits, even recommends, rational inquiry, but it does not require it. For most people there is simply no need to philosophize: they either have no ability for the subject or are uninterested in it. This weakening of the obligation to do philosophy is based upon a strict application of a "division of labor principle," according to which philosophy and revealed religion constitute two very disparate disciplines, whose methods and goals are quite different. Del Medigo speaks of philosophy and religion as having procedures and purposes that are domain-limited. In general the two domains do not overlap, and hence there is usually no need nor justification for interference or intervention. Here the biblical commandment in Deuteronomy 19:14 not to transgress boundaries is most relevant. Harmony between religion and philosophy is not obtained by eliminating theology and the theologian, as urged by Averroes, but by making sure that the philosopher and theologian are each separately doing what they are supposed to do.[11]

However, things are not always so peaceful between religion and philosophy, even when the philosopher and the theologian are minding their own stores, and del Medigo is aware of this fact. There are, he claims, situations where the philosopher has the right, indeed the duty to correct what the theologian has said. Let us consider a doctrine that vexes del Medigo a great deal, the kabbalistic theory of the ten *sefirot*.[12] According to del Medigo, this doctrine impugns and impairs divine unity. Since the latter has been proved philosophically and is the basic principle of Judaism, the doctrine of the *sefirot* is to be rejected, no matter how it is interpreted. Here del Medigo exhibits considerable courage, since the kabbalah had achieved great authority at this time, and not only amongst Jews.[13] Religion must be immune from absurdity. And it is part of the business of the philosopher to point out the irrationality of beliefs that are nonsensical. Religion is not philosophy, but it cannot hide behind the division of labor principle in order to preach nonsense, even if the nonsense is "Jewish."[14]

Let us return to the aforementioned remarks concerning individual immortality. Del Medigo seems to suggest that philosophy holds death to be the end of the individual, whereas Judaism presumes individual immortality. In general, such divergence on specific issues is the considered doctrine of the Christian Averroists, who were willing in the final analysis to sacrifice reason on the altar of religious faith.[15] On this very issue of immortality Averroes himself maintained that it does not matter too much which doctrine of the afterlife one adheres to, as long as one believes in some such doctrine. If the masses prefer the resurrection doctrine, that is acceptable; if the philosophers believe in intellectual conjunction, that too is acceptable. What matters is how one behaves: if the philosopher and the ordinary person behave rightly, both will be rewarded; it is God's business how this reward is to be realized.[16] It is tempting to read del Medigo on this issue in this way. Like his philosophical mentor, he too is concerned only with the general principle of reward and punishment, which he takes to be central to Judaism. How this principle is to be interpreted is another question, one that does not have to be decided in a dogmatic manner. Since it is a belief that is action-oriented, as long as the desired behavior is achieved, it matters little how the principle is interpreted. God is here not in the details.

It is not easy to understand del Medigo's real beliefs on this matter. Perhaps he "was not above dissimulating," as Herbert Davidson and Kalman Bland have suggested.[17] His earlier appeal to religious tradition may have been just advocacy of a belief that had some political and pedagogical use, as both Averroes and Maimonides suggested with respect to some religious dogmas. It may have been that he denied individual immortality. Or, perhaps he is simply inconsistent. According to Julius Guttmann, del Medigo wavers between the original position of Averroes and the "double truth theory" of the Christian Averroists. At times he sounds like Averroes and seems prepared to minimize any apparent conflict as a relatively minor matter that could be resolved. But, as we have seen, on occasion he seems to recoil from this position in the manner of a Christian Averroist.[18] This ambivalence seems to have been a feature of some of his Paduan colleagues as well, such as Pietro Pomponazzi, who also wavered between a "radical" philosophical position and traditional religious affirmation, especially on the question of immortality.[19]

BETWEEN ARISTOTLE AND PLATO: ISAAC ABRAVANEL

In 1492, two years after Elijah del Medigo left Italy for his native Crete, Isaac Abravanel and his family went into Italian exile from their native Iberia. All his financial and political connections and experience could not save him and his fellow Jews from expulsion or forced conversion. Settling first in Naples and then eventually living the last decade of his life in Venice, Isaac Abravanel spent these years in Italy primarily in intellectual pursuits. Although he had begun or completed several works in Spain or Portugal, most of his vast output was initiated or completed in Italy. Abravanel's main concerns were exegetical and theological, although his first work was a purely philosophical essay on a topic in Aristotle's natural philosophy, *The Forms of the Elements (Tzurot ha-Yesodot)*. As he was to say at the end of his life, the two axes around which his thinking and writing revolved were the Bible and Maimonides' *Guide of the Perplexed*, on both of which he wrote commentaries. Although he was not a philosopher in the sense that Elijah del Medigo was – indeed, as we shall see, he would have been angered by such an attribution – his writings are deeply entrenched in the medieval Aristotelian framework, even when he is critical of this tradition. In this respect we can see him as well as del Medigo as among the last remnants of Aristotelianism in Jewish thought.

Although he was not unfamiliar with some Renaissance literary and philosophical trends, Abravanel's intellectual outlook was essentially medieval. Enormously erudite and well read in Latin classical and medieval literature, he presents a kind of philosophical skepticism or "weariness" that has led some interpreters to label him as an "antirationalist." There are indeed arguments in Abravanel against philosophy in general and in particular against Aristotle and his followers, both Jewish and Muslim; but his criticisms are almost always philosophical. Moreover, when he advances his own views, especially on the more vexing problems in medieval religious thought, such as creation of the universe, his treatment is highly philosophical. In some very important respects he can be considered a moderate Maimonidean. Although he shared some of the criticisms leveled against Maimonides by Hasdai Crescas, he rejected some of the more extreme views of the latter on such questions as divine omniscience and creation of the universe. Like Maimonides and Crescas, he saw himself as a defender of the faith, but he performed this role in a more conservative manner, carefully using philosophy to serve as a "handmaiden" to theology without casting her out of the house when the job had been done. This can be illustrated by examining his discussions of two of the more vexing issues in medieval philosophical and theological literature: creation of the universe and immortality of the soul. Unlike Elijah del Medigo, who showed little interest in the former question, Abravanel was obsessed with it. In addition to his lengthy discussion of creation in his commentary on Genesis, he wrote two monographs devoted to this subject: *The Deeds of God (Mifalot Elohim)* and *New Heavens (Shamayyim Hadashim)*.

Abravanel defends explicitly and vigorously the traditional doctrine of creation *ex nihilo*, which theory he believed was inadequately defended by Maimonides, unjustifiably rejected by Gersonides, and betrayed by Crescas' eternal emanation interpretation of it. He defends the traditional version of this theory, according to which God, employing no intermediaries, created the entire universe from no preexisting matter at the first instant of time, which itself was created with the creation of the world.

After canvassing and criticizing the various views on creation, especially Gersonides' rejection of creation *ex nihilo*, Abravanel then proceeds to develop his own defense of this doctrine. He first argues that the concept is not logically absurd, as the philosophers had maintained in their dictum *ex nihilo nihil fit*. Here he relies heavily upon the principle of God's infinite power, defined as his ability to do whatever is logically possible. He then distinguishes between that which is absolutely, or logically, impossible and that which is impossible relative to some agent. Michelangelo needs marble to make his statue of David, since his creative power is finite, no matter how great. But God's creative power is unlimited; hence, he can make a world without requiring any pre-mundane eternal matter.[20] Indeed, in doing the latter God exhibits his omnipotence most clearly. Once Abravanel has shown that creation *ex nihilo* is logically possible, he then proceeds to argue that the universe has been created, as follows: If physical bodies are essentially corruptible, as was shown by Plato and John Philoponus, then sooner or later the physical world will self-destruct. But, as Aristotle himself proved, whatever has an end has a beginning.[21]

Abravanel's conservatism is also evident in his account of individual (human) immortality. If he had known of Elijah del Medigo's sympathetic, perhaps sincere, defense of Averroes' doctrine, he would have sharply disagreed with his coreligionist on this matter. Not only does he defend the traditional doctrine of individual immortality, but he rejects the whole Averroist psychology upon which the denial of individual immortality rests. Most important, in several places he expresses doubts about the doctrine of the Agent Intellect. There is no conjunction with the Agent Intellect, according to Abravanel. Nor is immortality achievable through intellectual perfection, especially through philosophy and science, as Maimonides and Gersonides had maintained. Love of God through observance of the commandments is the *summum bonum*.

Indeed, Abravanel is much closer to Plato's psychology than he is to Aristotle's doctrine of the soul, for he holds that the human soul is a separate (incorporeal) substance, not just an embodied set of capacities, or faculties, for cognition, as many of the medieval Aristotelians had believed, including Maimonides, according to Abravanel's reading of the *Guide*. Although God created all human souls, these souls are inherently incorruptible by virtue of incorporeality; their domicile in the body is only temporary. Abravanel is clearly wedded to Plato's dualistic psychology: the soul and the body are two ontologically distinct entities.

Upon death each human soul survives and returns to God, its source (Ecclesiastes 12:8). However, at some time in the future each soul will return to its own original body, which will be resurrected and then both will be judged. If God can create the world *ex nihilo*, why cannot he revive the dead? Further, the traditional doctrines of individual immortality and resurrection of the dead are joined by another (Greek) idea – transmigration of souls. This doctrine entered Judaism fairly late, but was rejected by Saadya and is ignored by Maimonides and Gersonides. Nevertheless, it found its way into Jewish mystical literature, and by Abravanel's time it became a widely held view in the kabbalah. Abravanel is open to it and uses it to explain the biblical practice of levirite marriage: the soul of the dead brother comes to inhabit the body of the son of his widow and living brother, who has married his widow.[22] Abravanel rejects, however, those versions of this doctrine that allow for transmigration of human souls into animal bodies, and conversely.

Abravanel's discussions of creation and immortality manifest his ambivalence toward Platonism. Whereas his cosmology is anti-Platonic, his psychology is Platonic. In several of his writings there are other favorable comments about Plato and the Platonists. There is even perhaps a reference to Plotinus, whom he refers to under the name "Polotino."[23] However, as his comments show, Abravanel's familiarity with Plotinus' thought is at best superficial. For example, he considers Plotinus to have been a student of Aristotle. It is true that in these scattered and not always accurate or consistent comments about Platonic philosophy Abravanel was cognizant of the newer Platonic philosophy of the Renaissance. But he was not a Platonist in his philosophy, to the extent that he had a consistent philosophical framework; nor was he familiar with some of the newer translations of Plato's dialogues, especially those that were unknown in the Middle Ages, such as the *Symposium*. He made use of Plato, to the extent that he knew Plato, when it suited his purposes. But for a more genuine and thoroughgoing assimilation of Platonic philosophy into Judaism we must turn to some other Jewish thinkers, one of whom was Isaac Abravanel's own son Judah.

THE REVIVAL OF PLATONISM: YOHANAN ALEMANNO, JUDAH ABRAVANEL, AND JUDAH MOSCATO

Perhaps the earliest of the Renaissance Jewish Platonists was Yohanan Alemanno (1434–1504). Born in France but residing in Italy for most of his life, Alemanno represented precisely the new trend in philosophy that Elijah del Medigo resisted and criticized: Neoplatonic kabbalah. In his writings one finds a complex blend of ideas drawn from a variety of sources, but mainly from the medieval Arabic and Hebrew Platonic literature and the kabbalah. Yet, he was also open to the newer Plato of the Florentine circle, since he became one of Pico's Jewish teachers. It is, however, noteworthy that his knowledge of the newer Plato and the Neoplatonists is less influential upon his thinking than that of the medieval Jewish and Muslim Platonists. Although he mentions Plotinus, Porphyry, and Proclus, his knowledge of their writings is not deep, and probably only secondhand. What was of primary interest to him was the compatibility, indeed identity of Platonism, as he understood it, and kabbalah. And this was what interested Pico as well. Both harnessed these two thought systems to produce a practical philosophy that was explicitly magical and theurgic. In this regard he reflects another aspect of Renaissance thought: the marriage of philosophy, mysticism, and the occult.

One of the more Platonic themes in Alemanno's thought is his conception of the ideal political leader. This is expressed in a laudatio dedicated to Lorenzo de' Medici. The laudatio was a common literary form throughout the Renaissance, and it was cultivated by Jewish, as well as Christian, intellectuals.[24] In Alemanno's panegyric we find a blend of Platonic and biblical motifs centered around the figure of King Solomon, the "wisest of all kings." Wanting to flatter and placate his political patron, Alemanno presents Lorenzo as a modern King Solomon, indeed as Plato's ideal philosopher-king. Relying heavily upon Averroes' *Commentary on Plato's Republic*, Alemanno portrays Solomon (and Lorenzo by implication) as the ideal prince, whose practical wisdom, as well as theoretical knowledge, was manifest throughout his long reign and in many ways. Not only did Solomon master all the standard sciences, he was also most skilled in magic, astrology, and mysticism, all of which he used in his role as king. But as great as his theoretical and political virtues were, Solomon was primarily motivated by his love of God, which reached such a level of passion that he attained the *summum bonum* – conjunction with God. It is no wonder that he wrote Song of Songs, on which Alemanno himself wrote a commentary. In that biblical book the beloved is God and the lover is King Solomon, who, as the prototype of the perfect ruler and the perfect philosopher, attains immortality through his intense passion for God. The intellectual conjunction with the Agent Intellect, which for the Averroist-minded Jewish philosophers such as Elijah del Medigo constituted immortality, even though it meant the obliteration of individuality, is now replaced with the Platonic-kabbalistic idea of love. As Solomon's song teaches, love is stronger than death (Song of Songs 8:6). And in this passionate conjunction, which is a reunion with God, human individuality is preserved.

Jewish Platonism is more evident and more philosophically represented in Judah Abravanel (c. 1460–1523), who went into Italian exile with his father. Unlike Isaac, Judah Abravanel was not a financier or diplomat but a physician, and continued to practice this profession in Italy, primarily in Naples, although he spent some time in Genoa. It was probably in the latter city that he began the book that made him famous, *The Dialogues of Love (Dialoghi d'Amore)*.[25] Penned under the name of "Leone Ebreo," it is still uncertain in which language he originally wrote this work. It has been alternatively maintained that he initially wrote it in Spanish, Hebrew, or Latin. Whatever the original language, it became a bestseller throughout the Renaissance, translated into Spanish (three times), French (twice), Latin, and Hebrew.[26] Written in dialogue form with two characters Philo (love) and Sophia (wisdom), whose names already set the tone and thrust of the book, the work discusses a variety of topics, many of which clearly manifest the newer Plato of the

Florentine Platonic Academy of Marsilio Ficino, who himself also wrote a *Book of Love* (*Libro d'Amore*), as well as a lengthy commentary upon Plato's main dialogue on love, the *Symposium*. Indeed, Leone's work itself is in many respects a commentary on and a sympathetic critique of the *Symposium*.

Both the title, style, and content of the work mark major departures from the intellectual outlook of his father, Isaac Abravanel. Other than the traditional idea of the *summum bonum* as man's love of God, love as such was of no interest to Isaac. Moreover, even though Isaac was well read in Latin, he had no real interest in classical belles lettres. Judah's work abounds in discussions of Greek mythological themes, with overt references to Homer and Ovid. Indeed, the *Dialoghi d'Amore* may be the first Jewish work to exhibit such an interest in pagan religion and literature. In these discussions Judah attempts to find philosophical significance in the Greek myths and to show the similarities, as well as differences, with biblical analogues. Nor is there in Judah any real worry about one of the main preoccupations of medieval philosophy, the relationship between reason and revelation. Whereas his father Isaac was most concerned to draw the lines sharply and to limit the scope and power of reason, Judah sees no problem. He assumes that philosophy is the key to human happiness and does not worry at all about conflicts between philosophy and prophecy. Any apparent or putative conflict would be resolvable through interpretation. Although Judah makes it quite evident that he is a faithful Jew and makes plentiful references to the Bible and postbiblical authors, such as Solomon ibn Gabirol and Maimonides, for the most part the *Dialoghi* is a philosophical book, addressed to philosophically literate readers of any religion. In part this explains its success throughout the sixteenth and seventeenth centuries.

Before we examine the Platonic dimension of the *Dialoghi*, we must note the presence of a medieval remnant in Judah Abravanel's thinking. This is his Aristotelian-Averroist conception of the nature of human immortality. Still wedded to Aristotle's psychological theory and its ramifications for the survival of the human intellect, Abravanel offers a summary of the various medieval accounts of the human intellect, all couched in the language of Aristotle and Averroes. What is especially noteworthy is his conclusion: he eventually opts for a modified Alexandrian theory of the intellect, whereby our immortality consists in conjunction with the Agent Intellect, who is none other than God. Although some of the medieval Jewish and Muslim philosophers, such as Gersonides and al-Farabi, were sympathetic to Alexander's psychology, they refused to identify the Agent Intellect with God. Not so Abravanel. His Agent Intellect/God is both the formal and efficient cause of all reality: the formal, insofar as it contains all the ideas of all things; the efficient insofar as it is the productive cause of things. Yet even in this most Aristotelian digression, he cannot help but introduce a Plotinian theme: the ultimate cause of things is also the "home" to which all things return to find their final felicity.[27] This return is achieved by love, as Alemanno had emphasized; but Abravanel gives this love a distinctly intellectual cast. His love is identical with knowledge of God. It is admittedly a passion, but it is an emotion stimulated and governed by cognition. Echoing Maimonides and anticipating Spinoza, Abravanel enunciates the goal of the "intellectual love of God." Like Maimonides and Alemanno, Abravanel too links this motif to King Solomon's Song of Songs; but for him the guide back to God is furnished by philosophy, not prophecy or mysticism.[28] The "circle of being" is identical with the circle of love, and both are expressed and activated through intellectual love, a theme that pervades Abravanel's cosmology as well as his psychology.[29]

Abravanel's cosmological speculations constitute the bulk of the third book, the longest of the extant three books of the *Dialoghi*.[30] In his discussions of the question of the creation of the world, Abravanel is clearly aware not only of Plato's *Timaeus*, but of the later Platonic interpretations of this work, including that of Plotinus, whom he mentions by name.[31] But unlike his father, Abravanel is quite convinced that the world was created out of some kind of formless matter, which he likes to call "chaos," following the practice of Ovid and Boccaccio.[32] Interestingly, Abravanel makes no mention of Gersonides, the foremost advocate of this doctrine in medieval Jewish philosophy, but relies solely upon Plato. Although he is aware that this is not the accepted doctrine of traditional Judaism, it is clear that this is his view. The traditional doctrine of creation *ex nihilo* he attributes to the "faithful," who are represented by Sophia, the questioner in the dialogues. The doctrine of creation *ex nihilo*, although logically possible, is contrary to the widely accepted view of the philosophers that nothing comes from nothing.[33] Philo, who is the teacher of Sophia, adheres to the latter principle. However,

Abravanel does make one concession to tradition: he claims that according to Plato himself this matter is eternally created by God, an idea that one could get from the *Timaeus* if one reads it in a Plotinian mode, whereby everything, including matter, emanates eternally from the One.[34]

Once eternal matter is introduced into the story of creation, Abravanel proceeds to construct a philosophical midrash on the theme of God's creating the world from the primeval chaos. In this account God is called "the father," whereas matter, or chaos, is called "the mother."[35] Again, Abravanel is alluding to the *Timaeus*, especially Plato's characterization of the substratum of creation as a "receptacle," which in Greek is feminine in gender. As noted, he corrects this account, which he finds in Ovid as well, stating that matter too is created by God, albeit eternally. The world is produced by the father's fashioning a cosmos out of formless matter.

Later in the book, however, Abravanel proceeds to offer us a somewhat different cosmological scheme. It still preserves the key Platonic motif of eternal formless matter but introduces a new factor into the story. The stage-setting of this scene in the dialogue is an interesting analysis of beauty, which leads Abravanel to enter into a discussion of Platonic Forms. After reporting the state of the issue, especially Aristotle's critique of the Platonic hypostatization of the Forms, Abravanel again sides with Plato. But it is not with Plato himself, as it is with some of the later Platonists. For he now introduces a version of the Philonic Logos theory: between God and the physical world there is an intermediary agent containing all the Forms as paradigms. Abravanel labels this entity with different names: "the Idea of the universe" (407), "the first intellect" (414–15), "primary beauty" (405), and "wisdom" (415). In the language of Plotinus, Abravanel proceeds to characterize this entity as eternally emanating from God, who is "higher" than it.[36] Abravanel's first intellect is indeed none other than Plotinus' Nous.

Equally striking in this account of creation is Abravanel's revamping of the father–mother theme. The mother of creation is now this first beauty, intellect, or wisdom. Here he weaves together Platonic cosmology with Jewish midrashic lore, especially the interpretation of Proverbs and Song of Songs, especially Proverbs' elevation of wisdom as God's assistant in making the world (Proverbs ch. 8). One should keep in mind that in Hebrew, Greek, Latin, and the modern languages deriving from Latin, the term for wisdom is feminine in gender. Accordingly, in this midrash the world has, as its active cause, the father, God; the passive cause is its mother, wisdom or beauty.[37] The physical world is then "the son" produced from God and wisdom. In this midrash matter has been relegated to a back seat in favor of Intellect; but this too is good Platonism.

It is not obvious whether these two cosmological schemes can be made consistent. Indeed, it is not evident that Abravanel saw himself as propounding a systematic cosmology. His cosmological discussions may be just Platonic midrashim on Genesis 1, rather like Plato's own myth of creation in the *Timaeus*, which Plato confesses is just a likely story. If we simply ignore the metaphorical aspects of these midrashim and focus upon their more philosophical aspects, we can easily see the Platonic imprint. It is quite clear that Abravanel is committed to some kind of Platonic account of creation. Such an account acknowledges the eternity of matter and the role of an intermediary intellectual paradigm as God's "instrument" in creation.

Judah Abravanel is not alone in his Platonic–Plotinian conception of creation. It was echoed by a later Jewish thinker, Judah Moscato of Mantua (c. 1530–1593). Although mainly a pulpit rabbi, Moscato composed two works, *Qol Yehudah* (*The Voice of Judah*), a long commentary upon Judah Halevi's *Kuzari*, and a collection of sermons, entitled *Nefutzot Yehudah* (*The Dispersions of Judah*). The former is a virtual encyclopedia of medieval Jewish philosophy used to elucidate Halevi's work. The latter is a partial selection from Moscato's homilies on diffferent portions from the Bible and includes also several dedicatory sermons.[38] Since some of these sermons are quite philosophical, it is likely that they were intended to be read at leisure rather than to be heard on the spot in the synagogue. In addition to their philosophical interest, several of the sermons contain references, among the earliest in Hebrew literature, to the long-lost Jewish Platonist Philo of Alexandria. For over a millennium Philo was unknown to his coreligionists until he was rediscovered by Italian Renaissance Jews. Moscato not only mentions Philo by name but refers to several of his books.[39]

The Philonic presence in Moscato is not just window dressing. It is an important element in the overall Platonic cosmological imprint in Moscato's thinking about creation, which is found in several of his sermons. In Sermon 8 Moscato interprets the opening sentence of Genesis as follows:

First of all God emanated forth a created intellect as an effect, unitary and perfect; he endowed it with the patterns of all things...In the emanation of this effect not only did God create all things but he created them in the most perfect manner. This intellect has been called by the Platonists and other ancient philosophers "God's son," as is recorded by the sage Pico della Mirandola in a short essay that he wrote on the heavenly and divine love (Sermon 8, 21c [note Moscato's reference to Pico]; my translation).

This "intellectual son of God" is of course Philo's Logos and Plotinus' Nous. Not only is Moscato content to incorporate this Platonic motif into his exegesis of Genesis 1, but he is also not reluctant to label Plotinus' second hypostasis by the metaphor "son," despite the obvious Christian connotations of this term. And like Plotinus, Moscato mentions the vertical vectors of Intellect: it turns upward and imitates God, the One, and downward and produces the World-Soul, the third of Plotinus' hypostases. The latter too has both upward and downward vectors: by looking up it receives from Intellect the patterns, or Forms; in looking down it produces souls and the corporeal forms of earthly substances, the most important of which is humankind, who, unlike all other terrestrial substances, is capable of receiving intellect. Moreover, Moscato tells his audience that the light mentioned in Psalms 104 and in several midrashim refers to God's son, Intellect, which is "the place of the Forms" and the "glory of God's creation."[40]

In several of his sermons Moscato addresses another theme in Platonic philosophy. Most medieval epistemological discussions were dominated by Aristotelian empiricism. In Sermon 9, entitled "Man the Microcosm," Moscato develops Plato's theory of innate ideas and finds this theme in Psalms 19:9, where it is written: "the precepts of the Lord are right, rejoicing the heart." The Hebrew term for "precepts" in this verse is unusual: instead of one of the many biblical legal terms, the passage has the term *pequdei*, which literally means "deposited." Moscato interprets this passage in a Platonic vein: the teachings of the Lord are placed in humankind's mind by God. These teachings include not only the commandments, but also the first principles of knowledge. Moscato is quite aware that his adoption and adaptation of Plato's theory is anti-Aristotelian.

Moreover, he explains our cognitive career by utilizing both Plato's doctrine of recollection and the biblical story of Adam's and Eve's sin. Their choice to indulge in corporeal pleasure caused forgetfulness of their original intellectual endowment. Henceforth, the human species is continually striving to recall what it originally knew.

This incorporation of Platonic innatism is fortified by his claim that the human intellect is independent of the body. Moscato states:

[T]he intellect is not dependent upon the imagination, as if the latter were the instrument for its intellectual activity. In this regard the intellect's activity differs from the activity of perception ... the activity of the intellect is complete in itself without [the need of] an instrument ... (*Qol Yehudah*, 3:53a; my translation).

However, Moscato makes a concession to Aristotle: in our present condition the human mind needs sensory data for knowledge. Here Moscato sounds rather like Duns Scotus and William of Ockham, who claimed that in theory the human intellect could have intuitive, that is, direct apprehension of external objects, but in our present mortal state we need the help of sense-percepts.[41]

THE SCIENTIFIC REVOLUTION: JOSEPH SOLOMON DEL MEDIGO

Renaissance thought was marked not only by the rediscovery and assimilation of ancient philosophy. It also reflects some of the new ideas of the "scientific revolution" of the sixteenth and seventeenth centuries. Philosophy and science were not wholly distinct disciplines in the Middle Ages, nor were they completely separate during the Renaissance. It is not accidental that one of the major centers of philosophical activity in Italy at this time was also an important place for scientific and medical study – the University of Padua. We have already noted that Elijah del Medigo studied medicine and philosophy there. In the seventeenth century another Jew from Crete, perhaps a family relation of Elijah, studied at Padua with Galileo and became one of the earliest Jewish "converts" to the "new science" – Joseph Solomon del Medigo (1591–1655). (Henceforth I shall refer to him by his Hebrew acronym "Yashar.") However, what makes Yashar both perplexing and intriguing is his incorporation of Neoplatonic and kabbalistic elements into his new scientific approach to philosophy. These diverse elements are not always easy to disentangle in his writings. Moreover, his habit of hiding his views behind the voice of other spokesmen, some fictitious, makes it difficult to determine Yashar's real positions. Nevertheless, several salient strands in his thought can be discerned.[42]

Yashar's "new science" begins with a critique of Aristotelian natural philosophy and metaphysics. Like Hasdai Crescas, for whom he has the highest appreciation, Yashar rejects the basic assumptions and principles of Aristotelian philosophy, which by the seventeenth century was losing ground in Italy, even at Padua. But unlike Crescas, whose critique of Aristotle was theologically motivated, Yashar's rejection of Aristotle was based upon the adoption of an alternative physical theory and natural philosophy. Underlying his critique is a certain disappointment that Aristotle is insufficiently empirical and rigorous. Although he recognizes that Aristotle's philosophy is grounded in sense perception and the logical demands of strict proof, Yashar accuses Aristotle of not being faithful to his own methods. In language echoing Galileo's remarks, Yashar often chides Aristotle for not getting his hands dirty in the laboratory or going outside his study and looking at how falling bodies fall. If he had done so, he would have seen that his hylomorphic theory of nature was not based upon the facts. Skeptical of Aristotle's essentialism, which he sees as a form of disguised Platonism, Yashar opts for a physics based upon the observed properties of bodies, many of which would be regarded by Aristotle as "accidental" and thus non-essential. The whole notion of form or substance is replaced with the concept of separable, or transient, and inseparable, or semi-permanent, properties, both of which are observable. These properties are "effective," or causal, and there is no need to posit unobservable underlying "formal" causes, or essences. Referring to Galileo, Yashar claims:

Aristotle's principle of essential forms ... is based upon thin air and is nothing but wild dreams ... According to Aristotle himself, the qualities themselves are the causes of all changes ... The essences are not perceived; therefore, they are of no use (Yashar, *Sefer Elim* 49; my translation).

Not only is Yashar critical of Aristotle's terrestrial physics; he is equally hostile to the latter's theory of the celestial movers of the heavenly bodies, which in the medieval Aristotelian tradition were known as the "separate intellects." This doctrine had already been

challenged philosophically by Crescas, and now with the new astronomy of Copernicus and Galileo their postulation became otiose.
Yashar's criticism of this theory, however, was more scientific than
philosophical:

I heard from my teacher [Galileo] that the reason for positing the separate
intellects as the movers of the heavenly spheres was that these philosophers [the Peripatetics] observed that they had contrary motions...How-
ever, according to Copernicus, the heavenly motion is regular, not forced.
He believes that each sphere has only one motion...The same is true for
the Earth...One should not distort reality to fit Aristotle's theory, but the
theory should agree with reality...There is no need for separate movers and
intellects (Yashar, *Sefer Elim* 58, 61; my translation).

Convinced by Copernicus and Galileo of the heliocentric theory,
Yashar dismisses the whole Aristotelian–Ptolemaic cosmology, with
its elaborate doctrines of incorporeal movers of the heavenly bodies,
retrograde planetary motion, and the centrality of the Earth.[43]

As noted previously, Yashar's thought is not simple or mono-
lithic. Confounding his commentators, he moves continually between naturalistic arguments and doctrines, which he learned from
Galileo, and Renaissance Neoplatonism and kabbalah, which was
ever present. His knowledge of the ancient Platonists was quite extensive and based upon primary sources, since he was able to read ancient Greek. He refers to Plotinus' *Enneads*, citing book and chapter.
He is familiar with the later Greek Platonists as well; he also quotes
Philo.[44] Equally pervasive but more perplexing is his attitude toward and uses of kabbalah, a subject he treats in detail in his later
work *Sefer Ta'alumot Hokhmah*, the first part of which, *Matzref la-
Hokhmah*, is devoted to the kabbalah. To characterize his diverse
statements about kabbalah as ambivalent would be an understate-
ment. Some commentators have dismissed his positive statements
as just window-dressing to appease his mystically inclined audience; other commentators have contrarily argued for a more balanced
and nuanced approach, giving due consideration to his utilization of
kabbalah.[45]

An example of Yashar's amalgam of mysticism and science is his
adoption and adaptation of atomism. The once despised ancient theory of Democritus and Epicurus was now gaining respectability. In a
passage that anticipates Spinoza's denigration of Plato and Aristotle

in favor of Democritus and Epicurus,[46] Yashar reveals his atomist sympathies along with his willingness to interpret atomism within a kabbalist metaphysics. After expressing his commitment to an atomist physics, he comments:

Some of the philosophers thought that by the aggregation and segregation of the atoms all the things in the world are generated and corrupted. Their words seem strange at first glance ... But perhaps they intended the world of points of the Wisdom of kabbalah out of which the letters were formed and all the worlds.[47]

In another passage Yashar, referring to Lucretius' *On the Nature of Things* Book 4, discusses the atomist doctrine of light according to which light consists of subtle particles or atoms. He then identifies this theory with the kabbalist doctrine of the points, which had been developed by the great sixteenth-century kabbalist Isaac Luria.[48] No matter how the debate over Yashar's attitude toward the kabbalah will be resolved, it is clear that he and many of his contemporaries in both the Christian and Jewish worlds were not immune from its attractiveness and assimilated its doctrines in various and diverse ways.

THE END AND THE BEGINNING: SPINOZA

In his library Spinoza had copies of both Judah Abravanel's *Dialoghi d'Amore* in a Spanish translation and Yashar's *Ta'alumot Hokhmah*. But, as we shall see, whatever influence these books may have had upon his intellectual development, Spinoza was to transform radically the major motifs of medieval philosophy in general, and not merely medieval Jewish philosophy. Indeed, Julius Guttmann argues that Spinoza belongs to the history of European philosophy, and not to the history of Jewish philosophy.[49] Spinoza's life would seem to support this claim: he was excommunicated from the synagogue at the age of twenty-four and lived the rest of his short life only amidst Christians.[50]

Nevertheless, Spinoza's relationship to his medieval Jewish predecessors has been a major preoccupation of historians of philosophy, especially historians of medieval Jewish philosophy. In his commentary on Spinoza's *Ethics*, Harry Wolfson offers the student of Spinoza a history of medieval Jewish philosophy as well.[51] Indeed, several more recent Spinoza scholars, primarily medievalists, have labeled Spinoza a "Maimonidean."[52] An alternative to this approach is the perspective proposed by the "Hispanists," who stress the Sephardic, especially Marrano, background of Spinoza. Seen from this angle, Spinoza was the natural, if extreme, outgrowth of a heterodox Marrano environment in Jewish Amsterdam.[53]

This focus upon the Jewish background of Spinoza can, however, lead us away from the more immediate and relevant philosophical-scientific context of Spinoza's thought: the philosophy and physics of Descartes and the political thought of Hobbes. Spinoza was first and foremost a thinker in and of the second half of the seventeenth century. His conceptual framework was set by the Copernican-Galilean revolution in astronomy, the new natural philosophy of Descartes, and Hobbesian politics, rather than the assumptions of Maimonides, Crescas, and Judah Abravanel.[54] Although the notion of the intellectual love of God and the rejection of Aristotelian physics and metaphysics are to be found in Spinoza, the former has a completely different meaning for Spinoza than for Judah Abravanel, just as his commitment to modern science is devoid of any magical or kabbalistic interpretations. There are remnants of medieval thought in Spinoza, but they are to be understood more as obsolete relics to be discarded than as positive factors in his new philosophical system.

In several important respects it is useful to look at Spinoza as a philosopher of science. He, like his philosophical mentor Descartes, was deeply concerned with methodological issues, especially as they arose in the sciences.[55] There are in addition some critical analyses and revisions of Cartesian mechanics in Spinoza.[56] Although not a practicing scientist like Galileo or Descartes, except in optics, Spinoza was well versed in the scientific literature of his day and reflected philosophically about its implications for an understanding of nature and humankind. He concluded in the end that traditional paradigms of supranaturalism and cosmological dualism must be abandoned.

Cosmological dualism suggests that nature is in some way produced by or dependent upon a transcendent cause that is ontologically distinct from its effect. Whether we understand this ultimate cause as did Plato, Aristotle, Plotinus, or the medievals, it is clearly supranatural, "above" (outside of) nature. Moreover, in its standard medieval, even Cartesian, version, this model allows for divine intervention in the course of nature, for on this view nature exhibits design and goals. The natural order was created voluntarily and purposively by a supranatural cause and hence can be altered, albeit only momentarily, for a purpose. No matter how orderly, the regularity of the natural order is subordinate to a "higher" will, and hence is in this sense only accidental, or contingent. Spinoza rejects this whole conception of nature, and substitutes for it a naturalism that abolishes any form of cosmological dualism. For him, *everything* is literally "natural"; there is nothing that is above or beyond nature. The ultimate ground or cause of nature is not transcendent, but immanent (Spinoza, *Ethics*, I, 18; IV, Preface). God and nature are one.

This identification of God with the active forces within nature (*Ethics*, I, 29, Scholium) leads Spinoza to reject the traditional conception of God as an agent who acts in a way incomprehensible to humans. Spinoza has no tolerance for fideists or mystics. As Jonathan Bennett aptly puts it, Spinoza was absolutely committed to the principle of "explanatory rationalism": everything can be explained.[57] But this does not limit these explanations to those that are anthropocentric. Nature is neutral: it is devoid of any teleology, which for Spinoza is no more than a human imposition upon nature. As a fixed system of laws, nature precludes any (miraculous) interruptions or interventions. Indeed, to posit the possibility of miracles is to deny God; again, God is nature. A change in nature would be a change in God, and this is absurd.[58]

If cosmological dualism is to be rejected, is psychological dualism still possible? From Plato through Descartes, philosophers have maintained that the human soul or mind is a distinct ontological entity, incorporeal and immortal. This doctrine was an essential part of the medieval and Renaissance philosophical tradition, as we have seen in such thinkers as Isaac Abravanel and Judah Moscato. However, in the interactionist version of Descartes its difficulties became apparent, and different accounts of the human mind were proposed by Descartes' contemporaries and immediate successors. Some were monistic – either materialistic, such as Hobbes', or mentalistic, such as Berkeley's – others retained some form of dualism, but denied interactionism, such as Malebranche and Leibniz. Spinoza forged a new path. Just as the infinite God, or nature, exhibits infinite attributes, including extension, so too humankind manifests both physical and mental features. But these are not properties of two radically distinct substances or entities, as they are in Descartes' psychology; they are rather two different but complementary ways of understanding human nature. Mind and body are not two distinct entities; they are one and the same thing seen under two different attributes. Neither attribute is reducible to the other, but they do not designate two distinct entities (*Ethics*, II, 7–13).

Having established the metaphysical and psychological foundations of humankind's place in nature, Spinoza moves on to consider the human condition in the concluding two books of the *Ethics*. He sees humans as essentially in bondage, in servitude to their passions, emotions brought about through ignorance and submission to external force. Freedom (from submission) is achieved through an arduous and continuous process of self-education, whereby we overcome our passivity and become active through the acquisition of true beliefs ("adequate ideas") concerning ourselves and the world in which we live. Knowledge liberates us; it enables us to become autonomous agents, to the extent possible to us, rather than dependent beings. In developing this program Spinoza revises radically some of the more venerated values in traditional morality, especially in its religious version. Consider, for example, his analyses of the virtues of humility and repentance. Humility is the feeling one has of one's weakness; as such, it causes pain. But since pain is a loss of power, humility cannot be a virtue (*Ethics*, IV, 53). Nor is there any point to repentance. To repent is to express remorse over something done that could have been otherwise. But this is an illusion: what was done could not have been otherwise than it was. To think otherwise is to think that nature, or God, could have been different. But this is absurd (*Ethics*, I, 33 and IV, 54). It is not surprising that Nietzsche, the great "transvaluator of values," saw Spinoza as forerunner of his new ethical agenda.[59]

The culmination of the *Ethics* is its depiction of the free man, whom Spinoza describes as "blessed." With respect to such blessedness, Spinoza reverts to the notion we found in Judah Abravanel: the intellectual love of God. But Spinoza's *amor Dei* is not identical with that of his Jewish predecessor. His God is not the God of Abraham, Isaac, and Jacob. The free person's love of God is for Spinoza the knowledge of nature and its inexorable laws, an intellectual intuition engendering in us the highest form of mental contentment, or joy. This is our salvation, our eternity.

Spinoza's *Ethics* was not published in his lifetime; his *Theological-Political Treatise* (*TTP*) was. In many respects the *TTP* is just as radical as the earlier *Ethics*. Written in a more engaging and less formal style, the *TTP* was immediately controversial. Leibniz, who had met with Spinoza several times in The Hague a year before the latter's death, was extremely agitated when he learned of and later read the *TTP*. In it he correctly saw doctrines that were potentially even more disturbing than those of the *Ethics* precisely because they were political and theological. In the Preface Spinoza makes quite plain his agenda: to produce a theoretical framework within which political peace can be secured. Living during the religious wars that plagued Europe and being the offspring of victims of religious persecution in Iberia, Spinoza knew very well what happens when church and state form an alliance. Indeed, the Netherlands at this time was not at peace, with different religious factions struggling to influence politics and to gain political power for themselves. In the Preface to the *TTP* Spinoza puts forth his main thesis: there will be no civil peace unless church and state are divorced once and for all time. The unholy alliance between the secular and the ecclesiastical authorities has produced only civil discord and war. In short, what is needed is the separation of church and state, a revolutionary doctrine in the seventeenth century. But as he develops his argument, Spinoza makes it clear that he is also seeking another divorce: he wants to emancipate philosophy from religion, or theology. The marriage of philosophy and religion that characterizes, indeed defines, much of medieval thought has been for Spinoza an absolute disaster, to the detriment of both. Accordingly, the *TTP* wages war on two fronts: it argues for the separation of the state from religion and the autonomy of philosophy vis-à-vis religion.

Spinoza's strategy is to attack the very basis for both the unholy alliance between the church and the state and the marriage between philosophy and theology – the Bible. Why the Bible? First, the Bible was the model upon which several Protestant countries, especially those modeled after Calvin's Geneva, constructed their polities. Moses' theocracy was for them the paradigm for government pending the second coming of the Messiah. Second, one of the underlying assumptions of medieval philosophy was that the Bible was a book containing important philosophical teachings that could be extracted by intelligent exegesis. In this way it could be shown that revelation and reason are in harmony. Thus, the Bible was both politically and philosophically relevant and authoritative. Spinoza rejects both assumptions.

He does this by denying the supranatural origin and character of Scripture. Both the Old and New Testaments are only human documents, no different than Homer's *Iliad*. They are the products of many hands over many centuries, reflecting the diverse stages of development of the ancient Hebrews and their specific social, political, and cultural circumstances.[60] The prophets were people who spoke on the basis of imagination, not reason; they were not philosophers or scientists, but rather moral preachers and in some cases political pundits. Some of their pronouncements upon philosophical or scientific issues were false; even when true, these statements were not attained in a philosophical or scientific manner. This holds true even for Moses, who is in this respect no different from Amos, who was a shepherd. On the other hand, Spinoza has considerable respect for King Solomon, whose determinist (fatalist) speculations in Ecclesiastes are quite in accord with his own philosophy.[61]

In his secularization of Scripture Spinoza attacks not only the institution and nature of prophecy, but also the election of Israel, the importance of ritual law, the possibility of miracles, and the relevance of biblical law to the modern state. In the course of this critique he frequently attacks Maimonides by name, accusing him of not reading the biblical text literally. As a result of this error, heaps upon heaps of misleading and mistaken interpretations of the Bible have accumulated. Scripture has become Plato, Aristotle, or Plotinus speaking Hebrew (*TTP*, ch. 7). While the Bible is still a valuable guide for morality, especially the virtue of obedience, it is not philosophy or physics or even political science. It may have been a good political guide for the ancient Israelites, but now it is antiquated. Hobbes and Machiavelli are more relevant (*TTP*, chs. 18–19).

Spinoza marks not just the end of medieval philosophy, and much of Renaissance philosophy as well; he signals its complete obsolescence and irrelevance. He, not Descartes, is the first modern philosopher, one who has emancipated not only himself but also philosophy from religion, who is unafraid of the new science and its implications for philosophy and morals, and who welcomes the secular state as the locus of salvation. Religion is to be domesticated and privatized, so that it will do minimum harm. Philosophy and science need no legitimation from either the state or the church. If the latter mind their own stores, there will be peace; if they do not, war will ensue. Is it any wonder then that Spinoza became for many modern Jewish thinkers a model for their own untraditional philosophies.[62] Amsterdam Jewry may not have been fully cognizant of what was in Spinoza's heart or mind at the time of his excommunication, but they were quite prescient of where his heretical thoughts would take him. The community could not allow his kind of critique of the status quo; otherwise its existence as a tolerated minority would be jeopardized. Nevertheless, Spinoza persevered, and thus became a paradigm of the "free spirit" who suffers for his right to philosophize. He is a Socrates redivivus.

NOTES

1. H. Davidson, "Medieval Jewish Philosophy in the Sixteenth Century," in *Jewish Thought in the Sixteenth Century*, ed. B. Cooperman (Cambridge, Mass.: Harvard University Press, 1983), 106–45.

2. Some of the *Enneads* were known in the Middle Ages, first in Arabic translation and then in Latin as *The Theology of Aristotle*. Plotinus himself, however, was not known; see P. O. Kristeller, "Neoplatonismo e Rinascimento," in *Il Neoplatonismo nel Rinascimento*, ed. Pietro Prini (Rome: Istituto della Enciclopedia Italiana, 1993), 8–28.

3. The Renaissance also witnessed the rediscovery of Hellenistic philosophy, as the obsession with Cicero's writings indicates. Lucretius, Seneca, and Sextus Empiricus, among others, also reappear in the sixteenth and seventeenth centuries. Their influence upon Jewish thinkers of this period, however, was minor. Nevertheless, the Venetian rabbi Simha (Simone) Luzzatto (1582–1663) shows signs of the influence of Sextus Empiricus in his treatise *Socrate*; see D. Ruderman, *Jewish Thought and Scientific Discovery in Early Modern Europe* (New Haven: Yale University Press, 1995), ch. 5.

4. J. Blau, *The Christian Interpretation of the Cabala in the Renaissance* (New York: Columbia University Press, 1944). Since Blau, an enormous literature has arisen on this subject; see especially M. Idel, "Magical and Neoplatonic Interpretations of Kabbalah in the Renaissance," in *Jewish Thought in the Sixteenth Century*, ed. B. Cooperman (Cambridge, Mass.: Harvard University Press, 1983), 186–242.

5. On this subject the work of Joseph Sermoneta is most important. For a bibliography of his writings, see the *Joseph Baruch Sermoneta Memorial Volume*, ed. A. Ravitzky (Jerusalem: Hebrew University, 1998), 493–506.

6. Indeed, Padua was the center of the study of Averroes. See J. H. Randall, "The Development of Scientific Method in the School of Padua," in *Renaissance Essays*, ed. P. O. Kristeller and P. Wiener (New York: Harper & Row, 1968), 217–51.

7. P. Merlan, *Monopsychism, Mysticism, Metaconsciousness* (The Hague: Mouton, 1962), ch. 2; H. Davidson, *Alfarabi, Avicenna and Averroes on the Intellect: Their Cosmologies, Theories of the Active Intellect, and Theories of Human Intellect* (New York and Oxford: Oxford University Press, 1992), ch. 2.

8. A. Ivry, "Averroes on Intellection and Conjunction," *Journal of the American Oriental Society* 86 (1966), 76–85.

9. Quoted in K. Bland, "Elijah del Medigo, Unicity of the Intellect and Immortality of the Soul," *Proceedings of the American Academy for Jewish Research* 61 (1995), 17.

10. Averroes, *On the Harmony between Religion and Philosophy*, trans. G. Hourani (London: Luzac, 1961).

11. Elijah del Medigo, *Behinat ha-Dat*, ed. J. Ross (Tel Aviv: Rosenberg School of Jewish Studies, 1984), 75–84. D. Geffen, "Insights into the Life and Thought of Elijah del Medigo, Based upon his Published and Unpublished Works," *Proceedings of the American Academy for Jewish Research* 41–42 (1973–74), 69–86.

12. The doctrine of the *sefirot* is one of the more fundamental ideas in kabbalah. In general, the *sefirot* are the supernal powers that emanate from God. Some kabbalists understood them as the essential attributes of God; others construed them as instruments of divine activity. For a good introduction to this thorny topic, see E. Wolfson's entry, "Jewish Mysticism: A Philosophical Overview," in the *History of Jewish Philosophy*, ed. D. H. Frank and O. Leaman (London and New York: Routledge, 1997), ch. 19.

13. Elijah del Medigo, *Behinat ha-Dat*, 91; K. Bland, "Elijah del Medigo's Averroist Response to the Kabbalahs of Fifteenth-Century Jewry and Pico della Mirandola," *Jewish Thought and Philosophy* 1 (1991), 23–53.

14. Del Medigo believed that authentic Judaism contains very little of the irrational; herein lies one of its virtues, whereas Christianity is laden with philosophical and theological absurdities (*Behinat ha-Dat*, 81–2).

15. Boethius of Dacia, *On the Eternity of the World*, trans. J. Wippel (Toronto: Pontifical Institute of Mediaeval Studies, 1987).

16. Averroes, *The Incoherence of the Incoherence* (*Tahafut al-Tahafut*) trans. S. van den Bergh (London: Luzac, 1954), 1: 359–63.

17. Davidson, "Medieval Jewish Philosophy in the Sixteenth Century," 110. Bland, "Unicity of the Intellect," 18.

18. J. Guttmann, "Elia del Medigos Verhältnis zu Averroes in seinem *Behinat ha-Dat,*" in *Jewish Studies in Memory of Israel Abrahams* (New York: Jewish Institute of Religion, 1927), 202–3.

19. Pomponazzi, *On the Immortality of the Soul,* trans. W. H. Hay II, in *The Renaissance Philosophy of Man,* ed. E. Cassirer, P. O. Kristeller, and J. H. Randall, Jr. (Chicago: University of Chicago Press, 1948), 280–381, esp. 379–81.

20. Abravanel, *The Deeds of God (Mif'alot Elohim)* 4.4. Abravanel's distinction is similar to that made by some medieval thinkers between that which is logically impossible and that which is naturally impossible, above nature. Thus, miracles are instances of the latter, but not of the former (Maimonides, *Treatise on Resurrection,* chaps. 37, 41–3; Aquinas, *Disputed Questions on Power,* 1.3 and 7; *Commentary on the Sentences,* 4:17.1.5). Abravanel's argument for creation from cosmic destruction is based upon Plato, *Phaedo* 78b-c; *Republic* 478e–479a; *Timaeus* 41a-b; Philoponus, *De Aeternitate Mundi contra Proclum,* ed. H. Rabe (Leipzig: Teubner, 1899), 241–2. See H. Davidson, *Proofs for Eternity, Creation and the Existence of God in Medieval Islamic and Jewish Philosophy* (New York and Oxford: Oxford University Press, 1987), ch. 4.

21. Aristotle, *On the Heavens* 1:12. Abravanel, *The Deeds of God,* book 9.

22. Abravanel, *Commentary on Deuteronomy,* Parshat Tetze (New York, 1959), 107b–109a.

23. Abravanel, *Commentary on Genesis,* Parshat Bereshit, 24b.

24. Alemanno's laudatio has been studied by several scholars; see E. I. J. Rosenthal, "Some Observations on Yohanan Alemanno's Political Ideas," in *Studies in Jewish Religious and Intellectual History,* ed. S. Stein and R. Loewe (University: University of Alabama Press, 1979), 247–61; A. Melamed, "The Hebrew 'Laudatio' of Yohanan Alemanno in Praise of Lorenzo il Magnifico and the Florentine Constitution," in *Jews in Italy: Studies Dedicated to the Memory of Umberto Cassuto,* ed. H. Beinart (Jerusalem: Magnes Press, 1988), English section, 1–34.

25. The standard edition in Italian is still that of S. Carmella (Bari: Guis, Laterza, and Figli, 1929). An English translation was made by F. Friedeberg-Seeley and J. H. Barnes under the title *The Philosophy of Love* (London: Soncino, 1937).

26. A modern Hebrew translation was done by M. Dorman (Jerusalem: Mosad Bialik, 1983). It contains a comprehensive biographical and historical introduction by Dorman.

27. Leone Ebreo, *Philosophy of Love,* 38–46; Carmella, 36–43.

28. Although Abravanel makes several sympathetic salutes to kabbalah and links Plato to the latter, it is not altogether obvious that by the

term "kabbalah" he means anything more than "tradition." Moreover, specific kabbalistic doctrines, such as the theory of the *sefirot*, play hardly any role in his thinking.

29. M. Idel, "Sources of the Images of the Circle in the *Dialoghi d'Amore*," [Hebrew] *Iyyun* 28 (1980), 156–66.

30. It is maintained by several scholars that a fourth dialogue was planned; see Carmella (ed.), *Dialoghi*, 428–9.

31. *Philosophy of Love*, 277–87; Carmella, 236–46.

32. Ovid, *Metamorphoses* 1:1; Boccaccio, *Genealogie Deorum Gentilium*, proemium 3.

33. *Philosophy of Love*, 282–3; Carmella, 240–1.

34. *Philosophy of Love*, 278; Carmella, 237.

35. *Philosophy of Love*, 122–4, 283–5; Carmella, 108–9, 242–3.

36. *Philosophy of Love*, 415–23; Carmella, 348–51.

37. *Philosophy of Love*, 424; Carmella, 355.

38. I use the Warsaw edition of the *Nefutzot Yehudah*, published in 1871. For the *Qol Yehudah*, I use the Vilna edition of Halevi's *Kuzari* (1904).

39. It is not certain who was the first Jew to rehabilitate Philo. Perhaps it was Moscato's colleague, the Mantuan historian Azariah di Rossi. At any rate, Moscato refers to Philo in sermons 18, 31, and 36; he mentions Philo also in *Qol Yehudah*, Book 5, 123. On Philo's reappearance among Italian Renaissance Jewry, see J. Weinberg, "The Quest for Philo in Sixteenth-Century Jewish Historiography," in *Jewish History: Essays in Honor of Chimen Abramsky*, ed. A. Rapoport-Albert and S. Zipperstein (London: P. Halban, 1988), 163–87.

40. M. Idel gives an excellent analysis of this theme in his important essay, "Judah Moscato: A Late Renaissance Jewish Preacher," in *Preachers of the Italian Ghetto*, ed. D. Ruderman (Berkeley: University of California Press, 1992), 41–66. Idel points to the Hermetic and kabbalistic strains in Moscato's thought, as well as to the Platonic ones. See also I. Barzilay, *Between Reason and Faith: Anti-Rationalism in Italian Jewish Thought, 1250–1650* (The Hague and Paris: Mouton, 1967), 167–93.

41. See S. Day, *Intuitive Cognition: A Key to the Significance of the Later Scholastics* (St. Bonaventure: Franciscan Institute, 1947).

42. The most comprehensive and detailed study of Yashar is I. Barzilay, *Yoseph Shlomo Delmedigo (Yashar of Candia): His Life, Works, and Times* (Leiden: Brill, 1974).

43. Whether Yashar was the first Jewish thinker to adopt the new astronomy is not certain; but he was the first to promulgate it in writing. The Venetian rabbi Simha (Simone) Luzzatto (1582–1663) also had mathematical and astronomical interests, and in one of his works refers to the

observational discoveries of Galileo. However, unlike Yashar, Luzzatto uses these results to bolster his argument for epistemological skepticism. Moreover, Luzzatto was also uninterested in and mildly critical of kabbalah; see his *Treatise on the Jews of Venice* [Hebrew], trans. D. Lattes, ed. M. Shulvass and R. B. Bachi (Jerusalem: Mosad Bialik, 1950), 143. For a good discussion of Luzzatto's skepticism, see Ruderman, *Jewish Thought and Scientific Discovery*, ch. 5.

44. See his *Matzref la-Hokhmah*, Jerusalem (reprint of the Warsaw edition of 1890), on Philo, 53, 114; on Plotinus, 113; on Porphyry, 113; on Proclus, 113; on Iamblichus, 114.

45. Barzilay and the earlier commentators tend to minimize the importance of kabbalah for Yashar; see Barzilay, *Yosef Shlomo Delmedigo*, ch. 16. More recently Ruderman has argued for a more positive role of kabbalah in his thought; see Ruderman, *Jewish Thought and Scientific Discovery*, ch. 4.

46. Spinoza, letter 56. Although Spinoza was not an atomist, in this letter he clearly expresses more appreciation for the ancient atomists than for Plato or Aristotle.

47. *Novlot Hokhmah*, 7a, quoted in Idel, "Differing Conceptions of Kabbalah in the Seventeenth Century in Jewish Thought," in *Jewish Thought in the Seventeenth Century*, ed. I. Twersky and B. Septimus (Cambridge, Mass.: Harvard University Press, 1987), 185. Idel claims that Yashar's atomism was more indebted to Bruno than to Galileo (195 nn. 289–90).

48. Cited by Idel, "Differing Conceptions," 195.

49. J. Guttmann, *Philosophies of Judaism*, trans. D. Silverman (New York: Schocken Books, 1973), 301. However, this claim did not prevent Guttmann from devoting over twenty pages to a discussion of Spinoza's philosophy.

50. The specifics of his excommunication are still not clear or precise. There is a whole literature on this question. For recent discussions, see S. Nadler, *Spinoza: A Life* (Cambridge: Cambridge University Press, 1999), and S. Nadler, *Spinoza's Heresy: Immortality and the Jewish Mind* (Oxford: Oxford University Press, 2001).

51. H. A. Wolfson, *The Philosophy of Spinoza*, 2 vols. (New York: Schocken Books, 1969).

52. W. Z. Harvey, "A Portrait of Spinoza as a Maimonidean," *Journal of the History of Philosophy* 19 (1981), 151–72.

53. See the pioneering work of I. S. Revah, *Spinoza et Juan de Prado* (The Hague and Paris: Mouton, 1959). More recently, Y. Yovel has expanded upon this theme in his *Spinoza and Other Heretics* (Princeton: Princeton University Press, 1989), 1.

54. I agree with M. Gueroult, who characterizes Wolfson's approach as "l'obsession de la littérature juive"; see his *Spinoza I: Dieu* (Paris: Aubier-Montaigne, 1968), 445.

55. Spinoza discusses methodology in his early essay, *Treatise on the Emendation of the Intellect*, and also in several letters, especially those addressed (via Henry Oldenburg) to the English chemist Robert Boyle, letters 6 and 11.

56. See Part 2 of his *Principles of Cartesian Philosophy; Ethics*, Part 2, Proposition 13; Letters 81 and 83. A. Lecrivain's essay "Spinoza and Cartesian Mechanics" (in *Spinoza and the Sciences*, ed. M. Grene and D. Nails [Dordrecht: Reidel, 1986], 15–60) is most stimulating on this topic.

57. J. Bennett, *A Study of Spinoza's "Ethics"* (Indianapolis: Hackett, 1984), 29.

58. Spinoza, *Ethics* I, Appendix; *The Theological-Political Treatise (TTP)*, ch. 6.

59. Nietzsche, *Human, All-Too-Human*, paragraph 408; Yovel, *Spinoza and Other Heretics*, II, ch. 5.

60. Spinoza, *TTP*, chs. 8–11.

61. Spinoza, *TTP*, chs. 1–2.

62. On the importance of Spinoza for modern Jewish thought, see E. Schweid, *The History of Jewish Thought in Modern Times* [Hebrew] (Jerusalem: Keter, 1977), ch. 1; Z. Levy, *Spinoza's Interpretation of Judaism* [Hebrew] (Tel Aviv: Sifriyah Poelim, 1983).

GUIDE TO FURTHER READING IN ENGLISH

For more detailed bibliographies, including primary texts and material in foreign languages, see the notes to the individual chapters.

GENERAL WORKS

Frank, D. H. and O. Leaman (eds.), *History of Jewish Philosophy* (London and New York: Routledge, 1997).

Frank, D. H., O. Leaman, and C. H. Manekin (eds.), *The Jewish Philosophy Reader* (London and New York: Routledge, 2000).

Guttmann, J. *Philosophies of Judaism*, trans. D. Silverman (New York: Schocken Books, 1973) [originally published 1933].

Husik, I. *A History of Mediaeval Jewish Philosophy* (New York: Atheneum, 1976) [originally published 1916].

Hyman, A. and J. J. Walsh (eds.), *Philosophy in the Middle Ages*, 2nd ed. (Indianapolis: Hackett, 1973).

Lerner, R. and M. Mahdi (eds.), *Medieval Political Philosophy: A Source Reader* (Ithaca: Cornell University Press, 1963).

Sirat, C. *A History of Jewish Philosophy in the Middle Ages* (Cambridge: Cambridge University Press, 1985).

BIBLICAL AND RABBINIC BACKGROUND TO MEDIEVAL
JEWISH PHILOSOPHY

Eisen, R. *Gersonides on Providence, Covenant, and the Chosen People: A Study in Medieval Jewish Philosophy and Biblical Commentary* (Albany: State University of New York Press, 1995).

Elman, Y. "The Contribution of Rabbinic Thought to a Theology of Misfortune," in *Jewish Perspectives on the Experience of Suffering*, ed. S. Carmy (Northvale, N.J.: Jason Aronson, 1999), 155–212.

Halbertal, M. *People of the Book: Canon, Meaning, and Authority* (Cambridge, Mass.: Harvard University Press, 1997).

446

Harvey, W. Z. "Rabbinic Attitudes toward Philosophy," in *"Open Thou Mine Eyes": Essays on Aggadah and Judaica Presented to William G. Braude on his Eightieth Birthday and Dedicated to his Memory*, ed. H. Blumberg (Hoboken: Ktav, 1992), 83–101.

Kraemer, D. *Responses to Suffering in Classical Rabbinic Literature* (New York and Oxford: Oxford University Press, 1995).

Moore, G. *Judaism in the First Centuries of the Christian Era*, 3 vols. (Cambridge, Mass.: Harvard University Press, 1927–30).

Runia, D. T. *Exegesis and Philosophy: Studies on Philo of Alexandria* (Aldershot: Variorum, 1990).

Saperstein, M. *Decoding the Rabbis: A Thirteenth-Century Commentary on the Aggadah* (Cambridge, Mass.: Harvard University Press, 1980).

Schechter, S. *Aspects of Rabbinic Theology* (New York: Schocken Books, 1961).

Urbach, E. *The Sages: Their Concepts and Beliefs*, trans. I. Abrahams (Cambridge, Mass.: Harvard University Press, 1987).

Winston, D. *Logos and Mystical Theology in Philo of Alexandria* (Cincinnati: Hebrew Union College Press, 1985).

Wolfson, H. A. *Philo: Foundations of Religious Philosophy in Judaism, Christianity and Islam*, 2 vols. (Cambridge, Mass.: Harvard University Press, 1968).

ISLAMIC CONTEXT AND JEWISH *KALAM*

Alon, I. *Socrates in Medieval Islamic Literature* (Leiden: Brill, 1991).

Altmann, A. (ed. and trans.), *Saadya: The Book of Doctrines and Beliefs* (Oxford: East and West Library, 1946; reprinted, with new introduction by D. H. Frank, Indianapolis: Hackett, 2002).

Ben-Shammai, H. "Studies in Karaite Atomism," *Jerusalem Studies in Arabic and Islam* 6 (1985), 243–98.

Ben-Shammai, H. "Kalam in Medieval Jewish Philosophy," in *History of Jewish Philosophy*, ed. D. H. Frank and O. Leaman (London and New York: Routledge, 1997), 115–48.

Black, D. *Logic and Aristotle's Rhetoric and Poetics in Medieval Arabic Philosophy* (Leiden: Brill, 1990).

Brody, R. *The Geonim of Babylonia and the Shaping of Medieval Jewish Culture* (New Haven and London: Yale University Press, 1998).

Chiesa, B. and W. Lockwood, *Ya'qub al-Qirqisani on Jewish Sects and Christianity* (Frankfurt am Main: Peter Lang, 1984).

Chittick, W. *The Sufi Path of Knowledge: Ibn al-'Arabi's Metaphysics of Imagination* (Albany: State University of New York Press, 1989).

Chodkiewicz, M. *An Ocean without Shore: Ibn Arabi, the Book, and the Law* (Albany: State University of New York Press, 1993).

Cohen, B. (ed.), *Saadia Anniversary Volume: Proceedings of the American Academy for Jewish Research* (New York: Jewish Publication Society, 1943).

Corbin, H. *History of Islamic Philosophy*, trans. L. Sherrard (London: Kegan Paul International, 1993).

Daftary, F. *The Isma'ilis: Their History and Doctrines* (Cambridge: Cambridge University Press, 1990).

Davidson, H. *Proofs for Eternity, Creation and the Existence of God in Medieval Islamic and Jewish Philosophy* (New York and Oxford: Oxford University Press, 1987).

Davidson, H. *Alfarabi, Avicenna, and Averroes, on Intellect: Their Cosmologies, Theories of the Active Intellect, and Theories of Human Intellect* (New York and Oxford: Oxford University Press, 1992).

Fakhry, M. *A History of Islamic Philosophy*, 2nd ed. (New York: Columbia University Press, 1983).

Goodman, L. E. *The Book of Theodicy: Translation and Commentary on the Book of Job by Saadiah ben Joseph al-Fayyumi* (New Haven: Yale University Press, 1988).

Gutas, D. *Greek Thought, Arabic Culture: The Graeco–Arabic Translation Movement in Baghdad and Early 'Abbasid Society (2nd–4th/8th–10th Centuries)* (London and New York: Routledge, 1998).

Hourani, G. (ed.), *Essays on Islamic Philosophy and Science* (Albany: State University of New York Press, 1978).

Kraemer, J. L. *Philosophy in the Renaissance of Islam: Al-Sijistani and his Circle* (Leiden: Brill, 1986).

Kraemer, J. L. *Humanism in the Renaissance of Islam: The Cultural Revival during the Buyid Age*, 2nd ed. (Leiden: Brill, 1992).

Lameer, J. *Al-Farabi and Aristotelian Syllogistics: Greek Theory and Islamic Practice* (Leiden: Brill, 1994).

Leaman, O. *A Brief Introduction to Islamic Philosophy* (Cambridge: Polity Press, 1999).

Leaman, O. *An Introduction to Classical Islamic Philosophy* (Cambridge: Cambridge University Press, 2002).

Malter, H. *Saadia Gaon, his Life and Works* (New York: Jewish Publication Society, 1921).

Morewedge, P. (ed.), *Neoplatonism and Islamic Thought* (Albany: State University of New York Press, 1992).

Nasr, S. *An Introduction to Islamic Cosmological Doctrines*, rev. ed. (Albany: State University of New York Press, 1993).

Nasr, S. and O. Leaman (eds.), *History of Islamic Philosophy* (London and New York: Routledge, 1996).

Netton, I. *Muslim Neoplatonists: An Introduction to the Thought of the Brethren of Purity* (London: George Allen & Unwin, 1982).

Netton, I. *Allah Transcendent: Studies in the Structure and Semiotics of Islamic Philosophy, Theology and Cosmology* (London: Routledge, 1989).

Rashed, R. (ed.), with R. Morelon, *Encyclopedia of the History of Arabic Science*, 3 vols. (London: Routledge, 1996).

Rescher, N. *Studies in Arabic Philosophy* (Pittsburgh: University of Pittsburgh Press, 1966).

Rosenthal, F. *The Classical Heritage in Islam* (London and New York: Routledge, 1975).

Schwarz, M. "Who were Maimonides' Mutakallimun?: Some Remarks on *Guide of the Perplexed* Part 1 Chapter 73," *Maimonidean Studies* 2 (1992), 159–209; 3 (1995), 143–72.

Sklare, D. *Samuel ben Hofni Gaon and his Cultural World: Texts and Studies* (Leiden: Brill, 1996).

Stroumsa, S. (ed. and trans.), *Dawud ibn Marwan al-Muqammis's "Twenty Chapters" (Ishrun Maqala)* (Leiden: Brill, 1989).

Wolfson, H. A. *The Philosophy of the Kalam* (Cambridge, Mass.: Harvard University Press, 1976).

Wolfson, H. A. *Repercussions of the Kalam in Jewish Philosophy* (Cambridge, Mass.: Harvard University Press, 1979).

JEWISH NEOPLATONISM

Altmann, A. "Creation and Emanation in Isaac Israeli, a Reappraisal," in *Essays in Jewish Intellectual History*, ed. A. Altmann (Hanover: University Press of New England, 1981), 1–15.

Altmann, A. and S. Stern (eds. and trans.), *Isaac Israeli: A Neoplatonic Philosopher of the Early Tenth Century* (London: Oxford University Press, 1958).

Dillon, J. "Solomon ibn Gabirol's Doctrine of Intelligible Matter," in *Neoplatonism and Jewish Thought*, ed. L. E. Goodman (Albany: State University of New York Press, 1992), 43–59.

Goodman, L. E. (ed.), *Neoplatonism and Jewish Thought* (Albany: State University of New York Press, 1992).

Hyman, A. "From What is One and Simple only What is One and Simple Can Come to Be," in *Neoplatonism and Jewish Thought*, ed. L. E. Goodman (Albany: State University of New York Press, 1992), 111–35.

Ivry, A. L. "Neoplatonic Currents in Maimonides' Thought," in *Perspectives on Maimonides: Philosophical and Historical Studies*, ed. J. L. Kraemer (Oxford: Littman Library, 1991), 115–40.

Ivry, A. L. "Maimonides and Neoplatonism: Challenge and Response," in *Neoplatonism and Jewish Thought*, ed. L. E. Goodman (Albany: State University of New York Press, 1992), 137–56.

Katz, S. T. (ed.), *Jewish Neoplatonism* (New York: Arno, 1980).

Rudavsky, T. "Conflicting Motifs in Ibn Gabirol's Discussion of Matter and Evil," *The New Scholasticism* 52 (1978), 54–71.

Wolfson, H. A. "The Meaning of Ex Nihilo in Isaac Israeli," *Jewish Quarterly Review* 50 (1959), 1–12.

Wolfson, H. A. "The Meaning of Ex Nihilo in the Church Fathers, Arabic and Hebrew Philosophy, and St. Thomas," in his *Studies in the History of Philosophy and Religion*, 2 vols., ed. I. Twersky and G. Williams (Cambridge, Mass.: Harvard University Press, 1973), I: 207–21.

JUDAH HALEVI

Baneth, D. "Judah Halevi and al-Ghazali," in *Studies in Jewish Thought: An Anthology of German-Jewish Scholarship*, ed. A. Jospe (Detroit: Wayne State University Press, 1981), 181–99.

Berger, M. S. "Toward a New Understanding of Judah Halevi's *Kuzari*," *Journal of Religion* 72 (1992), 210–28.

Davidson, H. *Alfarabi, Avicenna, and Averroes on Intellect: Their Cosmologies, Theories of the Active Intellect, and Theories of Human Intellect* (New York and Oxford: Oxford University Press, 1992).

Goitein, S. D. "Judeo-Arabic Letters from Spain (Early Twelfth Century)," *Orientalia Hispanica* 1 (1974), 331–50.

Goodman, L. E. "Judah Halevi," in *History of Jewish Philosophy*, ed. D. H. Frank and O. Leaman (London and New York: Routledge, 1997), 188–227.

Green, K. "Religion, Philosophy, and Morality: How Leo Strauss Read Judah Halevi's *Kuzari*," *Journal of the American Academy of Religion* 61 (1993), 225–73.

Kreisel, H. *Prophecy: The History of an Idea in Medieval Jewish Philosophy.* Amsterdam Studies in Jewish Thought, 8 (Dordrecht: Kluwer, 2001).

Lasker, D. "Judah Halevi and Karaism," in *From Ancient Israel to Modern Judaism: Intellect in Quest of Understanding: Essays in Honor of Marvin Fox*, 4 vols., ed. J. Neusner et al. (Atlanta: Scholars Press, 1989), III: 111–25.

Lobel, D. *Between Mysticism and Philosophy: Sufi Language of Religious Experience in Judah Halevi's Kuzari* (Albany: State University of New York Press, 2000).

Pines, S. "Shi'ite Terms and Conceptions in Judah Halevi's *Kuzari*," *Jerusalem Studies in Arabic and Islam* 2 (1980), 165–251.

Silman, Y. *Philosopher and Prophet: Judah Halevi, the Kuzari, and the Evolution of his Thought* (Albany: State University of New York Press, 1995).

Strauss, L. "The Law of Reason in the *Kuzari*," in his *Persecution and the Art of Writing* (Glencoe: The Free Press, 1952; reprinted, Chicago: University of Chicago Press, 1998), 95–141.

Wolfson, H. A. "The Platonic, Aristotelian and Stoic Theories of Creation in Hallevi and Maimonides," in *Studies in the History of Philosophy and Religion*, 2 vols., ed. I. Twersky and G. Williams (Cambridge, Mass.: Harvard University Press, 1973), I: 234–49.

Wolfson, H. A. "Maimonides and Hallevi: A Study in Typical Attitudes Towards Greek Philosophy in the Middle Ages," in *Studies in the History of Philosophy and Religion*, 2 vols., ed. I. Twersky and G. Williams (Cambridge, Mass.: Harvard University Press, 1977), II: 120–60.

MAIMONIDES

Benor, E. *Worship of the Heart: A Study of Maimonides' Philosophy of Religion* (Albany: State University of New York Press, 1995).

Buijs, J. (ed.), *Maimonides: A Collection of Critical Essays* (Notre Dame: University of Notre Dame Press, 1988).

Burrell, D. *Knowing the Unknowable God: Ibn-Sina, Maimonides, Aquinas* (Notre Dame: University of Notre Dame Press, 1986).

Cohen, R. and H. Levine (eds.), *Maimonides and the Sciences* (Dordrecht: Kluwer, 2000).

Diamond, J. *Maimonides and the Hemeneutics of Concealment* (Albany: State University Press of New York, 2002).

Dobbs-Weinstein, I. *Maimonides and St. Thomas on the Limits of Reason* (Albany: State University of New York Press, 1995).

Fox, M. *Interpreting Maimonides: Studies in Methodology, Metaphysics, and Moral Philosophy* (Chicago: University of Chicago Press, 1990).

Frank, D. H. (ed.), *Maimonides* (special issue), *American Catholic Philosophical Quarterly* 76 (2002).

Goodman, L. E. *On Justice: An Essay in Jewish Philosophy* (New Haven: Yale University Press, 1991).

Goodman, L. E. *God of Abraham* (New York: Oxford University Press, 1996).

Guttmann, J. (ed.) and C. Rabin (trans.), *The Guide of the Perplexed* (London: East and West Library, 1952; reprinted, with new introduction by D. H. Frank, Indianapolis: Hackett, 1995).

Halbertal, M. and A. Margalit, *Idolatry* (Cambridge, Mass.: Harvard University Press, 1992).

Halkin, A. (trans.) and D. Hartman, *Crisis and Leadership: Epistles of Maimonides* (Philadelphia: Jewish Publication Society, 1985).

Hartman, D. *Maimonides: Torah and Philosophic Quest* (Philadelphia: Jewish Publication Society, 1976).

Hartman, D. *A Living Covenant: The Innovative Spirit in Traditional Judaism* (New York: Free Press, 1985).

Kellner, M. *Maimonides on Human Perfection* (Atlanta: Scholars Press, 1990).

Kellner, M. *Maimonides on Judaism and the Jewish People* (Albany: State University of New York Press, 1991).

Kellner, M. *Maimonides on the Decline of the Generations and the Nature of Rabbinic Authority* (Albany: State University of New York Press, 1996).

Kraemer, J. L. (ed.), *Perspectives on Maimonides: Philosophical and Historical Studies* (Oxford: Littman Library, 1991).

Kreisel, H. *Maimonides' Political Thought: Studies in Ethics, Law, and the Human Ideal* (Albany: State University of New York Press, 1999).

Lachterman, D. "Maimonidean Studies 1950–86: A Bibliography," *Maimonidean Studies* 1 (1990), 197–216.

Langermann, Y. "The Mathematical Writings of Maimonides," *Jewish Quarterly Review* 75 (1984), 57–65.

Langermann, Y. *The Jews and the Sciences in the Middle Ages* (Aldershot: Variorum, 1999).

Leaman, O. *Moses Maimonides* (London: Routledge, 1990).

Leibowitz, Y. *The Faith of Maimonides* (New York: Adama Books, 1987).

Novak, D. *The Image of the Non-Jew in Judaism: An Historical and Constructive Study of the Noahide Laws* (Lewiston, N.Y.: Edwin Mellen Press, 1983), 275–318.

Novak, D. *Natural Law in Judaism* (Cambridge: Cambridge University Press, 1998).

Ormsby, E. (ed.), *Moses Maimonides and his Time* (Washington, D.C.: The Catholic University of America Press, 1989).

Pines, S. and Y. Yovel (eds.), *Maimonides and Philosophy* (Dordrecht: Nijhoff, 1986).

Robinson, I., L. Kaplan, and J. Bauer (eds.), *The Thought of Moses Maimonides: Philosophical and Legal Studies* (Lewiston, N.Y.: Edwin Mellen Press, 1990).

Rudavsky, T. M. *Time Matters: Time, Creation, and Cosmology in Medieval Jewish Philosophy* (Albany: State University of New York Press, 2000).

Seeskin, K. *Jewish Philosophy in a Secular Age* (Albany: State University of New York Press, 1990).

Seeskin, K. *Maimonides: A Guide for Today's Perplexed* (West Orange, N.J.: Behrman House, 1991).

Seeskin, K. *Searching for a Distant God: The Legacy of Maimonides* (New York: Oxford University Press, 2000).

Stern, J. *Problems and Parables of Law: Maimonides and Nahmanides on Reasons for the Commandments* (Albany: State University of New York Press, 1998).

Strauss, L. *Philosophy and Law: Contributions to the Understanding of Maimonides and his Predecessors*, trans. E. Adler (Albany: State University of New York Press, 1994) [originally published 1935].

Twersky, I. (ed.), *A Maimonides Reader* (New York: Behrman House, 1972).

Twersky, I. (ed.), *Introduction to the Code of Maimonides (Mishneh Torah)* (New Haven: Yale University Press, 1980).

Twersky, I. (ed.), *Studies in Maimonides* (Cambridge, Mass.: Harvard University Press, 1991).

Weiss, R. *Maimonides' Ethics: The Encounter of Philosophic and Religious Morality* (Chicago: University of Chicago Press, 1991).

Weiss, R. and C. Butterworth (eds. and trans.), *Ethical Writings of Maimonides* (New York: New York University Press, 1975).

MEDIEVAL JEWISH POLITICAL THOUGHT

Berman, L. V. "A Reexamination of Maimonides' 'Statement on Political Science'," *Journal of the American Oriental Society* 89 (1969), 106–11.

Biale, D. *Power and Powerlessness in Jewish History* (New York: Schocken Books, 1986).

Elazar, D. (ed.), *Kinship and Consent* (Ramat-Gan: Turtledove, 1987).

Elon, M. *Jewish Law: History, Sources, and Principles*, trans. B. Auerbach and M. J. Sykes (Philadelphia and Jerusalem: Jewish Publication Society, 1994).

Fox, M. *Interpreting Maimonides: Studies in Methodology, Metaphysics and Moral Philosophy* (Chicago: University of Chicago Press, 1990).

Frank, D. H. "Idolatry and the Love of Appearances: Maimonides and Plato on False Wisdom," in *Proceedings of the Academy for Jewish Philosophy*, ed. D. Novak and N. Samuelson (Lanham, London, and New York: University Press of America, 1992), III: 155–68.

Funkenstein, A. *Perceptions of Jewish History* (Berkeley: University of California Press, 1993).

Goitein, S. D. *A Mediterranean Society: The Jewish Communities of the Arab World as Portrayed in the Documents of the Cairo Geniza*. II. *The Community* (Berkeley: University of California Press, 1971).

Hartman, D. *Israelis and the Jewish Tradition: An Ancient People Debating its Future* (New Haven: Yale University Press, 2000).

Kellner, M. *Dogma in Medieval Jewish Thought: From Maimonides to Abravanel* (Oxford: Littman Library, 1986).

Kellner, M. *Maimonides on Judaism and the Jewish People* (Albany: State University of New York Press, 1991).

Kellner, M. "Chosenness, not Chauvinism: Maimonides on the Chosen People," in *A People Apart: Chosenness and Ritual in Jewish Philosophical Thought*, ed. D. H. Frank (Albany: State University of New York Press, 1993), 51–75.

Kreisel, H. "Judah Halevi's Influence on Maimonides: A Preliminary Appraisal," *Maimonidean Studies* 2 (1992), 95–121.

Kreisel, H. *Maimonides' Political Thought: Studies in Ethics, Law, and the Human Ideal* (Albany: State University of New York Press, 1999).

Lorberbaum, M. *Politics and the Limits of Law: Secularizing the Political in Medieval Jewish Thought* (Stanford: Stanford University Press, 2001).

Macy, J. "The Rule of Law and the Rule of Wisdom in Plato, al-Farabi, and Maimonides," in *Studies in Islamic and Judaic Traditions*, ed. W. M. Brinner and S. D. Ricks (Atlanta: Scholars Press, 1986), 205–32.

Melamed, A. "Medieval and Renaissance Jewish Political Philosophy," in *History of Jewish Philosophy*, ed. D. H. Frank and O. Leaman (London and New York: Routledge, 1997), 415–49.

Melamed, A. *The Philosopher-King in Medieval and Renaissance Jewish Political Thought* (Albany: State University of New York Press, 2003).

Netanyahu, B. *Don Isaac Abravanel: Statesman and Philosopher* (Philadelphia: Jewish Publication Society, 1982).

Pines, S. "Truth and Falsehood versus Good and Evil," in *Studies in Maimonides*, ed. I. Twersky (Cambridge, Mass.: Harvard University Press, 1991), 95–157.

Pines, S. "Spinoza's *Tractatus Theologico-Politicus*, Maimonides and Kant," in *The Collected Works of Shlomo Pines*, ed. W. Z. Harvey and M. Idel (Jerusalem: Magnes Press, 1997), v: 687–711 [originally published 1968].

Ravitzky, A. *History and Faith: Studies in Jewish Philosophy*, Amsterdam Studies in Jewish Thought, 2 (Amsterdam: J. C. Gieben, 1996).

Scholem, G. *The Messianic Idea in Judaism and Other Essays on Jewish Spirituality* (New York: Schocken Books, 1971).

Schorsch, I. "On the History of the Political Judgment of the Jew," in his *From Text to Context: The Turn to History in Modern Judaism* (Hanover, N.H. and London: Brandeis University Press, 1994), 118–32.

Silman, Y. *Philosopher and Prophet: Judah Halevi, the Kuzari, and the Evolution of his Thought*, trans. L. J. Schramm (Albany: State University of New York Press, 1995).

Smith, S. B. *Spinoza, Liberalism, and the Question of Jewish Identity* (New Haven: Yale University Press, 1997).

Strauss, L. "On Abravanel's Philosophical Tendency and Political Teachings," in *Isaac Abravanel: Six Lectures*, ed. J. B. Trend and H. Loewe (Cambridge: Cambridge University Press, 1937), 95–129.

Strauss, L. *Persecution and the Art of Writing* (Glencoe: The Free Press, 1952).

Strauss, L. *What is Political Philosophy?* (New York: The Free Press, 1959).

Strauss, L. *Philosophy and Law: Contributions to the Understanding of Maimonides and his Predecessors*, trans. E. Adler (Albany: State University of New York Press, 1995) [originally published 1935].

Twersky, I. (ed.) *Introduction to the Code of Maimonides (Mishneh Torah)* (New Haven: Yale University Press, 1980).

Walzer, M., M. Lorberbaum, and N. Zohar (eds.) and Y. Lorberbaum (co-ed.), *The Jewish Political Tradition*. 1. *Authority* (New Haven: Yale University Press, 2000).

Weiler, G. *Jewish Theocracy* (Leiden: Brill, 1988).

SUFISM, PIETISM, AND KABBALAH: JEWISH MYSTICISM

Altmann, A. *Studies in Religious Philosophy and Mysticism* (Ithaca, N.Y.: Cornell University Press, 1969).

Altmann, A. "Lurianic Kabbalah in Platonic Key: Abraham Cohen Herrera's *Puerta del Cielo*," *Hebrew Union College Annual* 53 (1982), 317–55.

Cohen, G. "The Soteriology of Abraham Maimuni", *Proceedings of the American Academy for Jewish Research* 35 (1967), 75–98; 36 (1968), 33–56.

Fenton, P. B. "Some Judaeo-Arabic Fragments by Rabbi Abraham he-Hasid, the Jewish Sufi," *Journal of Semitic Studies* 26 (1981), 47–72.

Fenton, P. B. *The Treatise of the Pool, al-Maqala al-Hawdiyya by 'Obadyah Maimonides* (London: Octagon, 1981).

Fenton, P. B. "The Literary Legacy of David II Maimuni," *Jewish Quarterly Review* 74 (1984), 1–56.

Goitein, S. D. "A Jewish Addict to Sufism in the Time of Nagid David II Maimonides," *Jewish Quarterly Review* 44 (1953–54), 37–49.

Goitein, S. D. "A Treatise in Defence of the Pietists," *Journal of Jewish Studies* 16 (1965), 105–14.

Goitein, S. D. "Abraham Maimonides and his Pietist Circle," in *Jewish Medieval and Renaissance Studies*, ed. A. Altmann (Cambridge, Mass.: Harvard University Press, 1967), 145–64.

Goldziher, I. "Ibn Hud, the Muhammadan Mystic, and the Jews of Damascus," *Jewish Quarterly Review* 6 (1893), 218–20.

Heller Wilensky, S. O. "Isaac ibn Latif: Philosopher or Kabbalist?" in *Jewish Medieval and Renaissance Studies*, ed. A. Altmann (Cambridge, Mass.: Harvard University Press, 1967), 185–223.

Huss, B. "*Sefer ha-Zohar* as Canonical, Sacred and Holy Text: Changing Perspectives of the Book of Splendor between the Thirteenth and Eighteenth Centuries," *Journal of Jewish Thought and Philosophy* 7 (1998), 257–307.

Idel, M. "The Magical and Neoplatonic Interpretations of the Kabbalah in the Renaissance," in *Jewish Thought in the Sixteenth Century*, ed. B. Cooperman (Cambridge, Mass.: Harvard University Press, 1983), 186–242.

Idel, M. "Hitbodedut as Concentration in Ecstatic Kabbalah," in *Jewish Spirituality: From the Bible to the Middle Ages*, ed. A. Green (New York: Crossroad, 1986), 405–38.

Idel, M. "Differing Conceptions of Kabbalah in the Early Seventeenth Century," in *Jewish Thought in the Seventeenth Century*, ed. I. Twersky and B. Septimus (Cambridge, Mass.: Harvard University Press, 1987), 137–200.

Idel, M. *Abraham Abulafia and the Mystical Experience* (Albany: State University of New York Press, 1988).

Idel, M. *Studies in Ecstatic Kabbalah* (Albany: State University of New York Press, 1988).

Idel, M. *Language, Torah and Hermeneutics in Abraham Abulafia*, trans. M. Kallus (Albany: State University of New York Press, 1989).

Idel, M. "Jewish Kabbalah and Platonism in the Middle Ages and the Renaissance," in *Neoplatonism and Jewish Thought*, ed. L. E. Goodman (Albany: State University of New York Press, 1992), 319–51.

Idel, M. *Kabbalah: New Perspectives* (New Haven: Yale University Press, 1994).

Idel, M. "Encounters between Spanish and Italian Kabbalists in the Generations of the Expulsion," in *Crisis and Creativity in the Sephardic World: 1391–1648*, ed. B. Gampel (New York: Columbia University Press, 1997), 190–222, and nn. 336–51.

Idel, M. *Messianic Mystics* (New Haven: Yale University Press, 1998).

Liebes, Y. *Studies in the Zohar*, trans. A. Schwarz, S. Nakache, and P. Peli (Albany: State University of New York Press, 1993).

Matt, D. "The Mystic and the Mizvot," in *Jewish Spirituality: From the Bible through the Middle Ages*, ed. A. Green (New York: Crossroad, 1986), 367–404.

Rosenblatt, S. (ed.), *The High Ways to Perfection of Abraham Maimonides* (New York: Columbia University Press, 1927).

Ruderman, D. *Kabbalah, Magic, and Science: The Cultural Universe of a Sixteenth-Century Jewish Physician* (Cambridge, Mass.: Harvard University Press, 1988).

Scholem, G. *Major Trends in Jewish Mysticism* (New York: Schocken Books, 1941).

Scholem, G. *On the Kabbalah and its Symbolism* (New York: Schocken Books, 1965).

Scholem, G. *Origins of the Kabbalah*, trans. A. Arkush, ed. R. J. Z. Werblowsky (Philadelphia: Jewish Publication Society, and Princeton: Princeton University Press, 1987).

Tirosh-Rothschild, H. "Theology of Nature in Sixteenth-Century Italian Jewish Philosophy," *Science in Context* 10 (1997), 529–70.

Tishby, I. *The Wisdom of the Zohar*, 3 vols., trans. D. Goldstein (London: Littman Library, 1998).

Wirszubski, C. *Pico della Mirandola's Encounter with Jewish Mysticism* (Cambridge Mass.: Harvard University Press, 1989).

Wolfson, E. *Through a Speculum that Shines: Vision and Imagination in Medieval Jewish Mysticism* (Princeton: Princeton University Press, 1994).

Wolfson, E. "Jewish Mysticism: A Philosophical Overview," in *History of Jewish Philosophy*, ed. D. H. Frank and O. Leaman (London and New York: Routledge, 1997), 450–98.

Wolfson, E. *Abraham Abulafia – Kabbalist and Prophet: Hermeneutics, Theosophy and Theurgy* (Los Angeles: Cherub Press, 2000).

THE THIRTEENTH CENTURY: PHILOSOPHY IN HEBREW AND THE MAIMONIDEAN CONTROVERSY

Baer, Y. *A History of the Jews in Christian Spain*, 2 vols. (Philadelphia: Jewish Publication Society, 1978) [originally published 1945].

Halbertal, M. *People of the Book: Canon, Meaning, and Authority* (Cambridge, Mass.: Harvard University Press, 1997), 109–19.

Halkin, A. "Why was Levi ben Hayyim Hounded?," *Proceedings of the American Academy for Jewish Research* 34 (1966), 65–76.

Halkin, A. "Yedaiah Bedershi's Apology," in *Jewish Medieval and Renaissance Studies*, ed. A. Altmann (Cambridge, Mass.: Harvard University Press, 1967), 165–84.

Harvey, S. *Falaquera's "Epistle of the Debate": An Introduction to Jewish Philosophy* (Cambridge, Mass.: Harvard University Press, 1987).

Harvey, S. "Did Maimonides' Letter to Samuel ibn Tibbon Determine Which Philosophers Would be Studied by Later Jewish Thinkers?" *Jewish Quarterly Review* 83 (1992), 51–70.

Harvey, S. (ed.), *The Medieval Hebrew Encyclopedias of Science and Philosophy*, Amsterdam Studies in Jewish Thought, 7 (Dordrecht: Kluwer, 2000).

Ravitzky, A. "Samuel ibn Tibbon and the Esoteric Character of the *Guide of the Perplexed*," *AJS Review* 6 (1981), 87–123.

Saperstein, M. *Decoding the Rabbis: A Thirteenth-Century Commentary on the Aggadah* (Cambridge, Mass.: Harvard University Press, 1980), 47–158.

Saperstein, M. "The Conflict over the Rashba's Herem on Philosophical Study: A Political Perspective," *Jewish History* 1 (1986), 27–38.

Saperstein, M. "The Social and Cultural Context: Thirteenth to Fifteenth Centuries," in *History of Jewish Philosophy*, ed. D. H. Frank and O. Leaman (London and New York: Routledge, 1997), 294–330.

Sarachek, J. *Faith and Reason: The Conflict over the Rationalism of Maimonides* (New York: Hermon Press, 1970).

Septimus, B. *Hispano-Jewish Culture in Transition: The Career and Controversies of Ramah* (Cambridge, Mass.: Harvard University Press, 1982).

Stern, G. "Philosophic Allegory in Jewish Culture: The Crisis in Languedoc (1304–6)," in *Interpretation and Allegory: Antiquity to the Modern World*, ed. J. Whitman (Leiden: Brill, 2000), 187–207.

Twersky, I. "Aspects of the Social and Cultural History of Provençal Jewry," in his *Studies in Jewish Law and Philosophy* (New York: Ktav, 1982), 180–202.

THE FOURTEENTH CENTURY: GERSONIDES, AND THE IMPACT OF
SCHOLASTICISM ON JEWISH PHILOSOPHY

Baer, Y. *A History of the Jews in Christian Spain*, 2 vols. (Philadelphia: Jewish Publication Society, 1978).

Dales, R. C. *Medieval Discussions of the Eternity of the World* (Leiden: Brill, 1990).

Eisen, R. *Gersonides on Providence, Covenant, and the Chosen People: A Study in Medieval Jewish Philosophy and Biblical Commentary* (Albany: State University of New York Press, 1995).

Feldman, S. "Levi ben Gershom (Gersonides)," in *History of Jewish Philosophy*, ed. D. H. Frank and O. Leaman (London and New York: Routledge, 1997), 379–98.

Freudenthal, G. "Gersonides," in *History of Islamic Philosophy*, ed. S. Nasr and O. Leaman (London and New York: Routledge, 1996), 739–54.

Freudenthal, G. (ed.), *Studies on Gersonides: A Fourteenth-Century Jewish Philosopher-Scientist* (Leiden: Brill, 1992).

Funkenstein, A. *Theology and the Scientific Imagination from the Middle Ages to the Seventeenth Century* (Princeton: Princeton University Press, 1986).

Glasner, R. "Levi ben Gershom and the Study of Ibn Rushd in the Fourteenth Century," *Jewish Quarterly Review* 86 (1995), 51–90.

Grant, E. "The Effect of the Condemnation of 1277," in *The Cambridge History of Later Medieval Philosophy*, ed. N. Kretzmann, A. Kenny, and J. Pinborg (Cambridge: Cambridge University Press, 1982), 537–40.

Kellner, M. *Dogma in Medieval Jewish Thought: From Maimonides to Abravanel* (Oxford: Littman Library, 1986).

Kellner, M. "Bibliographia Gersonideana: An Annotated List of Writings by and about R. Levi ben Gershom," in *Studies on Gersonides: A Fourteenth-Century Jewish Philosopher-Scientist*, ed. G. Freudenthal (Leiden: Brill, 1992), 367–414.

Langermann, Y. *The Jews and the Sciences in the Middle Ages* (Aldershot: Variorum, 1999).

Levine, H. "Paradise not Surrendered: Jewish Reactions to Copernicus and the Growth of Modern Science," in *Epistemology, Methodology and the Social Sciences*, ed. R. S. Cohen and M. W. Wartofsky (Dordrecht: Reidel, 1983), 203–25.

Manekin, C. "Hebrew Philosophy in the Fourteenth and Fifteenth Centuries: An Overview," in *History of Jewish Philosophy*, ed. D. H. Frank and O. Leaman (London and New York: Routledge, 1997), 350–78.

Manekin, C. "When the Jews Learned Logic from the Pope: Three Medieval Hebrew Translations of the *Tractatus* of Peter of Spain," *Science in Context* 10 (1997), 395–430.

Pines, S. *Scholasticism after Thomas Aquinas and the Teachings of Hasdai Crescas and his Predecessors*, in *The Collected Works of Shlomo Pines: Studies in the History of Jewish Thought*, ed. W. Z. Harvey and M. Idel (Jerusalem: Magnes Press, 1997), v: 489–589 [originally published 1967].

Rosenberg, S. "The Concept of *Emunah* in Post-Maimonidean Jewish Philosophy," in *Studies in Medieval Jewish History and Literature*, ed. I. Twersky (Cambridge, Mass.: Harvard University Press, 1984), ii: 273–307.

Rudavsky, T. M. *Time Matters: Time, Creation, and Cosmology in Medieval Jewish Philosophy* (Albany: State University of New York Press, 2000).

Ruderman, D. *Jewish Thought and Scientific Discovery in Early Modern Europe* (New Haven: Yale University Press, 1995).

Thijssen, J. M. M. H. *Censure and Heresy at the University of Paris 1200–1400* (Philadelphia: University of Pennsylvania Press, 1998).

THE FIFTEENTH CENTURY: CRESCAS, AND THE JEWISH–CHRISTIAN
PHILOSOPHICAL DIALOGUE

Baer, Y. *A History of the Jews in Christian Spain*, 2 vols. (Philadelphia: Jewish Publication Society, 1978).

Baron, S. *A Social and Religious History of the Jews* (New York: Columbia University Press, 1965), x: 167–219.

Davidson, H. "Medieval Jewish Philosophy in the Sixteenth Century," in *Jewish Thought in the Sixteenth Century*, ed. B. Cooperman (Cambridge, Mass.: Harvard University Press, 1983), 106–45, esp. 110–14.

Davidson, H. *Proofs for Eternity, Creation, and the Existence of God in Medieval Islamic and Jewish Philosophy* (New York and Oxford: Oxford University Press, 1987).

Davidson, H. *Alfarabi, Avicenna, and Averroes, on Intellect: Their Cosmologies, Theories of the Active Intellect, and Theories of Human Intellect* (New York and Oxford: Oxford University Press, 1992).

Feldman, S. "The Theory of Eternal Creation in Hasdai Crescas and Some of his Predecessors," *Viator* 11 (1980), 289–320.

Feldman, S. "Crescas' Theological Determinism," *Da'at* 9 (1982), 3–28.

Feldman, S. "A Debate Concerning Determinism in Late Medieval Jewish Philosophy," *Proceedings of the American Academy for Jewish Research* 51 (1984), 15–54.

Feldman, S. "On the End of the Universe in Medieval Jewish Philosophy," *AJS Review* 11 (1986), 53–77.

Gutwirth, E. "Towards Expulsion: 1391–1492," in *Spain and the Jews*, ed. E. Kedourie (London: Thames & Hudson, 1992), 51–73.

Harvey, W. Z. "Hasdai Crescas' Critique of the Theory of the Acquired Intellect," Ph.D. dissertation, Columbia University, 1973.

Harvey, W. Z. "Albo's Discussion of Time," *Jewish Quarterly Review* 70 (1980), 210–38.

Harvey, W. Z. "Crescas vs. Maimonides on Knowledge and Pleasure," in *A Straight Path: Studies in Medieval Philosophy and Culture, Essays in Honor of Arthur Hyman*, ed. R. Link-Salinger, R. Long, and C. Manekin (Washington, D.C.: The Catholic University of America Press, 1988), 113–23.

Harvey, W. Z. "The Philosopher and Politics: Gersonides and Crescas," in *Scholars and Scholarship: The Interaction between Judaism and Other Cultures*, ed. L. Landman (New York: Yeshiva University Press, 1990), 53–65.

Harvey, W. Z. "Nissim of Gerona and William of Ockham on Prime Matter," *Jewish History* 6 (1992), 88–98.

Harvey, W. Z. *Physics and Metaphysics in Hasdai Crescas*, Amsterdam Studies in Jewish Thought, 6 (Amsterdam: J. C. Gieben, 1998).

Idel, M. "Jewish Thought in Spain," in *The Sephardi Legacy*, ed. H. Beinart (Jerusalem: Magnes Press, 1992), 1: 261–81.

Kellner, M. *Dogma in Medieval Jewish Thought: From Maimonides to Abravanel* (Oxford: Littman Library, 1986).

Kreisel, H. *Prophecy: The History of an Idea in Medieval Jewish Philosophy*, Amsterdam Studies in Jewish Thought, 8 (Dordrecht: Kluwer, 2001).

Lasker, D. *Jewish Philosophical Polemics against Christianity in the Middle Ages* (New York: Ktav, 1977).

Lasker, D. "The Impact of Christianity on Late Iberian Jewish Philosophy," in *In Iberia and Beyond: Hispanic Jews between Cultures*, ed. B. Cooperman (Newark: University of Delaware Press, 1998), 175–90.

Rudavsky, T. M. *Time Matters: Time, Creation, and Cosmology in Medieval Jewish Philosophy* (Albany: State University of New York Press, 2000).

Tirosh-Rothschild, H. "Jewish Philosophy on the Eve of Modernity," in *History of Jewish Philosophy*, ed. D. H. Frank and O. Leaman (London: Routledge, 1997), 499–573, esp. 500–12.

Tirosh-Rothschild, H. "Human Felicity – Fifteenth Century Sephardic Perspectives on Happiness," in *In Iberia and Beyond: Hispanic Jews between Cultures*, ed. B. Cooperman (Newark: University of Delaware Press, 1998), 191–243.

Wolfson, H. A. *Crescas' Critique of Aristotle* (Cambridge, Mass.: Harvard University Press, 1929).

Wolfson, H. A. *The Philosophy of Spinoza*, 2 vols. (New York: Schocken Books, 1969) [originally published 1934].

THE END AND AFTEREFFECTS OF MEDIEVAL JEWISH PHILOSOPHY

Barzilay, I. *Between Reason and Faith: Anti-Rationalism in Italian Jewish Thought, 1250–1650* (The Hague and Paris: Mouton, 1967).

Barzilay, I. *Yoseph Shlomo Delmedigo (Yashar of Candia): His Life, Works, and Times* (Leiden: Brill, 1974).

Bennett, J. *A Study of Spinoza's "Ethics"* (Indianapolis: Hackett, 1984).

Bland, K. "Elijah del Medigo's Response to the Kabbalahs of Fifteenth-Century Jewry and Pico della Mirandola," *Jewish Thought and Philosophy* 1 (1991), 23–53.

Bland, K. "Elijah del Medigo, Unicity of the Intellect and Immortality of the Soul," *Proceedings of the American Academy for Jewish Research* 61 (1995), 1–22.

Blau, J. *The Christian Interpretation of the Cabala in the Renaissance* (New York: Columbia University Press, 1944).

Davidson, H. "Medieval Jewish Philosophy in the Sixteenth Century," in *Jewish Thought in the Sixteenth Century*, ed. B. Cooperman (Cambridge, Mass.: Harvard University Press, 1983), 106–45.

Feldman, S. "Isaac Abravanel's Defense of Creation ex Nihilo," in *Proceedings of the Eleventh World Congress of Jewish Studies*, Division C, vol. 2 (Jerusalem: World Union of Jewish Studies, 1994), 33–40.

Feldman, S. *Philosophy in a Time of Crisis: Don Isaac Abravanel, Defender of the Faith* (London and New York: RoutledgeCurzon, 2003).

Garrett, D. (ed.), *The Cambridge Companion to Spinoza* (Cambridge: Cambridge University Press, 1996).

Geffen, D. "Insights into the Life and Thought of Elijah del Medigo Based upon his Published and Unpublished Works," *Proceedings of the American Academy for Jewish Research* 41–42 (1973–74), 69–86.

Grene, M. and D. Nails (eds.), *Spinoza and the Sciences* (Dordrecht: Reidel, 1986).

Husik, I. *Judah Messer Leon's Commentary on the "Vetus Logica"* (Leiden: Brill, 1901).

Idel, M. "Magical and Neoplatonic Interpretations of Kabbalah in the Renaissance," in *Jewish Thought in the Sixteenth Century*, ed. B. Cooperman (Cambridge, Mass.: Harvard University Press, 1983), 186–242.

Idel, M. "Differing Conceptions of Kabbalah in the Seventeenth Century in Jewish Thought," in *Jewish Thought in the Seventeenth Century*, ed. I. Twersky and B. Septimus (Cambridge, Mass.: Harvard University Press, 1987), 137–200.

Idel, M. "Judah Moscato: A Late Renaissance Jewish Preacher," in *Preachers of the Italian Ghetto*, ed. D. Ruderman (Berkeley: University of California Press, 1992), 41–66.

Kaplan, Y. *Isaac Orobio de Castro: From Christianity to Judaism* (Oxford: Littman Library, 1989).

Kristeller, P. O. *Renaissance Thought and its Sources* (New York: Columbia University Press, 1979).

Lesley, A. "'The Song of Solomon's Ascents' by Yohanan Alemanno: Love and Human Perfection According to a Jewish Associate of Pico della Mirandola," Ph.D. dissertation, University of California, Berkeley, 1976.

Lesley, A. "The Place of the *Dialoghi d'Amore* in Contemporaneous Jewish Thought," in *Ficino and Renaissance Neoplatonism*, ed. K. Eisenbichler and O. Pugliese (Ottawa: Dovehouse Editions Canada, 1986), 69–86.

Melamed, A. "The Hebrew 'Laudatio' of Yohanan Alemanno in Praise of Lorenzo il Magnifico and the Florentine Constitution," in *Jews in Italy: Studies Dedicated to the Memory of Umberto Cassuto*, ed. H. Beinart (Jerusalem: Magnes Press, 1988), English section, 1–34.

Nadler, S. *Spinoza: A Life* (Cambridge: Cambridge University Press, 1999).

Nadler, S. *Spinoza's Heresy: Immortality and the Jewish Mind* (Oxford: Oxford University Press, 2001).

Preus, J. S. *Spinoza and the Irrelevance of Biblical Authority* (Cambridge: Cambridge University Press, 2001).

Ravven, H. and L. E. Goodman (eds.), *Jewish Themes in Spinoza's Philosophy* (Albany: State University of New York Press, 2002).

Rosenthal, E. I. J. "Some Observations on Yohanan Alemanno's Political Ideas," in *Studies in Jewish Religious and Intellectual History*, ed.

S. Stein and R. Loewe (University: University of Alabama Press, 1979), 247–61.

Ruderman, D. *Jewish Thought and Scientific Discovery in Early Modern Europe* (New Haven: Yale University Press, 1995).

Smith, S. *Spinoza, Liberalism, and the Question of Jewish Identity* (New Haven: Yale University Press, 1997).

Tirosh-Rothschild, H. *Between Worlds: The Life and Thought of Rabbi David ben Judah Messer Leon* (Albany: State University of New York Press, 1991).

Tirosh-Rothschild, H. "Jewish Philosophy on the Eve of Modernity," in *History of Jewish Philosophy*, ed. D. H. Frank and O. Leaman (London and New York: Routledge, 1997), 499–573, esp. 512–29.

Wolfson, H. A. *The Philosophy of Spinoza*, 2 vols. (New York: Schocken Books, 1969).

Yovel, Y. *Spinoza and Other Heretics*, 2 vols. (Princeton: Princeton University Press, 1989).

INDEX